Personal Finance

SEVENTH EDITION

PERSONAL FINANCE

Harold A. Wolf

University of Texas

ALLYN AND BACON, INC.

BOSTON   LONDON   SYDNEY   TORONTO

To my parents

The first three editions of this book were authored by Maurice A. Unger and Harold A. Wolf.

Library of Congress Cataloging in Publication Data
Wolf, Harold Arthur, 1923–
  Personal finance.

  Bibliography: p.
  Includes index.
  1. Finance, Personal. I. Title.
HG179.W573 1984   332.024   83–22346
ISBN 0-205-08060-X

Printed in the United States of America

10 9 8 7 6 5 4 3 2   88 87 86 85

CONTENTS

x   Contents

PREFACE

This, the seventh edition of *Personal Finance*, represents a significant and substantial revision in response to the increasing complexity and rapid changes taking place in today's economic and financial environment. Personal financial planning was complex enough in 1964 when the first edition was published; it is infinitely more so today.

Inflation is one of the major reasons for this situation. Not too many years ago it was not as difficult as it is today to keep ahead of inflation and to maintain and even improve your standard of living. In 1964 the Consumer Price Index stood at 92.9 (the base year of 1967 being 100); in August 1983, at 301.1. In 1964 the inflation rate was 1.7 percent; in March, 1980 the figure was 18 percent per year. Since then the rate of inflation has declined substantially—down to about a 3 percent per year rate by late 1983. What the future holds in store no one knows, but some fear inflation may begin to rise again in 1984 and 1985 and approach double-digit levels. The total amount of inflation during this book's life so far has been 225.2 percent.

It is obvious that whatever one's individual life-style and goals are, a better understanding of the principles of personal finance is absolutely vital today. The goal of this book remains the same: to provide the reader with the information necessary for understanding these principles and to help the reader develop better skill in making financial decisions that will bring the most personal satisfaction.

CHANGES IN THE SEVENTH EDITION

The organization format and the content of this edition have been substantially changed. After securing the comments and suggestions from many users of the book over the years, the following changes were made.

In Chapter 2 the sections on record keeping and personal financial data (the balance sheet and income statement) were strengthened, and new material on career planning was added. The important topic of budgeting is now given its own chapter.

Many users of the book suggested that the chapters on personal taxes and home ownership (housing) be presented earlier. These subjects, after all, are expenditures and belong in the part dealing with managing your income. These two chapters (formerly Chapters 16 and 17) are now Chapters 8 and 9, respectively. The material formerly found in Chapter 7, Part Two (*Savings through Thrift Institutions*) is now included in Chapter 14, Part Four, at the suggestion of many users of the book, because savings do become investments.

Not only was the material in Part Three (insurance) brought up to date but a short introductory chapter (Chapter 10 on risk management) was added as well to set the stage for a more meaningful presentation of the various kinds of insurance in Chapters 11 through 13.

Part Four, *Managing Your Investments*, now begins with a chapter on investing indirectly through thrift institutions (Chapter 14). In earlier editions this part only presented material on direct investments.

Part Four (through Chapter 18) has been completely rewritten and updated because of the rapid changes that have taken place in this area.

Part Five was also changed substantially. In the older editions, this part included material on home ownership and taxes. Since these two chapters are now included under Part Two, Part Five is now about retirement and estate planning. In previous editions, retirement planning was included in the part on insurance, because annuities are an insurance concept. However, because retirement planning encompasses far more than just insurance and annuities, an entire new chapter, Chapter 19, was written on that subject. This chapter includes not only Social Security and traditional annuities, but also other retirement arrangements. It discusses corporate pension plans and individual retirement plans that provide substantial tax benefits. The final chapter on estate planning was completely rewritten to take into account the 1981 and 1982 changes in the tax laws.

The goal in this revision was to provide the most up to date discussion of personal finance topics possible, given the almost daily changes in today's world. The data, statistics, and details concerning inflation, prices, interest rates, and innumerable other information was current when this book went to press.

New questions and cases have been added to the end of each chapter, and the list of suggested readings has been thoroughly revised, expanded, and updated. For the first time a student study guide is now available.

ORGANIZATION AND APPROACH

All individuals are consumers. As such, they are almost constantly engaged in spending money for all kinds of things; spending on food takes place almost daily, while expenditures on big items like a car or household furniture less frequently.

People also constantly engage in borrowing money; using credit cards; investing savings; paying taxes; buying houses and life, home, and auto insurance; and many other activities that may involve some financial pitfalls. I hope this book will help the reader avoid some of these pitfalls.

As people grow older their income and patterns of expenditures change. Many young couples just starting out are heavy consumers and light savers. Not only is their income lower, but they are (or soon will be) buying housing and household furniture. With the coming of children, consumption will remain high. However, as income rises, savings hopefully will grow. Later, after a house full of furniture is acquired, and the children are through college, savings should rise further as the heavy consuming years are left behind.

This changing pattern of expenditure may be thought of as the family financial cycle. This cycle includes earning income, borrowing, making many different types of expenditures, acquiring consumer assets, making plans for retirement, and planning an estate. In the process of going through the financial cycle many complex situations may arise.

The book now is divided into five parts with twenty-two chapters. However, almost any chapter can be read out of sequence, and the topics can be studied in any order.

Part One, *Introduction to Financial Planning*, has three chapters. Chapter 1, *The Purpose of Personal Financial Management*, begins with a discussion of the goals of personal finance and the economic environment in which we must live. It then discusses inflation, how inflation is measured, and how it affects our lives, and ends by introducing aggregate income, and noting what is to come in the rest of the book. Chapter 2 deals with record keeping and financial and career planning, Chapter 3 introduces the personal budget. An analysis is made of funds flowing into the budget in the form of income and of funds flowing out of the budget in the form of expenditures.

Part Two, *Managing Your Income*, is designed to give you more consumption per consumer dollar. The first chapter in this part (Chapter 4), *Depository Institutions and the Services They Provide*, discusses the role of these institutions and the services that they provide. Next comes Chapter 5, which deals with using consumer credit. This chapter covers the sources of consumer credit as well as the cost of using credit—interest. Next comes Chapter 6, *Consumer Spending*, which is about consumerism narrowly defined. It discusses how to get more utility from consumer expenditure—covering buying strategies and consumer protection. This is where the consuming side (as opposed to the savings side) of the individual's income is discussed.

Chapter 7, *Consumer Laws and Consumer Protection Agencies*, presents all of the various consumer protection laws and agencies in one chapter rather than at various points in several chapters as in previous editions. Chapter 8 deals with personal taxes, a sort of an expenditure in the sense that they represent monies flowing out of the budget. Chapter 9 examines in detail homeownership (or housing), which represents the largest single expenditure (investment) and the largest asset for most individuals.

Part Three deals with all types of insurance. Chapter 10, *Risk Management: Principles of Insurance*, introduces the concept of risk management. The various risks in life must be handled somehow, and insurance is one way of doing so. This chapter also presents some general principles of insurance and an overall view of how insurance works. Then life insurance, health insurance, and property and casualty insurance are examined in Chapters 11, 12, and 13. In each of these chapters an attempt is made to shed some light on the questions of how much and what kind of insurance to buy and when to buy it.

Part Four, *Managing Your Investments*, covers investments of all kinds. If a budget calls for savings, the individual must decide where to invest them. Thrift institutions may be selected as an investment medium, in which case one invests in fixed assets, indirectly through these institutions, as discussed in Chapter 14. Many individuals invest directly in corporate stocks and bonds; when doing so, however, they must still choose between fixed assets (bonds) and variable assets (such as stock). Consequently, Chapters 15 through 17 discuss securities. Mutual funds are also presented for those who would like to invest in common stock indirectly. I hope the material will aid investment decision making.

Chapter 18 includes some material on other (nonsecurity) outlets for saving such as investing directly in rental income-producing property like duplexes or apartment buildings. This chapter also covers unusual (exotic) investment outlets such as gold and silver, antiques, paintings, works of art, and the like.

Part Five deals with retirement and estate planning. Chapter 19, *Social Security, Annuities, and Other Pension Plans*, deals with the accumulation of assets in order to provide income at retirement. The chapter begins with Social Security, which is the foundation on which a wise planner builds supplementary retirement programs. There are a good many ways to reduce your federal income taxes when planning your supplementary retirement program. These tax-saving devices (sometimes called tax shelters) are all discussed in some detail.

Part Five ends with Chapter 20, *Estate Planning, Wills, Gifts, and Trusts*. This chapter deals with what might be called the preservation of accumulated assets and the allocation of assets to specific individuals after death. It begins by introducing wills, which are for everyone, not just for the rich. This chapter also includes a discussion of trusts, and gift and estate taxes. Trusts are one of several means of reducing taxes.

ACKNOWLEDGMENTS

In the preparation of any project of this nature there are many who need to be thanked for having so graciously given of their time and encouragement.

Particular credit is due Professor Lee Richardson, Martin Marietta Eminent Scholar in Marketing at the University of Baltimore, who made many valuable contributions throughout the manuscript and who authored Chapter 6. I also wish to single out for special recognition Professor Patricia Tengel of Carnegie Mellon University and Jerry Jorgensen of the University of Utah for their valuable aid. Bette Grubbs of the Social Security District Office, Austin, Texas, was helpful in the ever-changing field of Social Security. Dick Dexter, agent for Penn Mutual, and Morgan Brenner of the Educational Training Department at the Penn Mutual home office were advisors for the chapters on insurance. Lorrain Walker of the University of Texas School of Nursing, who is also an avid horsewoman, provided assistance on horses as an exotic investment. Grant J. Wells of Ball State University must be cited for graciously giving his time and energy in thoroughly critiquing the manuscript.

I am grateful for the benefit of the in-depth reviewers of this the seventh edition, including: James O. Hill, Vincennes University; Delmer Hylton, Wake Forest University; Bryce D. Jordan, University of Southern Mississippi; Jagdish R. Kapoor, College of DuPage; Peggy D. Keck, Western Kentucky University; Bruce Lytton, University of Tennessee at Martin; Joseph C. Samprone, Jr., Georgia College; Bobby H. Sharp, Mississippi University for Women; Lawrence Shepard, University of California, Davis; Robert A. Strong, Pennsylvania State University; Stanley H. Walker, Brigham Young University, and Utah County Treasurer; and Raquibus Zaman, Ithaca College.

The following individuals have made a real contribution with their thoughtful comments on various portions of the manuscript: Sam Andrews, University of Southern Maine; Sheldon Balbirer, School of Business, University of North Carolina, Greensboro; Robert Berry, Department of Business, Mt. San Antonio College; Margaret A. Charters, Director of Consumer Studies, Syracuse University; Ginny Dickinson, Oregon State University; Sue A. Greninger, University of Texas at Austin; K. P. Hill, School of Business, Wichita State University; Ralph Marini, St. Joseph's University; Cynthia Needles, Iowa State University; Sue Peterson, Northern Illinois University; and Esther Williams, Idaho State University.

In writing a book covering such a wide range of related but somewhat different areas, it was necessary to consult various experts on the firing line in the business and financial community. They are too numerous for all of them to be mentioned here, but I do wish to specifically cite the following:

Donald Noser, Director Public Relations, Standard and Poor's Corporation; Denise Chiarello, Argus Research Corporation; Kenneth W. White, Health Insurance Association of America; Mike Bigley, Southwest Regional Manager of the Farmers Insurance Group; Bill Thurman, President of Gracy Title Company, Austin, Texas; Lynn M. Wyrick, American Automobile Association; Ysabel M. Burns and Thomas Durkin, American Financial Services Association; Robert N. Chiappetta, American Council of Life Insurance; George P. Masot, United States Treasury, Bond Division; Dr. William L. Anthes, President, College of Financial Planning, Denver, Colorado; Scott L. Spitzer, American Stock Exchange; Dick Perkins, E. F. Hutton and Co.; John Wolf, John Onken, John Eccles, William Armer, and Patricia O'Neil, all of City National Bank of Austin, Texas; Leona Paycen and Dan R. Bullock of InterFirst Bank, Austin, Texas; Linda Arnold, Dow Jones and Company, Inc.; Jack Rubinson, Director, Department of Research and Economics, National Association of Mutual Savings Banks; Howard Cosgrove, Credit Union National Association, Inc.; Barbara Wheeler, New York Stock Exchange; Suzanne K. Stemnock, American Council of Life Insurance; Harry J. Guinivan, Investment Company Institute; Fred C. Cohn, President and Editor, Johnson's Charts, Inc.; Judy Dunn, Stewart Title Co.; David K. Fortt, Executive Vice President, Vernon Publishing Services, Inc.; Thomas J. Wolff, C.L.U., Vernon, Connecticut; Stephen Sanborn, Vice President, Standard and Poor's Corporation; Paul A. Johnston and Kathleen Q. Lantero, Wiesenberger Investment Service.

In addition, I wish to acknowledge the many students who have made valuable criticisms while using the book and some additional colleagues at colleges throughout the country who have shared their experience with the book in the classroom. While the full list of those to whom I am in debt is too lengthy to be spelled out here, a number of them must be mentioned: Albie Rasmussen of Kansas State University; Martha Muncrief of N. L. Industries; Linda Hiniker of West Virginia University; Carol C. Fedrke of the University of Iowa; Leonard P. Vidger of San Francisco State University; Ronald B. Pruet of the University of Mississippi; Elizabeth Dolan of the University of New Hampshire; Sharon Garrison of North Texas State University; J. L. Hafstrom of the University of Illinois; Eugene Kosy of Central Washington University; David W. Weber of the University of Montana; Daniel L. Schneid of Central Michigan University; Carl H. Pollach, Jr. of the School of Business Administration, Portland, Oregon; J. Richard Becker of Indiana State University; and James E. Wert of the University of Arizona.

Last but not least I give credit to my typists, who have labored over the manuscript. Judy Brown, Andrea Cunningham, Joan Dana, Sharen Lackey, Kathleen Middleton, Leona Sparks, and Mary Wingo deserve special recognition.

PART ONE

INTRODUCTION TO
FINANCIAL PLANNING

CHAPTER ONE

THE PURPOSE OF PERSONAL FINANCIAL MANAGEMENT

The Goals of Personal Finance
The Current Economic Environment
Society and National Income
What Is to Come

Financial planning, money management, personal finance, and personal financial management are terms that are all used interchangeably. Moreover, nearly everyone engages in the above activities. Ours is a money—as opposed to a barter—economy; everyone who has money at his or her disposal must do some financial planning or money management. Some of us do a better job of it than others. Financial planning—or personal finance—has to do with the allocation of scarce resources (money income) among alternative and competing ends. Human wants are virtually unlimited, while money income, the means to satisfy these wants, is limited. A dollar spent on clothing cannot be spent on food. Consequently, choices must be made and priorities established.

For a few wealthy individuals almost all wants can be satisfied, although even such cases must be qualified because a vast fortune could be dissipated quickly. Most of us must manage our personal financial affairs, and if we do this wisely we accomplish several things: enlarge our income; improve the mileage we get out of each dollar of expenditures; and protect that which we already have.

THE GOALS OF PERSONAL FINANCE

Personal financial management is intended to help people plan their financial affairs intelligently. People are consumers, and personal finance is the finance of and for the consumer. However, it is more than that. People are also producers (by participating in the labor market or by household activities) and hence income earners, savers, and investors. Thus, personal financial management must also take cognizance of money income, savings, and investments. Nor does the list end there.

You will from time to time engage in borrowing money; using credit cards; investing your savings; paying taxes; buying insurance, automobiles, houses, and furniture; and other things. You may also be planning your retirement. Carrying out these activities well requires technical knowledge, which the study of personal finance provides you with. These activities may also expose you to some financial pitfalls; once more, knowledge about personal finance will enable you to cope and to achieve many of your goals.

Maximizing Satisfaction

When they talk about the "good life" most people mean the standard of living, which in turn is determined, in large part, by their purchasing power. They also think about consumption. We are a hedonistic people living in a materialistic age. We like to enjoy good food, nice clothes, automobiles, fine homes. We also enjoy leisure, travel, and entertainment. To be sure, tastes vary, and different people want different combinations of a variety of goods and services. Some would consume a larger part of a given income and save less than others. Nevertheless it is probably safe to say that most of us strive to maximize personal satisfaction by applying our own set of values, and we generally associate the degree of satisfaction as positively related to our level of income.

In recent years, a new term, *measure of economic welfare* (MEW), has come into use. MEW is an attempt to refine income into a meaningful concept of how well off we are. In earning our income, certain social costs are created that cannot always be measured, such as pollution, congestion, and noise, which reduce the quality of life. Economists refer to these social costs as negative externalities, i.e., costs generated by some but borne by all. Therefore, while our money income is a measure of our standard of living, it is an imperfect gauge of the quality of life.

It has been suggested that MEW is equal to income adjusted for a number of things. First, it would be reduced by the cost of maintaining clean air and water. Also subtracted would be the estimated costs of noise and urban congestion, both money costs and an estimate of the value of the psychological pain. To this reduced figure would be added an estimate of the value of household activities for which there is no market value and also an estimate of the value of leisure time. This would be MEW. When this is first done, MEW is an abstraction that means little. However, comparing MEW from one year to the next could be an indication of how life is improving. It could be that income is growing and MEW is declining. If so, this suggests that the amenities of life are worth more than additional material things and that amenities are being reduced by population and economic growth.

The difficulty with MEW is that it must be an estimate. True measures of the cost of pollution cannot always be obtained. The value of increased leisure must also be an estimate. The same is true of noise and congestion. In addition, not only must some of the concepts be estimates, but the value judgments of the estimator are crucial in determining the final figure. For this reason, one cannot cite valid figures for MEW, but it is an interesting and thought-provoking concept.

Nonpecuniary Income and Fringe Benefits

Related to MEW but different is nonpecuniary income. Some jobs are more pleasant than others, and the degree of pleasure or unpleasantness provided by any given job varies. Thus there is often an element of nonpecuniary (or psychic) income involved. Some people are willing to accept a lower money income for the prestige attached to a job. Other people may prefer to live in sunny Florida or California and attach some return to being able to do so. If a person wants to live in the crisp cool air of Colorado and be within a few miles of the fine skiing slopes, he or she no doubt will have to sacrifice some money income.

Statistics on money income usually exclude fringe benefits, even though their monetary value can be calculated in many cases. Such things as free, or reduced cost, health insurance, sick leave, paid vacation, and retirement benefits often vary from job to job. Employers view these costs as legitimate costs of obtaining labor, and employees should also include them in their total income.

Consumer Spending

Generally, we maximize our satisfaction by spending our income on a variety of goods and services. This is consumption, and expenditures on consumer items are consumption expenditures. When you buy food, clothing, an automobile, or household furniture, when you take a vacation trip, or when you buy thousands of other so-called *end products* (also called *final goods and services*), you are making consumer expenditures.

We must differentiate between consumer expenditures and other expenditures, which consist of investment expenditures and government expenditures made on our behalf with our tax dollars by the various levels of government. Expenditures, therefore, can be broken down into (1) consumption expenditures, already discussed; (2) investment expenditures; and (3) government expenditures.

Investment Expenditures or Wealth Accumulation

Most actual investment expenditures are made by businesses. But you might be financing them. If you save part of your income (i.e., do not spend it on consumption), you may make it available to business for investment expenditure.

If you put your savings into a bank, the bank will lend these savings to a business that will spend it by making an investment.

When you pay your insurance premiums, the insurance company will lend the money to a business that will spend it on investments. However, it is not until a business builds a new plant, or buys machinery or inventory, that it is actually making the investment. Investment expenditures, then, may be defined as expenditures made on goods that will be used to produce other goods—for example, a new factory. Such an expenditure may in turn yield an interest (or investment) return.

Individuals, as opposed to businesses, make investments when they purchase homes. A new house, while it will not produce other goods, will produce services, housing for the owner; thus it must be considered an investment expenditure.

Government Expenditures

The federal government spends billions of dollars on our behalf. State and local governments spend billions more. They provide us primarily with services: law and order, education, national defense, mail services, roads, and so on. But they too are part of overall expenditures, which benefit us and which we pay for with our taxes. Our taxes then are also spending on the services of governments.

Money in the Scheme of Things

Money is the name of the game. You earn your income in the form of money; you make your consumption and investment expenditures (wealth- or asset-accumulating expenditures); and you pay your taxes in the form of money Money, therefore, is a medium of exchange. Money is used in virtually all transactions because it is much more convenient than barter; hence, it is also a standard of value. It is also a store of value. You can convert your work effort into money, store (save) it, and later use the money for personal consumption expenditures.

THE CURRENT ECONOMIC ENVIRONMENT

The trinity of groups that make up most of the U.S. economy consists of governments, businesses, and consumer-producers.[1]

1. There are others: for example, there are churches, various nonprofit institutions, farmers, self-employed professionals, and labor unions. However, farmers and self-employed professionals are really businesses, and the members of labor unions are also part of the consumer-producers. Churches and certain nonprofit organizations, while important, account for only a small part of the total output of goods and services.

Government

At one time it was believed that the government's main role was that of umpire. It was to see that the law was carried out, and it enforced contracts between individuals. In addition, it provided for the national defense. To carry out its function, the government levied taxes and made certain expenditures.

Today the role of the government has been expanded to include regulation of businesses and even individuals. More restrictions are imposed than formerly to protect the public and the environment. The philosophy is that the government is to do those things that citizens cannot do for themselves, or cannot do as well. The government has more of a welfare function now. While how large a role the government should play is still a controversial question, there is little doubt that most agree it must have a larger role than it did forty or fifty years ago. As the government's role has expanded so has its size, and the dollars in taxes it needs. While the government itself produces little in the way of goods, it is inexorably wrapped up in the productive process via taxes and regulations. In the process it produces a service.

Businesses

Most of the goods and services produced in the United States today are produced by the business sector. There are hundreds of thousands of business firms, some large like General Electric, some small like many one- or two-owner corner grocery stores. Business firms employ the majority of the labor force and are the means through which most of the income of the American people is earned. Business entities are probably the most important single factor in the economic environment.

Consumers-Producers

As noted above, everyone is a consumer. However, every consumer who is in the labor force is also a producer. Many consumers thus serve in a dual capacity in our economy; they buy goods and services and sell their labor services. Consumers are demanders of output and suppliers of labor to produce it. To enjoy the good life you have to earn an income. In the short run you have to operate within a given economic environment. But as a group (for example, through unions or consumers groups) you can also affect, to some extent, the economic environment.

The economic environment, then, consists of an interrelationship between the governments, businesses, and consumer-producers. This is illustrated in Figure 1–1, that shows consumer-producers providing labor services to business firms in exchange for money incomes. These money incomes are then used to make

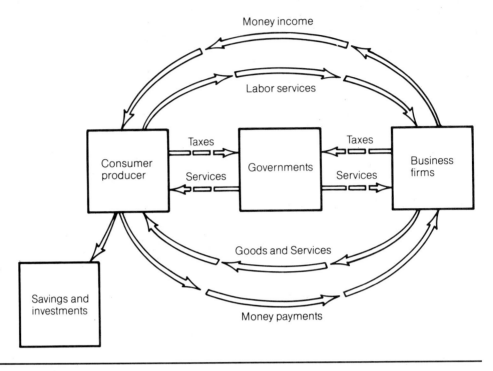

Figure 1-1   The economic environment

money payments to business firms in exchange for goods and services, which are purchased. These are consumption expenditures. The diagram shows the circular flow of money (represented by the outside arrows), which finances the flow of real goods and services depicted by the arrows on the inside. The diagram also shows the payments of taxes by businesses and consumer-producers (individuals) to governments in return for the services supplied by various levels of government. Also shown is a withdrawal in the form of savings from this income stream. These savings will flow back into the system when one buys bonds or stock or deposits money in a savings account. In doing this, one is making an investment expenditure or accumulating wealth in the form of earnings assets. Money, then, is the oil in the system, which is necessary for the interrelationships and permits the production and exchange of real goods and services.

Inflation

Inflation is also part of the economic environment, and it can affect your well-being or your standard of living because it can affect how much your income can purchase. Inflation may be defined as a continuous increase in the overall price level; many prices must be considered. During periods of inflation the dollar purchases less and less; its value declines. Inflation can be defined in two ways: a rise in the overall price level, or a decline in the value of the dollar. The amount of the decline in value of the dollar is equal to the reciprocal of the rate of inflation.

Deflation, or an appreciation in the value of the dollar, is the opposite— a continuous decrease in the overall price level. But deflation happens less frequently than inflation; in recent years it has not occurred. During periods of inflation, those having fixed incomes find themselves with less and less buying power while those whose incomes rise more rapidly than prices are better off. Inflation is inequitable since it harms some and benefits others.

Adjusting money income to take into account the effects of inflation provides what is known as real income. If prices are rising by 5 percent per year, an individual must obtain a 5 percent annual increase in income just to stay even. If the person's income is fixed, he or she is about 5 percent worse off every year in the above situation. This has happened to some people but others have had wage and salary increases that have more than offset inflation. A person earning $40,000 in 1975 and still earning that today would have had a real income reduction equivalent to $21,750 by the end of July 1983.

In 1975 average family money income in the United States was about $15,546; by midyear 1983 this had grown to about $28,100. Most of this was due to inflation. In real terms, average family income had increased only to about $15,000.

Even persons whose incomes keep pace with inflation become worse off as time passes because they move into a higher marginal tax bracket. For example, a person earning $40,000 in 1975 whose income had just kept pace with inflation would be earning $73,560 in 1983. Table 1–1 summarizes this by showing money income, real income, taxes, after-tax money income, after-tax real income, and economic deterioration for such a hypothetical person. It also shows the same things for a person whose income has remained constant over these years. The person whose income kept up with inflation earned $73,560 (up from $40,000 in 1975), but after-tax real income declined by $4,253 because of higher taxes. The person whose income remained at $40,000 over the period suffered a loss in real income due to inflation of $15,391 ($33,736–$18,345). Finally, the table illustrates that to have kept up with both inflation and higher taxes, the hypothetical person would have needed an income of $87,527.

In addition to changing people's incomes in real terms, inflation erodes savings held in the form of fixed assets. The dollars held in bank accounts, bonds, and insurance policies will buy less and less as prices rise. Even the interest earned by these investments must be adjusted for inflation. For example, if savings accounts can earn 8 percent interest and prices rise (inflation) at a rate of 6 percent per year, the real interest rate is only 2 percent per year. In some years, the rate of inflation has been higher than the money interest rate, making the real return on fixed investment negative.

Inflation also changes the debtor-creditor relationship. For example, if an individual assumes a $50,000 mortgage in 1984 at the 1984 price level, and if

Table 1—1   How inflation and taxes affect income

	1975 A,B,&C	1984 A	1984 B	1984 C
Money Income	$40,000	$73,560	$40,000	$87,527
Real Income	40,000	40,000	21,750	47,595
Taxes	6,264	19,340	6,264	25,486
After Tax Money Income	33,736	54,220	33,736	62,041
After Tax Real Income	33,736	29,483	18,345	33,736
Real Loss in After-Tax Income	—	4,253	15,391	—

Taxes were calculated using 1984 rates for both years, and with the assumption that the individuals were married and filed a joint return, had 4 dependents, and did not itemize deductions.

Source: Calculated by author from official U.S. Government statistics.

prices then double, the mortgage is paid off in dollars of only one-half the purchasing power of the dollars originally borrowed. The debtor (borrower) benefits from this situation, while the creditor's position is worsened.

Finally, inflation, if it is rapid and continues long enough, may produce undesirable psychological and political effects. People may expect inflation to continue and spend energy attempting to hedge against it rather than in productive activities. If enough people are aroused, it may even affect their vote, the results of which may or may not be beneficial.

Factors Contributing to Inflation

There are many causes of inflation. One is a situation where there are too few goods and a great demand for those goods that forces prices up. This is commonly called *demand-pull* inflation. This situation occurred immediately following World War II. During the 1950s and 1960s this factor disappeared but in the 1970s shortages (especially in energy, food, and commodities) again drove up prices.

A second cause is the easy availability of credit, resulting in an oversupply of money. If there is a large increase in the quantity of money without a concomitant increase in production, prices are bid up.

Third, there could be a rise in the costs of production to where manufacturers or producers of goods see their profits threatened, and they might raise the price of their product. This is called *cost-push* inflation.

Fourth, inflation may be caused by excessive government expenditures, especially if they are financed via a deficit in the national budget. This government demand adds to aggregate demand and pulls prices up.

Government regulations are a fifth cause. Not only do the regulations cost the government money to enforce but they also impose additional costs on business in meeting the regulatory requirements.

Institutional factors are a sixth cause. By this we mean that some businesses and unions have such market power that they can often impose wage and price increases not warranted by market considerations.

Recently some economists have cited a new cause—that both taxes and inflation discriminate against the saver and investor in favor of consumption. This causes savings and hence investment capital to dry up, which in turn forces the economy to grow more slowly. This, after a lag, causes the supply of goods and services to be less than otherwise.

An eighth cause concerns foreign trade and the international value of the dollar. If the international value of the dollar declines, imports cost more, and this alone adds to inflation. That imports cost more makes it easier for domestic suppliers of like goods to raise their prices, causing a secondary inflationary jolt from this source. Finally, widespread expectations that inflation will continue may contribute to its continuation as people react in ways calculated to protect themselves or to minimize the harm they will suffer. "Buy now before the prices rise" represents this attitude.

The above causes of inflation suggest what we as a nation might do to control or halt inflation. If we have expanded the money supply and credit excessively, this can be halted. If the government taxes and spends too much, this can be stopped. If business and labor contribute to inflation, greater restraint by these groups can lessen upward price movements. If taxes discriminate against savers, changes can be made in the tax laws to remedy this. If government regulations have now gone too far, this can be changed. If the dollar is too weak internationally, it can be strengthened by importing less. We as individuals can do little, but as a group we can do a great deal.

Consumer Price Index; Measuring Inflation

The method used to measure the degree to which prices have risen is the statistical device known as *index numbers*. The Department of Labor calculates and publishes what it calls the *consumer price index*, a barometer of inflation. If a person's income does not keep up with the rise in this index, the individual is falling behind in what his or her income will purchase. This consumer price index is commonly called the *cost of living index*, an index issued monthly by the United States Department of Labor's Bureau of Labor Statistics, the full title being "Consumer Price Index for All Urban Consumers." To construct this index, the prices of some four hundred goods and services are gathered in 85 cities. The index, according to the Bureau of Labor Statistics, covers

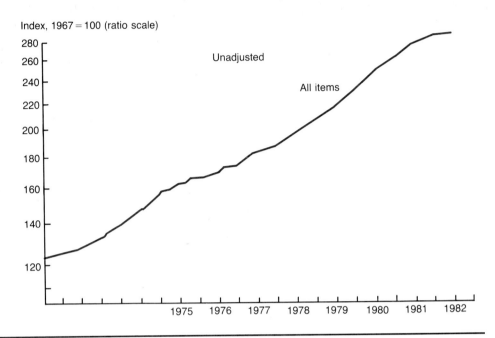

Figure 1-2   **Consumer prices.** (*Source*: Economic Indicators, Oct. 1982, Council of Economic Advisers, U.S. Department of Commerce, p. 23.)

prices of everything people buy for living—food, clothing, automobiles, homes, house furnishings, household supplies, fuel, drugs, and recreational goods; fees to doctors, lawyers, beauty shops; rent, repairs costs, transportation fares, public utility rates; etc. It deals with prices actually charged to consumers, including sales and excise taxes. It also includes real estate taxes on owned homes, but does not include income or social security taxes.[2]

The prices are weighted and averaged. The index is now figured on a base period of 1967 as being equal to 100. If the base period is 100 and the index is now (late 1983) 302.4, the cost of living has risen 202.4 percent since the base period. The same number of dollars now will purchase 66.9 percent less than during the base period. This calculation measures the degree of inflation and the reduction in the purchasing power of the dollar.[3]

2. U.S. Department of Labor, Bureau of Labor Statistics, *Supplement to Economic Indicators* (Rev. January 1967), Washington: U.S. Government Printing Office, 1967, p. 94.
    3. When prices rise, the value of the dollar falls but not by the same amount. The value of the dollar falls reciprocally. For example, if prices rise by 100 percent, say from an index of 100 to 200, obviously the value of money cannot fall 100 percent to zero. In this case the value of money fell by 50 percent. In order to calculate how much the value of money has declined with a given increase in prices, we use the following formula:

$$\frac{\textit{Base year prices}}{\textit{Current year prices}} = \frac{\textit{Value of money in current year}}{\textit{Value of money in base year}}$$

Figure 1–2 shows how prices have risen over the past few years' base period. The cost of living can be classified into food items, nonfood items, and services such as medical services; a composite can be made up of all these items.

SOCIETY AND NATIONAL INCOME

We have examined some of the factors that will influence individual personal income. If we put all of the millions of individuals' incomes together, we have the nation's income. Some knowledge of the nation's income is important in studying personal finance because it will teach you about the overall economy and how it is behaving. You will need to have an understanding of two terms that economists and businesspersons use in analyzing what is happening to the entire economy. They are: *national income* and *gross national product*.

National income is the sum total of all the *income* of all the people in the United States for a given accounting period. It tells how well off we are as a group; individual income is the individual's share of national income. Then there is gross national product. It is somewhat larger than national income because the government takes something off the top (excise taxes) and because machinery, plant, and equipment used by industry wear out and must be replaced. *Gross national product* (usually referred to simply as GNP) is the market value of all final goods and services produced in the United States per year. It is the dollar sum of all Tootsie Rolls, all Ford cars, all tomatoes, and thousands of other products. To this figure must be added the cost of the services of doctors, lawyers, government workers, ministers, and all others who do not make goods but render services.

In 1984, GNP amounted to more than $3.3 trillion. Figure 1–3 illustrates the growth in GNP since 1974. National income is somewhat smaller than GNP (about $700 billion smaller in 1983) because national income does not include the annual replacement of worn-out machinery or certain other items such as the federal excise taxes. National income has been defined as the return (or income) to all of the factors of production. The factors of production produce output and are paid an income to do so. There are four factors of production:

1. Land
2. Labor
3. Capital
4. Ownership or risk assumption

---

or, in the illustration,

$$\frac{100}{302.4} = \frac{X}{100} \text{ or } 302.4X = 10{,}000X = 33.1$$

Then $100 - 33.1$ gives us 66.9, which is the decline in the value of money.

Billions of dollars (ratio scale)

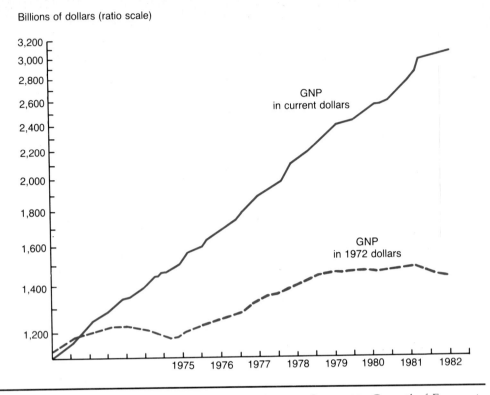

Figure 1–3   Gross national product. (*Source:* Economic Indicators, Oct. 1982, Council of Economic Advisers, U.S. Department of Commerce, p. 1.)

Each of these four factors gets a return, and this return respectively is

1.   Rent to the owners of land
2.   Wages and salaries to labor
3.   Interest to lenders of capital
4.   Profit to owners who assume the risk of business failure

These four types of income are the only kind anyone can earn. Labor and wages and salaries are broadly defined. Salaries include the incomes made by the managers and executives of all business firms. Labor includes all human effort. The phrase "wages and salaries," then, includes the salary of the president of General Motors as well as that of the president of the United States. They are specialized and highly skilled workers. Figure 1–4, along with Table 1–2, illustrates the distribution of the four types of income earned by the American people in 1983.

Note that the total return of the four factors of production in Table 1–2 comes to only $2,375.3 billion, whereas national income amounted to $2,504.5

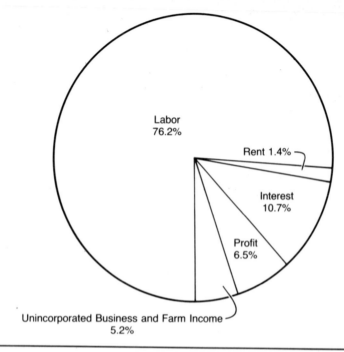

Labor
76.2%

Rent 1.4%

Interest
10.7%

Profit
6.5%

Unincorporated Business and Farm Income
5.2%

Figure 1—4   Distribution of types of income earned by Americans, 1982.

billion in 1983. How do we explain the difference? A fifth category includes a mixture of all four of the above-mentioned types of income: farm income and the income of the self-employed. Their income cannot be separated into wages and salaries, rent, profit, and the like, and is lumped together. This income was $129.2 billion in 1983, which, if added to the $2,375.3 billion in Table 1—2, gives us $2,504.5 billion.

Table 1—2   Distribution of U.S. income, 1982

	Dollars in billions	Percent
Wages and Salaries	$1,908.5	76.2
Rent	35.3	1.4
Interest	266.9	10.7
Profit	164.6	6.5
Unincorporated Business and Farm Income	129.2	5.2
TOTAL	$2,504.5	100.0

WHAT IS TO COME

The material in this book is organized into five parts. The sequence in which they appear was chosen after a great deal of planning, experimentation, and pedagogical research. Since the book was first published 20 years ago, hundreds of students, college professors, and others have given us feedback, which has proven invaluable in reorganizing the material in this major revision. The unit and chapter titles indicate their content, and their sequence is designed to give the instructor greater flexibility in teaching the course.

The five units are:

One	Introduction to Financial Planning
Two	Managing Your Income
Three	Managing Your Insurance Program
Four	Managing Your Investments
Five	Retirement and Estate Planning

Part One, "Introduction to Financial Planning," consists of three chapters which are designed to set the tone of things to come.

This first chapter will help you plan your financial affairs more intelligently. The following chapters will elaborate on how to become a better money manager. The first step toward intelligent personal financial management is to get a clear idea of where you are and where you want to go. The next chapter discusses record-keeping and financial and career planning, two techniques that will help greatly in achieving these goals. Budgeting, a powerful planning tool, is introduced in chapter three.

Part Two, "Managing Your Income," is intended to increase the mileage you get out of each dollar spent. It starts out with "Banking Services" (chapter four) and "Using Consumer Credit" (chapter five). These two important areas affect us all since we all need checking accounts and most of us use certain other services that banks provide. Chapter four introduces you to the world of banks and their services.

When you buy "big ticket" items (cars, household furniture, and the like), you will probably borrow money (use credit), and when doing so, you should shop around as not all lenders will give you the same deal. Chapter five deals with "Using Consumer Credit" and with "Shopping for Money."

Chapter six, "Consumer Spending" is designed to help you become a wiser shopper. It discusses not only how to avoid certain pitfalls by sophisticated shopping and how to get the most for your consumer dollar, but also how to obtain redress of grievances if you have been victimized in the marketplace. Chapter seven reviews the various laws designed to protect the consumer.

We are all affected by taxes. Another way of increasing your assets (and stretching your income) is by minimizing your taxes, and in chapter eight material on that subject is developed. A home is the largest single expenditure (investment) for many families. Homeownership is a good investment. Increasing your assets via homeownership is also a means whereby you may hedge inflation. However, some people rent, so material is developed on housing in the broad sense, covering both renting and owning, in chapter nine.

Part Three, "Managing Your Insurance Program," introduces all of the kinds of insurance protection you will need. Chapter ten explains how the various risks we face may be managed and how insurance works in general. Chapter eleven deals with life insurance, which in a sense protects your income stream for your beneficiaries. We provide guidelines and step-by-step suggestions to help you determine your insurance needs in terms of both the amount and the type. It is here that we explore insurance as a savings vehicle and as a means of protecting the income stream.

Then in chapter twelve, health insurance, the modern way of financing medical needs, is introduced. Since you no doubt drive a car, you will need to know about protection for yourself and your assets in the event of an accident. You will also need to protect your home and personal belongings from all kinds of hazards. Consequently, a chapter on property and liability insurance is included as the final chapter in part three.

Part Four, "Managing Your Investments," is concerned with investments of all kinds. Chapter fourteen explores investing indirectly through a thrift institution. The first savings you accumulate should be put into deposits in thrift institutions. In recent years a wide variety of new types of deposits have been developed and chapter fourteen explores them all. There are also a number of different kinds of thrift institutions. They are all examined and their similarities and differences are explained. When investing indirectly, you deposit your money in these thrift (also called depository) institutions, and they invest your funds for you. You should certainly keep a number of emergency or nest-egg dollars in these institutions in those kinds of deposits which are highly liquid and easily accessible. Others could be kept in less liquid but higher yielding accounts in the thrifts.

Greater diversification can and should be achieved by investing some funds directly. Therefore the next chapter (chapter fifteen) discusses the fundamentals of direct security investments. Then in chapter sixteen the array of available securities will be presented. For most people, investments should be made in more than one security; a diversified portfolio of both stocks and bonds is desirable. To present a wide range of possibilities we will examine the securities markets and the brokers and dealers that operate them and mutual funds. Chapter eighteen begins with a discussion of investment companies (also called mutual funds), explores owning rental property, and ends with some material on other unusual (or exotic) investments.

Part Five, "Retirement and Estate Planning," has two chapters—covering social security, annuities, and pension funds; and wills, gifts, and trusts. Chapter nineteen begins with a discussion of social security, which is the foundation or base everyone has and upon which you should build your own retirement program. This can often be done in a way that simultaneously reduces your personal income taxes, and chapter nineteen will show you how. The final chapter (chapter twenty) introduces the complex area of wills, gifts, and trusts—the entire area of estate planning. Wills are not just for the rich; they are for everyone. The chapter also deals with gift and estate taxes and how to minimize them. This chapter, in short, deals with keeping what you have earned.

Your personal finance problems and needs will change as the years pass (you may need more or less insurance as you grow older). Because personal financial needs vary throughout the life cycle, personal financial planning is an ongoing task.

You may find it useful to retain the text as a handy reference after the semester is over. While the data and statistics presented will change, the principles and concepts of personal financial management are likely to endure.

QUESTIONS FOR REVIEW

1. What are the goals of personal finance? How can personal finance help you to achieve these goals?
2. How is the degree of satisfaction related to the level of income?
3. What is meant by the measure of economic welfare?
4. What is nonpecuniary income?
5. How do consumption expenditures differ from investment expenditures?
6. What is meant by the term *consumer-producer*?
7. What is inflation? How would you expect inflation to affect those on fixed incomes?
8. What does it mean to state that the cost of living index has gone from 100 to 210?
9. How is the cost of living index a barometer of inflation?
10. Are an increase in prices and a decline in the value of money the same thing?
11. How do you calculate how much the value of money has declined from a given increase in prices?
12. What are some of the factors contributing to inflation?
13. How is inflation measured?
14. What is the difference between national income and GNP?
15. What are the four different sources of income?

CASES

1. Debra Patrick has a salary of $26,000, which is $2,000 more than what she earned last year. However, inflation during that same period was 6

percent. What was Debra's increase in real income? What is her increase in real after-tax income?

2. Connie Brashear has $25,000 of investments in the form of bank accounts, bonds, and insurance policies. Her total investment income last year amounted to $2,325; what is her overall yield in both nominal and real terms? Also calculate it after taxes.

3. Linda Jann Lewis is self-employed. She has her own secretarial and accounting business. Last year she had a net income after all expenses of $23,425. What portion of that represents salary and what portion consists of interest and profit?

4. Claire Baldwin and her husband Bob both recently graduated from a veterinary school and started their own animal hospital. They rent the building but spent $3,000 on medicine and supplies, $5,000 on special equipment, and $1,500 on furniture. What portion of the $9,500 is an investment expenditure, and what part is consumption? Did they contribute to wealth accumulation?

SUGGESTED READINGS

Batten, Dallas S. "Inflation: The Cost Push Myth," *Federal Reserve Bank of St. Louis Review,* June, 1981.

Brown, James, and Wolf, Harold A. *Economics Principles and Practices.* Columbus, Ohio: Charles E. Merrill Publishing, 1979.

Campbell, Claudia R., and Lovati, Jean M. "Inflation and Personal Savings," *Federal Reserve Bank of St. Louis Review,* August, 1979.

Credit Guide, Federal Reserve Bank of Chicago, April, 1982.

Credit Overview, Standard and Poor's, 1982.

Economic Indicators. Washington, D.C.: Council of Economic Advisers for the Joint Economic Committee. A monthly publication.

Economic Outlook U.S.A. Ann Arbor, Mich.: University of Michigan Survey Research Center. Quarterly publication.

Feldstein, Martin. "Inflation and the American Economy," *The Public Interest.* Spring, 1982.

National Consumer Finance Association. *Finance Facts Yearbook.* Washington, D.C. An annual publication.

People and Productivity, A Challenge to Corporate America. A study of the New York Stock Exchange, 1982.

Resler, David H. "The Formation of Inflation Expectation," *Federal Reserve Bank of St. Louis Review,* April, 1980.

Roos, Lawrence K. "Is It Time to Give Up the Fight Against Inflation?" *Federal Reserve Bank of St. Louis Review,* October, 1982.

Samuelson, Paul A. *Economics: An Introductory Analysis,* 11th ed. New York: McGraw-Hill, 1980.

U.S. Census, Income of Families and Individuals in the U.S. in Current Population Reports, Consumer Income. Series P-60. Get latest series of this quarterly publication.

CHAPTER TWO

RECORD-KEEPING AND FINANCIAL AND CAREER PLANNING

The Tools of Financial Planning
The Individual and His or Her Income
Career Planning

With today's inflation one must run as fast as one can just to stay in the same place. In order to do this a person must keep adequate financial records and understand the basic facts involving financial statements.

Most people have to live within their incomes. While this is not completely true in any one year (for example, a person may borrow to finance a large item such as a car), it is true for most people most of the time. A person who consumes more than his or her income in one year will probably be forced to consume less while repaying during the next year what was borrowed. Over a lifetime if one consumes more than one's income one can only get out from under debts through court action—that is, through bankruptcy.

While persons have command over their money income, they have only two main alternatives as to what to do with it: consume it or save it. Most people divide their income, and while they consume most of it, they save some. Once they have committed a part of their income to consumption, they must make further decisions regarding what type of items to buy. Once a person has decided to save, say, 20 percent of his or her income, a second decison regarding where and how to invest it must be made. In this consuming and investing process, a person must constantly choose between alternatives. A limited income can never stretch over all the alternatives, so priorities must be assigned and choices made. This is more effectively carried out if you engage in financial planning.

THE TOOLS OF FINANCIAL PLANNING

Business firms as well as the various levels of government keep financial records and develop financial statements to aid them in their planning, and you can too. Government and many businesses have full-time planning and budgeting staffs, but at the personal level, only a few minutes per day are needed for financial planning once a system is set up. After making a few suggestions regarding record keeping we shall examine the two financial statements that are useful: the balance sheet and the income statement.

Record-Keeping

Record-keeping is necessary for tax purposes as well as for planning your financial affairs. All canceled checks should be retained for a time. Canceled checks and receipts for items that are tax deductible should be filed separately so that they will be easily accessible at tax time. After your taxes have been paid, keep these receipts and checks as well as other checks for large amounts for four years, because that is the time the statute of limitations runs out. Less important checks can be destroyed once a year. If items are charged on a credit card, and one check pays for many purchases, separate the charge receipts and treat them just like the checks. Learn which items are tax deductible, and keep records of these items to the penny. Many people, fearful of the Internal Revenue Service, have consistently overpaid their taxes. If you keep adequate records, you may take all of your legal deductions without fear.

Keeping records, paying bills, and reconciling the monthly bank statement is something in which both members of a married couple should be involved. The same is true regarding all major financial decisions. Then in the event one of the partners is left alone in the future, he or she will not be inexperienced in these matters. One way this could be done is for the husband to keep the books one month and the wife the next.

You should keep a file of manila folders. Classify the major items such as taxes, insurance, investments, household expenditures, and the like. A small filing cabinet where all the papers could be kept in one place is useful.

The Personal Balance Sheet

A balance sheet is a financial statement that depicts your financial position at a particular moment in time. It is like a photograph. Its three main components are assets, liabilities, and the difference between the two, called net worth.

Assets

The terms *wealth* and *assets* mean the same thing; anything of value is wealth and can also be looked upon as an asset. Moreover, something of value to you may not be of value to somebody else and therefore is not wealth to that person. Assets, then, are the good things you own. Assets can be broken down into earning and nonearning assets.

1. Earning assets are those that yield a return. Stocks, bonds, savings accounts, and real estate that you can rent are earning assets in that they yield a return in the form of interest, dividends, or rental income.
2. Nonearning assets consist of personal automobiles, clothing, jewelry, household furniture, and the like. They yield no money return, but they are valuable and are wealth or assets.

Assets can also be classified as financial and nonfinancial.

1. Financial assets include such things as stocks, bonds, bank accounts, and cash or currency.
2. Nonfinancial assets include clothes, real estate, automobiles, and so on.

There is some overlap between these classifications. For example, all financial assets except checking accounts and idle currency are also earning assets. Most nonearning assets are also nonfinancial assets, but there are exceptions. For example, a cattle ranch or a wheat farm is an earning asset, but it is not a financial asset. However, the piece of paper proving ownership of the ranch or farm can be considered a financial asset. The largest single asset for most families is their home, and the largest single liability is the mortgage on it.

When you construct your personal balance sheet, list your assets on the left and attach a dollar value to them that reflects their fair market value. You should list and value all of your assets even though you may not have fully paid for some of them; the amount that you still owe will be listed later under your liabilities.

Liabilities

Liabilities are the debts you owe others. The amount you still owe on your car, the sum you have run up on your gasoline credit card and other charge accounts are examples. The unpaid balance (mortgage) on your family home is another example. Generally speaking, you will have to pay interest on the debts you owe.

Net worth

Net worth is equal to total assets minus total liabilities. As such, it is the truest reflection of what the person is actually worth. If you were to sell all of your assets and pay off all of your debts, that is what would remain. Assets are nearly always greater than liabilities, but in those relatively rare cases where they are not, the person is, technically speaking, bankrupt. We will examine bankruptcy in the next chapter. Table 2–1 shows a balance sheet for a hypothetical person.

Table 2–1   Balance sheet

Assets	Example	Your personal entry	% return	Liabilities and net worth	Your personal entry and % cost
Cash					
Currency	$ 50	_____	0	Unpaid bills	
Checking account	500	_____	0	Bank credit card	$150 _____
Savings deposit	1,000	_____	9%	Other charge cards	75 _____
Investments				Repair bill on car	125 _____
Government bonds	1,200	_____	9%	Telephone bill outstanding	12 _____
Corporate bonds	1,000	_____	12%	Installment loan	800 _____
Corporate stock	1,500	_____	10%		
Mutual funds	1,200	_____	10%	Mortgage loan	
Cash value of life insurance	1,200	_____	8%	Owner-occupied	50,000 _____
				Other rental	35,000 _____
				Total liabilities	86,162 _____
Real estate		_____			
Owner-occupied	70,000	_____			
Rental property	50,000		12%		
Personal property					
Automobile	5,000	_____		Net worth	$52,688
Household furniture	4,000	_____			
Clothes	1,500	_____			
Jewelry	200	_____			
Other assets	500	_____			
Total assets	$138,850	_____			

The financial assets are the ones listed first, through life insurance. The earning assets have been given an estimated percentage return.

The Personal Income Statement

The income statement is another important financial tool useful in planning your personal financial affairs. The balance sheet depicts your financial condition at a given point in time; the income statement shows what has happened to your financial position over a period of time, say a year. It is a flow concept. It can be compared to a stream of water that is measured in terms of flow: so many gallons of water per minute. The income statement measures dollar income inflows and dollar expenditure outflows. In the case of business income statements, sales usually measure gross inflows, and the various expenses (labor costs, raw material costs, and so on) indicate the outflows. The difference between the two represents profits. Your personal income statement measures your salary and other income inflows and your cost of living outflows. The difference between the two is called *savings* and may be looked upon as your yearly surplus or something similar to business profits.

Income

The income statement has three main parts: income, expenditures, and savings. Your income includes not only wages and salaries but all investment income such as interest and dividends. It should also include gifts, inheritance, and any other cash inflow.

Outgo—expenditures

Expenditures consist of all the items on which you spend money. You should develop a number of major categories and keep track of them, but it is not necessary to account separately for every penny spent. There should be a category for food, clothing, transportation, and the like.

Savings

Finally, the income statement should have an item for savings. This item should be planned for; if you assume savings will emerge as a residual, you will often

Table 2–2   Income statement

	Annual	Monthly	Your personal income statement
Income			
Wages and salaries	$24,000	$2,000.00	_____
Interest	200	16.66	_____
Dividends	100	8.33	_____
Christmas bonus	500	41.67	_____
Other	—	—	_____
Total	$24,800	$2,066.66	_____
Expenditures			
Food	$ 5,600	$ 466.66	_____
Clothing	1,258	104.83	_____
Transportation	2,100	175.00	_____
Housing	5,200	433.33	_____
Medical care	1,300	108.33	_____
Recreation	1,000	83.33	_____
Other	1,400	166.66	_____
Taxes			
Social security	1,642	136.83	_____
Personal income tax	4,100	341.66	_____
Savings and investments	1,200	100.00	_____

Table 2-3   Yearly income flow

	Jan.	Feb.	March	April	May	June	July	Aug.	Sept.	Oct.	Nov.	Dec.*	Annual
After-tax wages or salary of breadwinner	$2,000	$2,000	$2,000	$2,000	$2,000	$2,000	$2,000	$2,000	$2,000	$2,000	$2,000	$2,500	$24,500
Dividend	$25			$25			$25			$25			$100
Interest income	$50			$50			$50			$50			$200
Other possible income													
Total	$2,075	$2,000	$2,000	$2,075	$2,000	$2,000	$2,075	$2,000	$2,000	$2,075	$2,000	$2,500	$24,800

*Includes Christmas bonus.

end up with nothing. To be sure, savings are not held in the form of idle cash but are invested, and they flow out of the income statement. Nevertheless, they are different from other outflows, which are mostly consumption items. Two simple annual and monthly income statements are shown as Tables 2–2 and 2–3. You should develop your income statement on either a monthly or an annual basis, and multiply or divide in order to obtain the second one.

THE INDIVIDUAL AND HIS OR HER INCOME

Your money income will in large part determine your standard of living. A few people inherit great wealth, but most of us do not. The amount that an individual earns is directly related to education, occupation, age, property ownership, where you live, ability, drive, family connections, and plain luck.

Income and Education

Statistics indicate that over a lifetime persons with more schooling tend to earn more money. In general, it may be said that the time, effort, and money invested in education increase the productivity of the individual and yield a return in the form of additional compensation. An alternative explanation, however, is that in acquiring an education a person invests a great deal in what has been called *human capital*. Just as ordinary capital (plant and equipment) yields a return called interest and profit because it is productive, so too does human capital. According to this theory, part of the high wages and salaries made by the highly educated is a return on human capital and is analogous to interest and profit.

Some experts have expressed concern that colleges are turning out too many graduates who expect elite occupations but who are really not prepared for them. There may not even be enough elite occupations to go around. Generally in such cases, it would be expected that many of these individuals would enter other less prestigious occupations. Some might become skilled craftspersons and work with their hands.

Income and Occupation

The income of individuals also varies greatly with occupations. However, there is also a high correlation between higher-income jobs and level of education. For example, professional and managerial workers have the highest incomes, and these people, generally speaking, are also college graduates. Private domestic household servants have the lowest income and are usually the most poorly educated. Many occupations require a college education or a lengthy training period for a person to be qualified for admittance; others do not. However, for any given level of education a number of different occupations are possible, and earnings within these occupations vary substantially. Many high school graduates can choose between more highly paid clerical and sales occupations and more poorly paid service and laborer occupations. Or if they are willing to spend a rather lengthy period as relatively low-paid apprentices, they may enter the ranks of the highly skilled, highly paid building trade craft occupations.

Income and Age

Generally speaking, the low-income groups are concentrated among the very young and the very old. The young have low incomes because they have not yet learned a skilled trade or worked their way up the ladder; the old are either retired or hold only part-time jobs. In 1981, for example, families whose head was in the forty-five to fifty-four-year-old bracket earned an average of $32,070, the highest average income of any age classification.

Most family heads reach their maximum earning capacity between the ages of thirty-five and fifty-four. The greatest percentage of those with incomes of $50,000 a year or over are the forty-five to fifty-four-year-olds. As an observer put it: "The trouble is you don't get into the really high income group until you're too old to carry your suitcase."

Income and Property Ownership

The Internal Revenue Service (IRS) classifies income into earned and so-called unearned. According to their definition, earned income consists solely of wages and salaries; it is a payment made in return for services rendered by individuals, or work. The so-called unearned income consists of income derived from property.

Although precise statistics are unavailable, economists have long known that there is a positive correlation between property ownership and income because most property yields a return. Indeed, nearly all of the truly high incomes in the United States today are derived from property. Real estate yields rent; stocks and bonds yield dividends or interest; oil wells yield royalties; and a theater yields income in the form of revenue from ticket sales.

Two ways of acquiring income-yielding property are inheritance, or saving current income and using it to acquire property. One who inherits property benefits from the savings of a previous generation. One who acquires property makes a sacrifice today by investing current savings (giving up consumption) in order to enjoy a higher income and higher consumption in the future.

While it is true that the more property you own, the more income you receive, it is also true that the more income you receive, the more you are able to save and the more property you are able to acquire to enhance your income in the future. Low-income groups find it difficult to save and acquire property to increase their future income. High-income groups are more likely to save and acquire property and to enjoy an even higher income in the future. However, even higher income groups do not find it painless to save and acquire assets. Real effort is usually involved; it means giving up current consumption, saving money, and buying assets. It is also true that property is even more unequally distributed than income, and this contributes further to inequality of income.

Regional Differences in Income

Horace Greeley's admonition, "Go West, young man, go West," is still valid insofar as earnings are concerned. Assuming that two persons equal in all respects (such as age and education) are working in the same occupation, but one works in the northern or western part of the United States and the other in the South, the person in the North or West will earn more. It should be noted, however, that incomes are growing more rapidly in the South than in the rest of the country.

Other Factors Affecting Your Income

Luck

Being in the right place at the right time often determines a difference in income between people of equal ability. One of the richest silver strikes in the state of Idaho resulted from a jackass taking the wrong trail and by pure chance knocking off a piece of outcropping that turned out to be high-grade silver ore.

Talent and brains

Some people are born with talent and "brains"; others are born with just talent and others just "brains"; some have ability, others little or none. A low IQ may force a person into jobs that are menial labor. Some with talent are able to rise to the top of the income stratum through pure natural ability. A few noted actors and actresses have been known to get by on less. On the other hand, unfortunately, a number of persons have talents that never see the light of day. Still others have physical handicaps that may decrease their earning power.

Hard work

There is little doubt that some people are more industrious than others. Some people will only do enough to get by; others will do more in the hope that their hard work and energy will win them a promotion to a better paying job. Related to hard work is incentive. Without an incentive to succeed, people will not work hard. One of the most powerful incentives to work hard is the monetary reward that hard work brings, but different people respond to it with different levels of work intensity.

Family connections

One way to get ahead might be to marry the boss's daughter—or son! Or if you are just out of law school and the member of a socially prominent family, you might get employment in a prestigious law firm. If so, your income is likely to be higher than if you are the son or daughter of an average family and hang out your own shingle.

Discrimination

Discrimination has historically been one of the chief causes of inequality of income. The two major groups that have been discriminated against in jobs were minority groups and women. This is now changing. There is very little overt discrimination based on race or sex today, but subtle forms still exist. The results of past discrimination may still affect income today because certain groups have not yet had time to develop the skills needed to compete effectively for better-paying jobs.

The differences in income between white families and those from minority groups, while lessening, are still substantial. In 1982, median family income in the United States was $22,388. The median income of white families was $23,517, but for nonwhite families the median was $14,598.[1]

CAREER PLANNING

Since income is determined in large part by ability, drive, education, and chosen occupation, the individual has some control over it, particularly if the individual is young. There are also nonmonetary rewards in many occupations. Therefore, the choice of a vocation is not usually made on the basis of money income alone.

Aptitude must be given some weight in choosing a career. Not many can choose a career as a concert pianist. This takes a rare talent, and only a few have it. The same may be said of certain other so-called glamorous vocations such as acting or professional athletics. While many people would like to make careers in these areas, and many even try to do so, only a few succeed. However, there is nothing wrong with testing talents in these areas at the amateur level (often in high school and college) to see whether enough talent exists to warrant professional training. Moreover, one does not need acting talent to go into radio and television. There is room for producers, directors, technicians, and various other behind-the-scene jobs. If one has a liking and an aptitude for this kind of work, it can be a rewarding career.

If you are a blue collar worker, it is a good idea to develop a skill. Carpenters, electricians, mechanics, plumbers, bricklayers, and electronic technicians are not only in greater demand, but also their earnings are higher than those of the nonskilled or semiskilled worker. In some cases, these blue collar workers' earnings rival those of college graduates.

College students have many options open, and they often make commitments when selecting a major. The student can choose to be prepared for a career in engineering, law, medicine, accounting, and a wide variety of other professions.

1. U.S. Department of Commerce, Bureau of the Census, Series P-60, No. 134, March 1982, p. 9.

In the professions particular care should be given to aptitude. Even a bright student should not go into engineering if an aptitude for mathematics and technology is lacking. Various aptitude tests can determine the likelihood of success in a number of different professions such as law, medicine, and accounting. Information on these tests can be obtained at the counseling and guidance centers that most colleges and universities maintain.

Before finally choosing a career (and an employer), college students should also touch base with their college placement center. These centers are constantly receiving information about various careers as well as various companies. In many cases, the placement centers work with the counseling and guidance centers in career counseling.

Choosing a Marketable Major

In the old days many thought that college was to provide a liberal education. After that you carved out your career on an equal footing with all others. There were, of course, exceptions; some students studied the professions—law, medicine, engineering, accounting, and the like. In recent years, more students have selected their college major with an eye on the employment and income potential it would provide. For this reason, in recent years, majors in business, engineering, computer sciences, and certain other fields have soared. Enrollment in liberal arts has declined. While one should not select a major solely on its marketability, this is a competitive world, and there is nothing wrong with preparing yourself to earn a good income while in college. To be sure, you should also take some electives in other fields to broaden your horizons.

Recently, one of the most popular majors has been accounting, because it is one of the most sought-after business specialties, especially tax accounting. The facts are that the tax laws and other governmental regulatory provisions have become the "full employment act" for accountants.

It's a technical world. Engineering enrollment, too, has been rising because of the greater employment opportunities in that field. Because of the economic realities of today, business and engineering majors command a higher starting salary than do liberal arts majors.

While law school enrollments have soared over the past decade, there seems to be a surplus of lawyers. If you get in with the right law firm, you will do well.

People getting a degree in one of the health sciences—medicine, dentistry, pharmacy, and nursing—have also done well in recent years. However, there is now a surplus of dentists in some areas of the country, and it is predicted by government experts that there will be a surplus of doctors by the end of the 1980s, a surplus likely to be limited to the urban centers in the more desirable parts of the country.

Nursing has always been a relatively low-paying profession relative to the skills and training a nurse must have. There are institutional reasons for low salaries in nursing, but because of the nursing shortage this is now changing. If you are a man and have the inclination and personality, you might want to consider becoming a male nurse, one of the fastest growing professions, but with a small supply.

In medicine, law, and dentistry, of course, advanced professional schooling is required. In the other fields described above, advanced (graduate) training is not required, but often is helpful.

The master of business administration (M.B.A.) has been the magic degree over the past decade, but there are now signs that supply is beginning to catch up with demand. One of the best combinations in recent years has been an undergraduate engineering degree and an M.B.A. Whether this will hold true in the future no one knows, but it is today still a useful combination.

All of the above does not mean that if you are a liberal arts major, you should rush out and switch. There is still room for the liberal arts major. (If you are a business or engineering major, take all the liberal arts electives you can; in the long run they are likely to serve you as well as your technical specialties.) If you are a liberal arts major, take some business and science electives. They will make you more marketable, and also will permit you to advance more rapidly in the business world. A knowledge of accounting, finance, statistics, mathematics, and computers will provide you with invaluable tools in this technical world.

To be a productive member of society, you must have the capacity to sell a skill in the marketplace, that is, to produce goods or services that someone wants. The decade of the 1980s is likely to be different than were the 1970s. No one knows just what the differences will be but it appears that there will be more competition. The view that society owes everyone a job seems to be eroding, and the view now emerging places greater reliance on the individual to develop a marketable skill.

Career Opportunities; Sources of Information

Students should become familiar with a number of publications on career opportunities. First, there is *The Occupational Outlook for College Graduates*, compiled by the U.S. Department of Labor and published by the U.S. Government Printing Office, Washington, D.C. This publication surveys the general outlook of the job market for college graduates and discusses various professions such as accounting, engineering, and actuarial sciences. It describes each of these professions with respect to the nature of the work, the training required, salaries and working conditions, and the employment outlook.

The second publication is the *College Placement Annual*. This is a yearly publication of the College Placement Council, Incorporated (P.O. Box 18017, Bethlehem, Pennsylvania), the official placement organization serving various college placement centers throughout the United States and Canada. The publication gives general information for college graduates, and it provides an alphabetical list of all the major private employers in the United States as well as all government agencies. It also contains an employment index in which all employers are listed by the occupations they need and the region they serve.

The Occupational Thesaurus is a two-volume work that lists various areas of employment for which college majors would be qualified. It describes the various industries that have a need for people with specific job skills. This publication can be obtained from Everett A. Teal of Lehigh University (Bethlehem, Pennsylvania), or, like the others noted above, it is likely available at your college placement center or library.

The student should become familiar with *The Encyclopedia of Careers and Vocational Guidance*, a two-volume work published by J. G. Ferguson Co. of Chicago, Illinois (distributed by Doubleday and Company). It provides general information about how to find a job, interviewing, and vocational testing. This publication covers all possible jobs and professions, not only those requiring college training. It has a section on "the future world of work," which discusses current job trends and makes some projections into the future. It classifies the various career fields from advertising to truck transportation.

Everybody's Business, An Almanac: The Irreverent Guide to Corporate America by Harper and Row is another valuable book. It analyzes several hundred corporations from A&P to Zenith. It classifies them by industries and then discusses what they do, the history of the company, what they own, their reputations, who runs each company, their stock performance, and their major employment centers.

If you are interested in a career with the federal government you should examine *Federal Career Directory; A Guide for College Students*. It is published by the U.S. Civil Service Commission, Washington, D.C. This publication lists various federal jobs and describes what each job entails and indicates to whom to write for more information. In a section entitled "Job Briefs by College Major," the book lists various jobs for which each college major could qualify, including many jobs that any major could fill.

Writing a Resumé

At most colleges the placement center will sponsor various employers who visit the campus to recruit degree candidates. During your senior year you should arrange for interviews with employers from the career fields you have chosen. This is also the time to write your resume. The resume is to introduce yourself and your qualifications to prospective employers; it is a summary of your worthwhile accomplishments to date. While there are several formats for a resume, a fairly standard form has evolved.

Its heading should include your name, address, date of birth, marital status, degree, and graduation date.[2] Next state your career objective. This is often

---

2. Your date of birth and marital status legally are optional; an employer cannot require them because of the Equal Employment Opportunity Commission guidelines.

where students are at a loss for words. A one- or two-sentence statement can indicate the type of career you are seeking. List your degrees in reverse chronological order; include the dates degrees were awarded, your major, the institutions, your grade-point average, and any academic honors you may have received. If you speak, read, or write a foreign language, this is to be noted next; note too your proficiency—are you fair, good, or fluent in the language?

Then list your work experience in reverse chronological order. Include all summer and part-time jobs no matter how menial, and regardless of whether they were paying jobs. Some students also put, at this point, the percentage of their total college expenses they themselves have earned. Honors, activities, elected offices held, and hobbies should then be noted, and finally references, although some students merely state, "references will be furnished upon request." Some students put their date of birth and marital status at the end of their resumé, together with their location preferences, if any. A typical college student resumé is shown in Figure 2–1.

The Cover Letter

In many cases if you are interviewed on campus, you may not need a cover letter, but you should prepare one in the event it is needed. If you mail your resumé to a prospective employer, a cover letter is absolutely necessary to introduce yourself and your resumé; it should be short and to the point. State that you would like to have a career with the firm in question, your qualifications, (e.g., accounting major), refer to your resumé, and indicate your willingness to be interviewed.

Your cover letter and your resumé should be sent to the person who has the authority to hire you. If you do not know who that is, write to a person who is in a supervisory position in your area of interest, or send it to the personnel director.

The Interview

Most prospective employers will want to interview you—and you, them—either on your college campus or at their place of employment. Often the company recruiter will screen candidates at the college interview and then bring those in whom they are interested to the company office for a second interview and perhaps a tour of the facilities. The interview is where you must sell yourself to the company and the company must sell itself to you.

First impressions can be important. Your appearance will make the first impression on the interviewer. Therefore, your clothes and grooming are important. Wear neat, well-fitting clothes in subdued colors to create a look of confidence. Your hair should be cut to a reasonable length; if you have a beard or a mustache, be sure it is well trimmed.

```
                          Shirley Ann Jones
                           BBA/Management
                            April 1984

      PRESENT ADDRESS                  PERMANENT ADDRESS
      2900 Pearl                       33061 Belfast Drive
      Austin, Texas 78712              Port Sam, Texas 79716
      (512) 478-1739                   (213) 488-7922


      CAREER OBJECTIVE: (Optional)
      Position in the area of personnel or employee relations
      with opportunities for advancement and remuneration
      predicated on ability and effort.


      EDUCATION:
      University of Texas at Austin      1982-1984
        Major: Management    GPA in Major: 3.25  GPA overall: 3.01
      Bee County Junior College, Beeville, Texas     1980-1982
        GPA: 3.65
      Port Sam High School, Port Sam, Texas      1976-1980


      FOREIGN LANGUAGE ABILITY: Speak, read and write Spanish


      ADDITIONAL INFORMATION: (Optional)


      EMPLOYMENT:
      Waitress, Pecan Street Restaurant, Austin, Texas 1982-
        Present (evenings)
      Grader, Dept. of Economics, Bee County College, Beeville,
        Texas 1980-1982 -- Graded and administered tests for Eco.
        302 & 303 courses while attending Bee County College.
      Cashier, Joske's, Port Sam, Texas  Summers 1976-1978


      PERCENT OF COLLEGE EXPENSES EARNED: 60%


      HONORS AND ACTIVITIES: Who's Who Among Students in American
      Universities and Colleges, U.T. Student Government, Alpha Phi
      Social Sorority, American Marketing Association.  Athletic
      Interests Include: Tennis, Sailing, Jogging.


      PERSONAL DATA:
      Date of Birth: April 24, 1960
      Marital Status: Single
      Location Preference: Dallas, Southwest, Open

               References Available on Request
```

Figure 2-1   Sample resume

During the interview be calm, and maintain eye contact with the interviewer. Be sure to remember his name. Let him or her set the pace and lead the interview; answer all questions directly and honestly. Don't try to bluff. Let the interviewer decide when the interview is over. While you may be nervous, especially if it is your first interview, relax and be yourself. After all, you are not on trial for your life.

QUESTIONS FOR REVIEW

1. What are the alternative uses to which a person may allocate his or her income?
2. What are the tools of financial planning?
3. Why is it important to keep good financial records?
4. What is a balance sheet? Why is it important?
5. What is an income statement? Why is it important?
6. What is meant by the phrase *human capital*?
7. In terms of occupational groupings, where does it appear that the opportunity for highest personal income lies? What does your answer suggest in terms of education?
8. If your career follows the expected norm, what can you expect regarding your income as you pass through the various age groups?
9. What is the relationship between income and property ownership?
10. How can the place in which one happens to live affect one's income?
11. How is it that a woman with ability is frequently unable to earn as much on the same job as a man?
12. What aid can you obtain in choosing a career?
13. What are some of the sources of information on various careers?
14. Why is it important to write a good resumé?

CASES

1. John Brown is twenty years old and has just completed his military service. He has a high school education but no college education, and he has two career alternatives in his uncle's trucking firm. An offer to drive a truck will pay him $400 per week to start and will provide for periodic increases to a maximum salary of $500 per week after five years; moreover, if he can educate himself at night, he will be given an opportunity to move into a managerial position with the firm. The other possibility is to go to the state university and get a degree in business administration. This will take him four years, during which he will probably have to go into debt. At

the end of four years, his uncle has promised him a job in the management training program at $400 per week.

John thinks it would be unwise to forego over $80,000 of income over the four years, especially since he believes he can educate himself at night. Hence he is contemplating taking the truck-driving job. Do you agree? Why?

2. Betty Balinski, age twenty-two, has just received her degree from a large midwestern university and has several offers of teaching jobs. She would like your help in deciding which to accept. One is the school system in a midwestern metropolitan area that includes her hometown. It pays $18,000, and she could live at home and save considerably on her expenses. Another job is in a smaller town in the South at a salary of $16,000, but she has heard that the cost of living is much lower there. Finally, she could go to California and accept a job at $20,000.

    In two years, Betty's fiancé will be discharged from the Navy and they plan to marry. She would like to save as much as possible during those two years. Which job should Betty accept and why?

3. Tom Doley has just graduated from high school with better than average grades and has been accepted as a freshman at the college of his choice. Although he has very little money, he has two alternatives for financing his education. By working part-time during the summer, and perhaps dropping out of school for a semester to work occasionally, he could finish his education in five to six years. The other possibility would be to accept the offer of his uncle, Bruce Gelt, who is willing to lend him the money to enable him to finish college in four years. Tom does not care whether he finishes in four or in six years, but he wants to do what is financially most advantageous for himself. He knows that his income will be greater after he receives his B.A. degree, but he is not sure that receiving it one or two years earlier would offset being in debt. What should he do?

4. Albert Buckboard, who has just graduated from a large eastern law school, has two job opportunities: (1) to work for the United States government in Washington, D.C., or (2) a job with a law firm in New Jersey. Albert does not care where he lives but is concerned about the income he can earn. He requests your advice with respect to the advantages and disadvantages of the two positions.

5. Sally Hollsack is about to graduate from college with a degree in accounting. She has been offered a job with a CPA firm and would like your advice whether to accept it or go on and get her MBA.

SUGGESTED READINGS

Bolles, Richard. *The Three Boxes of Life.* Berkeley, Calif.: Ten Speed Press, 1978.
Bolles, Richard. *What Color Is Your Parachute? A Practical Manual for Job Hunters* (revised). Berkeley, Calif.: Ten Speed Press, 1981.

Bostwick, Burdette. *Finding the Job You've Always Wanted*. New York: John Wiley and Sons, 1977.

College Placement Annual, 1983. The College Placement Council, P. O. Box 2263, Bethlehem, Pa.

Crystal, John, and Bolles, Richard. *Where Do I Go from Here with My Life?* New York: Seabury Press, 1974.

The Encyclopedia of Careers and Vocational Guidance, two vols. Chicago: J.G. Ferguson Publishing Co., 1981.

Figler, Howard. *The Complete Job Search Handbook*. New York: Holt, Rinehart and Winston, 1979.

Fox, Marcia R. *Put Your Degree to Work*. New York: W.W. Norton, 1979.

Ginn, Robert J., Jr. *The College Graduate's Career Guide*. New York: Charles Scribner's Sons, 1981.

Gootnick, David. *Getting A Better Job*. New York: McGraw-Hill, 1978.

Jackson, Tom, and Mayleas, Davidyne. *The Hidden Job Market*. New York: New York Times Book Company, 1981.

Kocher, Eric. *International Jobs: Where They Are, How to Get Them, A Handbook for Over 500 Career Opportunities Around the World*. Reading, Mass.: Addison-Wesley, 1979.

Mitchell, Joyce Slayton. *I Can Be Anything: Careers and Colleges for Young Women*. New York: College Entrance Examination Board, 1978.

Munschauer, John L. *Jobs for English Majors and Other Smart People*. Princeton, N.J.: Peterson's Guides, 1981.

National Consumer Finance Association. *Finance Facts Yearbook*. Washington, D.C. An annual publication.

Occupational Outlook Handbook. 1982-83 Edition. Bulletin 2200. Washington, D.C.: U.S. Department of Labor, 1983.

Rogers, Edward J. *Getting Hired*. Englewood Cliffs, N.J.: Prentice-Hall, 1982.

Schill, William J., and Nichols, Harold E. *Career Choice and Career Preparation*. Danville, Ill.: Interstate Printers & Publishers, 1979.

Stewart, Charles J., and Cash, William B. *Interviewing: Principles and Practices*, 3rd ed. Dubuque, Iowa: Wm. C. Brown, 1982.

Thompson, Melvin R. *Why Should I Hire You?* San Diego, Calif.: Venture Press, 1981.

U.S. Bureau of the Census. *Income of Families and Individuals in the U.S. in Current Population Reports, Consumer Income*. Series P-60. Get latest series of this quarterly publication.

U.S. Department of Labor, Bureau of Labor Statistics. *The Occupational Outlook Handbook, 1983-84 Edition*. Washington, D.C.: U.S. Government Printing Office, 1983.

CHAPTER THREE

THE PERSONAL BUDGET

Benefits of a Budget
Some General Rules of Budgeting
Budgetary Variations over the Life Cycle
Some Major Expenditures
Some Notes on Budgeting

To do an effective job of managing your money and financial affairs, it is necessary to budget. The budget is a type of income statement. However, while many business income statements represent a look backward to see what has happened, a budget is a look forward to allocate expected future income among alternative expenditures. It is a financial plan in the form of an income statement that uses current and future operations to achieve certain goals that might otherwise be beyond one's reach, and it must often be an estimate of future receipts and disbursements.

BENEFITS OF A BUDGET

Since a budget is a financial guide to spending, establishing a budget will enable one to run one's personal financial affairs better than can those persons who fail to keep a budget. By using it, one can make a real attempt to live within one's income.

A budget will also enable an individual to estimate more effectively his or her income than can a person who does not use a budget. It will force the individual into a more acute consciousness of the sums that must be set aside to meet future expenses. The individual will learn to allocate available funds among specific expenses and to estimate what may be left over for savings. Sometimes, through good habits, savings are voluntarily set aside; sometimes they are forced, as when one purchases a home or life insurance. In either case, a budget makes the situation clear. Furthermore, a budget may help one identify alternative ways of spending that can lead to additional savings and concomitant financial security.

If the budget is for a family rather than for an individual, the entire family should be brought into the budgetary process. The budget now becomes a group budget. While some members of the family may not contribute much to family income or be directly involved in making expenditures, they should nevertheless be brought into the decision-making process. Expenditures are made on behalf of all members of the family. All members should have input in setting goals and establishing priorities. If it is decided that certain items are to be cut, this can be done more effectively if all members of the family are consulted. Disagreements may exist among family members. There may be different priorities, and compromises will have to be made by all members. There may be a number of different trade-offs, but if agreements can be reached and differences hammered out, all members of the family are more likely to accept any sacrifices necessary to live within the budget.

SOME GENERAL RULES OF BUDGETING

The Form of the Budget

The form of the budget is not critical, and almost any type can be used. Table 3–1 may serve as a budget. It was left blank so that you may develop a personal budget. Many financial institutions have variations of similar forms and will be delighted to furnish a copy. Remember, a budget has two main parts, income and expenditures.

A person can plan a budget on weekly, monthly, or annual bases. Some experts feel it is best to plan a budget period equal to the period between income receipts—a weekly budget if one is paid weekly, and a monthly budget if one is paid monthly. Others feel this can lead to problems if the pay period (and hence the budget) is less than one month because some monthly expenses are greater than the weekly take-home pay. A person in this situation might want to budget monthly and also break the budget down by the week in order to set aside some money each week to meet large expenditures on a monthly basis. Some people, however, have a yearly and a monthly budget as well as the pay-period budget; for those whose income does not come in uniform amounts at regular intervals, the monthly or yearly budget is probably best. People who have a fluctuating income will find a budget particularly useful, since they may have a problem estimating their income accurately over whatever time period they select.

No budget will be the same for any two families or any two individuals, even assuming that both have the same income. There is no magic formula for budgeting; however, there are some rules of thumb:

1. Set your goals. The budget should be reasonable and planned toward a reasonable goal. For example, if savings must be increased to provide funds

Table 3–1   A budget plan

Item	Amount
Money income after taxes	$_____
Savings:	
Future goals and emergencies	$_____
Seasonal and large irregular expenses	_____
Regular monthly expenses:	
Rent or mortgage payment	$_____
Utilities	_____
Installment payments	_____
Other	_____
Total	_____
Day-to-day expenses:	
Food and beverages	$_____
Household operation and maintenance	_____
House furnishings and equipment	_____
Clothing	_____
Transportation	_____
Medical care	_____
Education and reading	_____
Recreation	_____
Personal and miscellaneous	_____
Gifts and contributions	_____
Total	_____
Total	$_____

for a child's education, other items must be trimmed. Different preferences, income, age, and size of a family will result in different goals for different families.

2. The fixed items of expenditure must be provided for first; such items as rent or mortgage payments, life insurance premiums, and installment loan repayments are first priority "must" items. Only after these items are included can luxuries and other "comforts" be planned.

3. Big-expense items paid less frequently than the budget period have to be spread so that each income period bears a share of these expenses. For example, property taxes not included in monthly mortgage payments must be set aside monthly.

4. A major expense cannot necessarily be cut just because it is large. For example, food may take a sizable part of the budget, and that item may appear easy to cut—on paper.

5. A budget should help to develop a set of priorities on general items of expenditure, but it need not consist of a detailed set of accounts indicating where every penny is spent. While there are some rules of thumb on major items, there are also value judgments involved in choosing among different

items. One person or family, because of different preferences, will spend more on clothes and less on housing than another similar family.

6. Adequate records should be kept indicating how much has been spent on each major category.

Income

Every budget begins with income. If the only source of income is in the form of salary or wages earned by the head of the family, there is no problem except to make a realistic estimate of the income available to the individual. Just because the head of the family is employed at $25,000 per year does not necessarily mean that income can be listed as $25,000. Instead, you might want to list take-home income after all deductions have been made, such as withholding taxes, Social Security, health insurance premiums that are withheld at the source, and the like. On the other hand, if you are self-employed you might want to take your gross income and budget your taxes and Social Security payments.

If both spouses work, another question arises in planning the budget. Should both spouses' incomes be included as permanent "family" income? Some families treat the lesser income as permanently built into the budget; other families treat it as transitory income and do not include the additional income in the budget. Such families live on the greater salary, and the lower salary can all be saved or periodically used to purchase specific items.

If income derives from a business or profession, a more difficult problem arises. Frequently the breadwinner's annual or weekly income can be estimated, based on the volume of business the previous week, month, or year. However, some types of businesses might be called "feast or famine." In some months or even certain years, income is exceedingly high, and in other months or years, very low. If this is so, it is probably best to make a low estimate and attempt to live within that amount.

Expenditures

The reverse side of the budget coin is the expenditures. There are certain "must" items over which the individual has little control, such as rent or mortgage payments. In the long run you can move to a cheaper apartment or sell your home and reduce these payments; in the short run these expenditures are fixed. Certain other expenditures such as food and clothing outlays can be controlled more readily. While it is difficult to reduce the food item in a budget, some reductions can be made by wiser shopping and by buying less expensive grades of food. It is also true that different families will spend different amounts for the same items. Family size differs, as noted above.

Another problem arising in budgeting concerns large annual or semiannual expenditures. If all expenditures were neatly broken down into monthly bills and if all paychecks were received monthly, one problem of budgeting would be eliminated. Unfortunately, necessary payments are frequently not so easily broken down. One might have to pay an insurance premium of $500 every September. (Semiannual or annual insurance premiums are less costly than payment on a monthly basis, and consequently one might decide to take advantage of this saving. The budgeting problem, however, becomes a bit more difficult.) It is necessary to meet the payment when due. A sound psychological reason for this is that many people tend to allow the future to take care of itself and, in the case of insurance premiums, to hope that somehow the money will be available. Some individuals authorize their bank to deduct one-twelfth of their annual insurance premium from their checking account and automatically put it into a special savings account. Then at the end of the year, the premium dollars are available and in the meantime a few dollars of interest will have been earned.

Savings

Finally, in addition to consumption expenditures, a budget should contain an item to assure that the individual (or family) will have some savings. Not all income should be consumed. In the absence of a carefully planned savings program, all too often savings will not materialize. Many people feel that they can budget their expenditures and generate savings as a residual. But conscious effort is usually required to generate savings.

Table 3–2 Annual budgets for a four-person family at three levels of living in the urban United States; Autumn, 1981

	Lower budget	Intermediate budget	Higher budget
Total budget	$15,323	$25,407	$38,060
Total consumption	12,069	18,240	25,008
Total food	4,545	5,843	7,366
At home	3,894	4,866	5,788
Away from home	651	977	1,578
Total housing	2,817	5,546	8,423
Shelter	2,114	4,348	5,851
House furnishings and operations	703	1,199	2,266
Transportation	1,311	2,372	3,075
Clothing	937	1,333	1,947
Personal care	379	508	719
Medical care	1,436	1,443	1,505
Other family consumption	644	1,196	1,972
Other items	621	1,021	1,718
Social Security payments	1,036	1,703	1,993
Personal income taxes	1,596	4,443	9,340

Source: Bureau of Labor Statistics. *News,* U.S. Department of Labor, "Urban Family Budgets."

Table 3–3   Annual budget for four-person family at three levels of living in various cities

	Lower	Intermediate	Higher
Boston	$15,402	$29,213	$44,821
New York	15,705	29,540	47,230
Philadelphia	15,116	26,567	39,560
Chicago	15,587	25,358	37,368
Cleveland	15,176	25,598	37,487
Detroit	15,107	25,208	37,721
St. Louis	15,112	24,498	35,965
Atlanta	14,419	23,273	34,623
Baltimore	15,315	25,114	38,090
Dallas	14,392	22,678	33,769
Washington, D.C.	16,702	27,352	41,137
Denver	15,093	24,820	36,979
Los Angeles	16,618	25,025	38,516
Seattle	17,124	25,881	37,396
Honolulu	20,319	31,893	50,317
Anchorage	22,939	31,840	45,119
U.S.	15,323	25,407	38,060

Source: Bureau of Labor Statistics, News, U.S. Department of Labor, "Urban Family Budgets."

Sample Budgets

Table 3–2 shows some sample budgets developed by the Bureau of Labor Statistics for a four-person family; there is a budget for a lower, intermediate, and higher income family. Each budget applies to the urban United States as a whole. Table 3–3 gives some budget figures developed for different cities which have different costs of living. Anchorage, Alaska, is the most expensive of all U.S. cities, according to the Bureau's figures. It should be noted that these budgets reflect a certain level of well-being, but this should not be taken as a minimum level set by the government as desirable. You will note that the budgets contain only consumption items and Social Security and personal income taxes. You should allow for savings as an additional item in your personal budget. Figure 3–1 gives you a blank worksheet on which you can calculate your personal spending and savings.

BUDGETARY VARIATIONS OVER THE LIFE CYCLE

It was noted previously that expenditures vary somewhat from family to family because of differences in family sizes, tastes, priorities, and preferences. Expenditures also vary substantially for any given family as the years pass. To some extent, income, too, varies for any given family over the years. These variations are reflected in the budget and are referred to as *life cycle variation.*

See item-by-item explanation accompanying this worksheet.

To convert weekly figures into monthly figures, multiply by 4.33.

Name: _____

Date: _____

LINE NO.		COL. #1 "CASH WEEKLY"	COL. #2 "OTHER MONTHLY"	LINE NO.		COL. #1 "CASH WEEKLY"	COL. #2 "OTHER MONTHLY"
1.	FOOD			51.	SHELTER		
2.	Grocery store			52.	Rent or mortgage		
3.	School lunches			53.	Maintenance on home		
4.	Lunches for working hus. & w.			54.	Property taxes		
5.				55.	Home insurance		
6.				56.			
7.	Total			57.			
8.	HOUSE OPERATION			58.	Total		
9.	Electricity			59.	TRANSPORTATION		
10.	Gas			60.	Auto pyts. (or saving for new car)		
11.	Heating fuel			61.	Bus, taxi or train		
12.	Telephone			62.	Gas & oil for car		
13.	Water			63.	Auto tires & repair		
14.	Household help			64.	Auto insurance		
15.	Furniture and equipment			65.			
16.	Children's allowances			66.			
17.	Newspapers & magazines			67.	Total		
18.	Dues & fees			68.	PERSONAL		
19.	Payments on old bills			69.	Personal allowances (hus. & w.)		
20.				70.	Family entertainment		
21.				71.	Vacation fund		
22.				72.	Education		
23.	Total			73.	Medicine & medical care		
24.	CLOTHING			74.	All insurance (health, life, etc.)		
25.	Clothes for all family			75.	Dues and fees		
26.	Cleaning & laundry			76.	Income taxes not deducted		
27.				77.	Payments on old bills		
28.	Total			78.			
29.	CONTRIBUTIONS			79.			
30.	Holiday gifts			80.	Total		
31.	Non-family gifts			81.	SAVINGS & INVESTMENTS		
32.	Family gifts			82.	Savings		
33.	Charities, Church, Synagogue			83.	Regular investments		
34.				84.	Self-paid retirement plan		
35.				85.			
36.	Total			86.	Total		
37.	SUMMARY: EXPENSE			87.	SUMMARY: EXPENSE		
38.	Food			88.	Shelter		
39.	House operation			89.	Transportation		
40.	Clothing			90.	Personal		
41.	Contributions			91.	Savings and Investment		

92.	Total expense		
93.	Total cash × 4.33		
94.	Total monthly expense		
95.	Plus monthly expense		
96.	Average monthly expense		
97.	Average monthly income		

Figure 3–1   Worksheets for family spending

When persons reach their peak earning period, income will vary with the job or profession. A person employed as an unskilled or semiskilled worker will reach the maximum within a year or two of initial employment. Unskilled or semiskilled laborers who go to work at age eighteen or twenty will have achieved their maximum income by their early twenties. This maximum (or ceiling) will rise a little bit each year as the union wins cost-of-living wage increases, as well as increases based upon additional productivity (better tools and machinery will permit workers to produce more), and workers will remain at their rising ceiling until they retire.

Skilled laborers like carpenters or electricians will reach their maximum income somewhat later in life. They have long apprenticeships to serve at a relatively low income. They will achieve their maximum income in from four to six years, sometimes even longer. (Again, this maximum ceiling rises as the years pass.) For example, pilots who bring supertankers into Houston harbor have to serve an apprenticeship of fourteen years.

Professional people like doctors, lawyers, and corporate executives generally have the longest training period of all. Doctors and lawyers are usually about thirty years old before they can practice, and then it takes additional years before they develop a clientele. Doctors and lawyers generally achieve their maximum income during their fifties. This is also generally true of corporate executives. These professional people's income often declines a bit during the last few years before they retire, especially if self-employed.

People's expenditures also follow a life cycle pattern. Young, single adults generally have no real responsibilities and usually save little. While they consume most of their income, it tends to be relatively low. Later, as they marry and start to raise families, they will begin to save as they build up an equity in houses and life insurance. However, the years between the late twenties and about forty or forty-five are also years of heavy consumption, because the family is growing up and needs to acquire durable consumer goods to fill the house it is buying. By this time incomes usually have risen substantially. After about age forty-five, consumption (certainly as a percentage of income, and perhaps absolutely) may begin to decline and savings rise. By now the children are on their own and the house is nearly paid for and is stocked with paid-for furniture and appliances. The years of heavy forced consumption are over. Individuals at this stage may begin to consume more services like travel, but they also can save more, and they will have an incentive to do so because of the approaching retirement years.

During the retirement stage of the life cycle, both income and expenditures usually decline. The standard of living does not necessarily decline. Often retired couples move to a less expensive section of the country. Also, certain payments need no longer be made. The house should be fully paid for, and life insurance no longer needed. Older people also receive a double tax exemption. On the other hand, people over sixty-five have higher medical expenses than younger people. Not only is their budget lower, it also contains different items. However, if they budgeted properly and were able to make substantial savings during the heavy savings years (age forty-five to sixty-five) of the life cycle, their retirement years can be pleasant.

SOME MAJOR EXPENDITURES

Major items in any budget will vary in size not only with income but also with family size, the stage of the life cycle, and personal preferences.

Housing

In general, it can be said that low-income groups tend to spend a greater percentage of their income for housing than high-income groups. Extremely low-income groups spend between 25 and 35 percent of their incomes for housing, while many very high-income groups spend less than 10 percent. Interestingly enough, there is a considerable variation in money spent on housing within any income group, for the following reasons:

1. The size of the family. Within any income group, large families tend to spend a smaller percentage of their incomes for housing than do smaller families. This is probably because large families have to spend more on food, clothing, and other necessities than do smaller families.
2. Scales of preference. Some people prefer to spend more on housing than do others within the same income group.
3. The wealth of the family. Some families within any one income group can afford to spend more for housing than others because of their ability to draw from savings and other assets.
4. Length of time that families have been in any one income group. There is frequently a time lag in the adjustment of housing expenditure to change in income.

Whether renting or purchasing a home under the terms of a mortgage, this is a fixed or "must" payment, for which money must be set aside. The mortgage payments always include interest and reduction of principal. The payments may or may not include taxes and insurance. If, in purchasing a home, provision is not made for annual tax payments or insurance protection, then a sum should be set aside each month.

The person who rents also pays these four items indirectly because they are included in rental payments. That portion of the mortgage payment that consists of interest is a deductible item on the federal income tax form. However, the renter who pays interest indirectly cannot take this deduction. The same is true of the property tax payment on a home. Therefore, there is a tax advantage to home ownership. That portion of the mortgage payment that is reduction of principal is really a savings, generally referred to as building an equity in a house.

Some rules suggest what the expenditures on housing should be. Some bankers suggest that the monthly mortgage payment be no more than 25 percent of the person's monthly income. A monthly rent equal to about one week's take-home pay is probably right. These rules of thumb, however, are not sacred, and they can be modified in accordance with one's priorities, especially today because the rapid inflation during the last half of the 1970s caused housing costs to rise more rapidly than the average level of prices.

Household Operations

Household operations consist of such services as fuel, water, electricity, gas, and telephone. These items vary from family to family, to a large degree depending upon geographical location. In most cases such items as the phone bill are fairly uniform from month to month. Fuel bills, on the other hand, are higher during the winter months. The family may better budget for this type of item by setting aside funds during the summer to pay the higher bills during the winter.

Food

Since food is a major item of the family budget, estimates should be made not only for food consumed at home, but also for meals that are to be eaten out. The size of the family will have a major bearing on what proportion of any budget will be devoted to food. As food prices rise, those on fixed incomes are forced to spend a larger portion of their budget on this item. In recent years food price increases have been among the most rapid. While incomes have also risen, expenditures on food are nevertheless the largest single item in most budgets.

Life Insurance

Nearly all adults in the United States have some form of life insurance. In the budget life insurance is a necessary fixed cost. Where possible, it is desirable to pay the premiums annually because this will result in a modest savings by reduced premiums of from 2 to 6 percent.[1] Where this is not practical and premiums have to be paid on a semiannual, quarterly, or monthly basis, a smaller amount of the monthly premiums can often be saved by giving the company

---

1. Technically speaking, premiums are not reduced when they are paid annually. Rather, a service charge of from 2 to 6 percent is added for monthly premiums.

permission to withdraw the monthly premium from the premium holder's checking account. This can be done by signing a form supplied by the insurance company. Since the premium has to be paid, this is a painless way of reducing the cost of the insurance.

Other Insurance

Other fixed items in the budget may include health insurance, property and casualty insurance, personal property insurance, and possibly specialty insurance such as malpractice insurance for professional people. If some of these items are deduced from the paycheck, they don't have to be taken into the budget as fixed expenses. But if they are not automatically deducted, they must be budgeted for; one-twelfth of the annual premium should be set aside each month in order to make these annual payments when they are due.

Regular Payments

Regular payments on loans and furniture and other installment payments should be regarded as fixed expenditures until paid. These expenditures will be discussed in greater detail in chapter five.

Medical Care

The American people spend billions of dollars on health care every year, and the amount is rising rapidly. This figure includes not only health insurance premiums and physicians' services but also dental care, drugs and medicines, eyeglasses, and hospital accommodations. Women spend more than men for medical services, and, as might be expected, medical expenses tend to rise with age. Medical expense varies greatly from person to person, and it becomes difficult to set aside arbitrarily a sum in the family budget to provide for this sort of expense. Health insurance costs, on the other hand, are readily determinable and constitute a fixed item in the budget.

Health insurance is the modern method of paying medical bills. Over 185 million Americans had some form of private health insurance in 1981. While health insurance may pay part of your medical bills, it does not pay them all because of its deductible and co-insurance features.

Transportation

A recent study showed that, on the average, about 13 percent of personal consumption expenditures went for transportation, most of it in owning and operating the family automobile. Furthermore, with the growth of suburbia, many families find two cars a necessity. If you own or partially own an automobile, you must take into account in the budget the monthly payments, which may or may not include the insurance. If insurance is not included, you must set aside an amount each month or week to take care of the annual premium. Furthermore, as the car depreciates with age, new tires and other repairs will become necessary. The weekly or monthly amount spent for gas and oil must also be considered.

The American Automobile Association (AAA) broke the costs into variable costs (those that vary with the number of miles driven) and fixed costs (those that do not vary with the number of miles driven). The study was made on several 1983 Chevrolet four-door sedans with automatic transmission and power steering. Table 3–4 summarizes the results of the AAA's findings.

With gasoline becoming more and more expensive, it is well to remember that for every 10 cents per gallon increase in the price of gas, the per mile cost of running a car increases by one cent if the car delivers 10 miles per gallon, or one-half cent if the car delivers 20 miles per gallon.[2]

Clothing

Expenditures for clothing, according to a recent study by the Department of Commerce, amount to about 6.9 percent of total consumption expenditures. Generally, the large expenditures for clothing are seasonal; every family with children is faced with buying clothing during the fall. The ideal way to handle this expense is to set something aside monthly in anticipation.

Savings

No family budget would be complete without an item for savings. In mid-1983 aggregate personal savings in the United States were running at about $150 billion per year, or about 6.7 percent of disposable personal income, which is personal income after taxes. Percentagewise, this is low relative to that of other industrial nations.

A savings feature built into a budget will assure that a person ends up a net saver; relying upon savings to develop as a residual often results in no savings. While the volume of savings is influenced, to a large extent, by the size of a person's income, a budget will usually increase savings. Possible uses for savings will be discussed in detail in subsequent chapters of this text. Developing a budget will show you whether your savings are too low. If they are and if you find it difficult to save, you can make arrangements with your bank to have

2. From *Your Driving Costs*, 1984 Edition, American Automobile Association.

Table 3–4   The cost of driving

	1983 Chevrolet Chevette 4-cyl. (98 CID) 4-door hatchback	1983 Chevrolet Malibu 6-cyl. (229 CID) 4-door sedan	1983 Chevrolet Impala 6-cyl. (229 CID) 4-door sedan	Average Cost
Details of Car Costs				
VARIABLE COSTS	**COST PER MILE**	**COST PER MILE**	**COST PER MILE**	**COST PER MILE**
Gasoline and oil	5.14 cents	6.64 cents	6.98 cents	6.13 cents
Maintenance	.87 cents	1.04 cents	1.04 cents	.98 cents
Tires	.61 cents	.68 cents	.77 cents	.69 cents
	6.62 cents	8.36 cents	8.79 cents	7.80 cents
FIXED COSTS	**COST PER YEAR**	**COST PER YEAR**	**COST PER YEAR**	**COST PER YEAR**
Comprehensive insurance ($100 ded.)	$ 58.00	$ 80.00	$ 63.00	$ 67.00
Collision insurance ($250 ded.)	169.00	201.00	174.00	181.00
Property damage and liability ($100/300/50M)	222.00	222.00	222.00	222.00
License, registration, taxes	85.00	102.00	105.00	97.00
Depreciation	1,121.00	1,343.00	1,432.00	1,298.00
Finance charge (20% down; loan@ 15%/4 yrs.)	450.00	558.00	578.00	529.00
	$2,105.00 (or $5.77 per day)	$2,506.00 (or $6.87 per day)	$2,574.00 (or $7.05 per day)	$2,394.00 (or $6.56 per day)
ADD-ONS				
Air conditioning	.20 cents per mile and 36 cents per day	.30 cents per mile and 38 cents per day	.30 cents per mile and 39 cents per day	.25 cents per mile and 38 cents per day
Depreciation for excess mileage per 1,000 miles over 15,000 miles annually	$51.00	$67.00	$69.00	$62.00

Cost Per Mile

Based on the above figures, the motorist driving 15,000 miles a year would pay:				
15,000 miles	@ 6.62¢ $ 993.00	@ 8.36¢ $1,254.00	@ 8.79¢ $1,319.00	@ 7.80¢ $1,170.00
365 days	@ $5.77 2,105.00	@ $6.87 2,506.00	@ $7.05 2,574.00	@ $6.56 2,394.00
	$3,098.00	$3,760.00	$3,893.00	$3,564.00
Cost per mile	**20.6 cents**	**25.1 cents**	**25.9 cents**	**23.8 cents**

The same person driving 10,000 miles a year would pay:				
10,000 miles	@ 6.62¢ $ 662.00	@ 8.36¢ $ 836.00	@ 8.79¢ $ 879.00	@ 7.80¢ $ 780.00
365 days	@ $5.77 2,105.00	@ $6.87 2,506.00	@ $7.05 2,574.00	@ $6.56 2,394.00
	$2,767.00	$3,342.00	$3,453.00	$3,174.00
Cost per mile	**27.7 cents**	**33.4 cents**	**34.5 cents**	**31.7 cents**

The same person driving 5,000 miles a year would pay:				
5,000 miles	@ 6.62¢ $ 331.00	@ 8.36¢ $ 418.00	@ 8.79¢ $ 440.00	@ 7.80¢ $ 390.00
365 days	@ $5.77 2,105.00	@ $6.87 2,506.00	@ $7.05 2,574.00	@ $6.56 2,394.00
	$2,436.00	$2,924.00	$3,014.00	$2,784.00
Cost per mile	**48.7 cents**	**58.5 cents**	**60.3 cents**	**55.7 cents**

The same person driving 20,000 miles a year would pay:				
20,000 miles	@ 6.62¢ $1,324.00	@ 8.36¢ $1,672.00	@ 8.79¢ $1,758.00	@ 7.80¢ $1,560.00
365 days	@ $5.77 2,105.00	@ $6.87 2,506.00	@ $7.05 2,574.00	@ $6.56 2,394.00
Added depreciation per 1,000 over 15,000 miles	@ $51 255.00	@ $67 335.00	@ $69 345.00	@ $62 310.00
	$3,684.00	$4,513.00	$4,677.00	$4,264.00
Cost per mile	**18.4 cents**	**22.6 cents**	**23.4 cents**	**21.3 cents**

Source: Your Driving Costs, 1983 Edition, American Automobile Association.

a specific amount transferred automatically from your checking to your savings account.

Contributions

Contributions consist of monies given to church, charities, and certain civic groups. In some cases, the contribution is weekly and can be easily budgeted. In other cases, the contribution is annual, and money should be set aside monthly to take care of it. Where pledges are made to charities, arrangements can be made to pay over a period of time to make budgeting easy. A later chapter on taxes will point out that contributions made to certain organizations are tax deductible within certain limitations.

Gifts, Entertainment, and Recreation

This category includes sums set aside for birthday and holiday gifts for family and friends. Included here should be a reserve for those having children in the family, for sooner or later they will be invited to birthday parties given by their friends, and over a year's time the amount spent on this item is likely to be startling.

Recreation is important for health and in the long run may save physicians' bills. Recreation relaxes one and tends to release tension; certain types of recreation also give release to hostilities that, if repressed, might lead to the psychiatrist's couch.

Education

Since taxes finance public education, the personal budget need not make an additional allowance for it. However, colleges are not entirely financed with tax funds; if there is a college-aged boy or girl in the family, parents may need to budget for college expenses. The budget should probably reflect this expectation before the person reaches college age so that the funds will be available when needed.

Some of the more expensive private colleges now charge tuition and fees in excess of $10,000 per year. In addition to tuition, another $3,000 or so is required for room, board, and personal expenses. The cost of a year of college can run over $12,000. If a state university is selected, the tuition cost is greatly reduced. Nevertheless, a college education can easily cost in excess of $5,000 per year even at a state university. Because of these high costs, it is suggested that a college fund be started for each child at birth. Your personal budget will then contain a monthly item for college for about eighteen years for each child.

If $20 per month is put into a college fund at a bank or savings and loan association at 5 1/2 percent interest, in eighteen years it will amount to about $7,000. While this sum is hardly enough to pay for four years of college at most schools, it will help. However, the college trust fund should be invested in higher yielding deposits than 5 1/2 percent as soon as it is large enough dollarwise (See Chapter 13). It is also possible for the boy or girl to help pay for part of college expenses by taking part-time jobs and by working in the summer.

Enrollment in graduate school or in some professional schools requires even more funds. Moreover, for certain careers, graduate or professional school is absolutely mandatory. Of these schools, medical schools in general are the most costly. Tuition and other fees in the more expensive private medical schools can be about $12,000 per year, and in private law schools as high as $8,000 or $11,000. State-run law and medical schools generally have somewhat lower tuition, but it too can be close to $10,000 for nonresidents and about half that for state residents in medical schools. State-financed law schools generally have tuition charges that are close to or only slightly lower than those of their medical schools.

Other Personal and Miscellaneous Expenses

Anything that cannot be budgeted for as a specific item can be included under "other expenses," and perhaps here one might put something aside as a cushion in the event of an emergency. A special savings account might be set aside and, in the fortunate event that the emergency does not arise, this amount could be added to the permanent savings account.

Certain budgetary items are often forgotten—bank service charges, legal fees, investment counseling fees, and interest on personal debts. Some of these costs, such as interest payments, are included in fixed items like installment payments. If such expenditures are not fixed and can be foreseen, however, they should be taken into account

SOME NOTES ON BUDGETING

A few other things about budgeting with which you should be familiar are such things as the envelope budget, surplus and deficit budgets, and how a computer can be a budgetary tool.

The Envelope Budget

For those of us who have a mental block against budgeting there is a way of phasing into it through the use of the "envelope budget." Take a number of envelopes and label one for each major expenditure item. Mark one "food," one "clothing," "recreating," "transportation," and so on. Keep records by putting each bill into the proper envelope. At the end of the month you can total them up to see where you spent your money. This type of arrangement will quickly let you see which items are out of line and should be cut.

The next month use this information to draw up a budget. Then place some money—or a piece of paper on which you have written the dollar amount allocated for each major expenditure—into the various envelopes. As you spend money on these items, subtract it from the sum in each envelope. When you have exhausted the sum in any envelope, expenditures on that item should cease. Such a system will aid you in controlling expenditures.

Surplus and Deficit Budgets

Do not be a slave to your budget. It is permissible to exceed budgeted expenditures in a given category in any one month if there is a sale or another legitimate reason. For example, if you have a freezer, you might buy a side of beef and lay in a supply of vegetables during the growing season. In future months this should reduce your expenditures on food. Or a family may exceed its clothing expenditures in, say, September, if there are children to equip for school. To some extent these overbudgeted expenditures may be offset by reductions in other categories during the same month, but it is also possible that they will throw the entire budget into a deficit. There should, then, be some monthly budgetary surpluses later to offset them. After all, in the case of sales you exceeded your budgeted sums to save money in the longer run. Over a number of months your personal budget should be balanced with an allowance for some savings

The Personal Computer as a Budgetary—and Other—Tool

Most college students, or people generally, do not as yet have a personal computer. However, in five or six years they may; many students have a pocket calculator, whereas ten to twelve years ago they did not. Computers are becoming smaller and less expensive. Therefore, it is worthwhile to learn to use a computer while you are young so as not to be intimidated by it later in life.

Using a personal computer to help manage your personal financial affairs will not only enable you to perform this task more efficiently, but will save you a great deal of time. So get ready—the day of the personal computer is coming fast, and there is almost no limit to what you may computerize. For example, you may computerize your budget and also reconcile your bank statement with your computer. You simply punch in your income from all sources, and the major categories of expenditures such as food, clothing, housing, transportation, and the others, and the computer will do the rest. As you punch in the expenditures on the various items, the computer can give you a running total on each one, and tell you whether you are running ahead or behind your budget, and which items are out of line and by how much.

In the case of your bank statement you can tell the computer your beginning balance, feed in your deposits and checks, and get an itemized list and a new balance. No longer is a laborious hand-reconciliation calculation needed.

Your computer can do an almost unlimited number of things. It can analyze and monitor your security investments. It can show the yield, capital gain or loss, price of each individual security, and the total value of your portfolio, and the change from a previous period. To do all this you will need the capability of tying into a telephone system line to connect to a brokerage house and get current stock quotations—no problem with today's technology. Your computer can also become your filing cabinet; by keeping your record of expenditures classified according to the various tax-deductible items it can speed the preparation of your tax returns, and in so doing, can make sure you don't miss any legal deductions. If you are in a high tax bracket (or expect to be in the future), your computer can aid you in tax planning and help you decide how many tax shelters will profit you and by how much. Possible alternative strategies can be first tested on a computer before deciding which one to choose.

Your personal computer can also store other information for instant retrieval; for example, its memory can hold all the names, addresses, zip codes, and telephone numbers that you feed in, as well as your Christmas list, and even recipes.

A Budget and Personal Bankruptcies

A budget may also help you to avoid bankruptcies. Most personal bankruptcies come about because people are careless in their financial planning. Often they overextend themselves by the careless use of credit. There has been a growing trend to bankruptcies over the past twenty years. If you should ever be so unfortunate as to have to declare bankruptcy, there is a regular procedure to follow.

Bankruptcies can be classified into business and personal bankruptcies. Each in turn can be broken down into voluntary and involuntary bankruptcies; involuntary ones are forced on a person by creditors. Bankruptcy proceedings are conducted under federal law, but this law does allow for some variations from state to state. Nevertheless, a good deal of uniformity exists. The first step in filing for bankruptcy is to buy a bankruptcy kit, available for a few dollars at any store handling legal papers. This kit contains forms on which must be listed all assets, liabilities, and the creditors; the forms are then filed in federal district court. A $50 per person fee must be paid to the court upon filing. If the case appears to be complex, an attorney should be retained. After the filing, all the creditors are notified and a hearing is held before a bankruptcy referee who is acting under the jurisdiction of the federal court. While the creditors can contest the bankruptcy, it is virtually impossible to prevent a personal bankruptcy from being made effective.

A person may file for personal bankruptcy under Chapter 7 or Chapter 13 of the federal bankruptcy laws. Under Chapter 7, you get out from under your debts by letting your creditors have those assets which they may legally seize. Under Chapter 13, you work out a new repayment schedule over several years. Even under Chapter 13, however, debts are usually scaled down, and creditors do not receive full payment. Therefore, many people who have substantial assets choose Chapter 13.

After the bankruptcy is granted, a trustee usually is appointed to take over what assets remain and pay off those debts that can be paid. The debts are classified into an order of priorities; the administrative costs of handling the bankruptcy have first priority. They are followed by wage claims, up to a point, and then taxes. These debts are paid first and then if any assets are left, general claims receive a prorated payment.

In October 1979 the new federal bankruptcy law went into effect. It significantly changed the relationship between the creditor and the debtor filing for bankruptcy. It did this by making the federal law more sympathetic toward the debtor. There are now certain assets that federal law protects from seizure to satisfy creditors' claims. The federal law also provides that if the state law is more lenient in the state where the bankruptcy is filed than is the federal law in protecting assets from seizure, the person filing bankruptcy may choose the state exemptions if he or she wishes to do so. The federally protected assets become the starting point and establish a minimum on the assets that are protected. Federally exempt assets include up to $7,500 equity in homestead property ($15,000 if you file jointly with your spouse), $1,200 in a motor vehicle, and $300 each in furniture, clothing, and other household goods. Exempt assets vary from state to state, but generally they include the homestead, a car (in some states two cars) regardless of its value, and the "tools of your trade." A house or car, however, is not protected if it has been pledged to pay off a specific debt. Therefore, a house can be seized to pay off a mortgage or a car to pay off the loan that financed the car.

There was formerly a stigma attached to personal bankruptcies, but this is less true today. Bankruptcy relieves the person of debts, and the logic behind this is that a person who has too many debts becomes economically unproductive. Relieving the individual makes him/her productive again, and hence benefits society as well as the individual. While many lenders no doubt would not lend to anyone who has ever declared bankruptcy, the person is not as bad a credit risk as one might imagine. The bankrupt person is debt-free, and the law does not permit bankruptcy to be filed again for six years. While some people have, no doubt, deliberately run up large debts and then taken the easy way out, most bankruptcies appear to be due to poor planning and poor budgeting.

Taking a Financial Inventory

All competing businesspersons take a periodic inventory of their assets, liabilities, and net worth. In this way they are able to tell from year to year whether their financial positions are improved. If net worth has increased, they know that they are going forward.

With a rising cost of living, most families feel that everything is going out and nothing is coming in, but this is not necessarily the case. The only way to tell is to make a family balance sheet and compare present status with that of a year ago, of five years ago, or of any other period. A family balance sheet can be used to plan ahead, especially in the purchase of big items such as automobiles, homes, and life insurance. A balance sheet can provide clues as to whether new life insurance is needed, a larger home is within a family's financial means, or it would be desirable to increase savings. (See Table 2–1, p. 23.) The assets (shown on the left in Table 2–1) are plus items; they represent property that has value. The items on the right (liabilities in Table 2–1) are negative items; they represent debts that you eventually will have to pay. The difference between the two is net worth, the best measure of what you are actually worth.

QUESTIONS FOR REVIEW

1. What are some of the benefits of a budget?
2. Discuss briefly a personal budget and the real purpose of a budget.
3. Should you have a weekly, monthly, or annual budget?
4. Comment on the statement that everyone must live within his or her income.
5. Discuss the guidelines or rules of thumb that you believe can be followed when preparing a budget.
6. What are some of the problems that occur when preparing the income side of the budget?
7. What are the major expenditures in a personal budget?
8. Why are some items in a budget fixed and some variable?
9. Discuss the personal budget and the life cycle.
10. Discuss food in the family budget.
11. Discuss briefly why life insurance premiums must be budgeted.
12. Discuss the importance of savings in a budget.
13. Should an allowance be made in the budget for taxes if your employer withholds taxes from your weekly salary? Explain.
14. What role can the budget play in financing a college education?
15. Why is the tuition charged by professional schools like law and medical schools generally higher than that charged by undergraduate colleges?
16. What is an envelope budget?

17. What are surplus and deficit budgets?

18. How can a personal computer serve as a useful tool in budgeting?

CASES

1.   John and Helen Moonan, who are in their early thirties, have two children, a boy of five and a girl of three. John works for Exxon and earns $26,000 per year after taxes. Having recently discovered that they are saving very little, they have decided to start a budget. John would like to buy at least $50,000 more life insurance, which would cost them $330 per year. This would amount to a total life insurance premium payment of $460 per year because John already has $20,000 of life insurance. In addition, they would like to save part of their income for the purpose of financing their children's college education and for a nest egg for themselves.

Prepare a budget to help them achieve their goal.

2.   Archie and Priscilla Ford are looking forward to Archie's retirement next year from the Ford Motor Company, where he has worked on the assembly line for forty years. The company will provide him with a pension of $400 per month. In addition, he will receive social security payments of $910 per month, and he has a contract with a life insurance company that will pay them $200 per month for as long as they both live. This represents their total retirement income.

They have no dependents, and they own a modest home, fully paid for, in a pleasant Detroit suburb. The taxes on their home are $916 per year.

They request your help in planning a budget for their retirement.

3.   Joan Rider and Mary Lou Miller, both twenty-five years old, are United Airlines flight attendants flying the Denver-to-Newark run. They share an apartment in Ivy Hill in Newark that costs them $450 per month. They each make $1,500 per month take-home pay plus an allowance for uniforms. Joan has an old Ford that is fully paid for, but Mary has payments of $220 per month to make on her new car. They have agreed to share the common expenses of keeping up the apartment, including the food consumed there.

Prepare a joint budget for Joan and Mary Lou and then a separate personal budget for each of the women for the income they will have left over after meeting their joint expenses.

4.   Captain Bob Warning, the pilot of the Boeing 707 on which Joan and Mary Lou fly, has seen the budget you prepared for them and is so impressed that he requests your help on a budget for his family. He is forty years old, has been flying with United for thirteen years, and as a pilot is making $80,000 per year. His take-home pay, however, is only $60,000. Bob is married and has four children: two girls aged two and six and two boys aged twelve and ten.

Bob also lives in New Jersey and is buying a house in South Orange on which the payments are $650 per month (including interest, reduction of principal, taxes, and insurance). He has a monthly life insurance premium of $150 he must pay but no other fixed expenses.

5. Mary Rivers has just graduated from Odessa High School in Odessa, Texas. She is going to the university next fall on a full-tuition scholarship. She will, however, have to pay her room and board, buy her own clothes and books, and meet other personal expenses. Mary has decided to live in the dormitories, where she pays a flat fee of $3,000 for room and board for the entire academic year. She can pay this sum in six equal installments, which are due on September 30, October 31, November 30, January 31, February 28, and March 31. Mary has saved $3,400 from various summer jobs, and she will use that money to help finance her education. She would like to stretch this money as far as possible. Also, her uncle has agreed to pay one-half of her room and board fees. Prepare a budget for Ms. Rivers that will minimize her expenses.

6. Sally Holsack is a twenty-two-year-old New Jersey woman who has just graduated from Wesleyan College with a B.A. in chemistry. This morning a letter informed her that she has won a scholarship to the University of Utah Medical School starting next fall. The scholarship will pay only her tuition; she will have to pay her own lab fees and her room and board and miscellaneous expenses. Sally has some money saved, but not a great deal. Her parents have promised to help her with a loan if needed, but Sally would like to minimize her indebtedness when she graduates. Therefore, she would like a bare bones budget to get her through four years of medical school. Can you prepare a hypothetical budget for her?

SUGGESTED READINGS

Better Business Bureau. *Getting More for Your Money.* New York: Grosset & Dunlap, 1982.

Bohn, Robert F. *A Budget Book and Much More.* Provo, Utah: Brigham Young University, 1980.

The Buying Guide—Consumer Reports. Mt. Vernon, N.Y.: Consumers Union. A yearly publication.

Consumer Guide Editors. *Home Repair Money Saver.* New York: Fawcett Book Group, 1981.

Cost of Personal Borrowing in the United States. Boston, Mass.: Financial Publishing Company. Published annually.

Credit. Washington, D.C.: National Consumer Finance Association. Published bimonthly.

Credit Research Center Monographs, Working Papers and Reprints: West Lafayette, Ind.: Credit Research Center, Purdue University. A series of research studies on topics significant to consumer credit.

Finance Facts Yearbook, Washington, D.C.: Research Services Division, National Consumer Finance Association. Published annually.

Huber, Roger, ed. *Where My Money Is Going: Income and Expense Budget*. W. Newton, Pa.: Lankey Publishing, 1980.

International Credit Union Yearbook. Madison, Wis.: Association of Credit Union Members, International, Inc. Published annually.

The Kiplinger Washington Letter, Washington, D.C. A weekly newsletter with a good deal of material on business and finance.

Money Management. A series of pamphlets published by the Household Finance Corporation. Topics include (1) your food dollar; (2) your clothing dollar; (3) your housing dollar; (4) your home furnishing dollar; (5) your equipment dollar; (6) your shopping dollar; (7) your automobile dollar; (8) your recreation dollar; and (9) your savings and investment dollar. Contact your local Household Finance Company Office for more information on these booklets.

"1979 Gas Mileage Guide," *EPA Fuel Economy Estimates*. Consumer Information Center, Pueblo, Colo.

Pierre, Melvin. *How to Manage Your Family Budget During These Troubled Times*. New Orleans: RMP Financial Consultants, 1978.

U.S. Department of Agriculture. *Family Economics Review*. Washington, D.C.: Consumer and Food Economic Research Division, U.S. Department of Agriculture. Published quarterly.

———. *A Guide to Budgeting for the Family*. Home and Garden Bulletin. Washington, D.C.: U.S. Government Printing Office.

———. *National Food Review*. Washington, D.C.: Economic Research Service of the U.S. Department of Agriculture, U.S. Department of Labor, Bureau of Labor Statistics. *News*, a quarterly publication.

———. *National Food Situation*. Washington, D.C.: Economic Research Service of the U.S. Department of Agriculture, published quarterly.

U.S. Department of Labor, Bureau of Labor Statistics. *News*, an annual publication on budgeting.

Your Driving Costs, 1984. American Automobile Association, 8111 Gatehouse Road, Falls Church, Va. An annual publication.

PART TWO

MANAGING YOUR INCOME

CHAPTER FOUR

DEPOSITORY INSTITUTIONS AND THE SERVICES THEY PROVIDE

Cash Balances, Liquidity, Money and Checks
Other Services Provided by Depository Institutions
Depository Institutions Deregulation Act of 1980

Originally checking accounts did not pay interest, but recently a number of kinds of checking accounts have evolved, some of which now do. Four types of payment media (coins and currency, checking accounts, credit cards, and debit cards) are currently what we use to pay for day-to-day transactions. Credit and debit cards will be discussed in Chapter 5—credit cards because they involve the use of credit or borrowed money since payment is delayed, and debit cards because they are new and are similar to credit cards. Coins, currency, and checking accounts will be discussed in this chapter as will be the various depository institutions that issue checking accounts.

CASH BALANCES, LIQUIDITY, MONEY AND CHECKS

Liquidity is a relative concept indicating how close something is to money.[1] Money is the most liquid thing in the world, and an old pair of shoes that still has value is perhaps one of the least liquid things. Cash balances—or money—consist of currency, coin, and checking accounts. Savings accounts, while liquid, are not used to settle day-to-day transactions and hence are *near money*; they will be discussed with investments.

You should minimize your cash balances because they earn a relatively low

---

1 Some financial experts have defined liquidity as being how quickly and easily an asset can be converted to money without making a price concession.

rate of interest or none at all. However, you carry some coin and currency for convenience in making small payments and because some people may not accept your checks. Checks are often more convenient than currency in making payments.

The Traditional Checking Account

A check is a written order, drawn on a bank by a depositor (the new types of check may be drawn on other depository institutions) ordering the bank to pay on demand and unconditionally a definite amount of money to bearer or to the order of a specific person or business firm named on the check. Funds in traditional checking accounts are called *demand* deposits, and they earn no interest. Checks are always payable on demand, and you must demand payment (cash your check) within a reasonable length of time; of course, you can deposit it into your own account, if you have one. The Uniform Commercial Code states that a check is not to be paid after six months have elapsed since it was written. For this reason checks are dated.

There are three parties to a check. The person drawing the instrument is called the *drawer;* the party requested to pay the stated amount is known as the *drawee;* and the person to whom the instrument is made payable is known as the *payee.*

There are also specialized checks referred to as *drafts.* Drafts are specialized checks written by one bank on its account in another bank. They are usually sold to a person who wishes to pay someone in a different section of the country. For example, a person in Denver might buy a draft written on a New York bank from a Denver bank and use it to pay for purchases in New York. A bank draft can be a *sight draft* (payable on demand) or a *time draft* (payable at some predetermined future time).

The New (Interest-Bearing) Checking Account

This is called a *NOW Account* (Negotiated Order of Withdrawal), a specialized checking account that bears interest or a specialized savings account on which checks may be written. The NOW Account was originally authorized in 1972 but only for certain institutions in Massachusetts and New Hampshire. In March 1980, a federal law was passed that makes these accounts legal for all depository institutions throughout the United States. This specialized account is not restricted to commercial banks, but may also be issued by credit unions, mutual savings banks, and savings and loan associations. While these accounts are all NOW accounts, they are referred to by a variety of names—share drafts, save-or-spend, net worth checking, investor checking, check action, paymaster, and many others. They pay interest at the passbook rate, but often there are substantial monthly service charges, unless a fairly high minimum balance is maintained.

The Depository Institutions

Four main institutions provide some form of checking accounts—commercial banks, savings and loan associations, mutual savings banks, and credit unions.

Banks

The financial institutions we call banks are technically defined as commercial banks to differentiate them from more specialized savings banks that exist in some states. Commercial banks have been called "the department stores of financial institutions" because they can do under one roof almost everything that the more specialized financial institutions do all together. Banks make loans to businesses, farmers and ranchers, individuals, and all levels of government. Banks perform the role of trustee, make available strongboxes for safekeeping valuables, and administer the nationwide credit card system that some of them have developed. But the most important role of banks for the general public is to establish and service checking accounts, including clearing checks, which in turn permits our complex society to function.

Since banks perform a fiduciary function and are depositories of other people's moneys, they are closely regulated by the government. This regulatory power includes the ability to grant bank charters. A bank cannot be established by anyone wishing to do so as can most businesses. To obtain a charter and go into the banking business, the group wishing to do so must first prove to the regulatory agencies that the establishment of the proposed bank would serve the convenience and need of the public and that it would not unduly harm an existing bank.

Savings and loan associations

Savings and loan (S and L) associations (also called building and loan associations in some states) are evolving rapidly and are becoming more like commercial banks. At one time savings and loans performed, for the most part, only two functions, accepting savings deposits and making mortgage loans. Now S and Ls make consumer loans, provide trustee services, and accept checking accounts. They, too, are closely regulated by the government because they are a depository of the public's funds. The government also controls the granting of S and L charters.

Mutual savings banks

Mutual savings banks (MSB) are much like savings and loan associations. The MSBs, however, are all true "mutuals," they have no stockholders, and in theory the depositors are the owners. At one time they too limited their activities to accepting savings deposits and making mortgage loans, but have now expanded into other areas, and accept interest-bearing checking accounts. They, too, are tightly regulated by the government of the state in which they operate.

Credit unions

Credit unions are voluntary cooperative associations. Members have a common bond—usually this consists of the employees of some enterprise. They still specialize in making consumer loans to their members, using these same members' savings deposits to finance the loan. They may now make a wide variety of loans, and may accept the new interest-bearing checking accounts.

Industrial banks

Industrial banks, or "Morris Plan banks," are another type of thrift institution; they are found in about twenty states and accept both passbook savings and certificates of deposit (CDs). In some states they are also permitted to accept the interest-bearing account, the NOW account. There are not many statistics about industrial banks so most comments are only generalizations. Industrial banks are typically regulated by state banking commissions, and to a degree the regulations vary from state to state. They are specifically forbidden to act as trustees. Frequently they are required to establish reserve accounts, often as high as 15 percent of their savings deposits. In some states the law prohibits borrowing by any of the bank's officers or stockholders, and usually the state banking commissioner conducts periodic examinations of the bank. Industrial banks do not exist in many states.

Financial centers

You may soon be able to meet all your personal financial needs under one roof. There has been a blurring of the differences among the various financial institutions. Until recently commercial banks were considered the department stores of financial institutions because they made all kinds of loans. The other institutions specialized in, for example, home mortgages or consumer loans. All this has now changed; under recently passed legislation different institutions can now provide many similar kinds of services. They are rapidly evolving into financial service centers.

Indeed, even nonfinancial organizations have become financial centers. Sears, Roebuck and Company, for example, is now a financial institution as well as a giant retailer. Sears now owns banks, savings and loan associations, an insurance company, an investment firm, a real estate firm; it has a national credit card and a tie with an accounting firm that will prepare tax returns for you. Several large investment firms, such as Merrill Lynch, have also expanded their range of financial services. Large commercial banks, in order to compete, have also developed broader financial services. Today, particularly in metropolitan areas, you have access to at least one such financial center.

Opening a Checking Account

Opening a checking account is simple. The new customer is given a card on which to fill in his or her name, address, phone number, occupation, employer, and signature. The signature on the card is identical to that to be later used on the checks. A specimen signature card is shown in Figure 4–1.

The new customer is assigned a number and given a checkbook with the customer's account number and name and perhaps address and phone number printed on each check. The customer is also given some deposit slips with the same account number on them. Usually when the account is opened an initial deposit is made. When future deposits are made, two deposit slips are filled out, one for the bank and one that is kept by the depositor and serves as a receipt.

Before you open a checking account, you must decide what kind. If you go to a commercial bank, you will have at least two choices—the NOW account and the traditional checking account. Some banks even have two different kinds of traditional (noninterest-bearing) checking accounts. Most other depository institutions will provide only the NOW account.

Most institutions have service charges, which vary not only from institution to institution but also with the type of deposit. You should shop around before opening an account. Thus you can obtain the type of account that is best for you and can minimize the cost.

Service charges are generally higher on the NOW account than on others. However, you earn interest on your dollars, which tends to offset the service charges. If your minimum monthly balance is fairly high, you will usually come out ahead with a NOW account; if it is small, it is generally best to use a traditional account.

Many institutions require a minimum monthly balance of as high as $2,000 before they waive monthly service charges on a NOW account. Credit unions, however, as a rule require much less, as do some other institutions. If service charges are assessed, they generally run from $3 to $7 per month. Some institutions also charge 10¢ or 15¢ per check.

If you establish a regular checking account, usually no service charges are assessed if the minimum monthly balance does not fall below a certain level (usually $300, but sometimes $500). If the account falls below the minimum, a service charge is levied, usually a flat fee of $3, $4, or $5 per month. In some cases, if the minimum balance falls even lower, say below $200, this flat fee may rise a dollar or two; and if the balance falls below $100, the service charge may rise another dollar. Some institutions also add a 10¢ or 15¢ fee per check to their flat fee service charge if the balance falls below a specified minimum.

Some banks also have special noninterest-bearing (traditional) checking accounts. In such a case, usually no minimum balance is required. Rather, there is a monthly service charge of 50¢ or $1.00 and a further charge of 15¢ or 20¢ per check. Special accounts are not very popular, but they appeal to certain groups such as students who write few checks and whose balance either is low all the time or fluctuates a great deal.

In recent years, some banks have developed a third type of noninterest-bearing checking account. To obtain it you must usually join a "bank club" or some other arrangement. This usually costs $6 to $7 per month; it varies from

Account No._____

Account Name _____

No. of Signatures

TEXAS STATE BANK
AUSTIN, TEXAS

Required _____

All the conditions on the reverse side of this card pertaining to this agreement have been read and agreed to by the undersigned. The Texas State Bank is authorized to recognize the following signatures in the payment of funds and all other transactions dealing with this account.

1._____ Soc. Sec. No. _____

2._____ Soc. Sec. No. _____

3._____ Soc. Sec. No. _____

4._____ Soc. Sec. No. _____

Res.
Address _____ Res.
Phone _____

City _____ State _____ Zip Code _____

Employer _____

Bus.
Address _____ Bus.
Phone _____

Perm.
Address _____ City _____

Prev.
Bank _____ City _____

Identification _____

New A/C
Clerk _____ Date _____ Initial
Deposit _____

Type Account ☐ Comm ☐ Reg ☐ Tex ☐ 2 + Ck
☐ Reg Sav ☐ S/I Sav ☐ 2 + Sav

Corresponding 2 + No. _____

Checks Ordered _____ Passbook Issued _____

Comments: _____

JOINT ACCOUNT BECOMING PROPERTY OF SURVIVOR UPON DEATH OF OTHER PARTY

We agree and declare that all funds now, or hereafter, deposited in this account are, and shall be, our joint property and owned by us as joint depositors with right of survivorship, and not as tenants in common; and upon the death of either of us any balance in said account shall become the absolute property of the survivor. The entire account or any part thereof may be withdrawn by, or upon the order of, either of us or the survivor and the bank shall have the right to pay the entire balance to said survivor and upon such payment shall be discharged of all liability.

NOTICE: This agreement is not effective between a husband and wife as to community funds.

NOTICE: Read Additional Terms and Conditions on Reverse Side

Figure 4–1   Example of signature card. (*Source:* Texas Bank of Austin.)

bank to bank. But if you join this club, you then have free checking privileges. Belonging to such a club may also provide a few other benefits such as free travelers' checks. Some banks even include a few thousand dollars of life insurance. Whether this is worth the $6 or $7 per month is a matter of individual opinion. In addition to the above fees, you have to buy the checks you use from your bank.

Clearing Checks

Virtually all checks in the United States are now cleared by computer, using "magnetic ink character recognition" (MICR). This is possible because each customer has an account number on his or her checks. It is printed with special ink and characters so that a computer can read it. When the customer writes a check, the bank deducts that amount from the account, and the person receiving the check has that sum added to his or her account. If two different banks are involved, then one bank has a claim on the other. Since hundreds of checks are presented for payment each day, all banks have funds flowing both in and out. Hence, in net terms, a bank will lose (or gain) very little on any given day. The clearing of checks is usually carried out by a clearinghouse association or by the Federal Reserve System. It nets the checks and then debits and credits the accounts of the proper bank.

Clearing checks takes time; the period can range from one day if the banks are in the same city to several days or longer if they are on opposite sides of the country. One should be careful not to write checks against a deposited check until sufficient time has elapsed for the first check to clear. Otherwise the written one may clear before the deposited one.

Figures 4–2 and 4–3 show how clearing works. Sometimes the banks involved are in two different cities, perhaps many miles apart. In such a case, a third institution is involved, and the clearing process is more complicated. This third institution is the Federal Reserve System, established by the U.S. Congress in 1913 as a federal banking institution. This federal bank does not deal directly with the public, however. It clears checks for banks if they are in different cities. Figure 4–3 illustrates this intercity check clearing process.

Joint Accounts

It is often desirable for a married couple to open a joint account. To do this, both individuals must endorse the signature card. A specimen of this type of card is shown in Figure 4–1. Once the account is opened, both persons may write checks or, more precisely, draw against the account.

There are a number of advantages in opening a joint account. The bank regards it as one account; therefore, the service charges are less than they would

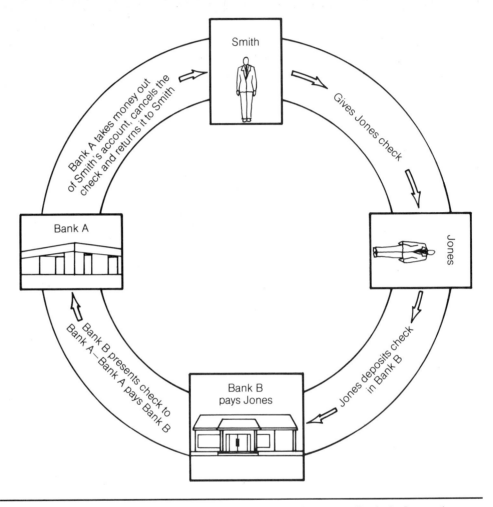

Figure 4–2   Smith pays Jones some money owed with a check drawn on Bank A. Jones deposits it in Bank B.

be if the husband and wife had separate accounts. The most important advantage, however, arises in the event of the death of one of the parties. If the husband has an individual account and the wife has an individual account and the husband dies, then, until the estate of the deceased is probated, the bank will refuse to honor any checks drawn against the husband's account by the man's wife. However, when the husband and wife have a joint account, because of the nature of a joint tenancy with the right of survivorship, title to the fund passes immediately upon death to the survivor. The practical effect is that the wife can draw checks on the joint account after having obtained a release from the tax commission in those states having state inheritance taxes. The release can be arranged by a bank for the survivor within a few days. The major disadvantage

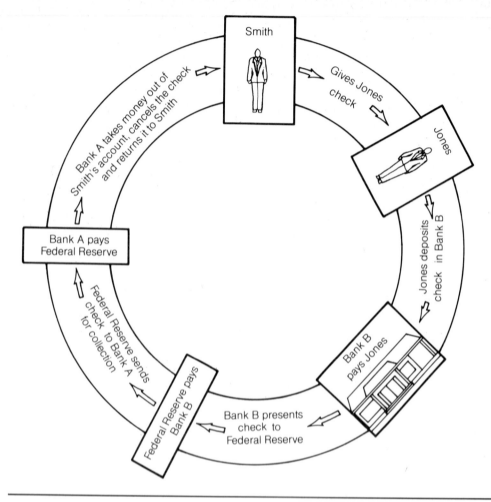

Figure 4–3   Smith pays Jones, who lives and banks in another city

to a joint account is that neither party knows what checks the other has drawn, and the account might be overdrawn.

Certified Checks

Contracts frequently call for payment by certified check. A *certified check* is one signed by the drawer and made payable to the payee in the same way any other check is drawn; however, the drawer takes the check to his or her bank and asks to have it "certified." The cashier or some other employee of the bank takes the check to the bank's bookkeeping department, and the amount of the check is subtracted from the balance of the drawer's account. The bank employee then stamps the check "certified." The bank is substituting its credit for that of the drawer, so that even if the drawer attempts subsequently to withdraw the amount from the account, he or she cannot. Furthermore, the payee of an uncertified check may have the check certified by requesting that the bank do so. Certified checks are a means of assuring the payee that the check is good in those cases where he or she lacks confidence in the drawer.

Cashier's Checks

A cashier's check is drawn by a bank on its own order to a designated payee or to his or her order. It differs from the certified check in that it is a liability of the bank, not of an individual. A person wishing to buy a cashier's check goes to the bank and pays the face value of the check, which the bank will write on itself. There is a small fee for this service. The cashier's check serves the same purpose as the certified check. It gives the payee absolute assurance that the check can be converted into cash. However, a cashier's check can be bought from a bank by a nondepositor, whereas certified checks can be obtained only by a depositor. Some banks will sell only cashier's checks and not certified checks. Figure 4–4 shows a cashier's check.

Using a Checking Account

All checks must be written clearly and legibly. The uppermost line on a check is for the date. Immediately below this is a line for the name of the person to whom the check is written and a place to put the dollar amount of the check in figures. Below is a third line to write out the dollar amount of the check in

Figure 4–4   A cashier's check. (*Source*: Texas Bank of Austin.)

words. The dollar amount expressed in figures and in words must agree. Then the check is signed on the line at the lower righthand corner. The signature there must agree with the signature on the signature card given the bank when the account was opened. For example, a person who sometimes uses the middle initial and sometimes does not will be in trouble. Each check must be signed the same way and precisely as on the signature card. Checks can, of course, be typed, with the exception of the signature. Some checks have another line to the left of the signature. On it can be written for what purpose the check was made out.

When a check is written or a deposit made, a corresponding entry must be made in the checkbook ledger that is provided by the depository institution. The ledger should include the same information that is on the check including the check's number. A sample check and deposit slip are shown in Figure 4–5.

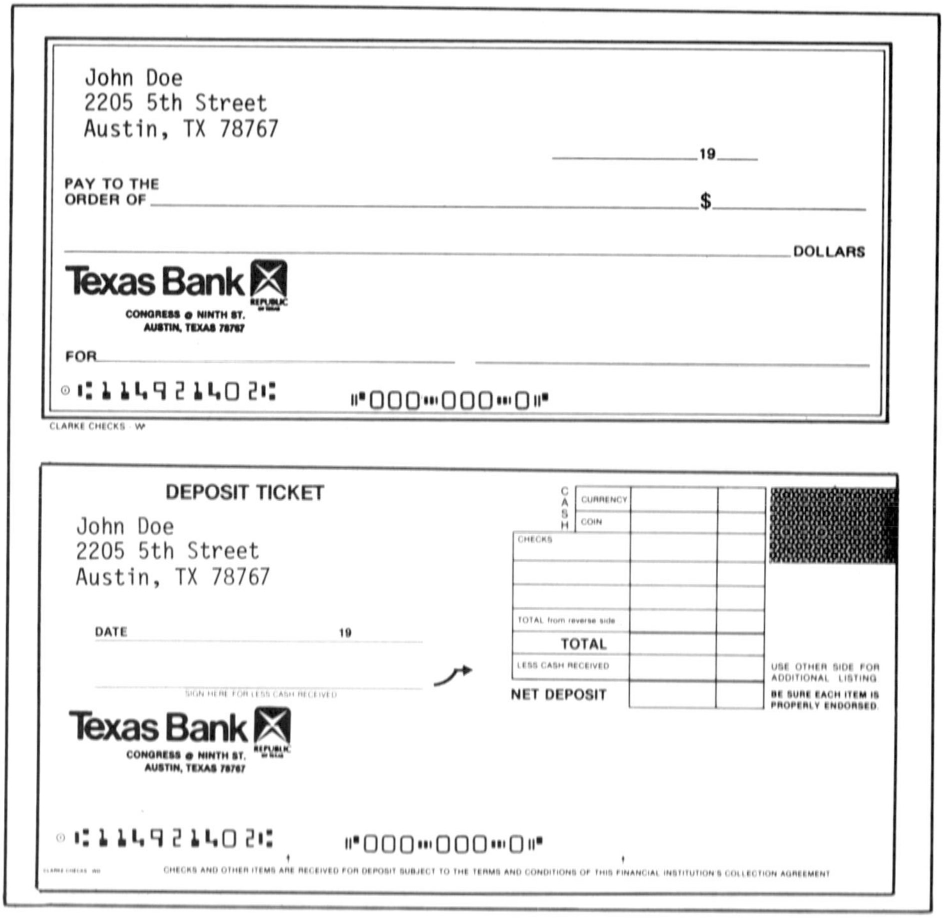
John Doe
2205 5th Street
Austin, TX 78767

19

PAY TO THE ORDER OF $

DOLLARS

Texas Bank
CONGRESS • NINTH ST.
AUSTIN, TEXAS 78767

FOR

CLARKE CHECKS

DEPOSIT TICKET

John Doe
2205 5th Street
Austin, TX 78767

DATE 19

SIGN HERE FOR LESS CASH RECEIVED

Texas Bank
CONGRESS • NINTH ST.
AUSTIN, TEXAS 78767

CASH: CURRENCY, COIN
CHECKS
TOTAL from reverse side
TOTAL
LESS CASH RECEIVED
NET DEPOSIT

USE OTHER SIDE FOR ADDITIONAL LISTING
BE SURE EACH ITEM IS PROPERLY ENDORSED

CHECKS AND OTHER ITEMS ARE RECEIVED FOR DEPOSIT SUBJECT TO THE TERMS AND CONDITIONS OF THIS FINANCIAL INSTITUTION'S COLLECTION AGREEMENT

Figure 4–5 A check and a deposit slip. (*Source:* Texas Bank of Austin.)

Monthly Statements

Most institutions send monthly statements to their depositors indicating the balance at that time. These statements show all deposits and withdrawals during the month, the balance at the beginning and at the end of the month, and the service charges, if any. The canceled checks are returned at the same time. Although such statements are usually sent toward the end of the month, some banks send them out over several days or even weeks to spread the work of preparing them. These monthly statements can be used by the depositors to reconcile their balances. This requires first an analysis of all checks written but not yet cleared as well as all deposits made but not yet shown on the statement.

Reconciliation of the Statement

A reconciliation form is often provided on the back of the bank statement. To reconcile a statement, use the following steps. First, enter the ending bank balance that appears on the front of the statement. Next, all checks that have been written but not yet cleared must be added. Third, subtract this amount from the balance. Fourth, add to the balance any deposits that have been made but do not appear on the statement. This should then be the true balance, which should be reconciled with the checkbook ledger balance. To do this, subtract any service charges on the statement from the checkbook ledger. The check ledger balance and the bank statement balance should now agree. If they do not, there has been an error. Go over all calculations again. The canceled checks should be compared to the check records to make sure the amounts agree. If the bank has made an error (and banks do make errors occasionally), the bank should be notified to correct it. Figure 4–6 is an example of a monthly bank statement.

Truncation—Coming Soon?

Truncation is a system where canceled checks are not returned to the drawer with the monthly bank statement. Rather the statement consists of a computer printout that lists each check, its number, the dollar amount, and to whom paid. This statement would serve as proof of payment. The checks would be retained by the bank for a time and later microfilmed and the checks destroyed. Approximately 40,000 checks can be stored on a cassette tape four inches in diameter. It is estimated that stopping this avalanche of paper would save financial institutions several billion dollars per year.

A few banks and savings and loan associations are experimenting with truncation, and it is being used successfully in a number of European countries. Some experts have expressed concern over whether or not the American people will accept truncation. Others point to Europe, and note that truncation will

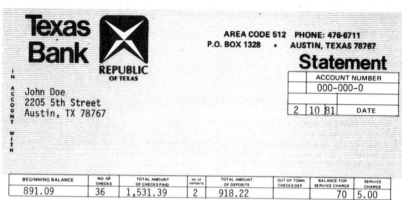

BEGINNING BALANCE	NO. OF CHECKS	TOTAL AMOUNT OF CHECKS PAID	NO OF DEPOSITS	TOTAL AMOUNT OF DEPOSITS	OUT OF TOWN CHECKS DEP.	BALANCE FOR SERVICE CHARGE	SERVICE CHARGE
891.09	36	1,531.39	2	918.22		70	5.00

DATE	CHECK	CHECK	DEPOSIT	BALANCE
7-23		BALANCE FORWARD		891.09
7-24	20.00	40.00		
7-24	171.58			659.51
7-25	40.00	160.00		459.51
7-28	8.66	21.00		
7-28	73.73			356.12
7-29	40.00			316.12
7-31	20.00			296.12
8-1	20.00			276.12
8-4	10.11	20.00		
8-4	33.00			213.01
8-5	20.00	40.00		153.01
8-6	40.00			113.01
8-7	40.00			73.01
8-8			469.77	542.78
8-11	58.70			484.08
8-12	6.70	25.00		
8-12	40.00	44.25		368.13
8-14	40.00			328.13
8-18	8.15	13.51		
8-18	50.00			256.47
8-19	4.00	20.00		232.47
8-20	110.00			122.47
8-21	20.00		448.45	550.92
8-25	6.30	8.00		
8-25	40.00	58.70		
8-25	160.00	5.00 SC		272.92

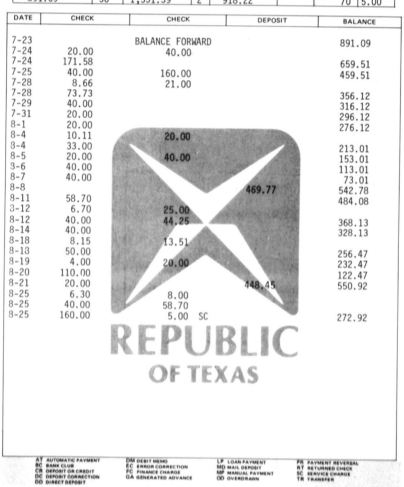

AT	AUTOMATIC PAYMENT	DM	DEBIT MEMO	LP	LOAN PAYMENT	PR	PAYMENT REVERSAL
BC	BANK CLUB	EC	ERROR CORRECTION	MD	MAIL DEPOSIT	RT	RETURNED CHECK
CR	DEPOSIT OR CREDIT	FC	FINANCE CHARGE	MP	MANUAL PAYMENT	SC	SERVICE CHARGE
DC	DEPOSIT CORRECTION	GA	GENERATED ADVANCE	OD	OVERDRAWN	TR	TRANSFER
DD	DIRECT DEPOSIT						

Figure 4—6   A monthly bank statement. (*Source*: Texas Bank of Austin.)

also save the public a good deal of time. Over fifty billion checks are expected to be written this year, and the figure is expected to rise further. With such a volume of paperwork, the public will have to accept either truncation or greatly increased service charges for their checking accounts.

Making Deposits

Deposits can be made in person or by mail. All banks have a special deposit slip bearing the customer's name, address, and account number. This slip has a spot on which to list all checks (or currency) being deposited. The amount should be totaled on the bottom. The depositor should make out two deposit slips, one for the bank and one that is stamped and returned to the depositor and becomes the receipt until the monthly bank statement is issued.

A word of caution to the mail depositor: currency for deposit should not be sent through the mail, and checks should be deposited promptly. If not, death of the drawee may delay collection, or the drawer may not have the funds available later for some reason. Finally, there is a time limit; after about six months banks do not have to honor checks.

Overdrafts

Sometimes checks are written for which there are insufficient funds. If the amount is small and the drawer is a good customer of the bank, the check will usually be paid and the drawer notified so he or she can deposit the needed funds. Banks charge a fee for this service ranging from $5 to $8 for each overdraft. If the amount of money involved is relatively large or the drawer is not a valued customer, the bank may refuse to pay the check. In such a case, the check is stamped "insufficient funds" and returned to the payee. Most overdrafts are innocent and come about due to clerical errors; a few are the result of fraud and may involve criminal action.

Endorsing Checks

Checks are transferred from one person to another by means of endorsement. Section 3-202(2) of the Uniform Commercial Code states, "An endorsement must be written by or on behalf of the holder and on the instrument or on a paper so firmly affixed thereto as to become a part thereof." Typically the writing is placed on the back of the instrument. However, if it is clear that the writing is an endorsement, it may be placed anywhere on the instrument or even on a separate piece of paper attached to the instrument.

There are five kinds of endorsements. One of the most common is called an endorsement in blank. The endorser merely signs his or her name on the back of the instrument. This makes the instrument legally payable to the bearer, and if it happens to be a check, anyone can cash it. A thief or a finder of a check endorsed in blank has no legal right to cash the check, but if he or she succeeds in doing so, the person who has endorsed it in blank has no rights against anyone except the person who has unlawfully cashed the check. Thus the blank endorsement is the name only:

J. J. DeFoe

The special endorsement names the person to whom the instrument is endorsed, for example, "Pay to the order of John Smith" (signed) "J. J. DeFoe." This means that only Smith can endorse the instrument to pass it to someone else or to collect on it. The special endorsement reads as follows:

Pay to the order of John Smith
J. J. DeFoe

The third kind of endorsement, the restrictive endorsement, prevents further negotiation of the paper. For example, an endorsement stating "Pay to John Smith, only" (signed) "J. J. DeFoe," means exactly that. A better illustration is, "Pay to John Smith, for collection only" (signed) "J. J. DeFoe," or it may read, "For deposit only" (signed) "J. J. DeFoe." When one cashes a check in a supermarket, the clerk immediately stamps the check "For deposit only." One of the reasons for this practice is that if the store is robbed and the checks stolen, there is no financial institution that will cash the check; and if the thief happens to bring the check to the institution carrying the account of the supermarket, the only thing he or she will accomplish is to deposit the check to the market's account. The restrictive endorsement also prevents the finder of a lost check from cashing it. The restrictive endorsement would read as follows:

Pay to the order of John Smith, only.
J. J. DeFoe

or

For deposit only
J. J. DeFoe

The fourth variety, the conditional endorsement, places a condition to the endorsement—for example, "Pay to John Smith after he completes painting my house" (signed) "J. J. DeFoe." Legally the condition is not binding on the person paying the instrument. For example, if the endorsement is on a check and the bank cashes the check before the condition has been complied with, the bank is not liable to DeFoe in the illustration given above. However, Smith would be liable to DeFoe for having violated the condition. It should be noted that the condition makes further negotiation impossible. The conditional endorsement would say the following:

Pay to the order of John Smith when he completes painting my house.
J. J. DeFoe

Finally, a qualified endorsement is an endorsement that limits the liability of the endorser. If a person endorses a check in blank and the maker fails to pay the note when the third party who has legal possession of it demands payment, the original payee is liable. Such a situation would typically arise in this manner: A signs a note promising to pay B. B endorses the note in blank to C. A fails to pay C upon proper demand. C may then collect from B. B as the endorser is said to be secondarily liable on the note. However, it may be that B wishes to limit his or her liability, and in this case, when passing the note to C, B may make a qualified endorsement. This B does by endorsing the note, signing on the back, "Pay to the order of C, without recourse" (signed) "B." The qualified endorsement is illustrated below:

Pay to the order of John Smith without recourse.
J. J. DeFoe

The meaning of this qualified endorsement is that in the event A, the maker, fails to pay C, then B is not liable to C, with the following exceptions:

1. B still guarantees that the instrument is genuine in all respects in what it purports to be.
2. B guarantees that all prior signers have contractual ability.
3. B has good title to the instrument.
4. B guarantees that at the time of the endorsement the instrument was valid.

Stopping Payment on a Check

If one wishes to stop a check from being collected after it has already been given to someone, one need merely notify the bank upon which it is drawn and the bank will refuse to honor it. If the check is lost or stolen, a stop order should be given the bank. Or if the check was given for defective merchandise or if some other part of a contract by the payee was not carried out, payment may be stopped.

The bank generally requires that a form be filled out giving the pertinent data regarding the check, such as the date, the check number, the amount of the check, and the payee, in order to put a stop order on a check. (See Figure 4–7.)

Some banks have a clause in their stop order relieving them of any liability in the event that they pay a check by mistake that has a stop order on it. In addition, some banks charge a $10 or $15 fee for a stop order. Whether or not a fee is charged usually depends upon how many stop orders a bank has. Many small town banks, where few stop orders are issued, do not charge a fee for this service.

With today's computerized operations, a stopped check is seldom paid due to error. The computer can read both the account number and the dollar amount of the check, which is stamped next to the account number, and it will be programmed to kick out the stopped check. In addition, all tellers are notified

```
STOP                                                                                              FILE COPY
PAYMENT                              Texas Bank    [X]
Please stop payment on check described below:    P. O. BOX 1328 • AUSTIN, TEXAS 78767   REPUBLIC      19
                                                                                        OF TEXAS
```

CHECK NO.	DATE	AMOUNT	PAYEE	REASON

DUPLICATE CHECK HAS BEEN ISSUED { Yes_____ Ck #_____ Dtd_____   Account No._____

                                 { No_____ .

Taken By_____ Dept._____ , Time_____

The bank accepts this stop payment order subject to the provisions contained in the Uniform Commercial Code as adopted in Texas. The customer must describe the item with certainty and allow the bank reasonable time to act on the order. This order will automatically become void at the end of six month from date hereof unless renewed in writing.

_____
CUSTOMER'S SIGNATURE

THE BANK ASSUMES NO RESPONSIBILITY IF THE DESCRIPTION OF THE ABOVE CHECK IS INACCURATE OR INCOMPLETE
LITHOPRINT CO., AUSTIN, TEXAS

Figure 4–7   Sample stop payment order form. (*Source:* Texas Bank of Austin.)

that this account has a stop order on it. They scrutinize all checks from that account that are presented for payment at the window.

Drive-In Banking

Most banks have drive-up windows where deposits and withdrawals may be made from within a car as a convenience to the bank's customers. Often these drive-in windows are open later than the regular banking hours, permitting people to meet most of their banking needs on their way home from work. However, a loan cannot be negotiated at a drive-in window; for this a trip to the bank and a meeting with the loan officer are required.

Automated Teller

In recent years, some banks and other depository institutions have installed a fully automated twenty-four-hour-a-day teller, a machine that will accept deposits or allow withdrawals. A special card is issued that has a magnetic strip on the back on which the customer's bank account number has been placed. The card also has a second number on it, and a third special number that is not on the card is assigned each customer. The card is placed into a slot, and the machine is activated by all three of the numbers. The number not on the card must be punched in on a keyboard as must the amount of money withdrawn or deposited. The automated teller then carries out the transaction. The special number is a safeguard. If it is given incorrectly, the machine tells the customer to try again. But if the number is given incorrectly three times, the machine keeps the card. The machine can also be programmed to keep lost or stolen cards. These automated tellers are placed outside the building of the institution issuing the card and are accessible at all times. In recent years they have also been placed in shopping centers, office buildings, and other places.

Deposit Safety

What would happen to a depositor's money if a bank should fail? In nearly all cases depositors are protected against such possibilities. The Federal Deposit Insurance Corporation (FDIC), a federal agency, insures deposits up to $100,000 against such loss. All banks in the United States are eligible for FDIC membership. Savings and loan associations, credit unions, and mutual savings banks have the same insurance, either with the FDIC or with a similar U.S. government agency. Only a few institutions have chosen not to have this deposit insurance. All insured institutions have metal signs indicating that they have insurance in prominent places or near the tellers' counters. If an insured bank should fail, depositors would be reimbursed by an agency of the U.S. government. Even if an institution is robbed or burns down, depositors do not lose their money because depository institutions carry private insurance against losses from such risks.

OTHER SERVICES PROVIDED BY DEPOSITORY INSTITUTIONS

There are a number of other services provided by depository institutions with which you should be familiar.[1] They are (1) accepting savings accounts; (2) providing safety deposit boxes; (3) providing trustee services (discussed in greater detail in Chapter 20); (4) nighttime depository lockbox; (5) automatic funds transfer; and a number of others.

Savings Accounts

Savings deposits are discussed in greater detail in Chapter 14 on thrift Institutions. Savings accounts are not as liquid as checking accounts and consist, in general, of funds that can be invested by the banks for the long run.[2] For this reason, institutions pay interest on savings deposits rather than charge service fees, as

---

1. Loans are not included in this discussion. These institutions make all kinds of loans, and they are discussed in Chapter 5.
2. Liquidity is a relative term, but it refers to how close something is to money, that is, how easily and quickly it can be converted to money. While anything of value can be sold and converted into money, some things can be converted more quickly and easily than others, hence they are more liquid. Money is the most liquid commodity of all.

in the case of checking accounts. Savings accounts are also sometimes called time deposits because they cannot be withdrawn by the depositor without prior notice. Technically, notice of thirty days must be given before the passbook savings funds can be withdrawn. This requirement is nearly always waived, and in fact savings deposits are highly liquid. Recall that earlier we referred to checking account deposits as "demand deposits." Checks cannot be written on savings accounts. In order to make a withdrawal it is sometimes necessary to make a trip to the institution, although most institutions provide for both deposits and withdrawals by mail and even by telephone.

Money Orders and Travelers' Checks

Although in terms of dollar volume these instruments rank low compared with checks, they should be mentioned briefly because some disbursements are made in this way. Money orders are a means of transmitting funds and serve much the same function as checks. There are three parties to the money order: the *payer*, who buys the money order; the *payee*, who receives it; and the *drawee*, which is the institution ordered to make the payment. One such institution is the U.S. Post Office. Postal money orders, which are purchased for a small fee from any United States Post Office, permit only one endorsement and are collected by presentation at either a post office or a commercial bank. Although postal money orders are very safe, they are not as convenient to use in paying bills as checks because they require a trip to the post office. In recent years, other institutions such as banks and savings and loan associations have begun to sell money orders. They are usually drawn on a large bank, not necessarily on the bank issuing the money order.

Travelers' checks are issued by the American Express Company and by Thomas Cook Company, both private corporations. They are issued in much the same manner as money orders; the basic difference between the two is that the express money order can pass from hand to hand by continuous endorsement. Travelers' checks are sold by many depository institutions, most travel agencies, and at the offices of the American Express Company, which can be found in any large city. They come in denominations of $10, $20, $50, $100, and $500. The fee charged is $1 per $100 of checks purchased. They are often used by people who travel, since they are universally known and accepted almost everywhere just like money itself. They are, however, safer than money because they must be endorsed before they can be exchanged. If they are lost or stolen, American Express will replace them. The checks are numbered, and the buyer should make a separate copy of these numbers since they will be needed if a lost or stolen claim is to be filed.

The American Express Company has offices in most foreign countries, and their checks are widely accepted abroad. In recent years a number of competitors (mostly large city banks) have entered this field. The Bank of America now has its own negotiable and nearly universally accepted money order. The First National City Bank of New York and a number of other large city banks now also provide this service. These travelers' checks are sold to the public nationally by banks and travel agencies having ties to the issuing banks. The purchase and use conditions of the American Express travelers' checks apply to these competitors' checks.

Automatic Funds Transfer (AFT); The Sweep Accounts

In 1978 the Federal Reserve authorized all national banks to transfer funds automatically from passbook savings accounts to checking accounts. Since then, some states have also permitted state banks to provide this service for their customers. This permits a person to hold the bulk of his or her money in a savings account, where it will earn interest, and minimize the amount of money in a noninterest-bearing checking account. Then as checks are written and come into the bank for clearing, the needed funds are transferred into the checking account by computer. In recent years the other depository institutions have also developed AFT systems.

An agreement is made that the checking account is not to fall below a certain minimum, a minimum that will vary according to the desires and needs of the customer. When checks come in which reduce the checking account below the minimum, funds are transferred. Some institutions will also provide two-way transfers. That is, if your checking account climbs above the minimum, the computer transfers funds from it to your savings account. How often the computer sweeps the account varies from institution to institution as well as with the size of the deposits. Some are swept daily, others weekly. The various institutions charge varying fees for these services. Some charge a few dollars a month, others charge 50¢ or $1 for every day a transfer is made (but not per transfer); others use some combination of the two. Some banks also provide the entire AFT service free of charge if a certain minimum (often $5,000) is kept in the savings account. Some also assess no service charge on the checking account if it never falls below, say, $1,000. In these banks if your savings account never falls below $5,000 or your checking account never falls below $1,000, all these services would be free. The AFT system then provides overdraft protection, and is also a means of keeping most of your deposits in interest-bearing accounts.

One word of warning: if you have an AFT system, your bank statement may be more difficult to reconcile. This is because most banks send a monthly statement in the case of the checking account, but only a quarterly statement in the case of the savings account.

Automatic (Computer-Assisted) Payment of Bills

In those cases where you have a regular monthly bill of a uniform size (like a mortgage or rent payment) you may authorize the payee to write a draft on your checking account on a certain day. All you need do is sign a card, and the bank will honor the draft and send a receipt to you indicating the bill has been paid.

More recently some banks and savings and loan associations have gone one step further and have developed computer-assisted check writing and bill payment systems. Sometimes these are also tied in with the automatic funds transfer system discussed above, and hence most of your funds can be kept in an interest-bearing savings account until your bills are due. You must furnish the financial institution with the names and addresses of all vendors whose bills you want them to pay. Each of these vendors is then given a number by the institution. You are given a secret code number which in addition to your account number enables you, but no one else, to talk to the bank's computer, if you have a 12-key touch tone phone. You call a special number, punch in your secret code number, your account number, the vendor's number, and the amount of money to be paid. The computer writes a check, your account is charged, and the check is mailed for you. Often you may do this 24 hours a day. If you have an old-fashioned telephone, you must call the personnel at the bank and they will punch the data into the computer for you. Often the fee for this is less (10¢ to 15¢ per check) than the postage required to send the check. The institution can still make money because their postage costs are small; they send one check (with one envelope) to pay hundreds and even thousands of people's bills to certain vendors, like the various credit card issuers, utilities, local governments, and the like.

Electronic Debit

Similar to the automatic payment of bills is the electronic debit; under this system a computer pays your bills for you automatically at the time of a purchase, usually through use of a debit card. A debit card, unlike a credit card, transfers funds immediately and automatically, and no check need ever be written. When you buy, say, a shirt, your debit card is inserted into a point-of-sale terminal (POST) and certain numbers are punched in. The computer then automatically transfers funds from your account to the merchant's account and gives you a receipt, eliminating the need for writing checks. The disadvantage is that you have to pay your bills immediately just as in a cash sale.

Safety Deposit Box

Safety deposit boxes are heavy steel boxes inside a special walk-in vault. The vault door is locked when the bank is closed. Inside the walk-in vault are individual boxes, each with its own separate lock, that may be rented by the bank's customers. These boxes come in several sizes, and rental fees vary with the size and range from about five dollars to about sixty dollars per year. Each customer has a key to the box he or she rents and the bank has a second key; both are needed to open the box. Safety deposit boxes are protected by alarms and heavy metal, and are fireproof insofar as possible. All valuables that could be lost by fire or burglary and that are compact should be kept in a safety deposit box. This includes such things as stock certificates, bonds, wills, insurance policies, and savings account passbooks. One must be careful where one keeps the key; if it is lost, the box must be opened by drilling through the lock because no other key exists. These boxes should be in the joint name of the husband and wife so that if one dies, the other can enter the box. Otherwise it is sealed until the estate is probated.

Trustee Services

Commercial banks are authorized by law to perform the role of a trustee. This involves managing the assets of someone else. Sometimes a will of a deceased person will set up an estate for the heirs. The trust department of a bank can manage the estate. The bank will look after the financial affairs of a minor. Large banks have well-established trust departments that invest billions of dollars of other people's money. If you need trustee service, a highly specialized service, go to a large bank. The trustee service is discussed in greater detail in Chapter 22. Recently, savings and loan associations have also been authorized to provide trustee services.

Nighttime Depository Lock

Most banks also have a nighttime depository lockbox built into the wall of the bank. The box can be used from outside the building. A special key opens the door. These are used primarily by business firms that may make deposits after banking hours. These boxes are not needed if the bank has a fully automated teller (discussed above) unless the deposits are too bulky to fit into a legal-size envelope.

DEPOSITORY INSTITUTIONS DEREGULATIONS ACT OF 1980

In March 1980 a federal act (Public Law 96-221) was signed into law by the President. Its provisions go into effect at various times in the future. Its main impact, however, will be to eliminate many of the current differences between commercial banks and other depository institutions. Generally speaking the act provided for the following:

1. Authority for all depository institutions throughout the U.S. to establish NOW accounts for their individual customers.
2. The automatic transfer of funds from savings to checking accounts.

3. Permission for depositor institutions to provide for overdraft protection. That is, an automatic loan would be granted if a check were written in excess of the amount of funds a depositor had in his or her account.
4. Increased insurance on deposits from $40,000 to $100,000.
5. Permission for federal savings and loan associations to make consumer loans.
6. Authority for federal savings and loan associations to issue credit cards.
7. Authority for federal savings and loan associations to exercise trust and fiduciary powers.
8. Authority for mutual savings banks to make some commercial loans and to provide checking accounts for these corporate customers.
9. Preemption of state usury laws on mortgage loans made by financial institutions. However, the federal law does provide that the various states have the right to reimpose their ceilings.
10. Phasing out over the next 2 years of the legal ceilings on the interest rate that financial institutions pay on all savings deposits.

Some of the above provisions had been granted piecemeal before in some or all states. The 1980 act provided for more uniform treatment of all institutions throughout the United States. Some observers believe that as time passes the new NOW account will replace both the checking account and the passbook savings account. This is unlikely. First of all, the NOW account is not for everybody because of service charges and/or minimum balances. People will continue to need regular checking accounts. Also with the elimination of regulation Q and the freeing of interest rates on savings deposits, the interest that will be paid on NOW accounts may turn out to be lower than that on all other interest-bearing accounts. The 1980 act will, however, as noted above, lessen the differences among the various depository institutions and, in so doing, increase competition in the industry.

QUESTIONS FOR REVIEW

1. What is liquidity?
2. Are cash balances highly liquid? Why should you minimize your cash balances?
3. What (or whom) are the three parties to a check?
4. How do the "new" checking accounts differ from the traditional accounts?
5. What role do the depository institutions perform?
6. What is a financial center?
7. How do you go about opening a checking account? What are service charges?
8. How do banks clear checks?
9. What are the advantages of a joint checking account between husband and wife?
10. How does a certified check differ from a cashier's check?

11. What is truncation?
12. What is likely to happen if your account has insufficient funds to clear a check?
13. Explain the five different kinds of endorsements found mainly on checks.
14. How do you stop payment on a check?
15. Explain the value of a safety deposit box.
16. How does the automatic teller work?
17. What are money orders and travelers' checks?
18. How does the automatic funds transfer work?
19. How is a depository institution able to pay your bills automatically?
20. What are the trustee services which some banks provide?

CASES

1. Bill and Mollie Donnell are newly married and up to now have been paying their bills in cash. They feel now, however, that the convenience of a checking account is worthwhile. They believe that they will write on the average about fifteen checks per month and that their account, although modest, will not fall below the bank's minimum requirements. They are uncertain whether to open a regular or a special checking account but do want to minimize the service charges. Can you advise them?

2. Jim and Katherine Center are a young couple who have recently moved to town. They have decided to open a checking account but are undecided whether they should open a joint account or whether each should have a separate account. Can you outline the advantages and disadvantages of each?

3. Wilfred and Dorothea Brown have just moved to Omaha, Nebraska, and their furniture is due tomorrow. The truck driver has phoned them explaining he will have to be paid $1,050 before he can unload it and that an ordinary check will not do. He has agreed, however, to accept either a cashier's check or a certified check. What is the difference between an ordinary check, a cashier's check, and a certified check?

4. Alfred White works in a supermarket, and one of his duties is to deposit the numerous checks in the bank handling the store's account. He notices that they are all stamped on the back "For deposit only." The bank clerk told him this was a restrictive endorsement and prevented someone else from cashing the check if it were lost. Can you explain the various other types of endorsements?

5. Rebecca Ann Wagoner has both a savings account and a checking account at the First National Bank, and transfers funds from one to the other as needed. She would like to minimize her checking account balance and maximize her savings deposit balance so as to maximize her interest yield. Recently she learned about the NOW account which has been described

as both an interest-bearing checking account and a savings account on which checks can be written. Ann is a bit confused. Could you explain the difference between a savings account, a checking account, and a NOW account?

SUGGESTED READINGS

Bankers Magazine. Boston: Warren, Gorham and Lamont. This journal is published every other month.

Crosse, Howard D., and Hempel, George H. *Management Policies for Commercial Banks.* Englewood Cliffs, N.J.: Prentice-Hall, 1980.

The Electronic Fund Transfer Commission and Finance Companies: Report of the NCFA Task Force. Washington, D.C.: National Consumer Finance Association, 1978.

Electronic Fund Transfers: Current Legal Developments, 1981. New York: Practicing Law Institute, 1981.

Finance Facts Yearbook. Washington, D.C.: Research Services Division, National Consumer Finance Association. Published annually.

Garcia, F. L. *How to Analyze a Bank Statement.* Boston: Bankers Publishing, 1979.

Gup, Benton E. *Financial Intermediaries,* 2nd ed. Boston: Houghton Mifflin, 1980.

Hutchinson, Harry D. *Money, Banking, and the U.S. Economy.* Englewood Cliffs, N.J.: Prentice-Hall, 1980.

Journal of Bank Research. Published quarterly by the Bank Administration Institute, 303 South Northwest Highway, Park Ridge, Ill.

Money and Credit Management Education: A Descriptive Catalogue of Educational Materials for the Classroom Teacher or Counselor 1972–73. Washington, D.C.: National Consumer Finance Association, 1977.

Money and Your Marriage. Washington, D.C. Educational Services Division, National Consumer Finance Association, 1977.

"Monitor, A Summary of Current Research in Consumer and Mortgage Credit," West Lafayette, Ind.: Credit Research Center, Krannert School of Management, Purdue University. Semimonthly report.

Wyatt, John W., and Wyatt, Madie B. *Business Law,* 4th ed. New York: McGraw-Hill, 1979.

CHAPTER FIVE

USING CONSUMER CREDIT

The Classification of Consumer Credit
Why Consumers Borrow
Benefits and Dangers of Consumer Credit
How Much Do You Pay?
Sources of Consumer Credit
Other Things to Know about Consumer Credit and Consumerism
Financial Documents Accompanying Consumer Loans
Some Dos and Don'ts of Consumer Credit

Why do people buy on the installment plan? It would be cheaper to pay cash for all items because interest and service charges would be eliminated. Interest costs are also incurred when you borrow money at a bank in order to buy an item. Why do most people not save enough money through a budget to pay cash for large items like cars or household furniture? They are impatient. The money for a car would probably take several years to save. Some people, even if they had a budget, would never be able to save enough to pay cash for a car. So they go into debt, buy the car, and then engage in a negative form of savings when liquidating the debt.

To be sure, some people's incomes are so high that they can easily pay cash for any purchase and this group borrows little money. At the other extreme are the very low-income groups who are unable to borrow much money because their credit rating is such that lenders are hesitant to lend to them. The great bulk of consumer credit, as it is called, is extended to the middle class, those whose incomes are high enough to give them a good credit rating and enable them to borrow, but too low to pay cash.

THE CLASSIFICATION OF CONSUMER CREDIT

Consumer credit is credit extended to individuals for the purchase of final consumer items. Consumer credit is sometimes classified into *sales credit* and *loan credit. Sales credit* is extended by a merchant, and the person gets goods and promises to pay later. *Loan credit* is extended by a financial institution, and the person gets money (credit) with which to buy something and must then repay the loan. A second classification is perhaps superior; it is used by the Federal Reserve Board and consists of (1) installment credit and (2) noninstallment credit.

Installment Credit

Installment credit consists of all credit extended to individuals which is to be repaid in two or more installments. It can be broken down into the type of product that it finances, such as:

1. Automobile Loans
2. Revolving Charge Accounts
3. Mobile Homes
4. Other

Credit extended for the purchase of autos is the largest single category. Most automobiles sold in the United States are financed through the use of installment credit. Revolving consumer credit is that which is extended through the use of credit cards. Only a portion of the balance need be paid every month, and it finances a wide variety of goods such as gasoline, clothing, and some household items.

Credit extended for the purchase of mobile homes is self-explanatory. Most of this credit is extended by commercial banks and finance companies, but in some states savings and loan associations also make it available.

Other consumer credit finances all other durable goods such as television sets, household appliances, home improvements, and other items. It also includes personal loans which may be made to individuals to purchase other goods and services, even a vacation. Table 5–1 shows these classifications, the dollar amounts, and the institutions that extended the credit, over the past few years. Figure 5–1 shows the relative shares of the major consumer lenders.

Noninstallment Credit

Noninstallment credit consists primarily of single repayment loans and service credit. It also, however, consists of those few remaining old-fashioned charge accounts in which the entire sum charged was due and payable at the end of each month (there are very few of these left in the U.S. today).

Single repayment loans

Many upper-income and even upper-middle-income groups are able to borrow money to purchase durable consumer goods on their personal signature. They

Table 5–1   Consumer installment credit total outstanding (millions of dollars)

Holder, and type of credit	1980	1981	1982	1982					1983		
				Aug.	Sept.	Oct.	Nov.	Dec.	Jan.	Feb.	Mar.
				Amounts outstanding (end of period)							
1 Total	313,472	331,697	344,798	334,971	337,469	336,473	338,372	344,798	343,151	340,343	342,568
By major holder											
2 Commercial banks	147,013	147,622	152,069	148,438	149,801	149,528	149,651	152,069	150,906	150,257	151,319
3 Finance companies	76,756	89,818	94,322	93,207	93,357	92,541	93,462	94,322	95,080	93,859	94,817
4 Credit unions	44,041	45,954	47,253	46,154	46,846	46,645	46,832	47,253	46,946	46,757	47,081
5 Retailers*	28,448	29,551	30,202	26,751	26,829	27,046	27,639	30,202	28,859	27,734	27,472
6 Savings and loans	9,911	11,598	13,891	12,833	13,051	13,457	13,672	13,891	14,209	14,860	15,083
7 Gasoline companies	4,468	4,403	4,063	4,714	4,669	4,322	4,141	4,063	4,102	3,780	3,669
8 Mutual savings banks	2,835	2,751	2,998	2,874	2,916	2,934	2,975	2,998	3,049	3,096	3,127
By major type of credit											
9 Automobile	116,838	125,331	130,227	128,051	128,856	128,375	129,299	130,227	129,482	129,055	130,959
10 Commercial banks	61,536	58,081	58,851	57,992	58,542	58,552	58,701	58,851	57,740	57,971	58,567
11 Indirect paper	35,233	34,375	35,178	34,345	34,728	34,744	34,884	35,178	—	—	—
12 Direct loans	26,303	23,706	23,673	23,647	23,814	23,808	23,817	23,673	—	—	—
13 Credit unions	21,060	21,975	22,596	22,071	22,402	23,306	22,395	22,596	22,458	22,360	22,518
14 Finance companies	34,242	45,275	48,780	47,988	47,921	47,518	48,203	48,780	49,284	48,724	49,874
15 Revolving	58,352	62,819	67,184	61,293	61,845	61,836	62,362	67,184	65,562	63,372	63,091
16 Commercial banks	29,765	32,880	36,688	33,509	34,017	34,110	34,233	36,688	36,282	35,481	35,533
17 Retailers	24,119	25,536	26,433	23,070	23,159	23,404	23,988	26,433	25,178	24,111	23,889
18 Gasoline companies	4,468	4,403	4,063	4,714	4,669	4,322	4,141	4,063	4,102	3,780	3,669
19 Mobile home	17,322	18,373	18,988	18,918	19,011	19,043	19,049	18,988	19,291	19,374	19,379
20 Commercial banks	10,371	10,187	9,684	9,967	9,956	9,860	9,806	9,684	9,828	9,806	9,739
21 Finance companies	3,745	4,494	4,965	4,916	4,953	4,971	4,970	4,965	4,981	4,960	4,967
22 Savings and loans	2,737	3,203	3,836	3,544	3,604	3,716	3,775	3,836	3,984	4,112	4,174
23 Credit unions	469	489	503	491	498	496	498	503	498	496	499
24 Other	120,960	125,174	128,399	126,709	127,748	127,219	127,662	128,399	128,816	128,542	129,139
25 Commercial banks	45,341	46,474	46,846	46,970	47,286	47,006	46,911	46,846	47,056	46,999	47,480
26 Finance companies	38,769	40,049	40,577	40,303	40,483	40,052	40,289	40,577	40,815	40,175	39,976
27 Credit unions	22,512	23,490	24,154	23,592	23,946	23,844	23,939	24,154	23,990	23,901	24,064
28 Retailers	4,329	4,015	3,769	3,681	3,670	3,642	3,651	3,769	3,681	3,623	3,583
29 Savings and loans	7,174	8,395	10,055	9,289	9,447	9,741	9,897	10,055	10,225	10,748	10,909
30 Mutual savings banks	2,835	2,751	2,998	2,874	2,916	2,934	2,975	2,998	3,049	3,096	3,127

* Includes auto dealers and excludes thirty-day charge credit held by travel and entertainment companies.
Source: *Federal Reserve Bulletin*, May, 1983, Board of Governors of the Federal Reserve System, p. A42.

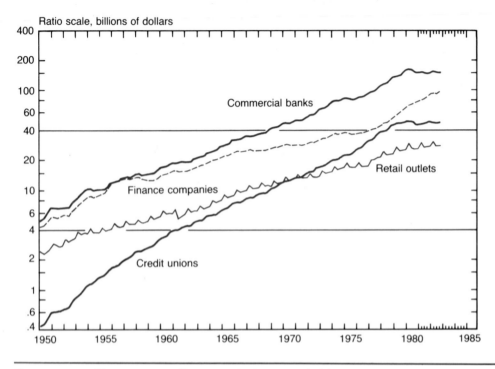

Ratio scale, billions of dollars

Figure 5–1   Consumer installment credit by major holders; amount outstanding, end of quarter. (*Source: 1982 Historical Chart Book*, Board of Governors of the Federal Reserve System, p. 67.)

may, for example, borrow several thousand dollars to buy household furniture, and then repay the entire amount in one lump sum, say six months later, together with the interest. They will have to do their own budgeting in the meantime and set aside a portion of the loan each month in order to have the wherewithal to liquidate the loan when it comes due.

Service credit

Service credit is that which is extended by professional practitioners and some establishments such as hospitals. Because of the growing use of medical insurance this type of credit is not as important as formerly, but it includes unpaid medical and dental bills, monies owed to hospitals or to the accountant who prepared your tax returns, and that unpaid bill of the plumber who unplugged your sink last week. The amounts owed to utilities after deducting deposits are also part of the statistics of service credit. Figure 5–2 shows how consumer installment debt (as well as that repaid) has risen over the last few years.

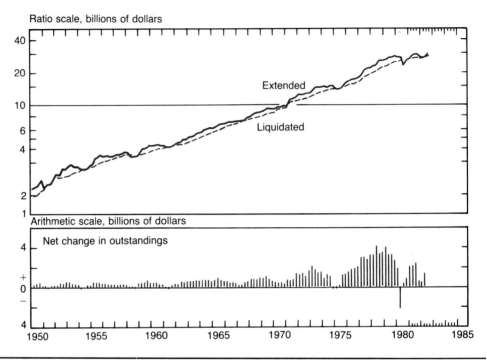

Figure 5–2   Total consumer installment credit; seasonally adjusted, quarterly averages. (*Source:* 1982 *Historical Chart Book,* Board of Governors of the Federal Reserve System, p. 65.)

WHY CONSUMERS BORROW

Consumers borrow or use consumer credit for different reasons just as savers save for different reasons. One individual may save to pay her son's tuition, while another may have to borrow to pay the tuition. Some people pay cash while on vacation; others use credit cards.

High Cost of Durables

A main reason for the use of consumer credit is the high unit cost of durable consumer goods. A *consumer durable* is a durable good having a relatively long life, such as a television set, household appliances, or an automobile. Of the $343 billion consumer debt in March 1983, about $131 billion or approximately 38 percent resulted from the extension of automobile credit. The cheapest and possibly the best way to buy this type of durable good would, of course, be to save and pay cash. But to save, one must abstain from present consumption. However willing the spirit may be, for most of us unfortunately (when it comes to saving) the flesh is weak. Suppose, for example, that we planned to save to buy an auto priced at $10,000; we would have to defer the use of the car and put aside, say, $2,000 per year for five years before we would be able to buy the car. For most of us, saving $2,000 per year for five years for the purpose of buying a car appears a formidable task. Once we have part of it saved, as the economists say, our consumption function tilts. Most of us tend to increase our cash-consumption expenditures if we feel we have a reserve to fall back on. Finally, we find that we are not saving, but are even tapping the funds we have already saved. So we find that when it comes to high unit cost durable goods, most of us buy on time. We are able to use the product immediately instead of having to defer its use until a future date and perhaps not get it at all. For this current use we are willing to pay interest.

Financial Emergencies

Unfortunately, many of us frequently are forced to borrow because of unforeseen emergencies. Unusually high medical and dental bills not completely covered by insurance are examples. Noninsured flood damage to a home is another. There are dozens of types of emergencies and other reasons for which consumer loans may be necessary.

Convenient Form of Payment

Consumer credit constitutes a convenient and easy method of paying for goods. A few dollars down and a few dollars a week appears attractive to many. The terms appear easy enough, and the individual may enjoy consuming the goods at the present time. The same is true of the use of credit cards. Charging things and then later paying one bill is more convenient than writing a separate check for each item.

Travel and Vacation

Many people finance their vacations with consumer credit. Not only do they make extensive use of credit cards while on their trips, but often they borrow money at a financial institution to spend at their destination and to finance their transportation costs. This is a growing segment of consumer credit. Ten or fifteen years ago very little consumer credit was used to finance vacations other than through credit cards. Now it is quite common.

BENEFITS AND DANGERS OF CONSUMER CREDIT

There are three groups who are benefited by the extension of consumer credit. These are the savers (who are also the lenders), the borrowers, and society as a whole. There are dangers as well.

The Savers

The accumulations of many individual savers make up total national savings. In 1983, for example, total personal income amounted to over $2,700 billion. After taxes and consumption expenditure, there remained a residual of about $150 billion in personal savings. These thrifty individuals make their money available for borrowers. These savers (lenders) receive the benefit of interest on their loans and thus derive additional income. In short, if it were not for borrowers, the savers would have no place in which to invest their savings and add to them through additional interest income. It is the borrowers who keep the savings institutions in business and keep money out of old socks and mattresses.

Not all individuals borrow to purchase final consumer goods. Business firms borrow an even larger amount than do consumers—they borrow to expand their businesses. In this way they bring about economic growth. Nevertheless, individual consumers make up an important part of total borrowings, which in turn must be large enough to provide an outlet for total savings.

The Borrowers

Consumer credit will enable the borrowers to consume certain items more quickly than otherwise would be the case. If you go into debt to buy an automobile, you are then forced to save out of future income to repay the loan. Without consumer credit you might end up with neither savings nor the car. With consumer credit you at least have the car.

Society as a Whole

Society as a whole may benefit from consumer credit provided that those granting it do not overdo it. Credit extension may lead to increased demand and hence increased production of goods and services and help to maintain full employment. The extension of consumer credit can lead to a lower unit cost of goods. For example, as a result of increased effective demand created by the extension of credit, certain firms are led to large-scale production. To a point, large-scale production brings about certain efficiencies that result in lower costs, and in a competitive economy these savings are frequently passed on to the consumer.

Economic Instability

Some years ago when the Federal Reserve Board concluded and published a monumental study on consumer credit, some controversial questions were left unanswered. One was whether the granting of consumer credit contributed to economic instability. Some economists feel that if the economy is operating at or near capacity, consumer credit must take something away from investment spending, thus perhaps contributing to economic instability and to a lower rate of economic growth.

Some economists also feel that overextension of credit has led to inflation, extravagance, and general lack of prudence. Consumer credit increases the demand for goods and services. If this demand is sufficiently strong, it can pull up prices. The demand on the part of individual consumers is by far the largest in our economy. It is this consumer demand plus business demand for investment expenditures on new plant and equipment plus government demand (expenditures) that together may be excessive and cause inflation. Since consumer demand is the largest of these three, however, it is often singled out for special treatment.

Higher Cost of Goods and Services

One argument against extension of consumer credit is that the resultant interest costs actually reduce the amount of consumer goods that persons might have purchased had they saved the money in the first place. As has been previously pointed out, however, it may be that the cost of borrowing is offset because credit extension increases sales and consequently has a tendency to lower unit costs as a result of mass production. This depends to some extent on the amount of competition involving a particular product and on whether or not any cost savings are actually passed on to the consumer in the form of lower prices.

Getting in Over Your Head

When you borrow money, you take on an obligation of making a fixed payment on a time schedule. This payment is interest and repayment of the principal. Such a fixed payment comes off the top of the budget before the remainder of your income is allocated among alternative wants. How large a fixed payment an individual can accept is determined largely by his or her income. But if credit is easy to obtain and a person lacks discipline, it is possible that he or she will have so many debts that it becomes impossible to meet the fixed monthly payments because they take too large a portion of income. Those who miss a payment or two may have their car or furniture repossessed. Worse still, they may be forced into bankruptcy. This is not really a danger of consumer credit but rather a danger that comes from *abusing* consumer credit. It is the unwise and excessive use of consumer credit that gets people in over their heads. Frequently, this may be just as much the lender's fault as the borrower's. Do not be afraid of consumer credit. Use it when needed, but only wisely and after careful planning. Use it only if you are sure you can take on the additional fixed payment required. One of the reasons for a budget, discussed in an earlier chapter, is to help you avoid getting "in over your head."

HOW MUCH DO YOU PAY?

When one borrows money or buys something on the installment plan, it is wise to take time and shop around. One should not buy the first item one sees from the first dealer one visits. Instead, visit several dealers and compare prices. If borrowing money from a lending institution, do not agree to the first terms that are offered but visit a number of lending institutions and compare their interest rates and the other terms of the loan. Remember that the item to be purchased or the money to be borrowed will still be there tomorrow. Do not be stampeded into a quick deal.

It is often less costly for consumers to purchase those items of merchandise they need for cash; however, for most of us, installment purchases or cash borrowing are often the alternatives. The difficulty most consumers have when they wish to borrow money is that they are suddenly overcome by a strong sense of inferiority. The first tendency is to feel that the loan will not be granted, and the second—because they frequently need the loan badly—to feel that they must take the first offer that comes along. Individuals would benefit if they would adopt the attitude that money is a commodity like beans and that financial institutions are in business much as are grocery or department stores, so that they often compete with each other in terms of cost.

Interest Rate Calculations

One of the fundamental problems of borrowing is to determine just how much interest is being charged. The borrower should be able to answer the question: What is the effective rate of interest that I must pay? or What is the real cost in percentage of interest charged?

Although the mathematics of obtaining a precise answer to "How much interest am I paying?" is complex, there are two formulas that will provide the approximate answer. The first formula is:

$$R = \frac{2 \times m \times I}{P(n+1)} \text{ or, transposed, } I = \frac{R \times P(n+1)}{2 \times m}$$

In the above formula:

R = annual interest rate in decimal form
I = dollar cost of the credit
m = the number of payment periods in a year
(twelve if paying monthly and fifty-two if weekly)
n = the number of payments scheduled in total
P = the net amount of credit or principal advanced

And the second is:

$$R = \frac{M(95N+9)F}{12N(N+1)(4P+F)}$$

where

R = annual percentage interest rate
M = number of payments in a year
N = number of payments over the life of the loan
F = dollar cost of the credit
P = the net amount of credit or principal advanced

You may borrow on a single repayment basis or on an installment basis. A loan may also be discounted, in which case the interest is taken out in advance. For example, a single repayment loan of $1,000 for one year discounted at 10 percent will result in the borrower receiving $900 and paying back $1,000 one year later. The interest rate is $100 divided by $900 or 11.11 percent. Discounting tends to increase the interest rate yield a bit above the discount rate.

If, on the other hand, a $1,000 loan at 10 percent is not discounted but is repaid in 12 equal monthly installments over a year, it is referred to as a 10 percent *add-on loan*. The so-called *add-on interest* must be converted to simple interest, or as it is also called, *annual percentage rate* (APR). The two above formulas will approximate this conversion.

Suppose that Ms. Stein borrows $1,000 at 12 percent, and must pay back $1,120 in twelve equal monthly installments of $93.33. The total cost is $120, but what is the interest rate? Substituting the figures into the formulas above:

$$I = \$120$$
$$M = 12$$
$$N = 12$$
$$P = \$1,000$$

$$R = \frac{2 \times 12 \times \$120}{\$1000\,(12 + 1)} = \frac{2880}{13,000} = 22.15 \text{ percent}$$

or

$$\frac{12\,(95 \times 12 + 9)\,\$120}{12 \times 12\,(12 + 1)\,4 \times \$1000 + \$120}$$

$$\frac{12 \times 1149 \times 120}{1872 \times 4120} = \frac{1,654,560}{7,712,640} = 21.45 \text{ percent}$$

As noted above, these two formulas only approximate the true annual percentage rate (APR), and this explains why they differ slightly.

A loan can be both discounted and repaid in installments, but the above formulas will still approximate the APR, if you use the net amount of the principal advanced. If the above $1,000 installment loan had also been discounted at 12 percent, the formulas would use:

$$I = \$120$$
$$M = 12$$
$$N = 12$$
$$P = \$880$$

and

$$M = \quad 12$$
$$N = \quad 12$$
$$F = \$120$$
$$P = \$880$$

The reason why the true interest rate (APR) is so much higher than the add-on rate is because when repaying a loan on an installment basis, the add-on interest applies to (and must be paid) on the original balance throughout the entire period of the loan. When loans are repaid on the installment basis, the amount of money actually owed declines with each repayment. To calculate the true interest rate, one must take into account this declining balance; otherwise the borrower is paying interest on money even after he or she has already repaid it. The formulas discussed above do this, but to understand the logic of how interest rates work, you must think in terms of the declining balance. An illustration will make this clear.

When you borrow money that is repaid on an installment basis, there are three balances: an original balance, a declining balance, and an average balance. We can illustrate this system with another method of calculating the true interest rate. Remember, however, that this second method of calculating the interest rate is somewhat cruder and hence a little less accurate than the formula explained above.

Let us assume that you borrow $1,200 from a bank to purchase a used automobile and agree to repay it in twelve equal monthly installments of $110. You will pay back a total of $1,320; $120 of that total is interest (the I in the formula above); the original balance you owe is $1,200. After one month you make your first payment and you still owe $1,100; a month later you again repay $100 and owe $1,000, and so on. The balance you owe declines each month, as shown in Table 5–2.

Table 5–2   Estimating interest costs

Original balance: The amount originally borrowed	Month	Balance	Average balance: The amount of money you actually have on the average for the full year
$1200	1	$1,200	
	2	1,100	
	3	1,000	
	4	900	
	5	800	$650.00
	6	700	
	7	600	
	8	500	
	9	400	
	10	300	
	11	200	
	12	100	

At the end of six months, you have repaid $600 and owe only $600; yet you are still paying 10 percent interest on the full $1,200. If you were to calculate and pay interest monthly, you could take 10 percent of the declining balance and divide it by twelve to get the true interest cost at 10 percent. But to approximate what rate you are actually paying, get the average balance over the year (the first and last month's balance divided by two, or $650) and calculate the interest rate on it. Since interest charges are $120 and you have really borrowed only $650, the interest rate is 18.46 percent.

Let us take another case, in which you borrow $1,800 at 10 percent add on, to be repaid in eighteen equal monthly installments. Ten percent of $1,800 is $180 per year, but since your loan is for a year and a half, an additional interest payment of $90 is called for. Your total interest cost, dollarwise, is $270. You could calculate an average balance for the first year and again for the next 6 months and get the true interest rate, but the formula introduced above provides us with an easier way.

$$I = \$270$$
$$m = 12$$
$$n = 18$$
$$P = \$1800$$

Thus:

$$\frac{24 \times 270}{1800 \times 19} = \frac{6480}{34200} = 18.95 \text{ percent}$$

The terms *add-on interest* and *simple interest* are two technical terms employed in the finance industry. Simple interest (also called true or actuarial interest) is what the actual interest rate, as it has been understood through the ages, really is. It is the interest as applied to a declining or average balance. Add-on interest, however, is the rate that is associated with the original balance even though the balance is declining. When one is discussing finance charges and interest rates, one must be sure to make clear to the lender one's awareness of the difference between add-on and simple interest.

In the past, lenders and merchants offering installment contracts found all kinds of devious ways of disguising the true interest rates. Often they would merely say, "so much down and so much per month," and the true interest cost (the I in the formula) or the net amount of credit advanced (the P in the formula) could not always be ascertained. If asked what the interest rate amounted to, lenders would often become evasive and sometimes even tell outright lies. In many cases, the borrower paid 12, 30, or 42 percent or even more without knowing it. All of this changed with the passage of the federal truth-in-lending law in 1968 (the Consumer Credit Protection Act). This law does not limit the rate that may be charged; it merely requires that the lender tell the borrowers what they are paying, both dollarwise and as a percentage of the loan. (A number of different agencies enforce truth in lending. See Chapter 7 for a complete list.) Lenders and merchants who extend credit do not work through

Table 5–3   Actuarial equivalents of add-on rates. The annual add-on rate is shown as the left hand index. If this rate is applied to the original amount for the full term and the loan is repaid monthly, then the body of the table shows the actuarial rate of return on the money actually outstanding.

Add-on rate per year	3 mo.	6 mo.	9 mo.	12 mo.	15 mo.	18 mo.	24 mo.	30 mo.	36 mo.	42 mo.	48 mo.	54 mo.	60 mo.	72 mo.	84 mo.	96 mo.	108 mo.	120 mo.
1.00	1.50	1.71	1.80	1.84	1.87	1.89	1.91	1.92	1.93	1.93	1.93	1.94	1.94	1.94	1.93	1.93	1.93	1.92
2.00	3.00	3.42	3.59	3.67	3.72	3.76	3.79	3.81	3.82	3.82	3.82	3.82	3.82	3.80	3.79	3.77	3.75	3.74
3.00	4.49	5.12	5.37	5.49	5.56	5.61	5.66	5.68	5.68	5.68	5.67	5.66	5.64	5.61	5.57	5.54	5.50	5.46
3.50	5.24	5.98	6.26	6.40	6.48	6.53	6.58	6.60	6.60	6.59	6.58	6.56	6.54	6.49	6.44	6.39	6.34	6.29
4.00	5.99	6.82	7.14	7.30	7.39	7.45	7.50	7.52	7.51	7.50	7.47	7.45	7.42	7.36	7.30	7.23	7.17	7.11
4.25	6.36	7.25	7.59	7.75	7.85	7.91	7.96	7.97	7.96	7.94	7.92	7.89	7.86	7.79	7.72	7.65	7.58	7.51
4.50	6.74	7.67	8.03	8.21	8.30	8.36	8.41	8.42	8.41	8.39	8.36	8.33	8.29	8.22	8.14	8.06	7.98	7.91
4.75	7.11	8.10	8.47	8.66	8.76	8.82	8.87	8.88	8.86	8.84	8.80	8.77	8.72	8.64	8.55	8.47	8.38	8.30
5.00	7.48	8.52	8.91	9.10	9.21	9.27	9.32	9.33	9.31	9.28	9.24	9.20	9.15	9.06	8.97	8.87	8.78	8.69
5.25	7.86	8.94	9.36	9.55	9.66	9.73	9.78	9.78	9.76	9.72	9.68	9.63	9.58	9.48	9.37	9.27	9.17	9.08
5.50	8.23	9.37	9.79	10.00	10.11	10.18	10.23	10.23	10.20	10.16	10.11	10.06	10.01	9.89	9.78	9.67	9.56	9.46
5.75	8.60	9.79	10.23	10.45	10.57	10.63	10.68	10.67	10.64	10.60	10.54	10.49	10.43	10.31	10.18	10.06	9.95	9.84
6.00	8.98	10.21	10.67	10.90	11.02	11.08	11.13	11.12	11.08	11.03	10.97	10.91	10.85	10.72	10.58	10.46	10.33	10.21
6.25	9.35	10.64	11.11	11.34	11.45	11.53	11.57	11.56	11.52	11.47	11.40	11.34	11.27	11.12	10.98	10.85	10.71	10.59
6.50	9.72	11.06	11.55	11.79	11.91	11.98	12.02	12.00	11.96	11.90	11.83	11.76	11.68	11.53	11.38	11.23	11.09	10.96
6.75	10.10	11.48	11.99	12.23	12.36	12.43	12.47	12.44	12.39	12.33	12.25	12.17	12.09	11.93	11.77	11.61	11.47	11.32
7.00	10.47	11.90	12.43	12.68	12.81	12.87	12.91	12.88	12.83	12.76	12.68	12.59	12.50	12.33	12.16	11.99	11.84	11.69
7.25	10.84	12.32	12.87	13.12	13.25	13.32	13.35	13.32	13.26	13.18	13.10	13.01	12.91	12.73	12.55	12.37	12.21	12.05
7.50	11.22	12.74	13.30	13.57	13.70	13.77	13.80	13.76	13.69	13.61	13.51	13.42	13.32	13.12	12.93	12.75	12.57	12.41
7.75	11.59	13.17	13.74	14.01	14.14	14.21	14.24	14.19	14.12	14.03	13.93	13.83	13.72	13.52	13.31	13.12	12.94	12.76

Term-months

8.00	11.96	13.59	14.18	14.45	14.59	14.65	14.68	14.63	14.55	14.45	14.35	14.24	14.13	13.91	13.69	13.49	13.30	13.12
8.25	12.33	14.01	14.61	14.89	15.03	15.10	15.12	15.06	14.97	14.87	14.76	14.64	14.53	14.29	14.07	13.86	13.66	13.47
8.50	12.71	14.43	15.05	15.34	15.48	15.54	15.55	15.49	15.40	15.29	15.17	15.05	14.92	14.68	14.45	14.23	14.02	13.82
8.75	13.08	14.85	15.49	15.78	15.92	15.98	15.99	15.92	15.82	15.70	15.58	15.45	15.32	15.07	14.82	14.59	14.37	14.16
9.00	13.45	15.27	15.92	16.22	16.36	16.42	16.43	16.35	16.24	16.12	15.99	15.85	15.71	15.45	15.19	14.95	14.72	14.51
9.25	13.82	15.69	16.35	16.66	16.80	16.86	16.86	16.78	16.66	16.53	16.39	16.25	16.11	15.83	15.56	15.31	15.07	14.85
9.50	14.19	16.11	16.79	17.10	17.24	17.30	17.29	17.21	17.08	16.94	16.80	16.65	16.50	16.21	15.93	15.67	15.42	15.19
9.75	14.57	16.53	17.22	17.53	17.68	17.74	17.73	17.63	17.50	17.35	17.20	17.04	16.89	16.58	16.29	16.02	15.77	15.53
10.00 →	14.94	16.94	17.66	17.97	18.12	18.17	18.16	18.06	17.92	17.76	17.60	17.44	17.27	16.96	16.66	16.38	16.11	15.86
10.25	15.31	17.36	18.09	18.41	18.56	18.61	18.59	18.48	18.33	18.17	18.00	17.83	17.66	17.33	17.02	16.73	16.45	16.20
10.50	15.68	17.78	18.52	18.85	18.99	19.05	19.02	18.90	18.75	18.58	18.40	18.22	18.04	17.70	17.38	17.08	16.79	16.53
10.75	16.05	18.20	18.95	19.28	19.43	19.48	19.44	19.32	19.16	18.98	18.79	18.61	18.42	18.07	17.74	17.42	17.13	16.86
11.00	16.43	18.62	19.39	19.72	19.86	19.91	19.87	19.74	19.57	19.38	19.19	19.00	18.80	18.44	18.09	17.77	17.47	17.19
11.25	16.80	19.04	19.82	20.15	20.30	20.35	20.30	20.16	19.98	19.78	19.58	19.38	19.18	18.80	18.45	18.11	17.80	17.52
11.50	17.17	19.45	20.25	20.59	20.73	20.78	20.72	20.57	20.39	20.18	19.97	19.77	19.56	19.17	18.80	18.46	18.14	17.84
11.75	17.54	19.87	20.68	21.02	21.17	21.21	21.15	20.99	20.79	20.58	20.36	20.15	19.94	19.53	19.15	18.80	18.47	18.17
12.00	17.91	20.29	21.11	21.46	21.60	21.64	21.57	21.41	21.20	20.98	20.75	20.53	20.31	19.89	19.50	19.13	18.80	18.49
12.25	18.28	20.70	21.54	21.89	22.03	22.07	21.99	21.82	21.60	21.37	21.14	20.91	20.68	20.25	19.85	19.47	19.13	18.81
12.50	18.65	21.12	21.97	22.32	22.47	22.50	22.42	22.23	22.01	21.77	21.53	21.29	21.05	20.61	20.19	19.81	19.45	19.13
12.75	19.03	21.54	22.40	22.76	22.90	22.93	22.84	22.64	22.41	22.16	21.91	21.66	21.42	20.96	20.54	20.14	19.78	19.44
13.00	19.40	21.95	22.83	23.19	23.33	23.36	23.26	23.05	22.81	22.55	22.30	22.04	21.79	21.32	20.88	20.47	20.10	19.76
13.50	20.14	22.79	23.68	24.05	24.19	24.21	24.09	23.87	23.61	23.33	23.06	22.79	22.52	22.02	21.56	21.14	20.75	20.39
14.00	20.88	23.62	24.54	24.91	25.04	25.06	24.92	24.68	24.40	24.11	23.82	23.53	23.25	22.72	22.24	21.79	21.38	21.01
14.50	21.62	24.45	25.39	25.77	25.90	25.91	25.75	25.49	25.19	24.88	24.57	24.26	23.97	23.41	22.91	22.44	22.02	21.63
15.00	22.36	25.28	26.24	26.62	26.75	26.75	26.58	26.30	25.98	25.64	25.32	24.99	24.68	24.10	23.57	23.09	22.64	22.24
15.50	23.10	26.10	27.09	27.48	27.60	27.60	27.40	27.10	26.76	26.41	26.06	25.72	25.39	24.79	24.23	23.73	23.27	22.85
16.00	23.84	26.93	27.94	28.33	28.45	28.43	28.22	27.89	27.53	27.16	26.80	26.44	26.10	25.46	24.88	24.36	23.88	23.45
16.50	24.58	27.76	28.79	29.18	29.29	29.27	29.03	28.69	28.30	27.91	27.53	27.16	26.80	26.14	25.54	24.99	24.50	24.05
17.00	25.32	28.58	29.64	30.03	30.14	30.10	29.85	29.48	29.07	28.66	28.26	27.87	27.50	26.81	26.18	25.62	25.11	24.65
18.00	26.80	30.23	31.32	31.72	31.81	31.76	31.46	31.04	30.59	30.14	29.70	29.28	28.88	28.13	27.46	26.86	26.31	25.82
19.00	28.28	31.88	33.01	33.40	33.48	33.41	33.06	32.60	32.10	31.61	31.13	30.67	30.24	29.44	28.72	28.08	27.51	26.99
20.00	29.76	33.52	34.68	35.07	35.14	35.05	34.65	34.14	33.60	33.06	32.54	32.05	31.58	30.73	29.97	29.29	28.69	28.14

the formulas presented above to determine the interest rates they charge. Rather they use tables that have been worked out in advance to tell the buyer the dollar amount of the finance charge and the annual percentage rate (APR) of these charges. Table 5–3 is such a table that can be used to obtain the true interest cost of any add-on rate. The various add-on rates are shown in the first column; to the right are shown the true rates for the various installment loans repaid monthly. For example, a 10 percent add-on rate is really 14.94 percent if paid back in three installments; 17.97 percent if paid back in twelve; and 17.92 percent if repaid in thirty-six.

Interest Rates and Consumer Loans

State laws set the maximum rates that may be charged on consumer loans; hence there is some variation from state to state. Some states have a number of different laws, each one applying to a specific lending institution. Others have only one or two laws which regulate all consumer lenders. The laws also allow for different rates for different items. For example, automobiles are generally financed at lower rates than other consumer goods. Also new autos are usually financed at lower rates than used autos. Rates on auto loans generally run from 12 percent all the way up to 30 percent depending upon the lender, the credit rating of the borrower, and the age and condition of the auto. The average, however, is probably about 13 or 14 percent on new autos and 17 to 18 percent on used.

Rates may be calculated on a monthly basis on the unpaid balance, say 1 to 3 percent, which of course is 12 to 36 percent per year. On very small loans for short periods of time, say of $100 or $200 for one month, some states allow rates in excess of 100 percent on an annual basis. For example, if you were to borrow $100 for 30 days there may be a minimum charge of, say, $10. You would pay back $110 in 30 days for a monthly rate of 10 percent. This amounts to 120 percent if annualized.

Loans to consumers may be secured or unsecured. If the loan is secured, something of value is pledged as collateral, such as an automobile or household furniture. This is accomplished by having the borrower give a security agreement to the lender. (See the end of the chapter for an example of a security agreement.) An unsecured loan is called a signature loan; no collateral is pledged, and the borrower has a good enough credit rating to obtain the loan by merely signing a promissory note to repay it.

The maximum loan that may be made under the various consumer finance laws varies from state to state. This runs as high as $25,000 in a few. However, with the exception of loans on automobiles and mobile homes, very few consumer loans are in excess of $2,500. Figure 5–3 illustrates average loan size over the past few years.

A typical consumer loan might work this way. The personable young television announcer informs you that you can borrow $600 for twenty-four months and repay it in monthly installments of *only* $32 per month. In terms of actual interest what does this mean? First, it means that the total amount you

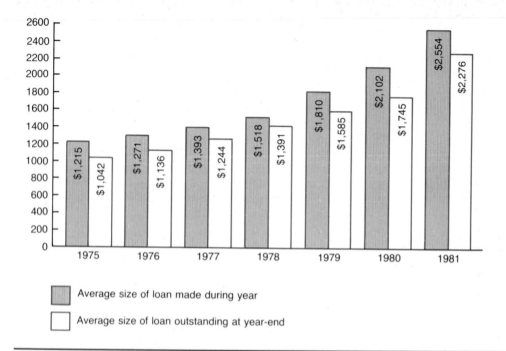

Figure 5–3   Average loan size, finance companies, selected years 1975–81. (*Source: 1982 Finance Facts Yearbook*, National Consumer Finance Association, p. 56, and updated data supplied by the National Consumer Finance Association.)

pay back is $768, of which $600 is principal and $168 is interest. It also means that, on the average, you owe the company over the twenty-four-month period about $300—because you are making monthly payments and constantly reducing the debt. Thus on the average unpaid balance of $300, which you had over two years, you are paying $168 in interest, or slightly over 27 percent interest on the average unpaid balance of your loan. This figure can be calculated using the formula described above, as follows:

$$\frac{2mI}{P(N+1)} = \frac{24 \times 168}{600 \times 25} = \frac{4,032}{15,000} = 27 \text{ percent}$$

The same young announcer will also say that there will be no additional handling charges, and this is true. Most state laws prohibit any additional charges such as fees, fines, or other handling charges.

SOURCES OF CONSUMER CREDIT

Consumer credit is made available by a number of financial institutions either directly or indirectly—directly when you go to an institution and borrow money and indirectly when you go to a merchant and buy something on the installment plan and the merchant arranges the financing. Sometimes the latter happens without your knowledge until after it takes place. For example, you sign papers promising to pay so much per month for so many months. Then, the merchant takes this paper to a financial institution, turns it over to the institution, and gets his money. This is called selling the paper or, more properly, discounting it. The institution gets the interest as the monthly payments are made, and you are told to make the monthly payments to the institution.

Financial institutions may also be extending credit indirectly when you use your credit card. This is because some banks issue credit cards, and also because merchants who have issued credit cards (e.g., Sears or a gasoline company) must borrow more money at a bank to carry you until you pay the bills you have on your card. Figure 5–4 shows the amount of consumer credit extended by the four main types of institutions over the past few years.

Financial Institutions

There are nine financial institutions which deal with consumer credit in the form of cash. They are:

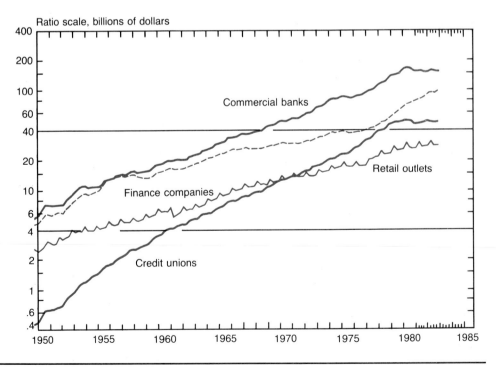

Figure 5–4   Consumer installment credit, by holder; amount outstanding, end of quarter. (*Source: 1982 Historical Chart Book*, Board of Governors of the Federal Reserve System, p. 67.)

1. Small loan companies
2. Credit unions
3. Industrial banks
4. Remedial loan societies
5. Life insurance companies
6. Commercial banks
7. Savings and loan associations
8. Mutual savings banks
9. Pawnbrokers

Small loan companies

The small loan company, also known as the consumer finance company or personal finance company, is a firm specializing in loans to consumers. Interest rates charged by finance companies are generally a bit higher than those charged by some other lenders because their loans are often smaller and they lend to poorer credit risks than do many other lenders. These companies make loans for almost any conceivable purpose, but personal loans and automobile loans constitute the bulk of their business. Figure 5–5 illustrates the outstanding credit of finance companies.

In 1911, the state of Massachusetts passed the first legislation enabling the operation of small loan companies. The other states gradually followed. Today forty-nine states and the District of Columbia have consumer finance laws; and

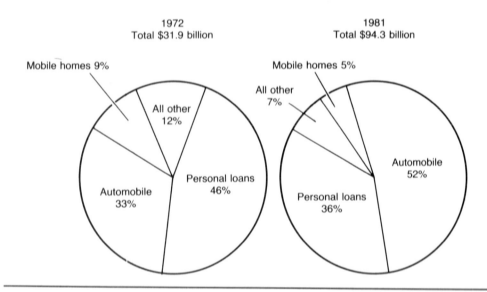

Figure 5–5   Consumer installment credit outstanding at finance companies at year end. (*Source: 1982 Finance Facts Yearbook*, National Consumer Finance Association, p. 54, and updated data supplied by the National Consumer Finance Association.)

only one state, Arkansas, has no similar legislation. On small loans a higher than normal rate of interest is actually necessary. The cost of servicing a small loan is frequently greater than that of servicing a large loan.

Credit unions

Credit unions are voluntary associations whose members have a common bond, usually that of having a common employer. However, some are organized by churches. They may have a federal or a state charter. In order to borrow from a credit union you must first join and to do so you must be eligible by having a common bond. Members may put their savings into the union and borrow from it, in effect pooling their savings and making loans to one another. Generally, credit unions charge between 9 and 18 percent on consumer loans, depending upon the size of the loan and the collateral offered. Sometimes, if the loan is secured by a savings deposit, they will charge only 3 percent above the deposit's earnings. Until recently, credit unions could make only consumer loans. But recently, federal credit unions (and some state-chartered ones) have been given permission to make mortgage loans. Some are slowly moving into this new area.

Industrial banks

These banks are found in only twenty states. When they were first organized, in the early part of the century, they specialized in making high-risk loans to industrial workers—hence the name. Today they are very much like commercial banks except that they do not provide trustee service. They also still make higher-risk loans than do commercial banks, however, and generally charge higher interest rates. Their rates are comparable to finance companies.

Remedial loan societies

There are still a few of these nonprofit organizations left in some of the big cities in the eastern United States. They operate very much like a pawnshop; that is, a watch, a camera, a diamond, or another article is pledged for relatively small loans. They generally charge interest rates of up to about 24 percent per year.

Life insurance companies

An individual with a savings-type insurance policy (which will be detailed in Chapter 8) may borrow the cash surrender value from the life insurance company or use the policy as security for a loan with a commercial bank. Generally after a policy has been in force for a minimum of two or three years, the insured builds up a "cash surrender value" in the policy. This means that if the holder wishes, he or she may give up the policy and be paid a sum in cash or may borrow an equivalent sum from the insurance company and permit the policy to remain in force. It is probably better to borrow against the policy than to cash it in.

As an alternative, the borrower may use the policy as collateral for a loan with another financial institution. Under these conditions, in the event the borrower fails to meet this obligation, the institution may cash the policy and pay off the loan, returning any surplus to the borrower. If the borrower should die prior to payment, the institution is paid the amount of the debt by the insurance company; any balance being paid to the beneficiaries.

Under the law, the insurance company *must* lend the cash surrender value to the insured if the latter so desires. From the viewpoint of the consumer, this sort of loan has a psychological drawback because one does not *have* to pay back the loan. Consequently, some people just ignore repayment and continue paying the interest. Upon the death of the insured, however, the beneficiary of the policy will receive the face value less the amount of the loan outstanding.

Borrowing from your life insurance company will probably result in as low a rate of interest as you can get anywhere. Insurance companies generally charge about 8 percent interest per year on the loan.

Commercial banks

Commercial banks make all kinds of loans including consumer loans. The cost of borrowing from commercial banks compares most favorably with that of other financial institutions. The rate generally begins at about 15 percent per year. Some banks tie it in to the prime rate, which is the rate banks charge their best customers. Usually, however, collateral is needed to get a loan at this rate and it must be a single-payment loan. On installment loans, higher clerical and administrative costs are involved and higher rates are charged. Most consumer loans are installment loans and only about one-half of the entire loan is usually borrowed for the entire period so the effective rate of interest ranges from 16 to 21 percent per year.

Usually, the interest rates charged by banks are lower than those charged by many other lenders, especially if you have a good credit rating.

Savings and loan associations

Savings and loan associations are in the business of accepting deposits and making mortgage loans. However, in some states they have long been permitted to make consumer loans if they are operating under a state charter (like commercial banks, savings and loan associations can operate under a federal or a state charter.) In 1980 federal legislation was passed which permitted federally chartered institutions to make consumer loans. They make both installment and single-payment loans. The interest they charge ranges from 15 to 18 percent if it is an installment loan and about 15 or 16 percent if it is a single-payment loan. Within these ranges, the actual interest charged on a given loan is determined by the size of the loan and the credit-worthiness of the borrower. These rates generally are comparable to rates charged by credit unions and commercial banks.

Mutual savings banks

Everything we have said about savings and loan associations in terms of consumer loans applies to mutual savings banks. Mutual savings banks are found only in seventeen states. They may make a limited number of consumer loans in some states, and the rates they charge are comparable to those charged by savings and loan associations.

Pawnbrokers

Pawnshop operators accept personal property which is pledged as collateral for the loan. The loans are never for more than 40 to 50 percent of the value of the property. The borrower receives a pawn ticket and has a certain period of time in which to repay the loan and redeem his property. If he doesn't do so, the pawnbroker may sell the article. The interest rate charged generally runs from 25 to 42 percent per year. For the most part, pawnshop customers are people in low-income groups who are frequently unable to borrow elsewhere.

One Final Word

When borrowing, shop around. Generally the institutions that charge the lowest rates are credit unions, commercial banks, savings and loan associations, and mutual savings banks, and rates vary among these four institutions, so my advice is to check several of them. However, if you are eligible to borrow from your life insurance company, this will probably be the cheapest source of funds of all the institutions, but unless you have the discipline to repay this loan, you should consider using your policy as collateral for a loan from some other financial institution.

Credit Cards

No discussion of consumer credit is complete without comments about credit cards. We are all familiar with gasoline credit cards and the credit charge plates of the major department stores; nearly all of us use them. Most of us are also familiar with national credit cards like American Express, Visa, and Master Card, although fewer of us use these.

Traditionally, the credit card permitted consumers to obtain merchandise without paying and at the end of the month one bill was sent for all purchases. Credit was extended for a few weeks at most. More and more department stores are using what is referred to as a rotating or revolving charge account, where the buyer is still permitted to liquidate the bill monthly but need not do this. Those who choose not to do so move into an automatic monthly payment plan. While these plans vary somewhat from merchant to merchant, they all are similar. They require a minimum monthly payment (usually $10 or 10 percent of the total amount due). They also have a maximum amount (usually $500 to $3,000) beyond which credit will not be extended unless special arrangements are made. Under these rotating charge accounts consumers need never liquidate their total bill. The only requirement is that they make the minimum monthly payment and do not exceed the maximum.

For this extension of credit, merchants charge interest on the unpaid balance. The rate charged varies. Until recently, it was 1.5 percent per month on roughly the first $1,000, 1 percent on the next $1,000, and .8 percent on amounts in excess of that. This amounts to 18 percent, 12 percent, and 9.6 percent annualized. Recently, however, more and more credit cards have begun to charge 1.75 percent per month in those states where the law allows such a high rate, which amounts to 21 percent per year. This interest is calculated not on the unpaid balance, but rather on the average daily balance from billing date to billing date. This has the effect of charging interest on future purchases. For example, suppose you are billed $200 on your credit card and pay $100. If you make no further purchases for, say, 10 days, your average daily balance for those 10 days is $100. If you now charge another $100, your average daily balance for the next 20 days is $200. To calculate your average daily balance, the bank would multiply $100 by 10 days and $200 by 20 days. These figures are added together ($5000) and divided by 30, which gives us the average daily balance of $166.67, on which interest is calculated. Many credit cards are calculating their interest rates on some version of this average daily balance method.

With certain national credit cards such as American Express, the credit card holder pays an annual fee of about $30. The card holder is billed monthly and must liquidate the bill monthly except for bills for airline tickets, where a twelve-month payoff is permitted. If a twelve-month payoff is chosen, an additional 1 percent per month interest on the declining balance is added. If the bill is paid every month, American Express does not assess interest.

The national credit card firms receive about 5 or 6 percent of the amount collected from the merchant for whom they collect it. This is their service charge and should be looked upon as a cost of credit. This fee is included in the price of the final goods and services, and, to a slight extent, those who do not have these credit cards subsidize those of us who do.

Two national credit cards have been developed by the commercial banking system: Visa, issued by the Bank of America, and Master Card, issued by CitiBank of New York. Various banks throughout the country have entered into an agreement with one of the two banks and are responsible for the credit cards within their region.

At one time credit cards were sent to people on an unsolicited basis, but this is no longer so. Now persons who want a credit card not only must apply, but must qualify. The criterion used to determine whether a person qualifies is primarily income; however, nearly anyone who has an annual income of $12,000 or more can obtain a national credit card upon application, if he has a good credit record.

The Checkless Society or Electronic Funds Transfer System; The Debit Card

Now that banks have developed national credit cards and they have been widely accepted, the next step will be to use the electronic computers of these banks to pay bills automatically. The result will be to do away with checks almost completely. This involves the use of what is known as the *debit card*.

Under the present system a bank does the bookkeeping and bill collecting. If you hold one of these cards, all participating merchants send your bills to the bank. The bank adds them up and sends you one monthly bill. You need to write only one check to the bank, which pays all your bills. In the event that you do not have the money to pay the bill, the bank will automatically make you a loan up to a predetermined maximum, if you have authorized this.

The next step, when it comes, will eliminate the need for you ever to write checks or make deposits in your bank account. One debit card is all you will need. Your weekly or monthly paychecks will be deposited automatically into your bank account by your employer. The bank will automatically pay your regular fixed monthly bills like your mortgage, your rent, or the payment on your car. This will be done by a computer. When you make any purchases, your debit card will be put into a special machine that all, or nearly all, merchants will have. This machine will be tied to the computer of your bank and the merchant's bank. When you make a purchase, the computer will automatically transfer the amount out of your bank account and into the merchant's bank account. The computer can do this immediately upon the purchase or at the end of the month in accordance with whatever arrangement is made. The computer, through the merchant's machine, will give you a receipt and a bank statement. You will get a bank statement each time you make a purchase (use your bank) rather than monthly. If the transfer of accounts is made at the end of the month rather than when purchases are made, you still get a monthly statement rather than a statement with each purchase.

Automatic loans will be granted by the computer as needed, in accordance with predetermined maximums. The computer will refuse to let us buy things if we don't have the money in the bank or are ineligible for a loan. The need for checks will virtually be over.

Why is all this likely to come about? Because of convenience. The number of checks being written daily (over one hundred million) is growing so large that the banking system is about to be buried in paper. It is also much more convenient for the public to be relieved of the necessity of writing checks and keeping records. What will all this checkless money cost? If the bank makes you a loan, its regular interest rate will be charged. The rate will vary with your credit standing.

What will the banks charge for the bill-collecting process? Presumably they will get about 4 or 5 percent of the bills they process and collect for a merchant. This 5 percent will be included in the final price of the goods. But that is also the case now. If we use credit cards now, the final price of the goods must be higher.

Recently critics have raised some concerns over this Electronic Funds Transfer System (EFTS). For example, how could a consumer do the equivalent of stopping the payment of a check if purchased goods were defective? Some mechanism would have to be built into the system to permit consumer retrieval of any fund transfer for a period of time. This problem has not been solved. Then too there is the problem of the monthly bank statement and canceled check. The computer could no doubt be programmed to provide for a periodic account to serve as a bank statement, but some critics feel persons could lose some degree of control over their bank transactions. If no canceled checks are available, what legal proof would there be that consumers had paid their bills?

Other critics are concerned about electronic fraud. Someone might be able to manipulate the master computer and steal almost limitless funds. While the new voice print and fingerprint systems might stop such fraud, the cost and inconvenience of this might be prohibitive. Finally, some are concerned about the possible invasion of privacy that EFTS would bring about. All of a person's financial transactions would be recorded for possible scrutiny by unauthorized individuals. Perhaps legislation could be enacted to control this and to prevent the widespread dissemination of personal financial data.

It should be noted that the checkless society is different from the automatic funds transfer (AFT) system discussed in the previous chapter, which merely transfers funds from your savings to your checking account or vice versa. It is also different from truncation (discussed in the previous chapter) which gives you a computer printout record of your canceled checks, but does not return them.

OTHER THINGS TO KNOW ABOUT CONSUMER CREDIT AND CONSUMERISM

The Credit Application

Whether one is going to open a charge account or apply for any other type of installment loan, one must make an application for credit. The credit application is a request for information concerning place of employment, address, size of income, bank account, assets and liabilities, and whether or not one has ever had credit (See Figure 5–6). From this information, the credit investigation is made.

The Credit Bureau's Report

After one has applied for credit, the information is generally forwarded to a local credit bureau for verification. Every credit bureau maintains records containing information on many individuals, much of it obtained from the office of the clerk of the county in which one lives. For example, the fact that any judgments have been recorded against one is entered in the record. In addition, home ownership and all existing mortgages and recorded bills of sale are included.

LOAN APPLICATION

Texas Bank
Austin
900 Congress
Austin, Texas 78767   REPUBLIC OF TEXAS

IMPORTANT: Read these directions before completing this Application.

Check Appropriate Box

☐ If you are applying for individual credit in your own name, are not married, and are not relying on alimony, child support, or separate maintenance payments or on the income or assets of another person as the basis for repayment of the credit requested, complete only Sections A and D.

☐ In all other situations, complete all Sections to the extent possible, providing information in B about your spouse or the person on whose alimony, support or maintenance payments or income or assets you are relying.

AMOUNT REQUESTED	NO. OF MONTHS	PURPOSE OF LOAN
	PAYMENT DATE DESIRED	

SECTION A — INFORMATION REGARDING APPLICANT

APPLICANT'S NAME		BIRTHDATE (MO./DAY/YR.)	NO. OF DEPENDENTS (Including Self)	PHONE (Area Code & No.)
ADDRESS	APT. NO.	CITY	STATE	ZIP CODE	HOW LONG? YR. MO.

PREVIOUS ADDRESS (If at Above Less than 5 Years)	CITY	STATE	HOW LONG? YR. MO.

BUSINESS EMPLOYER	GROSS MONTHLY SALARY $	POSITION	HOW LONG? YR. MO.

BUSINESS ADDRESS	CITY	STATE	BUSINESS PHONE

PREVIOUS EMPLOYER (If on Present Job Less than 5 Years)	CITY	STATE	HOW LONG? YR. MO.

CHECKING ACCOUNT - NUMBER - NAME OF BANK ☐ NO ☐ YES	SAVINGS ACCOUNT - NUMBER - NAME OF BANK ☐ NO ☐ YES

Alimony, child support, or separate maintenance income need not be revealed if you do not wish to have it considered as a basis for repaying this obligation.

ALIMONY, CHILD SUPPORT, SEPARATE MAINTENANCE RECEIVED UNDER
☐ COURT ORDER   ☐ WRITTEN AGREEMENT   ☐ ORAL UNDERSTANDING

SOURCE OF OTHER INCOME	NET AMT. YEARLY $	NET AMT. MONTHLY $

IS ANY INCOME LISTED IN THIS SECTION LIKELY TO BE REDUCED IN THE NEXT TWO YEARS OR BEFORE THE CREDIT REQUESTED IS PAID OFF?
☐ YES (Explain in detail on a separate sheet)   ☐ NO

NAME OF NEAREST RELATIVE, NOT LIVING WITH YOU	RELATIONSHIP	MOTHER'S MAIDEN NAME
ADDRESS OF NEAREST RELATIVE, NOT LIVING WITH YOU	CITY	STATE	PHONE

SECTION B — INFORMATION REGARDING SPOUSE OR OTHER PARTY *(Use separate sheet if necessary)*

FULL NAME	RELATIONSHIP TO APPLICANT	BIRTHDATE (M/D/Y)	PHONE
ADDRESS	APT. NO.	CITY	STATE	ZIP CODE	HOW LONG? YR. MO.

BUSINESS EMPLOYER	GROSS MONTHLY SALARY $	POSITION	HOW LONG? YR. MO.

BUSINESS ADDRESS	CITY	STATE	BUSINESS PHONE

Alimony, child support, or separate maintenance income need not be revealed if you do not wish to have it considered as a basis for repaying this obligation.

ALIMONY, CHILD SUPPORT, SEPARATE MAINTENANCE RECEIVED UNDER
☐ COURT ORDER   ☐ WRITTEN AGREEMENT   ☐ ORAL UNDERSTANDING

SOURCE OF OTHER INCOME	NET AMT. YEARLY $	NET AMT. MONTHLY $

SECTION C — MARITAL STATUS

APPLICANT
☐ MARRIED   ☐ SEPARATED   ☐ UNMARRIED (Including Single, Divorced or Widowed)

OTHER PARTY
☐ MARRIED   ☐ SEPARATED   ☐ UNMARRIED (Including Single, Divorced or Widowed)

SECTION D — DEBT INFORMATION

(If Section B has been completed, this Section should be completed giving information about both the Applicant and Spouse, or Other Person. Please mark Applicant-related information with an "A". If Section B was not completed, only give information about the Applicant in this Section.)

OUTSTANDING DEBTS (Include all charge accounts, instalment contracts, credit cards, etc. Use separate sheet if necessary.)

TYPE	NAME AND ADDRESS OF COMPANY	ACCOUNT NO.	NAME IN WHICH ACCT. CARRIED	BALANCE	MO. PMT.
AUTOMOBILE LOAN					
MASTER CHARGE					
VISA					
INSTALMENT LOAN OR ACCOUNT					
INSTALMENT LOAN OR ACCOUNT					
REVOLVING ACCOUNT					
REVOLVING ACCOUNT					
☐ BUYING HOME ☐ RENT	NAME OF LANDLORD OR MORTGAGE COMPANY				

ARE YOU A CO-MAKER, ENDORSER OR GUARANTOR ON ANY LOAN OR CONTRACT? ☐ YES ☐ NO	HAVE YOU BEEN DECLARED BANKRUPT IN THE LAST 14 YEARS? ☐ YES ☐ NO	ARE THERE ANY UNSATISFIED JUDGEMENTS AGAINST YOU? ☐ YES ☐ NO

Everything that I have stated in this application is correct to the best of my knowledge. I understand that you will retain this application whether or not it is approved. You are authorized to check my credit and employment history and to answer questions about your credit experience with me.

SIGNATURE OF APPLICANT	SOCIAL SECURITY NO.	DRIVER'S LICENSE NO.	DATE
SIGNATURE OF SPOUSE OR OTHER PARTY (Where Applicable)	SOCIAL SECURITY NO.	DRIVER'S LICENSE NO.	DATE

Figure 5–6   Example of a credit application. (*Source:* Texas Bank of Austin.)

Credit bureaus also keep records of all previous credit extended, going back generally seven years. Credit bureaus are the "middle men"; they receive information from all merchants and institutions that extend credit, store it, and then sell it to any legitimate third party. A legitimate third party is anyone entering into a business transaction involving credit with the person on whom a credit report is requested. If the person requesting credit has established credit elsewhere locally, generally a phone call to the credit bureau is all that is necessary. The bureau will give the merchant the necessary information over the phone, and the fee for this service is only a few dollars. If the person requesting credit is newly arrived in town, it may be necessary for the credit bureau to telephone a bureau in some other town. In such cases, the cost of a credit report can grow quickly.

When a credit bureau receives a request from a merchant or lending institution, it will pass on what information it has gathered; but the bureau usually will not assign a credit rating such as poor, fair, good, or excellent. Generally, the information the credit bureau will pass on includes the following:

1. The person's place of employment
2. Length of time with employer
3. Position with the firm
4. Income
5. Husband or wife's income, if any
6. All credit extended over the past seven years and the date it was extended
7. The dollar amount of the extension
8. How the loan was paid off (whether in accordance with the agreement)
9. What kind of security, if any, was required on past loans
10. Whether the person rents or owns his or her own home
11. Judgments, if any, recorded against the person
12. Bankruptcies, if any, that the person has filed

In the case of a young person requesting credit for the first time, no record exists and the credit bureau cannot help as much. The merchant must make a decision based upon the person's place of employment, position, income, and any other information the merchant can obtain. Generally, if the person has a responsible position and is not asking for more credit than his or her income warrants, it will be granted. Then a person begins to build a "track record"; if he or she repays credit in accordance with the agreement, these regular payments will be reported by the merchant and recorded by the credit bureau.

Generally, a credit investigation is made only the first time one applies for credit. Once one has used credit one will have established what is known as a "line of credit." The lending institution and merchants keep their own records and will extend credit up to a maximum amount almost routinely. In such cases, one may still have to fill out an application form but will not have to wait for a credit investigation.

Credit Scoring

Credit scoring is a method of appraising the credit-worthiness of potential borrowers. Numerical values are assigned to various factors. It is believed that good credit risks share certain characteristics and poor credit risks share other characteristics and that by analyzing these with a credit scoring report card, better decisions can be made regarding the granting of consumer credit.

Home ownership is a plus factor and a homeowner may receive, say, 20 points. A renter will receive less, but will receive some points for having lived at his or her present address for a certain number of years. A person will receive a certain number of points for the job he or she holds (say, for example, a supervisor 25 and a clerk 5), and some more for having held it five years or more. The level of income, assets, other debts outstanding, and marital status will all generate additional points. The total number of points will then be used to help determine whether or not credit will be granted. The credit scoring systems must ignore race, sex, and where a person lives, but can analyze his or her economic and financial strengths. Lenders give various weights to credit characteristics, and they have their cutoff point at various total points. A hypothetical credit score and the probability of repaying a loan are shown in Table 5–4.

Table 5–4   Credit scoring

Credit score	Probability of loan repayment
Below 60	.0
60–64	.0
65–69	7.9
70–74	15.2
75–79	20.3
80–84	33.0
85–89	34.2
90–94	45.4
95–99	45.9
100–104	61.9
105–109	70.4
110–114	73.5
115–119	76.0
120–124	80.6
125–129	82.3
130–134	89.5
135–139	92.6
140–144	91.8
145–149	94.5
150–154	96.0
155–159	97.9
160–164	98.4
170 and up	100.0

Using such a system, loan officers must now make decisions as to where to draw the line, and to help, they may personally interview the prospective borrower.

Credit Life Insurance

Sometimes the lender will insist that the installment buyer purchase life insurance in an amount equal to the debt. The lender is the beneficiary; and in the event of the death of the buyer, the balance of the debt is paid off by the insurance company. The cost of this life insurance is passed on to the installment buyer. In the case of lending institutions, this cost often shows up in the form of an extra 0.5 percent interest per month. In arrangements made with merchants, it either shows up as an added service charge or is included in the price of the item. In some cases, the lender actually keeps a portion of the insurance premiums; only part of them is necessary to buy insurance. This is another illustration of a price pack to enhance the return of the lender or dealer.

Not all lenders and dealers will insist that the buyer take the credit life insurance. In some states, it is against the law to require that the installment buyer buy credit life insurance. However, the buyer seldom knows this, and the law is very difficult to enforce. The lender can simply let it be known that the credit life insurance will have to be purchased as a condition to granting the loan.

Consumers who don't need or want the credit life insurance should try to negotiate it out of the package when discussing the terms of the contract. Showing evidence of knowledge of the subject being negotiated makes it more likely one will be successful in achieving one's goals.

Credit Card Abuse

All credit cards should perhaps have printed on them the warning, "financial experts have determined that credit cards are dangerous to your financial health." They are, if you abuse or overuse them. Then you can get in over your head and your income might be inadequate to liquidate the debt. One cardinal rule of thumb should be: use your credit card as a convenience and not as a source of funds. That is, never use your credit card if you could not immediately write a check for your purchase. Then when you are billed, liquidate your entire credit card charge each month. In this way you never build up an unpaid balance, and your credit card is not a source of borrowed funds for more than a few weeks. It is a convenience in that you need only write one check. You might also consider limiting the number of credit cards you own. Remember, if you need to borrow, go to a financial institution.

IF YOU USE A CREDIT CARD

Unsolicited credit cards

It is illegal for a card issuer to send you a credit card unless you ask or apply for one. However, a card issuer may send you, without your request, a new card to replace an expired one. You may also be sent an application for a card in the mail or be asked to apply by phone.

Lost or stolen credit cards

Your risk on lost or stolen credit cards is limited.
You do not have to pay for **any** unauthorized charges made **after** you notify the card company of loss or theft of your card. So keep a list of your credit card numbers and notify card issuers immediately if your card is lost or stolen. The most you will have to pay for unauthorized charges is $50 on each card—even if someone runs up several hundred dollars worth of charges before you report a card missing.

Prompt credit for payments

If you can avoid finance charges on your credit card account by paying within a certain time, it is obviously important that you get your bills, and get credit for paying them, promptly. Check your statements to make sure your creditor follows these rules:

- Prompt billing. Look at the date on the postmark. If your account is one on which no finance charge is added before a certain due date, then creditors must mail their statements at least 14 days before payment is due.
- Prompt crediting. Look at the payment date entered on the statement. In most cases creditors must credit payments on the day received.

Refunds for overpayments

If you overpay on your credit card account by $1.00 or more, a creditor must give you a refund at your request. Overpayments can occur when, for example, you overlook a return of merchandise to be credited to your account.

Discounts for cash payments

It is illegal for credit card companies to prohibit stores from offering discounts to people who pay by cash or check. Stores that do offer cash discounts must make this fact clear to all buyers. They may not add an extra charge (above the regular price) for those customers choosing to use credit cards.

For example, suppose you want to buy an item regularly priced at $50. The store offers discounts for cash of 5 per cent. If you pay in cash, your price should be:

$$\begin{array}{r} \$50.00 \\ -2.50 \text{ (5\% of \$50)} \\ \hline \$47.50 \end{array}$$

If you use a credit card, the price is $50.

Credit card costs

How much you pay for the use of a credit card depends on three important terms of the credit card arrangement, which differ for cards issued by banks, by retail stores, or for travel and entertainment. Creditors must tell you:

1. The annual percentage rate (APR).
2. The method of calculating the finance charge.
3. When finance charges begin to be charged to your credit account.

Some creditors also charge a flat annual membership fee for use of their card. Federal law does not set rates or tell the creditor how to calculate finance charges— it requires only that the creditor tell you the method. Be sure to ask for an explanation of any terms you don't understand.

Tips on credit cards

•   Shop around for the best terms. Remember that finance charges may differ depending on the method the creditor uses to assess them.
•   Make sure you understand all the terms of your credit card agreement before you sign.
•   Pay bills promptly to keep up your good credit rating and to avoid high finance charges.
•   Keep a list of all your credit card numbers in case of loss or theft, and keep a good record of your purchases and payments.

Source: Board of Governors of the Federal Reserve System, Washington, D.C. 20551

Why Interest Rates Vary

Why do interest rates on consumer loans vary from one institution to another? Aside from reasons involving legislative permissions enabling the various institutions to charge different rates for small loans, there are other considerations. Management expenses tend to vary greatly among the lending institutions. For a small loan company management expenses are fairly high, because many of their loans are small, and it costs just as much to manage a $200 or $300 loan as it does for a $2,000 or $3,000 loan. In addition, small loan companies make loans to people who are poorer credit risks. Because of this risk, they charge higher interest rates.

The management costs of the credit unions are low. Because they are mutual organizations, they have very little overhead; often they are given rent-free office space by their employers. Their record of losses is very low, and they are given a tax advantage over the commercial banks.

The insurance company suffers no risk of loss when making a policy loan, and its cost of collection is very low because these loans are single-payment loans that in many instances are never repaid.

Commercial banks generally make loans only to the better credit risks. Because of this circumstance, their loss record is low, a fact that their interest charges reflect. Savings and loan associations also accept only the better risks. Hence their rates are usually below those of finance companies and are comparable to those of commercial banks.

Industrial banks, on the other hand, accept more risk and charge higher rates than commercial banks. Also, industrial banks make more extremely small loans—$50 to $100 and even less—that result in high administrative cost per dollar loaned.

As a general rule, when borrowing money, first try a commercial bank, credit union, or insurance company. Usually they charge less than other lending institutions. One should also know that the maximum interest rate permitted on small loans (consumer loans) is higher than the rate permitted under the general usury laws. There are three reasons for this difference in interest rates:

1. Usually the cost of the credit investigation is higher per dollar lent. It takes just as much time to run a credit check and determine the credit-worthiness of a person borrowing $100 or $1,000 as it does of a person borrowing $10,000 or $20,000.
2. The bookkeeping and record-keeping costs are higher on a small loan than on a larger loan per dollar loaned.
3. There is often more risk to the lender because of the credit rating of many of the people borrowing from small loan companies. Because of the higher risk of default, the lender insists upon a higher rate of interest as compensation for assuming the greater risk.

This third point, high risk, is not always present; this is why, however, if your credit rating is good, you should shop around. Certain lending institutions such as commercial banks will lend only to those with solid credit ratings, so they are taking a relatively low risk. Personal finance companies will lend to those with poor credit ratings; they take more risk and charge higher rates of interest. While most interest charges, even those going up as high as 30 or 40 percent, are perfectly legal, there are a few lenders who break the law; they are the illegal "loan sharks."

Small loan laws attempt to protect both the borrower and the lender. The lender is permitted to charge higher rates to compensate for the credit investigation, bookkeeping, and risks. Borrowers receive some protection in that while they pay what may be a relatively high rate in some cases, there is a ceiling on the rate they may be charged. If it were not for the legal ceiling, borrowers might fall into the hands of an unscrupulous lender who might charge even more. The unwary consumer should note that where money has been lent at a usurious rate, most states provide for the forfeiture of the principal or interest or both.

Single Repayment Loans

You may enjoy substantial interest savings when you borrow if you agree to repay the loan in one lump at a specific future time. You will then, of course, need to do your own budgeting and set aside a certain amount each week or month in order to have the wherewithal to liquidate the loan when due. The major reason why a person can obtain a much lower rate on a noninstallment type consumer loan is because the lender incurs fewer bookkeeping, record-keeping, and collection costs. If you borrow from an insurance company on a noninstallment basis, the annual percentage rate will be about 8 percent. If you then set aside a sum every week or month in a passbook savings account, you will earn anywhere from 5 1/4 to 6 percent for a net cost of about 2 or 3 percent. A single repayment loan from a bank, savings and loan association, mutual savings bank, or credit union will cost about 13 to 15 percent depending upon the size of the loan and your credit rating. This amounts to a net cost of about 8 to 9 percent if you use a passbook savings account to budget the repayment. It should be noted that in order to borrow from many lenders on a noninstallment basis, your credit rating must be better than that of many installment borrowers.

The Family Life Cycle and Installment Credit

A definite pattern of installment debt depends upon the life cycle of the family. Relatively speaking, the young, the old, and, to a lesser extent, the unmarried make little use of installment credit. With marriage and young children comes installment debt. As one wag put it, the finance company holds hands with the bride and the groom as they slowly wend their way from the altar.

Seventy percent of those spending units under the age of forty-five, with the youngest children age six or older, have some installment debt. As the children grow up, the installment debt of the spending unit decreases. The years from twenty-five to about forty-five are the years when most of us accumulate our durable consumer goods and raise our families. After that, when we have a household of durables and the children have "flown the coop," we need only make replacements and there is less need for debt.

The family life cycle in relation to age and statistics on installment debt shows this pattern to be consistent. For example, a recent study indicates that 12 percent of those under twenty-five had $2,000 or more of consumer debt. At twenty-five to thirty-four years old, this figure was 19 percent; at thirty-five to forty-four, it was 15 percent; at forty-five to fifty-four, it was 20 percent; for ages fifty-five to sixty-four, it was 8 percent; and for those over sixty-five, it was only 3 percent.

Early Repayments: The Rule of 78

Supposing that sometime soon after assuming some consumer debt, a consumer experiences good fortune and discovers that he or she is able to repay it far in advance of the installment schedule. The question is, if the debt is paid off in advance, is an interest rebate given? The answer is yes, in most cases. Generally the method used to calculate this rebate is referred to as the *rule of* 78, but this figure is misleading. It could just as well be called the rule of 21 or the rule of 171. A few examples will make this clear.

Suppose that Mr. Wilson borrowed $1,200 to be paid off in twelve equal monthly installments at 12 percent. This makes his monthly payments $106.62. Then, when the third monthly payment is due he decides to liquidate the entire debt. How is the interest recalculated?

First, take the sum of all numbers from 1 to 12; they equal 78. If the loan is repaid in full after one month, the lenders receive 12/78 of the interest that they would have received had the loan been outstanding the entire year; if it is liquidated after two months, the lenders receive 12 + 11 or 23/78; if after three months, 12 + 11 + 10 or 33/78 and so on. Only if the loan is outstanding the full twelve months does the lender receive the full 78/78 of the agreed-upon interest. Calculating the interest for early repayments by this method results in the lender getting somewhat more than a strictly pro rata distribution of interest. For example, after three months on a pro rata basis, the lender would get only one-fourth of the total interest, which would be 19.5/78 in the example used above. This would be a true interest rate of about 6.6 percent for these three months. It is less than the annual 12 percent that would have applied if the loan had been amortized normally because the declining balance (and hence the average balance) is relatively high during the early months of the loan. But because of the sum-of-the-digits method, the lender gets 33/78, which in our example is 33/78 of $79.44 or a total interest payment of $33.59. This is about 12 percent per year simple interest over these three months. What the sum of the digits does is to increase the interest rate on installment loans to put it back up where it would have been had the loan been amortized normally.

Suppose that in another case $900 is borrowed to be paid back in six monthly installments of $150, but after two months the entire loan is liquidated. This could be called the rule of 21 (the sum of the digits from 1 to 6 = 21). The lenders would receive 11/21 of the total interest if the loan is repaid after two months. The sum of the digits is the rule, and it can be used to calculate the interest on an early repay for a loan of any length. All that is needed is to know the total number of payments and the total interest, in dollars, that would be paid if the loan were not liquidated early.

Assume, for example, that an eighteen-month installment loan is repaid in full after six months. The sum of the digits here gives us 171 (18 + 17 + 16 + 15, etc.). Since six months have elapsed, the lender receives 93/171 (18 + 17 + 16 + 15 + 14 + 13 = 93) of the interest that would have been received had the loan been outstanding the entire eighteen months.

To be sure, lenders do not calculate these rebates in this manner because tables have been prepared and the lender merely looks up the rebate from the tables. These tables have been prepared, however, by using the sum-of-the-digits method described here.

Credit Counselors

In recent years, an additional service has been developed in some states that some borrowers have found useful. It is a service known as *credit advisors* or *credit counselors*. Credit advisors are not a source of credit and they do not lend any money. They provide two useful services.

First, they help a person to manage his or her personal affairs; they may set up a budget and persuade the client to live within it. For example, if a person has monthly payments in excess of his or her ability to pay, the credit counselor will attempt to stretch out the debt over a longer time period and in this way reduce the monthly payments. Second, after having worked out a new payment plan that the individual can meet, the credit advisor will act as the middleman and attempt to persuade the lender to accept the new reduced monthly payments. As a disinterested third party, he or she can often do this more easily than the person involved.

No one who is capable of budgeting and managing his or her own financial affairs should have to use credit counselors. However, the growth of this group indicates that some people either cannot or will not do this for themselves.

Credit counselors charge a fee for their services, generally 12 percent of the outstanding debts (negotiated by them). This then is the fee one pays for not capably planning one's own affairs. Most lenders, too, will act as credit counselors for the borrower and, in most cases, will stretch out payments to keep the borrower afloat.

Certified Financial Planners

In recent years a somewhat more sophisticated personal financial planner and advisor has emerged. The certified financial planner (CFP) is able to assist the individual in virtually all aspects of personal financial affairs, including budgeting, restructuring excessive debt, insurance, investments, problems of home ownership, taxes, and even, in some cases, estate planning. Remember that if the CFP is not an attorney, he or she cannot legally draw up a will. Many CFPs are also either accountants, securities brokers, insurance agents, real estate brokers, or attorneys who have broadened the scope of their services.

Some of the planners have kept their former specialty and will aid the individual in financial planning for little or no fee, earning a commission by selling securities, insurance, or real estate to the person. Other planners charge a fee for their services; it can be either a flat fee or a percentage of the assets involved.

The concept of the certified financial planner was originally developed by the College of Financial Planning in Colorado, which was established by a group of financial planners. There is also an International Association of Financial Planners with headquarters in Atlanta, Georgia.

FINANCIAL DOCUMENTS ACCOMPANYING CONSUMER LOANS

A Typical Installment Contract

When you buy something or borrow money on the installment plan, you must sign some papers. The same is true when you borrow on a single repayment loan. Figures 5–7, 5–8, and 5–9 show this. The first is a typical security agreement and installment contract. It is the type generally used to finance the purchase of new automobiles in Texas, but it is drawn up in accordance with the Uniform Commercial Code and also conforms to the federal truth-in-lending law. Consequently, with slight variations, contracts similar to it are used for new cars throughout the United States. This type of contract is also employed to finance other durable goods.

This contract shows (as required by the truth-in-lending law) the number of payments, the fact that they are equal in dollar amounts, the total interest cost dollarwise as well as the true annual percentage rate (APR), and other pertinent facts.

It also has a default and delinquency clause, which spells out certain conditions of the agreement. It provides that the borrower pay all court and attorney's fees if they are necessary to collect payments. It also stipulates the penalty for late payments. The second document is a note for a 90-day single repayment loan. It is much like the first document. The third item is for a $200 30-day loan. In this case there is a $15 minimum fee. Over 30 days this amounts to 90 percent.

SOME DOS AND DON'TS OF CONSUMER CREDIT

The main advice we can provide when you use consumer credit is: "be careful." We can also summarize the things to do and not to do when using consumer credit, as follows:

Dos

1. Before you sign any credit application, decide how you are going to meet the payments when due.

PROMISSORY NOTE, DISCLOSURE STATEMENT AND SECURITY AGREEMENT
Chapters 3 or 4 — Precomputed Interest (Substantially Equal Monthly Payments)

ACCOUNT NO.

DEBTORS' NAME & ADDRESS (Last Name First)	LENDER/SECURED PARTY	DATE OF NOTE	OFFICER
Doe, John 2205 5th Street Austin, TX 78767	RepublicBank Austin 900 Congress P. O. Box 1328 Austin, Travis Co., TX 78767	2-10-84	

In this agreement the words "you" and "your" mean the Lender. The words "I," "we," "my," "our," "me," and "mine" mean each and all Debtors (and in the Security Agreement only they also mean any person who has signed the Security Agreement only but who has not assumed personal liability on the Note).

FEDERAL TRUTH-IN-LENDING DISCLOSURE

ANNUAL PERCENTAGE RATE The cost of my credit as a yearly rate.	FINANCE CHARGE The dollar amount the credit will cost me.	Amount Financed The amount of credit provided to me or on my behalf.	Total of Payments The amount I will have paid after I have made all payments as scheduled.
14.50%	$ 1,953.84	$ 8,170.08	$ 10,123.92

My payment schedule will be:

No. of Payments	Amount of Payments	When Payments Are Due	
36	$281.22	Monthly beginning	3-10-84

Insurance

Credit life insurance and credit accident and health insurance are not required to obtain credit, and will not be provided unless I sign and agree to pay the additional cost.

Type	Premium	Signature	
CREDIT LIFE	170.08	I WANT CREDIT LIFE INSURANCE	SIGNATURE
CREDIT ACCIDENT & HEALTH	n/a	I WANT CREDIT ACCIDENT & HEALTH INSURANCE	SIGNATURE
CREDIT LIFE & CREDIT ACCIDENT & HEALTH	n/a	I WANT CREDIT LIFE & CREDIT ACCIDENT & HEALTH INSURANCE	SIGNATURE

I may obtain property insurance from anyone I want that is acceptable to you. If I get the insurance from you, I will pay $ __n/a__
for the term of ____n/a____

Security: [Check applicable box(es).] I am giving a security interest in:
☒ the goods or property being purchased.
☐ _____

☐ this loan is unsecured.

Collateral securing other loans with you may also secure this loan.

Filing Fees: $ ____n/a____
Late Charge: If a payment is late for more than 10 days I will be charged 5¢ for each $1.00 of the payment.
Prepayment: If I pay off early, I will not have to pay a penalty and I may be entitled to a refund of part of the finance charge.

I will see my contract documents for any additional information about nonpayment, default, any required repayment in full before the scheduled date, and prepayment refunds and penalties.

e means an estimate

COLLATERAL & SECURITY AGREEMENT

Collateral will consist of:

1984 Buick Regal MVN 123456789

Collateral will be used by me primarily for:
☒ Personal, Family, or Household Purposes
☐ Agricultural   ☐ Business
Collateral will be located in ____Travis____ County at
☒ Debtors' Address ☐ Other Address:

I grant to you a security interest in the above described collateral, together with all parts and equipment used in connection therewith, additions, replacements, accessions, proceeds, products, and similar after-acquired property; provided this security interest shall not attach to after-acquired consumer goods, except accessions, unless I acquire rights in such after-acquired consumer goods within ten days after you give value. This security interest is given to secure payment of all my present and future indebtedness of any type to you, including without limitation: future advances; all expenditures by you for taxes, insurance, repairs to and maintenance of collateral; and the reasonable cost for repossessing, storing, preparing for sale, or selling the collateral.

The terms of this Security Agreement include the provisions printed on the reverse side.

SIGNATURES FOR PARTY SIGNING SECURITY AGREEMENT ONLY. I grant Lender/Secured Party a security interest in the collateral, but do not assume personal liability on the Note. (Warning: I will not sign here if I signed below):

X

PROMISSORY NOTE

Words in this Note have the meanings shown in the Federal Truth-In-Lending Disclosure box. To repay the loan you have made me, I promise to pay the Total of Payments to you or your order at your address shown above at the times and in the amounts shown in the payment schedule set out in the Federal Truth-In-Lending Disclosure box. I will pay each payment on the same day of each month.

PREPAYMENT: I may prepay this loan in full at any time without penalty and you will refund or credit any unearned finance charge based upon the method described in the Texas Credit Code and called the "Sum of the Periodic Balances Method." You will do this if the refund is one dollar or more. No refund will be made for partial payments. If I prepay in full before the first installment due date, you will retain for each elapsed day from the date the loan was made, one-thirtieth of the interest you could retain if the first installment period were one month and I prepaid the loan in full on the first installment period due date.

DELINQUENCY CHARGES: If I do not pay any installment in full within 10

Figure 5–7   Typical security agreement. (*Source*: Texas Bank of Austin.)

Itemization of the Amount Financed of $ ___8,170.08___

$ _____   Amount given to me directly

(_____ $ _____

_____ $ _____)

$ _____   Amount paid on my account with you

Amount paid to others on my behalf:

$ _____   to public officials

$ _____   to insurance companies

$ __8,170.08__   to ___draft_____

$ _____   to _____

[Check Applicable Box(es)]

[x] REQUIRED PROPERTY INSURANCE — IF THIS BOX IS CHECKED, PROPERTY INSURANCE IS REQUIRED IN CONNECTION WITH THIS LOAN AND I HAVE THE OPTION OF FURNISHING THE REQUIRED INSURANCE EITHER THROUGH EXISTING POLICIES OF IN-SURANCE OWNED OR CONTROLLED BY ME OR OF PROCURING AND FURNISHING EQUIVALENT INSURANCE COVERAGES THROUGH ANY INSURANCE COMPANY AUTHORIZED TO TRANS-ACT BUSINESS IN TEXAS. I WILL FURNISH THIS INSURANCE THROUGH:

_____
Agent/Insurance Company

_____
Agent's Address

_____
Agent's Phone Number

This Amount is Included in the Amount Financed for Property Insurance:

$ _____

[ ] INSURANCE NOT SOLD AT FIXED OR APPROVED RATE:

If this box is checked, the required property insurance is sold for a premium not fixed or approved by the State Board of Insurance, and I may cancel such insurance without charge within 5 days from the date of this Note and substitute other equivalent coverage in the manner described above.

[ ] INSURANCE INCLUDED IN THIS CONTRACT AT MY OPTION:

If this box is checked, charges in the amounts shown below for the insurance shown are included in the Amount Financed.

Credit Life	$ __170.08__
Credit Accident and Health	$ _____
Credit Life and Credit Accident and Health	$ _____

Please Charge My	Account Name:
Checking Account	Account Number:
for the Payments [ ]	Customer's Signature:

RPT-90-250-014-01

days after the scheduled due date, I will pay you a delinquency charge, not exceeding five cents for each one dollar of any such installment.

DEFERRAL CHARGES: If I ask, you may agree in your discretion to defer the payment of an installment for one or more full months, and if you do so I agree to pay deferment interest equal to the difference between the refund which would be required for prepayment in full as of the deferment date and the refund which would be required for prepayment in full one month prior to that date, multiplied by the number of months in the deferment.

ACCELERATION OF PAYMENT: You may accelerate payment or performance of this Note without prior written notice to me if: (a) I am in default on the per-formance of any of my obligations under this Note or the security agreement or (b) you in good faith believe that the prospect of payment or performance is impaired. If you do so, you will calculate the unearned portion of the finance charge on the date you accelerate the loan exactly as if I had prepaid the loan in full on that date and you will give me necessary credits so that in no event shall the amount of finance charge contracted for, charged or collected under this Note exceed the maximum finance charge permitted by law.

RIGHTS AFTER DEFAULT: After you accelerate the maturity of the Note or after the final scheduled maturity date, whichever occurs first, I agree to pay interest from that date calculated upon the amount legally owed by me at an annual rate of interest equal to 18%, provided that interest paid or agreed to be paid shall not exceed the maximum amount permissible under applicable law and, in any contingency whatsoever, if you shall receive anything of value deemed interest under applicable law which would exceed the maximum amount of interest permissible under applicable law, the excessive interest shall be applied to the reduction of the unpaid amount of Note or refunded to me. In addition you will have a right to set off any debt you owe me against the debt I owe you.

WAIVERS: I and anyone who endorses or guarantees this Note each and all waive presentment for payment, demand, notice of dishonor, and diligence in bringing or prosecuting any action under this Note and we agree you may renew or extend this Note, accept partial payments, and release or substitute collateral, all without notice to us, before or after maturity, and that you may also extend the time of payment, and that additional makers, comakers, guarantors, and sureties may become parties hereto without notice to us or any of us and without affecting my liability hereon. If you accept partial payments or performance it shall not operate as a waiver for any requirement of this Note.

ATTORNEY FEES AND COURT COSTS: If this Note is referred to an attorney for collection, I agree to pay the amounts actually incurred by you as court costs and attorney's fees assessed by a court.

OTHER COLLATERAL DOCUMENTS (If Any) USED WITH THIS CONTRACT:

DEBTORS' SIGNATURES

DEBTOR SIGNATURES FOR PROMISSORY NOTE & SECURITY AGREEMENT. I/We agree to the terms of this Promissory Note, Disclosure Statement, & Security Agreement ("this agreement") and acknowledge receiving a com-pleted copy of this agreement and all other documents signed by Debtor in connection with this loan. The terms and conditions on the reverse side are made a part of this agreement and are incorporated herein by reference.

X _____

Home Phone	Business Phone

X _____

Home Phone	Business Phone

NOTICE: See other side for important information.

Figure 5–7   (continued.)

2. Find out how much you have left after all your necessary expenses and payments are taken out.

3. Remember that credit costs money. Renting money is like renting a house or a car—you have to pay for its use. This means that an item bought on credit costs more than if it is bought for cash.

OFFICER	DATE	MATURITY DATE	AMOUNT OF NOTE	ANNUAL RATE OF INTEREST (AR)		LENDER'S PRIME PLUS	PERCENT-AGE POINTS	DAILY RATE

⊠ RepublicBank Austin PROMISSORY NOTE (Single Maturity)

NOTE NUMBER 9999   ACCOUNT NUMBER 1111-11-1

| OFFICER | DATE 2-10-84 | MATURITY DATE 5-10-84 | AMOUNT OF NOTE $2,000.00 | FIXED RATE OF 10 % | or | | 1/365 of AR |

Terms used in this note shall have the meanings indicated in the boxes above. ON DEMAND, or if no demand is made then on or before Maturity Date, for value received, Maker promises to pay to the order of Lender at Lender's address shown above the Amount of Note plus interest on unpaid Amount of Note from Date at the AR. Unpaid and past due Amount of Note and interest shall bear interest at the highest rate Lender lawfully may charge on this note. Until the earlier to occur of Demand or Maturity Date, interest shall be computed at the Daily Rate. If the AR is stated in terms of Lender's prime rate, the AR shall change with each change in such prime rate as of the date of any such change, but shall not exceed the highest rate Lender lawfully may charge on this note.

Each Maker, guarantor, surety and indorser waives demand, presentment, notice of dishonor, protest and diligence in collecting sums due hereunder; agrees to application of any debt of Lender to the payment hereof; agrees that extensions and renewals without limit as to number, acceptance of any number of partial payments, releases of any party liable hereon, and releases or substitutions of collateral, before or after maturity, shall not release or discharge his obligation under this note; and agrees to pay in addition to all other sums due hereunder reasonable attorney's fees if this note is placed in the hands of an attorney for collection or if it is collected through probate, bankruptcy, or other judicial proceeding. Reasonable attorney's fees shall be ten per cent (10%) of the unpaid balance unless either party shall plead and prove otherwise. The holder may accelerate the Maturity Date without prior notice to any party at any time he shall deem himself insecure, if Maker shall fail to pay any other debt to Lender when due, or if any default or event of default shall occur under any agreement securing, evidencing, guaranteeing, or providing for, debt of Maker to Lender. As used herein, where appropriate, the masculine gender includes the feminine and neuter and the singular number includes the plural.

Payment hereof is secured by:

John Doe
2205 5th Street
Austin, TX 78767

MAKER

FORM 320-154

Figure 5–8 Ninety-day single repayment note. (*Source:* Texas Bank of Austin.)

4. Be sure you find out how much more an item bought on credit will cost you. Insist that the salesperson give you a written statement showing all costs and charges *BEFORE* you decide whether or not you want to buy this item.

5. Be a good shopper. Compare cash and on-time prices for the same item in different stores.

6. If you get careless with credit and find your payments, when added to your necessary living expenses, are more than your paycheck, don't try to hide from your creditors. Ask about consolidating your debts. The lender may be able to lend you enough to pay the bills and to stretch out the payments so your monthly payments will be reduced to where you can handle them. But, remember, extra time costs extra money; so don't do it unless it is the only way you can pay your debts.

7. Analyze a deal before you sign for it. Look at total cost (purchase price plus interest) of the item you are considering. Would you pay that much in cash for it if you had the cash in your pocket? Would a cheaper model do just as well? Do you really need the item at all?

Don'ts

1. Don't let a smooth-talking sales representative pressure you into a final sale on credit to take advantage of a special bargain. If the "special bargain" is only going to last a few hours, it may not be so special.

2. Don't be a soft touch for a smooth salesperson who uses an emotional approach. *Example:* "You owe it to your kiddies to buy this set of encyclopedias

NOTE (SERVICE CHARGE)   Note No. _____

Name(s) and Address(es) of Borrower(s)	Name and Address of Bank
John Doe 458 West Rd. Harbor City, AN 068501	State Bank of Allston 7600 Brighton Road Harbor City, AN 068501

Date of Note	Total of Payments	Officer
8-10-79	$ 215.00	AB

For value received, Borrower(s) whose name(s) and address(es) appear above (hereinafter called "Borrower") hereby promises to pay to the order of the Bank whose name and address appear above (hereinafter called "Bank") at Bank's address shown above the Total of Payments shown below in a single payment due _____ 9-9-79 _____.

No default, delinquency or similar charges may be charged or received by Bank in connection with this Note.

In the event of prepayment of this Note in full or in part, Bank will **not** refund or credit to Borrower any of the Finance Charge.

1. Cash Advanced or Credit Extended $ 200.00	4. Service Charge $ 15.00
2. Prev. Bal. Renewed (Note #__n/a__) $ -0-	5. **FINANCE CHARGE** (same as 4) $ 15.00
3. Total Amount of Credit/ Amount Financed (1+2) $ 200.00	6. Total of Payments (3+5) $ 215.00
	7. **ANNUAL PERCENTAGE RATE** 90.00 %

All parties to this Note including endorsers and guarantors severally waive presentment for payment, notice of nonpayment, protest, notice of protest, demand, notice of dishonor, diligence in enforcement and indulgences of every kind.

Borrower agrees that the service charge disclosed above represents the reasonable value of the services rendered by Bank in connection with the loan evidenced by this Note.

I (We) acknowledge receipt of a copy of this Note executed on the Date of Note above written and completed as to all essential provisions and agree to its terms as set forth above.

Borrower: John Doe   Borrower:

_____(X)_____   _____

Figure 5–9   Thirty-day note.

(only $400)." By the time your kiddies are old enough to use them, the books will be outdated and worthless—and you will probably be in a much better position to afford the set they need than you are now.

3. Don't fall for the old sales gag about the "other buyer who is going to snap this bargain up" if you don't sign on the dotted line at once. If Salesman Sam really had a customer that eager, he wouldn't be trying so hard to sell you.

4. Don't buy anything—for cash or credit—that you don't really want or need just because it is cheap. *Example:* One eager customer signed up for a $260 super-model sweeper. Later, when creditors came around to see why he was behind in his payments, they found he didn't even own a rug. Of

course, few people are this eager to buy, but far too many seem unwilling to match their wants and needs with a realistic understanding of their ability to pay.

5. Don't buy anything just because you can get in on credit—or because no down payment is required or because payments are small. Remember, you will have to pay the full price in the end—plus the cost of credit, which is higher if no down payment is made or if payments are stretched over a long period of time to keep them low.

6. Don't count on a supplementary salary in any long-range credit plans (over six months). Layoffs may occur or a wife may become pregnant; then earnings may be cut off.

7. Don't take unnecessary chances. Buy from dealers in whom you have confidence. When you pledge a part of your earnings for the next several months, you want at least to know that you are dealing with a reputable businessperson who has an established place of business and one you can find in case the merchandise is faulty.

8. Don't expect to erase your debt by returning the merchandise. In most cases you have signed two contracts: one for the purchase of the goods and one for the loan of funds. In many cases, your loan contract will be sold to a bank or finance company at once and you will owe it instead of the dealer. Dealers should stand behind the goods they sell, but you still have to pay the loan in full, even if the car you bought won't run.

9. Don't sign a contract that a salesperson offers to hold until you make up your mind. Chances are it will be executed before you are out of sight. *Example:* A woman wanted to try out a used car and the obliging salesman agreed to let her use it for the weekend but "for her protection, insurance, etc." he insisted on having a contract signed that he promised to hold. When the woman took the clunker back on Monday and said she wouldn't buy it, she found she already had.

10. Don't sign your name to anything you have not read completely and carefully and that you do not understand fully. If a salesperson says the contract is standard and doesn't let you read it at your own pace, watch out.

11. Don't sign a contract that seems to be different from what the salesperson told you. In case of doubt, have the salesperson write out what he or she promises, sign it, and give it to you as a part of the agreement. If the salesperson refuses, take yourself away before this person takes you.

12. Don't let a smooth salesperson switch contracts so you read one and sign another. If the contract is taken away (for an OK) after you have read it, read it again when it is brought back to be sure it is the same one. Watch for different wording on carbons and for "short sheets" where you read one short page and actually sign a longer one hidden beneath it.

13. Don't overlook the fact that in some states you can't take mortgaged goods across the state line without permission of the mortgage holder. If you

might be moving before a major purchase is paid for, check this point before you sign on the dotted line.

QUESTIONS FOR REVIEW

1. How is consumer credit classified for statistical purposes by the Federal Reserve Board?
2. Distinguish between an installment loan and a single-payment loan.
3. Distinguish between a charge account and what has been commonly labeled *service credit*.
4. The text gives a number of reasons for consumer borrowing; list three and explain each in detail.
5. How do individual savers benefit by consumer borrowing?
6. It is said that society as a whole may benefit from consumer credit. Rationalize this statement.
7. Explain how easy credit and the careless use of it may actually wreck your budget.
8. Explain in detail whether consumer credit "costs" anything.
9. What are the underlying reasons for permitting small loan companies to charge as high a rate of interest as they do?
10. Explain the manner in which credit unions are organized.
11. What is the difference between the industrial bank and a commercial bank?
12. Differentiate between the remedial loan society and the pawnshop.
13. How may it be said that borrowing on a life insurance policy has a psychological drawback for many consumers?
14. In order of the lowest cost of borrowing, list the seven financial institutions discussed in the text.
15. What are sales finance companies and what is their relationship to consumer lending?
16. Explain in detail the workings of the revolving credit plan.
17. Do you think the checkless society will be a reality soon? What are your views regarding it?
18. What is a credit bureau? What does it do?
19. What is credit life insurance?
20. Aside from permissive legislation, discuss the reasons for variations in loan charges among the various financial institutions that grant consumer loans.
21. How does the family life cycle relate to the volume of the family's installment debt?
22. If you pay off your loan early, is there an interest refund?
23. What are credit counselors, and how do they differ from sales finance companies?
24. Discuss the dos and don'ts of credit.

CASES

1. Mary Rupp recently opened a revolving charge account at a large department store. The clerk told her she could always have some balance outstanding. However, every month she is billed for her entire account. She cannot reconcile these two facts. Can you help her?

2. In order to obtain consumer credit, it is generally necessary to make an application and undergo a credit investigation. What is the information for which you will be asked when you apply for credit? What will the credit investigation attempt to reveal?

3. Bob and Patricia Snelling, a young married couple, are recent arrivals in town. They rented a small apartment and have little savings left. Bob has a job at which he makes $400 per week and Patricia is seeking employment.

   Joe and Ellen Worth, on the other hand, have lived in the same community for twenty years. The Worths are in their forties, and Joe is a foreman at a local plant where his weekly salary is $600. Moreover, the Worths have a $20,000 mortgage on a $75,000 house.

   Both couples apply for a loan at the local finance company in order to buy a new car. Which applicant is more likely to receive a loan? Why?

4. Bill Brown has found a used car priced at $1,500 that he would like to buy. He has $1,000 in the bank and he can save $50 per month. Should he want until he has saved $500 and pay cash for the car, or should he borrow $500? What are advantages of waiting and paying cash? What are the advantages of borrowing and financing the car? Can you think of any disadvantages in borrowing the money?

5. Bill Hardy bought a used Ford valued at $2,400 and used his older car as a down payment. He agreed to pay off the balance of $1,600 over two years in twenty-four equal monthly installments of $79.50. What is the true interest rate on the loan?

6. Betty Canfield bought a used car valued at $1,800. The terms of the agreement provided that she make a down payment of $600 and pay the balance at $109 per month over twelve months. What is the actual dollar cost of the credit? What is the true interest rate she is paying for the use of the credit?

7. Helen Walker has decided to buy some new furniture for her apartment. One store has offered to finance it on the basis of $100 down and $20 a week for sixty-five weeks. Another store has offered her the same furniture at $100 per month for fourteen months with no down payment. The furniture is priced at $1,200 if sold for cash. Which of the two stores is offering Helen the better deal? What is the effective interest rate in both cases? Can you offer any suggestions that may save Ms. Walker some money?

8. Bob and Virginia, a young married couple, have decided to buy a television

set on the installment plan. The set they want costs $225 if bought outright for cash. The dealer has offered it to them for $20 down and $5 per week for fifty weeks. They think this makes the set rather expensive. Calculate what the set will cost them and what proportion of it is interest in absolute dollars. What is the true interest rate?

9. Jean and Dick are a young couple who recently purchased a color television set on the following terms. They paid $50 down and are paying $50 per month. They are to make ten payments. Yet the sum total which they must pay is $800. They don't understand how they can pay the total sum in ten payments. Can you explain it to them? If they had been able to pay cash, they could have obtained the set for $700. What interest rate are they paying?

10. Jim Hoffman earns $300 per week take-home pay. He has the following installment loans to pay off:

car $75 per month for ten months
refrigerator $25 per month for eight months
furniture $30 per month for twelve months
loan from bank $30 per month for six months

Jim's budget cannot meet these payments. Can you prepare a plan whereby Jim can pay off his debts? The most he can pay is $80 per month. Where can he go for such service?

11. Dorothy Jenkins is a young schoolteacher in Santa Ana, California, who borrowed $600 to repair her car after an accident and to meet other expenses. She agreed to pay it back in nine monthly installments of $74.70. What interest rate is this? However, after two months, Dorothy was reimbursed by an insurance company and was able to liquidate the entire loan. Calculate the actual dollar amount of interest Dorothy paid. What true annual percentage rate is this?

SUGGESTED READINGS

Banking Journal of the American Bankers Association. New York: American Bankers Association. Published monthly.

Cole, Robert H. *Consumer and Commercial Credit Management,* 4th ed. Homewood, Ill.: Irwin, 1980.

Consumer Credit and You. Greenfield, Mass.: Channing L. Bete Company, Inc., no date.

Consumer Finance News. Published monthly by the National Consumer Finance Association, Washington, D.C.

Consumer Finance Rate and Regulation Chart. Washington, D.C.: National Consumer Finance Association. Revised annually.

Consumer Loan and Sales Finance Rate and Regulation Chart. Washington, D.C.: National Consumer Finance Association. Revised annually.

Consumer Reports. A monthly publication of the Consumers Union of the United States, 256 Washington Street, Mt. Vernon, N.Y.

Cost of Personal Borrowing in the United States. Boston: Financial Publishing Company. Published annually.

Credit. Washington, D.C.: National Consumer Finance Association. Published bimonthly.

"Credit Research Center Working Papers." West Lafayette, Ind.: Credit Research Center, Purdue University. A series of research studies on topics significant to consumer credit.

Family Budget Guide. Washington, D.C.: National Consumer Finance Association.

Finance Facts Yearbook. Washington, D.C.: National Consumer Finance Association. Published annually.

Galanoy, Terry. *Charge It: Inside the Credit Card Conspiracy.* New York: G. P. Putnam's Sons, 1981.

International Credit Union Yearbook, 1984. Madison, Wis.: CUNA International, Inc. Published annually.

Let's Learn About Consumer Finance. Washington, D.C.: National Consumer Finance Association.

NCFA Research Report on Finance Companies. Washington, D.C.: Research Services Division, National Consumer Finance Association. Published annually.

Taylor, John. *Consumer Lending.* Reston, Va.: Reston Publishing Co., 1982.

U.S. Department of Agriculture, *Consumers All, The Yearbook on Agriculture.* Washington, D.C.: U.S. Department of Agriculture. Published annually.

Wood, Oliver G., Jr., and Barksdale, William C. *How to Borrow Money.* New York: Van Nostrand Reinhold, 1981.

CHAPTER SIX

CONSUMER SPENDING

Preliminary Comments on Consumerism
Prepurchase Analysis—Prevention
Making Purchases
Postpurchase Redress Procedures: How to Recover Your Losses
Consumer Protection Agencies

We are all consumers and would like to get the most for our dollar. Consumerism involves planning before we shop, then shopping around and comparing prices and values before we buy.

PRELIMINARY COMMENTS ON CONSUMERISM

While new legislation and business self-regulation now improve the bargaining position of the consumer in the marketplace, consumers must still use good judgment and be able to handle their money armed primarily with their own knowledge. If shoppers cannot solve their problems on their own, they should know where to get some help and how to complain and get results. *Caveat venditor* means "Let the seller beware." Persons who can enter the marketplace with the confidence that sellers of goods and providers of services should fear their presence are in a state of mind that few—if any—consumers can legitimately attain. Nonetheless, buyers should constantly seek to have knowledge equal to or better than their seller counterparts if they are to obtain adequate value for their limited dollars. *Caveat emptor*, "Let the buyer beware," is the traditional view taken of the buyer (by many sellers) in American popular culture. Its literal application could result in worthless medicines, dangerous cosmetics, and sky-high prices in those instances where the buyer is uninformed. Legislation, business self-regulation, high ethical standards of American businesses, and competition serve to prevent many of the hazards of pure *caveat emptor*. Still, within the law,

Grateful acknowledgment is extended to Lee Richardson, Martin Marietta Eminent Scholar, Professor of Marketing at the University of Baltimore and Vice President of The Consumer Federation of America for assistance with this chapter.

there is much latitude for the consumer to waste money or cause serious physical or psychological injury to self, family, or others as a result of ignorance. All is fair in love, war, and—to some extent—the marketplace.

The consumer's arsenal of knowledge and tactics can be divided into three areas: (1) prepurchase decision-making activities, which consist of analysis before making purchases; (2) making actual purchases, which requires some care; (3) postpurchase redress procedures, which deal with how to recover any losses. Customers must think of their financial position, budget, and priorities as well as choosing brands, comparing prices, and avoiding deceptive practices before spending any money. In the long run, successful prevention of difficulties through prepurchase decisions and the making of wise purchases will save more time, money, and sorrow than postpurchase redress treatment later, even if successful. Those who buy now and think later are blissfully ignorant of whether they correctly managed their money and got value received for value spent. Sometimes buyers who depend on treatment instead of prevention can only hope for satisfaction in the event they were legally wronged, often at the cost of legal assistance and considerable time and effort.

We Have Met the Enemy, and He Is Us

The critics of the consumer movement say it has gone too far, that often its adherents' complaints are not legitimate. Their complaints, it is alleged, often occur because something costs too much. The critics maintain that high cost are the results of inflation and not something over which businesses have control. While this may be true at times, it is not at others. Sometimes the consumer has legitimate complaints. Sometimes shoppers can also avoid problems by wise shopping. But if they cannot, they should know where to get help, or how to complain and get results.

In many cases the consumer is also a producer. As consumers we demand perfection; we want good quality products. As producers we are careless and often provide shoddy work. These are the opposite sides of the same coin.

Consumer Education

The education of the general public on consumer economics and finance is in its infancy. Various voluntary consumer organizations throughout the country are supporting educational efforts in consumerism both in and out of the public schools.[1] Nevertheless, the level of sophistication among the general public on consumer finance is not great, and therein lies part of the problem. A more informed consumer is a wiser consumer.

---

1. A group that works with consumer education nationwide is the Coalition for Consumer Education, 1314 14th Street, N.W., Washington, D.C. 20005.

Keeping Records (Receipts)

In Chapter 2 the importance of keeping records was discussed, for tax as well as other reasons. This is also important when you have a grievance with a merchant. Keep your purchase receipts. On "big-ticket" items especially, keep them for a year or two, or at least until the warranty has expired. On smaller items, or if there is no warranty, use your own judgment. Keep your receipts at least until you have used the item for a time and know it is functioning properly. One small manila folder will provide space for all of your receipts.

PREPURCHASE ANALYSIS—PREVENTION

Consumers may feel that good buying habits consist of bargaining for the lowest price on a stereo system or finding a sale on a pants suit. This may be misguided—much like worrying about deck chairs on the Titanic. Probably the most significant decisions about priorities and life-style are made with less conscious thinking effort than decisions about the details of the product or its price. For example, a family may argue more about the make of an automobile or which accessories to purchase than about its size or whether they need a new car or any car at all. These latter decisions are sometimes made with little regard to cost. A family may purchase a camper when it could save considerably by renting one for the few occasions it will use the vehicle. A parent may worry about the best buy in asparagus when the children would get by on highly nutritious spinach at one-third the price.

When buying services, the consumer must be even more wary because it is often even more difficult to judge quality. This is particularly true in buying professional services—those of lawyers, accountants, or physicians, for example.

Incompetent and Shoddy Workmanship

When you buy services, you may come directly in contact with incompetent or shoddy workmanship. Of course, when you buy an auto, television set, or any other item, you may obtain a product that has had shoddy workmanship embodied in it at the factory, and you have a lemon. But in such a case you must deal with the seller, and you have no direct control over poor workmanship as you do when you buy services.

Most repair services, whether for autos, household appliances, or general home repairs, are provided by small businesses. Not much capital is needed to open a repair shop, and consequently new firms are constantly entering this field. The casualty or failure rate is also high and firms from which to choose are in a constant state of flux. There are two dangers to guard against when dealing with repair firms: first, shoddy workmanship by people who don't care and, second, people who are incompetent, or there can be a combination of the two. In many cases a person wishing to become an artisan will work for an established shop for a year or two and then strike out on his own, long before he has experience in business or talent as an artisan.

To avoid incompetent and shoddy workmanship you should find out how long the business has been in existence and how many years' experience the individual workers have had. Often those firms that have advertisements as well as listings in the Yellow Pages of the telephone directory will indicate how long they have been in existence. You can also call your local Better Business Bureau (BBB) or Consumer Protection Agency.

When dealing with home repair services, realtors are a good source of information because they often deal with these people. Another source could be insurance adjusters, since they deal with roofers, plumbers, tile installers, and the like when they pay damage claims. Another way to ascertain which firms provide quality services is from personal experience and the experiences of friends and acquaintances. At a minimum, ascertain if the firm or its employees has the basic certification, licensing, or other credentials required by local or state government.

How to Pick an Expert; Choosing the Pros

Everyone is, from time to time, faced with the task of selecting an expert in a field in which he or she may be a novice. The following professional expert specialists are examples:

Dentist
Insurance Agent
Lawyer
Medical Doctor
Realtor
Stockbroker
Tax Accountant

If you need one of these experts how do you find one who is truly competent? This is especially true if you are new in town. To be sure, if you were dealing with one of these professionals in another city in a national firm, say Merrill Lynch or Arthur Anderson, you might be content to use the local office of the same firm, but this is not always possible. There is also the problem of the first-time user. If you are young and have never had an accountant, a lawyer, or a broker, how can you be assured of getting a good one when you need one for the first time?

When choosing a professional you need first to define and focus your need. If you need the services of a lawyer, what kind do you need? Lawyers specialize as do other professionals. There are tax attorneys, real estate attorneys, corporate attorneys, and others. A tax attorney may be completely ignorant about real estate. And as we all know, dentists and doctors also specialize.

Some firms have several specialties under one roof. If you visit a large law firm, brokerage house, or bank, there are many specialists to work with. At a large brokerage house, there are some who specialize in commodities and some in municipal bonds.

Even after you have defined the type of expert you need, you still have to decide which one to use. As before, sometimes your friends and acquaintances may be able to help. As before, you should find out how long any expert has been in this sort of work. Try to find out who other clients or customers are.

You may also sometimes be able to use one expert to help pick another one. Experts know experts in related fields. For example, if you know a corporate lawyer but need a tax expert, the corporate lawyer may be able to recommend one. Your banker too may be able to recommend various experts. Banks use a wide variety of experts and know which ones are the best. Many bankers, when they recommend an expert, will give you several from whom to choose.

For more important cases—especially if you are going to establish a permanent relationship with, say, a tax accountant who will compute your taxes year after year—you may wish to secure a face-to-face interview with several experts before choosing one. Set up an appointment for an interview and have all of your questions ready so as not to waste the expert's time. Probably 10–15 minutes is all the time he or she will grant without charging a fee. Incidentally when you telephone to arrange for an appointment, ask whether there is an interview fee and how much it is. Most reputable firms will grant a prospective client a free interview. If the one you call charges a fee, be a bit suspicious.

During the interview you should find out about the person's credentials, the experience he has had, and what degrees he or she has earned. You should also inquire regarding his or her fees. Trust your instincts to some extent. If the expert is candid and can answer all technical questions, this means a great deal. After the interview you should be able to form a good opinion regarding the extent of the person's expertise. If you interview two or three experts, you will also probably have an opinion about which one would be best for you.

Choosing a Brand

When buying goods, consumers frequently and incorrectly equate brand image with quality. If a product is well known, they presume it will have met the test of previous consumer satisfaction, but that is not necessarily the case. The name brand or well-known brand may simply be the most heavily advertised and promoted brand rather than a superior product. Particularly where taste is a matter of individual preference or stylish products have different appeals to different individuals, the brand image may be an unreliable guide to quality and value.

Brands have different values to different people. Every buyer should know the particular significance of a brand being considered for purchase; he or she should not rely on an intuitive feeling. The following guidelines will help clarify vague feelings.

1. Guide to popularity of the product. What is the significance of popularity? Is it important to the buyer to use a popular soft drink, especially if it is more expensive?

2. Guide to quality. What quality features are important to the buyer, and does this brand have them? Does the buyer want light weight or durability in a bicycle?

3. Guide to style. Does the buyer want the stylish features represented by this brand? Is the furniture style important for a television set in the basement?

4. Guide to service and follow-up by the maker. Does the foreign make of automobile have adequate parts and service facilities where the buyer plans to drive?

5. Guide to price. Does the product represent a high-priced or a moderately priced line? Does this brand of jeans have a discount reputation because it is constantly being offered on sale or because it is consistently lower in price?

6. Guide to prestige. Does the choice of watches make the buyer appear affluent or successful or does it represent the buyer as a penny-pinching bargain hunter? Is prestige or the time of day more important in a watch?

7. Guide to status. Does the choice of a certain type of winter coat appropriately represent the buyer's occupation, social class, or general standing in the community? Does the appearance of middle-class social status symbols or protection against the weather count more?

Consumers base some choices between brands on poor information. Of the hundreds of brands found in a supermarket, consumers will be unable to do much more than merely recognize some proportion of them. While recognition at least means that the consumer has run into the brand some time in the past through experience, conversation, advertising, or other promotion, familiarity with the brand alone doesn't make a logical argument for purchase.

The brand problem is not completely understood without an investigation of the private label brand. The national or regional manufacturers' brands are usually better-known; however, the consumer will benefit from lower prices and comparable qualities in certain private labels or a store's own brands. Today, chain department, general merchandise, food, and specialty stores have excellent values in their own lines of goods, made by the retailer's own plants or more often to specification in the factories of other nationally known name brand companies. On frequently purchased products such as food, over-the-counter drugs, and toiletries, a consumer should experiment in the hope of finding an adequate brand that could result in savings of as much as 50 percent on all future purchases. Pain relievers, canned fruits and vegetables, toothpastes, mouthwash, facial tissues, and audio cassette tapes are good beginning points for inexpensive experiments.

Choosing the Store or Vendor

Often the food buyer's first question in a discussion of saving money in the supermarket is, "Which store has the lowest prices?" The question reveals a major gap in consumer understanding of good spending habits because the questions of product choice and brand choice should be given some weight in the budget. Other pertinent questions about the store or vendor include the varieties and qualities of the products, the types of sales, various services such as delivery and credit, and the convenience of shopping.

The discount store is deceptively labeled in those instances where product quality is inferior to that in higher-priced stores. Regular department stores and discount stores have in many cases evolved to the point where only their names distinguish them. Some discount stores have legitimate overall savings opportunities, while the same is true of discount departments in otherwise higher priced department stores. Knowledgeable shoppers will find good values and lower prices on particular items in any store except those in Alaskan mining towns, isolated tourist souvenir shops, or railroad car dining rooms.

Sources of Information

Newspaper advertising

This is a reliable and low-cost source of information for price-conscious buyers because of the frequent use of price advertising and sales information. Department stores, drug chains, record shops, and grocers have regular advertisements on a daily, weekly, or other schedule that customers can expect. Wednesday or Thursday grocery advertisements and Sunday department store advertisements are reliable recurrent events in large and small cities. End-of-month, semiannual, and annual sales are common to other stores. Seasonal and holiday sales are expected from such merchants as sporting goods stores, clothiers, and toy stores. The January white sales, George Washington birthday sales, Labor Day sales, and day-after-Christmas sales are well known to American consumers. Each of the seasonal sales provides an opportunity to those who plan purchases for them; on the other hand, they can be financial disasters for persons who make unplanned and unnecessary purchases even at low, low prices. A $150 lawn mower purchased for $100 can be either a $50 savings or a $100 violation of a tight budget. Too, some merchants seem to advertise one gigantic sale after another, leaving the false impression that they never sell at regular prices.

Special directories

The telephone directory's Yellow Pages provide names of many services and retail businesses, particularly those that the consumer does not visit often. For someone needing to call a plumber, electrician, or photographer, the Yellow Pages provide a reasonably current and complete listing. Unfortunately for consumers, unreliable dealers and professional services are listed side-by-side with reputable firms, although sometimes the advertisements will show when the business was established or whether it is licensed.

Another special directory is the classified newspaper section. Besides its role as intermediary between consumers and businesses selling particular items, classified newspaper advertising provides a forum for consumers to buy and sell goods among themselves. *Caveat emptor* is the rule of classified selling because its advertising carries no guarantees of reliability and fair dealing and to some extent is similar to a laundromat bulletin board. Only a few other special directories exist in retail selling. Some large cities have specialized entertainment, restaurant, or tourist guides of varying quality. Many guides recommend all of their advertisers; the more independent gourmet guides—which may carry no advertising—feel free to criticize the biggest restaurants in town. Newspapers and magazines published for residents of certain cities contain information about current entertainment options, service firms, and other vendors.

Better business bureaus (BBBs) and consumer protection offices

Found in many U.S. cities and counties, semiautonomous BBBs and public consumer agencies have unique resources in their permanent files to assist consumers before they make their purchases. Consumers generally expect such offices to assist them in times of trouble after unwise purchases, whereas they emphasize preventive inquiries from potential buyers, both to benefit the consumer and to protect honest merchants from sales lost to disreputable sellers. Such agencies can provide prevention and treatment for consumer problems of certain types. Moderate-sized offices in smaller cities record tens of thousands of instances of service or service requests. Some serve 100,000 or more requests each year. Most of the work of these organizations concerns the handling of phone, letter, and personal visit inquiries directly from consumers who want to know whether they can rely upon a particular merchant, product, charity, service company, or repairman. Because of various legal complications, these offices do not directly recommend or condemn a business or other organization. However, consumers can accurately interpret a statement such as, "We suggest you contact an attorney before doing business with ABC company," or "We have no cases of unresolved complaints against the firm."

Educational work is extensive in the consumer offices and BBBs. Free pamphlets are provided on subjects ranging from the purchase of carpets to participation in multilevel sales organizations. Many also use newspaper publicity, mobile van exhibits, and other means of reaching people to educate, alert, and warn them about consumer problems. They are not exclusively concerned with assisting persons in selecting merchants, but their local orientation makes them expert in this area of consumer concerns. Nearly all are well informed, professionally managed organizations that attempt to serve legitimate businesses and consumers at the same time.

Consumer Protection Agencies differ from BBBs. Consumer offices are publicly financed, whereas BBBs derive support from businesses directly. As a consequence, some Consumer Protection Agencies are more independent than BBBs in their pursuit of wrongful practices by some sellers. Another limitation of BBBs is their general association with business organizations such as Chambers of Commerce, with a consequent reluctance to follow up aggressively against fellow merchants charged with undesirable sales practices.

Private industry's rating and evaluation systems

Rating systems such as Underwriter's Laboratories, National Electrical Manufacturers Association, Society of Automotive Engineers, and Good Housekeeping's seal can be useful aids in their particular areas of concern. These evaluators also have limitations: There are too few of these systems, and they tend to evaluate only a limited amount of information, such as UL's electrical safety standards, NEMA's electrical input and output, or SAE's service qualities for motor oil. They do not directly compare all brands, and sometimes their standards of acceptability represent only minimum satisfactory performance. These sources are not of uniform quality, and their ratings may have been influenced by the industries that pay for their services. These private industry sources may provide little assurance of quality or reliability even where they appear to offer general blanket endorsement. Good Housekeeping's seal, for example, does not actually give unqualified approval to products, but will only assure replacement or refund if the product is defective and then under limited conditions only.

Consumers Union

Consumers Union, a unique and reliable organization, uses valid tests in most cases and makes competent recommendations directly measuring and comparing brand performances. But such service has limited applications: While it makes tests of many appliances and other major purchases such as cars, its coverage of most other products such as foods, medicines, clothes, or furniture is spotty. Consumers Union evaluates quality, safety, and convenience, but rarely style and other factors of varying importance to consumers. It publishes an annual *Buying Guide* and a monthly magazine, *Consumers Reports*.

Labels and packages

The consumer has an opportunity to evaluate the qualities of products through information obtained from examination of the package or the product itself. Information content of packages varies widely between classes of products, and much of it is required by federal and state law.

Inspection of products, often indicated by labels or stamping marks, is required of some food and nonfood products. Grade, quality, and condition must all be certified in some instances. Eggs, for example, are graded for age, sorted by size, checked for other qualities and the quantity contained in the package, and sometimes are required to show the name and address of the packer. Fresh produce labels show weights, grades, and specific varieties of vegetables and fruits. "U.S. No. 1 red potatoes" is a typical designation on a ten-pound sack of potatoes. Be careful not to assume inspection means maximum quality; it usually is only a minimum. Grading standards are often based on shipping needs or sizes rather than qualities such as taste.

Listing of ingredients for prepackaged food, drug, and certain chemical products is required. The amount of each ingredient is not usually shown, but the ingredients are listed in descending order of amount on the labels. Confusion may result in cases where "beef and pork" is listed as one ingredient because the relative proportions of each are not clear. Such a list must include special additives like artificial color, artificial flavor, preservatives, and other chemicals. Some food products like cola drinks do not list ingredients because a special exemption has been granted. Minimum criteria must be met for standardized products like ice cream, strawberry jam, and mayonnaise, but ingredients are not required to be shown. Imitation products such as nondairy coffee creamer or imitation cream cheese must be so labeled. A description of nutritional qualities is missing from most food product labels. Pet foods labels usually give percentages for each nutrient, and processors of human foods have begun adding nutritional information in some cases.

Labels rarely show cost per unit of measure or weight. Unit pricing, increasingly found in large supermarket chains, gives the cost per ounce, pound, quart, or other measure for certain varieties of products regardless of the size of the package. For example, if a six-pack of twelve-ounce bottles of soft drinks costs $1.92 and an eight-pack of sixteen-ounce bottles costs $2.88, the cost per ounce is $.026 in the first case and $.022 in the second. Unit pricing shows the cost per ounce so that the consumer will not have to carry a calculator.

Standardized packaging helps consumers make better price comparisons if the weight or other measure of two packages is identical. If two packages of similar toothpaste brands are 6 3/4 ounces each, then a $.99 purchase is better than an $1.03 one. When two sizes or more are found, the consumer then must make the calculation per unit of measure.

Some packages are too big for the product. While standards for size and slack fill allowed in many food and nonfood products have been established, the consumer is advised to read the label for the weight rather than judge volume by the size of the carton, can, or bottle.

Packages containing hazardous ingredients or having hazardous uses are normally labeled to that effect. Some advise remedies in case of misuse or swallowing, and others have prominent warnings on proper handling. Special packaging to protect contents against contamination or adulteration is becoming more frequent.

Labels contain information on the use of the product. A lawnmower may have permanent metal plates showing how to start it. A prescription label has the dosage directions. Some labels exaggerate ease of use. Most consumers are familiar with the "easy open" carton or can that requires pliers and ice pick. Other examples of suggested uses that appear on labels are recipes for foods and ideas for applications of glue. The over-the-counter medicine with the label promising cures for cancer, gout, and insomnia fortunately is disappearing.

MAKING PURCHASES

When making purchases, you should exercise care so as not to be deceived and so as to get the most for your money. People are constantly being subjected to false and misleading advertising, deceptive trade practices, and other pitfalls. There are also some money-saving tips with which you should be familiar.

Common Deceptive Practices and Other Pitfalls

"Wholesale prices" advertisements

Many retailers advertise items at "wholesale prices." Retail establishments cannot sell you merchandise at wholesale prices, by definition. There is no standard to determine a true "wholesale price" or the meaning of claims such as "at wholesale" or "wholesale to everyone."

"Free tapes, books or records"

Books are by no means free if customers buy a set of additional books at inflated prices equal that of the regular price of the books plus the normal cost of the additional books. "Four books for $1.00" or "12 albums for $1.00" are variations on this kind of promotion.

Improvements and repairs

Homeowners are annually bilked out of thousands of dollars by con men with phony "improvements" to homes or property. Often itinerant peddlers will claim expensive repairs are necessary to prevent furnace explosions or termite damage.

Free merchandise with a redemption coupon

The offer of "free" merchandise with a redemption coupon is often a trap baited with low-quality merchandise, such as plastic steak knives. Such gimmicks bring customers face to face with a salesperson, where they may obligate themselves for costly and possibly unneeded merchandise, such as a sewing machine.

Close-out sales

There are fire sales, water-damage sales, going-out-of-business sales, removal sales, lost-our-lease sales, and other dubious reasons for holding sales. Some of these types of sales are legitimate, while others are not.

Charity promotions

Promoters often prey upon sympathies of citizens to raise funds for charities. While the charity may be legitimate, the fund-raising expense or promotion fees may consume as much as 90 percent of the gifts. Penny bubble gum machines sometimes are touted as charities, but the charities may see very few pennies.

Vanity biographical listings

There are several publications of famous-person reference books that charge listed consumers by requiring them to purchase a copy of the publication in order to be listed. No one reads them. Libraries don't buy them.

Illegitimate training schools

Many individuals with modest savings are induced to buy a correspondence course to become a writer or artist or to enroll in a school that trains truck drivers. Some of these courses will not improve the income of the student but will enrich the school.

Private sale offers

Dealers may use classified ads without identifying themselves and offer overpriced used furniture or even jewelry and furs.

Obituary exploiters

A con artist may send bills to the bereaved family for nonexistent obligations or purchases.

Pigeon drop

Incredible numbers of persons still meet strangers who offer to share a large cash treasure they have found if the dupe will put up "good faith" money until the treasure is delivered to be divided among the lucky group. The good faith money is never seen again.

Neighbor's deliveries

Don't pay for products sent to a neighbor who isn't home. The neighbor may not have ordered them.

Unordered merchandise

Generally, unsolicited mail orders or other unwanted deliveries of products do not have to be paid for in spite of the repeated bills and collection notices that may follow. Check with a consumer agency, BBB, or post office when in doubt.

Auto gas mileage saver

The thousands of special additives and assorted devices sold to improve auto performance are almost all useless or unproven. They may harm the engine, too.

Inheritance search

The person who claims to be able to help locate deceased wealthy relatives is operating a service for a fee. The fee becomes a means of increasing the wealth of the fee collector.

Health cures

Numerous persons are subject to chronic illness or the fear of major disease and disability and become the object of quack medicine men. Mexican cancer cure resorts and the fountain of youth are sad illusions to those who turn to them for help. Hair restorers, bust developers, and weight-reducing creams are cheaper but more common forms of health quackery.

Referral sales

It makes little sense to spend $300 for an $80 vacuum cleaner in the hopes of securing $10 payments for each of the persons who are referred to the salesperson and who decide to buy. It still happens.

Chain letters

Many people don't mind sending $1 to the person whose name is on top of a list of persons, if $10,000 may be forthcoming someday. Supposedly, the $1 contributor's name will rise to the top of the list that he or she is asked to reproduce and mail to ten friends with similar instructions. While illegal, chain letter games still flourish.

Vacation dream resorts

Expensive brochures with artists' conceptions of future development may create illusions of Shangri-La. It is obviously unwise to invest in undeveloped, unseen property sold by unproven promoters; but it is easy to let dreams guide our checkbooks.

Dancing instructions

Lonely men and women desire companionship, and persuasive salespersons are aware of this frailty of human nature. As a result, the prospective dancer can be swept into two years and $1,800 worth of unnecessary lessons.

Multilevel marketing pyramids

Some high-pressure sales organizations offer unwary buyers of distributorships an opportunity to sell cosmetics, wigs, taped self-improvement courses, or almost anything at big discounts if they invest heavily. Unfortunately no one buys the products.

The psychological price

A price of $4.95 appears smaller than $5.00, but the difference is minute; $4.73 appears to be a carefully cut price that was shaved to the lowest penny. Possibly the $4.73 or the $4.95 item will be a $4.00 value rather than a $5.00 value.

The inflated list price

Far too many merchants use artificial prices—often stated as regular or list prices—that were not the prevailing price for the product at any time in the past. The list price becomes the basis of discount price claims. Videotape recorders, record albums, and personal computers are rarely sold at list. Very few automobiles are sold at the list or "sticker" prices that must be shown on the windows of new cars. Superinflated list or suggested prices are common in the markets and bazaars of foreign countries, where the customer is expected to pay as little as 25 percent of the original price after a round of haggling.

The oversold discount

Furniture and appliance stores may spend more time explaining what money buyers are saving rather than what money they are spending. A consumer may enjoy saving $30 from the original price, but the $199 remaining price on a refrigerator is the price to evaluate closely and to compare to prices of other refrigerators.

Multiple pricing

Items are difficult to compare if one brand of canned applesauce is 27¢ and three of another similar-sized can sell for 83¢. A temptation is to buy three because of the suggestion of the pricing method.

Trade-in price

Automobiles are easy to trade to a dealer. The important figure in a trade is the difference between the sale price and the trade-in price. A dealer who gives $300 more discount on a new car but a trade-in price of $400 less on the trade is not offering as good a value as a competitor. Some appliance or auto supply dealers offer trade-ins on mostly worthless used appliances, tires, or batteries as disguised price discounts.

Slightly used-product discounts

The demonstrator car with a few miles of dealer use or the floor sample stove with a slight scratch may both possibly be sold at significant discounts. Sometimes, however, "like new" products have been badly abused and repaired.

Repossessions

Some stores frequently reclaim merchandise from debtors who cannot pay for it and, for surprising discounts, will resell the merchandise in very good condition. Customers should wonder about both the physical condition of the product and their own financing arrangements with the dealer who has many repossessed goods for sale.

"Loss leader" pricing

Stores use considerable amounts of price discounting, but they also expect to make a profit. There may be adequate profit even in a discounted item; but probably the seller expects to sell other products at regular, profitable prices to persons who come to the store to buy the special leader items.

Bait-and-switch pricing

Unethical dealers will try to persuade the customer to buy other products rather than the specially priced one. A "bait and switch" prospect is told that the "bait" is very poor, out-of-stock, or difficult to show. Furniture dealers may place their special bait in a fourth-floor storage room. A carpet salesperson may arrive for a home demonstration without samples of the bait item but well stocked with expensive substitutes.

There are many new schemes being invented each year to lure the unwary consumer. The only solution is to investigate thoroughly before spending money on any unusual opportunity or offer. Often a simple investigation resulting from a single moment of lucid thinking can save hundreds and thousands of dollars for a consumer who makes a mistake under pressure or false impression.

Money-Saving Tips

The tips one can receive from various sources to stretch buying power are endless. Extensive literature from public and private sources must be culled to obtain useful facts on the great variety of products available to American consumers.

Families can save as much as 25 percent on their food spending by using common sense alone. If a family is really interested in conserving its dollars, then even more substantial reductions can be made in the food bill.

Consider the nutritional aspects of your food.

- Look at the calorie count of the foods that you're eating. Most middle-income Americans can do without a lot of the foods that they eat, but they refuse even to consider doing it.
- Eliminate unnecessary snack foods such as cookies, candy, and potato chips that are generally expensive and nutritionally deficient. A nutritionally deficient food simply does not have to be eaten unless nothing else is available to stop that hunger pang.
- Cut down on expensive beverages such as soft drinks of doubtful nutritional value. The only nutritional defense for some soft drinks is that they contain water, an essential in human diets.

Examine your need for meats, especially expensive beef, lamb, and pork; you may be able to make substantial savings in just this type of food.

- Buy some lower-cost cuts and learn many interesting ways of cooking them. In the final analysis, consider the cost per serving.

- Switch your meat buying to cheaper fish, poultry, and organ meats, which have generally good nutritional value and may be appealing if cooked properly to persons who may now think they are not.
- Avoid convenient quick-service stores unless the extra 5 to 20 percent cost of foods in these stores is necessary. Surveys show some items in these quick-service stores can cost 50 percent over supermarket prices, and these stores rarely have good sale prices.

All consumers need to discover among the various stores where they shop which of the important items on the shopping list are available in those stores at good bargain prices.

- Do not waste money going to many markets, but shop one or two different stores each week, alternating among the several stores with which you are familiar. You do not want to waste precious gas; on the other hand, vary your stores every now and then to get the best values.
- Select a particular store or stores to shop in each week, primarily on the basis of major bargains you will be able to stock up on during that week. Use weekly or semiweekly newspaper advertisements to make your decisions, but don't overlook a no-frills store that doesn't spend money on advertisements.
- When real bargains come along, be ready to spend above your budget. Even if it is going to take another $5, $10, or even $50 for a particular week to take advantage of a few unusually good bargains, you should violate your budget to do so. After stocking up on some of these key items, future budgets are going to be easier to meet because you are living off the stocked-up items that you bought at good sale prices. The principle is not to miss bargains that will save you a lot of money just because you have some artificial limit on how much you spend at the grocery store each week.
- Do not be embarrassed or afraid to ask for huge quantities of bargain items when they are available, such as a case of food or fifty cans or twelve chickens when the price is unusually good.
- Buy as much as you can store or freeze until the next bargain comes along. For example, chicken sales are quite regular, and you do not need to stock up for as many weeks' supply of chicken as you would for items such as canned asparagus, which is rarely put on sale. If you estimate that the next bargain will come along in one or two months, buy enough at a sale price to carry you through until the next sale.
- In season, buy yearly quantities of seasonal fruits and vegetables where possible if you are able to can or freeze them. If you do not like to can or freeze items because it takes time to do it, reconsider.
- Invest in a freezer to save money only after a realistic look at the operating and depreciation costs of a freezer. Usually you will not save money unless you have a large family. Consider also if you want to pay a little more

for the convenience that you get for the extra $10 to $30 a month that the freezer and electricity combined are going to cost you.
- Keep trying new low-cost alternatives including generic brands.

In trying to choose between different brands of foods, consider the following principles:

- Be willing to switch brands when prices shift up and down. Do not get into a habit of buying the same brand. Many widely used products change prices regularly due to special promotion or sales that the alert consumer can take advantage of.
- Do not judge a bargain by its advertised price. In supermarket advertisements, there are more regular prices being advertised than there are sale prices. Check this out, and you will see that many of the advertisements carry only 10 percent of items that are on sale; the rest are regular prices.

Here are some hints on drug store and prescription prices:

- Some identical prescriptions are sold at different prices by the same drug store—price is at the druggist's discretion. The druggist may lower the price to help the poor, but don't count on it.
- Do not be afraid to ask your doctor to prescribe generic products. Often the generic equivalent can save you a great deal compared to the brand name product.
- Pharmacies may tell you whether a prescription can be purchased more cheaply off the shelf without going through the process of having the prescription filled. In other words, not every prescribed item has to be prescribed.
- If a drug store says it "will not be undersold," make the druggist meet the price that you pay at other drug stores. The same principle applies to other types of merchants with the same claim.
- Learn some home remedies, like salt gargle, and ask your doctor whether the claims of the television commercial for mouthwash and other modern concoctions are really valid.

Among many suggestions that have been offered to energy consumers (households and others) are the following:

- Use one large bulb rather than several smaller ones. For example, one 100-watt incandescent lamp usually produces more light than two 60-watt lamps.
- Turn off lights, heat, and air conditioning in unoccupied rooms and closets.
- Unplug electric clocks and even some televisions (which use electricity when turned off) when on vacation.
- Weatherstrip and caulk all houses.

- Plant deciduous trees and vines on the south and west sides of homes to provide protective shade against summer sun.
- Service gas and oil furnaces regularly to improve efficiency.
- Shut off gas furnace pilots in summer.
- Use washing machines and dishwashers only when a full load has accumulated.
- Eliminate yard lights where security is not a factor.
- Select more efficient appliances for purchase.
- Install radial tires on all automobiles.
- Do not overfill gas tanks on cars.
- Drive at a steady, moderate speed.
- Buy products made of recycled materials wherever possible.
- Buy articles made of those materials that present best opportunities for recycling.
- Ban smoking in public buildings so that the amount of fresh air intake can be reduced.

Miscellaneous Tips for Consumers

- Watch for people who are selling second-hand items in garage and moving sales. Many people are in a hurry to move out of town and have to get rid of items that may be useful to you, but some may overprice. Beware.
- Be on the lookout for white elephant sales and similar sales of schools and civic groups.
- Buy a cheap postage scale; one that sells for about $1 is a bargain. With today's postal prices, you can't afford to overestimate.
- Special delivery is only a help when you send mail to regular addresses. There is nothing gained when mailing special delivery to a post office box number.
- Do not ever pay postage due unless you know what you are paying for. You are under no obligation to pay postage due unless you want to accept the letter or package.
- Do not spend extra money on gasoline grades; on the other hand, do not spend too little if doing so will damage your engine. Follow the car manufacturer's recommendations.
- Consider the labor costs of rotating your tires; you may often find that it is cheaper and just as safe not to have your automobile tires rotated every few thousand miles.
- Check chain outlets for blemished tires sold at much lower prices due to minor imperfections.
- Save coupons that give you a few cents off on purchases. Keep an envelope available and start collecting them when you receive them in newspapers, magazines, and in the mail.
- When a special is out of stock, insist that the merchant give you the right

to come back and purchase it later at the sale price. Even if they do not usually offer a so-called rain check, they will probably give you one anyway if you insist on fair play.

- Standardization in clothing sizes is yet to come. When comparing sizes in different brands, do not assume that one size is going to be identical to that of another brand of clothing.

- As soon as you get home, change from your good clothes. Good clothes can be thus saved, and it would be more economical to wear cheaper house clothes.

- Learn how to shop a sale. At the beginning of the sale, you get a better selection, but at the end you may get further markdowns on the sales items that are moving too slowly.

- Don't overlook rebates, mail-in refunds, and other special offers. Check store bulletin boards or shelves for such offers, often worth several dollars apiece.

- During party season, run your parties back to back, to take advantage of the leftovers from previous parties.

- Why be extravagant when you wrap gifts? White tissue may be adequate for certain small gifts or children's gifts at any time of the year.

- To avoid paying a surcharge every month for an unlisted phone number, use a special name of your own choosing and give it out only to close friends.

- Just as a combination lunch of sandwich and drink may be less expensive than each ordered separately, the prices on several major complementary items will be less than their individual prices added together. Rooms of furniture, place settings of silverware, or stereo component collections may be sold at combination prices. It is common to find a minor accessory given away to the buyer of a major product. Ice trays or ice makers given to refrigerator buyers or batteries with a radio are common examples.

- Fashion goods or overstocked items are severely cut by many merchants to free capital for other purchases or to clear out products that are becoming worthless. Some stores specialize in buying markdowns from better, well-known stores that do not want to gain the reputation of being price cutters themselves. Styles may change, but consumers who do not worry about style in clothes or other merchandise can find 30 to 75 percent savings. Christmas cards may be stored for 11 1/2 months, and 50 percent savings on December 26 makes their purchase so far in advance worthwhile. Buy Christmas and greeting cards by the box when you know you'll be using them.

- Some firms will give an immediate discount to a customer who shows any interest in a product. This discount price is perhaps only the beginning of the bargaining. Small, owner-managed firms are good places to attempt to bargain. Owners may bargain whereas hired employees are usually not authorized to negotiate prices.

- While a retailer may offer only one price, another firm of a different type will sell the same item at a much lower price because it pays a wholesaler's price to the manufacturer. Building supply houses, among others, may sell to other retail dealers or even consumers at a discount because of their status as wholesalers. Farmers' prices may vary from those of retailers, and by buying fertilizer from a farmers' supply store instead of a city hardware store, significant savings can be realized.

Other Things You Should Know About Consumerism

The discount house

While cash discounts are difficult to obtain, in recent years the discount house store has developed, and in many cases better bargains can be obtained in the discount house than in more traditional stores. There are several reasons for these savings.

First, in many cases these stores are located in the suburbs or outlying areas and in plain buildings. This may result in lower land and construction costs than the traditional store has even if it moves to the suburbs.

Second, the discount house relies on self-service to a greater extent than the traditional store, reducing its labor costs. The discount house tries to lower costs even more by hiring part-time help such as students and others whom they pay less. Lower wages result in more labor turnover, but the stores do not mind. This turnover may reduce costs because a larger proportion of the employees are at the starting and hence minimum wage than is the case in a traditional store. Employees in a discount house are trained to do only a very few things, so the service is generally of a slightly lower quality, but usually adequate. Finally, discount houses often carry fewer lines of big items such as refrigerators, which they can buy in larger lots, reducing costs further. Because of lower costs, discount houses can pass some of their savings on to the consumer.

Warranties

Warranties are usually granted by the manufacturer, not the retailer or the lender. The retailer, however, is usually the one who will repair (or occasionally replace) a defective product. For example, automobile dealers are the agents through which manufacturers make the warranty good. However, some of the large retailers like Sears Roebuck and Company provide their own guarantee, or warranty. Sometimes the warranty provides only for the replacement of defective parts and does not cover the labor costs. In other cases both labor and parts are covered. Read any "limited warranty" carefully.

Retailers and lenders are, technically speaking, not liable for warranties granted by the manufacturer. But they do have to cooperate to make the manufacturer's warranty viable, and usually they do. Consumers may now also legally withhold future payments for defective goods until they are replaced or repaired. See Chapter 7 for a more detailed discussion of the legal aspects.

Service contracts

Many durable goods retailers are now offering service contracts that normally begin after the warranty expires. For a yearly fee the seller will repair the item covered without further charges. Some of these contracts cover both labor and parts, others only parts. Generally, the annual fee is determined by the age of the appliance and the historical repair record of the retailer on that particular item. It is because of the historical repair record that the annual service fee for a $300 item, say a washing machine, may be higher than for a $500 item, say a refrigerator. It is generally true that the fee is the same on two different models of the same item such as a $500 color television set and a $300 set. However, there are exceptions to this generalization.

If the service contract is renewed at the end of a year, the initial fee is increased. It is difficult to generalize as to whether these service contracts are a good buy; some fees seem excessive, others do not. Since the fees vary a good deal from retailer to retailer and from item to item sold by the same retailer, you should examine closely any contract you are considering. Remember, a new item built properly and working correctly should not need repair for some time. Consider, too, how often and how gently you will use the product.

The cash discount

Years ago many merchants would grant a 2 to 3 percent cash discount because it saved them paper work and they would get their money immediately. Sometimes the cash discount applied if the person paid within ten days rather than the traditional thirty. A 2 percent cash discount for payment within ten days (rather than the traditional payment within thirty days) means one is saving 2 percent over a twenty-day period. This amounts to about 35 percent if converted to an annual basis.

There are two reasons why fewer and fewer retailers will give a cash discount. First, they are geared to handle credit sales, and cash sales save them few, if any, expenses. Second, if they are engaged in the financing process, they actually earn a substantial amount (interest) in the financing operation. The common interest that retailers charge is 18 percent. This may be as much or more than their profit margin. Indeed, one wit once remarked he would gladly sell merchandise at cost if he could finance it on his terms.

On the other hand, merchants not having their own credit cards will sometimes grant a cash discount because credit is expensive to the merchant. Even bank credit cards charge fees to sellers, which means the merchant doesn't keep 100 cents out of each dollar charged in the store.

The one disadvantage of a cash discount is that it is more difficult to bring pressure on a merchant to correct a defective product if you have already paid him. See chapter 7 on consumer legal protection for the current legal status of cash discounts.

The acceleration and balloon clauses

The acceleration clause states that if one payment is missed, all remaining payments are immediately due and payable. In the absence of the acceleration clause, the creditor often could sue only monthly as each payment came due. Typically an installment purchaser signs the *note*, which is the promise to pay, and a *security agreement* under the Uniform Commercial Code, which makes the merchandise collateral for the purchase. Unscrupulous dealers can take advantage of the acceleration clause and repossess an item even if only one payment has been missed.

The balloon clause is designed to mislead buyers into thinking they are paying less than they really are and to keep them on the hook longer, to get them to pay more interest. For example, a contract may call for the payment of $50 per month for six months and then a single seventh payment of $300 more. When the seventh payment comes due, the buyer cannot pay and either has to refinance or may even lose the item. If, on the other hand, the contract had called for six monthly payments of $100 each, the buyer might well have been able to afford the payments.

Assigning wage clause

It is possible in some states for the creditor to get a court order garnisheeing the wages of a debtor. Then the employer must pay the lender so much per month directly. However, there are limits as to how large a portion of a person's wages may be garnisheed, and often it is bothersome to get the court order. Therefore, some dealers and financial institutions have inserted wage assignment clauses in their contracts. In such a case, the creditor can go directly to the employer and get a portion of the debtor's wages without first having to obtain a court order.

The add-on clause

The add-on clause ties several different sales together. For example, if you purchased a television set, the seller would retain title until it was paid for. But if you had only one more payment left to make on the television set when you purchased a refrigerator, the dealer would retain the title of both items until you had paid for both of them. If then, still later (when the television was fully paid for and you only had one or two payments left on the refrigerator) you purchase a sofa, all three items would be tied together; the dealer would retain title to all three. If afterward, when you only owed a few more payments on the sofa (and the television set and the refrigerator were fully paid for), you missed a payment because of an emergency, all three items could be repossessed.

Reputable dealers would not do this, but unscrupulous ones might. Obviously you should be careful and not have an add-on clause in your contract.

Trade-ins, price packing, and dealer participation

Trade-ins and price packing are related to the amount of the down payment and frequently cause the consumer to pay more for the product than he or she should. Price packing means jacking up the price in excess of what is expected in order to be able to reduce it later during a bargaining session or to enable the dealer to give an unusually large trade-in allowance.

Historically, price packing was resorted to most frequently by automobile and appliance dealers to impress the customer with large and unrealistic discounts or trade-in allowances. One evil of price packing most common among automobile dealers is the practice of charging different prices for the same autos on the same day. However, since 1958 an effort has been made to eliminate this evil; dealers are now required by law to place a list price tag on the auto. This is only the legally required "suggested list price." There is still room for bargaining, and almost no one pays the list price. Moreover, this bargaining can take place in the form of getting more for your trade-in or in getting the list price reduced.

An example of how the down payment is related to a packed price and the trade-in allowance is the following. Suppose an item has a "true" price of $1,000. The dealer may pack it an additional $500, giving it a price of $1,500. The dealer allows the buyer $1,000 trade-in on an item worth $500, and there remains a balance to pay of $500. It could be said that the down payment is 66.6 percent. If the dealer were realistic and did not pack the price and allowed a $500 trade-in and if this were the "true" worth of the item being traded, then the balance owed is still $500 but the down payment would be only 50 percent. Consequently the down payment can be misleading. Moreover, sometimes the price packing is greater than the added trade-in allowed, and the consumer ends by paying more.

In the automobile business the consumer should be aware of what is called "dealer participation," "dealer reserve," or "dealer bonus." Sometimes an auto dealer will attempt to persuade you to finance the purchase of your auto with a particular finance company. You will have to pay a finance charge on the loan, plus interest. The interest is paid to the financial institution making the loan, while the finance charge is split between the dealer and the financial institution that has purchased the installment paper. From the consumer's viewpoint, it is frequently more desirable to arrange for a bank or credit union loan before attempting to purchase a new car to avoid having to pay the additional dealer participation finance charges.

When buying a new car, the buyer is aware of the "suggested list price," but does not know the dealer's cost. So the buyer does not know really how much bargaining room exists. There are a number of car buying guides that publish the FOB factory price and estimated freight costs, information enough to enable a potential buyer to estimate the dealer's cost. However, these published figures are only estimates; often they contain errors or may not take into account dealer's make-ready costs. Sometimes as much as $100 is spent by a dealer in getting a newly received car in full running condition.

On the other hand, sometimes there are sales contests, and the auto manufacturers reduce the price of their products if dealers meet their sales quota. This can result in the opposite kind of error from the one noted above, and dealers' costs would be below the person's estimate.

When buying a car, two well-known guides that you should consult are:

1. NADA. This is the "blue book" and is published by National Auto Dealers Used Car Guide Co., 8400 Westpark Dr., McLean, VA 22101.
2. *New Car Cost Guide*, published by Auto Invoice Service, Division of Gousha

(a Times Mirror Company), 2001 Alameda (or P.O. Box 6227), San Jose, CA 95150.

Most financial institutions that finance cars have these books.

Auto repair protection—coming soon?

Many consumers have long complained that auto repair is one of the biggest consumer "rip offs" around. The most frequent complaints concern repairs not made or not made properly, and charges made for work not done or, if done, not needed. Some experts believe that about $20 billion per year is wasted due to faulty and unnecessary auto repairs. In a survey made by the U.S. Department of Transportation in 1979, it was found that 53¢ of each repair dollar was wasted.

Many states and localities have taken steps to provide the public with some protection from unscrupulous or incompetent auto repair shops. Many state automobile dealer groups have established an "Autocap" panel. This is a committee made up of car dealers and consumers which tries to resolve auto repair complaints. Some states have gone further. California has established a bureau of automotive repair within its Department of Consumer Affairs. Among other things, it has over a dozen "rigged" test cars constantly checking the competency and honesty of repair shops. In New York the Motor Vehicles Department is charged with monitoring repair shops. These activities are designed to keep the repair shops on their toes. If you have an actual complaint that you cannot resolve, check to see if your state or community has an Autocap Panel.

If you move, what will it cost?

Before moving, you should get a rate schedule from several different companies. The cost of any move is based on the weight of the goods shipped and the distance. It is important that you get an honest accounting of the weight. The truck is weighed both before and after loading, and you are entitled to a ticket

---

The law now provides that you may withhold payment of any balance due on defective merchandise or services purchased with a credit card, provided you have made a good-faith effort to return the goods or resolve the problem with the merchant from whom you made the purchase.

If the store that honored the credit card was not also the issuer of the card, two limitations apply to this right:

- The original amount of the purchase must have exceeded $50; and
- The sale must have taken place in your state or within 100 miles of your current address.

Figure 6–1 Defective merchandise or services. (*Source:* Board of Governors of the Federal Reserve System, Washington, D.C. 20551. December 1976.)

showing the weight in each case. If you have any doubt about the honesty of the company, be at the scales when the loaded truck is weighed. Make sure that only the weight of your goods is added to the final amount. Dishonest crewmen may add things on the way to the scale. Also make sure the weight of the loading crew is not added to your bill. Your shipping ticket should, in addition to the weight, include a list of all the items shipped. Don't misplace this because it will be needed for insurance claims should some items be lost or damaged. Before you select a mover you should try to find out the number of claims filed against the company (the lower the better) and the frequency with which the truck arrives at its destination on time.

POSTPURCHASE REDRESS PROCEDURES: HOW TO RECOVER YOUR LOSSES

Despite education and other preventive measures, consumers will make mistakes. Fortunately, many problems can be partially or fully resolved. Ethical businesses do not want dissatisfied customers to hurt their reputations. Various government agencies can also offer help when the customer has a problem. Some of the principal problems and their remedies are presented below. The National Association of Manufacturers advises that when a complaint is made, it is helpful to the seller or any other party contacted in behalf of the consumer if the buyer follows these procedures.[2]

- Make a habit of keeping receipts, hangtags, warranties, and care labels in one convenient place so they are readily available in case you need to return merchandise.
- Read and follow instructions carefully as to using, washing, oiling, or other general care. This may eliminate the need for a return.
- If you find it necessary to return an item or make a complaint, think through the reasons why you are dissatisfied so that you can present your case well.

When You Want a Refund

Some sellers will provide 100 percent satisfaction to consumers who desire to return merchandise, but most have a more limited policy on returns. Some may even bend over backward to avoid embarrassing the customer even if the customer brings in soiled clothes ("too small"!?), half of a ham ("odd taste"!?), or a non-functioning radio ("my wife already had bought one"), and a thinly veiled excuse for the refund request. It is unfair to the seller for the buyer to request refunds on some things that have been already used or misused, but many customers

---

2. "The Concern For Quality," National Association of Manufacturers. Undated pamphlet.

often fail to make requests for refunds when they would be welcomed. The National Association of Manufacturers makes the following suggestions when one returns merchandise to a store.[3]

- Return merchandise to the store where you bought it and to the department where it was purchased.
- Avoid making returns near closing time or during rush hours, when you may not be able to see the person who can do the most for you. If the person has no authority to service your complaint to your satisfaction, ask to see a person higher in authority.
- If you are leaving the item for repair or if a refund will be mailed to you, be sure to obtain a receipt.

When You Get the Clerk's Runaround

If an employee fails to offer a refund, provide a service, or give necessary information, the best rule is to go to the top of the organization. The manager of a store, rather than the public relations manager, personnel manager, or assistant manager, can usually break red tape better than anyone else in the establishment. Otherwise the customer may be frustrated by advancing slowly up the chain of command in a large store.

When You Can't Get Local Satisfaction

If the local sales representatives or local store will not resolve the problem, the top management of a large business will sometimes act. Customers may get satisfaction plus gift packages, samples, or other bonuses from the well-intentioned home office.

A little detective work may be necessary to find the higher authorities. The local representatives of a store may tell you their own company's home office and names of key executives; if the problem centers around a faulty product, they may not be able to supply this information.

Manufacturer addresses can be found on labels and packages of many products. Zip codes are required by law on labels in some cases. Local stockbrokers will have corporation home office addresses in their investment literature. These and other reference books with the pertinent information may be found in any good library. When writing to a company without the name of a particular officer, the president should be addressed. The National Association of Manufacturers advises that when writing a company or returning a purchase by mail, a consumer should do the following:

---

3. Ibid. "The Concern For Quality."

- Try to find the proper name of the company, the right department, address, and zip code. Improperly addressed letters are delayed. (The librarian in your local library will be able to help you.)
- Write a businesslike letter. Keep a carbon copy, even if the letter is handwritten. Write legibly.
- Give brand name, model number, size, color, and any other information that will help to identify the product.
- Try to explain exactly what is wrong. If you are returning a product, send it in the original package if possible. If the product is small, send the letter with the package and insure it. With certified mail, you can specify a return receipt so you will know it was received. Include your name, address, zip code, and telephone number on your correspondence.
- If you should not hear from the company, send a second letter. Most companies try to acknowledge complaint letters within two or three weeks.

When the Merchant or Manufacturer Won't Help: Voluntary Action

If the problem is serious or the firm cannot or will not resolve the situation, the consumer faces a multitude of possible actions—sometimes none of which is satisfactory. There are legal actions as well as other avenues open to the customer, depending upon the particular nature of the complaint.

Independent BBBs in many communities remain the leading complaint-handling agencies. BBBs try to resolve disputes between business and a consumer primarily by trying to present to each side the views of the other. A cooperative merchant may resolve a complaint quickly because of the intervention of the influential BBB in a particular case rather than because of the merits of the consumer's complaints. Few merchants will totally ignore the BBB's request for the company's reaction to a complaint. The BBB will not arbitrate a case or attempt to negotiate a settlement between two parties in the complaint situation, but it will undertake stronger measures where the facts warrant. Business and trade associations are increasingly becoming involved in complaint handling for their members or an entire industry. The Major Appliance Consumer Action Panel (MACAP), primarily supported by the Association of Home Appliance Manufacturers (AHAM), is a leading example of an industry response to consumer complaints. Member companies of AHAM let the consumer-operated but AHAM-sponsored MACAP group resolve the more difficult individual cases as well as advise AHAM members of general consumer problems. The Gas Appliance Manufacturers Association and American Retail Federation also participate in the MACAP program. Industrywide complaint systems are rare, but check to see.

Finally, if your complaint is not taken care of, you may go to one of the consumer protection agencies described below or take legal action against the business establishment (these could be governmental or private consumer protection agencies). Obviously, it would not be worthwhile for an individual to sue in most cases, but if, for example, a major defect exists in a car, it might be.

Consumer groups or public interest law firms may sometimes take legal action on behalf of consumers. Moreover, in recent years courts have leaned more in the direction of favoring the consumer if there is a legitimate complaint. Some consumer groups or law firms may choose to sue, even if the amount involved in the specific case is too small to warrant the action, on the grounds that such a suit will encourage the retailer and manufacturer to be more responsible in the future. Any publicity that may be generated by a lawsuit or by government action may also serve to increase the responsibility of the seller.

Small Claims Courts

Legal action should probably be used as a measure of the last resort. In most cases where small dollar amounts are involved, such action should be taken through a small claims court, which is often able to handle claims effectively, quickly, and at a much lower cost than regular legal action. However, the amount of damages for which a person may sue is limited in a small claims court, in most states under $1,000. If you have suffered damages (and would like to collect) in excess of that amount, you will probably have to hire an attorney and go to a regular court. The effectiveness of a small claims court depends on particular state laws and the availability of the courts in particular locations. But you do not need a lawyer. Procedures are usually handled in an informal manner, and the legal rules of evidence and procedure are often waived. You simply tell the magistrate what happened in your own words.

In some states the small claims courts are under the jurisdiction of the justice of the peace (J.P.), and in others under the alderman. Both of these are elected officials at the lowest (precinct) political subdivision.

The cost of filing a claim in a small claims court is only a few dollars. Actual court costs are also modest, and as a rule are paid by the loser. If you need more information about the small claims court in your area, call your county clerk. Or you may call the justice of the peace or alderman for your precinct. These telephone numbers will be found in the directory.

CONSUMER PROTECTION AGENCIES

Federal Consumer Protection Agencies

While more than forty separate federal agencies perform significant consumer functions, few of them are easily accessible to ordinary citizens seeking information and assistance. Most of these agencies assist consumers without the necessity of consumer participation because they are given specific authority to regulate the actions of business and professional groups. While they are charged with protecting the consumer interest, they need only work with groups they can regulate. Critics such as Ralph Nader charge that the constant contact between regulators and the regulated has caused regulators to lose sight of their objectives to serve the consumers they rarely meet.

In any event, consumers seeking assistance from federal agencies should recognize that the agencies serve many individuals and groups in the nation. They cannot be expected to fulfill all demands of individual consumers; they do work with organized groups such as labor, agriculture, and commerce. See Chapter 7, which discusses consumer protection laws, for a further comment on the federal protection agencies and a table showing what each one does and which one you should contact for a legitimate grievance.

State and Local Consumer Protection Agencies

Consumers can often obtain assistance from agencies of their state government. In rural areas of any state and in many smaller states, however, the limited resources of state consumer protection activities are not conveniently available except by telephone or mail or are missing altogether. All states now claim to have some type of consumer protection bureau, agency, or other unit. Some of these agencies are considered ineffective or are just beginning to breathe life into their activities.

The absence of consumer protection agencies with notable staff or budget does not mean that *caveat emptor* rages totally unchecked in a state. Many of the agencies of all state governments have partial responsibilities in consumer affairs, and they have had these assignments for many years. For example, advertising, personal selling, door-to-door sales, packaging, and other business practices affecting consumers are regulated to a limited extent by the states. Local district attorneys rarely consider consumer cases as primary responsibilities, but state attorneys-general, on the other hand, often have special consumer protection divisions. A number of states have "little FTC" laws resembling the Federal Trade Commission regulations on deceptive practices, and the state attorneys general usually enforce them.

Voluntary Consumer Organizations

In most states and many communities, voluntary groups of consumers have developed various programs to help themselves and advance their version of the consumers' cause. These groups generally have been assisted in their growth and activities by the Consumer Federation of America (CFA), a Washington, D.C. based coalition of over two hundred national, state, and local organizations. CFA's affiliates have their own memberships of more than thirty million persons in consumer, farmer, cooperative, labor, and other endeavors. The National Consumers League has been in existence since 1899. Ralph Nader has founded a number of specialized consumer organizations, and others have arisen in recent years to deal with problems in individual industries such as food, electric utilities, broadcasting, and housing.

Consumer groups developed rapidly following the activities of homemakers a few years ago in a well-publicized eruption of sentiment, pickets, and boycotts of supermarkets over rising prices. The activities of the groups that emerged reflect particular interests and special conditions of the urban, suburban, or rural areas in which they flourish.

Some groups make frequent statewide and local area comparisons of store prices for drugs, household items, and food. Others demand financial settlement for members who have received poor treatment. Voluntary consumer organizations generally do three things: (1) they engage in lobbying at all levels of government to obtain stronger consumer protection laws; (2) they engage in consumer education by sponsoring seminars and lectures on many topics of interest to consumers; (3) they provide consumer counseling. If you have a legitimate complaint, they will explain to you what your legal rights are and how you might go about obtaining relief, but they are often operated by volunteers unable to devote time to help resolve individual disputes or complaints.

QUESTIONS FOR REVIEW

1. Explain *Caveat emptor* and *Caveat venditor,* emphasizing which is justifiable and why.
2. Does *caveat venditor* mean consumers will always get their money's worth?
3. Why is prevention of consumer problems more desirable for consumers than is treatment?
4. Where could you go to find a good tax lawyer?
5. Discuss brand name products, pointing out why they are or are not superior to less well-known products.
6. Discuss the relative merits of the brand name product and the private label product.
7. Discuss how a consumer should choose a store or vendor.
8. Better Business Bureaus can be helpful before the purchase or after the purchase. Contrast these two categories of services of BBBs.
9. Contrast bait pricing with loss leader pricing.
10. When is a trade-in just a price discount?
11. What is meant by the psychological price? The inflated list price?
12. Why do some merchants engage in deceptive practices? How would you define a deceptive practice?
13. Why can discount houses sometimes sell items at a lower price than conventional stores?
14. Discuss briefly the balloon clause.
15. Explain in detail some of the intricacies of trade-ins, price packing, and dealer participation.

16. Explain how a rigid adherence to a weekly or monthly budget can be unwise.
17. Explain why, in your opinion, it is better to shop wisely than to develop skills at recovering any losses you may have suffered.
18. What strategy would you employ if a clerk were deliberately trying to prevent you from getting a complaint adjudicated?
19. What would you do if you could not get a dispute settled with the management of a local or a national chain?
20. Discuss the conditions under which it might be worthwhile to sue a store to settle a dispute.
21. The rising concern for consumer protection seems to be emanating from many sources and for many reasons. Discuss some of these sources and reasons for development.
22. Explain why the consumer does or does not, in your opinion, need protection.
23. What state agencies might a consumer in need of information or action appeal to? Do you think such agencies could do more than they presently do?
24. What possible problems do you see in the doctrine of "Let the Buyer Be Informed"?
25. Why is the consumer generally at a disadvantage when dealing with business firms?
26. Why have most legislative acts relating to consumer protection been at best only partially effective?
27. What types of activities do voluntary consumer organizations perform?
28. How can consumer education help in providing consumer protection?

CASES

1. Visit several supermarkets and compare their prices for common food products. Visit several department stores and discount houses and compare the prices of identical or similar products. What might account for some of the price differentials?
2. Watch newspaper advertisements for one week and note all of the deceptive or misleading advertising that you can find.
3. John and Jean Sargeant bought a set of four new radial tires for their station wagon recently at a price of $210.50 excluding tax. They were guaranteed against blowout for the life of the tire and for thirty thousand miles tread wear. After one year with just less than ten thousand miles on them, Jean hit a chunk of ice in the road and blew out one of the tires. What kind of settlement are they likely to get? What can they do if the dealer refuses to settle?
4. Make a list of the things you have purchased recently and then make a

second list of those things you have purchased but really didn't need. What were the subconscious reasons for buying these products? Were you influenced either directly or indirectly by advertising? Would you buy these products again?

5. Hi and Harriett Hansen were debating the value of their new automobile's brand name. She said it was worthless to her because she couldn't drive anywhere just because of the product name. Hi said that he felt the brand was valuable because their position in the community as upstanding citizens was enhanced by the purchase. Who was right? Was either or both right?

6. Florence argues that anything selling for $17.73 is bound to be cheap-quality merchandise since it is discounted. Ferdinand argues that such prices often turn out to be inflated. Fitzhugh feels that this price is a typical cut-rate discount price for a $20 item. Evaluate each argument.

7. Ask a large store in your area to indicate how it takes care of customer complaints. Does the store work with the Better Business Bureau, trade associations, voluntary consumer organizations, or government agencies in resolving any customer complaints?

8. Investigate and report on any consumer organization in your area.

9. Jan Burk recently had a problem with the front of his car and took it to the dealer for repairs. The mechanic aligned the front end, performed other work, and pronounced the car fit. On his way home, Jan tested the car at high speed and found the malfunction was still present. Jan took the car back again without explaining what had happened; the repair shop once more aligned his front end and performed other work and pronounced the car fit. This time the repairs actually were made, and the car functioned properly at high speed. A short time later Jan received two bills from the car dealer that were similar but not identical. How should Jan handle the matter?

SUGGESTED READINGS

Aaker, David A., and Day, George S. Consumerism: Search for the Consumer Interest. New York: The Free Press, 1978.

Annual Buying Guide, Consumer Reports. Published in December of each year by Consumers Union of the United States, 256 Washington St., Mt. Vernon, N.Y.

Changing Times, The Kiplinger Magazine. A weekly publication with a good deal of material of interest to the consumer.

Consumer Information Catalog. Pueblo, Colo.: Consumer Information Center. Published quarterly.

Consumer News. Washington, D.C.: Office of Consumer Affairs.

Consumer Newsweek. A weekly magazine published by Consumer News, Inc., 601 National Press Building, Washington, D.C.

Consumer Reports. Mt. Vernon, N.Y.: Consumer's Union of the United States.

Consumers Bulletin. Washington, N.J.: Consumer's Research, Inc.

Epstein, David G. *Consumer Law in a Nutshell.* St. Paul, Minn.: West Publishing Co., 1981.

Everybody's Money. Published quarterly by CUNA International, Box 431, Madison, Wis. 53201.

Federal Trade Commission. *FTC News Summary.* Available from the Commission, Washington, D.C. 20580.

Ford Motor Company. *Car Buying Made Easier.* Annual edition free by writing to Ford Motor Company, Dearborn, Mich. 48121.

Gilson, Christopher, et al. *Consumer Revenge: How to Handle Greedy Landlords, Shoddy Sellers, Crooked Contractors, and Other Consumer Frustrations.* New York: G. P. Putnam's Sons, 1981.

Goodman, Joel, and Huggins, Kenneth. *Let the Buyer Be Aware: Valuable Skills for Consumers, Parents and Teachers in the Eighties.* San Diego: The Wright Group, 1981.

Horowitz, David. *Fight Back—And Don't Get Ripped Off.* New York: Harper & Row, 1980.

Myerson, Bess. *Consumer Guidelines to Shopping by Mail.* Direct Mail Marketing Association, 6 East 43rd St., New York, N.Y. 10017.

Richardson, Lee. *Consumer Newsletter.* 10465 Waterfowl Terrace, Columbia, Md. 21044.

Rosenbloom, Joseph. *Consumer Complaint Guide.* New York: Macmillan, 1978.

Rowse, Arthur, ed. *Help: The Indispensable Almanac of Consumer Information.* New York: Everest House Publishers, 1981.

U.S. Office of Consumer Affairs. *A Consumer's Shopping List of Inflation-Fighting Ideas.* Pueblo, Colo., Information Center, 1978.

CHAPTER SEVEN

CONSUMER LAWS AND CONSUMER PROTECTION AGENCIES

Federal Consumer Protection Laws
Enforcing Agencies

In recent years legislation has been passed to protect the consumer. There is, however, no uniformity among various states' laws. Many states have usury laws that have been on the books for years. In some states these usury laws apply to consumer credit, and special laws have been passed that set the upper limits on consumer credit interest rates. Regular usury laws do, however, usually apply to mortgage loans made to individuals, and to business loans.

In most states there is a consumer credit commission or a similar office that regulates consumer credit lenders and enforces state laws that cover, among other things, the maximum interest rate that may be charged. In a few states this office may listen to consumer complaints and even take action if the complaint is legitimate. But an official state agency to help the consumer is the exception rather than the rule, and generally an individual must initiate legal action unless a federal or state statute has been violated. Private voluntary consumer organizations also exist in some areas. Some groups may aid an individual and bring strength of numbers to bear, or they may provide financial and legal aid in the event of a lawsuit. These groups may also lobby for stronger consumer protection laws. But unless a law has been violated there is often little that can be done, even if one has been treated shabbily. Consequently, read carefully any installment contract before signing it.

Nevertheless, consumer organizations can help sometimes. If there are none in your area and you wish to start one, contact the Consumer Federation of America, a Washington, D.C.-based coalition of seven hundred state and local consumer organizations and it will assist other state and local groups in getting started.

FEDERAL CONSUMER PROTECTION LAWS[1]

When you borrow money or buy something on the installment plan, there are certain federal laws that protect you. You should be familiar with this protection and know where you can go if a law has been broken. Currently, federal legislation covers the following general areas:

Truth in Lending
Fair Credit Reporting
Equal Credit Opportunity
Fair Credit Billing
Consumer Leasing
Fair Debt Collection Practices

Truth in Lending

Officially known as the Consumer Credit Protection Act, the federal truth-in-lending law was passed in 1968 and has been amended several times since then. "Truth in Lending" does what its title suggests: it requires that certain facts be disclosed when consumer loans are made.

Interest costs

The lender must inform the borrower of the "true" or actuarially correct percentage interest rate that he or she is paying. As pointed out in a previous chapter, this is called the annual percentage rate (APR) and must be distinguished from the so-called add-on interest rate. The add-on rate is misleading because it is calculated on the original balance, which is actually declining if paid off in installments. The borrower must also be told the total dollar amount of interest together with any service charges, extra loading fees, and points. If a product is being financed (rather than money being borrowed at a bank), the cash price as well as credit price must be spelled out.

Balloon clause and credit life

If there is a balloon clause in the contract, this must be disclosed. The cost of any credit life insurance must be explained; the same is true of accident, health, or loss of income insurance written in connection with any credit transaction. While the lender may require that the borrower accept credit life insurance, if he or she does, its premium is included in the cost of the loan (APR), which is subject to the various states' usury laws.

---

1. This material is drawn from Wolf and Associates, "Financial Seminars." Copyright, 1983 by Harold A. Wolf. Used by permission.

Right of rescission

The truth-in-lending law also requires that the "right of rescission" clause be inserted into every contract in which the borrower's home is used as collateral (including mobile homes). This gives the borrower three business days in which to nullify any such contract. The borrower's home is frequently used as collateral when a major repair or remodeling job is being done. In such a case, work may not begin until the three days have passed unless you, in writing, waive the right of rescission. If you cancel during the three days, you must also do so in writing.

Lost or stolen credit cards

This law also protects the borrower in the event a credit card is lost or stolen. Once the missing card has been reported, the cardholder is not liable for bills stemming from its unauthorized use. It is up to the issuer to block its illegal use. Even if the missing card is not reported, the maximum liability is $50.00 per card. Consequently, report any missing cards immediately, first by telephone and then by registered letter. To do this you will need to know the number of the card; it is suggested that you keep a record of all your credit card numbers. Some credit card issuers have a special form which you may use to report a missing card, or you may report it in an ordinary letter. In any event, treat your credit card like money; never take it out of your purse or wallet except when using it.

Garnishment of wages

In 1970 an amendment to the truth-in-lending law spelled out the maximum amount of a person's income that may be garnisheed to meet unpaid debts. This maximum is now either 25 percent of a person's weekly take-home pay or the amount by which his or her weekly take-home pay exceeds 30 times the minimum hourly wage, whichever is smaller.

The federal law then sets the maximum penalty with respect to garnisheeing wages. Moreover, it provides that in those states that have a garnisheeing law more lenient to the debtor than the federal law, the state law shall prevail. The law also prohibits an employer from firing an employee whose wages were garnisheed to satisfy any one debt. Formerly, firing was frequent because garnisheeing wages meant extra bookwork for the employer.

Fair Credit Reporting Act

This act guarantees certain consumer rights in reporting credit information about consumers to credit granters. For example, it gives you the right to see your credit file. All cities of any size have professional credit bureaus that collect and store pertinent financial data on virtually all individuals in the community. They then sell these data to institutions and individuals who extend credit. They also sell reports to prospective employers and life insurance companies that are considering you for life insurance. Your credit file includes personal data as well as data on where you work, your position, how long you have held that position, your annual income, spouse's income, assets, whether you rent or own your home, previous job and address, number of dependents, credit history and experience, and any judgments that may have been recorded against you.

Checking your file

If you merely wish to check your credit file routinely, you will have to pay the regular fees a lender pays—a few dollars. If you have been denied credit because of a credit report, the lender or merchant must tell you this. In such a case you have thirty days during which you may see your credit report free of charge; all data in it must be revealed and its source disclosed. Any errors you find must be corrected, and any falsehoods deleted. If your file contains information subject to two or more interpretations, your interpretation must be added and included in all future reports. The corrected version must also be sent to all possible creditors who have received a report on you during the last six months, and all prospective employers who have received a report during the past two years, at no cost to you.

Adverse information limitation

The limits to how long adverse information in your credit file may be made available in a credit report are as follows:

> Information on bankruptcies—14 years.
> Suits and judgments against you—7 years or until the statute of limitations has expired, whichever is the longer.
> Paid tax liens, collection acounts, accounts charged to bad debts, arrests, indictments, convictions, and other damaging information—7 years.

However, none of these limitations applies if the credit reports are to be used in connection with a credit or life insurance transaction involving $50,000 or more, or employment involving an annual salary of $20,000 or more.

Who may see your file

Although you may see your credit file, it is strictly confidential to almost all others. Those who have a legitimate need may see a credit report as may those whom you authorize. Those who may receive a report without your authorization because they have a legitimate need are: prospective creditors, creditors or their agents trying to collect past debts, prospective employers, and employees of life insurance companies considering you for life insurance. For anyone else a court order is needed. Even the government cannot see your file or receive a report unless it is considering employing you, granting you a license of some kind, considering you for security clearance, or thinks you owe back taxes. For

---

SUMMARY OF CONSUMER CREDIT LAWS

The Federal Consumer credit laws offer you these major protections:

1. The *Truth in Lending Act* requires disclosure of the "finance charge" and the "annual percentage rate"—and certain other costs and terms of credit—so that you can compare the prices of credit from different sources. It also limits your liability on lost or stolen credit cards.
2. The *Equal Credit Opportunity Act* prohibits discrimination against an applicant for credit because of age, sex, marital status, race, color, religion, national origin, or receipt of public assistance. It also prohibits discrimination because you have made a good faith exercise of any of your rights under the federal consumer credit laws. If you've been denied credit, the law requires that you be notified in writing and gives you the right to request the reason for the denial.
3. The *Fair Credit Billing Act* sets up a procedure for the prompt correction of errors on a credit account and prevents damage to your credit rating while you're settling a dispute.
4. The *Fair Credit Reporting Act* sets up a procedure for correcting mistakes on your credit record and requires that the record be kept confidential.
5. The *Consumer Leasing Act* requires disclosure of information that helps you compare the cost and terms of one lease with another and with the cost and terms of buying on credit or with cash.
6. The *Real Estate Settlement Procedures Act* requires that you be given information about the services and costs involved at settlement, when real property transfers from seller to buyer.
7. The *Home Mortgage Disclosure Act* requires most lending institutions in metropolitan areas to let the public know where they make their mortgage and home improvement loans.

Pamphlets describing some of these laws in more detail are available from the Board of Governors or from the Federal Reserve Bank in your District.

Source: Board of Governors of the Federal Reserve System.

---

the IRS to receive a report on you, it must have a legitimate case; it cannot go on a fishing expedition.

Equal Credit Opportunity Act

The Equal Credit Opportunity Act (ECOA) became effective in October, 1975, and it banned discrimination in the granting of credit on the basis of sex or marital status. In 1976 this act was amended so that it now also prohibits discrimination on the basis of race, color, religion, and age. The act also bans discrimination against welfare or other public assistance recipients and borrowers who exercise their rights under consumer protection laws. Moreover, it provides that if people are denied credit, they must be told why in writing.

Women and credit

Prior to the passage of ECOA, women had more difficulty getting credit than men. A married woman often had to rely on her husband's credit. In addition, single and divorced people often had a more difficult time getting credit than married couples. Now this discrimination as well as other types is unlawful.

Women should establish credit in their own name if they have an income, even if they are married. If a woman relies upon her husband's credit, then upon death or divorce she may be without it temporarily. To be sure, ECOA will permit her to establish credit in her own name in such a case, but this takes time.

Age and credit

Prior to the passage of ECOA, it was alleged that lenders sometimes refused to grant credit to older people. This act prevents the arbitrary denial of credit to the elderly, who for the purpose of the provision in this act are defined as persons 62 and older. Credit may still be denied on the basis of inadequate income, excessive debts, a person's credit record, and the like, but the reason for refusing credit must be spelled out in writing.

Fair Credit Billing Act

The Fair Credit Billing Act (FCBA) does three things: It permits merchants who so desire to grant cash discounts, it permits you to withhold payments for defective merchandise purchased with credit cards, and it provides some safeguards in the case of billing errors.

Cash discounts

Twenty or thirty years ago cash discounts were often granted by merchants to people who paid cash. This practice had all but ceased until very recently, when there has been a reemergence of the cash discount. Because of this, some major credit card companies included a provision in their contract with retail merchants prohibiting cash discounts. The FCBA prohibits such "no cash discounts" provisions. The act does not require cash discounts; it merely says that merchants may grant them if they wish. Consequently, if you pay cash rather than use your credit card, you should ask for a discount. This discount is limited to 5 percent because otherwise it would be in violation of the truth-in-lending law.[2]

Merchants granting cash discounts must have signs so stating in clear sight, such as near cash registers or on doors at entrances. Moreover, merchants

---

2. Discounts in excess of 5 percent would constitute a finance charge under the truth-in-lending law and hence would necessitate further regulations and red tape.

granting cash discounts must grant them to all buyers, not just to credit card holders.

Withholding payments

The FCBA permits the consumer to stop making payments for defective merchandise or service purchased with credit cards. If the merchant who sold you the merchandise is also the issuer of the credit card, all you need first do is make a good faith effort to return the merchandise or resolve the problem by having the merchant replace or repair the item. In the event that a third party issued the credit card (for example, Visa or Master Card), you may still withhold payment, but now there are two additional restrictions. First, the purchase must have exceeded $50, and, second, it must have taken place in your state or within 100 miles of your current address.

By withholding payments you can generate pressure to have the grievance resolved. If a third party's credit card is involved, you can, by withholding payment, enlist that party as an ally in bringing pressure on the retailer.

WHAT IS EQUAL CREDIT OPPORTUNITY?

The law says that a creditor may not discriminate against you—treat you less favorably than another applicant for credit—because of your sex or marital status.

Just because you are a woman, or single, or married, a creditor may not turn down a loan application.

The rules that follow are designed to stop specific abuses that have limited women's ability to get credit.

The most important rules

- You can't be refused credit just because you're a woman.
- You can't be refused credit just because you're single, married, separated, divorced, or widowed.
- You can't be refused credit because a creditor decides you're of child-bearing age and, as a consequence, won't count your income.
- You can't be refused credit because a creditor won't count income you receive regularly from alimony or child support.
- You can have credit in your own name if you're credit-worthy.
- When you apply for your own credit and rely on your own income, information about your spouse or his cosignature can be required only under certain circumstances.
- You can keep your own accounts and your own credit history if your marital status changes.
- You can build up your own credit record because new accounts must be carried in the names of husband and wife if both use the account or are liable.
- If you are denied credit, you can find out why.

Source: Board of Governors of the Federal Reserve System.

Billing errors

In some cases you may be billed incorrectly because of accounting errors, goods that were delivered to the wrong address, goods returned or not accepted, or other reasons. The FCBA makes it easier to settle such disputes. You have sixty days after receiving such a bill to report an error. This must be done in writing and the nature of the dispute explained. The creditor has thirty days in which to send you a written reply. While the dispute is being settled, the creditor may not collect any disputed amount, nor add interest charges. During this time the creditor may not close your account nor give you a bad credit rating because of your claim.

This provision of the law also spells out the time period during which a legitimate bill may be paid without an additional finance charge. Generally this so-called "free ride" (between when a bill is received and when it must be paid without incurring additional charges) is now fourteen days.

What these provisions of the FCBA have done is to make the creditor more cooperative in settling disputes; complaints must now be investigated. Even though legally complaints must be in writing, in many cases disputes can be settled on the telephone. National credit card companies have established regional offices throughout the country with full-time people who handle only complaints. Often the address and phone numbers for complaints are listed on the monthly bills, and the numbers are sometimes toll-free.

Consumer Leasing Act

While fewer consumers are involved in leasing than in purchasing, there is some legal protection for those who do lease automobiles, furniture, and other items. The leasing act covers only goods leased for personal, family, or household use; it does not cover goods leased to businesses. The act requires full disclosure, and it also is applicable in only those cases where the lessee either must buy or has the option to buy after a specific period of time. All payments including official fees must be spelled out in advance. In addition, the lessee must be told the market price and the appraised price of the leased item at the end of the lease. The act does not cover lease or rental agreements of less than four months.

Fair Debt Collection Practices Act

The Fair Debt Collection Practices Act (FDCPA) became effective in March 1978. It spells out the maximum amount of harassment that may be used to collect bills. It limits the number of phone calls that may be made and the time of day during which they may be made. Phone calls must be made at convenient times, which generally are defined as between 8:00 A.M. and 9:00 P.M. The debtor, however, cannot be contacted at his or her place of employment, if it is known that the employer prohibits or discourages this. The total amount of contacts of any sort is fixed, and of course threats, overt or implied, are prohibited.

This act, however, has one loophole. It does not apply to the lenders directly, but only to third parties collecting for them. A creditor can call you anytime, but a collection agency cannot.

Holder-in-Due-Course Doctrine

The Federal Trade Commission (FTC), which enforces many of the federal consumer protection laws, has by means of regulations weakened (but not completely eliminated) the holder-in-due-course doctrine. Holder-in-due-course is the legal concept that, if a merchant entered into a credit relationship with a consumer to finance, say, a refrigerator and then sold the installment contract to a third party (say, a finance company), a legally binding contract existed between the consumer and the finance company. The payments were then made to the finance company which bought the paper on good faith and was not a party to the agreement. In short, under the old holder-in-due-course doctrine you had to pay for the refrigerator even if it was defective. Normally you can generate great pressure to have a defective item repaired or replaced by withholding payments; this was not possible formerly if a third party was involved.

FTC regulations now permit the consumer to stop making payments to third parties (even if a credit card is not involved) for defective merchandise or services. Both the seller and the third party may now be held partly liable. This permits the consumer to generate greater pressure. If it comes to legal court action, she or he can go after both the seller and the financial institution, since both are equally liable. The person now has the same rights against the third party as against the seller.

The FCBA strengthens the hand of the consumer somewhat by permitting payments to be withheld. However, if it comes to a legal battle, sellers and creditors are often not liable. This is because often the warranty is granted by the manufacturer, not the seller. While the lender and the retailer share any warranty granted at that level, neither is liable if it is granted by the manufacturer. This is especially true if a disclaimer clause is inserted into a contract. The retailer and creditor are then freed of liability for defective products if there is a court case. Nevertheless, the new law is a plus for the consumer because he or she can now withhold payments, generate some additional pressure on the retailer and creditor, and enlist them as allies against the manufacturer.

The FTC's regulations now also prohibit the waiver of defense clauses in installment contracts. These were formerly used by some retailers and protected them against action on the part of the consumer.

ENFORCING AGENCIES

There are a number of federal and state enforcing agencies. If you have a complaint and the law has been violated, the correct agency to use depends on

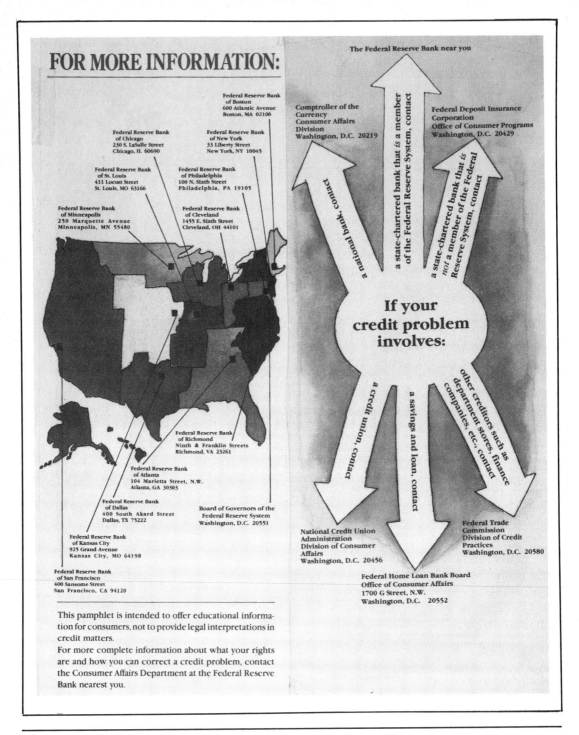

Figure 7–1   **Where to go for help.** (*Source:* Board of Governors of the Federal Reserve System.)

the creditor involved. The following illustration summarizes where you may take your complaints.

Federal Agencies

The federal laws are enforced by the agencies summarized below:

Creditor	Federal agency
National commercial banks	The Comptroller of the Currency United States Treasury Department Washington, D.C. The Comptroller has regional offices in a number of major cities. Check the telephone directory.
State banks that are members of the Federal Reserve System	The Federal Reserve Bank serving the area in which the bank is located
State nonmember banks that are insured by the Federal Deposit Insurance Corporation	The Federal Deposit Insurance Corporation Washington, D.C. The FDIC has regional offices in a number of major cities. Look in the telephone directory.
State nonmember noninsured banks	Division of Consumer Credit The Federal Trade Commission Washington, D.C. The Federal Trade Commission has regional offices in a number of major cities. There are very few such noninsured banks, however
Federal savings and loan associations	The Federal Home Loan Bank Board Washington, D.C. The FHLBB has regional offices in a number of major cities.
State savings and loans associations insured by the Federal Savings and Loan Insurance Corporation	The Federal Savings and Loan Insurance Corporation Washington, D.C. The FSLIC has regional offices in a number of major cities.
State savings and loan associations that are not insured	Division of Consumer Credit The Federal Trade Commission Washington, D.C. The FTC has regional offices in a number of major cities. Look in the telephone directory. There are very few such noninsured savings associations.
Mutual savings banks	The Federal Deposit Insurance Corporation Washington, D.C. The FDIC has regional offices in a number of major cities. Virtually all mutual savings banks are insured by the FDIC and hence regulated by them.

Federally chartered credit unions and insured state-chartered credit unions	The National Credit Union Administration Washington, D.C. The NCUA has regional offices in a number of major cities.
State-chartered non-insured credit unions	Division of Consumer Credit The Federal Trade Commission Washington, D.C. The FTC has a number of regional offices. There are very few noninsured credit unions.
Retail merchants, including department stores, finance companies, nonbank credit card issuers, and most others	Division of Consumer Credit The Federal Trade Commission Washington, D.C. The FTC has a number of regional offices.
Airlines and other creditors subject to Civil Aeronautics Board	Director, Bureau of Enforcement Civil Aeronautics Board
Meat packers, poultry processors, and other creditors subject to Packers and Stock-yards Act	Nearest Packers and Stockyards Administration area supervisor.
Creditors subject to Interstate Commerce Commission	Office of Proceedings Interstate Commerce Commission Washington, D.C.

The Federal Reserve System and the Comptroller of the Currency have established an Office of Consumer Affairs at all of their regional offices, as have many of the other federal agencies, where you should take your complaints. You may do so by mail. Write the Office of Consumer Affairs at the Regional Federal Reserve Bank of your district of the Federal Reserve System. They will send you a complaint form which you can fill out and return to them. A sample of such a complaint form is shown below (Figure 7–2).

The Department of Health, Education and Welfare (HEW) has also established an Office of Consumer Affairs. Although this office has no power of enforcement, it listens to complaints from consumer organizations. It plays the role of advocate and will report any violations of federal law to the proper enforcement agencies.

State Agencies

There are state agencies to enforce state laws. All states have banking commissioners by that or some other name. Some have credit union commissioners, savings

COMPLAINT FORM   **Federal Reserve System**

Name _____   Name of Bank _____

Address _____   Address _____
          Street   City   State   Zip

_____
  City   State   Zip

Daytime telephone _____   Account number (if applicable) _____
        (include area code)

The complaint involves the following service: Checking Account ☐   Savings Account ☐   Loan ☐

   Other: Please specify _____

I have attempted to resolve this complaint directly with the bank: No ☐   Yes ☐

   If "No", an attempt should be made to contact the bank and resolve the complaint.

   If "Yes", name of person or department contacted is _____
                                  Date

MY COMPLAINT IS AS FOLLOWS (Briefly describe the events in the order in which they happened, including specific dates and the bank's actions to which you object. Enclose copies of any pertinent information or correspondence that may be helpful. Do not send us your only copy of any document.):

_____

_____

_____

_____

_____

_____

_____

_____

_____

_____

_____

This information is solicited under the Federal Trade Commission Improvement Act. Providing the information is voluntary; complete information is necessary to expedite investigation of your complaint. Routine use of the information may include disclosing it to bank(s) or others involved or to other governmental agencies as deemed appropriate.

Date _____   Signatures _____

_____

Figure 7–2   Complaint form. (*Source:* Board of Governors of the Federal Reserve System.)

and loan commissioners, and consumer credit commissioners. Some have a similar state agency to enforce all state laws dealing with consumer credit including the maximum interest rates that may be charged. Some states also have deceptive trade legislation on the books, and some have established offices of consumer protection or consumer affairs, either within the Attorney General's office or elsewhere. Look in the telephone book of your state's capital city to find the proper state agency.

QUESTIONS FOR REVIEW

1. Does the federal law or state law govern the maximum interest rate that may be charged on consumer loans?
2. What do private voluntary consumer organizations do? Are there any in your area?
3. Discuss the truth-in-lending law. What is its purpose?
4. What does the truth-in-lending law say about credit life insurance?
5. What is meant by the right of rescission? What law grants it?
6. What should you do if your credit card is lost or stolen?
7. Which federal law deals with garnishment of wages? Summarize briefly what it provides.
8. What does the Fair Credit Reporting Act do?
9. Are you permitted to see your credit file?
10. How long may adverse information be kept in your credit file?
11. Who besides yourself may obtain a credit report on you without a court order?
12. What happens if a woman relies on her husband's credit, and they then separate?
13. Which law covers cash discounts? What does it provide?
14. May you legally withhold payments for defective merchandise?
15. What should you do if there is a billing error in your account?
16. What is the holder-in-due-course doctrine?
17. What groups are covered by the Fair Debt Collection Practices Act? Which groups are not covered?

CASES

1. Barbara Hudson applied for a loan at a bank so that she could buy a car. If the loan is granted, what information must the bank provide Barbara? If Barbara is turned down, what must the bank do?
2. Philip and Virginia Kidd recently purchased a new Cadillac. One day while Virginia was driving it, the motor literally exploded. Upon examination the dealer discovered a push rod had come through the block and the motor was damaged beyond repair. What recourse does Virginia have?
3. Dee Van Antwerp of Ogallala, Nebraska has been admitted to the Nebraska bar and has joined her husband in the practice of law. Dee doesn't have any credit cards of her own but uses her husband's. She feels perhaps she should get some cards in her own name, and seeks your advice.
4. Anita Garcia had a flight reservation from Austin, Texas to New Orleans via Dallas. But the flight to Dallas was late, so to avoid missing her connection there she purchased a ticket from another airline via Houston.

There was not time to cancel her flight via Dallas at the time but she did so later. She had charged all these flights on her Visa card and later both airlines billed her. What should Anita do?

5. Rusty Snow lost her purse, which had little of value in it except three credit cards. Rusty is concerned that someone might find them and run up a lot of bills. What should she do?

6. Blanche Wright wanted to buy some furniture for her apartment, but the store would not sell it to her on the installment plan because of an unfavorable report from the credit bureau. What are Blanche's rights?

SUGGESTED READINGS

Alice in Debitland; Consumer Protection and the Electronic Fund Transfer Act, Board of Governors of the Federal Reserve System, Washington, D.C. 20551, June, 1980.

Arbetman, Lee P., et al. *Law and the Consumer.* St. Paul, Minn.: West Publishing Co., 1982.

Charting Mortgages, Department of Consumer Affairs, Federal Reserve Bank of Philadelphia, 1982.

Consumer Handbook to Credit Protection Laws. Board of Governors of the Federal Reserve System, Washington, D.C. 20551, December, 1981.

Consumers, Credit Bureaus, and the Fair Credit Reporting Act. Associated Credit Bureaus, Inc., 6767 Southwest Freeway, Houston, Tex., no date. Check with your local credit bureaus; they may have similar publications by credit bureaus near you.

Credit Guide. Federal Reserve Bank of Chicago, 1982.

The Equal Credit Opportunity Act . . . and Age. Washington, D.C.: Board of Governors of the Federal Reserve System, May, 1977.

The Equal Credit Opportunity Act and . . . Credit Rights in Housing. Washington, D.C.: Board of Governors of the Federal Reserve System, January, 1978.

The Equal Credit Opportunity Act and . . . Doctors, Lawyers, Small Retailers, and Others Who May Provide Incidental Credit. Washington, D.C.: Board of Governors of the Federal Reserve System, May, 1977.

The Equal Credit Opportunity Act and . . . Women. Washington, D.C.: Board of Governors of the Federal Reserve System, May, 1977.

Fair Credit Billing. Washington, D.C.: Board of Governors of the Federal Reserve System, December, 1976.

The Fair Debt Collection Practices Act. Department of Consumer Affairs, Federal Reserve Bank of Philadelphia. No date.

Give Yourself Credit; A Consumer's Guide to Credit Protection Laws. Federal Reserve Bank of San Francisco, 1981.

How to File a Consumer Credit Complaint. Washington, D.C.: Board of Governors of the Federal Reserve System, July, 1978.

If You Borrow to Buy Stock. Washington, D.C.: Board of Governors of the Federal Reserve System, no date.

If You Use a Credit Card. Washington, D.C.: Board of Governors of the Federal Reserve System, December, 1978.

Staff Guidelines on Trade Regulations Rule Concerning Preservation of Consumers' Claims and Defenses.

Washington, D.C.: Federal Trade Commission. Bureau of Consumer Protection, 1976.

Truth in Leasing. Prepared jointly by the Federal Trade Commission and the Board of Governors of the Federal Reserve System, March, 1978.

What Truth in Lending Means to You. Washington, D.C.: Board of Governors of the Federal Reserve System. Revised April, 1978.

Your Credit Rating. Department of Consumer Affairs, Federal Reserve Bank of Philadelphia. No date.

CHAPTER EIGHT

TAXES

Government expenditures at all levels have risen sharply in recent years. Federal expenditures were $96.5 billion dollars in 1965. In 1983, they will exceed $800 billion. To be sure, today's dollars have been eroded by inflation so that today's $800 billion is only about $295 billion. Among the reasons are growth in population and the increase in the demand for more government services. Along with greater government expenditures came an increase in taxes.

TAXES AND EXPENDITURES

Tax Expenditures and National Income

The big increase in government expenditures (and hence taxes) started with World War II for the federal government and shortly after the war for state and local governments. Taxes have grown with expenditures. Total federal taxes were $620 billion in 1982; this amounted to 25.2 percent of national income. Expenditures of $730 billion amounted to 29.7 percent of national income. (See Table 8–1.) For 1983 taxes and expenditures will be about $650 billion and $800 billion respectively.

Comparing taxes and expenditures with national income and gross national product is one indicator of the cost (or burden) of government, since we pay our taxes out of our income.

Table 8–1   U.S. taxes, expenditures, and national income

Year	Taxes	Expenditures	Fiscal Year National Income	Taxes National income	Expenditures National income
1971	$188.4	211.4	858.1	22.0%	24.6%
1972	208.6	232.0	951.9	21.9	24.4
1973	232.2	247.1	1,064.6	21.8	23.2
1974	264.9	269.6	1,136.0	23.3	23.7
1975	281.0	326.2	1,215.0	23.1	26.9
1976	300.0	366.4	1,359.8	22.1	27.0
1977	357.8	402.7	1,525.8	23.5	26.4
1978	402.0	450.8	1,724.3	23.3	26.1
1979	465.9	493.6	1,924.8	24.2	25.6
1980*	532.2	572.7	2,117.1	25.1	27.1
1981*	599.3	657.2	2,352,5	25.4	27.9
1982	617.8	728.4	2,436.6	25.3	29.8
1983*	598.3	808.5	—		
1984*	653.7	843.9	—		

* Estimate.

The above figures were aggregates; for your personal share, you can compare your personal taxes with your personal income. The percentage of your income tax is called the effective tax rate. This only includes federal taxes; and state and local taxes add to the burden.

Principles of Taxation

There are five general principles of taxation, some of which are controversial.

1. *Ability to Pay.* For example, there is the ability-to-pay principle, that is, that high-income groups should pay more than low-income groups. This principle has been used to justify the income tax and even the progressive income tax. A tax based on ability to pay is the most equitable tax, it is argued. While most would probably agree, at least to some extent, with the ability-to-pay principle, there is some disagreement as to who has the most ability. Not all agree that income is the sole test. Also, even if the ability principle (and hence the income tax) were accepted, there is disagreement as to how progressive the tax should be. There is no final answer. Some groups say any income tax should be proportional (everyone being taxed at the same percentage rate).

2. *The Benefit Principle.* This concept suggests that taxes should be levied so that their burden is apportioned with the distribution of the services that the taxes finance. This, too, has the ring of equity to it until it is examined critically. This principle is sometimes used to defend the view that only

people with school-age children should be required to finance the schools since they are the beneficiaries of schools. This is not true because all of society, hence all citizens, benefit from schools. The benefit principle breaks down very quickly. How can the benefits of roads, schools, a system of courts, law enforcement, defense, or any other government service be allocated differently to different people?

3.   *The Political Expediency Principle.* Some argue that if taxes have to be raised, then whichever taxes that it is politically possible to raise should be selected. This view holds that all taxes are diffused throughout the system, and all of them are paid out of current income. Since economically it doesn't matter, politicians should select any one they can. While this principle can neither be proved nor disproved, political leaders give it some weight.

4.   *The Principle of Convenience and Certainty.* Taxes should be as simple as possible to make them easy to pay. The time needed to calculate the tax bill should be minimized and complexities in tax forms should be avoided. The income tax is the most complex tax. Its complexities are defended on the basis that equity requires some complexities. Taxes should also be definite and the dollar amount not subject to various interpretations. This is difficult to achieve.

5.   *The Ease of Administration Principle.* This is similar to principle number 4 above, except that it applies to the collecting agencies. Taxes should be easily collectible, and the cost of collection as small a portion of the tax revenues as possible.

While some of these principles may be inconsistent, they must nevertheless be considered by the tax authorities. Probably the concept of equity is the most troublesome.

STATE AND LOCAL TAXES

While some states and even some cities impose income taxes, the bulk of state and local tax revenues are from sales and property taxes. The largest single portion of the property tax goes to support the schools, but city and county governments also derive some revenue from it. Many cities today also have a sales tax. The bulk of sales tax receipts, however, flow into state treasuries. Other major sources of revenue for states in addition to income taxes are gasoline, liquor, and cigarette taxes.

Sales Taxes

Most of the revenue generated by the sales tax goes to the states, but some local governments receive some sales tax revenue. In some states, there are certain exempted or nontaxed items, and in others there are none. The most commonly exempted items are food consumed in the home and services such as doctors' fees, haircuts, laundry bills, and the like. Generally, rates vary from 3 to 7 percent for the states' share, and some cities add a bit more to this, usually 1 or 2 percent. The retail merchant must collect this tax and usually can keep a small part of it (this varies from state to state but generally is 1 percent of the taxes due) to cover collection cost.

The sales tax is considered to be regressive because it takes away a larger portion of a low income than a high one. It is a tax on consumption, and low-income persons consume more (save less) of their income than do high-income persons. For example, let us assume that Mr. A has $20,000 after withholding tax take-home income per year, and let us say he saves $1,000 and consumes $19,000 and lives in an area that levies a 5 percent sales tax. Depending on whether or not food and services are taxed, he will pay about $950 in sales taxes per year. This is 4.75 percent of his take-home pay. Let us assume Ms. B is earning $40,000 take-home pay per year and lives in the same town. But she saves $4,000 of it; hence, she pays about $1,806 in sales taxes, which is 4.5 percent of her income.[1] As incomes rise further, the percentage taken away under the sales tax generally declines further. Even though sales taxes are taxes on consumption, most citizens seem to prefer this kind of tax to a state or local income tax. This may be because it is paid in small amounts and seems more painless. The sales tax has the virtues of being broad-based and raising a lot of revenue; the administrative and collection cost is low relative to the revenue it raises.

Property Taxes

While some state and local governments impose a personal property tax—on automobiles, boats, and the like—and some even on intangible personal property—on bank accounts and securities—these taxes do not raise much revenue. The biggest single property tax for most individuals is on real estate, that is, on the person's home. The real property tax is an ancient device. It is not considered the best tax, but it will no doubt remain with us because it raises a good deal of revenue.

Criticisms of the property tax

1. It is costly to administer. A good deal of manpower is devoted by the taxing agency to keeping records, collecting the taxes, and appraising property for tax purposes.
2. It is inequitable. Not all property of equal value is equally assessed. Often

---

1. A sales tax of 5 percent may result in taxes of more than 5 percent of total consumption, because most purchases are in small amounts and fractional dollars are taxed at a higher rate. There are breaking points on the tables that the merchants use to calculate the tax and often the five cents per dollar tax is reached at seventy cents.

older property of equal value, not having been reappraised for many years, is on the tax rolls at a lower value than newer property. Moreover, in many cases the assessors are poorly trained.

3.   It violates the ability-to-pay principle. This is often true because the size of one's income, not the value of one's property, is the best measure of ability to pay. While there may be a relationship between income and the value of a person's property, the relationship is always valid.

4.   It penalizes pride of home ownership. Persons who maintain their property well and maintain or improve its value often must pay a higher tax than the persons who allow their property to become run down. Some critics even maintain that the property tax helps to create slums.

5.   The tax base does not automatically expand to provide for added tax revenues as the local government's need for revenue grows.

6.   It encourages flight from the central cities to the suburbs where taxes usually are lower.

7.   The tax is sometimes regressive. Larger and more valuable property is often assessed at a lower percentage of its market value than is cheaper property.

Critics of the property tax are willing to admit that it raises revenue, and that since it is an old tax people understand it and will accept it. On the other hand, there is grumbling about the property tax, and many observers believe most cities have reached the limit to the amount of revenue their property tax can raise. Yet local governments often have their hands tied. Not being sovereign, they have to receive permission from their state government before they can impose a sales or an income tax. In some cases a constitutional amendment would have to be passed before local governments could impose an income tax.

Paying the tax

The property tax is generally shared by the city government, the county government, the state government, and the school system, with the latter getting the largest share. Sometimes, however, a portion of the tax is also earmarked for specific items such as a sewer or water district. In some areas, the tax is paid to one of the above governments (usually the city or the county) and is then disbursed to the other unit in accordance with the predetermined percentage share each is to get. In other areas, various local governments cannot get together and the homeowner must write two (or more) checks and pay the county's share and the city's share separately. In most cases, if you are paying off a mortgage loan on a home, the lending institution will add 1/12 of the estimated annual tax to the monthly payment and then pay this tax for the homeowner when due.

Computation of the property tax

The computation of the property tax is roughly the same everywhere. The only variables are the appraised (or assessed) value and the tax rate or millage rate.

The assessed value generally varies from about 20 percent to 75 percent of the market value of the property.

The tax rate applied to assessed value to obtain the actual tax liability is stated either as a percentage (so much dollarwise per $100 of assessed valuation) or in mills (a mill is one-tenth of one cent). A house with a $20,000 assessed value could be taxed at 6 percent of its assessed valuation or 60 mills per hundred dollars of assessed valuation. In both cases the tax on it is $1,200.

State and Local Income Taxes

A growing number of states and a few cities have an income tax (in some states income taxes are unconstitutional). A few years ago most of the states having income taxes had laws that did not take advantage of the federal income tax. Therefore, after filing federal taxes, one had to go file again at the state level. Recently, more states have tied their income taxes into the federal government's. Consequently, after filing the federal form, a copy of it could be sent to the state authorities as verification of earned income and only a relatively simple additional state form would be needed. The only shortcoming of this system is that many of the inequities in the federal income tax law are incorporated into the state income taxes.

Other State and Local Taxes

A number of other taxes are levied by state and local governments. The most important of these are gasoline and tobacco taxes, taxes on liquor and hotel rooms, the personal property tax, personal intangible property tax, license and fees on a car, estate and inheritance taxes, and corporate income taxes. These are the major ones in use today.

FEDERAL PERSONAL INCOME TAXES

Although there are other federal taxes (for example, on corporations), the federal income tax is the largest revenue producer and the tax that has the biggest impact on the average citizen. In fiscal 1983 the federal government collected about $300 billion through personal income taxes. In fiscal 1983, personal income taxes generated about 46¢ out of each dollar that the government received. (The second largest source of revenue is the Social Security tax; and the third largest, the corporate income tax.) Figure 8–1 illustrates where the federal dollar comes from and where it goes.

The federal income tax has been described as a house of horrors. It is that—not only because of its complexities but also because of some inequities in it. However, people do not agree on what is equitable.

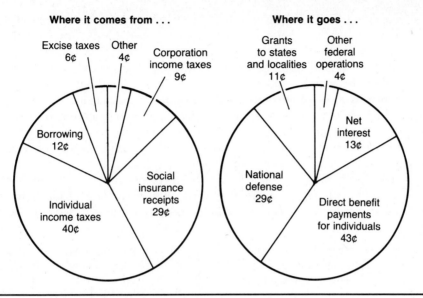

Figure 8–1   The budget dollar, fiscal year 1983 estimate. (*Source: The United States Budget in Brief, Fiscal Year 1983,* Office of Management and Budget.)

Cash Versus Accrual Basis

All taxpayers are required to account to the federal government and to keep such records as will enable them to render a true account. In accordance with the tax regulations, individuals may keep their records on either a cash basis or an accrual basis.

Most taxpayers keep their accounts—or render their returns—on a cash basis. Under the cash basis any income received is taxable during the year in which it was received even though it may have been earned in the previous year. This is usually only a factor to be considered by some self-employed professionals who may render a service in, say, December and receive their fees in January. The same is true of legitimate deductible expenses; they must be deducted in the year actually paid, even though they may have been incurred earlier.

Some businesses and self-employed individuals have chosen an accrual basis of accounting. With this system income is placed on the books when earned even though it is not received until later. The same is true of expenses; they count for tax purposes when incurred, not when paid.

Who Must File a Return and Pay a Tax?

Generally speaking, any individual must file an income tax return for any year in which he or she had a gross income of $3,300 or more, if single. If married and filing jointly, the figure is $5,400. The first $2,300 a single taxpayer earns is not taxed; it is called the *zero bracket amount*. In addition, the taxpayer has a $1,000 exemption for him- or herself. For a married couple filing jointly the zero bracket amount is $3,400, and this together with the two $1,000 exemptions makes the first $5,400 tax free. There is a second $1,000 exemption for any person over sixty-five and another one for blind persons. An additional $1,000 exemption is allowed for each dependent. The zero bracket amount and exemptions you have determine whether or not you must file a return. The exemptions you have for other dependents do not count in determining whether you must file, but count in determining whether you pay taxes. In some cases, then, a person must file a return even if he or she owes no tax. If a person is entitled to a refund he or she must file a return to get it. Table 8–2 illustrates the income levels at which a person must file a return regardless of whether or not a tax is due.

> The zero bracket amount, the amount allowed as an exemption for dependents, and many things discussed here will be changed almost yearly. You should get the latest instructions for the form 1040, issued by the Internal Revenue Service in early January every year and available at most post offices. Beginning in 1985, for example, all of the tax brackets including the zero bracket amount and the $1,000 exemption per dependent will be adjusted annually to offset the increase in the cost of living.

Earned Income Credit

In 1975, Congress began extending relief to low-income taxpayers by means of the earned income credit, a credit against taxes due amounting to 10 percent of a person's earned income up to a maximum credit of $500. Earned income

Table 8–2   Who must pay a federal income tax

Category	Income
Single	$3,300
Single, Over 65	4,300
Married, Joint Return	5,400
Married, Joint Return, One Spouse Over 65	6,400
Married, Joint Return, Both Spouses Over 65	7,400
(Add another $1000 for blindness). For Example:	
Married, Joint Return, Both Spouses Over 65 and Both Blind	9,400
Married, Joint Return, Both Spouses Under 65 with 5 minor children*	5,400

* Minor children do not count in determining who must file a return; they do count in determining who must pay a tax.

includes wages and salaries, but not interest and dividends. A taxpayer with an annual salary of $5,000 would be entitled to a credit of $500. The earned income credit is unique in that it is refundable. If the above taxpayer with a credit of $500 had a "precredit" tax liability of $200 and had not had any taxes withheld, he or she would receive a payment of $300. However, the amount of the earned income credit is reduced by 12.5 percent of the earned income in excess of $6,000. Therefore, the credit is reduced to zero for earned incomes above $10,000. This earned income credit applies only to heads of households who also have dependent children, and some taxpayers therefore do not benefit. This credit is also different from most tax credits which are taken on page 2 of Form 1040. This is calculated from special tables and is also taken on page 2 of the same form under the heading called "Payments."

Income Subject to Tax (Gross Income)

All income unless specifically excluded by law is considered taxable income; that is, wages and salaries, bonuses, tips, commissions—everything. It is the gross amount, not the net amount after withholding that counts. The following items are included.

1. All wages and salaries including tips and bonuses.
2. Interest and dividend income, except interest on bonds issued by state and local governments and their political subdivisions, which is specifically exempt by law. Interest on savings deposits is taxable in the year it is credited to your account, not when it is entered into your passbook. Interest on corporate and U.S. government bonds which pay the coupon rate is taxable when it is paid. Interest on series E (and EE) bonds is obtained via an appreciation in their price over the years. If the taxpayer is on an accrual basis, their increase must be reported and a tax paid on it annually. A taxpayer on a cash basis may report and pay a tax on the annual increase or may elect to report it only when it is realized upon the redemption of the bonds. Beginning in 1985, however, there will be an interest exclusion of 15 percent of net interest earned up to $450 on a single return and up to $900 on marrieds filing jointly. Net interest is defined as interest earned less interest paid on consumer loans.
3. All cash dividends on corporate stock (both common and preferred) must be reported. However, the first $100 ($200 on a joint return) is not taxable. Beginning in 1982, and continuing for the next four years, individuals may exclude from income up to $750 per year ($1,500 on joint returns) of dividends on *domestic public utility corporations*. To receive this benefit the shareholders must agree to receive the dividends as stock rather than cash.
4. Alimony awarded by a court is taxable although one-lump-sum settlements are not.
5. All rent and royalty income is taxed. If you own an apartment house, you

must report and pay a tax on the rent you receive. If you receive royalties from an oil well, you must report them. The same is true of royalties received by an author of a book. However, in the case of rent and royalties, only net income is taxed. You may first deduct all legitimate business expenses incurred (including depreciation where applicable) in generating the rent or royalty income.

6. Profit from a business or profession is taxable; again, you may first deduct expenses incurred in generating the income. If you are self-employed, this applies to you. If you own and run a corner grocery store, rent and so on are legitimate business expenses. The salaries a physician in private practice pays a nurse and a receptionist as well as the rent on his or her office are deductible from the physician's gross to obtain net or taxable income.

7. Gains from the sale or exchange of property are capital gains and are taxable. This includes gains on the sale of stock or bonds and real estate. However, capital gains are taxed under a special section of the law, usually at a lower rate than regular income. The taxation of capital gains is complex and is explained in greater detail below under "Capital Gains and Losses."

8. Payments received from pensions or annuities are often taxable at least in part. The taxation of pensions and annuities is complex and is discussed below.

9. Income from farms, estates, and trusts is taxed as ordinary income. This applies to farm income received by an absentee tenant who shares in the proceeds of the crop. As before, the expenses incurred in raising the crop (such as fertilizer, tractors, local taxes on the land) are deducted first. Income received from a trust is taxable, but it must actually be received. Income earned by a trust on behalf of a beneficiary, but retained by the trust, is not taxable to the individual. However, the trust itself may be subject to a tax. This complex issue of trust is explained in Chapter 20.

10. Generally sick pay is now included in gross income and is subject to taxation. There are two exceptions, however. First, if the sick pay is financed through an insurance company and the premiums are wholly paid by the employee (the insured) and not by the employer, the sick pay is not taxable. Second, if the person is permanently and totally disabled, the sick pay is excluded from taxation, but only up to a limit of $100 per week or $5,200 per year. This exclusion, however, is reduced dollar for dollar by adjusted gross income in excess of $15,000, and hence at an income of $20,200 it disappears. Sick pay is not listed separately, but is included with your regular wage or salary.

11. Unemployment compensation is included in gross income in some cases. If total adjusted gross income, together with unemployment compensation, is more than $20,000 ($25,000 if the taxpayer is married and filing jointly), it is subject to taxation. In such a case you must pay a tax on whichever of the following is the smaller: (1) total unemployment compensation, or (2) one half of that portion of other total adjusted gross income and

unemployment compensation, which together exceed $20,000 if the taxpayer is single and $25,000 if married and filing jointly.

12. Income from most other miscellaneous sources is also taxable. Normally, prize money or the fair market value of noncash prizes must be reported as income. Any money made from gambling must be included as income· gambling losses, on the other hand, may not be deducted—except from the winnings themselves, to arrive at a net gain.

13. State and local income tax refunds must be reported as taxable income in the year they are received, if the refund is for a year in which the taxpayer itemized deductions because state and local income taxes are legitimate itemized deductions.

Nontaxable Income

Some items that need not be included as income. Among these, but not altogether inclusive, are scholarships and prizes for scholarly works. If you were to win the Nobel Prize, for example, you would not need to pay taxes on it. While scholarships and honoraria are not taxable, the stipend received by college students who hold teaching or research assistantships is. Tax authorities do not consider gifts, honoraria, or scholarships as income; but do consider the stipend from a teaching or a research assistantship as income. Most government payments made to veterans and their families, worker's compensation payments, interest from state and municipal bonds, casualty insurance payments received, gifts, disability and death payments awarded by the courts, and inheritances are not subject to the income tax. There are separate gift and inheritance taxes at both the state and federal levels, but at the federal level there are high exemptions. Moreover, loopholes exist by which inheritance and gift taxes can be avoided legally. Gift and inheritance taxes are explained in Chapter 9. Table 8–3 illustrates various sources of income and whether or not they are subject to the federal income tax.

The above income items subject to taxation are together referred to as gross income. It is one of the first entries made on the personal income tax forms. It can be reduced somewhat before you calculate your tax.

Joint Returns or Income Splitting

Historically, those married persons living in the community-property states (namely Arizona, California, Idaho, Nevada, New Mexico, Texas, and Washington) had a tax advantage over married persons living in the other states. In the community-property states, the legal concept is that one-half of the earnings of any spouse belong to the other spouse. If a married person earns $20,000 per year, $10,000 of this is the wage earner's and the other $10,000 is the spouse's. This made a

Table 8–3   Checklist of taxable and nontaxable income

Item	Taxable	Nontaxable
Accident insurance proceeds		X
Alimony and separate maintenance payments periodically received	X	
Bad debt recovered, to extent of prior tax benefit	X	
Bequests		X
Board furnished for convenience of employer		X
Bonuses received as compensation for services rendered	X	
Capital gains	X	
Clergymen		
Rental value of parsonage furnished as part of compensation		X
Salaries, fees, contributions, etc., received for personal services	X	
Commissions received as compensation for services rendered	X	
Damages awarded by a court		X
Dismissal pay received	X	
Dividends		
In cash or property from corporate earnings (there is a partial exclusion; see above)	X	
In stock of corporation where proportionate interest of stockholders is not affected		X
On life insurance policies		X
On money market funds	X	
Executors' fees	X	
Farmers' income including government payments received under A.A.A. and other acts	X	
Gambling winnings	X	
Gifts		X
Inheritances		X
Interest on		
Bank savings accounts	X	
Bonds of a state, city, or other political subdivision		X
Savings and loan accounts	X	
Federal securities including bonds	X	
Corporate bonds	X	
Notes	X	
Tax refunds	X	
Insurance benefit payments		X
Jury fees	X	
Legacies		X
Marriage settlement, lump-sum payment received		X
Moving expenses of family paid by employer (in some cases. See below.)		X
Notary public fees	X	
Old age benefits		
Under Railroad Retirement Act		X
Under Social Security Act		X
Partnership income, distributive share of partnership profits	X	
Political campaign contributions received by candidates		X
Prizes won in contests, exhibits, fairs, raffles, etc.	X	

Item	Taxable	Nontaxable
Professional fees	X	
Rents	X	
Royalties received	X	
Salaries and wages	X	
Scholarships		X
Sick pay (Taxable in most cases)*	X	
Social Security benefit payments		X
State and federal employees' salaries	X	
Strike benefits from labor unions	X	
Teachers' salaries	X	
Tips	X	
Unemployment benefits under		
Railroad Unemployment Insurance Act		X
State Unemployment Compensation Laws		X
War veterans		
Bonuses		X
Pensions		X
Workers' compensation benefits		X

* Sick pay is not taxable in the case where the person is totally disabled, or if it is financed through an insurance company and the premiums were paid by the individual rather than by the employer.

substantial difference in the amount of tax paid by the couple, the reason being that the income tax is graduated, or progressive as some people call it. Thus the tax on a single return of $20,000 is greater than that on two $10,000 returns.

To put all married couples on an equal footing taxwise, Congress in 1948 wrote into the Internal Revenue Code a statement that gives married taxpayers the option of income splitting by filing a joint return. Ordinarily when a married couple files a joint return, they save substantially in taxes. Whether a couple is married for tax purposes is determined by their status on December 31 of the year in question. There is one exception to this rule; if one of the members of a marriage dies, the survivor may elect to file a joint return that year.

The tax savings arising from income splitting can best be shown by an illustration (see Table 8–4). Let us assume two individuals, each with an income

Table 8–4   Tax savings from income splitting

Joint return		Single return	
Income	$20,000	Income	$20,000
Dependents	2,000	Dependents	2,000
Taxable income	18,000	Taxable income	18,000
Tax	2,448	Tax	3,133
	Savings = $685		

Note: Zero bracket amount is not shown because it is built into both the tax tables and the tax rate schedule.

of $20,000 per year, two dependents, and each taking zero bracket amount. One splits income and one does not.

Different tables are available for those who file a joint return than for those filing a single return, and the benefits described in the example just above and shown in Table 8–4 are built into them. Moreover, the higher a person's income, the greater the tax saving from income splitting; the joint return has reduced the progressiveness of the tax.

The Discrimination against Married Couples

The above example suggests that the tax law discriminates against unmarried individuals by permitting income splitting because two individuals earning the same income, even if they have the same dependents, pay differing amounts of taxes if only one of them is married. However, recently many married couples have complained that they are discriminated against if both members hold jobs, because if each of them earns $20,000, their $40,000 total income is taxed more heavily than the $40,000 represented by two single individuals each earning $20,000; the married couple is taxed at the $40,000 tax bracket and the singles at $20,000. Both of these charges are true because of the progressive nature of the tax structure. The purist would say that a single person earning $40,000 per year should not have a heavier tax burden than a married person earning $40,000, as the joint return allows, and that a married couple each of whom earns $20,000 per year should not have a heavier tax burden than the combined burden of two singles each earning $20,000. In some cases singles have a heavier tax burden; in other cases married persons do. It is mathematically impossible to eliminate both of these types of discrimination under a progressive tax structure unless some formula is developed to give relief to a married couple both of whom work. As was pointed out before a congressional committee holding hearings on this subject, it is impossible for both ends of a see-saw to be up at the same time. Congress has recognized this and made an allowance for two-income families in the Economic Recovery Act of 1981. Beginning with 1982's income, married persons filing jointly may claim a deduction of 5 percent of the lower-earning partner's income up to an income of $30,000. This makes the maximum deduction $1,500 in 1982. In 1983 and subsequent years, this deduction becomes 10 percent, making the maximum dollar deduction become $3,000.

Head of a Household

Many persons who are unmarried are nevertheless the head of a household with many of the same expenses as a married person. Prior to October 31, 1951, individuals fitting into that category could file only individual returns and were thus placed in an unfair position compared with married persons who were able to file joint returns. After 1951, persons qualifying as heads of households were granted approximately 50 percent of the benefits given to married couples filing a joint return.

To qualify as head of household, an individual must be unmarried at the end of the tax year. He or she must further have maintained a household in which lives any closely related person for whom the taxpayer would ordinarily be entitled to a deduction. The taxpayer must contribute over half the cost of maintaining the home, which has been interpreted to mean property taxes, maintenance costs, mortgage payments or rent, and the like, plus the cost of food consumed on the premises.

Declaration of Estimated Tax for Individuals

If you have income not subject to withholding, you may have to file a declaration of your estimated income and pay a tax on it quarterly. People who are self-employed and those with substantial interest, dividend or other so-called nonearned income have to do this. If you have only a small amount of income not subject to withholding, you may avoid filing this form by increasing the amount withheld from your salary over what it normally would be. The rule is that if your withholdings are 80 percent or more of your total tax liability, there is no penalty for not filing a declaration on your other income.

Tax Exemptions

All taxpayers have at least one $1,000 exemption for themselves. If they attain or are over the age of sixty-five before the end of the taxable year, they are entitled to a second exemption. If they are blind, they are entitled to a third exemption. Thus an individual can have three exemptions totaling $3,000.

A married taxpayer is entitled to an exemption for his or her spouse if a joint return is filed. If a separate return is filed, each would probably take his or her own $1,000 exemption, although one could take it, and then the other would have zero exemptions. Further, if the spouse is over the age of sixty-five, an additional exemption may be claimed for him or her, and another possible exemption for the spouse if he or she is blind—unless of course these exemptions are claimed in his or her own behalf.

Further exemptions may be claimed in the amount of $1,000 for each dependent. However, a child or other dependent must have received more than half his or her support from the taxpayer (or from husband and wife if a joint return is filed). But if the child is married, in order for the parent to claim him or her as an exemption, the child must not file a joint return with a spouse. A further qualification is that the child must have been either a resident of the United States, Canada, Mexico, the Republic of Panama, or the Canal Zone or an alien child adopted by and living with the United States citizen abroad.

In the case of a child not over nineteen or a student over nineteen (including college students), sometimes a double exemption is possible. If individuals earn more than $3,300 (the zero bracket amount plus the $1,000 exemption), they must file a return and use themselves as an exemption. But if they are your children and you furnish more than one-half of their support, you can count them as dependents also, and deduct a full $1,000 for each. Children not over 19 and college students over 19, can, in these cases, provide a double exemption. However, to obtain a double exemption for full-time students they must be unmarried, or if married, must not file a joint return.

Tax Withholding

Employers are required to withhold a portion of their employees' wages for income tax purposes. This is referred to as collection at the source, or pay-as-you-go. Its purpose is both to assure the government that the taxes will be paid and to make it easier for the taxpayer. Before the enactment of the withholding tax law, many taxpayers had to borrow to pay their income taxes on time.

When persons begin work with an organization, they file with the employer a withholding tax exemption certificate (the W-4 form), which contains a statement of the number of exemptions to which they are entitled. Employees may if they desire claim fewer exemptions than they actually have to make sure they do not owe any taxes when the year is over. The employer will then withhold a percentage of wages based on the number of exemptions and the level of the wage or salary.

At the end of the year the employer gives the employee two or three copies of a W-2 form, showing the amount paid in wages, the amount of income tax withheld, and the amount of Social Security tax withheld, if any. (You will get three copies if you live in a state that has a state income tax and two if you live in a state that does not have a state income tax.) The W-2 form is the basis for the tax returns of those persons working for wages and salaries. The original copy of the W-2 form is submitted with the tax return and a duplicate is retained for the taxpayer's files.

The Taxation of Annuities and Pensions[2]

Annuities

An annuity is ordinarily thought of as an insurance contract providing for regular payments to the insured at a fixed rate and continuing throughout the life of the insured or for a certain number of years. Thus a prize fighter who has a high income during the early years of his career might pay an insurance company a lump sum, the agreement being that at the age of forty the fighter is to receive

2. Annuities and pensions are further discussed in Chapter 19.

$500 per week for the rest of his life. The problem from the tax point of view is

1. The lump sum given in exchange for the insurance annuity contract has already been taxed, and it would be unfair to tax it again as the fighter receives the $500 per week after reaching age forty.
2. However, if a prize fighter were to invest X dollars in corporate bonds, he would receive interest, which is taxable. The same logic applies to annuities; only part of the $500 per week that he receives each week after reaching forty until he dies is really interest on the lump sum that he invested with the insurance company. Part of the $500 return is principal and part of the return is income; the problem is to determine which part is income so that it may be taxed.

To determine the tax, the Internal Revenue Code has worked out a formula that provides for what is known as an exclusion ratio, determined by dividing the amount invested in the contract (and on which taxes have already been paid) by the expected return from the contract. For example, suppose $20,000 is the amount invested in the contract and, purely hypothetically, the annuitant is to receive $150 per month for life, and further that his age is such that his "expected" return will be $30,000. Then

$$\frac{\$20,000}{\$30,000} = 66\frac{2}{3} \text{ percent}$$

The annuitant can exclude 66 2/3 percent from the gross income of each $150 monthly payment that he receives, or $100. On an annual basis, of the $1,800 received, $1,200 is excluded from gross income and $600 is reportable as gross income subject to taxation. This is true even if the annuitant outlives the estimated life on which the exclusion ratio is based.

Pensions

A pension plan may also involve an annuity. This comes about in a number of ways. First, the entire cost of the annuity may be paid by your employer. In this case the entire amount received by you each year must be included in gross income, and this amount is fully taxable. However, generally what happens is that the employer contributes part of the payment of the annuity and the employee contributes the other part. The manner in which it is taxable depends on how the payments are made.

1. If the plan provides that you will recover your total cost, or the amount you contributed over the years, within the first three years after the first payment to you starts, then the proceeds received by you are not taxable until after you have received your total cost. After that, the total pension payment is treated as income and must be reported on your return as gross income.

2.   If you are not expected to recover your cost within three years, the pension is treated in the same manner as was outlined above under annuities. Your exclusion ratio must be established, this being your investment divided by the expected return.

In some cases, however, depending on the type of pension, you may be required to include the contribution of your employer in your gross income (and pay a tax on it) at the time the employer's contribution is made. This is the case where the pension plan is fully vested but is not what is considered "qualified" by the Internal Revenue Service. If this is the case, then, when determining the amount of the investment, your contribution plus the contribution of the employer are included in the investment, which has already been taxed. This is the figure employed to determine the exclusion ratio. Since this increases the investment figure and since the expected return figure remains the same, the percentage to be excluded rises and the net effect is that a lower amount of your pension is included in your gross income after the pension payments begin. Suppose the expected return is $10,000 and the investment is $5,000.

$$\frac{\$5,000}{\$10,000} = 50 \text{ percent}$$

Therefore 50 percent of the annuity payment can be excluded from gross income.

If the payments made on your behalf had been taxable at the time your employer made them and if over the years they totaled $4,000, the total investment is $9,000.

$$\frac{\$9,000}{\$10,000} = 90 \text{ percent}$$

Ninety percent of the annuity may be excluded from gross income after the annual payments of the annuity begin.

If the pension plan is referred to as "qualified" by the Internal Revenue Service, the payment made by the employer into the pension fund on behalf of the employees while they are working is not taxable as income to the employees. Moreover, the employers can take the payment as an expense when calculating their tax. But when these employees retire, that portion of their pensions that comes from the employer's contribution is fully taxable as income. Just how the plan must be set up to be considered qualified is too complex to examine here. If your firm has a pension plan, you can find out whether it is qualified or not and what is required for qualification from your personnel department.

There are many types of annuities and pension plans, and the tax treatment depends on the type of plan. Finally, the whole purpose is to exclude from the tax any amount on which you have already paid a tax and to include in gross income any monies you will receive and on which you have paid no income tax.

Two types of pension payments paid to retired persons are not subject to any form of federal taxation. The first of these is Social Security payments;

income from this source need not be reported.[3] A second type not subject to the federal income tax is the veteran's pension, paid because of a service-connected disability. Regular military retirement pay, however, is taxable.

Income Averaging

You can save money by income averaging if your income fluctuates sharply or if your income rises rapidly from a relatively low level. A special schedule—Schedule G—is used for this. It puts the taxpayer in a lower tax bracket by allowing the high-income years to be averaged (and hence reduced) with low-income years. It works as follows: First, average your taxable income for the four preceding years and add 20 percent to that average. That average plus 20 percent is considered your base income. If your current year's taxable income is $3,000 more than your base income, you may average. For example, if your average taxable income over the preceding four years is $20,000, then your base income is $24,000. Adding $3,000 to that gives $27,000. If your current year's income is more than $27,000, you may save taxes by averaging. This is because in a sense you are pushing some of your high current income back to lower income years and hence reducing the bracket at which you are taxed. In the above case, if your income is just over $27,000, you may or may not save by averaging. You should figure your tax both ways to determine this. If your current year is significantly more than $3,000 over your base income, you will save by averaging.

The Maximum Tax Provision

There is also a maximum tax rate on all income of 50 percent. No one need pay more than a 50 percent rate on taxable income. At what income level you reach the 50 percent bracket is, of course, determined by the number of exemptions you have and the amount of your itemized deductions, if any.

The Limited Charitable Contributions

The 1981 tax law allowed for a limited deduction for charitable contributions "above the line," as it is called. They become valuable even if you do not itemize. There is a limit during the phase-in years from 1982 to 1986. In 1982 and 1983, 25 percent of the first $100 of charitable contributions may be so treated, providing for a maximum deduction of $25. In 1984, this 25 percent will be applied to the first $300 of contributions; in 1985, 50 percent of *all* contributions,

3. The 1983 change in the Social Security law provided that high-income groups who also receive social security benefits will be taxed on a portion of their benefits. However, most people's social security benefits will remain tax free. See Chapter 19.

and in 1986, 100 percent of *all* contributions may be deducted. This deduction is taken on page 2 of the 1040 form where the tax computation is made. Contributions above this limited amount may be included under itemized deductions.

ADJUSTMENTS TO INCOME; ADJUSTED GROSS INCOME

There are certain page one deductions. These may be taken from gross income to arrive at adjusted gross income. There are also certain expense items similar to page one deductions in that they reduce gross income, such as expenses attributable to a business or to the generation of rent and royalty income. These include cost of travel, meals and lodging, and depreciation. However, these are taken on different schedules and reduce gross income to net business income.

Certain other expense items may be taken in order to further reduce adjusted gross income—called itemized deductions. I will examine them below, but first I will note those items that may be taken in moving from gross to adjusted gross income. These may be taken even if you do not itemize your deductions.

Moving Expenses

Moving expenses may be deducted in many cases. If you move to a new job location, you may be able to deduct some or all of your moving expenses. To obtain the deduction you must meet two tests: (1) the new job must be at least 35 miles further from your old home than your old job was, and (2) you must be employed full time at the new job for at least 39 weeks during the 12 months immediately following the move. Temporary moves do not count.

If you qualify, every penny of your direct moving costs may be taken, including cost of moving household and personal goods and reasonable travel costs for you and your family, including food and lodging.

Indirect moving costs include: househunting expenses; the cost of meals and lodging in temporary quarters up to 30 days; and the costs of selling, buying, or leasing a home, including brokers' and attorneys' fees and the like. There is, however, an overall limit on indirect cost deductions of $3,000, of which no more than $1,500 may be for househunting and temporary living expenses.

Employee Business Expenses

If your job requires you to travel, you may deduct travel costs (including an allowance for your car), meals and lodging, and necessary entertainment of clients. You may take these expenses only to the extent that your employer does not reimburse you. Your travel costs must be necessary travel costs and may not include commuting to and from work.

Payments to a Keogh and an Individual Retirement Account (IRA)

The Keogh Plan and the Individual Retirement Account (IRA) are discussed in Chapter 19. They are a means whereby you may set aside and earmark funds for your retirement and not pay a tax. They are deducted from gross income to arrive at adjusted gross income.

Penalty on Early Withdrawal of Savings

There is a penalty assessed in some but not all cases when you withdraw savings early from banks and savings and loan associations. The penalty is assessed in the form of reduced interest on early withdrawals, before maturity (see Chapter 14). The penalty is tax deductible and taken on page one of the 1040 form.

Alimony Paid

Periodic alimony payments or separate maintenance payments made under a court order may be deducted. You may also deduct payments made under a written separation agreement. You may not deduct lump-sum cash or property settlements, voluntary payments, or amounts specified as child support.

Marriage Penalty Deduction

As noted above, marrieds filing jointly may claim a deduction of 5 percent of the lower-earning partner's income up to an income of $30,000. This makes the maximum deduction $1,500 in 1982. In 1983 and subsequent years, this deduction becomes 10 percent, the maximum dollar deduction becoming $3,000. This deduction is taken in moving to adjusted gross income.

Disability Income Exclusion (Sick Pay)

This replaced the old sick pay exclusion. Sick pay is now fully taxable in most cases. Sick pay (disability pay) received by a person totally and permanently disabled is not taxable up to $5,200 per year. However, this $5,200 income exclusion is reduced dollar for dollar for other income in excess of $15,000; hence, at $20,000 it drops out. Sick pay financed by an insurance policy, the premiums of which were completely paid by the individual and not the employer, is also not taxable.

ITEMIZED DEDUCTIONS

Certain other deductions may be taken by the taxpayer who qualifies in moving from *adjusted gross income* to *net income*, also called taxable income. These are the itemized deductions. Some people do not wish to itemize or are not permitted to itemize because their legitimate deductions do not exceed the zero bracket amount.

The Zero Bracket Amount

The zero bracket amount replaced what used to be called the standard deduction. The federal income tax is progressive and the rates technically start at zero; and a zero rate applies to the following income:

Taxpayer's status

1. Single taxpayer or unmarried head of household $2,300
2. Married, filing jointly   3,400
3. Married, filing separately   1,700

In addition, there is a $1,000 exemption for the taxpayer and another $1,000 for each dependent. The zero bracket amount is built into both the tax tables and the tax schedule. The $1,000 exemption is built into neither, and you must take it on the 1040 form. The election to itemize deductions may be made only if these deductions exceed the zero bracket amount. It should also be noted that under current law, beginning in 1985, both the zero bracket amount and the personal exemption of $1,000 will be indexed for inflation. They will be adjusted upward to offset increases in the consumer price level.

If you use the so-called "short form" (1040A), the IRS will calculate your taxes for you if you so request. You may use the short form only if your income is $50,000 or less and if all of your income is from wages, salaries, tips, dividends, interest, pensions, and annuities; and if you don't itemize, income average, or want your refund applied to next year's tax.

Itemized Deductions

The itemized deductions that can be taken only on Schedule A are of no value unless they exceed the zero bracket amount. If the taxpayer has a few large items, however, such as interest on a mortgage and property taxes, these alone will often give a deduction in excess of the zero bracket amount. If this is the case, it is worthwhile to keep records so that all of the various smaller items can be added.

Taxes

Most general state and local taxes paid by the taxpayer during the taxable year are deductible. The major taxes involved are state and local income taxes, retail sales taxes, real estate taxes, and personal property taxes such as on automobiles and boats. Tables are available that can be used to establish the sales tax deduction for every state (sales taxes vary by state). If you bought a big item during the year such as a boat, car, or airplane, you can deduct the sales tax on it in addition to what the tables allow.

Real estate taxes are probably the most important single tax for the average person. If an individual has an adjusted gross income of $20,000 per year and his or her real property tax is $1,200, that alone will reduce the taxable income to $18,800.

Interest

Interest is another big deduction for many taxpayers, especially if they are paying off a mortgage. All interest paid on personal debts—such as mortgages, notes, loans on life insurance policies, and personal loans from finance companies—is deductible. There are a few exceptions; for example, interest on money borrowed to purchase tax exempt securities is not deductible.

During the first few years when an individual is making payments on a mortgage, much of the money is for the payment of interest and will constitute a major deduction. Of a hypothetical $600 a month paid during the first year of a mortgage, as much as $400 a month may constitute interest, and this amount is deductible. Over a full year, this can amount to $4,800 or more.

Contributions

A limited charitable deduction may be taken even if you do not itemize. It is deducted from adjusted gross income. Contributions over that limited amount may be itemized. Contributions to approved institutions operated for religious, charitable, literary, scientific, educational, or eleemosynary purposes may be deducted, although such deductions must not exceed 50 percent of the taxpayer's adjusted gross income (in some cases it cannot exceed 20 percent).

Casualty and theft losses

These items are deductible to some extent. Loss of value of property as the result of accident, fire, theft, riot, rebellion, uprising, or other casualty loss not covered by insurance is sometimes deductible. All of the various losses must first be added together and the amount of loss computed by determining the value of the property just before the loss. From this figure, to determine the net loss for tax purposes, the taxpayer must deduct the salvage value plus any insurance received. Then that portion of this net aggregate loss in excess of 10 percent of adjusted gross income may be deducted.

Medical and dental expenses

A taxpayer may deduct certain medical expenses on Schedule A of the tax form, but only when they exceed 5 percent of adjusted gross income. Health insurance premiums are included as deductible items. You may also add a mileage allowance of 9 cents per mile to your medical expenses if you drive your car to the doctor's office or other treatment center.

Expenses for medicines and drugs are included in the other medical expenses to the extent that the total cost of medicines and drugs exceeds 1 percent of the adjusted gross income until 1983. After 1983 drug expenses no longer are deductible separately, but are to be added to other medical expenses.

The following example illustrates how the medical deduction works.

Adjusted Gross Income (AGI)		$20,000
Medical Insurance Premiums	$ 875	
Total Medical Bills not Covered by Insurance	$1,500	
Dental Bills	$ 200	
Total Medical	$2,575	
5% of AGI	$1,000	
Medical Deduction	$1,575	
Drugs	$ 350	
1% of AGI	$ 200	
Drug Deduction	$ 150	

Auto expense

If you use your car for business purposes or to generate other income, the expense of running it can be deducted. If you have some rental property, and you use your car to manage it, part of your auto expenses are a legal deduction. If your car is used for both business and pleasure, you must prorate the expense in accordance with the ratio of business to pleasure mileage per year. The cost (or mileage) of driving to and from work is not considered a business expense and hence is not deductible. If you prorate your expenses, be sure to keep good records, and include all of them. The cost of all oil and gas, repairs, taxes, insurance, parking fees, tolls, and so on—everything, including an allowance for depreciation. (Depreciation is explained in greater detail below.) Also keep accurate records of miles driven for both business and pleasure. If 60 percent of the mileage driven was for pleasure (which, remember, oddly enough includes to and from work), and 40 percent was for business, you may deduct 40 percent of your total auto expenses.

An alternative method of calculating your auto expenses is to take so much per mile of business or other legitimate driving. This includes business mileage as well as mileage incurred in charitable work and trips to and from hospitals and doctors' offices if they were medically necessary. If you take a mileage expense, you may take 20¢ per mile for the first 15,000 miles, and 11¢ per mile for mileage in excess of 15,000 miles of business use. This figure is increased almost yearly.

Educational expenses

With greater attention being paid to higher education, there is a greater need for the explanation of deductible educational expenses. They are deductible only for maintaining your skills or improving your skills in your employment or other trade or business or for meeting the express requirements of your employer or the requirement of applicable law or regulations imposed as a condition to the retention of your salary or employment. Educational expenses are only deductible if necessary to keep your job.

Remember that expenses incurred for obtaining a new position, meeting minimum requirements, obtaining a substantial advancement in position, or for personal purposes are not deductible. If a middle-aged woman decides to take a night course in American literature for her own amusement, the expenses are not deductible. However, if a lawyer takes a refresher course to maintain skills, this is deductible. College tuition is not deductible, although Congress periodically discusses the possibility of allowing tuition as a deductible item.

Depreciation

Although most people have only one source of income, many have income other than that from wages and salaries and consequently may become involved with depreciation. A person who owns rental property may depreciate the home and take the depreciation·as a deduction. An accountant, lawyer, physician, or other professional person may recover the cost of books and certain other equipment through depreciation only.

Depreciation is defined as wear and tear on property used in a trade or business as well as obsolescence. To take depreciation as a deduction on the income tax you must have certain kinds of property; one cannot claim depreciation on land, stock, bonds, or securities. You must also know the date the property was acquired, because its life is figured from that date, and you must know the cost or other basis of the property.

Depreciation is computed on the fair market value of the property as of the date purchased. The useful life of the asset must be ascertained, for that may be the number of years over which depreciation may be charged. For tax purposes, however, the depreciation period may be less than the actual useful life; this period varies from asset to asset. For a rental house it may be fifteen years; for an auto used for business purposes, three years. The value of the asset may then be written down (depreciated) so much per year over the period of years agreed upon, at which time the asset is carried on the books at its scrap value, if any. The dollar write-down is then a legitimate itemized deduction.

There are two main methods of computing depreciation: the so-called straight-line method and the accelerated method. The straight-line method works as follows: Assume that a typewriter used for profit has an original cost of $400, that the estimated life of the machine is ten years, and that it has no scrap value. In such a case the machine is depreciated at the rate of 10 percent or $40 per year, and its original cost will be recaptured at the end of the ten-year period. Hence, the taxpayer will be allowed to deduct $40 per year. If a given machine costs $1,000 and has a useful life of ten years, the taxpayer would be permitted to deduct 10 percent per year, or in this case $100 per year.

Accelerated depreciation could be double declining balance (also called "200 percent of straight line") or it could be 175 percent or 150 percent of straight line. The following example illustrates how it works: Suppose you have a $20,000 machine that has no scrap value and that you are going to depreciate over twenty years. Using the straight-line method would give you $1,000 the first (and each of the following) year. Under the double declining method, however, after calculating the first year's depreciation you simply double it; hence you get $2,000 the first year. The second year the machine is only worth $18,000, one-twentieth of that value is $900, which you double and get your depreciation of $1,800. The third year it is valued at $16,200 ($20,000 less $3,800) for purposes of depreciation, and one-twentieth of that number doubled is $1,620, which is your third year depreciation. So it continues through the life of the asset.

If you use 175 percent of straight-line depreciation, it works as follows. If you have a $50,000 rental house to be depreciated over fifteen years, the straight-line method would give you $3,330 per year. If you use 175 percent, you simply jack up the depreciation charge by that amount and the first year's depreciation becomes $5,825. The second year the house is only worth $44,175. The normal straight-line depreciation would give you $2,942, but 175 percent of that value is $5,149, and so on as the years go by.

There are a few gray areas in the case of depreciation. For example, can a self-employed consultant deduct depreciation on his home, if he has an office in it? If the office is used primarily for consulting, he can deduct a prorated part of his house. If his house has nine rooms and he uses one for his office, and his house is valued at $50,000, he may depreciate his house as explained above in the case of a rental, but only take one ninth of the final figure (or he may make the proration on the basis of square feet).

If the consultant's office is not used primarily (and this has been interpreted as almost solely) for consulting, he may not charge a depreciation allowance on it. The same gray area exists for a musician who gives piano lessons in her home. If she gives enough lessons on her piano in her home, she may be able to depreciate part of her piano as well as part of her home. She has to prorate her piano in accordance with its use, and the room it is in as explained above.

Miscellaneous deductions

If you are a member of a union or professional society, you may deduct union and professional society dues. You may also deduct any fee you paid to have your tax return prepared the previous year. In addition, you may also deduct the following:

1.   The cost of renting a safe deposit box in which you keep income-producing securities;
2.   The cost of any investment or tax advice;
3.   Subscriptions to professional journals;
4.   Employment agency fees;
5.   Tools, supplies, and special equipment needed in your work; and
6.   Uniforms and special clothes not suitable for regular wear, including the cost of cleaning and repairing them.

Table 8—5 includes a listing of deductible and nondeductible items to use when itemizing your deductions on Schedule A. This quick reference checklist can aid you in deciding whether an item may be deducted or not.

TAX CREDITS

After you have itemized all of your deductions, you can use them to reduce your adjusted gross income, presumably by more than the zero bracket amount. Then you obtain your taxable income and calculate your tax liability. But then there are tax credits, which are better than deductions because they reduce not your income subject to tax, but rather the actual tax itself. After you have calculated the taxes due, every tax credit you have will reduce them dollar for dollar.

Political Contributions

You may take as a tax credit contributions to candidates for political office. One-half the contribution may be taken but this is limited to $50 for singles and $100 for marrieds filing jointly.

Tax Credit for the Elderly

The tax credit for the elderly (formerly called the retirement income credit) is a limited exemption in the form of a credit against the tax. It is designed to give low-income elderly a modest tax break. Its determination is somewhat complicated, and you can qualify only if you are sixty-five or over or if you are under sixty-five but have retired under a public retirement plan, set up for public servants, such as city officials and schoolteachers. In both cases, only the taxable portion of any pension is considered in computing the tax credit.

Table 8–5   Checklist of deductible and nondeductible items

Items	Deductible	Nondeductible
Alimony and separate maintenance payments taxable to recipient	X	
Automobile expenses (car used exclusively for pleasure)		
Gasoline taxes imposed on consumer	X	
Interest on finance loans	X	
License fees (property tax portion only)	X	
Ordinary upkeep and operating expenses		X
Burglary losses, if not covered by insurance	X	
Casualty losses not covered by insurance (fire, flood, windstorm, lightning, earthquakes; only if they exceed 10 % of adj. gross income	X	
Charitable contributions to approved institutions (limited to 50% of adjusted gross income; in some cases 20%)		X
Domestic servants, wages paid		X
Dues, social clubs for personal use		X
Employment fees paid to agencies	X	
Federal income taxes		X
Fines for violation of laws and regulations		X
Funeral expenses		X
Gambling losses, to extent of gains only	X	
Gift taxes		X
Gifts to relatives and other individuals		X
Income tax imposed by state	X	
Inheritance taxes		X
Interest paid on personal loans	X	
Investment advice	X	
Life insurance premiums		X
Medical expenses in excess of 5% of adjusted gross income (including the cost of artificial limbs, artificial teeth, drugs and medical supplies prescribed by a physician, eye glasses, hearing aids, dental fees, hospital expenses, to extent not covered by insurance).	X	
Old-age benefit tax withheld by employer		X
Professional dues and subscriptions to professional journals	X	
Property taxes, real and personal	X	
Residence for personal use		
Improvements		X
Insurance		X
Interest on mortgage loan	X	
Loss from sale of		X
Rent paid		X
Repairs		X
Taxes	X	
Termite damage		X
Safe deposit box	X	

Items	Deductible	Nondeductible
Sales tax, state and local	X	
Special tools	X	
State gasoline taxes		X
Teachers		
Fees paid to employment agencies	X	
Traveling expenses attending professional meetings	X	
Traveling expenses to and from place of business or employment		X
Unemployment taxes imposed on employees under state law	X	
Uniforms for personal use including cost and up-keep, if not adaptable for general use (nurses, policemen, jockeys, baseball players, firemen, trainmen, etc.)	X	
Union dues	X	
Use taxes imposed on consumers under state law	X	

If you qualify, the credit for the elderly is calculated on all income received (including earned income) except Social Security and other tax-exempt pensions and annuities. The credit is 15 percent, but the maximum amount of income on which the credit may be calculated is $2,500 for singles and married persons filing jointly if only one spouse has reached age sixty-five. If both spouses are sixty-five or older, the 15 percent credit can be calculated on up to $3,750 of income. The income on which the tax credit is calculated (the $2,500 and $3,750) must be reduced by one-half of the taxpayer's adjusted gross income above $7,500 in the case of a single individual and $10,000 in the case of a married couple, and by the amount of Social Security or other pensions that are excluded from gross income received. Because the maximum income base is $3,750 or $2,500, the maximum credit comes to $375 for a single individual and $562.50 for a married couple both of whom are sixty-five or older. Table 8–6 illustrates the retirement income credit. In the example in the table, the individual would calculate his or her taxes in the regular way on the 1040 form and then reduce the tax due by $262.50 if married and if each person is over sixty-five.

If the taxpayer had other income of $5,000, providing a total taxable income of $11,600, he or she would (if married) have to subtract half of that in excess of $10,000 from the $3,750 maximum tax credit base in addition to subtracting Social Security. In the above case, that would necessitate subtracting another $800 from $3,750, making the credit base $950 and 15 percent of that would make the actual tax credit $142.50. At an income level of $17,500, then, the income credit disappears.

A word of warning: This is a simplified example, and those eligible for

Table 8-6   Tax credit for the elderly

Source	Income	
Earnings	$3,000	
Rent	2,000	
Interest and dividends	100	
Taxable portion from annuity	1,500	
Social Security	2,000	(must offset other credit base income)
Total taxable income	6,600	
Maximum credit base	3,750	
Less Social Security	2,000	
Credit base	1,750	
Income tax credit is $262.50, 15% × $1,750 =	$262.50	

the credit should consult the Internal Revenue Service or their tax accountant if they have reason to believe that theirs might be a more complicated situation.

Child and Other Dependent Care

Child care expense is another tax credit to which many taxpayers are entitled. The same is true of expenses for other dependents if they are disabled. The child care or care of other dependents must be incurred in order to enable the taxpayer to be gainfully employed. The person being cared for must be under fifteen years old or disabled. The credit may be taken by a couple even if only one works full-time, if the other works part-time, or is a full-time student. The credit includes the cost of services received outside the taxpayer's home such as in a day care center. It is allowed even if the care is provided by a relative or member of the household if such person is not a dependent of the taxpayer.

There are, however, limits to how large a child care credit may be taken. First, the credit may not exceed 30 percent of the total cost of the care, up to $2,400 for one individual and $4,800 for two or more. This makes the maximum credit $720 and $1,440 respectively. The above amounts, however, apply only if your adjusted gross income (AGI) is $10,000 or less. The 30 percent is adjusted downward by 1 percent for each $2,000 (or fraction thereof) of income in excess of $10,000. The maximum downward adjustment, however, will not go below 20 percent.

Foreign Tax Credit

If you paid income tax to any foreign country, you may be able to claim a credit against the U.S. tax for the foreign taxes paid. To obtain this credit, use Form 1116 and attach it to your return.

Investment Tax Credit

The investment tax credit (ITC) generally applies only to those engaged in some business venture, but it may apply to some self-employed as well. This credit is 10 percent and applies to any business investment you make except most buildings. (The law now allows this credit for certain single-purpose agricultural structures.) If you invest $10,000 in expanding your business (say, you buy a couple of pickup delivery trucks), you may take a 10 percent credit and reduce your taxes by $1,000.

This credit applies to a self-employed person who has business assets. For example, if an author buys a new typewriter, he or she is eligible. Or a music teacher who buys a new piano on which he or she gives lessons may take the 10 percent credit on the new instrument. To obtain the full 10 percent credit, you will need to adopt a 5-year (or more) cost recovery (formerly called "depreciation") schedule. For certain assets which have a shorter life, the credit is only 6 percent. If the credit is to be taken on used property acquired, then the limitation on the value of the asset to which the credit applied is $125,000 in tax years beginning in 1981 and $150,000 in tax years beginning after 1984.

Residential Energy Credit

Homeowners, and renters as well, may take a tax credit of 15 percent of expenditures on energy-saving devices up to $2,000. Covered are expenditures on insulation, storm windows and doors, weatherstripping and caulking, and automatic thermostat set-back devices. Fifteen percent of the above expenditures up to a maximum credit of $300 may be taken on houses that have been substantially completed after April 20, 1977.

Solar heating and cooling equipment, wind energy devices, and geothermal energy installation expenses may be taken as a credit under a different provision of the law. In this case 40 percent of the expenditures, but not to exceed a credit of $4,000 may be taken. The expenditure must also have been made on the taxpayer's principal residence to be available for the tax credit. This credit is a lifetime amount, not an annual credit amount.

CAPITAL GAINS AND LOSSES

Capital gains and losses under the income tax law are frequently given special treatment.

Capital Assets

Capital assets consist of certain property held by the taxpayer. It may be income-producing such as rental houses, stocks, bonds, and the like, or it may be nonincome-producing such as the owner-occupied house of the taxpayer or his or her personal boat or auto. If you have a capital loss on a personal boat, car, or house (nonincome-producing assets), you have no deduction; on the other hand, capital gains on such personal assets are taxed.

Most income-producing assets, on the other hand, may generate both capital gains and losses for tax purposes. If the income-producing capital assets are used as stock in trade or business, any gain or loss they generate is treated as ordinary income. That is, stocks and bonds held by a security dealer do not qualify, but if they are held by an ordinary individual they do. The same is true of inventory held by a business, and houses held by a builder or realtor that are for sale. If these capital assets appreciate in price while being held by the dealer, realtor, builder, or other business person dealing in them, the resulting gain is considered income, when realized, and taxed as such. The words *when realized* are important. A capital gain (or loss) is not considered a gain until the capital asset is sold and the gain is realized.

Capital gains come about when qualified capital assets are sold at a price in excess of their acquired price. Capital loss comes about if assets are sold at below their acquisition price. It should be noted that many capital gains are illusory because they are solely the result of inflation. Others are real because they are not the result of inflation and their price appreciation has been in excess of inflation. The tax law does not differentiate between real and inflationary capital gains.

Short-term and Long-term Gains and Losses

Short-term gains and losses are those on capital assets that were held one year or less before being sold. Long-term gains (and losses) are those realized on assets held more than one year before being sold. The asset must actually have been sold and the gain or loss realized. Paper gains and losses do not count. Generally short-term gains or losses are treated like income whereas long-term gains and losses receive more favorable treatment.

Merging of All Gains and Losses

A taxpayer may have some or all of the following:

1. Short-term capital gain
2. Short-term capital loss
3. Long-term capital gain
4. Long-term capital loss

You must merge the short-term gains and losses to get a net short-term position. You must also merge the long-term gains and losses to get a net long-term

position. Next, the net short-term position is merged with the net long-term position to get a net capital gain (or loss) position. If this net capital gain position
is short-term, it is treated and taxed as ordinary income. If the total capital gain
position is long-term, it is treated differently.

Tax Treatment of Capital Gains and Losses

If all of your merged short-term and long-term capital gains and losses result in
a net short-term gain, they are taxed as ordinary income. If all of your merged
short-term and long-term capital gains and losses result in a net short-term loss,
they can be used to reduce your other income by a like amount before you
calculate your taxes on it.

If your net position (as described above) is a long-term capital gain, 60
percent of it can be excluded; that is, you pay no tax on it. The other 40 percent is taxed as regular income. Since the maximum tax rate is now 50 percent,
the maximum tax rate on long-term capital gains is 20 percent because only 40
percent of the gain is taxable (40% × 50% = 20%).

If all of your merged long-term and short-term capital gains and losses
result in a net long-term capital loss, they can be deducted from your other
income, but $2 of net long-term loss are needed to offset $1 of other income.
The maximum income offset is $3,000 per year, but any loss in exccess of that
can be carried forward until it is exhausted. If, for example, you have a $10,000
long-term capital loss, $6,000 could be used to reduce your otherwise taxable
income by $3,000. The other $4,000 of loss could be carried forward to next
year and reduce your income for tax purposes by $2,000.

There are four possible gain or loss positions, which I shall illustrate. Let
us assume in each case that the taxpayer has an income of $20,000 exclusive
of the gain or loss.

First, there may be a gain because the net short-term gain is greater than
the net long-term loss. If an individual has a net short-term gain of $5,000 and
a net long-term loss of $4,000, he or she merges them and adds $1,000 to the
$20,000 of other income and pays a tax on $21,000.

Second, the net long-term gain may be in excess of the net short-term
loss. In this case only 40 percent of the merged long-term gain over the net
short-term loss is included in income and is fully taxed as income. In the above
case, if we reverse our figures, there is a net long-term gain of $5,000 and a
net short-term loss of $4,000. Merging them provides a $1,000 net long-term
gain. But, because of the exclusion provision, only 40 percent of that gain, or
$400, is added to the $20,000 and the tax is computed on $20,400.

Third, there may be a net short-term capital loss after merging net long-
term and net short-term positions. The taxpayer may deduct the entire sum of
such loss up to a limit of $3,000 from other income dollar for dollar. (Amounts
in excess of $3,000 may be carried forward and deducted in future years until
exhausted.) If, for example, the taxpayer has a net short-term loss of $5,000

and net long-term gain of $4,000, he or she may deduct $1,000 from other income. In our hypothetical case of a taxpayer with income of $20,000, it declines to $19,000 for tax purposes.

Fourth, there may be a net long-term capital loss in excess of the net short-term capital gain. Using the same figures in the case above there is a long-term loss of, say, $5,000, which after being merged with a $4,000 short-term gain results in a net long-term loss of $1,000. This $1,000 net loss may be deducted from ordinary income, but $2 of long-term loss are needed to offset $1 of income. Consequently, the hypothetical taxpayer who has $20,000 adjusted gross income will have his or her tax computed on $19,500.

Capital Gains on Owner-Occupied Homes

With capital gains on the sale of owner-occupied houses, if the gain is reinvested in another house within twenty-four months, one need pay no capital gains tax whatsoever on this transaction. However, if the former house sells for more than the cost of the new, then the differential is taxable as a capital gain.

Congress also provided a once-in-a-lifetime exclusion in some cases. Any taxpayer, age 55 or over, may take a once-in-a-lifetime tax exclusion of $125,000 capital gain on the sale of a house which has been his or her principal residence for at least three years during the last five years ending on the date of sale of the house. This provision applies to homes sold after July 26, 1978.

ALTERNATIVE MINIMUM TAX (AMT)

If you are a high-income taxpayer, you may also have to pay an alternative minimum tax. It was imposed because Congress felt everyone should pay some taxes. A few high-income people have so arranged their affairs that they pay little or no taxes. Congress has provided certain beneficial provisions in the tax laws (sometimes called "loopholes"); if you take excessive advantage of these, the tax law attempts to recapture part of your gain. The alternative minimum tax, then, generally affects people who have a lot of tax-sheltered income, through what is called *tax preference items*, and capital gains relative to regular taxable income.

Tax Preference Items

Tax preference items include:

1. The excess of accelerated depreciation over straight-line depreciation in some but not all cases. This, of course, shows up as capital gain when the asset is sold.

2. The 60 percent capital gains which is excluded from the regular income tax laws. This applied to all capital gains, not just to those generated by accelerated depreciation.
3. The $100 ($200 on a joint return) divided exclusion noted above under the section entitled "Income Subject to Tax (Gross Income)."

Computation of the Alternative Minimum Tax

Other things besides tax preference items affect the AMT. To calculate it, you begin with adjusted gross income (AGI).

1. Increase AGI by certain (but not all) tax preference items. (You will need professional help here if this applies to you because of the complexities.)
2. Next, decrease AGI by certain "alternative tax" itemized deductions.
3. Reduce AGI further for any income it included due to a distribution from a trust.
4. Reduce AGI further for the exemption allowed under the AMT, which is $30,000 if single and $40,000 if married and filing jointly.
5. What you now have is the alternative minimum tax income base (AMTI). The alternative minimum tax (AMT) is 20 percent of that base. It may be reduced by only one tax credit—the foreign tax credit. You have now calculated your AMT; compare it with your regular tax calculated earlier. You will pay the higher.

The alternative minimum tax is complex. If you believe you are subject to it, you should probably seek professional help.

OTHER THINGS YOU SHOULD KNOW ABOUT TAXES

Legal Tax Avoidance

In 1982, national income was $2,425.2 billion and total personal income tax receipts were about $298.1 billion. This means that if the entire income had been subject to taxes, an average rate of only about 12 percent would have provided the same revenue. But the entire income is not subject to taxes. There are the normal deductions of $1,000 per person and all the other exemptions and deductions noted above. Over the years the tax base has eroded seriously because of legal loopholes discovered in the law by tax accountants or opened up by the courts or by Congress.

Loopholes apply to many individuals, such as deductions for interest on mortgages, local property taxes, and income splitting. Congress has in addition provided special loopholes for the wealthy, and a battery of clever accountants and attorneys is constantly developing others. These are too complex to describe in detail, but the more obvious ones are noted here.

Certain groups that have expense accounts have an obvious advantage over the rest of us. They can live lavishly, and the company deducts their expenses for tax purposes. You and I, in effect, pay for their lavish living. Capital gains is another loophole. High-income groups devise ingenious schemes for converting ordinary income into capital gains, which are taxed at a lower rate.

There are other tax loopholes (or tax shelters as some prefer to call them) such as cattle-feeding operations, rental property, leasing of business assets, and tax-exempt interest-bearing bonds. If you have rental residential property, you can take accelerated depreciation on it. If you own your own business and expand it, the 10 percent investment tax credit is available. You can take 10 percent of the dollar amount by which you expand your business and reduce your taxes by that. This, together with accelerated depreciation, may enable you to shelter a good deal of income. Corporate pension plans, the personal service corporation, Keogh plans, and the IRA are other methods of sheltering income from taxes (see Chapter 19). Many of these tax shelters that permit legal tax avoidance (as opposed to illegal evasion) are complex; if they apply to you, you should check with your tax accountant.

Tax Saving Tips

If you are a person with a modest income, you cannot hire a high-priced accountant to save taxes for you. There are, nevertheless, some things you may do that will save you money. In some cases where you never seem to have enough deductions to exceed the zero bracket amount, you might be able to do so every year by proper planning.

Consider the following suggestions:

1. Keep good records. Then you will not forget to take all the deductions that are legally yours.
2. Don't forget to include the sales taxes you pay on big items such as cars, boats, and airplanes.
3. Plan ahead especially when making certain big expenditures. If, for example, you have large noninsured dental (e.g., orthodontist) bills, which are often financed on the installment plan over several years by the dentist as the service is rendered, consider telescoping as many of them as possible into one year. This may be beneficial even if you have to borrow to do so.
4. Pay your auto and other personal property taxes every other year. These are usually due early in the year, but generally the bill comes in December of the previous year. In one year pay them at the normal time such as, say, January or February. Then pay next year's in December of the same year. This is referred to as bunching in alternative years when you itemize

to exceed the zero bracket amount; the other year you use the zero bracket amount.

5. Do the same with other deductible items which are beginning-of-year or end-of-year expenses, if flexibility permits, for example, such things as union and professional association dues.

6. Other year-end planning can also save you taxes. Any deductible items coming due in early January can be paid in late December, if you can get the bill a bit early.

7. If you are planning on taking some large long-term capital gain, consider taking part of it in December and part in January, if this is possible. That portion of your capital gain that will be taxed is subject to a progressive rate up to 20 percent. By taking your gain piecemeal, you may be able to lower the tax rate that applies.

8. If you are eligible for a Keogh plan or an IRA, be sure to establish one.

Using a Professional Tax Preparer

If your income consists solely, or even mostly, of wages and salaries, your return will be simple enough for you to prepare yourself. Even if you have substantial interest and dividend income you probably will not need professional tax help, but if you have such income, it is not subject to withholding and you will need to report your estimated income quarterly and pay a tax quarterly.

Only if your tax return is truly complex will you need professional help. If, for example, you have income property subject to depreciation, if you have made investments and qualify for the investment tax credit, or if you have other complex tax shelters, then you should consider a professional tax preparer.

In such a case, get a qualified certified public accountant (CPA) who has had tax experience, and one who does tax work on a regular basis. Only an accountant who is involved in tax matters at all times will be able to keep up with all the complex changes in the tax laws that take place constantly. Not only does Congress change the law frequently, but court decisions and IRS rulings result in changes.

It is also suggested that once you have established a relationship with a competent tax advisor, stay with the same one. After he or she has done your return once of twice, he will become familiar with your unique problems and conditions. This will save time (and hence money) when he prepares your return and also will enable him to do a better job.

If You Are Audited

If you have filled out your tax return correctly, the chances of being audited are remote. But if you are audited, don't panic. If you have kept good records and can prove every deduction, you have nothing to fear. Even if there are some gray areas and the IRS auditor absolutely won't allow a given deduction, all you need to do is pay the extra tax, with interest of 12 percent from the time the taxes were due (normally April 15) until the audit. If the IRS feels you were negligent in making out your tax return (as opposed to having made an honest mistake), they can assess a 10 percent penalty over and above the 12 percent noted above.[4] If you disagree with the auditor, you may appeal to the next higher level within the IRS, which is the Appeals Office of the IRS. After that you have to go to court if you cannot agree.

There are two kinds of audits. First, the simple audit where several items might be questioned does not usually take much time. If the items are in a gray area, there may be some bargaining. The IRS may compromise and allow some but not others.

Second, the Taxpayer Compliance Measurement Program (TCMP) is a more thorough audit. This may be an item-by-item examination of your return. There is a general feeling that if you are picked for this it is because the IRS believes there is something drastically wrong with your tax return. This is not usually true. Many of the people picked for the TCMP are picked at random. The purpose of the TCMP is to give the IRS a feeling for the various legitimate expenses of various income groups in order to update their computer, which scans millions of tax forms to spot irregularities.

If you are audited, all you have to do is to prove your tax return. Experts do not agree on whether you should take your tax preparer with you to an audit. If it is a simple audit and only a few items are questioned, many feel your tax accountant is not needed. However, if it is a TCMP, you should probably take your tax preparer along. If you are audited, abide by the following rules:

1. Be on time.
2. Dress neatly and conservatively.
3. If your tax accountant accompanies you, let him or her do most of the talking. You should only fill in details the accountant may have overlooked in your personal affairs.
4. Come armed with all your records.
5. Don't volunteer any information and supply only that which is requested.
6. Sit silently unless spoken to.
7. Don't make small talk or be overly chatty.
8. Never lose your temper or raise your voice.
9. Smile, and be polite and courteous, but not overly friendly, that is, act very professional.

4. The interest on past due taxes and sometimes even the penalty are adjusted periodically to reflect changes in the market rate of interest. The rates noted above were correct at mid-year 1983.

The statute of limitations is three years in the case of taxes. If the IRS has not audited you within three years of your filing your return or of the due date of your return, they may not do so unless they suspect fraud (in which case the statute of limitations never expires). In the case of the three year limitation, however, sometimes the IRS will request that a taxpayer grant them an extension after, say, two years and ten months only have elapsed. If this happens to you, I recommend strongly that you grant them the extension as they may (and probably will) file a deficiency claim against you if you do not. Such a deficiency claim is challengeable only in the courts.

The Tax Forms

There are three forms from which certain individuals may choose when filing their taxes. They are the 1040 form, the so-called "short form" 1040A, and the new 1040EZ form. If the taxpayer is eligible to use the so-called "short form" (1040A), and elects to do so, the Internal Revenue Service will calculate the tax if requested to do so. You need only fill out the first 17 lines. The IRS will then automatically send any refund, or bill the taxpayer for any deficiency. The 1040EZ form may only be used by single taxpayers with no dependents, whose taxable income is less than $50,000 and which consists only of wages, salaries and tips, and interest income of $400 or less. This form has only 11 lines.

The 1040 consists of a two-page form and may be used without any attachments by many taxpayers. If a person had income solely from wages, salaries, and tips; interest and dividends; or certain miscellaneous income; and does not itemize deductions, the basic two-page form is all that need be completed. If the taxpayer had income from other sources, wishes to itemize deductions, or wishes to claim certain credits (such as the investment tax credit mentioned above), supplementary schedules must be filled out and attached to the 1040.

If the taxpayer has an adjusted gross income of more than $50,000, he or she cannot use the tax tables, but must use the appropriate tax rate schedule (either Schedule X, Y, or Z) furnished by the IRS and included in the 1040 tax form instruction booklet. You calculate your taxes from these schedules, which have the zero bracket amount built into them but not the exemptions.

If your itemized deductions are in excess of the zero bracket amount ($2,300 for singles and $3,400 for joint returns), you simply take the difference between the two and subtract it from your adjusted gross income before going to the tax tables or tax rate schedules.

An example of one page of these tax tables is shown in Table 8–7. Shown, too, are the tax forms 1040, 1040A, and 1040EZ, and the Tax Rate Schedules S, Y, and Z, one for single taxpayers, one for married taxpayers, and one for unmarried heads of household. These sample forms follow as Tables 8–8 through 8–11.

Table 8–7

1982 Tax Table

Based on Taxable Income
For persons with taxable incomes of less than $50,000.

Example: Mr. and Mrs. Brown are filing a joint return. Their taxable income on line 37 of Form 1040 is $25,325. First, they find the $25,300–25,350 income line. Next, they find the column for married filing jointly and read down the column. The amount shown where the income line and filing status column meet is $4,247. This is the tax amount they must write on line 38 of their return.

At least	But less than	Single	Married filing jointly *	Married filing separately	Head of a household
			Your tax is—		
25,250	25,300	5,458	4,233	6,774	5,010
25,300	25,350	5,476	4,247	6,796	5,026
25,350	25,400	5,493	4,262	6,818	5,042

If line 37 (taxable income) is—		And you are—				If line 37 (taxable income) is—		And you are—				If line 37 (taxable income) is—		And you are—			
At least	But less than	Single	Married filing jointly *	Married filing separately	Head of a household	At least	But less than	Single	Married filing jointly *	Married filing separately	Head of a household	At least	But less than	Single	Married filing jointly *	Married filing separately	Head of a household
			Your tax is—						Your tax is—						Your tax is—		
0	1,700	0	0	0	0							5,500	5,550	452	256	549	410
1,700	1,725	0	0	a2	0	**3,000**						5,550	5,600	460	263	557	417
1,725	1,750	0	0	5	0	3,000	3,050	87	0	165	87	5,600	5,650	468	270	565	424
1,750	1,775	0	0	8	0	3,050	3,100	93	0	172	93	5,650	5,700	476	277	573	431
1,775	1,800	0	0	11	0	3,100	3,150	99	0	179	99	5,700	5,750	484	284	581	438
1,800	1,825	0	0	14	0	3,150	3,200	105	0	186	105						
1,825	1,850	0	0	17	0	3,200	3,250	111	0	193	111	5,750	5,800	492	291	589	445
1,850	1,875	0	0	20	0							5,800	5,850	500	298	597	452
1,875	1,900	0	0	23	0	3,250	3,300	117	0	200	117	5,850	5,900	508	305	605	459
1,900	1,925	0	0	26	0	3,300	3,350	123	0	207	123	5,900	5,950	516	312	613	466
1,925	1,950	0	0	29	0	3,350	3,400	129	0	214	129	5,950	6,000	524	319	622	473
1,950	1,975	0	0	32	0	3,400	3,450	136	c3	221	135						
1,975	2,000	0	0	35	0	3,450	3,500	143	9	228	141	**6,000**					
2,000						3,500	3,550	150	15	235	147	6,000	6,050	532	326	631	480
2,000	2,025	0	0	38	0	3,550	3,600	157	21	242	153	6,050	6,100	540	333	641	487
2,025	2,050	0	0	41	0	3,600	3,650	164	27	249	159	6,100	6,150	548	340	650	494
2,050	2,075	0	0	44	0	3,650	3,700	171	33	256	165	6,150	6,200	556	347	660	501
2,075	2,100	0	0	47	0	3,700	3,750	178	39	263	171	6,200	6,250	564	354	669	508
2,100	2,125	0	0	50	0												
2,125	2,150	0	0	53	0	3,750	3,800	185	45	270	177	6,250	6,300	572	361	679	515
2,150	2,175	0	0	56	0	3,800	3,850	192	51	277	183	6,300	6,350	580	368	688	522
2,175	2,200	0	0	59	0	3,850	3,900	199	57	285	189	6,350	6,400	588	375	698	529
2,200	2,225	0	0	62	0	3,900	3,950	206	63	293	195	6,400	6,450	596	382	707	536
2,225	2,250	0	0	65	0	3,950	4,000	213	69	301	201	6,450	6,500	604	389	717	543
2,250	2,275	0	0	68	0	**4,000**						6,500	6,550	612	396	726	550
2,275	2,300	0	0	71	0	4,000	4,050	220	75	309	207	6,550	6,600	621	403	736	558
2,300	2,325	b2	0	74	b2	4,050	4,100	227	81	317	213	6,600	6,650	629	410	745	566
2,325	2,350	5	0	77	5	4,100	4,150	234	87	325	219	6,650	6,700	638	417	755	574
2,350	2,375	8	0	80	8	4,150	4,200	241	93	333	225	6,700	6,750	646	424	764	582
2,375	2,400	11	0	83	11	4,200	4,250	248	99	341	231						
2,400	2,425	14	0	86	14	4,250	4,300	255	105	349	237	6,750	6,800	655	431	774	590
2,425	2,450	17	0	89	17	4,300	4,350	262	111	357	243	6,800	6,850	663	438	783	598
2,450	2,475	20	0	92	20	4,350	4,400	269	117	365	249	6,850	6,900	672	445	793	606
2,475	2,500	23	0	95	23	4,400	4,450	276	123	373	256	6,900	6,950	680	452	802	614
2,500	2,525	26	0	98	26	4,450	4,500	284	129	381	263	6,950	7,000	689	459	812	622
2,525	2,550	29	0	101	29	4,500	4,550	292	135	389	270	**7,000**					
2,550	2,575	32	0	104	32	4,550	4,600	300	141	397	277	7,000	7,050	697	466	821	630
2,575	2,600	35	0	107	35	4,600	4,650	308	147	405	284	7,050	7,100	706	473	831	638
2,600	2,625	38	0	110	38	4,650	4,700	316	153	413	291	7,100	7,150	714	480	840	646
2,625	2,650	41	0	113	41	4,700	4,750	324	159	421	298	7,150	7,200	723	487	850	654
2,650	2,675	44	0	116	44	4,750	4,800	332	165	429	305	7,200	7,250	731	494	859	662
2,675	2,700	47	0	119	47	4,800	4,850	340	171	437	312						
2,700	2,725	50	0	122	50	4,850	4,900	348	177	445	319	7,250	7,300	740	501	869	670
2,725	2,750	53	0	125	53	4,900	4,950	356	183	453	326	7,300	7,350	748	508	878	678
2,750	2,775	56	0	128	56	4,950	5,000	364	189	461	333	7,350	7,400	757	515	888	686
2,775	2,800	59	0	131	59	**5,000**						7,400	7,450	765	522	897	694
2,800	2,825	62	0	135	62	5,000	5,050	372	195	469	340	7,450	7,500	774	529	907	702
2,825	2,850	65	0	138	65	5,050	5,100	380	201	477	347	7,500	7,550	782	536	916	710
2,850	2,875	68	0	142	68	5,100	5,150	388	207	485	354	7,550	7,600	791	543	926	718
2,875	2,900	71	0	145	71	5,150	5,200	396	213	493	361	7,600	7,650	799	550	935	726
2,900	2,925	74	0	149	74	5,200	5,250	404	219	501	368	7,650	7,700	808	558	945	734
2,925	2,950	77	0	152	77	5,250	5,300	412	225	509	375	7,700	7,750	816	566	954	742
2,950	2,975	80	0	156	80	5,300	5,350	420	231	517	382	7,750	7,800	825	574	964	750
2,975	3,000	83	0	159	83	5,350	5,400	428	237	525	389	7,800	7,850	833	582	973	758
						5,400	5,450	436	243	533	396	7,850	7,900	842	590	983	766
						5,450	5,500	444	249	541	403	7,900	7,950	850	598	992	774
												7,950	8,000	859	606	1,002	782

*This column must also be used by a qualifying widow(er).

Continued on next page

a If your taxable income is exactly $1,700, your tax is zero.   c If your taxable income is exactly $3,400, your tax is zero.
b If your taxable income is exactly $2,300, your tax is zero.

Source: U.S. Department of the Treasury—Internal Revenue Service.

Form **1040**	Department of the Treasury—Internal Revenue Service	**1982**	(0)		

U.S. Individual Income Tax Return

For the year January 1–December 31, 1982, or other tax year beginning _____ 1982, ending _____ , 19 ____ . | OMB No. 1545-0074

Use IRS label. Otherwise, please print or type.	Your first name and initial (if joint return, also give spouse's name and initial)	Last name	Your social security number
	Present home address (Number and street, including apartment number, or rural route)		Spouse's social security no.
	City, town or post office, State and ZIP code	Your occupation ▶	
		Spouse's occupation ▶	

Presidential Election Campaign ▶ Do you want $1 to go to this fund? . . . . Yes ☐ No ☐ **Note:** Checking "Yes" will not increase your tax or reduce your refund.
If joint return, does your spouse want $1 to go to this fund? . . . Yes ☐ No ☐

Filing Status

Check only one box.

For Privacy Act and Paperwork Reduction Act Notice, see Instructions.

1 ☐ Single
2 ☐ Married filing joint return (even if only one had income)
3 ☐ Married filing separate return. Enter spouse's social security no. above and full name here ▶ _____
4 ☐ Head of household (with qualifying person). (See page 6 of Instructions.) If the qualifying person is your unmarried child but not your dependent, enter child's name ▶ _____
5 ☐ Qualifying widow(er) with dependent child (Year spouse died ▶ 19 ____). (See page 6 of Instructions.)

Exemptions

Always check the box labeled Yourself.
Check other boxes if they apply.

6a ☐ Yourself   ☐ 65 or over   ☐ Blind   ) Enter number of boxes checked on 6a and b ▶ ☐
 b ☐ Spouse   ☐ 65 or over   ☐ Blind   )
 c First names of your dependent children who lived with you ▶ _____   Enter number of children listed on 6c ☐

d Other dependents: (1) Name	(2) Relationship	(3) Number of months lived in your home	(4) Did dependent have income of $1,000 or more?	(5) Did you provide more than one-half of dependent's support?

Enter number of other dependents ▶ ☐

e Total number of exemptions claimed . . . .   Add numbers entered in boxes above ▶ ☐

Income

Please attach Copy B of your Forms W–2 here.

If you do not have a W–2, see page 5 of Instructions.

7	Wages, salaries, tips, etc.	7	
8	Interest income (attach Schedule B if over $400 or you have any All-Savers interest)	8	
9a	Dividends (attach Schedule B if over $400) _____ , 9b Exclusion _____		
c	Subtract line 9b from line 9a	9c	
10	Refunds of State and local income taxes (do not enter an amount unless you deducted those taxes in an earlier year—see page 9 of Instructions)	10	
11	Alimony received	11	
12	Business income or (loss) (attach Schedule C) . . . . ▶	12	
13	Capital gain or (loss) (attach Schedule D)	13	
14	40% capital gain distributions not reported on line 13 (See page 9 of Instructions)	14	
15	Supplemental gains or (losses) (attach Form 4797)	15	
16	Fully taxable pensions, IRA distributions, and annuities not reported on line 17 . .	16	
17a	Other pensions and annuities. Total received	17a			
b	Taxable amount, if any, from worksheet on page 10 of Instructions	17b	
18	Rents, royalties, partnerships, estates, trusts, etc. (attach Schedule E)	18	
19	Farm income or (loss) (attach Schedule F) . . . . ▶	19	
20a	Unemployment compensation (insurance). Total received	20a			
b	Taxable amount, if any, from worksheet on page 10 of Instructions	20b	
21	Other income (state nature and source—see page 10 of Instructions) ▶ _____	21	
22	**Total income.** Add amounts in column for lines 7 through 21 . . . . ▶	22	

Please attach check or money order here.

Adjustments to Income

(See Instructions on page 11)

23	Moving expense (attach Form 3903 or 3903F) . . .	23		
24	Employee business expenses (attach Form 2106) . .	24		
25	Payments to an IRA. You **must** enter code from page 11 (_____)	25		
26	Payments to a Keogh (H.R. 10) retirement plan . . .	26		
27	Penalty on early withdrawal of savings	27		
28	Alimony paid	28		
29	Deduction for a married couple when both work (attach Schedule W)	29		
30	Disability income exclusion (attach Form 2440) . . .	30		
31	**Total adjustments.** Add lines 23 through 30. . . . . ▶	31		

Adjusted Gross Income

32	**Adjusted gross income.** Subtract line 31 from line 22. If this line is less than $10,000, see "Earned Income Credit" (line 62) on page 15 of Instructions. If you want IRS to figure your tax, see page 3 of Instructions . . . . ▶	32	

☆ U.S. GOVERNMENT PRINTING OFFICE 1982—O—363-302 48-0627165

Table 8-8   (continued)

Form 1040 (1982)   Page **2**

Tax Compu-tation (See Instruc-tions on page 12)	**33** Amount from line 32 *(adjusted gross income)*	**33**	
	34a If you itemize, complete Schedule A (Form 1040) and enter the amount from Schedule A, line 30	**34a**	
	Caution: If you have unearned income and can be claimed as a dependent on your parent's return, check here ▶ ☐ and see page 12 of the Instructions. Also see page 12 of the Instructions if: • You are married filing a separate return and your spouse itemizes deductions, OR • You file Form 4563, OR • You are a dual-status alien.		
	34b If you do not itemize, complete the worksheet on page 13. Then enter the allowable part of your charitable contributions here	**34b**	
	35 Subtract line 34a or 34b, whichever applies, from line 33	**35**	
	36 Multiply $1,000 by the total number of exemptions claimed on Form 1040, line 6e . .	**36**	
	37 Taxable Income. Subtract line 36 from line 35	**37**	
	38 Tax. Enter tax here and check if from ☐ Tax Table, ☐ Tax Rate Schedule X, Y, or Z, or ☐ Schedule G	**38**	
	39 Additional Taxes. (See page 13 of Instructions.) Enter here and check if from ☐ Form 4970, ☐ Form 4972, ☐ Form 5544, or ☐ section 72 penalty taxes	**39**	
	40 **Total.** Add lines 38 and 39 . . . . ▶	**40**	
Credits (See Instruc-tions on page 13)	**41** Credit for the elderly (attach Schedules R&RP) **41**		
	42 Foreign tax credit (attach Form 1116) **42**		
	43 Investment credit (attach Form 3468) **43**		
	44 Partial credit for political contributions **44**		
	45 Credit for child and dependent care expenses (attach Form 2441). **45**		
	46 Jobs credit (attach Form 5884) **46**		
	47 Residential energy credit (attach Form 5695) **47**		
	48 Other credits—see page 14 ▶ **48**		
	49 **Total credits.** Add lines 41 through 48	**49**	
	50 **Balance.** Subtract line 49 from line 40 and enter difference (but not less than zero) . ▶	**50**	
Other Taxes (Including Advance EIC Payments)	**51** Self-employment tax (attach Schedule SE)	**51**	
	52 Minimum tax (attach Form 4625)	**52**	
	53 Alternative minimum tax (attach Form 6251)	**53**	
	54 Tax from recapture of investment credit (attach Form 4255)	**54**	
	55 Social security (FICA) tax on tip income not reported to employer (attach Form 4137) .	**55**	
	56 Uncollected employee FICA and RRTA tax on tips (from Form W-2)	**56**	
	57 Tax on an IRA (attach Form 5329)	**57**	
	58 Advance earned income credit (EIC) payments received (from Form W-2)	**58**	
06	**59** **Total tax.** Add lines 50 through 58 . . . . ■	**59**	
Payments Attach Forms W-2, W-2G, and W-2P to front.	**60** Total Federal income tax withheld **60**		
	61 1982 estimated tax payments and amount applied from 1981 return . **61**		
	62 Earned income credit. If line 33 is under $10,000, see page 15 of Instructions **62**		
	63 Amount paid with Form 4868 . . . . **63**		
	64 Excess FICA and RRTA tax withheld (two or more employers) . **64**		
	65 Credit for Federal tax on special fuels and oils (attach Form 4136) **65**		
	66 Regulated Investment Company credit (attach Form 2439) **66**		
	67 **Total.** Add lines 60 through 66 . . . . ▶	**67**	
Refund or Amount You Owe	**68** If line 67 is larger than line 59, enter amount **OVERPAID** . . . . ▶	**68**	
	69 Amount of line 68 to be **REFUNDED TO YOU** . . . . ▶	**69**	
	70 Amount of line 68 to be applied to your 1983 estimated tax . . . ▶ 70		
	71 If line 59 is larger than line 67, enter **AMOUNT YOU OWE.** Attach check or money order for full amount payable to Internal Revenue Service. Write your social security number and "1982 Form 1040" on it. (Check ▶ ☐ if Form 2210 (2210F) is attached. See page 16 of Instructions.) ▶ $	**71**	
Please Sign Here	Under penalties of perjury, I declare that I have examined this return, including accompanying schedules and statements, and to the best of my knowledge and belief, it is true, correct, and complete. Declaration of preparer (other than taxpayer) is based on all information of which preparer has any knowledge. ▶ Your signature Date ▶ Spouse's signature (if filing jointly, BOTH must sign)		
Paid Preparer's Use Only	Preparer's signature ▶ Date Check if self-em-ployed ▶ ☐ Preparer's social security no. Firm's name (or yours, if self-employed) and address ▶ E.I. No. ▶ ZIP code ▶		

Source: U.S. Department of the Treasury—Internal Revenue Service.

Table 8–9

1982 Department of the Treasury — Internal Revenue Service
Form 1040A US Individual Income Tax Return (0)   OMB No. 1545-0085

Step 1
Name and address
Use the IRS mailing label. Otherwise, print or type.

Your first name and initial (if joint return, also give spouse's name and initial) — Last name — Your social security no.

Present home address — Spouse's social security no.

City, town or post office, State, and ZIP code — Your occupation / Spouse's occupation

Presidential Election Campaign Fund
Do you want $1 to go to this fund?.................... □ Yes □ No
If joint return, does your spouse want $1 to go to this fund? □ Yes □ No

Step 2
Filing status
(Check only one)
and Exemptions

1 □ Single (See if you can use Form 1040EZ.)
2 □ Married filing joint return (even if only one had income)
3 □ Married filing separate return. Enter spouse's social security no. above and full name here. ____
4 □ Head of household (with qualifying person). If the qualifying person is your unmarried child but not your dependent, write this child's name here. ____

Always check the exemption box labeled Yourself. Check other boxes if they apply.
5a □ Yourself   □ 65 or over   □ Blind
 b □ Spouse   □ 65 or over   □ Blind   Write number of boxes checked on 5a and b □
 c First names of your dependent children who lived with you ____   Write number of children listed on 5c □

Attach Copy B of Forms W-2 here

d Other dependents: (1) Name (2) Relationship (3) Number of months lived in your home. (4) Did dependent have income of $1,000 or more? (5) Did you provide more than one-half of dependent's support?   Write number of other dependents listed on 5d □

e Total number of exemptions claimed ....   Add numbers entered in boxes above □

Step 3
Adjusted gross income

6 Wages, salaries, tips, etc. (Attach Forms W-2)................ 6
7 Interest income (Complete page 2 if over $400 or you have any All-Savers interest)...... 7
8a Dividends ____ (Complete page 2 if over $400) 8b Exclusion ____ Subtract line 8b from 8a 8c
9a Unemployment compensation (insurance). Total from Form(s) 1099-UC ____
 b Taxable amount, if any, from worksheet on page 16 of Instructions 9b
10 Add lines 6, 7, 8c, and 9b. This is your total income............. 10
11 Deduction for a married couple when both work. Complete the worksheet on page 17...... 11
12 Subtract line 11 from line 10. This is your adjusted gross income...... 12

Step 4
Taxable income

13 Allowable part of your charitable contributions. Complete the worksheet on page 18...... 13
14 Subtract line 13 from line 12...... 14
15 Multiply $1,000 by the total number of exemptions claimed in box 5e...... 15
16 Subtract line 15 from line 14. This is your taxable income...... 16

Step 5
Tax, credits, and payments
Attach check or money order here

17a Partial credit for political contributions. See page 19....... ■ 17a
 b Total Federal income tax withheld, from W-2 form(s). (If line 6 is more than $32,400, see page 19.)...... 17b
Stop Here and Sign Below if You Want IRS to Figure Your Tax
 c Earned income credit, from worksheet on page 21...... 17c
18 Add lines 17a, b, and c. These are your total credits and payments...... 18
19a Find tax on amount on line 16. Use tax table, pages 26-31...... 19a
 b Advance EIC payment (from W-2 form(s))...... 19b
20 Add lines 19a and 19b. This is your total tax...... 20

Step 6
Refund or amount you owe

21 If line 13 is larger than line 20, subtract line 20 from line 18. Enter the amount to be **refunded to you**...... 21
22 If line 20 is larger than line 18, subtract line 18 from line 20. Enter the **amount you owe.** Attach payment for full amount payable to "Internal Revenue Service."...... 22

Step 7
Sign your return

I have read this return and any attachments filed with it. Under penalties of perjury, I declare that to the best of my knowledge and belief, the return and attachments are correct and complete.

Your signature — Date — Spouse's signature (If filing jointly, BOTH must sign)

Paid preparer's signature — Date — Check if self-employed □ — Preparer's social security no.

Firm's name (or yours, if self-employed) ____ E.I. no.
Address and Zip code ____

For **Privacy Act and Paperwork Reduction Act Notice,** see page 34.

Source: U.S. Department of the Treasury—Internal Revenue Service.

Table 8–10

Department of the Treasury—Internal Revenue Service

Form 1040EZ Income Tax Return for
1982   Single filers with no dependents (0)

OMB No. 1545-0675

Instructions are on the back of this form.
Tax Table is in the 1040EZ and 1040A Tax Package.

Name and address

Use the IRS mailing label. If you don't have a label, print or type:

Name (first, initial, last)   Social security number

Present home address

City, town or post office, State, and ZIP code

Presidential Election Campaign Fund
Check this box ☐ if you want $1 of your tax to go to this fund.

Figure your tax

Attach Copy B of Forms W-2 here

1 Wages, salaries, and tips. Attach your W-2 form(s).   1 .

2 Interest income of $400 or less. If more than $400, you cannot use Form 1040EZ. 2 .

3 Add line 1 and line 2. This is your **adjusted gross income.**   3 .

4 Allowable part of your charitable contributions. Complete the worksheet on page 18. Do not write more than $25.   4 .

5 Subtract line 4 from line 3.   5 .

6 Amount of your personal exemption.   6   1,0 0 0 . 0 0

7 Subtract line 6 from line 5. This is your **taxable income.**   7 .

8 Enter your Federal income tax withheld. This is shown on your W-2 form(s). 8 .

9 Use the tax table on pages 26-31 to find the **tax** on your taxable income on line 7.   9 .

Refund or amount you owe

Attach tax payment here

10 If line 8 is larger than line 9, subtract line 9 from line 8. Enter the amount of your **refund.**   10 .

11 If line 9 is larger than line 8, subtract line 8 from line 9. Enter the **amount you owe.** Attach check or money order for the full amount payable to "Internal Revenue Service."   11 .

Sign your return

I have read this return. Under penalties of perjury, I declare that to the best of my knowledge and belief, the return is correct and complete.

Your signature   Date

X

For **Privacy Act and Paperwork Reduction Act Notice,** see page 34.

Source: U.S. Department of the Treasury—Internal Revenue Service.

Table 8–11

1982 Tax Rate Schedules

Your zero bracket amount has been built into these Tax Rate Schedules.

Caution: You must use the Tax Table instead of these Tax Rate Schedules if your taxable income is less than $50,000 unless you use Schedule G (income averaging), to figure your tax. In that case, even if your taxable income is less than $50,000, use the rate schedules on this page to figure your tax.

Schedule X

Single Taxpayers

Use this Schedule if you checked **Filing Status Box 1** on Form 1040—

If the amount on Form 1040, line 37 is: Over—	But not Over—	Enter on Form 1040, line 38	of the amount over—
$0	$2,300	—0—	
2,300	3,400	...........12%	$2,300
3,400	4,400	$132+14%	3,400
4,400	6,500	272+16%	4,400
6,500	8,500	608+17%	6,500
8,500	10,800	948+19%	8,500
10,800	12,900	1,385+22%	10,800
12,900	15,000	1,847+23%	12,900
15,000	18,200	2,330+27%	15,000
18,200	23,500	3,194+31%	18,200
23,500	28,800	4,837+35%	23,500
28,800	34,100	6,692+40%	28,800
34,100	41,500	8,812+44%	34,100
41,500	....	12,068+50%	41,500

Schedule Z

Unmarried Heads of Household

(including certain married persons who live apart (and abandoned spouses)—see page 6 of the instructions)

Use this schedule if you checked **Filing Status Box 4** on Form 1040—

If the amount on Form 1040, line 37 is: Over—	But not Over—	Enter on Form 1040, line 38	of the amount over—
$0	$2,300	—0—	
2,300	4,400	...........12%	$2,300
4,400	6,500	$252+14%	4,400
6,500	8,700	546+16%	6,500
8,700	11,800	898+20%	8,700
11,800	15,000	1,518+22%	11,800
15,000	18,200	2,222+23%	15,000
18,200	23,500	2,958+28%	18,200
23,500	28,800	4,442+32%	23,500
28,800	34,100	6,138+38%	28,800
34,100	44,700	8,152+41%	34,100
44,700	60,600	12,498+49%	44,700
60,600	....	20,289+50%	60,600

Schedule Y

Married Taxpayers and Qualifying Widows and Widowers

Married Filing Joint Returns and Qualifying Widows and Widowers

Use this schedule if you checked **Filing Status Box 2 or 5** on Form 1040—

If the amount on Form 1040, line 37 is: Over—	But not Over—	Enter on Form 1040, line 38	of the amount over—
$0	$3,400	—0—	
3,400	5,500	...........12%	$3,400
5,500	7,600	$252+14%	5,500
7,600	11,900	546+16%	7,600
11,900	16,000	1,234+19%	11,900
16,000	20,200	2,013+22%	16,000
20,200	24,600	2,937+25%	20,200
24,600	29,900	4,037+29%	24,600
29,900	35,200	5,574+33%	29,900
35,200	45,800	7,323+39%	35,200
45,800	60,000	11,457+44%	45,800
60,000	85,600	17,705+49%	60,000
85,600	....	30,249+50%	85,600

Married Filing Separate Returns

Use this schedule if you checked **Filing Status Box 3** on Form 1040—

If the amount on Form 1040, line 37 is: Over—	But not Over—	Enter on Form 1040, line 38	of the amount over—
$0	$1,700	—0—	
1,700	2,750	...........12%	$1,700
2,750	3,800	$126.00+14%	2,750
3,800	5,950	273.00+16%	3,800
5,950	8,000	617.00+19%	5,950
8,000	10,100	1,006.50+22%	8,000
10,100	12,300	1,468.50+25%	10,100
12,300	14,950	2,018.50+29%	12,300
14,950	17,600	2,787.00+33%	14,950
17,600	22,900	3,661.50+39%	17,600
22,900	30,000	5,728.50+44%	22,900
30,000	42,800	8,852.50+49%	30,000
42,800	....	15,124.50+50%	42,800

Page 40

Source: U.S. Department of the Treasury—Internal Revenue Service.

QUESTIONS FOR REVIEW

1. Discuss the ability to pay and the benefit principle of taxation.
2. It is said that sales taxes are regressive. Explain this statement.
3. How are state and local taxes on real estate calculated? Is the property tax a good or a poor tax in your opinion?
4. Why is it that two individuals with the same income and the same dependents do not necessarily pay the same amount of taxes?
5. Differentiate between the cash and the accrual basis.
6. Who must file a federal income tax return? Who might want to file even if they do not have to?
7. What is the earned income credit?
8. What is the earned income credit?
9. Is alimony subject to the federal personal income tax?
10. How does filing a joint return save you money?
11. How does the tax law discriminate against married couples? How did Congress try to alleviate this?
12. When is a person able to serve as a double exemption?
13. How are annuities and pensions taxed?
14. What is income averaging?
15. What is the maximum tax provision?
16. Are moving expenses deductible on your tax form?
17. What is the zero bracket amount on your tax return?
18. What are tax credits? Why are they more valuable than tax deductions?
19. It is said that capital gains receive special tax treatment. Can you explain how this works?
20. Why is it that most people who do not own a home are better off to take the zero bracket amount rather than to itemize?
21. What is the alternative minimum tax? How does it work?
22. What are tax preference items? How may they affect your taxes?
23. Make a list of all the deductions and loopholes in the tax law that apply to you but which you did not know about before.

CASES

1. Joe and Bette Madox earn $28,000 per year and have one child. They are buying a house and pay interest of $4,800 on their $50,000 mortgage. In addition, their property taxes are $1,100. The Madoxes have certain other expenses that were deductible on their tax form to the extent of $633. If they were renting, they would have taken the zero bracket amount as they always have in the past, but this year their expenses will be greater than the $3,400 zero bracket amount. Calculate their taxes on a nonitemized

deduction basis. Do the same with all their allowable deductions itemized. What is their tax saving from owning a house?

2. Bob and Joan Rider are a young couple with no dependents. Bob works as a salesman for a local manufacturer and earns $25,000 per year. Joan is a law student. They rent a modest apartment for $275 per month. They have never been able to itemize their deductions and get more than the zero bracket amount. Calculate the tax liability of the Riders using the zero bracket amount.

Bob would like to have you calculate his friend Jim's taxes for this year. He made the same income but had to pay more taxes. He was single but does not believe that one more exemption should make that much difference. What is the difference in the tax liability between the two men? How can you explain it other than by additional exemptions?

3. Kevin and Eleanor Kelley, aged sixty-seven and sixty-six, respectively, live in a large midwestern city where Kevin is a tool and diemaker earning $475 per week. They have no other income and no dependents. Their home is completely paid for, but the property taxes on it are $1,250. They also had expenses during the year as follows: $392 for medical bills; $189 for drugs; $975 for medical insurance; and $829 of traveling expense for Kevin when he went to the tool and diemakers' convention in Miami, Florida. What are their deductions? Explain. Calculate their tax liability.

4. During his summer vacation, Joe worked for nine weeks at the Super Service Station. His total wages were $2,160 and his employer withheld $105 in income tax. He had no other income. What is the simplest return form Joe may file, and how much refund will he receive?

5. Jan, who is twenty and a student, worked for the Paragon Builders, Inc., for twelve weeks during her summer vacation. She earned $3,840 and her employer withheld $665 for income tax. She had $300 interest income and her parents contributed more than half her support. What is the simplest return form Jan may file, and what is the amount of her income tax refund?

6. James Wingo has an annual salary of $26,000. His employer withheld $5,265 for income tax and $1,742 for Social Security tax. James was ill for one week and did not work during that time, but his employer has a qualified sick-pay plan and James received his regular salary that week.

James' wife Mary is self-employed; she has a secretarial and an accounting service, and earned $26,750 last year. Mary received $180 of dividends on stock she owned individually and $250 of interest income. During the year there was an auto accident in which Mary ran over a man who was so unfortunate as to get in front of her car. Mary suffered $300 damages to the grill and front end of her car. Her insurance policy has a $500 deductible clause. James and Mary also spent $910 in insulating their attic and weatherstripping all windows. Mary filed an estimated tax return and made four quarterly payments of $2,000 each on her estimated tax. As a self-employed person, Mary paid Social Security taxes of $2,504.

In addition to their own exemptions, they are entitled to claim an exemption for their two children. These are their other deductible items:

Contributions	$ 500
Interest	5,422
Taxes	1,545
Medical expenses paid (including $125 for medicine & drugs)	500
Professional dues	60
Medical Insurance	1,097

Compute James and Mary's additional tax or refund.

John and Bette Pasmack live on the West Coast, and John earned $22,750 last year. In addition, he received a bonus of $2,500 just before Christmas. His employer withheld $3,412 for income taxes and $1,524 for Social Security tax. John and Bette each had $60 of dividend income and, in addition, Bette received $170 interest income from a trust.

In addition to their own exemptions, John and Bette are entitled to exemptions for son Jack, daughter Jean, and Bette's seventy-year-old widowed mother. Their deductible items are:

Contributions	$ 510
Interest	3,476
Taxes	1,289
Loss on their summer cottage damage by fire ($900 minus $100 limitation)	800
Dues to professional societies	55
Medical expenses paid (including $225 for medicine and drugs and $750 for hospitalization insurance)	1,120

Compute their additional tax or refund.

Peter and Julie are considering marriage but have heard that their taxes would be much higher as a married working couple than if they were both single and they would like you to compute their tax liabilities under both assumptions.

Both are lawyers. His salary is $27,000 and hers is $35,000. Pete owns a home on which he will pay $4,200 in interest and $1,600 in taxes. They both have professional dues of $180 and medical insurance expense of $968. Julie lives in an apartment and has no other itemized deductions. Pete's interest income from CDs is $750.

SUGGESTED READINGS

Bittker, Boris. *Federal Income Taxation*. Boston: Little, Brown, 1980.

————, and Stone, Lawrence. *Federal Taxation of Income, Estates, and Gifts*. Boston: Little, Brown, 1981 (Supplement, 1982).

Cahill, Thomas D. *How to Save Tax Dollars As a Homeowner*. Oakland, Calif.: Rampart Publishing Co., 1981.

Commerce Clearing House. *Federal Tax Return Manual*. Chicago: Commerce Clearing House, 1982.

Crestol, Jack, and Schneider, Herman M. *Tax Planning for Investors: The Nineteen Eighty-Two Guide to Securities, Investments, and Tax Shelters*. Homewood, Ill.: Dow Jones-Irwin, 1982.

"Federal Tax Course." Chicago: Commerce Clearing House. Published annually.

"Federal Tax Courses." Englewood Cliffs, N.J.: Prentice-Hall. Published annually.

Internal Revenue Service. "Employer's Tax Guide, Circular E." Washington, D.C.: Internal Revenue Service. Published annually.

————. "Instructions for Preparing Form 1040." An annual IRS publication which can be obtained at any post office during tax time and at any regional IRS office at other times.

————. "Instructions for Preparing Form 1040A." An annual IRS publication which can be obtained at any post office during tax return time and at any regional IRS office at other times.

————. *Tax Guide for Small Business, 1983 Edition*. Washington, D.C.: U.S. Government Printing Office, 1983. Published annually.

————. *Your Federal Income Tax*. An annual IRS publication which gives a far more detailed explanation than the "Instructions for Preparing Form 1040." It can be obtained at any IRS regional office.

Levy, Michael E., et al. *The Federal Budget: Its Impact on the Economy*. New York: The Conference Board, 1980.

Mendlowitz, Edward. *Successful Tax Planning* (Revised). New York: Boardroom Books, 1982.

"The National Debt." Philadelphia: Federal Reserve Bank of Philadelphia.

"1984 M.S. Master Tax Guide." Chicago: Commerce Clearing House. Published annually.

Sommerfeld, Ray M., Anderson, Hershel M., and Brock, Horace R. *An Introduction to Taxation*, 2nd ed. New York: Harcourt, Brace & World, 1982.

United States Budget in Brief: Fiscal Year 1984. Washington, D.C.: U.S. Government Printing Office. Published annually.

CHAPTER NINE

HOUSING

Home ownership is important in a budget. Most people who own homes must meet a monthly mortgage payment that is a substantial proportion of the budget, a fixed payment that must be paid for many years. In addition, many people consider part of this monthly payment to be forced saving because with each monthly payment the individual's equity or ownership in the home increases. Others relate home ownership to the family budget because the interest paid as well as the real property taxes constitute large tax-deductible items.

The popularity of home ownership is shown by the fact that in the late 1970s about 64 percent of United States families owned their own homes. The rate of increase, however, has slowed down in the last few years, generally because of the greater availability of rental units, high interest rates, and increases in construction costs.

FACTORS TO CONSIDER

Advantages of Home Ownership

Personal factors

Some people attach great importance to the peace of mind, pride, security, greater privacy, and convenience that owning a home provides. Some also feel that homes are often located in a less congested area than apartments, and provide a better environment in which to raise children.

Tax advantages

There is a considerable tax advantage to home ownership. A homeowner pays interest on the mortgage and local property taxes on the home, while a person who rents an apartment pays rent. The latter, however, includes a sum to enable the landlord to pay the interest and tax; hence the renter pays these costs indirectly. Because of this hidden cost for the renter, homeowners have a tax advantage over renters. If their income, exemptions, and other deductions are the same as the renter's, they will pay fewer taxes. This is because homeowners may deduct from their incomes, when calculating their taxes, interest on their mortgage and property taxes. Rent, of course, cannot be deducted. This can best be illustrated by an example. Assume two childless couples whose circumstances are identical except that one rents and one is buying a house. Both have adjusted gross incomes of $15,500 and total deductions because of medical expenses, contributions to charity, church, and so forth, amount to $2,000. The couple buying a home, however, has additional deductions of $2,160 due to interest and property taxes ($50 per month taxes and about $130 per month interest is not unreasonable for even a modest home). The couple buying a home will take a total deduction of $4,160 while the one renting can take only $3,400. This is the zero bracket amount that married couples may take if filing jointly. The homeowners' taxable income is $760 lower. Moreover, the higher the tax bracket, the greater the tax advantage from home ownership. The nature of our tax laws enables the homeowner to pass part of the interest and property taxes on to Uncle Sam.

Even the homeowner who no longer has mortgage payments to make and lives in a community that has no property taxes is receiving favorable tax treatment because of imputed rent income received on which he or she pays no taxes. An example will illustrate. Assume two individuals working side by side for the Ajax Corporation, each making a salary of $20,000 per year. Each owns a home that is fully paid for, but while Ms. A lives in hers, Mr. B rents his and lives with relatives. Both have a $40,000 home free and clear. Mr. B receives $1,000 of net cash rental income after all expenses including his property taxes and depreciation. He pays a tax on $21,000. Ms. A in reality should look upon her cost-free living as worth about $1,000, which she really receives as income in kind. For these two individuals to be treated equally they should both pay taxes on either $20,000 or $21,000. But Ms. A pays on $20,000 and Mr. B on $21,000.

The same logic would apply if, while Ms. A invested her savings in her home, Mr. B rented and invested his savings in high-grade corporate bonds. After a time Mr. B would have interest income that is taxable, while Ms. A's rent income received in kind is not.

Homestead

In some states, laws have been enacted making it possible for persons to declare their home to be their homestead. This prevents the home from being seized to satisfy certain private debts. In some states, there is a dollar limit to the amount of real estate protected against seizure. The homestead act does not prevent the mortgage lender from foreclosing if mortgage payments are not made. Also, the government is not prevented from seizing the property if it has a valid claim against the owner. But with these two exceptions, the property is protected. In some areas, property taxes are also reduced by a modest amount if a homestead claim is filed.

A home as an inflationary hedge

A home is one of the best inflationary hedges. A person who rents and invests savings in a savings account or even in securities is likely to see them eroded as time passes and prices rise. Not so with a home, at least not usually. Generally, a home will appreciate as much, and sometimes more, than overall prices during times of inflation, because when prices rise, so too do building materials and labor costs. Consequently, during inflation, the cost of building new houses rises; this generally brings up the price of older houses as well.

Table 9–1 shows the sale of one-family homes and median price since 1970.

Disadvantages of Home Ownership

Some people consider maintenance as a disadvantage of home ownership. The house must be painted every few years, and from time to time the roof will need repairs. Occasionally, a plumber will have to be called, and certain built-in appliances like the hot water heater, furnace, and air conditioner wear out and must be repaired or replaced. These things can be avoided by the apartment dweller, as well as work like raking leaves, cutting the lawn, and shoveling snow. Since most people do these chores themselves, little monetary cost is involved, but the homeowner's time is committed.

It has been estimated that maintenance costs will be about 1 1/2 percent of the cost of the house per year. This is the average cost, and in some years

Table 9–1   Sales of one-family homes

Year	Number (thousands)			Dollar volume (billions)			Median price	
------	New homes	Existing homes	Total homes	New homes	Existing homes	Total homes	New homes	Existing homes
1970	485	1,612	2,097	$12.9	$ 41.4	$ 54.3	$23,400	$23,000
1971	656	2,018	2,674	18.6	56.5	75.1	25,200	24,800
1972	718	2,252	2,970	21.9	67.8	89.7	27,600	26,700
1973	634	2,334	2,968	22.5	76.8	99.3	32,500	28,900
1974	519	2,272	2,791	20.2	81.3	101.5	35,900	32,000
1975	549	2,452	3,001	23.4	95.6	119.0	39,300	35,300
1976	646	3,002	3,648	31.0	126.7	157.7	44,200	38,100
1977	819	3,547	4,366	44.4	169.9	214.3	48,800	42,900
1978	817	3,863	4,680	51.1	214.4	265.5	55,700	48,700
1979	709	3,701	4,410	50.9	237.6	288.5	62,900	55,700
1980	545	2,881	3,426	41.6	209.7	251.3	64,600	62,200
1981	436	2,351	2,787	36.2	184.1	220.3	68,900	66,400
1982	411	1,990	2,401	34.5	169.2	194.7	69,300	67,800

Source: 1983 Savings and Loan Sourcebook, p. 34.

the cost will be considerably higher. Some people consider the big investment required to be a homeowner a disadvantage. The fact that a home is not very liquid and requires time to sell reinforces this disadvantage.

To Rent or Own a Home

When comparing renting and buying, many people compare renting an apartment as opposed to buying a house. This is not completely valid because you are comparing two different things. Usually (but not always), a house is larger than an apartment. In addition, the homeowner has more privacy than a tenant in an apartment and a backyard, which the tenant lacks. Also, homeowners are building up an equity in their houses. Consequently, you cannot compare the monthly mortgage payment on a house with the monthly rental payment and reach a decision. You must also give some weight to all the things discussed above under advantages and disadvantages of home ownership.

To be sure, houses can also be rented. If you were to compare the monthly rent on a house with the mortgage payment on a like (or similar) house, you would have a more meaningful comparison.

You must look at the comparison in the long run and the short run. A homeowner does not build up much equity during the first few years of home ownership, because most of the monthly payments go for interest. Also, the first year will necessitate additional closing costs and possibly expenditures for putting in a lawn and other landscaping.

When buying a house as opposed to renting, you are almost certainly better off financially to buy, except possibly in the short run. That has been the case in the past, and it is likely to be so in the future. However, if you are only going to live in a community a year or two, you might want to rent for the somewhat greater convenience and possibly less expense: for example, no maintenance cost, no landscaping (needed on new homes only), no closing costs, no possible realtor's fee when you sell, and the like. In the long run, especially if your mortgage is lower than your monthly rent, probably you should buy.

If it does not matter whether you live in an apartment or buy a house and you want to make the decision between buying or renting strictly on a financial basis, then you have a more complex task. You will have to consider the following:

1. The monthly rent and the monthly mortgage payment
2. The dollar amount of property taxes and interest and your tax bracket, since these two items are tax deductible
3. How much your house is likely to appreciate in price per year
4. How long you are likely to be living in the community before you move

Whether you should buy or rent is a question that must be analyzed individually.

It will vary from time to time and place to place and person to person. You might be living in an area that is overbuilt with apartments. Hence, rents might be relatively low. If that is the case at a time when interest rates are very high and few homes are being built and hence very costly, you could be better off to rent at least for a time. If, later, apartments are no longer overbuilt and rents rise and at the same time interest rates decline, this might be the time to investigate home ownership.

When you decide whether to rent or buy you should review the material on the personal budget and on housing expenditures in Chapter 3. You should compare your housing expenses from renting and from buying in a budget. The following table (Table 9–2) is a beginning in making this analysis.

In the case shown in Table 9–2, the cost of owning a home would exceed the cost of renting if it were not for the tax benefits. But taking into account the tax benefits and the equity build-up, the person would be $516 better off by buying. In addition, the benefits would be even greater if the person were in a higher tax bracket, and besides the person has an inflationary hedge.

Tenant's Rights

If you rent, you have certain rights; however, you also have certain responsibilities. Although there are some apartment owners and homeowners who will rent on a month-to-month basis, most require a lease. Leases generally run for six months or a year. This means you are committed for that period; you cannot ordinarily break a lease, but there are exceptions. If you are transferred by your employer, most states have laws that will permit the lease to be broken by paying one month's rent. Indeed, you should state in the lease that if you are transferred or other mitigating circumstances occur, the lease shall become null and void.

Table 9–2   Expenses of renting versus buying a home

COST OF RENTING: $600/month × 12	$7,200 per year
COST OF BUYING A HOME:	
Mortgage payment $550/month × 12	$6,600 per year
Maintenance $50/month × 12	600
Interest foregone on $10,000 down payment ($10,000 × 9%)	900
Property taxes $75/month × 12	900
Insurance on house $30/month × 12	360
Total Cost	$9,360
Less tax benefits from deducting interest and property taxes:	
Interest $6,300	
Taxes 900	
$7,200 × 33% tax rate	− $2,376
Less equity build-up $25/month × 12	− 300
Net cost: $9,360 - $2,676	$6,684

Read your lease carefully. It will spell out all of your rights and responsibilities. Moreover, don't hesitate to request that certain things be added to your lease if you think it necessary: such things as when the rent is due, who will pay the utilities, that certain repairs are needed when you move in, the amount of the deposit, the condition of the rug, the broken patio door, and the like. Be a reasonable tenant, but know your rights. While there are unreasonable landlords, most of them will deal fairly with you if you do with them.

Most landlords will demand a deposit, which may vary from $100 to several hundred dollars or often the equivalent of one month's rent. Be sure the lease states you will get this back if you vacate the rental unit in as good and clean condition as you accepted it.

If you are a student, you may want your lease to run concurrently with the school year. Or, if you want it for a longer time, you may want a clause in it to permit you to sublease it, say during the summer.

A landlord who won't honor the terms of the lease can be held accountable. In most states, there are small claims courts or the equivalent where you can easily and inexpensively make the landlord fulfill the contract.

Many college students often complain they never get their deposit back; this is often their number one complaint. There is no need for this if you have not caused any damage. But treat the property as if it were your own. Many students are quite careful inside their unit, but careless about running over lawns, flowers, shrubs, and the like.

First of all, the decision must be made between renting and owning your home. There are some advantages to apartment living, and the same applies to rented homes. Some people are natural homeowners, some are not. Let us assume that the decision has been made to be a homeowner. Then you must decide what price range can you afford.

How Much House Can You Afford?

There used to be, and to some extent still are, four rules of thumb used by mortgage lenders to indicate how much of a house a prospective homeowner could afford. They are:

1. The price of the home (including the lot) should be no more than two and one-half times the purchaser's annual gross (before tax) income.
2. The amount borrowed to purchase a home should be no more than two times the purchaser's gross annual income.
3. The monthly mortgage payments of a homeowner (which includes reduction of principal, interest, taxes, and insurance—PITI) should be no more than 25 percent of the homeowner's gross income.
4. Total monthly housing costs should not exceed one week's take-home pay (net, not gross, income).
5. Total monthly payment on all debts (including consumer installment debt) should not exceed 36 percent of gross monthly income.

The first three rules all work out about the same. Under the first rule, a person making $25,000 per year could buy a house worth $62,500. He could also finanace about $50,000 of it under the second rule and hence would need a down payment of about $12,500. This is the often standard 20 percent.

Under the third rule, the person could pay $520 per month ($25,000 ÷ 12 = $2,083 × 25% = $520). Moreover, historically about 1 percent of the mortgage would cover the monthly payment needed for the reduction of principal, interest, taxes and insurance. In the $50,000 mortgage noted above, this amounts to $500. Since the person making $25,000 could pay $520, there would only be $20 per month left for taxes and insurance, which may not be enough.

Rule four has more often been applied to renters, but sometimes to homeowners. Under it, the person would not quite qualify. One week's gross pay is $480 ($25,000 ÷ 52). The net after taxes would be even less.

Under rule five the person making $25,000 per year could assume debts requiring montly payments of up to $750.

In recent years all of the rules have been stretched a bit, especially for two-income families. Obviously the higher a down payment you are able to make, the more house you can afford. But the rules have been modified in other ways. The 2½ times rule is now sometimes the 3 times rule. The 2 times rule is now sometimes the 2½ times rule, and the 25 percent has been modified to 28 percent in some cases. In such a case, the person making $25,000 could afford a monthly payment of $583. This has been done because interest costs and construction costs, and hence housing costs, have risen faster than income. In addition, many people have been willing to make a greater sacrifice to acquire a home because home ownership has proven to be a good investment. If you do this, do so with care, and budget wisely. If you are a two-income family, this is easier to do. This also partly explains why there are more and more two-income families.

New House or Older House?

Since you have decided to become a homeowner, you must choose whether you want to buy a new house or an older one or to build one from the ground up. Also you must decide whether to deal with a real estate agent or the owner directly. When buying a new house, you are at least usually assured of getting one in which everything works. If the wiring is wrong or the roof leaks, the builder will usually repair it at no cost. A greater degree of expertise is needed to evaluate an older house to determine that everything in it is in working order. If something goes wrong after you have bought it, the previous owner will not usually make an adjustment. On the other hand, if the house is relatively new, say two or three years old, most of the defects that appear in new houses (e.g., wiring) will have been repaired.

If the house is quite old, it may be more difficult to finance than a new one. Lenders generally require higher down payments on really old houses. If the house is used but relatively new, there will be an existing mortgage on it. There may be a problem if the new buyer is unable to take it over and a second mortgage may be required.

The Energy-Efficient Home

With today's high cost of energy you should consider the degree to which the home is energy-efficient. In the case of new homes minimum amounts of insulation are now required in the walls and ceiling by various local building codes. However, weatherstripping around doors and windows is not always included. If you live in the North, you should also check the cost of storm windows if they are not included.

Homes built prior to the 1970s, when energy was cheap, often did not have adequate insulation. If you are considering an older home you should check the insulation.

Remember too that if there are trees near your house that provide shade, they will reduce your air-conditioning bill if you live in a section of the country that has long hot summers.

Ceiling fans are returning. They will lessen substantially the amount of time your air conditioning will need to run, and fans use much much less energy than an air conditioner. If the home has two separate heating and air conditioning units, it is a more energy-efficient home, because a section of the house can be isolated and not heated or cooled if it is not being used. Even if your house has only one unit, you can reduce energy consumption somewhat by turning off the ceiling or floor vent and not heating or cooling a specific room.

Remember that a two-story house is more energy-efficient than a rambling one-story ranch style house with the same livable square footage, because there is less roof for heat or cold to escape. (It is also cheaper to build.)

While a house that is highly energy efficient will usually cost more than one that is less effficient, lower household operation costs offset the difference (see Chapter 2). A highly energy-efficient home will also have a higher resale value. You may make almost any home more energy efficient by adding more insulation, weatherstripping around windows and doors (or storm doors), and by planting shade trees.

Building a House to Specifications

In building a house, the owner will have a lot of headaches, but this may be the only way to get what one really wants. The headaches come from disagreements and misunderstandings with the contractor and because the average person does not have construction expertise. Also, the average person may not be able to read blueprints well enough really to visualize what the completed structure will look like. As construction takes place, owners will discover things they will want changed and this is expensive. If an architect is hired to take care of some of these things and draw up plans, there is, of course, the added expense of those fees.

It may be best not to make the first house you own one you build from the ground up. Buy an existing house first and learn something about houses. Later if you have the time to devote to it, and the patience, you may want to build your dream home. If you build, you will need a construction loan to build it and then a long-term mortgage after it is completed.

Does Your House Have a Warranty?

Some new homes have a warranty for a year or two against defects in workmanship and materials and against major structural defects. Some builders give these written guarantees, and then if defects do show up, the repairs are usually made by the same builder.

There is now also the Home Owner's Warranty (HOW), a national organization that insures some new homes against defects. HOW is recognized by the National Association of Home Builders, and many of these buiders issue their warranty through the HOW. The builder who issues a HOW through this group is still responsible for making needed repairs. However, if a homeowner and a builder cannot agree on what should be done, HOW has a dispute settlement procedure. If something should happen so that the builder cannot make the repairs, HOW will in some cases take care of the warranted items.

Using a Realtor

If you buy a house through a realtor, it may cost you more but it may be worth it. While the seller of a house pays the realtor's commissions, he or she will generally try to pass them on to the buyer in the form of a higher price.

Realtors' fees vary from state to state and even within towns in a given state but generally are from 5 to 6 percent. Usually in the bigger cities they are 6 percent, while in some of the smaller towns they are closer to 5. Many people wishing to sell their home find the market value (sometimes they deliberately set a price way above the market value) and then add the realtor's fees to this figure.

Most listings are now on a cross-listing basis, which means that listing it with any realtor will automatically list it with all realtors. A listing is for at least ninety days and during that time sellers must pay the realtor fees even if they sell the house to someone on their own. After the listing has expired, the homeowner may sell without paying the commissions if it is to a buyer who has not been shown the home by the realtor. If a prospective buyer has been shown the home by a realtor during the listed period, the commissions must be paid if it is bought within a given period, usually six months, after the listing has expired.

Whether realtors' fees are shifted to the buyer in the form of a higher price depends on the tightness of the housing market. But realtors are supposed to protect both the buyer and the seller. For example, a good realtor will discourage a homeowner from pricing the house unrealistically high. Also, a realtor will encourage a homeowner to make any necessary repairs to get the house in first-class condition.

The 6 percent realtor's fee has been standard for some time, but recently some agents have cut their fee because of the slow housing market. In some cases fees can be negotiated, especially with very expensive homes.

The Neighborhood

In considering proposed construction or the purchase of an existing structure, the buyer must consider the neighborhood. With the growth of a city or even a fairly small town, neighborhoods or districts are created. For the most part, they are the result of economic pressures, which cause them to be in a constant state of flux. As a result of changes in neighborhood—more often than not from a higher to a lower level of use—there develops what is known to the real estate appraiser as *economic obsolescence*, defined as the impairment of desirability and usefulness of property brought about by economic and environmental changes of a neighborhood.

In general, older sections of a city begin their decline soon after newer sections begin to make a strong appeal to home buyers. The prospective purchaser of a home should look for a neighborhood containing a high percentage of owner-occupied homes as distinguished from tenant-occupied homes. Neighborhoods containing a high percentage of the former tend to be more stable in value. Further, one should look for a neighborhood that contains well-planned and well-located homes of the same physical characteristics. It is also desirable if the residents have steady jobs with above-average income. Proximity to schools and good shopping centers is also important.

Contrary to what one would expect, in some older sections in some cities property values have held up well; often values have appreciated. This is because they are desirable places to live, for example, the Georgetown section of Washington, D.C., and Back Bay in Boston. In addition, urban renewal or restoration will usually enhance the value of older property.

The checklist below should be helpful in selecting the neighborhood. Consider each of the following items to determine whether the location of the property will satisfy your personal needs and preferences:

1. Convenience of public transportation
2. Stores conveniently located
3. School conveniently located
4. Absence of excessive traffic noise
5. Absence of smoke and unpleasant odors from factories
6. Play area available for children

7. Fire and police protection provided
8. Residential usage safeguarded by adequate zoning
9. Traffic patterns during the rush hours
10. Taxes and possible future assessments for sewers, water systems, for example
11. General stability of the neighborhood

The Lot and the House

In selecting a building site, the buyer must notice such details as whether it is located in the prevailing wind, which may carry noxious odors from factories and railroads. Will the lot be appropriate for the proposed structure? Is the drainage good enough to prevent standing water in the event of abnormal or even normal rainfall? Will the soil support the proposed structure? In the event septic tanks are necessary, have percolation tests been run to determine the ability of the soil to handle a septic tank? An important area of investigation is the availability of utilities, such as electricity, telephone, and water supply. In some parts of the country the need to drill for water would render many sites uneconomical. Probably one of the best ways to select a site after it has been determined that the neighborhood is satisfactory is to use such a checklist as the following, which can be expanded to meet local conditions.

Lot

Consider each of the following to determine whether the lot is sufficiently large and properly improved:

1. Size of front yard satisfactory
2. Size of rear and side yards satisfactory
3. Walks provide access to front and service entrances
4. Drive provides easy access to garage
5. Lot appears to drain satisfactorily
6. Lawn and planting satisfactory
7. Septic tank (if any) in good operating condition

House

Consider each of the following to determine whether the house is satisfactory:

Exterior construction

1. Wood porch floors and steps
2. Windows, doors, and screens
3. Gutters and wood cornice
4. Wood siding
5. Mortar joints
6. Roofing

7. Chimneys
8. Paint on exterior woodwork
9. Driveway and sidewalk

Interior construction

1. Walls free of excessive cracks
2. Walls and ceiling free of stains caused by leaking roof or sidewalls
3. Door locks in operating condition
4. Windows move freely
5. Fireplace works properly
6. Basement dry and will resist moisture penetration
7. Mechanical equipment and electrical wiring and switches adequate and in operating condition
8. Type of heating equipment suitable
9. Adequate insulation in walls, floor, ceiling, or roof
10. Wood floor finish
11. Linoleum floors
12. Condition of rugs
13. Sink top
14. Kitchen appliances
15. Bathroom fixtures
16. Painting and papering
17. Exposed joists and beams

Condominium or House?

Some people prefer a condominium to a house. A condominium provides some of the benefits of owning a house and some of the benefits of apartment living. Condominiums are apartment-like structures, but residents receive *title* to their units. They must make a down payment and arrange their mortgage, if financed, just as for a house. Moreover, they can sell at any time. Condominium owners have the same tax benefits as homeowners and build up equity like a homeowner. They have all the building maintenance problems to take care of in their unit.

A condominium owner is more like an apartment dweller in that there is no yard work to perform. There may be a common yard that can be enjoyed with other condominium owners in the building. Sometimes this includes a common swimming pool, tennis court, and putting green. Instead of maintaining these facilities, the individual is assessed a fee each month, and a maintenance crew is hired.

When buying a condominium, the owner joins the condominium association, and all members have one vote in deciding matters in accordance with the provisions as set forth in the condominium agreement that all members must agree to abide by. Generally speaking, condominium owners may sell their unit to anyone they choose. However, the condominium may contain a general statement requiring that new owners be acceptable to the members, and, if they are not, that the group will have the right to buy the unit back, if it chooses to do so.

Choosing between a house and a condominium is a personal matter. Those who want some of the benefits of home ownership but not all of the problems might choose this compromise, although they give up some backyard privacy.

Town House

This concept has several meanings. In the bigger eastern cities it may merely be a house in the city rather than in the suburbs. In some cases, older decaying areas have been renovated and have become fashionable residential sections of the city. In many cases town houses are expensive. The Georgetown area near Washington, D.C., is an example of an area with expensive renovated town houses.

In other cases, the town house may be a multifamily unit, with each resident owning the unit he or she occupies. In this case, the town house is similar to the condominium, although there may not be a common yard, swimming pool, and the like. All the tax benefits of home ownership apply.

Co-ops

In some cities, there are co-op apartments and even co-op homes. These co-ops are nonprofit corporations, and the residents of a co-op housing unit, technically speaking, do not own their unit. The corporation owns it, and each resident owns some stock (certificates of ownership) of the corporation. Often the number of apartments in a co-op is large, and home co-ops may cover an entire city block. Generally, the homes are connected and are built facing the street on all four sides of the block. The center then becomes a courtyard and serves as a common backyard.

Since the apartments (or homes) in a co-op are of varying sizes (and values), the amount of stock a co-oper has is prorated accordingly. The price residents have to pay for the stock is then similar to the down payment on a house. The co-oper makes a monthly payment (which varies in accordance with the value of the individual unit) to the co-op; this includes interest, taxes, insurance, and reduction of principal, and the co-op makes one mortgage payment to the mortgage holder. There is one common mortgage on twenty or thirty different rental units rather than each one being financed separately. As the years pass and the mortgage is reduced, the theoretical value of the co-op shares rises.

Since co-op housing is a relatively new development, few of them have been around long enough to have their mortgage paid off. However, when the common mortgage is paid, there is usually some arrangement for the co-op to be dissolved and all co-opers to obtain title to their units. Each co-oper may be expected to help in doing yard work, or there may be a monthly fee to have this done.

A co-op is similar to a condominium, but legally different. In a condominium, each unit has a separate mortgage and each resident has title to his or her property. In a co-op, there is one mortgage and the resident owns shares in the co-op. However, co-op owners may sell their shares to nearly anyone. Sometimes, however, the prospective owner must be acceptable to the group. If the person is not, the co-op corporation will usually buy the shares back.

That portion of the co-oper's monthly payment for the payment of interest or property taxes is fully deductible for tax purposes, just as in the case of the home or condominium owner. The co-op may offer one advantage over the individual residential unit, since on a mortgage often for hundreds of thousands of dollars (or even millions) the interest rate may be a little lower.

One question may have occurred to you. Since a co-op is a nonprofit corporation, who would have an incentive to establish one? The answer is realtors, builders, and land developers, who would stand to make a profit due to realtors' fees or in the construction of the building. One possible disadvantage to owning a co-op is that since there is one mortgage and since the value of the co-op shares rises as equity is built up, the new prospective buyer would need a large down payment to buy a co-op unit. In the case of an individual mortgage, it can be refinanced, but with a common mortgage this is not possible. This problem can be solved in some states where banks and savings and loan associations can make long-term loans using co-op stock as security.

Mobile Homes

Recently more and more people have been buying mobile homes. At one time these units appealed primarily to people whose jobs required that they move a good deal, such as construction workers. Today, however, primarily because they are so much cheaper than a conventional home, many young couples as well as older retired people are buying them.

There are two varieties of mobile homes. There is the true mobile home, which is on wheels and is moved from place to place. Many retired people have these trailers and go south during the winter. Then there is the so-called *mobile home*, which is on blocks and may have elaborate extensions built onto it. It can never again be moved and will remain permanently in a trailer or mobile home park.

In the past a mobile home was always a trailer with or without wheels. Recently, *motor homes* have been developed: self-propelled units generally built on a truck frame. Many of these units have become the second homes discussed below.

Mobile homes were financed like cars until a few years ago. Loans for them were considered consumer loans, the interest rates were similar to rates on cars, and they had to be amortized over several years like auto loans. Some lenders still feel this way; if they have wheels, they can be moved, and thus loans for them are similar to an auto loan. However, in the last few years, a number of changes have been made. Mobile home loans are now made for up to fifteen years. One reason is that the cost of a mobile home may now be as much as $30,000 and sometimes even more. Interest rates on mobile home loans are generally 2 to 3 points above regular home loans. In general at least a 15 percent down payment is required to obtain a mobile home loan.

Prefabricated Houses

Until recently, the use of prefabricated homes was greatly restricted by zoning laws. While still true in many areas this is slowly changing. Often prefabricated homes are found in the low-income areas of the community or are used as vacation homes. Until recently lenders did not finance them over more than ten years. This too is slowly changing. Prefabricated homes, while still cheaper than others, now sell for up to $50,000 and are a much better product than a decade ago. An advantage of buying a prefabricated home is that it takes much less time to assemble it than to construct a conventional home. The major disadvantage is that you will have less choice and flexibility as to style and design.

Second or Vacation Homes

Some of the more affluent members of society have summer or vacation homes. These are, if not mobile, usually located on a lake, at the beach, in the mountains, or at some other resort area. In some cases these homes are also an investment property. Arrangements can be made to rent them when they are not used by the owner. Most large resort areas have a service that makes the rental arrangements. People have purchased single-family units, condominiums, motor homes, prefabs, and trailers for their second homes. Of these single-family units, condominiums are the easiest to rent, since a service usually exists to do this for the property owner.

HOW MUCH IS A HOME WORTH?

When a person is purchasing a newly constructed home, there is little that one can do concerning the price; the builder sets the price and it generally remains at that level. Seldom will the builder bargain. The price is usually the cost of the house plus the builder's profit margin. A prospective purchaser can estimate the value of an older home that he or she is interested in purchasing. In addition, individuals placing their homes on the market should be able to estimate the selling price. Between the owner and the buyer who deals directly with the owner there may then be genuine bargaining. The total worth of a property is made up of three parts—the house itself, the land, and other improvements.

The House

The first step to determine the value of the house is to measure it. Each room should be measured, including closet space, but not including the garage or other unfinished space such as a patio. Ask your bank, local contractor, or real estate dealer for the current building costs in your area. If you have fifteen hundred square feet and building costs are $50 per square foot, the house would cost about $75,000 to build today. In this case $75,000 is the basic worth of the house—if it is in top condition. If it is not, the cost of the needed repairs such as new screens, painting, or a new roof, must be deducted. The basic cost, even if the house is in top condition, must be reduced somewhat on an older home to take into account an allowance for depreciation; the house is, after all, partly worn out. If the house is obsolescent or in a rapidly changing neighborhood, its value may be further affected. For example, if it lacks central heat or air conditioning or has high ceilings and major remodeling is required, this detracts from the value.

The value of the house is further lowered if it is in a decaying neighborhood. This is really discounting, to the present, the future expected decline in the area. Conversely, if the neighborhood is being restored, its future value is likely to rise because of this. After you have valued a house in this manner, you must then add an additional sum for the lot.

Another method of evaluating an existing house is to study the prices at which similar houses have been sold recently, a method that provides only a bench mark. First of all, few houses are precisely alike. Also other similar houses may be in better or in worse condition, and the location may make a difference. In addition, some sellers are in a hurry to sell, others are not, and this can affect prices. Consequently, analyzing the market price of recently sold similar houses will result in a range of prices. You must then make an allowance for any needed repairs or remodeling as well as an allowance for differences in the size of the lot and the desirability of the location. Nevertheless, analyzing the market price range of recently sold houses is a beginning. Applying judgment to that plus keeping in mind construction costs will enable you to appraise fairly a house that is for sale.

Land (Lot)

Using the market price as described above to evaluate real estate results in the house and the lot being appraised together. If you wish to evaluate a lot separately, you can read advertisements in the local newspaper and talk with real estate brokers to enable you to determine the current value of a lot accurately. Other lots of equal size and desirability in the same area would be worth about the same amount. The market price of similar lots recently sold is a good indicator of the value of a lot. Land value may also be increased substantially by a change in character of an area from rural to urban.

Other Improvements

Improvements enhance the value of the property and sometimes they should be evaluated separately, especially if you have added them yourself. Such items are landscaping, a garage or carport, a swimming pool, a basement made into a cozy playroom, an open attic transformed into bedrooms, a patio, or even a well-built barbecue pit. The value of these items should be estimated and added to the total cost of the house and the land, normally done by taking the original cost of the improvement adjusted by depreciation to take into account the wear and tear on it. During periods of rapid inflation some people use replacement cost and then adjust that down by depreciation. The grand total of the house, the land, and the improvements, after adjustments have been made as suggested above, will give an estimate of value. Table 9–3 provides a format for estimating the value of a home.

HOME FINANCING

About nine out of ten Americans who purchase or build a residence do so with the help of mortgage financing, the security for the debt. The borrower is called the mortgagor and the lender the mortgagee. The borrower gives the mortgage and the lender is said to take the mortgage. Most mortgage loans are made by financial institutions and a few individuals. The institutions involved are savings and loan associations, mutual savings banks, life insurance companies, mortgage banks, and some commercial banks. In addition, the trust departments of some commercial banks may finance a few mortgages, and recently credit unions were authorized to do so. However, up to now very few credit unions have been active in mortgage financing.

Historically there were three types of mortgages: conventional, FHA-insured, and VA-guaranteed. Recently, however, a number of innovative mortgages have been developed because of high interest rates.

In some states deeds of trust are used. This is a special kind of mortgage. The regular mortgage involves only two parties, the borrower (mortgagor) and the lender (mortgagee). In the deed of trust, the borrower conveys the realty not to the lender but to a third party, in trust, for the benefit of the lender, but for all practical purposes a deed of trust and a mortgage are the same.

Table 9–3 How to find the value of any house

Fill in the form below, one item at a time. As subtotals for such items as repairs are reached, add or subtract them as the case may be. The figures you will fill in at the end of the chart will be a realistic appraisal of what your house is worth at today's prices.

Room no. 1 Length _____ feet   Width _____ Feet   Length × Width _____ feet
Room no. 2 Length _____ feet   Width _____ Feet   Length × Width _____ feet
Room no. 3 Length _____ feet   Width _____ Feet   Length × Width _____ feet
           etc.

Total square feet:
Cost of construction today $ _____ per square foot.
Cost to build today: _____ sq. ft. × $ _____ (cost per square foot) =
   house value $ _____ .

Cost of needed repairs:
  1. Screens   _____
  2. Outside paint   _____
  3. Kitchen wallpaper   _____
  4. Gutters   _____
  5. Other   _____
                          Deduct $ _____ for repairs needed.

Functional obsolescence:
  1. Bathroom fixtures   _____
  2. Lighting   _____
  3. Lack of central heat
     or air conditioning   _____
  4. Other   _____
                          Deduct $ _____ for modernizing.

Changes in neighborhood affecting value:
  Add $ _____ (if neighborhood has improved)
  or
  Deduct $ _____ (if neighborhood has deteriorated)

Land value:
  Value of land by comparison $ _____ (add to total)

Improvements:
   1. Fireplace   _____
   2. Basement playroom   _____
   3. Finished attic   _____
   4. Patio   _____
   5. Storage wall   _____
   6. Under-stair closets   _____
   7. Full bath added   _____
   8. Enclosed porch   _____
   9. Landscaping   _____
  10. Insulated attic   _____
  11. Attached garage   _____
  12. Swimming pool   _____
  13. Other   _____
      Add: $ _____ for improvements

              Total value of property $ _____

The Conventional Mortgage

A conventional fixed-payment mortgage is an arrangement solely between the lending institution and the buyer of the home. The institution lends its money and, until a few years ago, assumed the entire risk of loss, but now there is insurance that pays any losses suffered by the lender due to a default. Conventional mortgage loans may be made for as long as thirty years, but many of them last much less than this.

In most states, savings and loan associations are now able to make loans up to 95 percent of the value of the home. Until recently, 80 percent was the maximum amount in most states because there was no mortgage insurance available on conventional mortgages. However, with the coming of private mortgage insurance (PMI), lenders are willing to make larger loans and the law allows it in most states. PMI works just like any insurance plan. A premium is assessed against the homeowner, and this goes into a fund used to pay any losses the lender might suffer if there is a default. To be sure, the interest charged on a 95 percent mortgage loan is usually a little higher than on a 90 percent loan, which in turn is higher than on an 80 percent one. While lenders may lend up to 95 percent of the value of the home, how much they actually advance varies. When money is scarce, they require a larger down payment than when money is plentiful.

The interest rate on mortgages varies from time to time and place to place. It varies from state to state because the demand for loans relative to the supply of mortgage money varies geographically. Generally speaking, all geographical areas have relative shortages of money at times and relatively plentiful supplies at others (but as noted above the relative degree varies regionally). Occasionally mortgage money is so scarce that it is very difficult and sometimes even impossible to obtain at any interest rate.

In 1981, mortgage interest rates hit an all-time high, and lenders responded by requiring a larger down payment and by tightening credit standards in other ways. In late 1982 and 1983, rates came down somewhat.

The FHA Mortgage

The FHA mortgage is a loan secured by a mortgage and given by an approved lending institution, but the loan is insured by the Federal Housing Administration. The government does not do the lending but merely acts as an insurance company. The borrower pays .5 percent (that is 1/2 of 1) annually of the unpaid loan balance as a premium for the "insurance policy." In the event of default in the payment of the loan by the buyer, the lending institution is paid for certain losses—not in cash but by long-term government bonds.

There is an upper limit to the insurance FHA provides. On a single-family dwelling, the insurance provided is equal to the loan but with a maximum of

$69,500. Because of this, if you buy a home under FHA financing for more than $69,500, you need a down payment for the difference.

For a prospective home buyer to qualify for an FHA-insured loan, he or she must meet certain credit and income requirements. In addition, the home must meet minimum appraisal standards as established by the FHA, providing the buyer with some protection. This necessitates FHA inspection of the home. This and other FHA red tape result in more time being required for a FHA loan to be approved than for a conventional loan. Although the maximum length of FHA loans changes from time to time, the current maximum maturity is thirty years. The minimum down payment required on an FHA mortgage varies as FHA regulations change and with the value of the house. At present, an approved lending institution may lend up to 97 percent of the first $40,000 of the appraised value of the house, and 95 percent of that portion over $40,000. On a $50,000 house then, a down payment of $1,700 would be required. Because these loan-to-value ratios are frequently changed by the FHA commissioner, it is necessary to obtain the current figures by asking a real estate broker or lending institution.

The maximum interest rate on an FHA-insured loan is set by the federal housing commissioner, subject to statutory limitations, and it too is changed from time to time. The current legal maximum rate is 12 percent—plus .5 percent for the insurance premium—making a total of 12 1/2 percent.

Sometimes FHA financing is more difficult to obtain than conventional, and sometimes the reverse is the case, because the legal ceiling on interest rates on these two types of mortgage loans is not always the same.

The VA-Guaranteed Mortgage

A VA-guaranteed mortgage is a loan on which the Veterans Administration guarantees payment to the lending institution or to an individual lender in the event of default by the veteran-buyer under the terms of the Servicemen's Readjustment Act of 1944 as amended. There are limits, however, and the VA can guarantee only up to 60 percent of the sales price of the house (since a VA loan does not require a down payment, the sales price and the loan may be the same) with a maximum guarantee of $110,000. To be eligible for a VA loan the person must be an honorably discharged veteran of the United States Armed Forces. The law also permits veterans who have had one VA loan who sold the house which it financed to obtain a second VA loan in certain cases.

The present legal ceiling on VA-guaranteed mortgages is 12 percent, but this changes periodically. The maximum maturity period is now thirty years. The maximum loan that a lender may make under a VA guaranteed loan is $110,000, but as noted above the maximum guarantee is only 60 percent of the sales price with a maximum guarantee of $66,000.

Billions of dollars of investors' money are tied up in various types of mortgages. Figure 9–1 and Table 9–4 illustrate total residential mortgages outstanding over the years, as well as mortgages outstanding by type of lender.

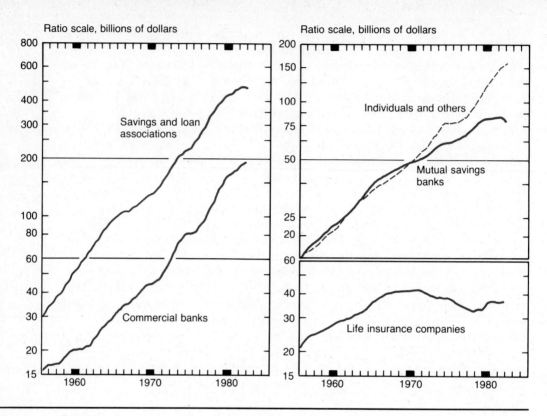

Figure 9–1   Residential mortgage debt, type of lender, amount outstanding, end of quarter. (*Source:* *Historical Chart Book,* Federal Reserve Board, 1982, p. 75.)

Table 9–4   Mortgage loans outstanding, by type of property and lender, year-end 1982*

| Lender | Residential properties | | | Commercial properties | Farm properties | Total mortgage loans |
	One- to four-family	Multi-family	Total			
Savings Associations	$ 400.6	$ 36.2	$ 436.7	$ 45.5	†	$ 482.2
Commercial Banks	177.1	15.8	$ 193.0	100.3	$ 8.5	$ 301.7
Mutual Savings Banks	63.7	14.9	78.7	15.2	†	93.9
Life Insurance Companies	17.0	19.1	36.1	92.3	12.9	141.3
All Others	447.2	62.3	509.4	41.4	85.7	636.6
Total	$1,105.6	$148.3	$1,253.9	$294.7	$107.1	$1,655.8

Note: Components may not add to totals due to rounding.
* Preliminary
† Less than $50 million
Source: Savings and Loan Sourcebook, 1983, p. 24.

Single-Payment Straight Mortgages

Prior to the 1930s, financing the purchase of a home was different. Usually the mortgage was for about five years and no provisions were made for monthly amortization payments. Rather, only the interest was paid every year, and at the end of the period, when the mortgage became due, the entire sum was to be repaid. Under such a system, of course, home buyers had to do their own budgeting and lay aside a sum every month. Few people, however, could save enough money to repay the entire mortgage in five years; consequently when the mortgage came due, at least part of it had to be refinanced. A mortgage usually had to be refinanced several times before it was finally liquidated.

One of the shortcomings of the single-payment mortgage arose over its refinancing. If it came due at a time when loans were hard to get, refinancing was often difficult. The process resulted in higher total interest costs than amortized mortgages. Interest had to be paid on the entire amount borrowed for the entire period, rather than monthly on the declining balance, as is now the case.

Second Mortgages

Sometimes second mortgages are needed to finance a home. Second mortgages come into existence when the purchaser does not have sufficient funds to make the necessary down payment to pay the owner his or her equity in an existing (not a new) home. The purchaser pays off what proportion of the equity he can and assumes a second mortgage for the remainder.

Second mortgages are more risky than first mortgages. In the event of a foreclosure and sale of a house on which the mortgagor has defaulted, the second mortgage is not paid off until after the first mortgagee has been completely repaid. An illustration will make the second mortgage clear. Assume that a buyer wishes to buy an older home for $75,000, and the home has a $40,000 mortgage on it. If the buyer could pay the seller $35,000 in cash, he could assume the old outstanding $40,000 mortgage. However, if he has only $25,000 for a down payment, he could pay that and give the seller a $10,000 second mortgage. Second mortgages are for smaller dollar amounts and run over fewer years than first ones. Generally they are for four, five, or perhaps up to ten years. The new homeowner now has two monthly payments to make. Interest rates are higher on second mortgages than on first because they are riskier.

Amortizing a Home Loan

A mortgage loan is paid off or amortized by having the homeowner make monthly payments, which pays off the mortgage loan in installments. A fixed monthly payment includes interest, reduction of principal, and perhaps taxes and insurance. A $50,000, 30-year mortgage at 12 percent would require a monthly payment of $514.31 to be amortized in 30 years, exclusive of taxes and insurance. Since the interest is calculated each month on the unpaid balance, that balance and the interest paid declines a bit each month on the unpaid balance. Inasmuch as the $514.31 payment is constant, the savings in interest are applied to reduce the principal more each month. These calculations have been made and printed in table form, and you can get such an amortization table from most banks or savings and loan associations.

The $514.31 monthly payment mentioned above includes interest of $500. the first month and $14.31 for the reduction of the principal. If we add $75 for taxes and $25 for insurance, the total monthly payment becomes $614.31. The second monthly payment would include less interest and a little more reduction of principal: for example, $499.86 and $14.45 respectively. The insurance and tax payments would presumably remain constant in the short run although every few years they are adjusted upward. These four monthly payments and the way they appear over time can be depicted graphically, as in Figure 9–2. Time is measured on the horizontal axis and the monthly payments on the vertical axis. This same relationship can be shown in a different manner, as illustrated by Table 9–5. You will note that after the last payment (the 360th payment) is made a principal of $53.38 remains. This is because a mortgage payment this long cannot always be made to come out exactly even.

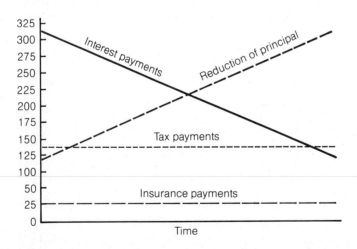

Figure 9–2   Relationships among the four payments included in single monthly loan payments. The graph is not geometrically accurate; it is only intended to illustrate the principle of amortization of mortgages. The tax and insurance payments may be adjusted upward periodically as taxes and premiums are raised.

Table 9–5   Relationship between payments and amount

Payment no.	Interest	Principal	Balance
1	$500.00	$ 14.31	$49,985.69
2	499.86	14.45	49,971.24
3	499.71	14.60	49,956.64
4	499.57	14.74	49,941.90
5	499.42	14.89	49,927.01
6	499.27	15.04	49,911.97
7	499.12	15.19	49,896.78
8	498.97	15.34	49,881.44
9	498.81	15.50	49,865.94
10	498.66	15.65	49,850.29
351	49.20	465.11	4,454.40
352	44.54	469.77	3,984.63
353	39.85	474.46	3,510.17
354	35.10	479.21	3,030.96
355	30.31	484.00	2,546.96
356	25.47	488.84	2,058.12
357	20.58	493.73	1,564.39
358	15.64	498.67	1,065.72
359	10.66	503.65	562.07
360	5.62	508.69	53.38

Final payment $53.38

Total payment $185,151.60

Total no. payments   360
Total principal $49,946.62
Total interest $135,204.98

Assumptions and Refinancings

The prospective buyer who has the necessary down payment to buy the equity in a house can take over an older existing mortgage. He or she then assumes all of the obligations of paying it off, often advantageous because by taking over an older existing mortgage the buyer may obtain funds at the interest rate prevailing several years before, which might have been lower. On the other hand, if rates were higher several years ago, the buyer might want to consider refinancing.

Sometimes lending institutions will not let a buyer assume an existing mortgage at the old interest rate. They will insist on refinancing at today's presumably higher rate, or in some cases they will permit the assumption but will escalate the interest rate to the current level. Whether or not lenders are able to force refinancing or escalate the interest rate is determined by the wording in the mortgage (deed of trust). Many (probably most) of the mortgages written during the last few years have a clause that permits the lender to require this. Some of the older ones do not.

If you have to refinance, not only must you pay today's (possibly high) interest rates, but also you must pay all the added *closing costs* which are considerable and which are avoided if you are able to obtain an assumption. Closing costs are discussed below.

It should be noted that the escalation of interest rates and forced refinancing are not permitted on FHA and VA mortgages.

Penalties

Since, in giving a mortgage loan, the lender has made an investment of a substantial amount of money at, say 12 percent for a long period of time, the lender wants to receive the interest income year by year. Over the years, interest on a mortgage may amount to thousands of dollars. Homeowners, on the other hand, might like to save this interest cost; if in the future their incomes should rise, they might want to make extra mortgage payments. Or if they should inherit a large sum of money, they might want to pay off the mortgage—perhaps even before the ink is dry. Other extra or windfall income might be used to greatly reduce or pay off a mortgage early.

To prevent or discourage the buyer from repaying the mortgage more quickly than agreed, the lender often insists on a penalty clause. Lending institutions defend these penalties on the basis that administrative and investment costs are involved in reinvesting early repayments, and that they partially compensate for lost income from interest.

In some cases, a penalty clause merely states that a fee, usually 1 or 2 percent, is charged for mortgage payments made in advance of the schedule. For example, if a person paid off in one payment a $20,000 mortgage, the penalty would be $200 or $400. Often, then, the penalty is small enough not to discourage greatly early repayment.

In other cases the penalty clause applies only to extra payments in excess of a given amount per year, say $1,000 or $2,000. In still other cases, penalties are calculated by applying the interest rate on the mortgage against the advance payment for so many months. There are three-month and six-month penalty clauses. If a 9 percent $20,000 mortgage carried a six-month interest penalty and you paid it off in advance, the penalty would be six months' interest on the amount paid off at 9 percent. If you paid off all $20,000, the penalty would be $900. In some cases the penalty clause drops out completely and automatically after a given period of time. The homeowner should, however, try to get a mortgage that does not contain a penalty clause. Usually the conditions in the money market will determine whether penalties are inserted into the mortgage. If funds are hard to obtain, not only will interest rates be higher but penalty clauses will more likely be inserted. If funds are plentiful, the homeowner will receive a lower rate of interest and can more easily avoid a penalty clause.

When Does It Pay to Refinance?

If one succeeds in avoiding a penalty clause, and in some cases even if one does not, it may sometimes pay to refinance. If, for example, you obtain a mortgage at a time when competitive conditions indicate a 15 or even 16 percent interest rate and a few years later rates are only 12 or 13 percent, it may pay to refinance. Remember that in doing this you have most of the closing costs to meet again, as well as the penalty, but if interest rates have declined enough the saving may more than offset these two items. For example, if you had a 16 percent, 30-year, $50,000 mortgage, the principal and interest would come to $672.50 per month. If the mortgage could be refinanced at 14 percent, the comparable monthly payment would be $592.50, a saving of $80 per month. Over just ten years, this would amount to a saving of $9,600. Whether it would pay to refinance would depend upon the size of the mortgage, the amount of decline in interest rates, and the dollar amount of closing costs. You would have to put a sharp pencil to your own case and figure it out.

Early Payoff Options; Be Careful

Recently some mortgage lenders have offered homeowners the option of paying off their mortgages early at rather attractive terms. These lenders offer substantial discounts to encourage early repayment to remove older, lower-yielding mortgages from their books. At first glance, both the lending institution and the homeowner would benefit from this. A mortgage made fifteen years ago and running over thirty years would yield about 7 percent as opposed to today's much higher rate. If the lender offered the homeowner a 15 percent discount on a $25,000 mortgage, the homeowner could pay it off completely for $21,250. He or she would have his or her home debt free and save $3,750 and all future interest. The lending institution, while it would be out $3,750, would have $21,250 to invest at today's higher market rate.

Everyone gains? Not really; the Internal Revenue Service has ruled that the $3,750 is ordinary income and fully taxable. While a bill has been introduced in Congress to amend the federal tax code to allow such early mortgage payoffs without taxing the imputed gain, until it passes do not do it.

Large Down Payment versus Small Down Payment

The size of the down payment individuals make is most often determined by the amount of cash available at the time they purchase the home. Assuming that one has a choice, however, the question is whether one should make a large or a small down payment. Note that even when persons are seeking FHA-insured or VA-guaranteed mortgages, they can, if they desire, make a down payment that is larger than the minimum. In any event, they should consider the following factors:

1. *The cost.* With a large down payment an individual may be able to reduce the time the loan will run before maturity, resulting in considerable interest savings. In addition, even if an individual places a large down payment on a property and the time to maturity remains the same, he or she will still save money on interest. For instance, a home buyer who borrows $50,000 at 12 percent interest for a twenty-five-year period will pay $107,986 in interest during the life of the mortgage. On the other hand, if the same borrower needed only a $40,000 mortgage for the same number of years at the same interest rate, interest payments would drop to $86,377—the person would save $21,609. In other words, the $50,000 mortgage will cost the borrower about 25 percent more than the smaller $40,000 loan. In addition, if a larger down payment is made, often the interest rate is reduced somewhat.

2. *Possibility of moving.* Each year nearly one out of every five American families moves to a new location. If there is a possibility that you are going to move, it is advisable to put as small a down payment on a home as possible when purchasing it. Many people consider that the competition between the sale of an older home and a newer home to a large degree rests with the size of the down payment, for it is easier to sell a home requiring a $5,000 down payment than it is to sell a home requiring a $20,000 down payment. Therefore, if one has a small equity in a home, it may be easier to sell if one has to move.

Interest on Mortgages

Both FHA-insured and the VA-guaranteed loans have maximum rates of interest set by law. Sometimes the rates you have to pay are at this maximum level, and sometimes they are below it. The interest rate on conventional loans fluctuates from time to time and also varies from one part of the nation to another, depending on the supply of money available for mortgage loans. Interest rates may also vary slightly with the amount of the down payment. If there is a substantial down payment, interest rates may be reduced from one-quarter to one-half of 1 percent from what the rate would have been with a lower down payment. Over the years, a quarter or a half of 1 percent difference can amount to a good deal of money, especially on a big mortgage. One half of 1 percent on $40,000, for example, is $200 per year.

For any given home, then, the size of the down payment will affect the size of the monthly payment as well as the total interest paid over the years (See Table 9–6). A $60,000 home is financed over twenty-five years at 12 percent with a large, a medium, and a relatively small down payment.

Table 9–6   Amortization of a $60,000 house with varying down payments over a twenty-five-year period at 12 percent interest

	A	B	C
House	$ 60,000.00	$ 60,000.00	$60,000.00
Down payment	10,000.00	20,000.00	30,000.00
Mortgage	50,000.00	40,000.00	30,000.00
Monthly payment (interest & principal only)	526.62	421.29	315.97
Total dollars paid	157,986.00	126,387.00	94,791.00
Total interest over the 25 years	107,986.00	86,387.00	64,791.00

Monthly Payments

The monthly payment varies not only with the amount of the mortgage but also with the length of the mortgage, the interest rate, and usually with the level of taxes and insurance premiums. A higher interest rate, all else being equal, tends to increase the monthly payments. The longer the number of years for which the mortgage runs, the lower the monthly payments with any given interest rate and dollar amount of the loan. However, if one reduces the monthly payments by increasing the length of the mortgage, one pays more total dollars in interest over the years.

When buying a house, the down payment is not always subject to variation; usually a person must have the $2,000 or $10,000 in cash, or whatever the figure is. The exception has been discussed previously. Buyers have some control over the length of the mortgage and, to a slight extent, over the interest rate if they shop around. If the house buyer wishes to save total interest costs, the person should select the amortization time period that makes the monthly payments as large as he or she can easily bear. On a $40,000, twenty-year, 12 percent mortgage, monthly payment (not including insurance and property taxes) would be $440.44. Total payments over the twenty years would be $105,705.60 and interest over the years would amount to $65,705.60. The same mortgage financed over twenty-five years would have monthly payments of $421.29 and total payments of $126,387, of which $86,387 would be for interest. By reducing monthly payments by $19.15, the buyer pays an additional $20,682 in interest over the years. This is not to say that mortgages should never be stretched out to reduce monthly payments. Sometimes such a step is necessary; one of the benefits of a thirty-year mortgage is that it reduces monthly payments to the point where people can buy homes who otherwise could not do so. One should make the decision with eyes open and not lengthen the mortgage just to reduce monthly payments. Table 9–7 shows the monthly payments necessary to amortize a given loan at 12 percent interest over a given number of years. It includes interest and reduction of principal only; taxes and insurance are omitted.

Table 9–7 Monthly payment necessary to amortize a loan at 12 percent

TERM AMOUNT	15 YEARS	16 YEARS	17 YEARS	18 YEARS	19 YEARS	20 YEARS	21 YEARS	22 YEARS	23 YEARS	24 YEARS	25 YEARS	26 YEARS	27 YEARS	28 YEARS	29 YEARS	30 YEARS	35 YEARS	40 YEARS
$22500	270.04	264.09	259.03	254.69	250.97	247.75	244.96	242.54	240.43	238.59	236.98	235.57	234.33	233.24	232.29	231.44	228.50	226.92
23000	276.04	269.96	264.78	260.35	256.54	253.25	250.41	247.93	245.77	243.89	242.25	240.80	239.54	238.43	237.45	236.59	233.58	231.96
23500	282.04	275.83	270.54	266.01	262.12	258.76	255.85	253.32	251.12	249.19	247.51	246.04	244.75	243.61	242.61	241.73	238.66	237.01
24000	288.05	281.70	276.30	271.67	267.70	264.27	261.29	258.71	256.46	254.50	252.78	251.27	249.95	248.79	247.77	246.87	243.74	242.05
24500	294.05	287.57	282.05	277.33	273.28	269.77	266.74	264.10	261.80	259.80	258.05	256.51	255.16	253.98	252.93	252.01	248.81	247.09
25000	300.05	293.44	287.81	282.99	278.85	275.28	272.18	269.49	267.15	265.10	263.31	261.74	260.37	259.16	258.09	257.16	253.89	252.13
25500	306.05	299.31	293.56	288.65	284.43	280.78	277.62	274.88	272.49	270.40	268.58	266.98	265.57	264.34	263.26	262.30	258.97	257.17
26000	312.05	305.17	299.32	294.31	290.01	286.29	283.07	280.27	277.83	275.70	273.84	272.21	270.78	269.52	268.42	267.44	264.05	262.22
26500	318.05	311.04	305.08	299.97	295.58	291.79	288.51	285.66	283.17	281.01	279.11	277.45	275.99	274.71	273.58	272.59	269.13	267.26
27000	324.05	316.91	310.83	305.63	301.16	297.30	293.95	291.05	288.52	286.31	284.38	282.68	281.20	279.89	278.74	277.73	274.20	272.30
27500	330.05	322.78	316.59	311.29	306.74	302.80	299.40	296.44	293.86	291.61	289.64	287.92	286.40	285.07	283.90	282.87	279.28	277.34
28000	336.05	328.65	322.35	316.95	312.31	308.31	304.84	301.83	299.20	296.91	294.91	293.15	291.61	290.26	289.07	288.02	284.36	282.39
28500	342.05	334.52	328.10	322.61	317.89	313.81	310.28	307.22	304.55	302.21	300.17	298.39	296.82	295.44	294.23	293.16	289.44	287.43
29000	348.05	340.39	333.86	328.27	323.47	319.32	315.73	312.61	309.89	307.52	305.44	303.62	302.03	300.62	299.39	298.30	294.51	292.47
29500	354.05	346.25	339.61	333.93	329.04	324.83	321.17	318.00	315.23	312.82	310.68	308.85	307.23	305.81	304.55	303.44	299.59	297.51
30000	360.06	352.12	345.37	339.59	334.62	330.33	326.61	323.39	320.57	318.12	315.97	314.09	312.44	310.99	309.71	308.59	304.67	302.56
30500	366.06	357.99	351.13	345.25	340.20	335.84	332.06	328.78	325.92	323.42	321.24	319.32	317.65	316.17	314.87	313.73	309.75	307.60
31000	372.06	363.86	356.88	350.91	345.78	341.34	337.50	334.17	331.26	328.72	326.51	324.56	322.85	321.36	320.04	318.87	314.83	312.64
31500	378.06	369.73	362.64	356.57	351.35	346.85	342.95	339.56	336.60	334.02	331.77	329.79	328.06	326.54	325.20	324.02	319.90	317.68
32000	384.06	375.60	368.39	362.23	356.93	352.35	348.39	344.95	341.95	339.33	337.04	335.03	333.27	331.72	330.36	329.16	324.98	322.73
32500	390.06	381.47	374.15	367.89	362.51	357.86	353.83	350.34	347.29	344.63	342.30	340.26	338.48	336.90	335.52	334.30	330.06	327.77
33000	396.06	387.33	379.91	373.55	368.09	363.36	359.28	355.72	352.63	349.93	347.57	345.50	343.68	342.09	340.68	339.45	335.14	332.81
33500	402.06	393.20	385.66	379.21	373.66	368.87	364.72	361.11	357.97	355.23	352.84	350.73	348.89	347.27	345.85	344.59	340.21	337.85
34000	408.06	399.07	391.42	384.87	379.24	374.37	370.16	366.50	363.32	360.53	358.10	355.97	354.10	352.45	351.01	349.73	345.29	342.90
34500	414.06	404.94	397.17	390.53	384.81	379.88	375.61	371.89	368.66	365.84	363.37	361.20	359.31	357.64	356.17	354.88	350.37	347.94
35000	420.06	410.81	402.93	396.19	390.39	385.38	381.05	377.28	374.02	371.14	368.63	366.44	364.51	362.82	361.33	360.02	355.45	352.98
36000	432.07	422.55	414.44	407.51	401.55	396.40	391.94	388.06	384.69	381.74	379.17	376.91	374.93	373.19	371.65	370.30	365.60	363.07
37000	444.07	434.28	425.95	418.83	412.70	407.41	402.82	398.84	395.37	392.35	389.70	387.38	385.34	383.55	381.98	380.59	375.76	373.15
38000	456.07	446.02	437.47	430.15	423.85	418.42	413.71	409.62	406.06	402.95	400.23	397.85	395.76	393.92	392.30	390.88	385.91	383.24
39000	468.07	457.76	448.98	441.47	435.01	429.43	424.60	420.40	416.75	413.55	410.76	408.31	406.17	404.28	402.63	401.16	396.07	393.32
40000	480.07	469.50	460.49	452.79	446.16	440.44	435.48	431.18	427.43	424.16	421.30	418.78	416.58	414.65	412.95	411.45	406.23	403.41
41000	492.07	481.23	472.00	464.10	457.31	451.45	446.37	441.96	438.12	434.76	431.83	429.25	427.00	425.02	423.27	421.73	416.38	413.49
42000	504.08	492.97	483.52	475.42	468.47	462.46	457.26	452.74	448.80	445.36	442.36	439.72	437.41	435.38	433.60	432.02	426.54	423.58
43000	516.08	504.71	495.03	486.74	479.62	473.47	468.15	463.52	459.49	455.97	452.89	450.19	447.83	445.75	443.92	442.31	436.69	433.66
44000	528.08	516.44	506.54	498.06	490.78	484.48	479.03	474.30	470.17	466.57	463.42	460.66	458.24	456.12	454.24	452.59	446.85	443.75
45000	540.08	528.18	518.06	509.38	501.93	495.49	489.92	485.08	480.86	477.18	473.96	471.13	468.66	466.48	464.57	462.88	457.00	453.83
46000	552.08	539.92	529.56	520.70	513.08	506.50	500.81	495.86	491.54	487.78	484.49	481.60	479.07	476.85	474.89	473.17	467.16	463.92
47000	564.08	551.66	541.08	531.92	524.24	517.52	511.69	506.64	502.23	498.38	495.02	492.07	489.49	487.21	485.21	483.45	477.31	474.00
48000	576.09	563.39	552.59	543.34	535.39	528.53	522.58	517.42	512.92	508.99	505.55	502.54	499.90	497.58	495.54	493.74	487.47	484.09
49000	588.09	575.13	564.10	554.66	546.55	539.54	533.47	528.20	523.60	519.59	516.09	512.91	510.32	507.95	505.86	504.02	497.63	494.17
50000	600.09	586.87	575.61	565.98	557.70	550.55	544.35	538.97	534.29	530.19	526.62	523.48	520.73	518.31	516.18	514.31	507.78	504.26
51000	612.09	598.61	587.12	577.30	568.85	561.56	555.24	549.75	544.97	540.80	537.15	533.95	531.14	528.68	526.51	524.60	517.94	514.34
52000	624.09	610.34	598.64	588.62	580.01	572.57	566.13	560.53	555.66	551.40	547.68	544.42	541.56	539.04	536.83	534.88	528.09	524.43
53000	636.09	622.08	610.15	599.94	591.16	583.58	577.02	571.31	566.34	562.01	558.22	554.89	551.97	549.41	547.16	545.17	538.25	534.51
54000	648.10	633.82	621.66	611.26	602.32	594.59	587.90	582.09	577.03	572.61	568.75	565.36	562.39	559.78	557.48	555.45	548.40	544.60
55000	660.10	645.55	633.17	622.58	613.47	605.60	598.79	592.87	587.72	583.21	579.28	575.83	572.80	570.14	567.80	565.74	558.56	554.68
56000	672.10	657.29	644.69	633.90	624.62	616.61	609.68	603.65	598.40	593.82	589.81	586.30	583.22	580.51	578.13	576.03	568.71	564.69
57000	684.10	669.03	656.20	645.22	635.78	627.62	620.56	614.43	609.09	604.42	600.34	596.77	593.63	590.87	588.45	586.31	578.87	574.85
58000	696.10	680.77	667.71	656.54	646.93	638.63	631.45	625.21	619.77	615.03	610.88	607.23	604.05	601.24	598.77	596.60	589.02	584.94
59000	708.10	692.50	679.22	667.86	658.08	649.65	642.34	635.99	630.46	625.63	621.41	617.70	614.46	611.61	609.10	606.88	599.18	595.02
60000	720.11	704.24	690.73	679.18	669.24	660.66	653.22	646.77	641.14	636.23	631.94	628.17	624.87	621.97	619.42	617.17	609.34	605.11
61000	732.11	715.98	702.25	690.50	680.39	671.67	664.11	657.55	651.83	646.84	642.47	638.64	635.29	632.34	629.74	627.46	619.49	615.19
62000	744.11	727.71	713.76	701.81	691.55	682.68	675.00	668.33	662.52	657.44	653.01	649.11	645.70	642.71	640.07	637.74	629.65	625.28
63000	756.11	739.45	725.28	713.13	702.70	693.69	685.89	679.11	673.20	668.04	663.54	659.58	656.12	653.07	650.39	648.03	639.80	635.36
64000	768.11	751.19	736.73	724.45	713.85	704.70	696.77	689.89	683.89	678.65	674.07	670.05	666.53	663.44	660.72	658.32	649.96	645.45
65000	780.11	762.93	748.29	735.77	725.01	715.71	707.66	700.67	694.57	689.25	684.60	680.52	676.95	673.80	671.04	668.60	660.11	655.53
67500	810.12	792.27	777.08	764.07	752.89	743.24	734.88	727.61	721.29	715.76	710.93	706.70	702.98	699.72	696.85	694.32	685.50	680.74
70000	840.12	821.61	805.86	792.37	780.78	770.76	762.09	754.56	748.01	742.27	737.26	732.87	729.02	725.63	722.66	720.03	710.89	705.96
72500	870.13	850.96	834.64	820.67	808.66	798.29	789.31	781.51	774.71	768.78	763.59	759.04	754.86	751.55	748.47	745.75	736.28	731.17
75000	900.13	880.30	863.42	848.97	836.55	825.82	816.53	808.46	801.43	795.29	789.92	785.22	781.09	777.47	774.27	771.46	761.67	756.38
80000	960.14	938.99	921.38	905.57	892.32	880.87	870.96	862.36	854.86	848.31	842.59	837.56	833.16	829.30	825.89	822.89	812.45	806.81
85000	1020.15	997.67	978.54	962.16	948.09	935.93	925.40	916.25	908.29	901.33	895.25	889.91	885.24	881.13	877.51	874.32	863.22	857.23
90000	1080.16	1056.36	1036.10	1018.76	1003.86	990.98	979.83	970.15	961.71	954.35	947.91	942.26	937.31	932.96	929.13	925.75	914.00	907.66
95000	1140.16	1115.04	1093.66	1075.36	1059.62	1046.04	1034.27	1024.05	1015.14	1007.37	1000.57	994.61	989.38	984.79	980.75	977.18	964.78	958.08
100000	1200.17	1173.73	1151.22	1131.96	1115.39	1101.09	1088.70	1077.94	1068.57	1060.38	1053.23	1046.95	1041.45	1036.62	1032.36	1028.61	1015.56	1008.51

Source: Austin Savings and Loan Association.

Monthly payments can include four items: interest, reduction of principal, insurance premiums, and local property taxes. Nearly all lenders will insist that insurance to protect the house against loss due to fire or other physical damage be obtained. Even if the lending institution did not demand it, no property owner should be without fire insurance. In addition to fire insurance, sometimes a life insurance policy is bought on the mortgage so that if the borrower dies before paying off the mortgage, the insurance company will pay it.

Although property taxes vary from community to community, they must be paid annually or semiannually in most cases. Since they usually run to several hundred dollars or more, a person who does not budget for them will have difficulty paying them. Many lending institutions include one-twelfth of the annual tax liability and add it to the monthly payments. These funds then go into a special account called the escrow account, which is used by the institution to pay the taxes when due. It may do the same with insurance premiums (both mortgage credit life insurance and hazard insurance premiums).

Some people object to these monthly payments for insurance and property taxes on the ground that they are paying in advance, and the financial institution has the use of their money for a time before it pays the bills. This is the same as an interest-free loan to the bank. However, the lending institution is providing a real service. It is doing your budgeting, and it also takes care of the paperwork involved in keeping the records and paying the taxes and insurance premiums. If you object to this advance payment, you should bargain with the lending institution and try to keep it out of your monthly payments. If the down payment is fairly large, you can probably keep the life insurance and the tax payments out, but it is more difficult to avoid including fire insurance premiums, which are, however, relatively small.

If you succeed in keeping some of the above items out of the monthly payments, you should do your own budgeting and set aside one-twelfth of the sum each month. Then not only will you be sure of having the funds when they are due, but you can put them in a savings account and receive interest perhaps from the very bank that has your mortgage.

INNOVATIVE MORTGAGES

In recent years, primarily because of very high interest rates but also because of a shortage of mortgage money, new ways of financing home ownership have been developed. These are referred to as the "new" or "innovative" mortgages. Even though there always have been (and still are) some long-term fixed-rate mortgages available (the mortgages discussed above), few would-be homeowners have been willing to lock themselves in at 18 percent interest for 30 years. Moreover, fewer would-be homeowners could qualify because high interest rates meant high monthly payments, which many people could not afford. Thus the real estate industry developed innovative mortgages. There may be dozens of such different mortgages, some with only slight variation from others, but they may be grouped into a number of general categories. Some of these mortgages, however, might be dangerous to your financial health, and you should stay away from them. We will note these pitfalls.

The Variable Rate Mortgage

The variable rate mortgage (VRM) is also referred to as the "adjustable mortgage" (ARM). With variable interest mortgages, the rate can be adjusted every six months or so, but only if certain other rates such as marketable U.S. government (or corporate) bond rates change. Normally there is a limit (usually two or three percent) on the overall upward or downward movement during the life of the mortgage. There are three methods of adjusting the variable interest rate: The first is to change the monthly payment with the maturity remaining constant. The second is to change the length of the maturity with the monthly payment remaining constant. The third is a combination of the first two.

The difficulty in using a variable rate is that when rates are high the borrower may be willing to sign a variable contract and hope that rates come down, but the lending institution is reluctant to do so. During times when rates are low, the reverse is the case: the lender favors variable rates, the borrower does not. Another problem with the VRM is that in some states there is no limit to how high rates may go. In addition, if the rates are adjusted to the extent that the life of the mortgage is lengthened, you really have a negatively amortizing mortgage which would in theory never be paid off. Sometimes the VRM is written so that when interest rates are escalated, the monthly payment stays the same and the principal is reduced, but only for, say, three or five years. After this time, the original amortization schedule returns. When this is so, it may require a large increase in the monthly payment.

Renegotiable Mortgages

A modification of the variable interest rate mortgage is the renegotiable mortgage, sometimes called the rollover mortgage. Under it, interest rates are fixed but renegotiated every three, four, or five years as the case may be. There would be a negotiated rate change as the market changed, but it would not be an automatic adjustment tied to some money market indicator. Under this mortgage the lender is obliged to renegotiate and renew the mortgage; he cannot cancel it. The borrower, on the other hand, may pull out at renewal time and get a new mortgage elsewhere. These new renegotiable mortgages were approved by federal regulatory agencies in April 1980, and all federally chartered savings and loan associations are now permitted to make them. The maximum interest rate adjustment (either up or down) is 1/2 of 1 percent per year for a total of 2 1/2 percent on a 5-year renegotiable.

In Canada renegotiable mortgages are much more common than in the

U.S. They are not an innovation, however. Prior to the 1930s this is how mortgages were typically financed.

The Rollover Mortgage

This is a variation of the renegotiable mortgage. It is generally written for five years, and it differs from the renegotiable in that when it comes due, the lender is not obliged to renew it. These are also sometimes referred to as "balloon" mortgages, because monthly payments are made for, say, five years, after which time the unpaid remainder is due in one large payment.

The Wrap-around Mortgage

Another way of financing a home if the buyer does not have enough funds to assume an existing mortgage is to use the wrap-around mortgage, often done if the seller is willing and able to finance the sale and assume the wrap-around mortgage; the new mortgage literally wraps around the old mortgage. This technique works particularly well if the existing mortgage is small. For example, suppose a seller has an older home for sale for $100,000 with only a $20,000 mortgage left on it. If the buyer has $40,000, he could pay that as a down payment, and the seller could take a $60,000 mortgage which includes (wraps around) the $20,000 due on the original. The seller would then continue to pay off the original $20,000 mortgage, and the buyer would need worry only about the new $60,000 one.

In some cases, however, the wrap-around mortgage may result in a violation of the usury laws. Consider the following situation. A house which has a $40,000 mortgage at 8 percent is sold for $100,000. The buyer pays $20,000 down and signs a mortgage of $80,000 with the seller at 12 percent and the seller continues paying off the old 8 percent $40,000 mortgage. This yields the seller about $9,600 the first year on the $80,000 mortgage but after paying 8 percent on the $40,000 (which amounts to about $3,200) the net return is $6,400. What percentage return is this to the seller? $6,400 is 8 percent of $80,000. But the seller only advanced $40,000, and $6,400 is 16 percent of $40,000; some attorneys feel that is what the courts may hold to be the true interest rate in such a case. Individuals are still subject to usury laws, which may be violated even though the federal government nullified usury laws for institutional lenders in 1980. Check this out carefully before you finance any mortgage, wrap-arounds or other types.

Wrap-arounds may also be illegal in some cases. Only if the mortgage is assumable or if the institution holding the original mortgage gives its permission is a wrap-around possible. Older mortgages often are assumable; but in the last seven or eight years, more and more insitutions have placed due-on-sale clauses in their loan contracts, and in such a case wrap-arounds are not possible.

The Blended Mortgage

If a wrap-around is not possible, you might be able to negotiate a blended mortgage. In the above wrap-around case, for example, if it had not been legal, the home might not have sold if the entire mortgage of $80,000 had to be financed at a higher rate. To get the old 8 percent loan off the books, many institutions will negotiate a new one at a favorable rate. The above $80,000 new mortgage could be an average of the $40,000 at 8 percent and $40,000 at a bit above the current market rate. This would make the blend somewhat below the market rate.

The Graduated Payment Mortgage (GPM)

Under this mortgage the monthly payments start out substantially below what they should be but then increase by $3 or $4 per month for a number of years. This increase usually levels off after five or ten, or sometimes even fifteen years. Since some of the principal is repaid later than under a straight fixed mortgage, the homeowner pays more interest. However, such a mortgage permits more young and lower-income people to qualify for home ownership, if their income is expected to rise in the near future. This mortgage may also have variable interest built into it. If it does, then how much monthly payments increase per month in the future is also in part determined by how much interest rates rise in the future. It is conceivable that during the first few years there could be negative amortization (increase in the principal borrowed) if interest rates rise rapidly enough.

The Buy-Down Mortgage

The buy-down mortgage is a misnomer, but it is a means of reducing the interest rate from, say, 13 percent to 10 percent. In reality, the buyer pays a lump sum (usually at closing) in return for which the lender will reduce the interest rate. This amounts to prepaying some of the interest and, upon closer examination, is not the best arrangement for the buyer. For example, a $50,000 mortgage at 13 percent over 30 years requires a $553.10 per month amortization payment. However, if the buyer pays an additional $4,115.16 at closing, the interest rate is reduced to 10 percent and the monthly amortization payment drops to $438.79. The buy-down was calculated by taking the difference between the two monthly payments ($553.10 − $438.79 = $114.31) and multiplying it by 36. The buy-down rate is therefore effective for three years, after which time the rate escalates to 13 percent or is renegotiated at the then market rate. The result may be that a buyer who did not qualify for a loan previously now does. Psychologically it may also be beneficial for the buyer to obtain 10 percent financing. In reality, however, it might have been better for the buyer to make a larger down payment, and finance a smaller principal sum at a higher rate. If the buyer does not have the required buy-down charges, the seller may provide it by means of a second mortgage. Many builders do this.

Equity Build-Up Mortgage (EBM); Shared Appreciation Mortgage (SAM)

More recently the equity build-up sharing mortgage has been developed. These are also called *shared appreciation mortgages* (SAM), and *shared equity mortgages* (SEM). With these, when the homeowner sells his home, a portion (say 20–25 percent) of the capital gain attributable to inflation is remitted to the mortgagee.

The Graduated Equity Mortgage (GEM)

The graduated equity mortgage (GEM) is not really an innovative mortgage designed to help people who otherwise could not purchase a home. Rather, it starts out as a straight conventional 30-year mortgage with a proviso that monthly payments will be escalated by a predetermined amount each month. This increased payment is applied entirely to the reduction of principal. The entire 30-year mortgage is then paid off over 13, 14, or 15 years rather than 30, saving a great deal of interest. This type of mortgage is fine for someone whose income is rising and who can afford the escalating monthly payments. This mortgage is no different than the traditional old-fashioned fixed 30-year mortgage which permits early repayments, except that a predetermined schedule of early repayment is worked out.

The Inflation-Indexed Mortgage

In this type the monthly payment is adjusted for inflation, fine for the person who is certain that his income will keep up with or do better than inflation. Since interest rates seem to move with inflation, real (adjusted for inflation) interest rates can be stabilized. A market interest rate is agreed upon at the time of consummation of the loan. Monthly payments are thereafter adjusted (up or down) so that the real interest rate is always a given amount (say 4 percent) above the rate of inflation.

Seller-Financed Mortgages

These mortgage loans are extended by the seller to the buyer, usually at lower than the going market rate, in order to expedite the sale of the home. These are sometimes called *purchase money loans*. Often these are second mortgages for five or ten years. Moreover, if they are for five years, they may have a final balloon payment. If this is the case, you should be certain that there is also a provision which will obligate the lender to refinance the balloon.

Reverse Mortgages

Older people whose mortgage is paid off and who wish to retire may sign a reverse mortgage whereby they sell their home back to a lending institution. Instead of making a monthly payment, they receive one. As time passes they own a smaller and smaller portion of their home; a larger and larger mortgage debt is built up on it again, as their equity in it declines. Usually only a portion of the value of the house (about 50 to 75 percent) can be reverse-mortgaged this way. While this can provide retirement income for a time, it is risky because after a number of years if the retirees are still living, they will have to sell their home to pay off the debt. Or they can try to refinance it and pay off another regular mortgage once again. However, if they were in such financial difficulty they had to reverse-mortgage their home, they probably could not now pay off a regular mortgage. If you need to sell your home to obtain retirement income, sell it outright and move into a smaller one, or into an apartment, and invest the difference.

Some Dangers of Innovative Mortgages

The major danger of innovative mortgages is that interest rates may escalate wildly. In the case of a fixed mortgage at least you know what the cost is—and will remain. To be sure, ceilings may be placed on the amount of interest escalation, but this is not always done. In the case of a variable rate mortgage, there is also the problem of what the rate should be tied to, i.e., what determines when rates are to rise. Probably the best indicator is the long-term U.S. government bond rate. The variable mortgage rate could be 1.5 or 2 points above the government rate. If a mortgage has a balloon on it and no guaranteed refinancing provision, the person may be in serious difficulty when it comes due.

The graduated payment mortgage is fine if the person's salary rises as expected, but not if it doesn't. The reverse mortgage is fraught with danger. This is not to say you should never use innovative mortgages; only go into such an arrangement with your eyes open, and be careful. Don't expect continued rise in home prices to bail you out if you get into difficulty. Rather, plan ahead, and don't get into difficulty.

OTHER THINGS TO KNOW ABOUT HOME OWNERSHIP

When buying something as expensive as a home, you should be alert to a number of other factors—for example, certain hidden costs you might face and how to go about making an offer on a home.

Points

Sometimes points are used when a loan is made. Generally, points are added during periods of tight money, and the tighter the money supply the greater the number of points added. A point is one percentage point of the mortgage loan and, technically speaking, is paid by the seller of the home. However, sometimes points are shifted to the buyer. On a $40,000 mortgage loan upon which 2 points are assessed, this amounts to $800. In theory, this sum is withheld from the amount the lending institution gives the seller. However, being aware that this is going to happen, the seller will attempt to raise the price of the house above its fair market value by this amount. While this price escalation is not always successful, if market conditions are tight and upward price pressures on homes exist, the seller may be successful in shifting this "point cost" to the buyer, at least in part. The lending institution receives this "points" sum, and it is a means of increasing interest rates the first year.

If an institution makes a $40,000 loan on a $50,000 house in which the seller has a $10,000 equity, and assesses 2 points, then the institution advances the seller only $9,200. The buyer assumes a $40,000 mortgage at 12 percent, but the lender really receives 14 percent return the first year.

Making an Offer on a House; Earnest Money

When a seller offers a house, he or she or the real estate agent draws up a sales contract. This piece of paper spells out the terms of the sale. It will describe the house, list the asking price and note the present mortgage. By signing this contract a prospective purchaser agrees to buy the house. However, usually the prospective buyer will make a counter offer by changing the terms somewhat, perhaps lowering the price.

To ascertain whether or not the offering price is reasonably close to the true market value, ask your realtor, who can give you a fairly good answer. Also check the selling price (not the offered price) of other comparable homes that have been sold recently. Many sellers will price their house above the realistic market value in the hope that they will find a naive person who will pay it. Often sellers will come down from their offering price. You can negotiate with the seller but only indirectly through the realtor. You should also find out from your realtor whether selling prices generally have been close to asking prices. How to ascertain the realistic market value of a house is discussed earlier in this chapter under "How Much Is a Home Worth?"

When you finally decide what you are willing to pay, you should make a counteroffer. This counteroffer is signed by the prospective buyer and conveyed to the seller by the realtor with a down payment (usually $500 to $1,000, depending on the price of the house) called earnest money. There may be several counteroffers between the buyer and seller; this is how you negotiate over the price. The buyer must sign any counteroffer he or she makes and present earnest money with it. If the seller signs the buyer's counteroffer, it is a binding deal.

In some states this earnest money goes to the seller immediately and in others it goes into an escrow account until the transaction is closed. In any event, when both buyer and seller have signed the contract, it is binding and either can force the other to comply. However, in practice the seller can nearly always back out by returning the earnest money, because it would require a lawsuit to force compliance. A buyer who wanted to back out, however, would generally lose the earnest money. That is why the offer (sales contract) must carefully spell out all the conditions desired by both parties. For example, the buy offer will always be a conditional offer and effective only if satisfactory financing can be arranged. An earnest money contract is shown in Figure 9–3. Note that under the heading "special conditions," a number of provisions have been written into the contract. This is more often done on older homes than on new homes.

Closing Costs

When the buyer and seller of a house have reached an agreement, they and the realtors involved get together to close the deal and sign the necessary papers. A representative of the lending institution also attends the closing which indeed may be held at the office of the lending institution. It is often at the closing that the surprised buyer first becomes aware that closing costs are involved. On a $60,000 house, there may be additional hidden closing fees of from $500 to $1,500. The question is, what do these costs consist of? The totals generally vary with the section of the country in which the loan is being made. Generally, however, they include the following:

1. Title insurance
2. Credit reports
3. Attorney's fees
4. Origination fee
5. Fire and other hazard insurance reserve
6. Tax reserve
7. Survey
8. Recording fee

Title insurance costs vary depending on the amount of the loan and the company with which the policy is placed. Fire insurance rates, credit reports, and attorney's fees all vary somewhat regionally. Furthermore, the closing costs differ depending on whether the loan is a conventional mortgage, a VA-guaranteed mortgage, or an FHA-insured mortgage; in general the same items are included.

In purchasing as important and expensive an item as a home, it is worthwhile for the buyer to engage the services of an attorney. The $100 or $150 cost is usually well spent. When entering into a legal agreement, it is best to have an expert explain all of the fine print. This is over and above the attorney's fees shown on the closing costs statement. The latter are for the fees of the lender's attorney who draws up the papers.

In past years it was also necessary to have a title search, to confirm the fact that the legal title of the property was vested in the seller and that he or she could legally transfer it to you. Presently most people buy title insurance

EARNEST MONEY**CONTRACT**

REALTOR®

RECEIVED OF ____William Jones_____ in the form of _check_ ,

the sum of ____FIVE HUNDRED AND NO/100----------------------- $500.00____

being earnest money deposited with the undersigned to be held by the undersigned in escrow in accordance with the terms and conditions stipulated herein.

The depositor, hereinafter called PURCHASER, agrees to purchase the following described real estate from SELLER, together with all improvements thereon in present physical condition unless otherwise specified herein, in Travis County, Texas:

Locally known as No.____2705 Ashdale_____

Property description: Lot ___17_____ Block_____

Addition:____Allandale Place, Section 1_____

____Austin, Texas_____

Total Price $ __40,000___to be paid by PURCHASER as follows: $ _500.00___ as earnest money which is hereby deposited with ___Don's Realty_____ then $_7,500____ cash on delivery of deed as herein provided, and

contingent upon Purchaser obtaining a loan at a Financial Institution in the amount

of $32,000

THE SAID EXECUTED note or notes to be secured by Vender's Lien and Deed of Trust, with the usual covenants as to taxes, Insurance, and default.

PRORATIONS: SELLER shall furnish tax certificates showing all taxes paid through the year 19_78_; taxes for the current year, current rents if any, and interest if any to be prorated as of date of delivery of deed.

TITLE EVIDENCE: SELLER agrees, at his option and expense, to furnish to PURCHASER an owner's title policy; or a complete abstract of title and to place order for same within ____10____ days from date _herein_.

CONTRACT UNDER TITLE EVIDENCE: If abstract is furnished, PURCHASER agrees within _not/app._ days from the receipt of said abstract either to accept the title as shown by said abstract or to return same to the SELLER with the written objections to the title. If the abstract is not returned to the SELLER with the written objections noted within the time specified, it shall be construed as an acceptance of said title. _as possible_

SELLER AND PURCHASER agree to consummate this sale within _as soon/_ days after title company, in event of title policy, or attorney, in event of abstract, approves the title, unless otherwise agreed herein. In the event abstract is furnished and valid objections to title are made, SELLER shall have _not/app_ days after written notice to remove such objections or furnish a policy of title insurance.

PURCHASER acknowledges that he has been advised that he should have the abstract examined by his attorney if furnished an abstract or in the alternative he should be furnished with or should obtain a policy of title insurance. Any restrictions, zoning ordinances, or conditions imposed by any addition, or subdivision, of which this property is a part, shall not be recited as objections to this title.

WARRANTY DEED: SELLER agrees, when any title defects have been cured, to deliver a General Warranty Deed, properly executed, conveying said property free and clear of all liens whatsoever except as herein provided, to said PURCHASER, or assigns; PURCHASER shall then and there pay the balance, if any, of said cash payment, and shall execute the note or notes and deed of trust herein provided for.

POSSESSION: SELLER agrees to give possession at time sale is consummated unless otherwise specified herein.

BREACH OF CONDITIONS: IF SELLER FAILS to comply with any of the above requirements, within the time specified, the earnest money may, at option of PURCHASER, be returned to PURCHASER UPON RETURN AND CANCELLATION of this receipt or PURCHASER may enforce specific performance. IF PURCHASER FAILS to consummate this purchase as specified for any reason except title defects or other reasons as set forth herein, SELLER shall have the right to retain said cash deposit as liquidated damages for the breach of these conditions or SELLER may enforce specific performance.

AGENT'S COMMISSION: It is agreed that ____Don's Realty_____of Austin, Texas, is the procuring cause of this sale and by acceptance of these conditions, SELLER promises to pay to said agent a commission of ___6%____of the sale price above set out (on the consummation of the sale or upon breach thereof.) If the PURCHASER fails to consummate this purchase as specified for any reason except title defects or other reasons as set forth herein, it is agreed that SELLER shall pay to agent one-half of the earnest money as his commission in such instance, provided, however, that agent's one-half shall never exceed ___6____% of the total sale price above stated. By SELLER'S signature to this contract, SELLER affirms Agent's right to sell the above described property.

SPECIAL CONDITIONS: Purchaser to have access to property for cleaning purposes prior to closing, effective upon date of agreeable contract. All plumbing, electrical, heating and cooling systems, appliances to be in good working order at time of closing. Purchaser to have opportunity to inspect same at Purchaser's convenience prior to closing. Seller to provide termite-free inspection certificate dated no earlier than 10 days prior to closing. Existing drapes, curtains, rods, carpet, refrigerator to remain. Patio door to be repaired to close and lock property.

ENTIRE AGREEMENT: This Contract contains the entire agreement. There are no other agreements, oral or written, and the terms of this contract can be amended only by written agreement signed by all parties hereto, and by reference made a part hereof. The terms and conditions shall not be effective unless accepted by both PURCHASER and SELLER.

EXECUTED IN _quadruplicate_ this _19_ day of _August_ , 19_78_ , at Austin, Travis County, Texas.

By_____

Escrow agent

Accepted:_____   Accepted:_____

Seller   Purchaser

Accepted:_____   Accepted:_____

Seller   Purchaser

Figure 9–3 **Earnest money contract.** (*Source:* Courtesy of the Austin Board of Realtors, Inc.)

F. 2853-01 R 7/76		Form Approved OMB No. 63-R-1501	Page 1

A.	B. TYPE OF LOAN

	1. ☐ FHA 2. ☐ FMHA 3. ☐ CONV. UNINS.
	4. ☐ VA 5. ☒ CONV. INS.

6. File Number:	7. Loan Number:
GF-81978	2323

SETTLEMENT STATEMENT
U.S. DEPARTMENT OF HOUSING AND URBAN DEVELOPMENT

8. Mortgage Insurance Case Number:
441 45 9090

C. NOTE: *This form is furnished to give you a statement of actual settlement costs. Amounts paid to and by the settlement agent are shown. Items marked "(p.o.c.)" were paid outside the closing; they are shown here for informational purposes and are not included in the totals.*

D. NAME OF BORROWER:	Bobby Buyer and wife, Betty Buyer
ADDRESS:	Austin, Texas

E. NAME OF SELLER:	Joe Doe and wife, Jane Doe
ADDRESS:	Austin, Texas

F. NAME OF LENDER:	XYZ Mortgage Company
ADDRESS:	Austin, Texas

G. PROPERTY LOCATION:	111 Express Avenue
	Austin, Texas

H. SETTLEMENT AGENT:	Gracy Title Company	I. SETTLEMENT DATE:
ADDRESS:	Austin, Texas	
PLACE OF SETTLEMENT:	Gracy Title Company	
ADDRESS:	Austin, Texas	2/1/83

J. SUMMARY OF BORROWER'S TRANSACTION		K. SUMMARY OF SELLER'S TRANSACTION	
100. GROSS AMOUNT DUE FROM BORROWER:		*400. GROSS AMOUNT DUE TO SELLER:*	
101. Contract sales price	100,000.00	401. Contract sales price	100,000.00
102. Personal property		402. Personal property	
103. Settlement charges to borrower *(line 1400)*	4,520.43	403.	
104.		404.	
105.		405.	
Adjustments for items paid by seller in advance		*Adjustments for items paid by seller in advance*	
106. City/town taxes to		406. City/town taxes to	
107. County taxes to		407. County taxes to	
108. Assessments to		408. Assessments to	
109.		409.	
110.		410.	
111.		411.	
112.		412.	
120. GROSS AMOUNT DUE FROM BORROWER	104,520.43	420. GROSS AMOUNT DUE TO SELLER	100,000.00
200. AMOUNTS PAID BY OR IN BEHALF OF BORROWER:		*500. REDUCTIONS IN AMOUNT DUE TO SELLER:*	
201. Deposit or earnest money	500.00	501. Excess deposit *(see instructions)*	
202. Principal amount of new loan(s)	95000.00	502. Settlement charges to seller *(line 1400)*	7,744.00
203. Existing loan(s) taken subject to		503. Existing loan(s) taken subject to	
204.		504. Payoff of first mortgage loan	54,000.00
205.		505. Payoff of second mortgage loan	
206.		506.	
207.		507.	
208.		508.	
209.		509.	
Adjustments for items unpaid by seller		*Adjustments for items unpaid by seller*	
210. City/town taxes to		510. City/town taxes to	
211. County taxes to		511. County taxes to	
212. Assessments to		512. Assessments to	
213.		513. Tax proration from	83.33
214. Tax proration from	to loan	514. 1/1/83 to 2/1/83	
215. 1/1/83 to 2/1/83	reserves	515.	
216.		516.	
217.		517.	
218.		518.	
219.		519.	
220. TOTAL PAID BY/FOR BORROWER	95,500.00	520. TOTAL REDUCTIONS AMOUNT DUE SELLER	61,827.33
300. CASH AT SETTLEMENT FROM/TO BORROWER		*600. CASH AT SETTLEMENT TO/FROM SELLER*	
301. Gross amount due from borrower *(line 120)*	104,520.43	601. Gross amount due to seller *(line 420)*	100,000.00
302. Less amounts paid by/for borrower *(line 220)*	(95,500.00)	602. Less reductions in amount due seller *(line 520)*	(61,827.33)
303. CASH (☒ FROM) (☐ TO) BORROWER	9,020.43	603. CASH (☒ TO) (☐ FROM) SELLER	31,172.67

Figure 9–4 Disclosure settlement statement. (*Source:* Courtesy of Stewart Title.)

Page 2

L. SETTLEMENT CHARGES

	PAID FROM BORROWER'S FUNDS AT SETTLEMENT	PAID FROM SELLER'S FUNDS AT SETTLEMENT
700. TOTAL SALES/BROKER'S COMMISSION based on price $100,000.00 @ 6% = 6,000.00		
Division of Commission (line 700) as follows:		
701. $2,000.00 to Sunshine Brokers		
702. $4,000.00 to Moonshine Brokers		
703. Commission paid at Settlement (Money retained by broker applied to commission $ 500.00)		6,000.00
704. Other sales agent charges		
705. Additional commission		
800. ITEMS PAYABLE IN CONNECTION WITH LOAN		
801. Loan Origination Fee 1 %	950.00	
802. Loan Discount 1 %		950.00
803. Appraisal Fee to A.A. Appraisers	250.00	
804. Credit Report to C.C. Credit	50.00	
805. Lender's Inspection Fee to FNMA	75.00	
806. Mortgage Insurance Application Fee to		
807. Assumption Fee		
808. photos	20.00	
809. Tax research fee	27.50	
810. amortization schedule	5.00	
811.		
900. ITEMS REQUIRED BY LENDER TO BE PAID IN ADVANCE		
901. Interest from 2/1/82 to 3/1/82 @ $35.63 /day	1068.75	
902. Mortgage Insurance Premium for 12 months to	950.00	
903. Hazard Insurance Premium for 1 years to I.I. Insurance Co.	581.00	
904. years to		
905.		
1000. RESERVES DEPOSITED WITH LENDER		
1001. Hazard insurance 2 month @ $48.42 per month	96.84	
1002. Mortgage insurance 1 month @ $22.00 per month	22.00	
1003. City property taxes 1 month @ $27.78 per month	27.78	
1004. County property taxes 1 month @ $13.89 per month	13.89	
1005. Annual assessments month @ $ per month		
1006. School 1 month @ $41.67 per month	41.67	
1007. month @ $ per month		
1008. month @ $ per month		
1100. TITLE CHARGES		
1101. Settlement or closing fee to		
1102. Abstract or title search to		
1103. Title examination to		
1104. Title insurance binder to		
1105. Document preparation to	100.00	75.00
1106. Notary fees to		
1107. Attorney's fee to		
(includes above items numbers:		
1108. Title insurance to Gracy Title Company	50.00	650.00
(includes above items numbers:		
1109. Lender's coverage $95,000.00		
1110. Owner's coverage $100,000.00		
1111. escrow fee	25.00	25.00
1112. Tax certificates		4.00
1113.		
1200. GOVERNMENT RECORDING AND TRANSFER CHARGES		
1201. Recording fees: Deed $7.00 ; Mortgage $9.00 ; Release $	16.00	5.00
1202. City/county tax/stamps: Deed $; Mortgage $		
1203. State tax/stamps: Deed $; Mortgage $		
1204.		
1205.		
1300. ADDITIONAL SETTLEMENT CHARGES		
1301. Survey to M.R. Surveyor	150.00	
1302. Pest inspection to P.E. Pest Control		35.00
1303.		
1304.		
1305.		
1306.		
1307.		
1400. TOTAL SETTLEMENT CHARGES (enter on lines 103, Section J and 502, Section K)	4,520.43	7,744.00

The above settlement statement is hereby approved, the disbursements indicated are authorized, and settlement may be completed by settlement agent.

Borrower _____   Seller _____

_____   _____

This form provided by CHICAGO TITLE INSURANCE COMPANY   HUD-1 Rev. (5/76)

Figure 9–4 (continued)

rather than have their attorney conduct such a search. This insurance policy protects the buyer against any loss because of a defect in the title. While this is typically paid for by the seller, sometimes the buyer also has to buy title insurance. In this latter case it is to protect the lender; that purchased by the seller protects only the buyer.

Another item under closing costs consists of what is called the origination fee (sometimes called finder's fee) or lender's fee. This is generally 1 percent of the mortgage, and if one is buying from a builder or a real estate broker it is supposedly a fee he or she receives for making the arrangements for the loan. Even if one is dealing directly with a financial institution, the fee is often charged. It is essentially then a means to increase the return to the broker, or the financial institution. Again conditions vary from one section of the country to another, but generally the only way to avoid paying the finder's fee is to make the arrangement for the loan yourself with a commercial bank. Commercial banks are not as liberal as other lenders with respect to whom they will make a loan, but they are less likely to charge a finder's fee.

Other typical costs are appraiser's fees, credit reports, the cost of hiring a surveyor to survey the property and ascertain its exact boundaries, and a fee for an amortization table. There may or may not be a charge for these. Sometimes hazard insurance is shown twice on a closing statement, once for the first year's premiums, which must be paid in advance, and again for a one-or two-month premium, which goes into an escrow account for next year's premiums. Property taxes must also be provided for. If it is an existing house, there may be extra funds in a tax escrow account which you will have to buy. If it is a new house, a tax payment may or may not be required; sometimes a one- or two-month tax payment is required at closing, sometimes not.

We discussed points above. They are assessed at closing but are assessed to the seller. All other closing costs except the premium on the title insurance, as discussed above, are paid by the buyer. Figure 9–4 shows a disclosure settlement statement. These are not standard forms; each is a sample and many variations exist.

QUESTIONS FOR REVIEW

1. Discuss the reasons for home ownership.
2. Explain in detail the current tax advantage of home ownership.
3. What is involved when persons declare their home a homestead?
4. Discuss the merits of renting or owning a home.
5. Discuss the relative merits of buying a new as opposed to an older house.
6. Why is it important to give some consideration to buying an energy-efficient home?
7. What factors should be looked into prior to purchase of a home?
8. What problems are involved in building a house from the ground up?

9. Discuss the advantages and disadvantages of buying a condominium.
10. Discuss co-op housing.
11. How can a home's value be ascertained?
12. Discuss the FHA mortgage.
13. How is a second mortgage different from a first mortgage? Does the second mortgage owner assume more risk than the first?
14. How is a home mortgage loan amortized?
15. When does it pay to refinance a mortgage?
16. What is a penalty clause in a mortgage?
17. Why is the size of the down payment on a house important?
18. How does the variable interest rate mortgage work?
19. How does the wrap-around mortgage work?
20. What is the buy-down mortgage?
21. What is earnest money?
22. What are closing costs?

CASES

1. Ernie and Eloise Johansen are presently living in an unfurnished apartment renting for $400.00 per month. They have saved $5,000, which they think is enough for a down payment on a $50,000 home. One lending agency has told them it will give them a twenty-year mortgage for $45,000 at 12 percent. Another financial institution has offered them a loan at 11 percent for twenty years if they can raise another $5,000. They can borrow $5,000 on their life insurance policy at 6 percent. Which offer should they take? What will be the total interest charges in both cases? They believe they can pay back the loan on their insurance over a two-year period.

2. Timothy and Martha Hennessey have found a home selling for $60,500 which they would like to buy. They have discovered they could finance it with a 10 percent down FHA loan for thirty years at 11.5 percent. Under these conditions what would be their monthly payments for interest and reduction of principal? They are now renting at $350 per month. Would you recommend that they buy? The Hennesseys could, however, easily make a down payment of 20 percent and if they did, the lending institution would charge them only 11 percent interest. Which should they do? How much interest would they save if they financed with the 20 percent down payment? What would the monthly payments be for interest and reduction in principal if they bought the home with a 20 percent down payment?

3. Samuel and Lillian Jelesberg are presently renting an apartment for $500 per month. They have discovered that they can buy a $65,500 home with a $13,500 down payment and assume a twenty-five-year mortgage at 9 percent interest. What would the interest on this loan be? The property

taxes on the home amount to $1,420 and insurance premiums are $240 per year. Sam and Lillian feel this is cheaper than renting. Are they right? Would you recommend that they buy or continue to rent? Why?

4. Howard and Patricia Jones would like to buy a new ranch-style house that is on the market for $75,000. The Joneses have two children, and Howard has an annual income after taxes of $20,000. They have $5,000 which they could use as a down payment and then assume a mortgage of $70,000. Can they afford to buy this home? Why or why not?

5. Frank and Myrtle Brodowski are thinking about buying a home. They have found a split-level house that will suit their needs for $54,975. They can get it for no down payment on a 30-year VA loan at 11.5 percent interest. However, they could afford to make a down payment of up to $5,000. Frank thinks they should do this and save interest charges. What would you recommend and why?

6. Carolyn and Bill Calkins have been renting a nice apartment for $350 per month. Most of their friends are homeowners and therefore are enjoying certain tax benefits that Carolyn and Bill cannot obtain. What are these benefits and how do they work? While Carolyn and Bill would like the above benefits of home ownership, neither of them enjoys yard work and the like. Is there a solution to their problem?

SUGGESTED READINGS

Anosike, Benji O. *How to Buy or Sell Your Own Home Without a Lawyer or Broker.* New York: Do-It-Yourself Publishers, 1981.

The Appraisal Journal. A quarterly publication of the American Institute of Real Estate Appraisers, 430 North Michigan Ave., Chicago, Ill.

Appraisal Review Journal. This journal is published three times per year by the National Association of Review Appraisers, Suite 410, Midwest Federal Building, St. Paul, Minn.

Bell, William W. *Secrets of a Professional Home Buyer.* Ashland, Ore.: World Wide Publishing Corp., 1983.

Bjelland, Harley. *How to Buy the Right Home.* New York: Cornerstone Library, 1980.

Boroson, Warren. *How to Buy or Sell Your Home in a Changing Market.* Oradell, N.J.: Medical Economics Books, 1983.

Cooper, James R., and Pyhrr, Stephen. *Real Estate Investments.* Boston: Warren, Gorham and Lamont, 1982.

Dawson, Joseph C. *Seeking Shelter: How to Find and Finance an Energy-Efficient Home.* New York: Quill, 1983.

Financial Real Estate Handbook, No. 512. Boston: Financial Publishing Co., 1980.

Gritz, Robert D. *The Complete Home Buying Guide.* Beverly Farms, Mass.: Kay Publishing Co., 1981.

Harwood, Bruce. *Real Estate Principles.* Reston, Va.: Reston Publishing Company, 1982.

"Homes: Construction, Maintenance, Community Development." Washington, D.C.: U.S. Government Printing Office, December, 1976.

Kau, James B., and Sirmons, C. F. *Tax Planning For Real Investments*, 2nd Ed. Englewood Cliffs, N.J.: Prentice-Hall, 1982.

Morton, Tom. *Real Estate Finance; A Practical Approach*. Glenview, Ill.; Scott Foresman, 1983.

The Real Estate Appraiser and Analyst. This is a bimonthly publication of the Society of Real Estate Appraisers, 645 North Michigan Avenue, Chicago, Ill.

Real Estate Review. This journal is published quarterly by Warren, Gorham and Lamont, 210 South Street, Boston, Mass. 02111.

Savings and Loan Fact Book. Chicago: United States Savings and Loan League. Obtain the latest edition of this annual publication.

Seller Services. This is a bimonthly publication on homeownership, published by the Federal National Mortgage Association, 3900 Wisconsin Avenue, N.W., Washington, D.C. 20016.

The Story of Modern Home Financing. Chicago: United States Savings and Loan League, latest edition.

Unger, Maurice A. *Real Estate Principles and Practices*, 4th ed. Cincinnati: South-Western, 1979.

What You Should Know Before You Buy a Home. Chicago: United States Savings and Loan League. Obtain the latest edition.

Wiedemer, John P. *Real Estate Investments*. Reston, Va.: Reston Publishing Company, 1982.

Wofford, Larry E. *Real Estate*. New York: John Wiley and Sons, 1983.

Wurtzebach, Charles H., and Miles, Mike E. *Modern Real Estate*. New York: John Wiley and Sons, 1984.

Your Housing Dollar. Chicago: Money Management Institute, Household Finance Corp., 1979.

PART THREE

MANAGING YOUR INSURANCE PROGRAM

CHAPTER TEN

RISK MANAGEMENT: PRINCIPLES OF INSURANCE

Risk Management
Concepts and Principles on Which Insurance Policies Are Based
Miscellaneous and Specialty Insurance
Summary and Conclusion

Life is full of risks. There are some risks you face that, if the event happens, will not result in serious consequences, such as having a flat tire, or oversleeping, or your furnace's pilot light going out. However, there are other risks that can cause serious consequences, and these concern us here. There is the risk that your house will burn down, blow away in a hurricane, or wash away in a flood, causing financial hardship. You may become ill or have an accident and be unable to work. You may then lose your income and have costly medical expenses. Your car may be wrecked or stolen. Your home may be burglarized and valuable possessions lost. You may become permanently disabled and unable to work and earn a livelihood. You may die prematurely, with your income stream cut off and your survivors left in dire financial straits. You may live too long; that is, you may outlive your income and your accumulated assets and spend your old age in poverty. You may be sued for damages you caused to others due to negligence or malpractice. The list of risks could continue, but we have covered the main ones. Risk, however, can often be insured against.

RISK MANAGEMENT

Some risk is insurable, some is not. The risk of loss while gambling is not insurable. Some risk is not worth insuring: for example, the risk of oversleeping.

Gambling versus Insurance

To understand the bare fundamentals of insurable risk, it is necessary to distinguish between gambling and insurance. A horse player visits Churchill Downs in Kentucky for the purpose of betting on horses. Although the gambler is becoming involved with the risk of loss, this risk is quite different from the risk borne by the person driving an automobile down an icy street or the risk assumed by everyone that he or she will die tomorrow. In the first instance, the individual has created his or her own hazard, namely, that of attempting to pick a winner, and in the latter case the individual has not created the hazard being faced. The driver is faced with a hazard inherent in the nature of things; so is every individual because no one knows when he or she is going to die. Here we have one important distinction between gambling and insurance. Gamblers create their risks, while those who face risks inherent in everyday living can make few choices about their fates.

The other difference between insurance and gambling is that the risk involved in insurance is predictable. Insurance actuaries can, if there are large numbers of drivers, predict to a high degree of accuracy how many of them will have accidents. They cannot predict which ones, but they can predict how many. They can also predict how many people will die each year, although they cannot tell which ones. The risk involved in gambling is not only self-created, but the possibility of winning is often sheer luck. How many times a person will win and lose, even over a long time, cannot be figured out mathematically with any precision.

Indeed, the authorities will not permit one to engage in gambling or semigambling activities by means of insurance. In the early 1600s, individuals did make insurance a form of gambling, mainly in the realm of maritime insurance policies. For example, a ship ready to set to sea and loaded with a valuable cargo would be inspected by various individuals hoping to make their fortunes. They would take out an insurance policy on a ship and a cargo in which they had no interest whatsoever. Then they would return home and hope, and probably sometimes pray, that the ship would sink. If they heard that the ship had sunk, they would immediately report to the insurance company, where they were paid the value of their policies. They had won their bet. This practice not only disturbed the insurance companies: it disturbed the members of the British Parliament even more. To prevent this sort of insured gambling, Parliament in the middle 1600s passed an act that prohibited individuals from obtaining insurance policies on *anything* unless they had in that thing what is today known as an "insurable interest." This "insurable interest" concept spread to other countries as well, including the United States.

Insurable Interest

For there to be an insurable interest, a relationship must exist between the insured and the event insured against so that the happening of the event will cause the insured some injury or loss. A person insured must in some way be actually interested in the subject matter of the insurance at the time of loss. For example, let us consider a young lady who is a professional ice skater. Her professional life depends on the soundness of her limbs (oddly enough, the same is true for a race horse). If she falls and breaks a leg, she will be unable to earn any money for a long time. Therefore, she has an interest in insuring her leg: that is, an insurable interest. For someone else to insure the skater's legs would be in the nature of a gambling contract; such an individual ordinarily would not have an insurable interest in her legs. However, an impresario who is managing the ice show and who stands a risk of loss in the event the star's legs are broken also may be said to have an insurable interest. The individual who can suffer no direct loss has no insurable interest whatever. For there to be insurance, therefore, one must have an interest in the thing or in the event being insured against.

The same is true of life insurance. One cannot, generally speaking, buy a policy on a stranger. (The exception is if one lends him money. Then one has an insurable interest up to the extent of the loan. This is discussed under credit life insurance.) One can, however, buy a policy on a direct member of one's family. Most life insurance is purchased by and on the breadwinner of a family.

Insurable Risk

For a risk to be insurable, the frequency of hazard insured against must be predictable. An insurable risk must also produce a monetary loss; it does not hold out the possibility of a financial gain, like gambling does. Pure insurance will merely restore value (reimburse for loss), not provide a profit. In addition, there must be an insurable interest for the risk involved to be insurable. There are three methods of managing insurable risk: minimize the risk, bear the risk yourself (self-insure), or transfer the risk to an insurance company. We will examine all of these things below.

Minimizing Risk

You may minimize (or lessen) risk to some extent. For example, if you neither drink nor smoke, and if you exercise regularly and watch your diet, you are minimizing the risk of a premature death. If you don't drive during a blizzard, you are minimizing (or lessening) the likelihood of an accident. In general, being an alert and careful driver and keeping your car in good working order will reduce the risk of an accident. Keeping a portable fire extinguisher will reduce the risk of loss due to fire in your home. Where your house is located and the type of material used in its construction have a bearing on risk. Some insurance companies charge a lower premium if the insured has reduced insurable risk.

Assuming Risk; Self-Insurance

Most people can and do assume some insurable risk themselves. For example, a deductibility on an automobile insurance policy indicates that the insured assumes some risk. If you have an old car, you might drop collision insurance completely and assume the entire risk in this area.

For health insurance, the insured virtually always assumes a portion of the risk; insurance companies do not pay the entire medical bill.

How much risk to assume is a question only you can decide; but the more risk you self-insure, the lower the premiums charged by life insurance companies. Before deciding how much insurable risk to assume, you should analyze your historical record and answer the following questions: In the case of health insurance, what have your medical expenses been in the past? What is the present condition of your health? For auto insurance, what kind of driver are you? Do you drive defensively? How many times have you been involved in an accident? Have you ever killed or injured anyone with your car?

For home insurance, is it near the fire station? Is it an old frame house or a new brick structure? In the case of life insurance, what would be the financial consequences of your premature death? How many dependents do you have? What are their ages? If your spouse is not now working, could she or he become employed if necessary? All of these factors will have a bearing on how much risk to self-insure. Finally, your financial strength will have a bearing on how much risk you can assume. How much self-insurance you should assume and how much you should transfer to an insurance company are discussed in greater detail in the next few chapters, where we will present some guidelines on how to determine the amount of the various kinds of insurance needed.

Transferring Risk; Buying Insurance

You may manage insurable risk by transferring it to somebody else, usually an insurance company, which pools the insurable risk of many individuals and manages the aggregate risk. Insurance is a device by means of which one party, through a contract (called the "policy") for a consideration (called the "premium") undertakes to assume for another party certain types of risk of loss. Insurance is social in nature since it represents cooperation for mutual protection. Through the payment of premium by many insured persons, the risk is spread over large numbers, and the few who suffer losses are reimbursed by the insurance company with the premiums paid by the many who do not suffer losses. You absorb a small but certain loss (the premium), but avoid the burden of a less likely but potentially much larger loss.

CONCEPTS AND PRINCIPLES ON WHICH INSURANCE POLICIES ARE BASED

There are numerous types of insurance; the main kinds are life insurance and property and liability insurance. Life insurance protects a breadwinner's income stream. For most people property and liability can be broken down into insurance on the home and on the car. The property portion is to reimburse the policy-holder for the physical destruction of the home or the car. The liability aspect is to protect the insured against lawsuits by others in the event of damage to others—either bodily injuries or the destruction of their property.

How Life Insurance Companies Spread Risk; Mortality Tables

The underlying principle of any type of insurance is the law of averages. Highly trained and specialized mathematicians called actuaries can, with an amazing degree of accuracy, determine how many young men thirty years of age, out of a large number of young men thirty years of age, will die within the coming year. Note that emphasis has been placed upon *large* numbers. No actuary or any other mortal can predict when any one individual thirty years of age is going to die. But an actuary working with large numbers can predict within limitations how many young men out of that large number will die within the year. In short, what cannot be predicted for the individual can be predicted in the mass. This can be done because we know a good deal about deaths at every age level from past experience.

Using past experience, insurance companies construct and use mortality tables to spread the risk of loss over large numbers. In this way they are able to absorb risk. Taking our thirty-year-old men again as an example, the actuaries who have for a great many years compiled life insurance statistics will predict that out of 100,000 thirty-year-old men in good health alive at the beginning of the year, 213 will die during the forthcoming year. Life expectancy is calculated the same way. Table 10–1 shows part of a mortality table and illustrates deaths per 100,000 as well as life expectancy in years.

In the most simple case (without attempting to figure in anything for the company's operating cost, profit, and the like), the premium for a thirty-year-old man under these circumstances would be $2.13 for every $1,000 of life insurance. The way this is calculated is simply that if 100,000 thirty-year-old men buy $1,000 life insurance policies, they would pay in a total of $213,000. In this simple case, then, the amount going into the company would be equal to the amount paid out to the beneficiaries of the 213 who died, and, at the end of the year, the company would have a total of zero remaining.

In real life things are not so simple. Just as in any other business, there must be additional sums included in the premium. In this case, the premiums include an amount to cover profits and operating costs.

It should be noted that some companies do not consider insurance age to

Table 10–1   Mortality tables

Age	American experience (1843–1858)		Commissioners 1958 standard ordinary (1950–1954)		Individual annuity table for 1971 male (1960–1967)		Individual annuity table for 1971 female (1960–1967)		United States total population (1969–1971)	
	Deaths per 1,000	Expectation of life (years)	Deaths per 1,000	Expectation of life (years)	Deaths per 1,000	Expectation of life (years)	Deaths per 1,000	Expectation of life (years)	Deaths per 1,000	Expectation of life (years)
0	154.70	41.45	7.08	68.30	—	—	—	—	20.02	70.75
1	63.49	47.94	1.76	67.78	—	—	—	—	1.25	71.19
2	35.50	50.16	1.52	66.90	—	—	—	—	.86	70.28
3	23.91	50.98	1.46	66.00	—	—	—	—	.69	69.34
4	17.70	51.22	1.40	65.10	—	—	—	—	.57	68.39
5	13.60	51.13	1.35	64.19	.46	71.69	.23	76.99	.51	67.43
6	11.37	50.83	1.30	63.27	.42	70.73	.19	76.01	.46	66.46
7	9.75	50.41	1.26	63.25	.40	69.75	.16	75.02	.43	65.49
8	8.63	49.90	1.23	61.43	.39	68.78	.14	74.03	.39	64.52
9	7.90	49.33	1.21	60.51	.39	67.81	.13	73.04	.34	63.54
10	7.49	48.72	1.21	59.58	.39	66.84	.13	72.05	.31	62.57
11	7.52	48.08	1.23	58.65	.40	65.86	.14	71.06	.30	61.58
12	7.54	47.45	1.26	57.72	.41	64.89	.16	70.07	.35	60.60
13	7.57	46.80	1.32	56.80	.41	63.91	.17	69.08	.46	59.62
14	7.60	46.16	1.39	55.87	.42	62.94	.18	68.10	.63	58.65
15	7.63	45.50	1.46	54.95	.43	61.97	.19	67.11	.82	57.69
16	7.66	44.85	1.54	54.03	.44	60.99	.21	66.12	1.01	56.73
17	7.69	44.19	1.62	53.11	.46	60.02	.22	65.13	1.17	55.79
18	7.73	43.53	1.69	52.19	.47	59.05	.23	64.15	1.28	54.86
19	7.77	42.87	1.74	51.28	.49	58.07	.25	63.16	1.34	53.93
20	7.80	42.20	1.79	50.37	.50	57.10	.26	62.18	1.40	53.00
21	7.86	41.53	1.83	49.46	.52	56.13	.28	61.19	1.47	52.07
22	7.91	40.85	1.86	48.55	.54	55.16	.29	60.21	1.52	51.15
23	7.96	40.17	1.89	47.64	.57	54.19	.31	59.23	1.53	50.22
24	8.01	39.49	1.91	46.73	.59	53.22	.33	58.25	1.51	49.30
25	8.06	38.81	1.93	45.82	.62	52.25	.35	57.27	1.47	48.37
26	8.13	38.12	1.96	44.90	.65	51.28	.37	56.29	1.43	47.44
27	8.20	37.43	1.99	43.99	.68	50.32	.39	55.31	1.42	46.51
28	8.26	36.73	2.03	43.08	.72	49.35	.41	54.33	1.44	45.58
29	8.34	36.03	2.08	42.16	.76	48.39	.44	53.35	1.49	44.64
30	8.43	35.33	2.13	41.25	.81	47.42	.47	52.37	1.55	43.71

31	8.51	34.63	2.19	40.34	.86	46.46	.50	51.40	1.63	42.77
32	8.61	33.92	2.25	39.43	.92	45.50	.53	50.42	1.72	41.84
33	8.72	33.21	2.32	38.51	.98	44.54	.57	49.45	1.83	40.92
34	8.83	32.50	2.40	37.60	1.05	43.58	.61	48.48	1.95	39.99
35	8.95	31.78	2.51	36.69	1.12	42.63	.65	47.51	2.09	39.07
36	9.09	31.07	2.64	35.78	1.20	41.68	.70	46.54	2.25	38.15
37	9.23	30.35	2.80	34.88	1.30	40.73	.75	45.57	2.44	37.23
38	9.41	29.62	3.01	33.97	1.40	39.78	.81	44.60	2.66	36.32
39	9.59	28.90	3.25	33.07	1.51	38.83	.87	43.64	2.90	35.42
40	9.79	28.18	3.53	32.18	1.63	37.89	.94	42.68	3.14	34.52
41	10.01	27.45	3.84	31.29	1.79	36.95	1.01	41.72	3.41	33.63
42	10.25	26.72	4.17	30.41	2.00	36.02	1.09	40.76	3.70	32.74
43	10.52	26.00	4.53	29.54	2.26	35.09	1.19	39.80	4.04	31.86
44	10.83	25.27	4.92	28.67	2.57	34.17	1.29	38.85	4.43	30.99
45	11.16	24.54	5.35	27.81	2.92	33.25	1.40	37.90	4.84	30.12
46	11.56	23.81	5.83	26.95	3.32	32.35	1.52	36.95	5.28	29.27
47	12.00	23.08	6.36	26.11	3.75	31.46	1.65	36.01	5.74	28.42
48	12.51	22.36	6.95	25.27	4.23	30.57	1.80	35.06	6.24	27.58
49	13.11	21.63	7.60	24.45	4.74	29.70	1.97	34.13	6.78	26.75
50	13.78	20.91	8.32	23.63	5.29	28.84	2.15	33.19	7.38	25.93
51	14.54	20.20	9.11	22.82	5.86	27.99	2.37	32.26	8.04	25.12
52	15.39	19.49	9.96	22.03	6.46	27.15	2.64	31.34	8.76	24.32
53	16.33	18.79	10.89	21.25	7.09	26.33	2.97	30.42	9.57	23.53
54	17.40	18.09	11.90	20.47	7.74	25.51	3.35	29.51	10.43	22.75
55	18.57	17.40	13.00	19.71	8.42	24.71	3.79	28.61	11.36	21.99
56	19.89	16.72	14.21	18.97	9.12	23.91	4.28	27.71	12.36	21.23
57	21.34	16.05	15.54	18.23	9.85	23.13	4.83	26.83	13.41	20.49
58	22.94	15.39	17.00	17.51	10.61	22.35	5.41	25.96	14.52	19.76
59	24.72	14.74	18.59	16.81	11.41	21.59	6.02	25.10	15.70	19.05
60	26.69	14.10	20.34	16.12	12.25	20.83	6.63	24.25	16.95	18.34
61	28.88	13.47	22.24	15.44	13.13	20.08	7.22	23.41	18.29	17.65
62	31.29	12.86	24.31	14.78	14.07	19.34	7.77	22.57	19.74	16.97
63	33.94	12.26	26.57	14.14	15.08	18.61	8.29	21.74	21.33	16.30
64	36.87	11.67	29.04	13.51	16.19	17.89	8.78	20.92	23.06	15.65
65	40.13	11.10	31.75	12.90	17.41	17.17	9.29	20.10	24.95	15.00
66	43.71	10.54	34.74	12.31	18.77	16.47	9.89	19.29	26.99	14.38
67	47.65	10.00	38.04	11.73	20.29	15.77	10.62	18.47	29.18	13.76
68	52.00	9.47	41.68	11.17	21.99	15.09	11.54	17.67	31.52	13.16
69	56.76	8.97	45.61	10.64	23.89	14.42	12.66	16.87	34.00	12.57
70	61.99	8.48	49.79	10.12	26.00	13.76	14.03	16.08	36.61	12.00
71	67.67	8.00	54.15	9.63	28.34	13.11	15.65	15.30	39.43	11.43
72	73.73	7.55	58.65	9.15	30.93	12.48	17.55	14.53	42.66	10.88

Table 10–1   continued

Age	American experience (1843–1858) Deaths per 1,000	Expectation of life (years)	Commissioners 1958 standard ordinary (1950–1954) Deaths per 1,000	Expectation of life (years)	Individual annuity table for 1971 male (1960–1967) Deaths per 1,000	Expectation of life (years)	Individual annuity table for 1971 female (1960–1967) Deaths per 1,000	Expectation of life (years)	United States total population (1969–1971) Deaths per 1,000	Expectation of life (years)
73	80.18	7.11	63.26	8.69	33.80	11.86	19.74	13.79	46.44	10.34
74	87.03	6.68	68.12	8.24	36.98	11.26	22.26	13.05	50.75	9.82
75	94.37	6.27	73.37	7.81	40.49	10.67	25.12	12.34	55.52	9.32
76	102.31	5.88	79.18	7.39	44.39	10.10	28.37	11.64	60.60	8.84
77	111.06	5.49	85.70	6.98	48.72	9.55	32.05	10.97	65.96	8.38
78	120.83	5.11	93.06	6.59	53.50	9.01	36.23	10.32	71.53	7.93
79	131.73	4.74	101.19	6.21	58.79	8.50	40.98	9.68	77.41	7.51
80	144.47	4.39	109.98	5.85	64.60	7.99	46.39	9.08	83.94	7.10
81	158.60	4.05	119.35	5.51	70.90	7.51	52.51	8.49	91.22	6.70
82	174.30	3.71	129.17	5.19	77.67	7.05	59.41	7.94	98.92	6.32
83	191.56	3.39	139.38	4.89	84.94	6.60	67.16	7.41	106.95	5.96
84	211.36	3.08	150.01	4.60	92.87	6.16	75.90	6.90	115.48	5.62
85	235.55	2.77	161.14	4.32	101.69	5.74	85.77	6.43	125.61	5.28
86	265.68	2.47	172.82	4.06	111.65	5.34	96.90	5.99	137.48	4.97
87	303.02	2.18	185.13	3.80	123.05	4.95	109.34	5.57	147.79	4.68
88	346.69	1.91	198.25	3.55	136.12	4.57	122.98	5.20	161.58	4.42
89	395.86	1.66	212.46	3.31	151.07	4.21	137.51	4.86	172.92	4.18
90	454.55	1.42	228.14	3.06	168.04	3.87	152.47	4.55	185.02	3.94
91	532.47	1.19	245.77	2.82	187.15	3.55	167.37	4.28	198.88	3.73
92	634.26	.98	265.93	2.58	208.46	3.26	181.78	4.04	213.63	3.53
93	734.18	.80	289.30	2.33	231.89	2.98	195.39	3.83	228.70	3.35
94	857.14	.64	316.66	2.07	257.15	2.73	208.07	3.63	243.36	3.19
95	1,000.00	.50	351.24	1.80	283.84	2.50	219.90	3.46	257.45	3.06
96			400.56	1.51	311.57	2.30	231.10	3.29	269.59	2.95
97			488.42	1.18	340.21	2.11	242.21	3.13	280.24	2.85

Age								
98	668.15	.83	369.77	1.94	253.82	2.97	289.77	2.76
99	1,000.00	.50	400.19	1.79	266.45	2.81	289.69	2.69
100			431.41	1.65	280.54	2.65	306.96	2.62
101			463.31	1.53	296.45	2.49	314.61	2.56
102			495.76	1.41	314.54	2.33	321.67	2.51
103			528.60	1.31	335.12	2.17	328.17	2.46
104			561.69	1.21	358.54	2.01	334.14	2.41
105			594.88	1.13	385.12	1.85	339.60	2.37
106			628.02	1.05	415.24	1.70	344.60	2.34
107			660.95	.98	449.27	1.55	349.17	2.30
108			693.50	.92	487.65	1.41	353.33	2.27
109			725.52	.86	530.79	1.27	357.12	2.24

Notes: Mortality rates contained in the 1958 Commissioners Standard Ordinary table were obtained from experience of 1950–1954, but contain an added element designed to generate life insurance reserves of a conservative nature in keeping with the long-term guarantees inherent in life insurance contracts. Premiums for life insurance policies, on the other hand, are based on assumptions that include expected mortality experience. Mortality rates for the 1971 Annuity Tables are, again, conservative as related to the actual experience on which they are based.

Source: 1979 *Life Insurance Fact Book,* American Council of Life Insurance, pp. 108–9.

be the same as actual age. Insurance age is one's nearest birthday. That is, the moment one is six months, one day old, one is one year old insurancewise. Persons remain one year old insurancewise until they are 1 1/2 years old chronologically, when they become two for insurance purposes. Other companies stick with the chronological age.

The 100,000 thirty-year-old men referred to above must be in good physical condition. Statistics upon which the actuaries determine the probability of the number of deaths in any age group are based on the assumption that those persons insured are in good physical condition and good mental health to begin with. If it were not for the requirement of good physical and mental health, obviously anyone with a disease would immediately rush out to the company and buy insurance, in which case the predictions of the actuaries would fall short of their mark and the companies would rapidly go out of business.

Loading Charges

In the hypothetical example given above, the rate or premium cost was $2.13 per $1,000 of insurance for a thirty-year-old male. It was also pointed out that nothing was added for costs or other expenses to the rate of $2.13 per $1,000 of insurance. This is called *pure insurance* or the pure rate. The premium cost to the individual is the pure rate plus other costs, and these other costs are called loading charges; in short, something is "loaded" onto the pure rate to make up the final premium cost. These other costs consist of commissions paid to the insurance agent and other operating costs of the insurance company. The greater percentage of the loading costs come from commissions paid. Generally speaking, life insurance agents receive two forms of commissions: first, the first-year sales commissions and, second, renewal service commissions. On the average, the life insurance agent's first-year sales commissions vary from 30 percent to about 55 percent of the premium, depending upon the company. In addition, the agent is paid a "renewal service commission" during the next nine years that the policy is in force. This rate varies, but generally amounts to 5 percent or less of the premiums during this time.

The mortality tables (or insurance permiums) are also loaded for fractional payments. Insurance premiums can be paid annually, semiannually, quarterly, or monthly. However, insurance companies make certain assumptions regarding the interest income they can earn and hence guarantee for their policyholders, and these assumptions call for annual payment of premiums. If one pays premiums on a basis other than annual the insurance company has these premiums for a shorter period of time and earns less interest. Therefore, the tables are loaded for semiannual, quarterly, and monthly payments of premiums to make up for the loss of interest. In general, it can be shown that the total loading charges increase the cost of insurance between 20 and 25 percent over and above the pure or net insurance rate.

How Insurance Companies Spread Medical Expenses

Medical expenses may also be predicted fairly accurately based on past experience and estimated current cost of treatment. Using large numbers of individuals, insurance actuaries are able to calculate the number of, for example, appendectomies or heart attacks per 100,000 individuals. In the case of health insurance, however, there is a variable. It is the cost of treatment. Drugs, hospital charges, and doctors' fees rise periodically. Consequently, health insurance premiums rise almost yearly. Nevertheless, health insurance companies spread health care costs over large numbers of individuals and the premiums paid by individuals who do not get sick and who are not injured are used to pay the claims of those individuals who do have medical bills.

How Property and Liability Companies Spread Risk

Like health insurance, property and liability insurance are financed over a much shorter time period than is life insurance. Insurance on a house, for example, is sold for a one- or two-year period and then renewed. For an automobile, the insured period is six months or one year. The reason is that there are more variables. Inflation will cause rates to go up annually. Even without inflation, the cost of auto and home repairs could rise. Jury awards and how these awards may have risen in the recent past will also affect premiums. Like other insurance companies, property and liability insurance companies make an allowance for their expenses and the interest they can earn on premium dollars when setting rates. Just as in the case of other insurance, when one transfers the risk on a car or a home to an insurance company, it is spread over large numbers of people, and the premiums of those who do not suffer misfortunes pay for the damages of those who do. The insurance companies base premiums on a probability distribution for each of the various losses, and they base premiums on that. Sometimes, auto insurance companies will raise premiums for those drivers who have had two or more moving violation traffic tickets, on the theory that they are higher-risk drivers.

MISCELLANEOUS AND SPECIALTY INSURANCE

There are a number of other types of insurance with which one should be familiar. Some of these fall in the category of property insurance, some into liability, and some into specialty. Some are a bit unusual. A number of companies sell unusual insurance. We have all heard of Lloyd's of London, who will insure prospective parents against having twins or triplets. Less unusual is insurance on the hands of a pianist or a professional football quarterback. A singer or a college professor can get insurance on his or her voice. Lloyd's also sells what they call livestock mortality insurance. This is really term insurance on farm animals. Indeed, Lloyd's will sell insurance on almost anything. The bulk of Lloyd's insurance in the United States, however, is the extrahazardous insurance that most American companies do not solicit. Examples are fire insurance on expensive buildings and equipment located outside of any town and far away from any fire-fighting equipment.

Boat Insurance

One can hardly venture out on the highway today without seeing someone speed past towing a boat. Consequently, there is both a growing need for and a concomitant growth in the number of insurance policies issued against a boating loss. These policies are designed, first, to protect against loss of boating equipment and, second, to protect against possible personal liability. The first category protects against such hazards as fire, theft, sinking, collision, capsizing, explosion, windstorm, hail, submerged objects, vandalism, and lightning. The policies, written in much the same manner as the automobile collision policy, are generally written as either $50, $100, $200, or $500 deductible policies.

In addition to the loss of equipment, the policies are also written to cover personal liability such as hitting a swimmer, injuring passengers as the result of a fire aboard your own boat, and ramming another boat with resulting personal injury to the persons aboard that vessel. The policies are generally written with a limit of $10,000 to $25,000, but go higher at an extra cost.

Trip Insurance

Most of these policies are a package that includes some term life insurance and some medical insurance. The life insurance could cover a person for all accidental deaths occurring while the insured is on the trip or (at a reduced premium) just accidental deaths occurring while the insured is on the airplane, in or around the airport, or in a limousine going to or coming from the airport. Some are written so that if the insured is killed while in a common carrier his or her beneficiary(ies) get a certain amount, but get somewhat less if the insured is killed while on the trip but not in a common carrier.

Most of these policies also have a medical insurance feature that pays up to 5 percent of the principal sum for medical bills due to an accident (but not due to an illness). There are a few exclusions regarding the medical insurance; for example, medical bills due to a skiing or hunting accident are not covered.

Generally these trip policies can be purchased in values from $5,000 to $300,000. A person who travels a lot may want to purchase continuous trip protection, which is available and which provides the same protection described above for any trips during the year, rather than to purchase it separately for each trip.

Crop Insurance

In the western states, specialized insurance companies sell crop insurance. Rates vary regionally and cost so much per acre, based on past hail damage experience. But crop insurance can be obtained only if sufficient historical weather information exists to establish premium rates with actuarial accuracy.

Malpractice Insurance

Malpractice insurance primarily protects doctors and nurses against personal liability damage suits arising out of actual or alleged professional carelessness; in recent years lawyers and accountants have been buying it in increasing numbers. This type of insurance is sold by some fire and casualty companies.

Malpractice insurance used to be quite cheap, but this has changed in some states recently. Because of a changing legal philosophy, not only are larger awards now being made in malpractice suits, but in addition the courts have been more liberal in making awards. In some states even hospitals have lost their immunity from lawsuit. Consequently, in malpractice suits in those states both the doctor and the hospital are sued. California and New York are two states in which more and larger awards have recently been granted. As a result, malpractice insurance rates are very high in those states. Nevertheless, most doctors and nurses feel they have to have this kind of protection. However, because of its high costs some doctors have dropped this insurance in recent years. This is called "going naked." In other cases, medical societies or groups of doctors have formed their own insurance pool. Each of them puts so much into a fund each month, which is then used to aid those doctors who are sued. This is really self-insurance.

Group Legal Insurance

Some experts believe that before too long insurance to pay for legal fees will be available on a group basis. Even today a few people have such protection, but generally it is financed through a labor union, credit union, or other organization; insurance companies are not yet involved.

Generally, a contract is negotiated between a group and a law firm, which provides certain legal services free to the individual members of the group. The group pays the fees, and the individuals pay indirectly through higher dues or some other such method. But this uses the insurance principle by spreading actuarially over large numbers the legal fees of the few unfortunate enough to get into trouble.

Major lawsuits are not covered, but such things as divorce, drafting of wills, minor disputes with landlords or finance companies, disagreements with retail merchants, and minor traffic violations are handled. In many cases relatively small sums of money are involved, and most persons are reluctant to spend money on attorney's fees (and possible court costs). The result is they often pay any claim made or represent themselves in court and invariably lose.

SUMMARY AND CONCLUSION

In this chapter, we have presented the various types of insurance available. Insurance can be purchased for almost all hazards. The average person, however, will be concerned primarily with life, health, property, and liability insurance. Therefore, the next three chapters will deal with these in greater detail.

QUESTIONS FOR REVIEW

1. What are some risks that, if the event happens, will result in serious consequences? What are some that will not cause serious consequences?
2. What is insurable risk?
3. What are the three methods of managing risk?
4. What is the difference between gambling and insurance?
5. Explain insurable interest.
6. What is self-insurance?
7. How do insurance companies spread mortality risk?
8. Explain the concept of pure insurance premiums.
9. Justify loading charges in life insurance.
10. How do property and liability insurance companies spread risk?
11. What is specialty insurance?
12. Describe malpractice insurance.

CASES

1. Connie Brashear is a literary agent for a number of successful authors. She receives 10 percent of all of their earnings and would like to take out a life insurance policy on several of the more successful ones. May she do that? Would it be a wise thing to do?
2. Joyce Faye Allen is a policewoman and wonders whether she should have malpractice insurance. Can you advise her?
3. Claire Baldwin is confused between minimizing risk, assuming risk, and transferring risk. Can you advise her?

SUGGESTED READINGS

Athearn, James L. *Risk and Insurance.* St. Paul, Minn.: West Publishing Co., 1981.

Bickelhaupt, David L. *General Insurance,* 10th ed. Homewood, Ill.: R. Irwin, 1979.

Crane, Frederick G. *Insurance Principles and Practices.* New York: John Wiley and Sons, 1980.

Dorfman, Mark S. *Introduction to Insurance.* Englewood Cliffs, N.J.: Prentice-Hall, 1978.

Elliot, Curtis M., and Vaughan, Emmett J. *Fundamentals of Risk and Insurance.* New York: John Wiley & Sons, 1978.

Greene, Mark R. "Risk and Insurance." Cincinnati: South-Western, 1981.

Harris, Louis. "Risk in a Complex Society," *The Journal of Insurance,* July-August, 1980.

Life Insurance Fact Book. Published annually by the Institute of Life Insurance, New York.

Mehr, Robert I., and Cammack, Emerson. *Principles of Insurance.* Homewood, Ill.: Irwin, 1980.

Rejda, George E. *Principles of Insurance.* Glenview, Ill.: Scott, Foresman, 1982.

Williams, C. Arthur, Jr., and Heims, Richard M. *Risk Management and Insurance,* 4th ed. New York: McGraw-Hill, 1981.

Williams, C. Arthur, Jr., Herd, George L., and Glendenning, William. *Principles of Risk Management and Insurance.* Malvern, Pa.: American Institute for Property and Liability Underwriters, 1978.

CHAPTER ELEVEN

LIFE INSURANCE

When you buy life insurance, you should ask yourself: "Why, when, what kind, how much, and where?" Premiums will vary depending on when you buy it (your age), what kind (type of policy), how much you buy, and where (from whom) you buy it.

WHY AND WHEN TO BUY LIFE INSURANCE

Why Buy Life Insurance at All?

There are only two reasons for most people to buy life insurance: for protection and for savings. In most cases protection is primary. We discussed risk management, which is what we have in mind when we talk about protection, in Chapter 10.

While you may buy life insurance with living benefits and hence a savings feature built in, insurance is usually a poor savings vehicle. Its return is modest and will be eroded by inflation. Only if you are not disciplined and find it impossible to save in any other way should you consider entering into a contract with a life insurance company in which you are forced to save. Some investment advisors suggest that if you are in a high tax bracket, insurance as a savings—and investment—scheme may not be so bad because of favorable tax treatment. (See "Taxes and Life Insurance Benefits" later in this chapter for a discussion of how insurance is taxed.) That may be partially true, but if you are in a high tax bracket, you would probably be better off buying insurance for protection alone and then investing the difference.

Insurance provides protection in the event of premature death, death that occurs before the person has reached his or her full life expectancy. Insurance protects the dependents of the insured against financial hardship in the event of death of the breadwinner. You are protecting your income stream. You are substituting insurance dollars for earned dollars. That gives us a clue as to how much insurance you need.

When to Buy Life Insurance

The best time to buy life insurance is the day before you die, if you know when that will be and if you can still buy it at that time. If you are in ill health at an advanced age, you are probably uninsurable.

When should you buy a refrigerator? Should you buy one for your children when they are, say, ten years old, on the theory that the price will be lower when they are ten than when they are twenty years of age? That's the logic some insurance salesmen will use; premiums are cheaper at age ten than age twenty. Yes, but not that much cheaper. Besides, you don't buy something you don't need just because it's cheaper. The only valid argument for buying insurance for children is that they may become uninsurable with a remote possibility of illness in young adulthood. Consequently, you should buy life insurance when you need it and can afford it—just like a refrigerator—that is, when you become a young adult and take on family responsibilities.

Probably you won't be able to buy all you will need or want at one time; hence, be prepared to buy several blocks over a few years as your income rises. Review your insurance program periodically because your needs will change as you grow older. Sometimes you will need more and at other times you may wish to let some term insurance expire, or surrender permanent insurance for cash.

DECIDING HOW MUCH LIFE INSURANCE TO BUY

There are four ways to decide. They are: the needs concept which depletes capital, the capital needs analysis which maintains capital, the present value of future income concept, and the multiple income concept.

Family Needs Concept—Depleting Capital

It is useful to list all possible family financial needs, to arrive at the total amount of insurance needed to produce enough capital to meet them, should the insured die:

1. *Funeral and other final expenses.* In addition to funeral expenses, there may be final medical and hospital bills to pay. There may also be administrative

expenses and attorney's fees associated with probating a will and settling an estate. These expenses will probably be a minimum of $2,000 to $3,000 and may be much larger, especially if the estate is fairly large.

2. *Paying off the mortgage and other debts.* If there is a mortgage on your house, you may wish to pay it off as well as liquidate any other installment debt outstanding. You may have special mortgage and credit life insurance for this, or it may be included in your regular insurance policy. There is no way of estimating the dollar amount of this item; it will vary greatly from person to person. An alternative way of handling the home mortgage is not to pay it off but to include the mortgage payments in regular family living expense needs. (See below.)

3. *Emergency fund.* You will no doubt want an emergency fund. You should already have this in a savings account, but if not it could be looked upon as part of your insurance needs. Many experts suggest this fund should be about twice your monthly take-home pay.

4. *College fund.* If there are college-bound children, college expenses become part of the insurance needs. You need not necessarily provide for full four-year college expenses because students can earn income to help defray the cost. On the other hand, it is difficult to calculate future college costs because of rapid inflation. College costs vary greatly even among state schools, but total costs (tuition, room and board, etc.) can easily reach $6,000 or $7,000 per year. At private schools this figure can go as high as or higher than $12,000 per year.

5. *Annual family living needs.* This consists of the day-to-day living expenses and is related to the personal or family budget discussed in Chapter 3. The amount will vary depending on the size of the family, its age makeup, and accustomed standard of living, or the level of livelihood that you would like to provide. Remember, however, this item will continue for a number of years. Moreover, this need will change; children will grow up and be on their own; this will be partly (or perhaps entirely) offset by inflation. The amount of insurance needed for family living would also need to be adjusted (presumably downward) to take into account other earning assets, Social Security benefits, and any private corporate pension payments to be received. Social Security benefits for children continue until the children reach age sixteen (twenty-one in the case of students, including college students). The Social Security benefits paid to a surviving spouse do not begin until she or he reaches age sixty. (The time between when the benefits for the children end and when they begin again for the surviving spouse is known as "the blackout years.")

Insurance to meet family living needs may also be reduced somewhat if it is reasonably certain that the survivor is willing and able to get a part-time (or full-time) job. You should also note that upon the death of the breadwinner, family living needs decline somewhat because the income earner is also an income spender.

A dollar figure cannot be suggested for family living needs; you must decide this from your personal budget. However, there are some bench marks. Studies have indicated that a certain percentage of the breadwinner's gross income will typically suffice upon the breadwinner's death. (See Table 11–1.)

6. *Retirement living.* Your insurance needs also include an amount for your own retirement, in case you do not die prematurely. To be sure, your retirement needs can be met by means other than insurance; we mentioned Social Security, private pensions, and other earning assets earlier. All of these factors reduce your insurance needs. It should also be noted that the retirement living really includes family living needs and a bit more. It is the added amount required if the insured is in retirement with the family.

7. *Totaling your insurance needs.* Adding up all of the above six points will provide you with an answer. Table 11–2 summarizes this. We left the first four blank; fill in whatever amount is appropriate and add it to the amount shown here to get your total insurance needs. We have also calculated a hypothetical figure for family living needs and retirement. Not all of the entries will necessarily have a dollar figure. You may or may not have debts to pay off; you may or may not already have an emergency fund; you may or may not need a college fund; and you may have other assets.

Remember also, however, that the last two items, the $20,000 for family living and/or retirement living, are annual and recurring expenses. You will have to multiply them by some figure that varies from person to person that should be the life expectancy of the individual. If we multiply one of those two figures by twenty years, or whatever is appropriate, we get the lifetime needs. If we multiply the $20,000 annual needs by 20 we get $400,000, but if you had that much money now it would also grow by whatever interest rate it could earn. Consequently, less than that amount would be needed. But the $20,000 per

Table 11–1   Approximate income needed upon the breadwinner's death

Annual gross Income	Income needed upon breadwinner's death (percent)
Up to $29,000	70%
$29,001 to $33,000	65%
$33,001 to $37,000	60%
$37,001 to $42,000	55%
Over $42,000	50%

Source: *Capital Needs Analysis*, Thomas J. Wolff, Certified Life Underwriter. Vernon Publishing Services, Inc., Vernon, CT. Used with permission.

Table 11–2   Worksheet

1. Final expenses		$_____
2. Payment of debts		_____
3. Emergency fund		_____
4. College fund		_____
5. Family living		
Current budget	_____	
Less reduction in expenses after death of insured	_____	
Less new income from other sources	_____	
Equals insurance for family living (annually)	$ 20,000	
times 20 years	$400,000	
6. Retirement living (annually)	$ 20,000	
times 20 years	$400,000	
7. Point 6 or 7 times 20 years and then adjusted to take into account 6 percent interest and 5 percent inflation		$360,920
8. Total insurance needs (Points 1 through 4 plus 8)	Total	$_____

Source: Capital Needs Analysis, Thomas J. Wolff, Certified Life Underwriter. Vernon Publishing Services, Inc., Vernon, CT. Used with permission.

year income would also be eroded by inflation. Therefore, if we wanted to provide $20,000 adjusted for inflation, we would have two variables in the calculation. We will assume an inflation rate of 5 percent and an interest rate of 6 percent. Now the problem becomes one of calculating how large a lump sum of money (insurance) is needed to provide for twenty annual payments of $20,000, adjusted for an inflation rate of 5 percent, if the remaining lump sum is also growing at 6 percent while being depleted by the annual payments. Any good insurance agent can give you the answer. The computation is complex but the agent can get the answer through the home office's computer. In our case it is about $360,900; that is to say, 360,900 dollars (insurance) invested at 6 percent, would provide twenty annual payments of $20,000, in real terms, if inflation is 5 percent per year, taking into account both interest income and principal withdrawals. The first year the recipient would get $20,000; the second year $21,000; the third year about $22,050, and so on. At the end of twenty years the $360,900 would be gone.

The above analysis of insurance needs has several shortcomings. First, it depletes capital. Also, in planning you cannot be certain of the future rate of inflation or the interest rate. In addition, twenty years might be too short a period of time, and you could outlive your capital. On the other hand, the $360,920 figure in the table assumes the family has no other assets or pension benefits, which is unlikely, and the figure may overstate the insurance needed. Nevertheless, it is a place to begin.

Capital Needs Analysis; Maintaining Capital

An alternative method of calculating the total amount of insurance you need is by means of "capital needs analysis."[1] This is similar to what was discussed above, but it does not deplete the insured's capital, and it takes into account any other assets which the family may have. It utilizes the individual's balance sheet, capital analysis, and income analysis (Tables 11–3 and 11–4) to calculate the amount of insurance needed. This is shown in the tables below for a hypothetical person A. (Blank capital needs analysis tables [Tables 11–5 and 11–6] to calculate your personal insurance needs follow Tables 11–3 and 11–4.) A's total assets as shown by the balance sheet are $218,000, with nonmortgage liabilities of $6,000. While this makes A's net worth $212,000, that is not the amount of capital available to A or to dependents in the event of A's death.

The capital analysis indicates that A's estate would have only $82,000 capital available for income-producing purposes. Taxes, the cost of administering the estate, and paying off a mortgage would reduce A's capital. A would also no doubt want to set aside something for a college fund, which would reduce further the capital available for investments. Finally, A's nonincome-producing property (such as house, car, household furnishings, and other personal property) has to be netted out to obtain the $82,000.

The income analysis makes an assumption regarding Social Security income and the return on the $82,000. A relatively low 8 percent return is chosen because a long-run view is taken. There is no assurance that today's somewhat higher interest rates will prevail. In addition, if more than 8 percent is earned in some years, it should be retained (added to capital rather than used) to offset future inflation. In any event, the total income provided falls $7,540 short of the goal. The goal in this case is 55 percent of present income. This 55 percent was chosen because economic and financial statistics indicate that upon the death of a breadwinner, if the mortgage payment and future college expenses are taken care of, about 55 percent of the income of a person at A's level is required to maintain the standard of living to which the family has become accustomed. The income analysis also shows that $94,250 of additional capital is needed to provide earnings equal to 55 percent of present income in the event of A's death. That capital can, of course, be provided by life insurance.

Present Value of Future Income Stream

Using the present value of your future income stream is another method of determining your insurance needs. It is your income stream you are protecting because that is what would be cut off in the event of death. This requires an estimate of your future lifetime income, which cannot be made precisely, but accurately enough.

---

1. This technique was developed by Thomas J. Wolff, Certified Life Underwriter, whose permission to use the material is gratefully acknowledged.

Table 11–3   Balance sheet of _____ A. _____ Date _____

Assets		Liabilities	
New equity in home			
Market value: 60,000			
Mortgage: 40,000	$ 20,000*	Current bills	$ 1,500
Other real estate	_____	Notes	2,500
Personal property	30,000*	Other debts	2,000
Death benefits under retirement plans	_____		
Listed securities	12,000		
Stock options	_____		
Life insurance	150,000		
Business interest	_____		
Checking and savings accounts	6,000		
Other	_____		
Total	$218,000	Total	$ 6,000
Satisfied with amount saved Yes ☐ No ☐			
Monthly amount that can be saved			$_____

Capital analysis		
Total assets		$218,000
Liabilities	$ 6,000	
Taxes and costs of administration	16,000	
Payment of mortgage	40,000	
Cost of education	24,000	
Nonincome producing property	50,000*	
Total deductions		136,000
Capital available for income		$ 82,000
Income-producing assets not owned by you (including non-owned personal life insurance on your life).		
Total capital available for income		$ 82,000
Expected earnings to age 65 ($_____ × _____ years)		$_____

* Nonincome producing property.
Source: *Capital Needs Analysis*, Thomas J. Wolff, Certified Life Underwriter. Vernon Publishing Services, Inc., Vernon, CT. Used with permission.

Let us assume a thirty-five-year-old individual making $20,000 per year after taxes. (You need not fence in with insurance Caesar's annual tribute since insurance benefit payments are not subject to the income tax.) If the person continues at this income level until age 65, he or she will earn $600,000 after taxes until retirement. However, the income will almost certainly rise above $20,000 per year, even if there are no promotions—for two reasons. First there

Table 11–4   Income analysis

Present income (all income of both husband and wife)	$42,000
Income objective (_55_ % of above) (See below)	$23,100

Income presently provided
  Capital available for income
    $ _82,000_ @ _8_ % $6,560 (A)
  Social security and other government
    programs   9,000 (B)
  Other income (if any) $_____ (C)

Total income provided now $15,560

Income shortage $ _7,540_ (D)

New capital required (divide income shortage (D) by assumed
  interest rate) $94,250 (E)

If there is an income surplus, reduce the "Capital Available for Income" by the amount necessary to eliminate the surplus. Enter the capital surplus on line E with a minus sign and continue on to the "Total Income Analysis."

Income objective

Based on a study by a group of economists, the following are typical income objectives in order to permit a family to "remain in their own world" after the death of the breadwinner. Assumption is that the mortgage on residence is paid and that educational expenses are provided for separately.

Annual gross income	*Percentage of gross income required*
Up to $29,000	70%
$29,001 to $33,000	65%
$33,001 to $37,000	60%
$37,001 to $42,000	55%
Over $42,000	50%

Source: *Capital Needs Analysis*, Thomas J. Wolff, Certified Life Underwriter. Vernon Publishing Services, Inc., Vernon, CT. Used with permission.

will be periodic productivity raises. Productivity increases are based on increased output per man-hour worked and are due to better tools, management techniques, and other innovations. The national average long-run productivity increase has been 2.5 to 3 percent per year. We will assume that level for our hypothetical person. In addition, most people will receive salary increases to offset inflation. Assuming inflation returns to its more reasonable and traditional level of 3 to 4 percent, the $20,000 will also grow by that amount. This gives us a growth rate of about 6 or 7 percent per year. Compounding the $20,000 by 7 percent over the thirty-year period gives us a lifetime income stream of about $1,889,220. However, future dollars must be discounted because they are worth less than

Table 11–5   Balance sheet of _____ B. _____   Date _____

Assets		Liabilities	
New equity in home			
Market value: _____			
Mortgage: _____	$_____	Current bills	$_____
Other real estate	_____	Notes	_____
Personal property	_____		
Other debts			
Death benefits under retirement plans	_____		
Listed securities	_____		
Stock options	_____		
Life insurance	_____		
Business interest	_____		
Checking and savings accounts	_____		
Other	=======		=======
Total	$_____	Total	$_____
Satisfied with amount saved Yes ☐ No ☐			
Monthly amount that can be saved			$_____
Capital analysis			$_____
Total assets			
Liabilities	$_____		
Taxes and costs of administration	_____		
Payment of mortgage	_____		
Cost of education	_____		
Nonincome producing property	$=======		
Total deductions			=======
Capital available for income			$_____
Income-producing assets not owned by you			
(including non-owned personal life insurance on your life).			=======
Total capital available for income			$_____
Expected earnings to age 65			
($_____ × _____ years)			$_____

Source: Capital Needs Analysis, Thomas J. Wolff, Certified Life Underwriter. Vernon Publishing Services, Inc., Vernon, CT. Used with permission.

present dollars. What we need is a figure which, if invested now and earning interest and with funds being withdrawn periodically, would provide a total income stream over the next thirty years of $1,889,220. If we assume that the funds are earning 8 percent interest while the amount being withdrawn annually is originally $20,000 but is growing at 7 percent, then we can calculate an answer. (This is the same problem we faced above when we calculated the sum

Table 11-6   Income analysis

Present income (all income of both husband and wife)	$_____
Income objective (_____% of above) (See below)	$_____

Income presently provided
  Capital available for income

$_____ @ _____%	$_____ (A)
Social security and other government programs	$_____ (B)
Other income (if any)	$_____ (C)

Total income provided now	$_____
Income shortage	$_____ (D)
New capital required (divide income shortage (D) by assumed interest rate)	_____ (E)

If there is an income surplus, reduce the "Capital Available for Income" by the amount necessary to eliminate the surplus. Enter the capital surplus on line E with a minus sign and continue on to the "Total Income Analysis."

Income objective

Based on a study by a group of economists, the following are typical income objectives in order to permit a family to "remain in their own world" after the death of the breadwinner. Assumption is that the mortgage on residence is paid and that educational expenses are provided for separately.

Annual gross income	*Percentage of gross income required*
Up to $20,000	70%
$20,001 to $24,000	65%
$24,001 to $28,000	60%
$28,001 to $32,000	55%
Over $32,000	50%

Source: Capital Needs Analysis, Thomas J. Wolff, Certified Life Underwriter. Vernon Publishing Services, Inc., Vernon, CT. Used with permission.

needed to provide $20,000 in real terms [or growing at 5 percent] for twenty years under family living needs in the discussion of insurance based upon need). Here the figure is $487,019. That is the present value of the future lifetime income stream of our hypothetical person aged thirty-five whose present $20,000 per year after-tax income is growing at a compound rate of 7 percent per year. That, in theory, is the amount of insurance the individual in question should have to protect the income stream fully. Moreover, with each passing year, insurance needs decline because there is less and less future income to earn. When the person is sixty-four years old, the insurance needed to protect future income is exactly the same as the final year's earnings.

If the thirty-five-year-old individual described above purchased all this insurance, the annual premiums would be about $4,062 if it were 20-year term, $6,204 if it were 30-year term, and $12,414 if it were the cheapest form of whole life. Consequently, we can conclude that virtually no one can afford to pay the premium necessary to purchase all the insurance needed in accordance with the future income criterion. However, it is an important bench mark; we can use it and modify it in accordance with the "family need" criterion and personal value judgments. The amount of insurance needed under the future income stream criterion is the theoretical upper limit of a person's insurance needs. It is higher than the amount calculated under the needs criterion because the latter assumes that when the breadwinner dies, family needs decline.

Multiple Income Approach

The final approach to calculating the amount of insurance you should buy is simply to take your after-tax income and multiply it by some factor, the most common ones being 3, 5, 7, and 10. The multiple selected will be determined by your age, the number of dependents, their ages, your total assets and liabilities, and income from property. Although this is an arbitrary way, it can also be looked upon as a rule of thumb based upon experience.

The Final Decision

The methods we have discussed of determining your insurance needs are only bench marks. You still have to make a decision based on what you can afford and your value judgments and priorities.

Insurance for Children

Insurance for children should be a low-priority item. Children are not breadwinners as a general rule. Some people buy insurance on their children, which builds up a cash value to give them a nest egg to start out when they reach young adulthood. If the budget can afford this, such a plan is fine. But saving via insurance should be compared with the yield on alternative investment outlets. In most cases, you could find an alternative that would yield more.

Insurance on a Nonincome-Earning Spouse

Although a spouse may not contribute money income to the family, the time and skills he or she provides for the family are valuable and would be costly to replace in case of death or disability. The cost of child care alone might justify some insurance for income protection.

For example, while the death of one parent may not decrease family dollar income, it may necessitate an increase in family expenditures if the household is to be properly operated and the children are to receive adequate care. Hence a case for some term insurance could be made where children are involved. To be sure, if a nonworking spouse died, there would be one less consumer in the family, and expenses would decline. You must decide what the net effect would be in your individual case.

If there are two breadwinners in the family, there is a reason for life insurance on both. Since there is a second income to protect, the analysis above regarding how much a person is worth applies to both husband and wife. The future income of both partners can be calculated as the beginning or "scaling down" point in determining how much insurance is needed.

TYPES OF ORDINARY LIFE INSURANCE

Most people who buy individual life insurance policies buy what is referred to as "ordinary life," and buy it from legal reserve life insurance companies. The terminology covering ordinary life is a bit confusing because not all companies use the same designations. There are only a handful of kinds of ordinary policies: term, whole life, endowment, combinations that include two or more of the above, and the recently developed universal and variable life policies. In addition there are two types of whole life policies, the straight life and the limited pay life policies, and they are not the same. The following classification illustrates the various ordinary policies.

Ordinary life insurance
      Term
      Whole life
            Straight life
            Limited pay life
      Endowment
      Combinations of two or more of the above
      Universal life
      Variable life

Table 11–7 shows ordinary life insurance in force in the United States.

Term Life Insurance

Term life insurance is the simplest type of ordinary life insurance, and is also the cheapest; it provides the most insurance coverage per dollar of premium. Term insurance is a contract that provides protection for a specific period of time, and, when that time has expired, the policy lapses. It has no savings feature built into it, hence no living benefits, only death benefits. Consequently, most of the premiums paid into the company are also paid out in the form of death benefits. For this reason, it is cheaper than all other insurance—which is also sometimes called "permanent" insurance as opposed to term. Many term

Table 11–7   Ordinary life insurance in force in the United States, by plan

Plan of insurance	1977			1981		
	Number of policies (000 omitted)	Amount (000,000 omitted)	% of Amount	Number of policies (000 omitted)	Amount (000,000 omitted)	% of Amount
Whole life						
Straight life,						
Premium paying	60,300	$ 616,900	47.8	68,600	$ 934,100	47.2
Limited payment life,						
Premium paying	28,300	123,500	9.6	25,400	152,200	7.7
Paid-up	20,200	45,200	3.5	22,900	61,500	3.1
Endowment	11,900	52,200	4.1	9,100	52,000	2.6
Retirement income						
with insurance	2,400	21,700	1.7	1,800	18,200	0.9
Term						
Extended	5,600	20,700	1.6	6,900	30,900	1.6
Regular						
Decreasing	6,100	114,800	8.9	6,600	153,700	7.8
Other	4,700	147,400	11.4	7,300	401,000	20.3
Other						
Decreasing	—	79,600	6.2	—	87,600	4.4
Other	—	67,300	5.2	—	86,900	4.4
Total	139,500	$1,289,300	100.0	148,600	$1,978,100	100.0

Source: 1982 Life Insurance Fact Book, American Council of Life Insurance, p. 19.

policies are renewable. When the term for which it is written has expired, it may be renewed at the option of the insured without the need for a medical examination.

A term policy may also be convertible. It can be converted to a permanent policy without a medical examination. There are several types of term policies, but they are basically the same in that they are financed over a specific but variable number of years.

One year renewable term

This type of policy expires after one year; it is the cheapest type to buy. At the end of the year you may renew it for another year, and so on. Each time you renew it, however, you are one year older, and you pay a higher premium. Refer to the mortality table in the previous chapter (Table 10–1). You will see that for a person age twenty, deaths per 1,000 are 1.79. This indicates that for every $1,000 worth of life insurance the pure premium for a twenty-year-old would be $1.79. If 1,000 twenty-year-olds paid that, it would raise just enough ($1,790) to pay the claims for those who died. To be sure, the premium would be more because the insurance companies add something for expenses and may even subtract a bit to take into account the interest they could earn before they had to pay it out in death claims. The mortality table referred to is a standard one; but not all companies use it. Each has developed its own, and it may be more favorable (lower premiums) because the company has had a more favorable mortality experience. Thus, you should shop around when buying life insurance.

The next year, the person is twenty-one years of age, and premiums would rise to $1.83 per $1,000 of insurance, and so on year after year with premiums rising. At age 40 they would still only be $3.53. Eventually premiums would get so high that they would be prohibitive. By then, however, you probably would no longer need insurance and would drop your policy. You should consider dropping your policy any time you no longer need it even if your premiums are not prohibitive (e.g., if your children are grown and on their own).

Level premium term

Level premium term may run for five years, ten years, or even twenty years or more. Premiums are merely averaged. If a twenty-year-old bought five-year level premium term, the deaths per thousand shown in the mortality table would be averaged for all ages 20 through 24. The premium ($1.86, adjusted for expenses and interest), which would be in excess of that needed in the early years, would build up a reserve to be used in later years when premiums would be deficient. Premiums can also be averaged over ten or twenty or any number of years, even over a lifetime. Figure 11–1 illustrates how a level premium policy works and how reserves are built up.

Until recently, ten- and twenty-year term policies were popular, but recently more people have switched to one-year renewable term. When you buy level premium insurance you are paying some premiums in advance. You can do your own budgeting and in theory bank the difference in premiums in the early years and develop your own reserve and earn interest, although the dollars saved in the early years by doing this may be small.

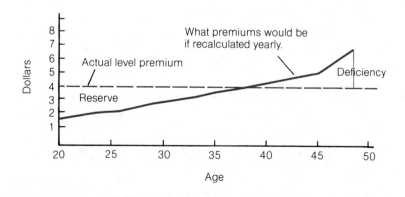

Figure 11–1 Sample of a level premium policy, and what the premiums would be if they were recalculated on an annual basis.

Decreasing term rider

It is also possible to buy a term policy, the face value of which declines as the years or even the months pass. These are sometimes used to pay off a mortgage if the insured dies. Suppose one has a $50,000 mortgage on a home and desires to protect the family or to keep them from the necessity of paying that mortgage in the event of one's death. Under some circumstances it might be desirable for the individual to turn to the decreasing term policy for this purpose. In the amortizing type of mortgage, where part of the principal and interest is paid each month, the amount paid on the principal increases with each monthly payment. Hypothetically, let us assume that when individuals take out a $50,000 mortgage, they make a payment of $550 a month. Assume further that out of the $550 monthly payment, in the first month, $500 is paid in interest and $50 to reduce the principal. This leaves a balance due of $49,950. It is obvious that for purposes of protection, by the end of the first month a $50,000 policy is no longer necessary. The mortgage could be paid off at the end of that first month if the individual or the estate had $49,950. The decreasing term policy can take care of this.

For this purpose, the companies will typically write or issue a level premium policy on a decreasing term contract for as long as the mortgage runs, and the policy will decline with the mortgage. Any payoff turned over to the beneficiary will be sufficient to pay off the mortgage. In short, the contract states in effect that as each month passes, the amount the company will pay on the policy decreases. If the insured dies when only $1,000 is due on the mortgage, this balance will be paid off; or if the insured dies at the end of the first month with a balance due of $49,950, this amount will be paid to the beneficiary. The net result is to cause the average monthly premiums to be considerably lower than they would be if a policy with a fixed amount due is purchased because, as each month passes, the amount the beneficiary will receive is reduced roughly in the same amount that the balance due on the mortgage is reduced.

Permanent Insurance Versus Term

If you buy permanent insurance, you are developing a savings and investment program via insurance. These savings earn only a modest return and are eroded by inflation. It is usually best to fill the bulk of your insurance needs with term. We will discuss whole life, which in turn may be broken down into straight life and limited payment life, the endowment policy, and others.

Straight Life Policy

Straight life builds up a cash surrender value and may pay dividends. If the dividends are left with the insurance company, a straight life policy may eventually become a paid-up policy. Otherwise premiums are paid for as long as the policy is in force.[2]

As was pointed out in the discussion of the term policy, the premium rates should rise each year as the insured grows older. However, to avoid changing the rates each year, insurance companies developed the idea of averaging the first five years' cost, the second five years' cost, and so forth. Thus in the five-year renewable policy, a constant level premium is paid during the first five years the policy is in force and a new and higher rate is paid during the second five years. The rate thus changes every five years. From this idea of averaging the rates every five years there grew the concept of averaging over an entire lifetime. For example, since it is possible to determine, on the average, the remaining life of a man aged thirty, it is possible to average what the cost of protection would be over the balance of his life. This is what is done. When the thirty-year-old man buys a whole life policy, his annual premium is greater than it would be if he were to purchase the same amount of term insurance. This, in part, because the policy never expires. All term policies eventually expire. Hence, in the averaging process a straight life policy has to take into account some very high premiums because of advanced age.

As a result of averaging premiums over a lifetime on a policy that never expires, a higher reserve is built up than in the case of a term policy that eventually does expire. Some premiums are paid in advance and are called a reserve, which are invested by the insurance company to earn interest income. This is the savings feature of a straight life policy and, because of it, the policy builds up a cash surrender value as the years pass. Cash surrender value is the amount available in cash if the owner voluntarily terminates the policy. The policy itself never expires, and premiums continue to be paid until the policyholder dies, at which time the beneficiaries are paid the face value of the policy. However, policyholders may choose to take the cash value (their living benefits) and surrender their policy. Many people do this at an advanced age because they have no one financially dependent upon them. They have had insurance protection when they needed it and they have used insurance as a vehicle to generate savings for their old age.

The savings feature built into a straight life policy can be described as modest, not heavy, but it is precisely this modest savings feature, together with insurance protection, that has made it appealing to some people. A straight life policy may become paid up if dividends are left with the company. A dividend is a return of part of the premium on participating insurance to reflect the difference between the premium charged and the combination of actual mortality, expense, and investment experience. It should also be noted that if a person lives long enough and the straight life policy remains in force long enough, it will eventually become an endowment policy.

---

2. A straight life policy pays dividends only if it is a participating policy. Most policies purchased from mutual companies and some purchased from stock companies are participating policies.

Limited Payment Life Policy

The limited payment life insurance policy is the second type of whole life policy. It carries the idea of the straight life policy a step further. If it can be determined what the annual rates or premiums should be for the straight life policy and what the average lifetime premiums will be, why not divide the lifetime premiums by twenty or thirty and get paid-up insurance? This really amounts to a limited number of installment payments of the premium on such a policy for ten, twenty, thirty years, or to age sixty-five.

This policy provides for permanent protection, but the premiums are paid only for a certain number of years though the protection afforded is for the *whole life* of the individual. The most popular forms are twenty-pay life and thirty-pay life policies. The premium calculation is the same as that for the straight life policy, but, because the payments are made over a shorter period, the yearly or monthly premiums have to be greater. The insured pays much less than the face value of the policy during the limited payment period because the company is able to invest the funds at compound interest from the time the initial payment is made until the time, on the average, when those insured will die. For example, an individual at the age of twenty might be said to have a life expectancy of an additional 51.20 years. Thus, on the average, the company will have the use of the money for many years before it has to pay it out. This also means that the cash value of the policy will continue to rise even after the period for payment of premiums has expired, until eventually, if the insured does not die first, the cash value will equal the face value, and could even rise above it. The main reason for purchasing this type of policy is that some people want to pay for their insurance during the time when their earnings are the highest.

Another reason for buying a limited payment life policy is that it has a heavier savings feature built in than does straight life. If a person wants to save systematically through life insurance, this type of policy provides a means. The savings feature is greater because the premiums are paid sooner than in straight life, hence more interest can be earned and more premiums per year are paid.

The Endowment Policy

The endowment policy provides protection for a specified number of years, at the end of which the insured will receive the face amount of the policy. If an individual purchases a $10,000 endowment policy and dies before the end of the specified number of years, his or her beneficiaries will receive the face amount of the policy. If this person lives for the number of years specified in the policy, the policy has matured and he or she will be paid the face value of the policy. At maturity, the face value and the cash surrender value are the same. An endowment policy has a limited number of payments. The most popular are twenty-year and thirty-year plans.

People who buy endowments usually do so because they want a specific number of dollars for a specific purpose sometime in the future. Funds to send a child to college or to provide for retirement income or a trip around the world might be financed through an endowment policy.

When the endowment plan is paid up, it is like money in the bank rather than like insurance. Beneficiaries are paid with the insured's own money after the endowment plan is paid up. When endowments become paid up, they are usually surrendered and the money used for some specific purpose. However, the policy can be left with the insurance company, where the cash surrender value builds up above the face value at some specified interest rate.

The emphasis in an endowment policy is on savings. Premiums on endowment policies are even higher than on the limited payment life policy. Because these premium funds are then invested and earn interest, the amount paid by the company when the policy matures—or to the beneficiaries if the policyholder dies—is greater than the amount paid in as premiums by the individual.

In summary, one can state that in progression from term, to straight life, to limited payment life, to endowments, the premiums rise with any given age because the savings feature also rises greatly. A second reason why the limited payment life and limited payment endowment policies have higher premiums than equal amounts of a straight life policy is because premiums are, in part, paid in advance. Endowment plans are no longer very popular, because of their high savings feature. Rather, people have chosen other media more immune to inflation, such as common stocks and real estate.

Other Types of Policies; Combinations

A number of other policies are variations or combinations of the above.

Modified plans

Some insurance companies also sell what they call "Mod. Three" and "Mod. Five" life insurance. These modified plans are simple and are designed for special groups. For example, suppose one feels the need for $40,000 of life insurance to protect one's family, but the premiums are more than can be afforded now because one is just out of college and starting out. In three or four years this insurance will be affordable. One could wait, but may not have to.

The Mod. Three and Mod. Five plans have reduced rates the first three and five years respectively, after which time they rise. Since the first few years' premiums are substantially below those indicated by the mortality tables, the later years' premiums must be above the mortality figures. This is exactly the case. This type of policy appeals to people whose income is low now but promises to be high in the future—for example, someone starting a career in medicine or a promising young lawyer.

Variable and universal life insurance

In recent years, two new life insurance policies have been developed: variable life and universal life policies. Both are attempts to protect both the cash value (e.g., the savings feature) and the death benefits of the policy from inflation by investing part of the premiums in high-yielding money market funds or common stock. If the investments do well and the return exceeds inflation, the cash value and the death benefits are increased. In this way, both living and death benefits it is hoped will be inflation proof. But it doesn't always work that way. With the premiums invested in common stock, there may be losses as well as gains, and both the cash value and the death benefit can decline. Some policies have a guarantee that the death benefit will never fall below the face value. Even if the premiums are invested primarily in high-yielding money market funds, your return may not be as high as it should be, because there may be high commissions and brokerage or loading fees. Also, money market interest rates may decline.

Universal life.   Universal life is a combination of annual renewable term insurance tied to an investment program. The premiums must more than cover the cost of the term insurance for there to be a surplus to invest on your behalf. Moreover, this premium rises as you grow older. Often a universal life policy is set up by making a fairly large lump sum payment, which is then invested in various securities and the insurance company deducts from that deposit once a month enough money from the fund to pay the premiums for your life insurance. You may make periodic payments into the fund at any time. You may also increase the face value of your term life insurance; but, if you do, monthly premium withdrawals will be increased. This makes the universal policy more flexible than most others. You have an investment fund that is managed by the insurance company and from which your insurance premiums are withdrawn.

You may also withdraw cash from your fund (after all, it's your money) without any penalty. The only requirement is that your fund always have sufficient money to pay the monthly premiums on your term life insurance. When you set up such a fund to finance your life insurance, there are fees, generally 7 to 8 percent, charged on the moneys you pay in. On a $1,000 payment, then, only $930 to $920 goes into the fund.

Such a fund has certain tax benefits; the interest that it earns is not taxed until you withdraw it. To be sure, this is true of all insurance policy interest income.

Is universal life a good investment? That depends on how well the company manages your funds, and whether or not the company earns more than you could with your own investment program. Generally universal life policies are superior to other permanent insurance policies—such as straight life, limited pay life, and endowments. But if you need more life insurance, it might be better to buy term directly, and invest the difference.

Variable life.   Variable life is similar to universal life and straight life. It differs from straight life in that premiums are invested primarily in variable assets— such as common stock—that fluctuate in price with inflation. It differs from universal life in that premiums are fixed and money cannot be withdrawn from the fund. Variable life also was developed to protect the policyholder from inflation. Both its face value and its cash value will rise (or fall) if the insurance company is successful in investing in assets that appreciate pricewise with inflation.

What Kind of Insurance—Permanent or Term?

What type of life insurance should be bought depends on the individual. Is it being bought primarily for protection or for a savings program? Persons who need protection primarily should weight their insurance program toward term, which gives the maximum amount of insurance for the money. It often appeals to young people who have small children and need a good deal of insurance but have a limited income. However, term insurance eventually expires.

It has been stated that one who can save on one's own should buy term insurance and then bank the differential in premiums between term and straight life. Would a person who did this be better off in twenty years? Whether this is true would depend upon how much interest one could earn. Probably in most cases one could earn a little more in a savings and loan association than in an insurance company, but this is not always true. Also, in some cases there is a tax advantage in saving through life insurance, because any interest earned in a savings and loan association is fully taxable as income.[3] There is no hard and fast rule regarding what type of insurance one should buy. Some people, however, feel they should save via several media, if for no other reason than that one is never sure what the return on a future investment will be. Therefore, they diversify their savings and investment portfolio and buy some permanent insurance for savings purposes.

Cash Value Buildup and Net Risk to the Insurance Company

We have seen why and how insurance policies, with the exception of term, build up cash surrender values. The cash surrender value should be looked on as savings by the policyholder; it is like money in the bank because the policyholder may surrender his or her policy, take the cash surrender value (the living benefits), and call it quits at any time. If the policyholder dies before surrendering the policy, the amount of funds the beneficiary receives, which come from the insurance company's pocket, is the difference between face value and cash surrender value. This difference is also the amount of risk the insurance company

3. How life insurance is taxed will be discussed later in the chapter.

assumes, a risk that declines dollarwise as the years pass. This cash surrender value and the risk the insurance company assumes are illustrated in Figure 11–2. The two bottom curves are for a straight life policy, the two middle are for a twenty-pay life, and the two top are for a twenty-year endowment. The cash surrender value was calculated for a $25,000 face value policy on a twenty-year-old person in each case. The annual premiums are $322.25, $539.75, and $1,047.25, respectively. Each policy has two possible buildups: one (the lower curve) if you take the annual dividends in cash, and one (the upper curve) if you leave them to accumulate more interest. The cash surrender value builds up over the years, as depicted by the curves, and the savings are represented by the surface under the curve. The risk assumed by the insurance company is depicted by the area above the curve, and this risk declines as the years pass. In the case of the twenty-year endowment policy, if the person were to die at

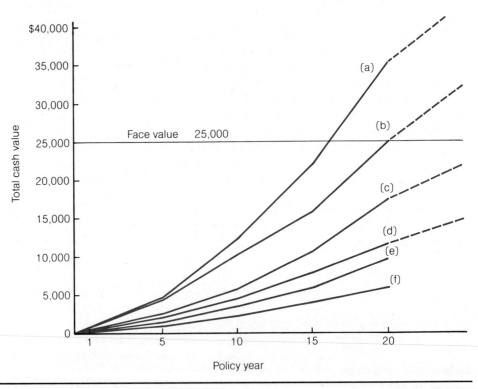

Figure 11–2 The relationships between cash surrender value and face value for each of three insurance policies for a female aged twenty. (a) Twenty-year endowment, dividends accumulated; (b) twenty-year endowment, dividends withdrawn; (c) twenty-pay life, dividends accumulated; (d) twenty-pay life, dividends withdrawn; (e) straight life, dividends accumulated; (f) straight life, dividends withdrawn. Dividends accumulated at interest are based on the 1982 dividend scale and are not guaranteed; dividends are withdrawn at guaranteed cash value. These graphs were furnished by a large eastern mutual life insurance company.

the end of the twentieth year, the company would simply give the beneficiary $25,000 of the policyholder's own money.

If the dividends are left with the company, the cash surrender value will build up more quickly and, with an endowment policy, will equal the face value in a little over sixteen years; if the policyholder dies about then, his or her beneficiaries are paid off with his own money. (In all cases, if there is a death claim the companies pay the face value or the cash value, whichever is the larger.) The amount of insurance a person has then declines as the years pass and the cash surrender value builds up.

At the end of twenty years the limited pay life (LPL) and the endowment policy are paid up and premiums are no longer paid. The cash surrender value if not taken by the policyholder will now build up more slowly because only interest return adds to cash value. This is depicted by the dotted line. In the case of a whole life policy, the cash surrender value continues at a more uniform rate because in theory this type of policy is never paid up. There are two exceptions to this statement, however. First, if the policyholder outlives the mortality tables—which happens when one reaches the age of one hundred—the policy is paid up. At age one hundred one is actuarially dead, and insurance companies will pay off the policy. One has not won without dying, however, because cash surrender value is equal to face value. The other exception is when dividends are left with the company. In such a case, a straight life policy may become paid up before a person dies even though the person is not one hundred years of age. Whether it does depends on the age of the person when the policy was bought and upon the interest rate the insurance company is able to earn. Any policy will build up more quickly if dividends are left with the company.

OTHER TYPES OF LIFE INSURANCE

Group Life Insurance

The major difference between life insurance sold to an individual and that sold to a group is one of administration. Insurance is often sold by the life insurance company to a business firm, and the business firm provides each insured employee with an insurance certificate. The premiums may be withheld from the employees' salary, they may be paid entirely by the employer, or they may be shared. A second difference between group life insurance and insurance sold to an individual is that group life involves neither an individual medical examination nor an individual application for insurance.

The group insurance package commonly consists of some term, which provides for benefits on the death of the policyholder, and some medical insurance (which is health, not life, insurance and is discussed in the next chapter) to pay for all or part of the medical bills of the employees covered. Usually employees automatically lose this group insurance when they leave the company, even by retirement. However, employees have the right to convert their group insurance to an individual policy within thirty days after leaving the employer, without a medical examination. If they do convert, they pay the higher premiums that individual policies require.

Group insurance is nearly always cheaper than individual insurance, for several reasons. First, the employer may pay all or part of the premiums. Even if not, the administrative cost to the insurance company is less, and part of these savings are passed on to the policyholder. Since only one policy is written for many individuals, underwriting costs are reduced. Clerical and accounting costs are less for the same reasons, and the costs of premium collection also are less because the company involved remits one check per month for all the employees. In addition, commissions to insurance salespeople are eliminated or greatly reduced, the contract being often negotiated directly by the insurance company and the business whose employees are to be covered. Finally, in some cases a person saves because the premiums are determined by the average age of the employees covered. Because of this the younger members of the group subsidize the older in some cases. In other cases, the group is broken into six or eight age categories, and the premium for each category is determined by the average age therein. Most group plans are sold via a common employer; if you are self-employed, check your professional organizations, which often have a group plan. Group life insurance is the modern way to buy life insurance because it is cheaper. However, there are limits, imposed by state law, on the maximum amount of group life insurance a person may buy, usually some multiple of the person's annual income. Because of this limit, group insurance cannot be looked on as a complete insurance plan.

Credit Life Insurance

Another type of life insurance policy is the so-called *credit life policy*. Many financial institutions require that anyone borrowing money on a personal note be insured for the amount of the note. Thus a bank or other lending institution will automatically sell a creditor enough insurance to cover the amount of the loan in the event the borrower dies before the debt is paid. The lender merely sells the borrower the credit insurance; the institution has an arrangement with an insurance company that actually carries the policy.

Credit life insurance is a specialized type of term policy. It is also most often sold on a group basis; the lender has an arrangement with an insurance company whereby all of its borrowing customers are covered by one plan.

Industrial Life Insurance

Industrial life insurance is commonly referred to as the "nickel and dime" life insurance business. Most of the policies are sold to people in low-income groups

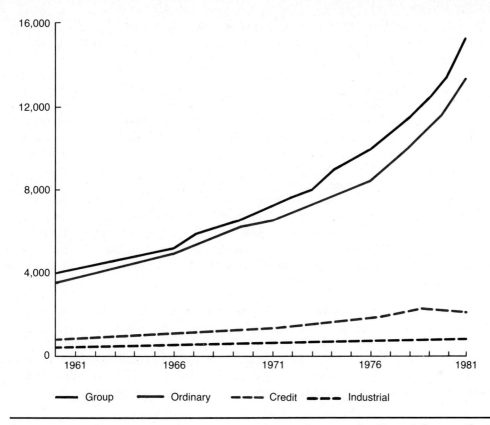

Figure 11–3. Average size life insurance policy in force in the United States. (*Source: 1982 Life Insurance Fact Book*, American Council of Life Insurance, p. 21.)

and have an average death benefit of about $600. Approximately 55 million of these policies are in force, with a total coverage of about $35 billion.

Collections of premiums are often made weekly by agents who in some cases literally go from door to door. As a result, the insurance is exceedingly costly and should be avoided wherever possible. The amount of industrial insurance in force in some recent years has actually declined. Figure 11–3 illustrates the average size of the various types of life insurance in effect.

GI Life Insurance (Government Insurance)

The United States government made insurance available to members of the armed forces for the first time during World War I. Term insurance, whole life, and endowment policies were offered. The limit was $10,000 face value.

During World War II the federal government once again provided insurance in the form of the National Service Life Insurance, the famous GI life insurance. It was issued as term insurance but the serviceman could convert it to permanent insurance within one year. When the serviceman was discharged, he could keep this insurance, and many did. The maximum amount of GI insurance that could be purchased was $10,000, and it was much cheaper than any insurance that any civilian company could provide, because the government paid for the administrative cost of the program, and, of course, there were no commissions.

The reason the government embarked upon these two insurance schemes was to provide protection against the risk of death due to war action. During both world wars private insurance companies inserted "war" clauses into all of their insurance contracts. If a person was killed in a war, the insurance would not pay off. During the Korean War, the "war clause" was again widely used, and the federal government again provided government insurance. Today the "war clause" is not in general use. During the Vietnam War, Servicemen's Group Life Insurance replaced the National Service Life Insurance, and it is in effect today.

Today military persons are eligible to buy up to $35,000 of term life insurance from the government. It is a group policy officially called Servicemen's Group Life Insurance, administered by the Veteran's Administration, with insurance provided by private insurance companies. The government acts just like an employer and buys a group plan for all service personnel. When people leave the service, they have one hundred twenty days in which to convert their insurance with a civilian insurance company without taking a medical examination. If they do not convert, the insurance lapses.

Mutual Savings Bank Life Insurance

There are limits to how much insurance you may buy under a group plan; if that is inadequate, you may wish to supplement it. In such a case, if you are fortunate enough to live in Massachusetts, New York, or Connecticut, investigate the life insurance sold by mutual savings banks, because in these states MSBs are permitted to sell insurance. While they don't solicit the business, their rates are generally below what you would pay when dealing with a life insurance company directly. The main reason for this is that commissions are not charged.

OTHER THINGS TO KNOW ABOUT LIFE INSURANCE

First, you have to select an insurance company. Not all companies are the same; premiums vary for a number of reasons. Life insurance benefits are taxed differently, and there are certain other benefits and options that a policyholder enjoys.

Selecting a Company; Why Premiums Vary

There are more than 1,700 life insurance companies in the United States, and they are not all the same. There are big and small, and stock and mutual companies. Therefore, when buying something so important, you should shop around.

Premiums of course vary with the type of policy and the age of the insured. Table 11–8 shows this variation; the premiums shown are annual premiums per $1,000 of insurance. Premiums must be set high enough to meet the expenses of running the company, expenses that are largely wages and salaries of the insurance company employees.

Premiums also vary from company to company for like policies on individuals of the same age. The following factors help explain this variation.

1. Some companies have a more favorable mortality experience, that is, their death claims are fewer (or come later) per ten thousand policyholders, and hence their mortality tables are more favorable than those of other companies.
2. Not all companies are equally efficient. Some have higher administrative and clerical costs than others.
3. Some companies earn a higher rate of return on their investments than others.

While there is an official mortality table (the Commissioners Standard Ordinary [CSO]), insurance companies are permitted to use their own mortality

Table 11–8   Annual premiums per $1,000 insurance

Age	Term 1 yr	Straight life OL	LPL 20L	LPE 20E
Male				
18	$1.79	$ 8.26	$19.15	$44.93
19	1.79	8.44	19.47	44.94
20	1.79	8.52	19.68	44.96
30	1.91	11.88	24.68	45.33
40	2.76	17.82	30.58	47.24
50	6.51	28.22	44.45	52.90
Female				
18	$1.58	$ 7.74	$18.63	$44.77
19	1.58	7.91	18.94	44.77
20	1.58	8.92	19.13	44.79
30	1.77	12.95	23.21	45.09
40	2.24	15.77	28.53	46.34
50	5.11	24.40	36.63	51.06

Figures furnished by a large eastern insurance company.

experience with only the proviso that it cannot be less favorable to the policyholder than the CSO. Consequently, with different mortality tables, premiums can vary somewhat from company to company.

Furthermore, not all companies are equally well managed and hence their costs are not the same. Even with companies that are equally well managed, the expense of running the insurance company, per $1,000 of life insurance in force, may vary with the size of the company and how fast it is growing. Generally newer and smaller companies have higher costs than older and larger companies, but there are exceptions. The percentage yield on the investments that a company earns will vary from company to company. A company that consistently earns more can either pay a higher dividend or charge a lower premium.

A final reason why insurance premiums vary is that two different policies from two different companies, while they appear about the same, may not be. Only one of them may have a dismemberment clause, which provides so much for the loss of an arm or a leg. You may or may not want this coverage, but if your policy has it you will pay more. Also the guaranteed cash surrender value buildup over the years may differ on two otherwise like policies. In such a case, different amounts of savings are built into otherwise similar policies. This can, of course, be done by varying premiums or dividends.

Thus, you will be able to obtain a better bargain by shopping around and comparing companies' policies. Some weight should also be given to the financial strength and financial soundness of the insurance company with which you deal. While total assets of the insurer are important, they are not the only factor to consider because there are also liabilities. It is difficult to compare the financial soundness of the various insurers, but one meaningful bench mark is referred to as the policyholder's "surplus ratio." It is simple—the insurance company's net worth (assets less liabilities) divided by liabilities. It can easily be calculated from an insurance company's balance sheet.

Insurance companies are regulated by the states. It is the task of the regulatory agencies to make sure that the insurers are sufficiently sound. However, the rigor of these agencies (and the stringency of the laws under which they operate) varies from state to state. You may place some confidence in an insurance company if it operates in many, and especially in all, states. Since New York state has the toughest (best from the consumer's point of view) insurance laws, some financial advisers suggest that a bit more confidence may be placed in an insurance company that operates in New York.

Comparing Different Companies' Policies

Comparing term policies is usually simple enough. Since often no dividend is involved and there is no cash surrender value, a simple comparison of premiums per $1,000 of face value is all that is required.

In the case of permanent insurance, the analysis is more complex, but two or more similar policies can be analyzed to see which appears to be the better buy. This can only be approximated. First you must subtract the likely dividends from the gross annual premiums. Since future dividends are unknown, they must be estimated based on past experience. This calculation will give you the approximate net annual premiums. You must now multiply this by, say, 5, and 10, and 20, to get your total premiums over the years. Then compare that to what the cash surrender value (which can be predicted with accuracy and which is stated in the policy) of the policy will be in 5, and 10, and 20 years. If you do this with several policies you will be able to spot the better buy. However, while this can give you a comparison among several policies, it ignores the interest you could have been earning with your premium dollars if you had invested them elsewhere. It also ignores the present value of dollars payable in the future, and future dollars are likely to be worth less than present dollars.

The recently developed interest-adjusted indexes attempt to consider factors and in so doing compare the cost of different policies. In the interest-adjusted method of calculating costs, each year's premium is assumed to earn interest (at, say, 5 percent). In calculating the index we first obtain the total (say 20 years) accumulation of premiums plus interest. From this we subtract, first, all dividends plus interest on them, and, second, the cash value of the policy at the end of twenty years. The result is the total (20 year) cost of the policy. It is then divided by the number of $1,000 units of coverage to get the 20-year cost per $1,000 of insurance. This cost per $1,000 is then divided again by a factor (34.57 in our case).[4] The final result is a dollar figure that if set aside each year at 5 percent would equal the net dollar cost of your policy. This will vary from company to company, but a recent random sample of nine different companies indicated that this interest-adjusted cost figure on a straight life policy on a thirty-five-year-old man varied from a low of $4.33 to a high of $6.68. While this interest-adjusted index is only an approximation, it is a useful measure of the difference in the cost of a policy.

Grace Period

After a premium is due but not paid, there is generally a grace period of twenty-eight to thirty-one days during which the premium may be paid without penalty. In the event that a policyholder dies during the grace period, the unpaid premium is collected from the amount paid to the beneficiary.

---

4. This ($34.57) is the amount of money you would have if you added one dollar per year for twenty years and these dollars were earning interest at 5 percent. In many tables this figure is 33.066, but this is because most tables accrue no interest until the end of the year, whereas in our case we earn interest continuously over the entire year.

Reinstatement

Most policies contain a provision for reinstatement. If your policy has lapsed, you may, within a stated period, put it into effect again provided that you are insurable, and of course this implies another physical examination. If you pass the physical, you must then pay the overdue premiums together with interest.

Incontestability

After two years, your policy will ordinarily be incontestable. This means that the company is given two years in which to check certain information given by you when you made your original application for the policy. If the company discovers that you made a materially false statement, it may seek to have itself released from the policy. After the incontestable period has passed, however, the company can no longer seek such release.

Nonforfeiture Value

What happens if one can no longer pay the premiums for some reason? Term insurance, which has no cash surrender value, will lapse after the grace period. If it is permanent life insurance and has built up a cash surrender value, one has four options. (Recall from the discussion that generally all policies except term build up a cash value after they have been in force for a few years and that this cash value increases as the years pass.) One's options are assured by the nonforfeiture values that in a sense guarantee the cash surrender value of your policy. These four options are:

1. *Cash value.* A policy can be surrendered for its cash value. This cash surrender value can be taken in one lump sum or in a number of regular payments if it is large enough (usually $1,000 or more). This cash surrender value is like money in the bank and builds up because many policies have a savings feature built into them.

2. *Extended term insurance.* Often a policy includes a provision that if the holder fails to pay the premiums during the grace period, the policy automatically will remain in force as a term policy for as long as the cash surrender value of the policy will permit. For example, suppose you have a $4,000 cash surrender value in a $20,000 ordinary life insurance policy and you have failed to pay your premium during the grace period. Under the terms of the policy, the amount of cash surrender value ($4,000) may be enough to keep that policy in force as term insurance for nine or ten years. Your $4,000 equity in the policy actually is used to pay the premium on what will now be an *extended term policy*.

3. *Reduced paid-up insurance.* If one no longer wishes to pay premiums, one can reduce the face value of life insurance but keep it in force as paid-up permanent insurance. Then your $4,000 cash surrender value on your $20,000 policy might provide a paid-up policy with a face value of $10,000. This is now paid up and in force, and the death payment would become $10,000 but you no longer need to pay premiums.
4. *Automatic premium loan* (APL). Some insurance policies have a provision that grants the insured an automatic loan used to pay the premiums after the grace period has expired if the policy has a cash value. This is designed to prevent the policy from lapsing due to the insured accidentally forgetting to pay the premiums, which might happen if he or she is on an extended trip. Then upon the policyholder's return the loan could be repaid and the insurance continue in its original form.

Borrowing on Your Life Insurance Policy

You may borrow the cash surrender value of your life insurance policy from the company, and often you can use the policy as security for a loan from a commercial bank. Most states have laws requiring these loans to be made by insurance companies. However, insurance companies may wait as long as several months before making the loan. In practice, however, they make the money available almost immediately.

Insurance companies charge about 8 percent (annual percentage rate) interest on these loans, as low a rate as you can get anywhere. The theory behind these loans and low interest rates is that the policyholder is merely using his or her own money. The insurance companies must obtain the small interest which they charge because were it not for the policy loan they would invest the money elsewhere and their investment income would be greater. Since the insurance contract is made with an assumption of certain interest income, they have to charge a rate on policy loans.

There can be a danger in borrowing from your insurance company. First of all, these loans are single repayment rather than installment loans. Therefore, you must do some budgeting and set aside a sum every week or month so that you will be able to liquidate the loan eventually. Moreover, there is no obligation ever to repay the loan. Some people just continue to pay the interest. If there is a death claim on a policy with a loan outstanding, it is deducted before the face value is paid. In some states the borrower is not even required to pay interest. In such a case, if the amount borrowed plus the accumulating interest grow to equal the cash surrender value of the policy, it is cancelled, and you end up with no insurance. Therefore, unless you are absolutely sure you will repay the loan, you should think twice before borrowing from your insurance company. It might be better to use your policy as collateral for a bank loan. Such a secured loan will permit you to borrow at a favorable interest rate, and the bank will make you repay the loan.

Assignment

It is frequently possible to use one's life insurance policy as collateral (and hence reduce the interest rate) when borrowing money from banks and others. Lenders may feel it desirable for them to be assigned the policy, so that if the borrower dies before repaying the obligation, the debt will be paid from the proceeds of the policy. To assign a policy, however, one must have the right to change the beneficiary; otherwise, it will be necessary to obtain the beneficiary's consent. Furthermore, the policy specifically states that no assignment will be binding on the company until the company has been notified.

Ownership of the Policy

In a life insurance contract, there are the insured, the beneficiaries, and the owner of the policy. The meaning of *insured* and *beneficiary* is clear and needs no further elaboration, but the term *owner* requires explanation.

Usually, but not always, the insured is also the owner. The insured can turn ownership over to the beneficiary. The owner of the policy, while living, has the right to modify the policy, change the beneficiary (if he or she has reserved that right in the policy), select the settlement options, surrender or cancel the policy, receive any insurance dividends, and any other rights which may exist. On the death of the insured (who may or may not be the owner) ownership of the policy is immediately and automatically transferred to the beneficiary.

One reason why a person may want to transfer ownership to the beneficiary prior to death is to avoid estate taxes. (Estate taxes are discussed in Chapter 20.) If the beneficiary is not the owner prior to the death of the insured, then although the beneficiary receives the insurance claim upon the death of the insured, it is subject to the deceased's estate tax (not income tax, but estate tax). If the beneficiary is the owner, this tax is avoided. To make certain that this tax savings is realized, however, the beneficiary–owner should have his or her own checking account and pay the insured's premiums with his or her own personal checks. The actual transfer of ownership to the beneficiary is also a gift; and if the cash surrender value of the policy is large, this could have gift tax implications. (See Chapter 20 for a discussion of gift taxes.)

One word of warning: if you transfer ownership of your policy, you lose all control over it and can never change the beneficiary or the settlement options, nor will you receive the dividends it may pay. In addition, if the owner–beneficiary dies before the insured, the cash value of the policy becomes part of the beneficiary's estate.

Change of Beneficiary; Third Party Rights

There may be many reasons why one might want the beneficiary in a policy changed, such as marriage, divorce, or newborn children. To effect such a change at any time, one must have reserved the right to change the beneficiary when originally taking out the policy; most policies contain a clause giving this right. The company will furnish the proper forms. In some cases, where the insured has failed to reserve the right to change the beneficiary when taking out the policy, he or she must first obtain the consent of the present beneficiary in writing before the company will permit the change to be made.

What happens if a named beneficiary dies before the policyholder? Normally the company pays the money directly to one's estate. However, one or more persons can be, and usually are, named in the policy as contingent beneficiaries. In this case, the contingent beneficiary or beneficiaries receive the proceeds of the policy should the first-named beneficiary die before the insured.

Settlement Options

Several different settlement options may be chosen that will determine how insurance benefits are to be paid. These options may be selected by the owner of the policy or the beneficiary, depending on the circumstances. The owner has first choice at selecting the options; if he or she does not do so, the beneficiary may. The owner of the policy is also usually the insured, but this need not be the case. If the payments are living benefits, the owner is also usually the beneficiary, and he or she will choose the options. If the owner has selected a certain option and then dies, the beneficiary must live with that decision. If, as is often true, the owner has not selected any option, upon his or her death the beneficiary may do so. If the beneficiaries are of sound mind and able to handle money, it is probably best not to select settlement options until the benefits are to be paid. If the beneficiary is a minor or has shown that he or she cannot handle money, then the owner might want to provide for certain specific installment payments rather than one lump sum settlement. Anyone who has the right to select an option has the right to change it during his or her lifetime. If an installment option rather than a lump sum is selected, arrangements can be made for the payments to be made on an annual, semiannual, quarterly, or monthly basis.

There are four general options from which to choose:

1.   *Lump sum.* In this case the entire sum is paid at once, and the beneficiary has the money management problem. However, when interest rates are high, this person might be able to earn more on his or her lump sum settlement than the insurance company.

2.   *Interest payment only.* The company holds the principal sum due under the terms of the policy. Arrangements are made with the company to pay interest at a guaranteed rate, the payments to be received for a stated number of years or for life. Upon the death of the beneficiary the principal could be paid to a secondary beneficiary. Or this option could have a proviso that at some predetermined future date the principal would go to the primary beneficiary if still alive. If only interest is paid, the principal

is never exhausted, and some provision must be made to pay it to someone eventually. Sometimes arrangements are made whereby the beneficiary can dip into the principal within limits. This would reduce future interest payments, but would provide flexibility and an additional source of money for the beneficiary in the event of an emergency.

3.   *Installment payments.* The company makes regular payments in equal amounts until the fund is exhausted. During the time that such regular payments are being made, the company will add interest to the part of the money not paid out. If each payment is for a specific amount—for example, $50 per month—then the length of time during which the payments will be made depends on the amount of the policy, the amount of the periodic income payment, and the rate of interest guaranteed in the policy.

If the payments are to be spread out over a given time period—ten or fifteen years—the amount of each payment depends on the amount of the policy, the number of years the income is to be paid, and the rate of interest guaranteed in the policy.

Thus one can decide that the payments are to be made as a stated sum per month or can elect to have the money paid for a stated time period. One may, furthermore, when electing installment payments for the beneficiary, permit the beneficiary to "commute" the remaining payments, or to stop the income payments and choose to take all the money that remains in one final payment. The policyholder may also arrange that any money left when the first beneficiary dies shall be paid in one sum or continued as income to one or more secondary beneficiaries.

4.   *Life annuity income.* One may elect to receive as a settlement a life annuity income. Briefly, a life annuity gives the beneficiary, or annuitant, a stated income for as long as he or she lives. (See Chapter 19.)

In some annuity plans, if the annuitant dies before the payments reach a stated total amount or before the payments have been made for a stated period of time, arrangements can be made to have the payments made to a secondary beneficiary. The amount of each payment depends on several factors, including the age of the annuitant when payment begins, the specified mortality table, the rate of interest guaranteed in the policy, the form of life annuity settlement used, and the amount of the policy.

Another variation of this option is sometimes chosen if there are two or more primary beneficiaries, the joint survivorship life income annuity. It is the same as life annuity income just described, except that payments are made until both beneficiaries are deceased.

Disability Premium Waiver

The waiver of premium, or what is more commonly referred to as a "disability clause" in a life insurance policy, means that any premiums that fall due after the beginning of a total and permanent disability will be waived. Thus if one is disabled, the life insurance policy will continue in force because the company will make the premium payments. Disability must occur before one has reached a certain age, generally age sixty, and before the policy is paid up. In some cases, the disability must last for at least six months before premiums will be waived.

To have such a disability clause written into the policy, the insured must request it and must pay a small additional premium. The disability clause written into a policy really amounts to taking out additional insurance to insure that the premiums will continue to be paid if the policyholder is disabled. The addition to the premium is so small that its inclusion is recommended.

Accidental Death Benefits

The clause relating to accidental death benefits is sometimes also called "double indemnity." Under the provisions of this clause, the company promises to pay twice the face value of the policy if death occurs by accidental means. If the death is to be construed as "accidental," it must occur within a certain time after one is injured. Suppose, for example, that an injury occurs that causes hospitalization for, say, one year, and after a year death can be directly attributed to the accident. In such a case, the accidental death benefit clause of the policy will probably not apply. Most policies state that death must occur within ninety days after the accident to be construed as accidental death. Furthermore, there is commonly a second limitation to the accidental death clause: the accidental death must have occurred before age sixty or sixty-five, depending on the policy.

The double indemnity clause further excludes from the meaning of "accidental" death death arising from certain kinds of accidents. The reason is either that these deaths result from risks that cannot be calculated or that the cause of death is not accidental in the legal sense. For instance, if a person jumps from a moving car, his or her death is suicide, not an accident, and the double indemnity will not hold. Of if a person has a heart attack while driving a car and is killed in an accident caused by the attack, that person is not covered even though the death is caused by the accident, not the heart attack.

It is even possible to obtain a triple indemnity clause in an insurance policy. In such a case, the company pays three times the face value in the event of accidental death as defined above. An added premium must be paid in order to obtain either a double or a triple indemnity clause. However, these added premiums are not high. A traveling salesperson or other frequent traveler might want to consider either a double or a triple indemnity clause.

Stock Insurance Companies Versus Mutual Companies

There has been much discussion over the respective merits of these companies. The *stock company* is a corporation, the ownership of which is in the hands of stockholders, and, as in any other corporation, the business affairs of the corporation are run by a board of directors. The profit, if any, is distributed to the stockholders much in the same manner as that of any corporation.

A *mutual life insurance company*, on the other hand, is owned by the policyholders. No stock is issued. The idea is that each policyholder is entitled to share in the profits of the company. On the other hand, policyholders can be assessed—in theory at least—in the event of losses in excess of their reserves. The assessment is usually limited to 100 percent of the annual premium. However, there has been a tendency on the part of the mutual companies to issue a nonassessable insurance contract, so the policyholder is virtually exempted from liability. The management of the mutual company is entrusted to experts in the insurance business just as the management of the stock company is placed in the hands of experts.

Insurance Dividends

The distinction between stock and mutual companies is important because of dividends. Historically, insurance dividends have been paid by mutual companies to their policyholders. These should not be confused with the stock dividends given as a share of the profits to the stockholders of the stock companies. In the mutual company, if the income exceeds the amount needed to pay beneficiaries and expenses, part of it is returned to the policyholders in the form of dividends. The policyholder is generally given a choice of receiving the cash, applying the amount to subsequent premiums, buying paid-up additional insurance, or leaving it with the company at interest.

To compete with dividends paid to mutual policyholders, some stock companies issue a participating type of policy, which provides that the policyholder will share in the profits of the corporation along with the shareholders. Generally the premium rates of the participating policies are higher than those of the nonparticipating policies.

Frequently, the premiums on policies issued by stock companies are lower than those issued by mutual companies. These are the nonparticipating policies. Some stock companies, then, issue both participating and nonparticipating policies. Both of these are a competitive device to offset wholly or partially the dividends paid by the mutual companies to their policyholders. Some stock companies argue that the dividends paid by the mutual companies are not all earnings being paid to the policyholders; these critics say that mutual companies charge too much in premiums in the first place and are thus merely returning the excess premiums. Mutual companies are quick to deny this charge.

Just under one-half of all life insurance policies are issued by stock companies and the balance by mutual companies. When buying life insurance and trying to choose between mutual and stock companies, keep in mind both the premiums and the dividends. The problem is often difficult because dividends are not guaranteed; however, a record of past dividends is usually available.

Keep in mind, when deciding between buying a policy from a mutual or stock company, the guaranteed buildup of cash surrender value. While the guaranteed cash buildup of stock companies is often somewhat higher than that guaranteed by mutual companies, the actual achieved cash buildup of the mutuals is usually better, especially in the long run. This is because if mutual companies earn more than they guarantee, they add it to the cash value, and in recent years this has happened. In the case of stock companies, any earnings in excess of that guaranteed may go to the stockholders, not the policyholders. Hence, the actual and the guaranteed cash buildups of a policy from a stock company are more likely to be the same.

Regardless of whether insurance dividends are a return of premiums or shared interest which the company earned with the policyholders' premiums, a policyholder receiving them must decide what to do with them.[5] There are several alternatives from which to choose.

1.   You may take the dividend in cash and use as any other income.
2.   You may apply the dividend toward the payment of future premiums. Your dividend will usually grow larger as the years pass because your cash surrender value grows larger, and after a time your dividends alone may pay your entire premium.
3.   You may elect to leave the dividend with the company to be compounded at the going interest rate and continue to pay your regular premiums; then the cash surrender value of your policy will build up more rapidly than if you select option 1 or 2, and it will become paid up more rapidly. However, under option 3 you will have to declare on your federal income tax the *added* interest that the company earns with your money. The dividend itself, however, is not taxable; but the interest earned with it is; the company will send you a statement indicating the amount of the interest.
4.   You may use the dividends to buy paid-up additional insurance. Then the face value of your policy goes up some every year, and this incremental amount is paid up. A person who needs more life insurance may want to select this fourth option because it will save commissions. However, buying paid-up additions is like buying a single-premium-payment life insurance policy. One is really paying all future premiums in advance, and while the companies make an allowance for this, it is not very high. Consequently, a single-premium paid-up policy is more expensive than buying insurance the usual way. However, one's dividends might very well add several hundred dollars of paid-up additions each year. This fourth option also results in your cash surrender value rising more rapidly than if you select option 1 or 2 but less rapidly than if you select option 3. Selecting option 4 also relieves you of having to pay federal income taxes on the interest that your dividend earns as in the case of option 3, because your dividend

5.   The Internal Revenue Service has ruled that the entire dividend is a return of premiums for tax purposes. Hence insurance policy dividends are not taxable.

earns no interest. You spend it on more insurance. Your dividend earns no interest if you select option 1 or 2. Only under option 3 does your dividend earn interest. If you select option 4, you will earn dividends on the insurance you bought with previous dividends.

5. You may use your annual dividend to buy one-year term. This will increase the face value of your policy by more than option 4 will for a number of years. After a time, however, option 5 may no longer be a means of providing the maximum anount of insurance because under option 4 the added insurance is permanent and the cumulative amount of it may surpass the amount of annual term you may purchase. If you select this option, your cash surrender value will build up at the same rate as under options 1 and 2.

Taxes and Life Insurance Benefits

Death benefits are not subject to the personal income tax but may be subject to estate taxes. Living benefits from a traditional policy are not taxable most of the time, but there are a few exceptions. There is no tax while the cash value builds up; when you surrender it, the cash value is taxable only if it is greater than the sum of the three following items:

1. The total of all of the premiums paid over the years, less any dividends taken in cash over the years.
2. The total of all of the dividends left with the company over the years.
3. The total of all the interest earned by dividends over the years and which was taxed along the way.

In such a case, the tax is on the excess. For example, if you surrender your policy for $15,000, after having paid over the years premiums—less dividends taken in cash over the years—totaling $12,000, and having left dividends with the company of $2,000, and having earned $500 with those dividends, your tax is levied on $500.

THE SEVEN DON'TS OF LIFE INSURANCE

After taking out insurance policies many people handle them badly. The following suggests that there are proper ways of handling policies.

1. *Don't let insurance go to the wrong people.* A family may take out a policy and name a specific child as the beneficiary. If a second child is born, they take it for granted that the second child will share in the benefits of the policy, but this is not so. It is necessary for a rider to be attached to the

policy specifically naming the second child as one of the beneficiaries, if that is desired. In the event of a divorce, it is necessary that the beneficiary be changed. If a man remarries and forgets to change the beneficiary, then the first wife will receive the proceeds of the policy in the event of his death. These two examples suggest that everyone's insurance program should be periodically reviewed. Every time a situation arises that changes the insurance needs, an individual should review his or her insurance program to make it conform with the changed circumstances.

2. *Don't let insurance dollars be foolishly dissipated.* The problem here is whether or not the beneficiaries should be given lump-sum payments or monthly payments. Some people cannot handle large sums properly.

3. *Don't forget to pay the premiums when they come due.* Most policies carry a thirty-one-day grace period, which means that even if one fails to pay on time, the policy will stay in force during that period. After that period, however, in order to reinstate the contract it may be necessary to take a new physical examination. In the event that an unsuspected change in one's health occurs, it may be impossible to reinstate the policy.

4. *Don't give up policies thoughtlessly.* Changing the kind of insurance one has by taking advantage of conversion privileges in one's policy is often a wise move but not so dropping one policy and buying another. A change in policies is very likely to turn out disadvantageously. Irreplaceable guarantees may be lost. Moreover, the cost of setting up policies is substantial, and since the insurance company applies this to the policyholder in the early years, no cash surrender value is built up on a new policy for a while.

5. *Don't hide policies in out-of-the-way places.* A mislaid policy delays prompt settlement of a death claim. Make sure the family knows where policies are kept.

6. *Don't ever throw away a policy, even if the premiums become unaffordable.* Many a supposedly worthless policy has been discovered to contain valuable benefits available to an individual or his or her heirs.

7. *Don't overlook the borrowing power of policies.* Insurance companies will lend money against the cash value of a policy at relatively low rates of interest.

QUESTIONS FOR REVIEW

1. What are the reasons why people buy life insurance? Who should buy it?
2. When is the best time to buy life insurance?
3. What is the only valid reason for buying life insurance on a child?
4. What are the two main factors to consider in determining how much life insurance to buy?
5. Why should a family's principal wage earner think of insuring his or her partner's life?

6. What is term insurance?
7. If insurance premiums rise with age, how can life insurance companies sell level premium insurance?
8. What is permanent insurance?
9. How is term insurance different from (1) straight life, (2) limited payment life, (3) an endowment policy?
10. What are variable and universal life insurance?
11. What is meant by guaranteed cash buildup? How do life insurance companies guarantee this?
12. Why is group insurance cheaper than ordinary life and industrial life insurance more expensive than ordinary life?
13. What is industrial life insurance, and why is it so costly?
14. What type of insurance would appeal to a young person with a very young family? Why?
15. Why do premiums vary from company to company?
16. How does the grace period in a life insurance policy relate to a policy lapse?
17. Explain the nonforfeiture value and how it works.
18. How does a person change the beneficiary of his or her life insurance policy?
19. Discuss the method and possible reason for an assignment of a life insurance policy.
20. What is a waiver of premium in a life insurance policy?
21. Discuss the age-old arguments between the stock companies and the mutual companies.
22. Discuss life insurance policy dividends. What alternatives does a person have as to how he or she disposes of dividends? Are they taxable?
23. How are life insurance benefits taxed?
24. What are the "seven don'ts" of insurance?

CASES

1. Myrtle and Alfred Newman are in their early thirties and have two children— a boy of six and a girl of four. Myrtle has not worked outside the home since their son was born. Alfred, who works for a large retail store, earns $20,000 per year take-home pay. They are buying their home and have a monthly payment of $450. Alfred has converted his $10,000 GI life insurance policy and is paying premiums on it. Also he has a $50,000 group life insurance policy on which his employer pays all the premiums. Recently an insurance agent suggested that Alfred buy more insurance and recommended term insurance. Should they take the agent's advice and buy more? If so, should they buy term? If more insurance is required, how much more would you recommend?

2.   Ellen Packer has a total of $50,000 of life insurance, which she purchased at various periods over the past twenty years. Ellen is now forty-five years old, and her youngest child will be graduating from college next year. Of the $50,000 of insurance, $20,000 is term insurance that will expire in one more year. Should she renew it? Why or why not?

3.   Donald and Sally McLaughlen are aged forty and thirty-five, respectively, and they have two children, ten and eight. Donald has an annual income after taxes of $25,000 per year and feels that his $35,000 of life insurance is adequate. However, Sally, who earns $18,000 a year, and the children have no life insurance. Do you recommend life insurance for them? Why or why not? If insurance should be purchased, how much?

4.   Archebald and Henrietta Brown are a newly married couple in their early twenties. Archebald has $20,000 of life insurance and plans to buy more later if and when he can afford it. However, Henrietta has a $10,000 policy on her life which she purchased some time ago when she was single. Archebald believes they should surrender this policy, which has a cash surrender value of $1,200, but Henrietta is not sure. They request your advice.

5.   Barbara Kidd is a 21-year-old senior in college. She is single and has no immediate plans to marry. She has accepted a job at $22,000 a year as an accountant with a large CPA firm when she graduates in June. She has no life insurance at present, but will have a health insurance plan and $30,000 of group term life with her employer. Barbara is uncertain whether or not she should buy an individual plan for either savings or protection. Work out an insurance plan for Barbara, and advise her as to how much and what kind of insurance she should buy.

6.   Mary Rupp has decided she should buy an additional $40,000 of life insurance. The insurance agent has told her she could have term, straight life, limited pay life, or a limited pay endowment plan. Mary has noticed a difference in the premiums and requests your clarification.

7.   Peter Calcins has a $20,000 straight life policy which has been paying dividends of about $100 per year recently. Peter has been taking the dividend in cash rather than leaving it to accumulate with the company because of tax reasons. What is this tax reason? What else could Peter do with his dividends? What else could he do and still not pay taxes on them?

8.   Gordon Wetherly works as a chemist for Du Pont and earns $40,000 per year. He is forty-five years old and expects to retire at sixty-five on a company pension plan plus Social Security. Although he does not expect to advance much more with Du Pont, he can look forward to a good steady job at his present income until he is sixty-five. He is not sure he should buy very much insurance for savings purposes, but he does feel he should have some protection for his family. How much insurance should he have for protection purposes? What would the theoretical limit be? What kind of insurance would you recommend?

9.   Wesley and Mary Roberts are a young couple in their early twenties. They

have two children, a girl aged four and a boy aged six. Wesley earns $18,000 at his job with a local manufacturing plant. Mary is a former schoolteacher and will probably go back to work when their daughter starts school. Wesley has a good group medical plan where he works but no life insurance; however, he is a veteran of the armed forces and has $10,000 of government life insurance. He is wondering whether he should buy more life insurance, and if so, what kind and how much. Can you help him?

10. Alfred and Ruth McLain are a young couple in their early twenties who have just graduated from college. They have no children yet but hope to in the future. Alfred has just taken a job as a traveling representative with a large book publisher. Alfred and Ruth would like to begin planning their insurance program now, even though they do not feel they can at this time afford all the insurance they would like. Alfred makes $16,000 per year. Although Alfred's salary is modest at present, he feels he will double it over the next ten years, after which time it will probably level off. Can you plan an insurance program for them? Note the kind and amount of insurance they should have today and ten years from today.

11. Barry Cohen is a millionaire in his thirties. He has inherited a vast sum of money, and since it is wisely invested in securities, Barry is able to live very comfortably on his investment income. He has never worked, and he plans never to do so. He does not think he needs any life insurance. Do you agree? Why or why not? Does he need medical insurance? Is there any other kind of insurance that you can think of that Barry might need?

SUGGESTED READINGS

American Society of Certified Life Underwriters (CLU) Journal. Published quarterly by the American Society of CLU, 270 Bryn Mawr Avenue, Bryn Mawr, Pa. 19010.

Best's Review, Life-Health Edition. Published monthly by A. M. Best Company, Inc., Oldwick, N.J. 08858.

Brown, Robert B. *Guide to Life Insurance.* Indianapolis, Ind.: Rough Notes Co., 1981.

Casey, William J. *Life Insurance Desk Book.* Englewood Cliffs, N.J.: Prentice-Hall, 1976.

Consumer Reports Editors. *The Consumer's Union Report on Life Insurance: A Guide to Planning and Buying the Protection You Need.* New York: Holt, Rinehart and Winston, Inc., 1981.

Finance Facts Yearbook. Washington, D.C.: National Consumer Finance Association. Published annually.

Huebner, Solomon S., and Black, Kenneth, Jr. *Life Insurance,* 8th ed. Englewood Cliffs, N.J.: Prentice-Hall, 1982.

The Journal of Insurance. Published bimonthly by the Insurance Information Institute, 110 William Street, New York, N.Y. 10038.

Kenton, Walter S., Jr. *How Life Insurance Companies Rob You and What You Can Do About It.* New York: Random House, 1983.

Life Insurance Fact Book. New York: Institute of Life Insurance. Published annually.

McEwan, Bruce. *Insurance: What's It All About?* New York: Vantage Press, 1980.

Mehr, Robert I. *Life Insurance.* Dallas: Business Publications, 1977.

A Shopper's Guide to Life Insurance; A Shopper's Guide to Term Life Insurance. Write to Pennsylvania Insurance Dept., Harrisburg, Pa., for a copy.

Understanding Life Insurance, A Basic Guidebook. Milwaukee: Northwestern Mutual Life Insurance Co.

CHAPTER TWELVE

HEALTH CARE AND HEALTH INSURANCE

Health care involves risk management. This risk can, in part at least, be assumed by the individual or shifted to an insurance company. We shall explain below what portion might be assumed by the individual—here we will merely note that the bulk of the risk should be transferred to an insurance company.

Among the hazards or risks of life is the possible loss of earnings and income because of accident and sickness. In addition, there may be heavy medical expenses resulting from doctors' and hospital bills. Physicians' fees and hospital costs have been rising rapidly in recent years and will no doubt continue to do so. It is possible, in the absence of insurance, for a major illness quickly to exhaust the savings of even the upper-middle income groups and force them deeply into debt.

The cost of a hospital room can easily run in excess of $300 per day. Expensive laboratory tests and the use of other expensive equipment are extra. Doctors' and surgeons' fees can in some cases amount to thousands of dollars. The American public spent over $300 billion on health care in 1982. In recent years the cost of health care has been rising more rapidly than the overall price level because of new, expensive, sophisticated equipment; more skilled personnel; better care; and an enormous increase in the demand for medical services generated by government programs. Figure 12–1 shows national health expenditures as a percent of gross national product over the last few years.

Some critics have suggested that a national health plan would reduce the

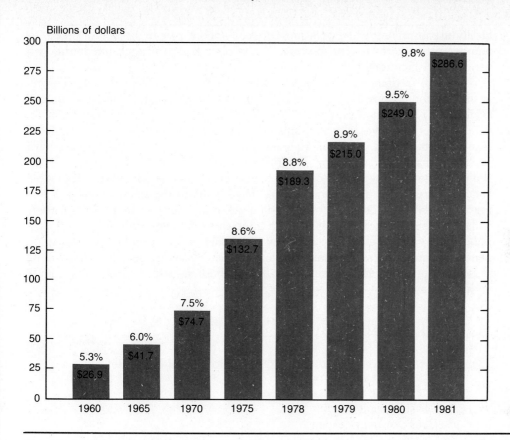

Figure 12–1 National health expenditures and percent of gross national product. (*Source: Source Book of Health Insurance Data, 1982–1983*, Health Insurance Institute, p. 40.)

cost of medical care. Whether this is true is controversial, as is the entire national health insurance proposal to be discussed later in this chapter.

Some maintain that health care costs will continue to rise unless the medical profession develops more paramedical services. Many routine things like giving injections, administering aid for minor ailments, and the like could be performed by medical personnel paid less than doctors. To some extent this has been done, but the medical profession is behind the dental profession in this regard. For example, there is no medical equivalent to dental technicians. Critics, however, maintain that this would lower the quality of medical care, with possible disastrous results at times.

Health insurance has been developed to protect the individual from such high medical costs, as well as against the loss of income. Health insurance, a broad term that covers all insurance in this area, can be broken down into two subclassifications, medical insurance and disability insurance. Medical insurance covers medical expenses including doctors' fees, cost of drugs, and hospital bills.

Disability insurance protects against loss of income while sick or disabled. A number of different health insurance packages can be obtained under the two general classifications.

Health insurance can be purchased on a group or individual basis. To buy group insurance, however, one must be eligible, and usually group insurance is available to the employees of a firm. The premiums on group insurance are lower than on individual policies, and for this reason people who are able to take advantage of a group plan should do so. Most insurance companies have several plans to choose from, differing in various amounts of coverage; some will pay virtually 100 percent of your medical bills, whereas others have deductible and coinsurance features. Some policies have limits to the amount they will pay for a hospital room, others do not. Some will not cover certain ailments, others will. The better the coverage, the higher the premium. Each of the various policies may be purchased to cover an individual or an entire family. There are generally three different premiums quoted for any given policy, one for a single person, another one for a couple with no children, and a third for a couple with children.

TYPES OF HEALTH INSURANCE COVERAGE

Types of health coverage can be classified into several categories:

- Medical expense
    Basic hospital expense
    Basic surgical expense
    Basic medical expense
    Hospital confinement indemnity
    Medical supplement
    Accident only
    Specified disease
    Short-term coverage
    Dental insurance
    Major medical expense
    Comprehensive medical insurance, a combination of all or some of the above
- Disability insurance or loss of income

Table 12–1 shows the number of people in the United States who are covered under some form of the more popular type of health insurance.

Basic Hospital Expense

This insurance covers basic hospital costs such as room and board, nursing care, x-ray costs, drugs, anesthetists and oxygen, laboratory work such as blood tests

Table 12–1   Number of persons with health insurance protection by type of coverage in the United States (000 omitted)

End of year	Hospital expense	Surgical expense	Physician's expense	Major medical expense	Disability income		Dental expense
					Short-term	Long-term	
1940	11,962	4,900	3,000	—	N.A.	N.A.	—
1945	32,072	12,602	4,713	—	N.A.	N.A.	—
1950	76,639	54,156	21,589	—	37,793	*	—
1955	101,400	85,681	53,038	N.A.	39,513	*	—
1960	122,500	111,525	83,172	32,590	42,436	*	N.A.
1961	125,825	116,376	90,393	41,974	43,055	*	N.A.
1962	129,407	119,766	94,717	48,393	45,002	*	N.A.
1963	133,472	124,105	100,095	55,382	44,246	3,029	N.A.
1964	136,304	127,092	106,007	62,112	45,092	3,363	N.A.
1965	138,671	130,530	109,560	69,666	46,927	4,514	N.A.
1966	142,369	133,995	113,986	73,843	49,931	5,068	N.A.
1967	146,409	138,898	119,913	81,550	51,975	6,778	4,570
1968	151,947	143,625	126,233	87,641	55,636	7,836	5,867
1969	155,025	147,774	131,792	95,528	57,770	9,282	8,858
1970	158,847	151,440	138,658	103,544	58,089	10,966	11,972
1971	161,849	153,093	139,399	108,813	59,280	12,284	15,263
1972	164,098	154,687	140,873	113,837	61,548	14,538	16,853
1973	168,455	162,644	151,680	124,627	64,168	17,011	20,418
1974	173,140	166,434	158,170	131,438	65,282	17,799	27,855
1975	177,980	168,895	161,854	134,092	62,971	18,396	30,246
1976	176,581	167,432	163,094	134,992	62,250	17,779	41,559
1977	178,968	167,220	160,429	139,362	64,627	19,364	50,301
1978	184,740	173,324	164,970	141,538	68,307	19,100	58,059†
1979	184,121	174,686	164,754	147,555	65,808	19,920	70,171†
1980	189,000	178,223	169,529	155,192	65,400	21,093	80,528†
1981:							
Under 65	172,726	165,638	153,319	154,513	N.A.	21,682	N.A.
65 and over	15,614	11,260	10,625	3,189	N.A.	—	N.A.
Total	188,340	176,898	163,944	157,702	60,306	21,682	86,302†

N.A.—Not available.

* Included in "Short-term," with the possibility of some duplication of disability income coverage for these years.

†Estimate.

NOTE: Some data are revised from previous years. For 1975 and later, data include the number of persons covered in Puerto Rico and other U.S. territories and possessions. The data refer to the net total of people protected, i.e., duplication among persons protected by more than one kind of insuring organization or more than one insurance company policy providing the same type of coverage has been eliminated.

Source: Source Book of Health Insurance Data, 1982–1983, Health Insurance Institute, p. 13.

and urinalysis, and certain other miscellaneous costs. Many hospital policies also cover other costs, for example, expenses incurred when the insured is treated in a nursing care facility. Also often covered is emergency room treatment in a hospital on an outpatient basis.

Room and board charges often are limited to a stated maximum amount, and a maximum number of days per illness may be stipulated. A person could choose a $100, $150, or $200 per day hospital room allowance with premiums varying accordingly. Some plans provide for full payment of a semiprivate room. Generally, most other hospital fees such as laboratory work are covered in full. If the patient is in intensive care, room costs are much higher, and some policies provide for a higher daily limit; others do not.

Basic Surgical Expense

Payment of surgical fees is not included in policies that cover hospital fees, and separate insurance plans have been developed to take care of them. Usually the company pays a given amount of dollars for certain types of operations. If the fee is above this figure, the person must pay the residual. The amount the policy will pay varies in accordance with the contract. Some policies state that reimbursable surgical fees will be based on reasonable and customary charges for the particular procedure in that area. This makes for uncertainty, but usually a reimbursement schedule is developed based on charges normally or most frequently made by doctors in the area for a similar procedure.

Basic Medical Expense

This type of insurance policy, meant to provide for general medical expenses not covered by surgical and hospital plans, covers such items as drugs and visits to a doctor's office, as well as laboratory work. There may be provision for a maximum number of visits to a doctor per year, and there are also maximum dollar amounts—if not per illness or accident, then per year. Many companies sell this type of coverage only on a group basis or as part of the package when selling comprehensive insurance.

Often these plans have a deductible of, say, $100 per year. The patient pays the first $100 of medical expenses per year and after that costs are usually shared, with the insurance company paying perhaps 80 percent and the patient 20 percent. This insurance will not usually cover visits to the doctor for regular checkups.

Hospital Confinement Indemnity

This relatively rare type of coverage provides for the payment of a specific cash sum of so much per day, per week, or per month while the person is in the hospital. It is similar to—but should not be confused with—disability insurance discussed below. This is short-term insurance, while disability insurance is long-term.

Medical Supplement Insurance

Medicare insurance, for older people, does not pay the entire medical bills of the insured. Supplemental insurance pays some or all of the expenses Medicare recipients are required to pay.

Accident Only

This insurance provides coverage for hospital and medical expenses caused by accident, but not covered by the person's regular hospital and medical policy. There is usually a maximum benefit amount—often $500 to $1,000.

Specific Disease

This is often called cancer insurance. However, it provides coverage for one or more catastrophic and/or devastating diseases stated in the policy, such as cancer or heart disease. It often pays substantial sums above what the person's regular insurance pays.

Short-Term Coverage

Short-term coverage of a few months takes care of the gap between permanent coverage being arranged for and the termination of previous coverage. This gap could arise during moves from one job to another, or for graduating students who have not yet taken their first job.

Dental Insurance

Many companies are now offering dental insurance covering examinations, fillings, extractions, root canals, oral surgery, and most other dental work. There is a limit to payments (usually $500) for expensive work such as orthodontics. There are also yearly limits applied separately to each member of the family. The plans have a deductible amount; usually 80 percent of the costs above the deductible are paid by the insurance company and 20 percent by the insured. Some plans also have a proviso that they will not cover a routine examination more often than once every six months. Figure 12–2 shows dental expense protection in the United States.

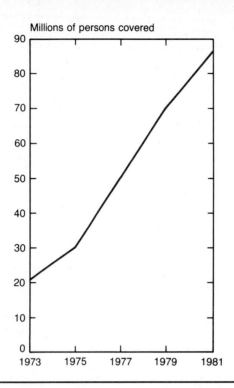

Figure 12–2   **Dental expense protection in the United States.** (*Source: Source Book of Health Insurance Data, 1982–1983,* Health Insurance Institute, p. 20.)

Major Medical Expense

Major medical insurance covers virtually all medical expenses except dental work. It covers hospital fees, physicians' and surgeons' fees, laboratory work, drugs, and nursing care. It is in effect catastrophe insurance; if a person has very high medical bills because of a serious illness or accident, major medical coverage comes into force. Also that portion of hospital, surgical, and basic medical expenses not paid by those policies can often be submitted under a major medical plan. Major medical insurance can be purchased on a group or on an individual basis, and can cover not only the individual but the entire family.

Deductible feature

Generally, the major medical policy has a deductible that the policyholder must pay which may range anywhere from $100 to $500 or even higher. The higher the deductible, the lower the premium. If a policy has a $500 deductibility clause, this means that the policyholder pays the first $500 of a medical bill. In most major medical policies, the deductible feature applies on a yearly rather than an illness basis. Therefore, once the person has paid a $500 deductible medical bill, all future medical expenses for the remainder of the year are submitted to the insurance company. This includes all bills not covered by regular medical or surgical insurance, because they too have a deductible feature. Sometimes there is also a family deductible which may be less than the sum of the deductibles of the individual family members. For example, if a family of four is covered and the policy has a $500 individual deductible, every member does not need to meet the $500 before he or she is covered. Rather, once that family as a group has reached $2,000 (and sometimes even less), the deductible is considered satisfied for all family members.

Coinsurance features

Most of the major medical policies contain a coinsurance as well as a deductible feature, in accordance with which the company agrees to pay only a part of the total expense. Most companies agree to pay up to 80 or 90 percent of the cost, with the insured paying the remaining 10 or 20 percent. For example, assume a bill of $2,500 with a $500 deductible clause and an agreement on the part of the company to pay 80 percent of the total cost above the deductible; the company would pay $1,600, with the remainder to be paid by the insured ($2,500 total bill, minus $500, or $2,000 × .80 or $1,600, which is to be paid by the company). Some major medical plans will pay 100 percent of all medical costs after a specific dollar amount has been achieved. The policy may pay 80 percent of the cost in excess of $500, and then 100 percent after the total yearly bill has reached $2,000. The maximum that the insured would then pay in such a case would be $800 (the first $500 deductible plus 20 percent on the next $1,500).

Benefits paid include virtually all kinds of health care prescribed by physicians. These include treatment given in and out of hospitals, special nursing care, x-rays, drugs, medical appliances, surgeons' fees, and many others. Major medical then covers many of the same things as does hospital insurance, surgical insurance, and regular medical insurance. However, major medical covers the big expenses that are above the maximums for basic policies.

Limitations

Most of the major medical policies contain a maximum amount that the company will pay. Generally, this figure ranges from $50,000 to $100,000, but it may go as high as $500,000, and even up to $1,000,000. These are usually lifetime limits. The limitation may also be written to cover any single illness or it may be written as a limitation for a year. The policy may read, for instance, that it will cover only $20,000 for any one illness, meaning that no matter how long the individual is hospitalized, the company will cease paying after the $20,000 has been used up. If the limitation applies to a policy year, then the company would make payments the following year in the event the policyholder was so unfortunate as to be hospitalized for that long. As an example, suppose the yearly limit of the policy was $20,000 and the total bill during one year was $25,000. The company would cease paying as soon as the $20,000 was used up; but as the next policy year started, the company would begin paying again if the illness continued. Generally policies are written so that as the second policy year starts, the insured must first pay the deductible amount before the company becomes liable. In addition, as noted above, most policies have a lifetime limit. This lifetime limit is usually several times the single illness or yearly limit. Generally, the lifetime limit is about $100,000, but it may vary; some go as high as $500,000 and even more. There is even the so-called jumbo major medical policy with a lifetime limit of $1,000,000. Figure 12–3 shows the growth of major medical insurance over the past few years.

Comprehensive Medical Insurance

An inclusive medical plan, comprehensive medical insurance, is an attempt to meet all health insurance needs with one package. Comprehensive insurance usually covers hospital expenses, surgical expenses, regular medical expenses, and major medical expenses. Some plans even include dental insurance. Major medical and the other type of insurance described above are put in one package. These policies are issued with the same sort of coinsurance feature. The deductible is usually somewhat lower under the comprehensive plan, and some plans do not have deductibility. More and more of the health insurance sold today is put into one comprehensive plan, reducing administrative and clerical costs and usually providing the policyholder a better return on his or her premium dollar.

Disability Insurance or Loss of Income

One of the hazards we all face is that we will lose our ability to earn a livelihood temporarily or permanently due to a serious accident or illness. Some jobs

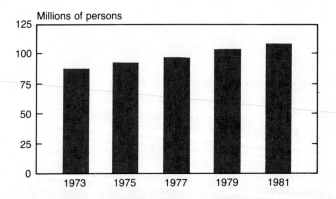

Figure 12–3. Major medical expense protection with insurance companies in the United States. (*Source: Source Book of Health Insurance Data, 1982–1983.* Health Insurance Institute, p. 18.)

themselves are dangerous and on-the-job accidents could cripple a person for life. Some illnesses can render a person incapable of working even after recovery. Even people in relatively safe occupations can suffer from accidents. Through no fault of one's own, a person might be crippled for life instead of killed in an automobile accident. Indeed, some insurance executives believe that disability insurance is needed even more than life insurance. The probability of partial or total disability is greater than the probability of loss of life for relatively young people. Because of this likelihood, disability (often called loss of income) insurance was developed.

The first of these policies was sold in 1847; modern policies began in 1898. However, very few people were covered prior to World War II. In general, the policies are designed to cover loss of income either as the result of a partial disability or as the result of permanent disability; in no case may the coverage be more than the actual earnings of the individual. If a person earns $500 per week, he or she cannot purchase a policy that would cover a loss of earnings of more than a certain percentage of that.[1]

The policies generally have two features: (1) payment as the result of loss of earnings from an accident, and (2) payment as the result of loss of earnings from sickness that prevents one from earning a living.

These policies are written in different ways. Most have a waiting period before benefit payments begin, and this waiting period varies. They pay a certain percentage (which varies) of earnings for various periods. Generally they can be grouped into those which provide short-term protection or long-term protection. The short-term policies provide benefits for various time periods up to two years, the long-term policies provide for protection for more than two years; some provide benefits for up to ten years and more. A few even provide benefits until the insured is age 65.

Premium rates vary in accordance with the above conditions; the longer the waiting period before payments begin, the lower the premiums, and the longer the period over which payments are made, the higher the premiums. The rates also vary with the occupation of the individual. Professional and certain types of businesspeople find the premiums lower and the benefits more liberal than those for persons in more hazardous occupations.

This type of policy also often contains a provision stating that for dismemberment the insured is to receive a lump sum equivalent to a stated number of weeks' indemnity in the case of being disabled permanently. For example, if an individual has a policy that provides for payment of $200 a week in the event of total disablement and then loses a leg in an accident, the policy may provide that the policyholder is to receive a lump-sum payment of one hundred weeks times $200, or $20,000. Where such a lump sum is received, the individual does not receive the weekly benefits provided for in the policy.

---

1. Insurance companies will not sell a person a disability policy that pays more than about 70 or 75 percent (it varies from company to company) of his before-tax income on the theory that if the person receives that much he has less (perhaps not any) incentive to overcome his or her disability.

More than a dozen varieties of limited disability insurance can be purchased to cover almost every situation imaginable. For example, an individual paying off a mortgage on a residence may purchase disability insurance to cover the mortgage payments. For a few dollars a month premium, depending on age, the company will agree to pay up to five years of the monthly mortgage payments after a waiting period of fifteen days.

HOW GOOD IS YOUR HEALTH INSURANCE PLAN?

There are all kinds of health insurance plans; some are excellent, some good, and some only fair. However, it is generally true that the quality of the policy is closely related to the premiums paid. Nevertheless, you can appraise the quality of your policy by studying the following checklist and answering each question.

Checklist to appraise the quality of your health insurance

1. What is your hospital room and board coverage?
   $100 to $125 per day?
   Full cost of semiprivate room?
   Is there an extra intensive care coverage?
2. Does it cover other hospital costs: x-ray, laboratory fees, drugs, anesthesia?
   Full coverage?
   Partial coverage?
3. What is your surgical coverage?
   Set fees for various procedures? What is it?
   Reasonable and customary fees with a limit?
   Reasonable and customary fees with no limit?
4. What is your basic medical coverage?
   Is there an overall dollar limit?
   What is the deductible?
   What is the coinsurance?
5. What is your major medical coverage?
   What is your deductible?
   What is your coinsurance?
   What is the annual limit?
   What is the per accident or per illness limit?
   What is the lifetime limit?
6. What kind of disability coverage do you have?
   What is the waiting period before you receive benefits?
   How long will benefits be paid?
7. What are the premiums on your policies?

OTHER IMPORTANT THINGS ABOUT HEALTH INSURANCE

Items Not Covered

Certain medical expenses are usually not covered by health insurance. Some policies cover psychiatric care, some do not. Those that do often set a special limit on this item. Abortions are generally not covered by most plans. The cost of regular checkups is usually not covered nor are the costs of eyeglasses and eye examinations, but treatment of eye disease or eye surgery is. Vasectomies and circumcisions may or may not be covered; the same is true of surgery to correct natural deformities, such as a clubfoot. The trend is toward broader coverage in these areas.

100 Percent Coverage

Since health insurance policies have a coinsurance clause that pays usually only 80 or 90 percent of the medical bills, can a person buy two policies and then receive benefits in excess of expenses? The answer is no, but one may collect more than if one had only one policy. There are, however, only a few cases where a person could get two group policies, although one could buy two individual policies; but individual policies have substantially higher premiums. Where both husband and wife work and both are eligible for group insurance, they could have two policies. Or in rare cases persons could have two group plans if they had one with their employer and another one with a professional association such as the American Accounting Association.

How would two such policies pay off if there were a claim? One policy would be classified as the primary policy; it would pay first in accordance with its terms, and the other policy would then pay part or all of the rest. In nearly all cases the primary policy is the one obtained with the employer. In the case of a husband-wife team, the primary policy would be the one from the employer of the person in the family making the claim.

Suppose a person has two policies, both with a $100 deductibility and an 80 percent coinsurance clause; assume a claim is filed for $1,100. The primary carrier would pay 80 percent of $1,000 or $800. The secondary carrier would then pay all or part of the remaining $300, depending upon what the contract said regarding secondary claims. It could be 80 percent of the $300; 80 percent of $200 ($300 less the deductibility), or 80 percent of $1,000, just as the primary carrier, with a limit of $300. In no case could a person get more than 100 percent coverage and in many cases it would be less. For this reason, it almost never pays to have two policies; a person pays double premiums and gets only marginal added protection.

Of course, if one doesn't tell the insurance companies one has two policies one might get a double payoff; but if the companies discover this, they will cancel. In the early days of health insurance, there was no question regarding whether a person had a second policy on the claim form, and some people did get double coverage. But now such a question appears on all forms for reimbursement.

Group Plans: The Modern Way to Buy Health Insurance

Any of the plans discussed above can be obtained on a group or individual basis. A group plan actually amounts to wholesaling insurance, and the features are the same as if an individual were to purchase his or her own policy. As a group member, however, one generally has the benefit of lower rates than if one were to purchase the policy on one's own.

There are a number of reasons why the rates are more favorable to the group, one being that there is a more favorable selection of risks. When it insures the group, the company usually insists that at least 75 percent of those eligible must join. Moreover, those who do join do not come with the idea that they will receive immediate benefits; and there are few cancellations. In some cases, the employee has no choice but to take the group insurance; it is a condition of employment. In other cases, it is voluntary, and it is in these cases that the insurance companies insist that the policy is not effective until 75 percent of the eligible employees have joined. Another reason for more favorable rates is that administrative costs are lower. As to collections, the employer customarily withholds the amount of the premiums from the employee's paycheck. The commission paid to the agent who sells the group policy is lower than if he or she were to sell the same number of policies to many individuals.

Frequently group health policies are a part of the so-called fringe benefits in labor-management contracts. Often the employer pays all or a part of the premiums and agrees to handle much of the paper work through the personnel office.

There is a growing trend toward the group method of meeting insurance needs, true not only of health insurance, but also of life insurance. The pattern today is to have one package negotiated on a group basis, which would then include some sort of a comprehensive health plan as described above together with some term insurance, all under one plan.

Guaranteed Renewable and Noncancellable Policies

In some cases, the insurance company retains the right to refuse to renew the policy when it expires. Indeed, sometimes the company has the right to cancel at any time during the term of the policy. It is, however, possible to buy guaranteed renewable and noncancellable policies. A guaranteed renewable policy can be renewed until some predetermined age is reached, generally age sixty-five. However, each time it is renewed, premiums can be increased if warranted.

A noncancellable policy is one that cannot be cancelled during the time it was originally stated to run, and during this time, premiums cannot be raised. Therefore, if a person buys a policy that is both noncancellable and renewable, the premiums cannot be raised during the period over which the policy runs. When the period is over, the policy must be renewed if the policyholder so chooses, but premiums can be raised.

How to Apply for Benefits

It is easy to apply for benefits under most health insurance plans. Every person with a health insurance plan receives a wallet-sized card from the insurance company. A person in a group plan has a group number and a certificate number on the card. With a hospital bill often the hospital staff will fill out the form and send it in. With a doctor's bill or reimbursement for drugs, the insured must often fill out the form, but it is self-explanatory. Since in many cases the insurance company pays only part of the bill, instructions are sent indicating how much the patient is to pay above the insurance claim. Until a few years ago, companies often paid the doctor directly. Now more and more companies are paying the patient who in turn pays the doctor.

When You Retire; Supplemental Plans

Most insurance companies, including Blue Cross-Blue Shield, now have supplemental plans for retired individuals who are covered by Medicare because Medicare does not pay all bills. These supplemental plans are designed to pay a portion of those costs not covered by Medicare. They work very much like regular plans in that they may have deductibility features and coinsurance, that is they treat that portion of the retired person's medical bill not covered by Medicare just as they would some other person's total bill. Because they provide less coverage, their premiums are, of course, lower.

NONPROFIT HEALTH INSURANCE PLANS

In addition to being able to buy health insurance policies from profit-making life insurance companies, one can purchase them from nonprofit organizations. The most widely known such nonprofit organization is Blue Cross-Blue Shield. The plans of this organization are set up to cover a certain geographical area; sometimes an entire state and sometimes only part of a state. Everyone in that area is theoretically eligible to join either through a group plan at the person's place of employment or as an individual.

Blue Cross is a cooperative nonprofit organization designed to pay hospital and other medical bills of its members, while Blue Shield is a similar nonprofit organization designed to pay physicians' expenses. The latter is sponsored by groups of physicians, and for the most part Blue Cross handles the details of selling, billing, and collecting for Blue Shield. Blue Cross-Blue Shield also provides major medical insurance, the comprehensive plan discussed above, and in some areas dental insurance and even disability insurance; in fact, most of the health insurance that other insurance companies provide.

Blue Cross

The payments for a Blue Cross policy depend on area; in some states, the cost of hospitalization is more expensive than in others. More important, the rates depend on the type of contract one purchases, for some contracts provide more benefits than others. In addition, rates vary depending on whether one purchases the insurance as a member of a group or singly. The period of hospitalization covered varies from plan to plan with the maximum being 365 days. There is also usually a limit to how much Blue Cross will pay per day for a hospital room, but generally it is the cost of a semiprivate room.

In addition, most of the plans pay all charges for operating room, recovery room, cast room, and cystoscopic room, plus all drugs in general use—with the exception of blood and blood plasma—as well as oxygen inhalations and physical therapy, all laboratory services, basal metabolism tests, electrocardiograms, and x-ray charges. If both husband and wife are covered, after nine months of membership maternity care is also included. If the entire family is covered, there is no extra cost for a newborn child; and when the mother is entitled to maternity benefits, the child is entitled to hospital nursery benefits. After the discharge of the mother and the child, the child thereafter is entitled to full benefits when he or she becomes a patient.

Under most Blue Cross and Blue Shield plans anyone under the age of sixty-five may enroll on an individual basis, and no physical examination is required. The policies are noncancellable except for nonpayment of dues or the fraudulent use of the membership.

When persons retire and draw Social Security, they may keep or lose their Blue Cross-Blue Shield depending on the local plan. However, more and more plans are adopting the modified Blue Cross-Blue Shield plan for retired people who wish to retain it, a policy consisting of reduced coverage (and reduced premiums), intended to complement Medicare.

Blue Shield

While Blue Cross is designed to cover hospitalization, Blue Shield is designed to cover physicians' fees, whether surgical, surgical-medical, or general medical.

Like Blue Cross, the basic rates of Blue Shield vary from state to state and from plan to plan. Most plans agree to pay the physician according to a basic schedule. The physician might charge $600 for services, and the Blue Shield payment schedule might call for a payment of $410. In such a case the subscriber would pay the balance of $190.

How much will be paid for a given operation varies from one section of the country to another. Also there are usually two or three different packages to choose from. A purchaser who is willing to pay a higher premium can obtain a higher surgical fee schedule. Some plans have even been sold that do not list the dollar amounts they will pay for a given operation but they state they will pay "reasonable and customary" surgical fees. That is, in effect they pay the entire bill the surgeon submits, unless it is deemed unreasonable.

Most Blue Cross-Blue Shield plans have a deductibility clause as well as a coinsurance clause on their plan, just like the private insurance company plans. They also have a family rate and a lower rate for only a husband and wife, and a still lower rate for a single person. As noted above, Blue Cross-Blue Shield also has a major medical plan which covers major illnesses. It too has a deductibility and a coinsurance clause; these clauses vary, but the most popular split is 80 percent-20 percent. The lifetime major medical limit may go as high as $1,000,000.

Health Maintenance Organizations (HMOs)

In recent years another type of medical expense protection has developed through health maintenance organizations. This method provides many of the same benefits as health insurance. It consists of group prepayment medical plans, often organized as nonprofit co-ops. These provide medical care for their members for a fixed fee per month. These groups own and operate clinics and hospitals and hire doctors, nurses, and other technicians. The professional medical personnel, including doctors, are paid an annual salary; consequently there is no set fee for such and such a service. Membership is on a volunteer basis; but in order to join a person obviously must live in a geographical area where there is an HMO. Some of the more well known plans are the Health Insurance Plan of Greater New York, Kaiser Foundation Health Plan, Ross-Loos Medical Group of Los Angeles, Community Health Association of Detroit, and the Group Health Cooperative of Puget Sound.

These group plans can provide most of the benefits that their members need from their own resources. If the services of a specialist are needed and none of the group's doctors qualifies, the group hires an outside specialist on a fee basis. The group cannot provide disability insurance internally, but most HMOs buy that for their members from an insurance company.

These organizations also practice preventive medicine, and have been established recently as a hopeful alternative to costly medical care. The theory behind this preventive medicine is that it is cheaper, both moneywise and in human suffering, to prevent illnesses than to cure them after they are well established. This process involves periodic medical checkups and screening programs to detect early warning signs of health breakdowns. Most of the HMOs offer more comprehensive coverage than most regular group insurance plans. Not only do they provide for regular medical checkups, but many of them have neither a deductibility feature nor a coinsurance clause. That is, 100 percent of all medical expenses are taken care of. The west coast Kaiser Foundation Health Plan was a pioneer in this field.

Before an HMO can be set up, the states must pass enabling legislation; by now twenty-six states have done so. There are currently about 270 HMOs in the United States, and their number is growing. Insurance companies are working with existing HMOs and have developed additional ones. HMOs are also sponsored by various governments, Blue Cross, hospitals, medical schools, consumer groups, employers' unions, and a number of other organizations. Since 1972 the federal government has provided grants and loans for the planning, development, and initial operating costs of HMOs.

Evidence suggests that HMOs reduce medical costs because the medical dollar goes directly to the doctor; there is no (or at least there is less) expensive bureaucracy siphoning off dollars. While the salaried doctors working for an HMO generally make less money than doctors in private practice, they seem happy because they work fewer hours and they have more regular schedules.

National Health Insurance

A number of proposals have been made that the federal government become more involved in health care. These range all the way from a complete government takeover to plans designed to supplement the present insurance plans. For example, some plans would provide complete cradle-to-grave coverage for everybody. They would replace all private health insurance plans. Life insurance companies would be out of the health insurance business. Blue Cross-Blue Shield too would go out of business. The more limited plans would merely offer additional benefits above what present health insurance now provides. Some of the supplemental plans would give mainly catastrophe coverage above what private major medical now provides. Others would pay some of the expenses now paid by the public due to deductibility and coinsurance clauses.

Those in favor of national health insurance maintain that the protection against catastrophic illnesses provided by most private major medical plans is inadequate. For example, upper limits exist per illness or per year, and for really serious and prolonged illnesses a person could exhaust the coverage. Also it is claimed the deductibility and coinsurance clauses are too high and hence medical care is still too expensive for many people. Then, too, some groups find it difficult to buy health care coverage, primarily people not covered by a group plan and whose health is too poor for them to buy an individual policy.

Those opposed to national health insurance maintain it is not needed or at most a supplemental plan is all that is needed. It is argued that not many will exhaust the benefits of a good major medical plan. If deductibility features or coinsurance are too high, the private companies can develop plans that have lower costs for such features. The critics maintain that the old are covered by Medicare, the poor by Medicaid, and most others by plans where they work. (Medicare and Medicaid are discussed in the appendix to this chapter.) The cost of medical care, they argue, will not be reduced by a national health plan; it will merely be financed differently. It will have to be paid by higher taxes rather than through insurance premiums. Indeed, the critics maintain that national health insurance will cause the cost of health care to rise further because of an enlarged bureaucracy needed to administer it. They point to the experience with Medicare and Medicaid to substantiate their claim.

A number of proposals have been made to finance national health insurance. Some would use regular funds from the general revenues of the Treasury. Others would finance it through the Social Security tax and raise rates to do so. Others would add a special health insurance tax to be paid in part by the employee and in part by the employer. A few years ago, national health insurance was a controversial issue. As this book goes to press, however, the issue has become dormant.

HOW MUCH HEALTH INSURANCE TO BUY

While much life insurance is designed to protect the family economically in the event of the premature death of the breadwinner, much the same sort of economic catastrophe can result from a serious illness or accident. Indeed, a permanent disability may be more of a disaster than a death; not only is the income stream cut off, but expenses may rise. Consequently, along with life insurance, the individual needs protection against such contingencies as these.

Medical Insurance Needs

It is strongly recommended that no breadwinner be without at least a major medical insurance policy. If one is able to obtain group insurance where one works, there is not really much choice in what kind of health insurance to buy. There is a package (sometimes two or three different packages with varying benefits) available and one can accept or reject it, and the worker should seriously consider accepting it.

Persons who are not members of a group and hence not eligible for a group policy should consider individual policies. At the very least, everyone should have a major medical policy. The cost can be kept within reason if the person puts the deductible feature at between $500 and $750. Shop around and compare the local Blue Cross-Blue Shield plan with what a private life insurance company can offer. Persons who live in an area with a health maintenance organization are indeed fortunate. This is often the cheapest type of health insurance protection, and it offers a means whereby an unattached individual can obtain group coverage.

Whether or not to buy hospital, surgical, and regular medical expense insurance, if one has the choice, is a matter of personal priorities. Certainly this should have a lower priority than major medical, and probably a lower priority than disability insurance. If the budget can afford it, fine; if not, a young and healthy individual might want to economize and take a modest risk here.

Disability Insurance Needs

Disability insurance should also be high on the list of priorities. Persons who have access to a good group plan should seriously consider it. Even if it must be bought on an individual basis, it should still be high on the list of priorities, to assure a monthly income in the event that regular income is cut off due to a lengthy illness or serious accident. Often professional and other groups are able to obtain this sort of insurance at relatively low rates. Consequently, this is one of the most rapidly growing areas in the insurance industry. Figure 12–4 shows the growth of private health insurance in the United States.

To calculate the actual dollar amount of your disability insurance needs you follow the same logic as when you calculated your life insurance needs. Since disability terminates the income stream (just as does death), the maximum amount of disability insurance would be the amount equal to your income stream. In theory as your income rises, your disability insurance needs also rise. Almost

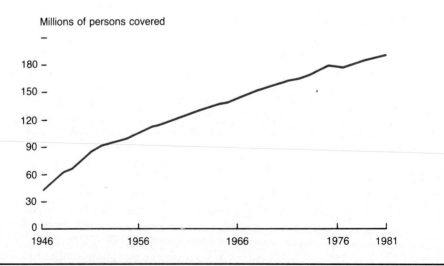

Figure 12–4. Growth of private health insurance in the United States. (*Source: Source Book of Health Insurance Data, 1982–1983*, Health Insurance Institute, p. 14.)

no one could afford this much disability insurance, but it is a bench mark where you can begin and then scale the amount down in accordance with your priorities and value judgments. Most people buy a policy that provides for the payment of a certain percentage of their income.

Or you could use the needs criteria in determining your disability needs. This method is similar but not identical to estimating your life insurance needs according to the needs principle. You should consider:

1. Gross annual living expense requirements.
2. Net annual living expense requirements. This is gross requirements less reduced expenses stemming from disability such as:
    a) Income taxes because disability insurance payments are nontaxable; neither are Social Security benefits.
    b) Transportation costs and other costs associated with holding a job which are reduced.
    c) Life insurance premiums which would be reduced by any disability premium waiver clause you may have.

This net annual living expense figure could be reduced further by the following items:

3. Sick pay if any.
4. Spouse's income; current or expected future income if spouse were to go back to work in the event of a disability.
5. Social Security disability payments.
6. Other disability benefit payments (such as corporate pension plan benefits where you work).
7. Investment income.

Actual net annual disability income needed which would have to be provided by disability insurance. This is item number 2 above less items 3, 4, 5, 6, and 7. You will note that, unlike the estimate of life insurance needs, we have made no allowance for

1. paying off the mortgage and other debts,
2. a college fund, and
3. an emergency fund.

These items could be taken care of under item 2, net annual living expenses, in which case they would remain part of the personal family budget, although conceivably they could be taken into account by insurance; then your disability insurance needs would be greater. Table 12–2 shows the disability insurance requirements of a hypothetical Mr. and Mrs. X.

It is also possible to calculate your disability insurance needs by using a rule of thumb and taking a certain percentage of your income, say, 60 per-

Table 12–2   Disability insurance needs of Mr. and Mrs. X

1. Gross Annual Living Expense Requirements		$ 16,000
Income tax on $16,000 *estimated	$2,000	
Transportation and other cost reductions	500	
Life insurance premium reductions	500	
2. Net Annual Living Expense Requirements		$ 13,000
3. Sick Pay (short term)	——	
4. Spouse's Income	——	
5. Social Security	$8,400	
6. Other Disability Benefits	——	
7. Investment Income	600	
8. Net Annual Disability Income Requirements		$ 4,000
9. Inflation Factor 33.066 (20 years at 5%)		
10. Twenty-year Income Stream of $4,000 per Year Adjusted for 5 Percent Inflation ($4,000 × 33.066)		$132,264
11. Average Yearly Income ($132,264.00 ÷ 20)		$ 6,613

cent. But going through the eight steps above will provide you with a more precise figure.

You may also wish to adjust your disability insurance needs to allow for future inflation. This is done in the table below. Actual net annual disability income requirements (current disability insurance needs) come to $4,000. If we assume a long-run inflation rate of 5 percent and a 20-year disability requirement, we can get the inflationary factor. It is 33.066 and is obtained from Table A14–3 (future worth of an annuity) in the appendix to Chapter 14, "Saving and Investing Through Thrift Institutions." It indicates that if you start with one dollar, and you add one additional dollar each year, and the entire sum is growing by 5 percent per year, it will amount to $33.066 at the end of twenty years. Multiplying that by $4,000, we find that the total disability payout over twenty years will amount to $132,264. Dividing this last figure by twenty years, we obtain $6,613, which is the average disability insurance payout per year over the entire period—that is, the disability insurance needs of Mr. and Mrs. X adjusted for inflation. Currently their needs are $4,000, but this will rise to $10,612 in the twentieth year, if inflation continues at 5 percent. If they make arrangements for $6,613.00 per year, they will have a surplus during the early years ($2,613 the first year). They should put this surplus in an interest-bearing account, and then it becomes a reserve that can be used in later years when their needs rise above $6,613. Providing for disability income of $6,613 yields slightly more than $4,000 in real terms over the years, assuming 5 percent inflation, because there will be interest on the surplus during the early years. However, this provides a hedge in the event that inflation rises above 5 percent.

QUESTIONS FOR REVIEW

1. What type of protection does health insurance provide?
2. Explain three types of coverage available in health policies.
3. What is basic hospital expense insurance?
4. What is hospital confinement indemnity coverage?
5. What is major medical coverage?
6. What is meant by coinsurance and the deductibility clause in health insurance?
7. Discuss comprehensive medical insurance.
8. What is disability insurance?
9. Does it pay to have two health insurance policies, both of which provide the same benefits? Why or why not?
10. What are some of the things that most health insurance policies will not cover?
11. Is it best to buy health insurance on a group or on an individual basis, assuming the person has a choice? Why?
12. What is the difference between Blue Cross and Blue Shield?
13. Discuss health maintenance organizations.
14. Is a national health insurance plan needed, in your opinion?
15. What is the difference between hospital insurance and medical insurance under the Medicare program?

CASES

1. William and Wanda Brown have health insurance coverage under the Blue Cross-Blue Shield plan. Now, however, William has an opportunity to join a group plan at his place of employment that is somewhat better. Should he join and keep both policies or should he drop his Blue Cross-Blue Shield?
2. Bill and Jeanette Jones had the following medical bills last year:

   a. $250 for Mark, their six-year-old son;
   b. $395 for Suellen, their five-year-old daughter;
   c. $250 for Jeanette; and
   d. $210 for Bill.

   They have coverage for all medical and drug bills up to $100,000 with a $100 deductibility feature and an 80 percent coinsurance clause. How much will their policy reimburse them?
3. John Brown, aged sixty-six, recently retired and is drawing Social Security. When he left his employer, he was told his group life and health insurance would lapse. He has since purchased an individual supplement plan from

Blue Cross-Blue Shield. What is a supplemental plan and how does it work? What other kind of coverage does John have?

4. Ann and Jim Clark both work for the same employer, and both are enrolled in a group plan there. Their plan is a comprehensive plan that covers everything up to $10,000 per illness with a $50 deductibility and a 90 percent coinsurance clause. Recently Jim had major surgery. The hospital bill was $175 per day for ten days. The surgical fee was $2,500, and all other expenses such as drugs and the like came to $250. How much of the total bill will his insurance pay, and how much will he pay? Will he benefit from the fact that he and his wife both have a policy? Are a primary and a secondary carrier involved? Would you recommend that the Clark family keep both of the policies they have?

5. Joan and Bill Rider both work for the same employer. They have a choice regarding their group health insurance. They can each buy a group policy for a single person or one of them can buy a policy for a husband and wife. Their benefits would be the same. What should they do?

6. While sliding down a water slide at a neighbor's swimming pool, Sara Scott hit her head at the bottom and knocked out one of her front teeth. Will Sara's parents' Blue Cross or Blue Shield pay for her dental surgery? Will the neighbor's homeowner's policy pay Sara's medical bills?

7. John and Alice Brown are a retired couple drawing Social Security benefits. Last winter John fell and broke his leg while shoveling snow; the fall also broke several teeth and he had to have oral surgery. While performing this surgery the dentist decided to remove two other teeth. John had the following bills:

Doctor's fees	$475
Hospital (emergency room; x-ray, and supplies)	$ 75
Rental of crutches	$ 40
Dental bill	$350

What proportion of this bill will Medicare pay, and how much will John have to pay?

SUGGESTED READINGS

Avedis, Donebedian. *Benefits in Medical Care Programs.* Cambridge, Mass.: Harvard University Press, 1976.

Beam, Burton T., Jr. *Group Insurance: Basic Concepts and Alternatives.* Bryn Mawr, Pa.: The American College, 1983.

Berstein, Joan Z., and Harris, Lucy R. *Health Maintenance Organizations: Opportunities and Problems.* New York: F&S Press, 1982.

Best's Review, Life-Health Edition. Published monthly by A.M. Best Company, Inc., Oldwick, N.J. 08858.

Birenbaum, Arnold. *Health Care and Society.* Totowa, N.J.: Allanheld, Osmun and Co., 1981.

Blue Cross-Blue Shield Fact Book, 1984. Published annually by the National Association of Blue Shield Plans, Blue Cross Association, 840 North Lake Shore Drive, Chicago, Ill.

Blue Cross Reports. Chicago: Blue Cross Association. Published quarterly.

Bonito, Grace. *Medical Insurance Billing Handbook.* Orange, Calif.: Career Publishing, Inc., 1983.

A Brief Explanation of Medicare. Washington, D.C.: Department of Health, Education and Welfare Publication No. (SSA) 73-10043.

Davidson, Stephen M., et al. *The Cost of Living Longer: National Health Insurance and the Elderly.* Lexington, Mass.: Lexington Books, 1980.

Davis, Karen. *National Health Insurance: Benefits, Costs, and Consequences.* Washington, D.C.: The Brookings Institution, 1975.

"Duplicate Coverage." Pamphlet published by Blue Cross-Blue Shield. No date.

Eusebio, Thomas C. *Guide to Health Insurance.* Indianapolis, Ind.: Rough Notes Co., 1981.

Follmann, J.F., Jr. "Dental Care Coverage." *Best's Insurance News.*

Galton, Lawrence. *The Patient's Guide to Surgery.* New York: Avon Books, 1977.

Health Insurance for People 65 and Older. Washington: U.S. Department of Health, Education and Welfare. You may obtain a free copy from a Social Security field office, which can be found in any large city.

"How to Shop for Health Insurance." HEW Publication, 1979. Consumer Information Center, Pueblo, Colo. 81009.

Inquiry, A Journal of Medical Care Organization, Provision and Financing. Chicago: Blue Cross Association.

The Journal of Insurance. A bimonthly publication of the Insurance Information Institute, 110 William Street, New York, N.Y. 10038.

Mehr, Robert I., and Cammack, Emerson. *Principles of Insurance.* Homewood, Ill.: Irwin, 1980.

Rosett, Richard N. (ed.). *The Role of Health Insurance in the Health Services Sector.* Washington, D.C.: National Bureau of Economic Research, 1976.

Source Book of Health Insurance. Published annually by the Health Insurance Institute, 277 Park Ave., New York, N.Y.

Your Medicare Handbook. Baltimore, Md.: Department of Health, Education and Welfare, 1982. Publication Number (SSA) 79-10050.

APPENDIX 12A: MEDICARE

Probably the most far-reaching of the 1965 amendments to the Social Security Law was the Medicare provision. It provided for two kinds of health insurance for those over age sixty-five: hospital insurance and medical insurance. The hospital insurance has come to be known as Part A of Medicare and the medical insurance as Part B. Practically everyone sixty-five or older is eligible for the entire Medicare program.

Certain individuals get Part A (hospital insurance) automatically and need not pay for it. Moreover, these people get this insurance even if they are still working and hence not drawing Social Security; the test is to be over sixty-five and eligible for Social Security. The following people are all eligible for Part A of Medicare.

1. Everyone over sixty-five and eligible for Social Security or railroad retirement benefits.
2. Disabled people under sixty-five who have been getting Social Security disability benefits for two years or more.
3. People insured under Social Security (but not yet getting benefits because they are under sixty-five) who need dialysis treatment or a kidney transplant. Wives, husbands, and children of insured people under sixty-five may also be eligible if they need kidney dialysis or transplants. Moreover, these people receive all the benefits of Part A until one year after they no longer have the above-described kidney problems, e.g., a successful kidney transplant.

Everyone who is covered automatically has hospital bills paid by Social Security as outlined below, and it also includes posthospital care.

People who are not covered automatically but who are over sixty-five may join Medicare on a voluntary basis and receive the same benefits, but they must pay a monthly premium. Those who buy hospital insurance (Part A) must also buy the medical insurance (Part B). The premium for Part A is fairly high, whereas it is quite cheap for Part B. These premiums are increased almost every year; contact the closest Social Security Field Office to obtain the current dollar figures. However, while people may not buy Part A without Part B, they may buy Part B without A. Indeed, this is what most of those over sixty-five and not eligible for Part A automatically have done. The high cost of hospital insurance has discouraged its use on a voluntary basis.

Those who are drawing Social Security and hence are automatically covered for Part A (hospital insurance) are not covered automatically with respect to Part B. However, they, too, may buy this coverage on a voluntary basis by paying the relatively modest monthly premium. The premiums are withheld from the retirement check of those drawing Social Security, whereas the others must send them to their Social Security Field Office.

Hospital Insurance (Part A)

The hospital insurance provides for the following three broad classes of benefits:

First, all but the first $304 of all covered hospital costs are paid for the first sixty days of what are called "benefit periods." Medicare will also pay all but $76 per day of all covered costs during the sixty-first through ninetieth day of each benefit period. A benefit period begins when a person enters a hospital and ends when the person has not been a bed patient in any hospital (or any facility that provides mainly skilled nursing care) for sixty days in a row. After this period, if a person is hospitalized again, he or she has a new "benefit period" and is entitled to coverage again. There is no limit to how many benefit periods a person may have.

On January 1, 1968, a "lifetime reserve" was included in the law. This provides that sixty additional days are added to the hospital insurance. Unlike the ninety days, which are renewed at the end of each illness, the "lifetime reserve" is not renewed after it is used. It means that if the ninety days have been used in a benefit period, the patient can be covered for an additional sixty days or part thereof. During the additional days the hospital insurance pays all but $152 per day of covered hospital expenses. One exception to this is mental patients. There is a lifetime limit of 190 days on payments for treatment in mental hospitals.

Second, Medicare will pay up to one hundred days in an extended care facility such as a nursing home. It will pay for all covered services for the first twenty days and all but $38 a day for up to eighty more days. Patients become eligible for the extended care payments, however, only if

- They need daily skilled nursing or rehabilitation care.
- A doctor determines they need this care and so orders it.
- They have been in a hospital for at least three days in a row before entering the nursing home.
- They are admitted to the nursing home within fourteen days after leaving the hospital.
- They were admitted for further treatment of a condition for which they were in the hospital.

Third, Medicare also will pay for up to one hundred home visits by nurses or other health workers from a home-health agency for each benefit period.

Hospital insurance covers the cost of room and meals (including special diets) in semiprivate accommodations (two- to four-bed), regular nursing services, and services in an intensive care unit of a hospital. It also covers the cost of drugs, supplies, appliances, equipment, and any other services ordinarily furnished to hospital or nursing home patients.

Hospital insurance does not cover doctors' bills, private duty nurses, the cost of the first three pints of blood needed, and convenience items such as a telephone or television set.

Medical Insurance (Part B)

The medical part of Medicare also has a deductible feature as well as a coinsurance feature. Basically, the medical insurance pays 80 percent of the reasonable charges after the first $75 in each calendar year. There are three exceptions to this general rule:

1. Home health services are covered at 100 percent with no annual deductible.
2. Payment for services of independent physical therapists is limited to a maximum, which is increased every year. See your local Social Security office for the current maximum.
3. Payment for physicians' psychiatric services outside a hospital cannot exceed a maximum, which also changes every year.

With the exceptions noted above, medical insurance will cover the following:

1. Physicians' and surgeons' services at home, in the doctor's office, in a clinic, or in a hospital.
2. Outpatient hospital service in an emergency room or an outpatient clinic.
3. Health-home services. These visits are in addition to the posthospital visits one gets with hospital insurance.
4. Outpatient physical therapy and speech pathology services.
5. A number of other medical and health services prescribed by the doctor such as diagnostic services; x-ray or other radiation treatments; surgical dressings, splints, casts, braces; artificial limbs and eyes; certain colostomy care supplies; and rental or purchase of durable medical equipment such as a wheelchair or oxygen equipment for use in the home.
6. Certain ambulance services, certain services by chiropractors, and home and office services by independent physical therapists.

In some cases, Medicare covers medical costs incurred outside the United States, but generally this is not the case. If help is needed regarding Medicare, contact the nearest Social Security office.

APPENDIX 12B: MEDICAID

Since 1966 there has also been a Medicaid program. Medicaid was authorized under a Title 19 of the Social Security Act amendment of that year. It provides for the medical expenses of the indigent regardless of age. It is administered by the states, and state funds are involved, although federal matching funds are also available on a 75 percent federal and 25 percent state basis. However, Medicaid is not mandatory; the states must pass enabling legislation. Also, benefits vary from one state to another, although there are minimum federal guidelines that the states must adhere to. The Medicaid program is administered by the various state departments of welfare or their equivalent.

CHAPTER THIRTEEN

PROPERTY AND LIABILITY INSURANCE

Insurance on the Home
Other Aspects of Home Insurance
A Home Insurance Program
Automobile Insurance
Other Aspects of Automobile Insurance

Property is subject to physical destruction from a number of hazards, such as fire, flood, theft, and others. Equally likely is the possibility that a person will destroy or damage someone else's property, as in an automobile accident. Once again we turn to insurance for protection. Property insurance reimburses for the value of destroyed property. A policyholder should have property insurance for both personal and real property. Personal property includes such things as furniture, automobiles, and clothing. Real property includes any buildings attached to land, such as a house or garage.

Liability insurance protects the insured against claims for death or injury suffered by other people. People can be killed or injured on the insured's property, and the policyholder is liable for these claims. Liability insurance is also necessary for those who drive automobiles, since automobile accidents often result in bodily injury as well as property damage.

This chapter covers the following insurance protection:

Home Protection
1. To protect property   (Both protected by a Homeowner's Policy)
2. To protect against
   liability
Automobile Protection
1. To protect property   (Both protected by Automobile Insurance
2. To protect against   Policy)
   liability

Property and liability insurance premium payments should be regarded as payment for the protection of family material assets. The premiums paid on an insurance policy on a home are protection in the event of the destruction of the home by fire or some other disaster. A person who runs over someone with an auto exposes the family assets to loss by lawsuit.

The principle of property and liability insurance is much like the principle behind term life insurance. The risk of loss is spread over many units, and those few who actually suffer a loss are reimbursed by the insurance company—but indirectly by those policyholders who do not suffer a loss. In the case of fire insurance, the companies know how many homes will burn down each year but cannot predict which ones. The insurance companies also know how many people will run over someone, but they do not know who they are.

INSURANCE ON THE HOME

If a home burns down, it could be a financial disaster for the owner. Consequently, a homeowner should have fire insurance. There are other hazards the homeowner faces that should also be insured against, such as damage due to wind, flood, smoke, theft, or people running over lawns and shrubs with cars. Until a few years ago, the homeowner had to buy a separate policy for protection against each of these hazards, but today most insurance companies sell the homeowner's policy which puts nearly all the homeowner's insurance needs into one package. Selling just one policy instead of several separate ones reduces the cost to the insurance companies by as much as 20 to 25 percent, and these reduced costs are passed on to the homeowner in the form of lower premiums.

Homeowner's Policy

The homeowner's policy provides for four kinds of insurance: (1) property insurance on the home, (2) personal property insurance, (3) liability insurance, and (4) medical payment insurance. Generally, the homeowner's policy includes the following protection for property damage:

1. Fire insurance on the house.
2. Extended coverage for damage from wind, hail, falling objects, smoke, motor vehicles, and others, plus an allowance for additional living expense in the event a homeowner has to live in a motel for a few days.
3. Personal property insurance for loss of personal property due to fire, theft, or mysterious disappearances.

The homeowner's policy also provides the following liability insurance:

1. Personal liability insurance to cover injuries occurring on the homeowner's property.

2.   Medical payment insurance to cover medical bills of persons injured on
      the homeowner's premises.

Most insurance companies have several types of homeowner's policy packages
to choose from, with names such as limited, basic, broad, all-inclusive, or all-
risk. They are referred to as policies HO-1, HO-2, HO-3, and HO-5. The
breadth of the extended coverage increases as one moves from policy 1 to policy
5; the premiums also increase.[1]

Property insurance

Homeowner's policy HO-1 (basic) covers the fewest items, but it covers more
than just fire. It usually includes damage due to wind, hail, falling objects, and
a number of others. With damage to a roof due to hail, however, the basic
policy will not pay for the cost of a new roof. Rather, the damaged roof will
first be depreciated, and the policy will pay for a lesser amount of damages.
For example, if the roof was ten years old when it was destroyed, and it is
assumed it had a useful life of twenty years, the policy will pay for one-half of
the cost of a new roof. Generally, under the broad and all-risks (HO-2 and
HO-5) policies, the destroyed roof is not first depreciated, and the policy pays
for the entire cost of a new roof.
      While nearly all homeowner's policies cover losses due to theft, in the case
of the *broad* and *all-risk* policies, coverage is more generous. For example, they
would pay for what is called mysterious disappearance, whereas the HO-1 would
not; HO-1 requires proof of theft such as a break-in or the like, whereas the
broad or all-risk policy does not.
      Some homeowners' policies also provide for living expenses if the homeowner
has to move into a hotel because the home has been so severely damaged that
it is unlivable. If it is a rental home, the fair rental value will be paid while the
tenant vacates the home during repairs.
      Generally in most states the HO-2 (broad) policy is the best buy. It costs
only slightly more than the HO-1 and provides a good deal more protection.
On the other hand, when moving from the HO-2 (broad) to the HO-5 (all-
risks) plan, premiums rise substantially while the protection rises only modestly.
However, check this carefully; this may not be true in your state.
      These all-risk plans cover everything except that which is specifically excluded,
and that varies from company to company. The all-risk plans do not usually
cover much more than the broad HO-2 form. A typical HO-5 would cover all
perils except war, nuclear radiation, earthquake, and flood. Table 13–1 summarizes
the perils against which property is insured under the various homeowner's
policies.
      There is also an HO-3 policy sold by some companies, with some of the
features of the HO-1 and the HO-2. It emphasizes personal property protection

---

1. There are also homeowner's policies for renters and for condominium owners. They are classified
as HO-4 and HO-6, respectively. The HO-1, etc. classification is generally used; however, in Texas and a
few other southern states, the HO-A, HO-B, etc. classification is used.

Table 13—1   Perils against which properties are insured (homeowner's policy)

Forms	Perils

Comprehensive { Broad { Basic (HO-1) {
1. fire or lightning
2. loss of property removed from premises endangered by fire or other perils
3. windstorm or hail
4. explosion
5. riot or civil commotion
6. aircraft
7. vehicles
8. smoke
9. vandalism and malicious mischief
10. theft
11. breakage of glass constituting a part of the building (not included in HO-3 & HO-4)

(HO-2) {
12. falling objects
13. weight of ice, snow, sleet
14. collapse of building(s) or any part thereof
15. sudden and accidental tearing asunder, cracking, burning, or bulging of a steam or hot water heating system or of appliances for heating water
16. accidental discharge, leakage or overflow of water or steam from within a plumbing, heating or air-conditioning system or domestic appliance
17. freezing of plumbing, heating and air-conditioning systems and domestic appliances
18. sudden and accidental injury from artificially generated currents to electrical appliances, devices, fixtures and wiring (TV and radio tubes not included)

(HO-5)   ALL PERILS EXCEPT: flood, earthquake, war, nuclear attack, and others specified in your policy. Check your policy for a complete listing of perils excluded.

less than protection on the house, and is more like basic coverage (HO-1) insofar as personal property is concerned and more like broad coverage (HO-2) insofar as the house is concerned.

Personal property coverage

Personal property is covered under a homeowner's policy along with real property. This covers loss of furniture, clothing, cameras, rugs, drapes, furs, books, paintings, jewelry, and the like. It provides protection not only against fire but also against loss due to theft, vandalism, and in some cases mysterious disappearance. This type of policy also insures for loss of items away from the home. For example, a camera stolen from an automobile is covered by the personal property clause.

This personal property coverage is written in different ways, but generally it will reimburse for losses up to 40 percent of insurance coverage carried on the home. If you have a $100,000 homeowner's policy, your personal property maximum protection would be $40,000. Most also have a deductibility clause, which amounts to 1 percent of the insurance carried on the house. That is, if the insured suffered a loss of $5,000 to personal property and has a $100,000 homeowner's policy, the insurance company would pay $4,000.

It is wise to have a written inventory listing all of your personal property and its value. For expensive items such as furs, jewelry, and the like the bills of sale should be kept so that you can prove their value. Photographs are also useful. If the value of your personal property exceeds 40 per cent of the value of your house, you may buy separate policy floaters on very valuable items such as furs, jewelry, and works of art. Insuring these items separately will probably reduce the value of your other personal property to about 40 per cent of the value of the house and hence it will be covered by the regular homeowner's policy. Even if the total value of your personal property is under 40 percent of the value of your home, many policies limit the coverage on furs and jewelry to $500 unless these items are specifically listed.

Personal liability coverage

Personal liability coverage protects the insured against claims from bodily injury to other people and against claims for damage to the property of others. The insured is protected against lawsuits because of injuries to others caused by pets, boats, and bicycles. The policy would even cover an accident where the insured strikes another with a golf ball. It will cover any type of accident except automobile accidents and accidents related to business pursuits. If a guest slips on the sidewalk and breaks his or her leg, the homeowner is covered. In the case of property damage, if you are burning leaves in your backyard and the fire spreads and damages your neighbor's house, you are covered. It even covers accidents away from home for which the insured or any member of the household is held responsible. If you have a swimming pool, this must be noted in your policy to be certain that you have coverage, since a pool is legally considered an attractive nuisance in some states. Therefore, if a neighborhood child fell in the pool while you were not at home, you could be sued.

The basic amount of personal liability insurance coverage is $25,000 in most states, but larger amounts can be purchased. Personal liability policy does not cover employees who are injured while working in the home. If a gardener, maid, or a television repairperson is injured, they are generally covered by workers' compensation, not the homeowner's policy.

Medical payments insurance

Medical expense coverage generally applies only to accidents that occur in the residence of the homeowner. Medical payments provide reasonable medical expense payments for injuries to people injured on the premises of the insured. For example, the medical bills of a person who slips and breaks a leg on the homeowner's sidewalk are paid. The coverage also applies to injuries occurring off the premises of the insured, but only if they were caused by the insured, a member of the insured's family, or their pets. Basic coverage is $500 for each person injured, but larger amounts may be purchased. Coverage is extended only to injuries of others and does not cover the homeowner or members of the family.

Just as in the case of the personal liability clause in a homeowner's policy, the medical payment part does not cover employees injured while working in or around the home. In such a case, workers' compensation takes over.

Renter's Insurance

Many people who rent rather than own their home feel that they do not need property insurance (other than on their car). This is not true. First of all, they need a personal property floater policy. In addition, renters need a personal liability policy. Even if you are renting a house and the owner has such a personal liability policy, it generally applies only if the landlord is living in the house and it does not always protect the renter. If someone were to trip on the sidewalk and break his or her leg, the renter could be held liable. Most insurance companies sell what they call renter's insurance in one package to cover the above items. This is the homeowner's policy for tenants, referred to as HO-4. Many insurance companies have more than one renter's package, and renters can choose between basic coverage or for a somewhat higher premium a more generous package similar to the broad coverage for owner-occupied homes.

Insurance on Condominiums

Some companies have developed a special homeowner's policy (HO-6) that applies to condominiums. Others use the HO-2 (broad) coverage to provide condominium protection. If the HO-6 policy is used, it provides essentially the same protection as the HO-2 plan.

Plain-English Policies

In recent years there has been a move to sell policies that are written in language the layman can understand. The legal terminology has been removed, and simple phraseology has been developed. These are similar to the various homeowner's policies in the protection they provide, and a person can buy basic, broad, or all-risks type of coverage. Only about twenty states currently have authorized plain-English policies, but they are becoming more popular. These policies are sometimes referred to as HO-76 because they were first introduced in 1976, but this is not an official designation.

Those who favor plain-English policies claim they are clearer and spell out more specifically what they cover; that is, the nonlegal language cannot be interpreted in several ways. The opponents of plain-English policies maintain that legal language, although more difficult, is also more precise and therefore the traditional policies are less subject to several interpretations.

Separate Individual Policies

As noted above, at one time a separate policy had to be purchased for each hazard: one for fire, one for hail, wind, personal property, liability, and so on. That made the total insurance cost more expensive. Today relatively few such policies are sold, but if you want only some of the hazard protection you can buy just that. Check that carefully. If you want only fire protection, that alone may cost you less than a homeowner's policy, but if you want coverage for two or three different hazards, you would probably save by buying a homeowner's policy. Most people need and should seriously consider the entire homeowner's package.

Flood Insurance

If you buy a homeowner's policy, you are covered for virtually all hazards, but you may need one for which you are not covered—flood insurance. Insurance companies will not sell flood insurance because they cannot actuarily spread the risk over large numbers—the reason being that only people living in a flood plain would buy flood insurance. You can buy flood insurance through an agency of the federal government, the U.S. Department of Health and Urban Development (HUD). The maximum amount of insurance you may buy is $185,000 on a single-family home and $60,000 on its contents. Premiums will vary depending upon where you live. Contact your homeowner's insurance agent if you need coverage.

Costs (Premiums) of Homeowner's Insurance

Premiums vary with the location of the property and type of construction. Certain areas are more susceptible to damage due to certain natural phenomena. Some areas are wind areas; others are in a hail belt; others, such as Florida and the Gulf Coast, are in the hurricane belt. Consequently, little can be said regarding costs regionally. Table 13–2 shows some data for a homeowner's coverage in four different areas.

Within a smaller area classified as having common hazards, rates vary primarily with the type of construction. There are generally three or four classifications and three or four rates per $1,000 of insurance. There is also variation

Table 13-2   Regional premium variation on a homeowner's policy

City	Premiums (annual rates)
Boston	$425
Austin, Texas	408
San Francisco	227
Small town in Arizona	159

Note: In all cases the house is a $100,000 home exclusive of the lot. This means, of course, that there is much more house in Arizona and Texas than in Boston or San Francisco. The premiums also include coverage on personal property, liability, and medical payments. In all cases there is an 80 percent coinsurance clause, and the deductibility is the same in all cases. The construction in all cases is the same: brick veneer. The houses are, then, the same in all respects except for size. Rates furnished by a large, well-known national company. Rates are as quoted in January 1983 and are subject to change due to rising construction costs and other factors over which the insurance industry has no control.

with what is built into the house. If it has central air conditioning and a fireplace, there is more value to be destroyed by fire. If there is a swimming pool, there is a greater hazard to small children. Rates will reflect this.

OTHER ASPECTS OF HOME INSURANCE

Actual Cash Value

One of the important clauses in some of the policies from the homeowner's viewpoint deals with actual cash value. The clause states that the company will reimburse for covered losses to personal property on the basis of actual cash value at the time of the loss but not to exceed the amount needed to repair or replace the property. In many cases the replacement cost is the higher, and hence the insured would have to bear some loss of his or her personal property. (A few companies offer replacement cost coverage for personal property, but at a considerably higher premium).

On the dwelling most policies will pay losses on the basis of replacement cost with no allowance for depreciation for partially damaged homes. However, the face value is the maximum a company will pay if a house is totally destroyed, even though the replacement cost may be the higher. This is explained in detail below under coinsurance.

Apportionment Clause

The standard policy has an additional clause that is important to the homeowner. It states, "This company shall not be liable for a greater portion of any loss, than the amount hereby insured against shall bear to the entire insurance covering the property against the peril involved, whether collectible or not."

The reason for this clause is that an individual may take out several policies with different companies. A person who has a home valued at $100,000 could conceivably take out a policy with company A in the amount of $60,000 and another with company B in the amount of $40,000. With the pro rata clause, however, company A would be liable only to the extent of three-fifths of any loss and company B to the extent of two-fifths of any loss. This clause also is effective in preventing a homeowner from getting more than the house is worth. If the person had two $60,000 policies on a $100,000 house and it was totally destroyed, each of the companies would pay $50,000.

Coinsurance

Most policies also have a coinsurance clause to discourage the homeowner from having too little insurance on the home. This is a statement that the company shall be liable, in the event of loss, only in the proportion that the actual amount of insurance bears to the insurance theoretically required. The required or proper amount of insurance is not 100 percent of the value of the house but usually about 80 percent, although some companies may require 90 percent. This 80 or 90 percent figure, which has been set after years of experience, reflects the fact that relatively few houses are completely destroyed by fire. The purpose of the coinsurance clause is to adjust rates equitably among the various policyholders. In the absence of a coinsurance clause, it might happen that an individual would be able to collect the full amount of the loss without paying much premium. Suppose a house is valued at $100,000 and a policy is placed on it for only $60,000. A loss occurs of $20,000, and in the absence of the coinsurance clause, the full $20,000 would be collectible. This award would be unfair to other people who had insured their property for the proper amount and who had therefore been paying higher premiums.

In an 80 percent coinsurance clause, it states, "This company shall not be liable for a greater proportion of any loss or damage to the property described herein than the sum hereby bears to 80 percent of the actual cash value of said property at the time the loss shall happen, nor for more than the proportion which this policy bears to the total insurance thereon." In other words, if you do not carry insurance amounting to 80 percent of the cash value of the property and if a partial loss occurs, you must share that loss with the company. You may recover only that proportion of the loss that the amount of insurance you actually have bears to the amount of insurance you should have under the coinsurance clause. This principle has long since been converted into the following formula:

$$\frac{\text{Amount carried}}{\text{Amount should carry}} \times \text{Actual loss} = \text{Recovery}$$

Suppose that the actual cash value of a home is \$100,000 and that there is an 80 percent coinsurance clause in the policy. You have insurance of only \$60,000, and there is a loss of \$10,000. How much of the \$10,000 loss can you collect? Substituting in the formula above:

$$\frac{\text{Amount carried } (\$60,000)}{\text{Amount should carry } (\$100,000 \times .80 \text{ or } \$80,000)} \times \text{Actual loss } (\$10,000)$$
$$= \text{Recovery of } (\$7,500)$$

On the other hand, assuming the same set of facts and assuming further that the proper amount of \$80,000 of insurance was carried, then:

$$\frac{\$80,000}{\$80,000} \times \$10,000 = \$10,000 = \text{(Recovery)}$$

It should again be emphasized that if a house is totally destroyed by fire, the insurance company will not necessarily pay for the entire value of the house. In most states the company will pay a sum equal to the face value of the policy or the actual cash value of the home, whichever is less. Therefore, if a homeowner has a house with an actual cash value of \$100,000 and because of an 80 percent coinsurance clause only carries \$80,000 of insurance, that is the maximum the company will pay. If the house is lost in a fire, the homeowner loses \$20,000. The coinsurance clause, then, protects the company against people who buy less fire insurance than they need but who still are fully protected against a fire that does not totally or almost destroy the house. For the homeowner to be fully covered in case a fire totally destroys the house, he or she needs 100 percent coverage. Indeed, many mortgage lenders require the homeowner to buy 100 percent coverage as a condition of making the loan.

It is also wise for the homeowner to reappraise the value of the house occasionally and change the insurance accordingly. The value of houses has risen substantially because of inflation. Many policies provide for an automatic increase yearly.

A HOME INSURANCE PROGRAM

Families who own their own homes should undoubtedly have one of the several available homeowner's policies that put all insurance needs in one package and save on premiums. Most insurance companies have three different homeowner's policies to choose from. These are usually referred to as basic (HO-1), broad (HO-2), and all-inclusive (HO-5).

Whether the homeowner's policy should be basic, broad, or all-inclusive is a matter of personal choice. Probably for most families, the basic plan (HO-1) or the broad coverage (HO-2) would be adequate. Which you select would be determined by your budget and your value judgments. In many states the HO-2 policy is not much more expensive than the HO-1, and it provides for much more protection. If you buy an HO-5 policy, you are paying more in premiums for only marginal additional protection.

Renters should consider the homeowner's policy for renters. The alternative would be to buy a straight personal property floater, but this would not provide liability protection for injuries to others on the premises which a renter's policy would provide.

Landlords who own a rental house might want an old-fashioned fire insurance policy with an extended coverage endorsement. Personal property coverage would not be needed if it is an unfurnished house, nor would medical payments coverage be needed. But a landlord would need liability coverage for the rental house. Both the tenant and the landlord need this since most policies cover only one or the other, and the provisions are not transferable. Someone who slipped and broke his or her neck on the sidewalk in front of the rental house could sue both the tenant and the owner. Each would need a separate policy; the policy of one would not cover the other. The landlord can buy this as a supplement to this same personal liability protection already owned on the house in which he or she resides. It is usually a little cheaper this way.

There remains the question of how much insurance to buy. This is largely determined by the value of the house. Since most companies have an 80 or 90 percent coinsurance clause, this sets the floor on the amount of insurance. For full protection, however, a person would need to buy a policy with a face value equal to 100 percent of the value of the house. One's own priorities will dictate whether to select 80, 90, or 100 percent coverage.

The amount of liability insurance you need to incorporate into your homeowner's policy will vary. The basic amount ($25,000 in most states) is what you will get in most homeowner's policies. You can obtain more than this, but in most cases this is enough. You need less liability insurance for your home than you do for your automobile, because there is less danger to guests and passersby. Also few of the injuries are as serious as injuries caused by autos can be.

AUTOMOBILE INSURANCE

In recent years there have been many press reports concerning "excessive" awards granted by juries to victims of automobile accidents. Some critics have placed the blame for rising automobile insurance rates directly on plaintiffs' attorneys and easily influenced juries. On the other hand, many individuals have been victimized by insurance company adjusters and insurance company attorneys. It is just as easy to generalize from these injustices as it is from the excessive awards. Then, too, a few state laws set an upper limit on the amount a jury may award for an accidental death. Oddly enough, since in most cases no limit is set for injuries, a person can collect more for a broken leg in these states than for a death.

In any event, automobile insurance is important. If an accident is due to the negligent operation of an automobile, the individual can be sued, and without insurance a resulting award might prove to be financially disastrous. Automobile insurance is of four types:

1. Liability insurance, which protects you from lawsuits if you kill or injure someone or damage their property
2. Collision insurance, which reimburses you if your car is damaged
3. Comprehensive insurance, which protects against loss due to fire, theft, wind, hail, and falling objects
4. Medical payment insurance, which will pay the medical expenses of all passengers injured while in your car. Your policy also covers all members of your family while riding in any car.

Liability Insurance: Bodily Injury and Property Damage

This type of policy protects the owner of the car from claims resulting from the negligent operation of an automobile. It covers the owner both from claims resulting from killing or injuring another person or from damaging property. These policies are generally referred to as "twenty/forty and ten" policies; $50,000/ $100,000 and $20,000; and $100,000/$300,000 and $50,000 policies, and so forth. The first two figures (twenty/forty and ten) refer to the bodily liability protection and the last figure to the property damage protection. Both the bodily liability protection and the property protection limits can go far above the limits described above. For example, one can buy $100,000/$300,000 and $50,000 coverage. The figures in a "twenty/forty and ten" policy mean that the policy covers bodily injuries up to $20,000 to any one person and bodily injuries up to $40,000 for any one accident injuring two or more persons.

For example, if one individual is run over because of the negligent operation of an automobile, that person can collect a maximum of $20,000 under the terms of the policy. If two or more persons are struck by the auto, the maximum coverage—or the most that the victims can collect—on the policy is $40,000. The final figure "ten" in the policy protects the insured for up to $10,000 in the event he or she is sued for damaging others' property. You may buy lower limits; for example a "five/ten and five" policy, but this is too low for most people.

In those states with financial responsibility laws (see below) the ten/twenty-five policy is the minimum a car owner must have to prove financial responsibility. Regardless of legislative action, a ten/twenty-five policy should be regarded by the individual as a bare minimum. Persons who have acquired wealth should certainly increase their coverage, and indeed many persons today carry $100,000/

$300,000–$50,000 policies. The reasoning is clear. Just because you carry insurance in the amount of $20,000 does not mean that this is all that you will be liable for; an individual may obtain a judgment against you for $50,000 or more. In this case, if your coverage is only ten/twenty, the company will pay $10,000 to the plaintiff and you will be personally liable for the balance.

The additional premiums required to finance a larger liability policy are not great. Therefore, it is recommended that you place a high priority on liability coverage. Coming up with a dollar figure is difficult, but some experts feel you should have, at least for bodily damage, protection of an amount equal to your net worth. Others would add somewhat more than this to take into account future earnings. Net worth is often used because that is what is in danger if a law suit is filed and you don't have insurance protection.

Others feel that the proper amount of liability insurance should be geared to the current pattern of jury award in the geographical area where the insured lives. According to this, you would need more insurance in New York or California, where awards are typically higher than elsewhere. On the other hand, in Mississippi, Arkansas, or North Dakota, you would need less. It is also true that sometimes there is no logical pattern to court awards, and hence it is somewhat arbitrary to determine your liability insurance this way. Nevertheless, a judgment could be based on both patterns of court awards and your net worth.

Collision Insurance

This type of insurance covers damage to the owner's car by collision with another car or with any other object, fixed or movable, and by upset. The policy usually has a deductibility feature, and the insurance covers the cost of repairs less the deductibility or the actual car value less the deductibility if the car is totaled. Thus if your car is demolished by a collision or by skidding off the road in a snowstorm, the company is liable—but only for an amount equal to the actual value of the automobile less the deductibility.

On some occasions, a car can be repaired after a collision, but the cost of repairing it is greater than the value of the car before the loss. In such a case, the cost of repairs does not enter into the matter. If the car was valued at $500 before a loss and has a junk value of $100 after the loss, and you have a $100 deductible in your policy, the company is liable only in the amount of $300, although it might cost $1,000 to restore the car to its original condition.

The greatest number of collision policies are issued on new automobiles, since most of the automobile purchases in the nation are made on the installment plan with a finance company or other institution financing the transaction. It is the financial institution that demands that the purchaser be insured. When a bank finances the purchase of a new car, the car itself is used as the collateral for the loan. If the driver runs the car into a telephone pole and wrecks it, the collateral is thereby reduced by an amount equal to the amount of the damages. Consequently, the bank is without collateral and, if the purchaser refused to pay the bank, it would have no other recourse than to sue on a promissory note that it holds; the purchaser might then have insufficient assets with which to pay off the judgment. To protect themselves, financial institutions demand that the auto be covered by collision insurance.

The deductible feature of a collision policy is written as $50, $100, $200, $250, and even $500 deductible. In the first instance the insured will bear the first $50 of loss and the company agrees to pay the balance. Consequently, if there is a loss of $300, with a $50 deductible policy the insured pays the first $50 of damages and the company is liable for $250. As the amount deductible increases, the premium rates decrease, because the risk of loss to the company is less.

One of the concepts that should be understood in connection with collision insurance is subrogation. Under the terms of the collision policy, the insured agrees that the company shall have the legal right to proceed against a negligent third party causing the loss and to prove damages in the name of the insured. The company has the right to step into the shoes of the insured, as it were, to proceed against a person causing the loss, and the insured agrees to cooperate fully with the company. Suppose a person is parked in a legal manner and another person driving negligently hits the parked car, causing damages of $1,000. If the insured has a $100 deductible collision policy, the company will pay the insured $900 and, under the terms of the policy, may commence a lawsuit against the negligent party to cover the $900 plus the $100 deductible. The insured person may in this manner recover his or her $100 out-of-pocket costs because the total amount of the suit will be $1,000.

Comprehensive Insurance

The comprehensive automobile insurance policy covers nearly all perils, with the exception of collision or upset and liability. Protection is given for any direct and accidental loss or damage to the automobile covered, as well as damage to the equipment usually attached to the vehicle. In addition, the automobile is covered for fire and theft. The important clause from the point of view of the insured states that the company shall be liable for "breakage of glass, and other loss caused by missiles, falling objects, fire, theft, explosion, earthquake, windstorm, hail, water, flood, malicious mischief or vandalism, riot, or civil commotion." The company limits its maximum liability to the actual cash value at the time of the loss. Although it has the option of repairing or replacing the damaged property, its maximum obligation is still limited to the actual cash value. Most comprehensive policies are written with a deductible provision, generally a $50 or $100 deductible.

One interesting coverage often put into some comprehensive policies is a clause providing for rental reimbursement for loss of use by theft. In this case, insured persons are paid, within limitations, for a vehicle that they may rent if their car is stolen. Sometimes car rental fees are also paid by the insurance company while a car is being repaired after it has been damaged in a collision. This, however, is usually taken care of by the liability section of the other driver's insurance company if he or she was at fault.

Rates on a comprehensive policy vary with the region where one lives, based on the past experience of loss. Rates in big cities are higher than in smaller towns or in rural areas because of the greater likelihood of vandalism, accidents, and the like. In certain rural areas of Colorado and Kansas, however, the lack of vandals is more than offset by the existence of hail or a combination of wind and dust, both of which will take the paint off a car.

Medical Payments Insurance

The basic endorsement calling for medical payments states that a company will pay within specified monetary limits, generally from $500 to $2,000, "all reasonable expenses incurred within one year from the date of the accident for necessary medical, surgical and dental services, including prosthetic devices, and necessary ambulance, hospital, professional nursing and funeral services" to persons injured "while in or upon, or entering into or alighting from the automobile . . . of the insured."

In recent years an extended medical payments insurance has appeared that in addition covers injuries as a result of "being struck, knocked down or run over by an automobile," or injured in a collision. If persons have this insurance, they and their family are covered while riding in another auto, or as a pedestrian, on a bicycle, or in any other way. People riding in the policyholder's car are also covered. The rates for this endorsement are low but vary with location and amount of coverage.

No-Fault Insurance

There is now much interest in no-fault auto insurance for bodily injuries. Under no-fault insurance, the victim's insurance company will pay regardless of who is at fault. The insurance company can then sue the other driver or his or her insurance company. Often much time and money are saved by avoiding going to court, particularly if it is not clear who is at fault.

At present about twenty-four states have some variation of no-fault laws on their books, but there is no agreement regarding what is meant by no-fault insurance. Purists insist that true no-fault would bar tort lawsuits for minor injuries. The injured party would be required to accept payment for injuries and not be permitted to sue.

The injured party would receive payments from his or her insurance company to compensate for these three types of losses:

1.   Income lost while injured
2.   Medical and hospital bills
3.   Expenses incurred in hiring maids and others to perform services formerly performed by the victim.

There is, however, an upper limit on the amount of lost income that could be recovered, which varies from state to state. Most states also set an upper limit on the amount of medical and hospital expenses that could be recovered (and this varies), but some states do not have a limit. Finally, the limit that all states have on the recovery of expenses incurred in hiring help to perform certain tasks for the victim varies. For loss of life, loss of limb, or for losses exceeding the maximums, lawsuits would be permitted, and no-fault would not apply. About fifteen states have such no-fault legislation on the books.

There are about nine states that have variations of no-fault laws. These states would permit no-fault settlements on a voluntary basis. The injured parties could sue for damages in any and all cases, even for minor injuries; but if they waived this right, the law would require that damages be paid regardless of who was at fault.

No-fault insurance does not apply to commercial vehicles, nor does it usually apply to property damages.

Since only about one-half of the states have no-fault insurance, there are numerous cases in which a driver from a non-no-fault (tort) state has an accident in a no-fault state with a driver covered by no-fault insurance, and vice versa. In such a case the no-fault driver is paid by his or her insurance company. Then that company and the other driver's insurance company settle the other driver's claim in the usual way. For example, if a Massachusetts driver (no-fault) has an accident in Texas (non-no-fault), the Massachusetts driver's claims are paid by his or her insurance company. This is because most no-fault policies are valid in all states. Then the Texas driver and his or her insurance company and the Massachusetts company settle the claim in the usual way, either amicably out of court or in court if necessary. If a Texas driver has an accident in Massachusetts, the same procedure is followed.

The advocates of no-fault insurance maintain that under it not only are settlements for injuries made more quickly, but they are more certain. Indeed, they are almost automatic. Under a tort (or fault) system usually lengthy legal battles must be fought. Also if the victim is partly at fault, the doctrine of contributory negligence prevents a settlement. Proponents also argue average no-fault settlements often result in the victim's getting more because there would be no court costs or attorney's fees to dilute the settlement. Under the tort system, less than one half of the liability insurance premium dollar is returned to the accident victim, according to a U.S. Department of Transportation study. Finally, proponents believe that no-fault saves time and money for the insurance companies, not only in the form of court costs and attorneys' fees, but in administrative expenses, which could reduce insurance premiums.

The opponents of no-fault say it is unfair in that it allows no settlement for pain and suffering or mental anguish. They also argue that by allowing damages automatically, many people who don't deserve them get them. (Presumably there are people who are at fault and have themselves caused, or at least contributed to, their injuries.) This, opponents say, increases insurance company costs and results in higher premiums.[2]

OTHER ASPECTS OF AUTOMOBILE INSURANCE

Financial Responsibility Laws

A few states have compulsory insurance laws, and many others have laws concerning financial responsibility even though they have no compulsory insurance laws. Financial responsibility means simply that when an accident occurs, the state requires the individual to post a bond or its equivalent. The term *bond* is usually taken to mean cash or high-grade securities in the amount of the estimated damages. As a substitute for the bond, individuals may prove that they are financially responsible by proving that they are adequately insured. There is no question of who was right or wrong in the accident; individuals must prove financial responsibility whether they were right or wrong.

The purpose of financial responsibility laws is to protect the victims of automobile accidents. The law attempts to do this by encouraging people to have at least the minimum amount of insurance and in this way increase the probability of the victim's being able to collect to compensate for the damages.

While the purpose of financial responsibility laws is admirable, in some states these laws are ineffective because of either court rulings or poor enforcement. In others they work fairly well. In some states, the car registration of a motorist who fails to prove financial responsibility is withdrawn. In others, it is common practice for the state police merely to remove the license plates from the vehicle, and the motorist is prohibited from driving it until they are returned.

The Uninsured Motorist Endorsement

Most states now require companies to offer policyholders the uninsured motorist endorsement for a slight extra premium. The uninsured motorist endorsement is simple and relatively inexpensive. It states that if you are injured as the result of an accident with an uninsured and negligent motorist or by a hit-and-run driver, your company will in effect insure that uninsured motorist for the "basic

---

2. Both sides maintain that their system would result in lower premiums. Neither side's case can be proven. The coming of no-fault insurance has not reduced premiums; indeed they have soared in recent years. However, much of this increase is attributable to inflation. A comparison of premiums in no-fault and tort states shows no discernible pattern.

sum" in accordance with the laws of the state. The term "basic sum" is the minimum of bodily liability insurance sold. In most states this is ten/twenty, but in some it is five/ten. If your policy has this endorsement, your own insurance company pays you, but generally only for bodily injuries and no more than the basic sum. A few companies, however, will also pay a collision claim under the uninsured motorist endorsement if you have a collision policy with them.

Your insurance company, after it pays you, has the right to sue the other motorist to recover what it paid. In practice this is often difficult because the uninsured motorist probably has no assets. Or if the driver injures someone without stopping, there is little the company can do unless he or she is subsequently apprehended.

Assigned Risk Plans

With the development of financial responsibility requirements, assigned risk plans were also developed to make financial responsibility possible. Liability insurance is one way of showing financial responsibility, but some drivers find it difficult to obtain insurance because of their driving record. Consequently, assigned risk plans were developed to take care of these people. When these plans were first established companies got together and set up a pool. Then the companies all issued some policies to these higher risk drivers. The idea was that if the assigned risks were spread over all of the companies, none of them would have an excessive amount. In some states it is still done this way, in others more informal methods are used to spread these risks over all companies. The amount of insurance the assigned risks may buy is limited to the basic sum, which varies from state to state, but most often ten/twenty bodily liability and five for property liability. In virtually all cases, the drivers who are assigned risks have to pay a much higher premium for their insurance than other drivers.

Preferred Risks

In a real sense, the preferred risk is the opposite of the assigned risk and came about as the result of competition among companies. Despite financial responsibility laws, many buyers, particularly in those parts of the country where rates are exceedingly high, began doing without insurance or purchasing only the minimum policies, such as a ten and twenty policy or even a five and ten in some states. Consequently, to increase their share of the market, some companies began issuing preferred risk policies at a lower rate, and other companies soon followed. In short, as a reward for safe driving the rate is lowered. Lowered rates are given only to selected risks, those who have had a safe record for a number of years. In addition, some companies emphasize that they specifically will sell insurance only to nondrinking drivers, and that because of this they can charge lower premiums.

Insurance Rates and Costs

Rates vary from one section of the country to another, in part, because juries typically grant larger awards in some areas. The cost of living is also higher in some sections of the country. Rates may also vary within any geographic region; generally they are higher in big cities than in small towns. Table 13–3 shows some of this regional variation for one national company.

Rates also vary somewhat with the age and sex of the driver. Male drivers under age 25 pay a higher premium because they have a higher accident rate. In some states if you are under 25 and married, you get some reduction from the general under-25 rate. Your driving record may also affect your rate. In some states if you have had several (the number varies from state to state but two to four is most common) moving traffic violations, your rates may be pushed above the regular rate even if you have had no accidents. If you have had an accident and you got a ticket, your rate could be adjusted upward even more. On the other hand, some companies reduce rates below regular rates for those drivers between age 30 and 60 who have good driving records. The age range 30 to 60 is dependent on the theory that drivers under 30 are less cautious than those over 30, and that the reflexes of drivers over 60 have slowed down. Finally, rates on collision and comprehensive coverage vary with the type of auto as well as the factors noted above. The more expensive the auto, the more expensive the insurance.

Table 13–3   Regional auto insurance premium variations

City	Premiums (semi-annual rates)
Boston	$518
Austin, Texas	195
San Francisco	333
Mesa, Arizona	152

Note: In all cases the cars are used only for pleasure and no driver is under twenty-five. The rates are for January 1983 and are subject to change at any time due to inflation, larger court awards, rising auto repair prices, and other factors beyond the control of the insurance industry. Rates furnished by a large, well-known national company. The rates apply to a 1983 Chevrolet purchased in January 1983 for $10,000 and are semi-annual.

While rates vary from place to place, and with differences among drivers, they are rising rapidly all over. Some attribute this to general inflation, others to more generous jury awards, still others to more costly cars that are more difficult (and hence costly) to repair. Rates vary from company to company even within a region, and you should shop around when buying insurance. Not all companies are equally prompt and fair in making settlement, and you should consider this when choosing a company.

In some states auto insurance pays dividends just like life insurance; these dividends vary. In some states rates are tightly controlled by state regulatory commissions; in others there is more competition. In many states the companies set rates which are then subject to approval by state regulatory agencies. Some critics maintain that the regulatory agencies contribute to higher rates by protecting the weaker companies.

Lately critics have suggested certain reforms they feel will reduce rates or at least halt the upward trend. The following reforms have been suggested:

1. Mass marketing through group plans
2. Better no-fault insurance laws
3. Open rating (a system in which insurance companies would set their own rates rather than rely on the regulatory agencies.)

It is hoped this would result in more competition and generate downward price pressure.

How Much Liability Insurance?

A person needs liability insurance; this is a must. The question is how much to have. The answer is a personal value judgment. However, as noted above, your net worth is what you are protecting, and this is the place to begin. You might also give some weight to your future earnings and future increase in net worth. If there is a pattern of court settlements in your area for seriously injured or killed automobile victims, consider that. You should have a fairly large liability policy even if your net worth is not very great. Rates do not rise rapidly as the amount of liability insurance purchased increases over the basic five/ten-five unit.

An Umbrella Policy

If you really need a large amount of liability insurance, buy an umbrella package. Most auto insurers do not write more than $100,000/$300,000–$50,000 of liability coverage, but many have a liability umbrella policy for as high as several million dollars. An umbrella policy normally has a $100,000/$300,000–$50,000 deductibility, so you need that coverage through your regular insurance. The umbrella covers all liability claims in excess of that for both your home and

your auto. For the coverge, premiums are relatively cheap, in most states, a
$1,000,000 umbrella can be purchased for less than $100 per year.

How Much Collision Insurance?

Should you have collision insurance, and if so how large a deductible should
you have? The answers depend upon the value of your car, how much you
drive, where you drive, and the kind of driver you are, factors that cannot be
measured mathematically.

Once a car depreciates below a given figure, collision insurance should be
dropped. The more you drive the more likely you are to have an accident. If
you drive mostly in the country or small towns, the likelihood of an accident
is less than if you live in a city and drive there, especially on freeways. Only
you know what kind of driver you are, hence only you can judge this point.
But if you drive defensively, you do not need insurance as much (or can live
with a higher deductibility) as would be the case if you drive offensively.
Premiums on collision insurance vary regionally as well as with the value of the
car. You should calculate the annual premium plus the deductibility as a percent
of your car's value. Remember this percent will go up as you increase the
deductibility, and this is a good way to save money. This ratio may also go up
as your car becomes older and loses its value. Check with your agent to see
what your saving would be if you increased your deductibility.

If you can reduce your premiums by $75 or $80 per year by increasing
your deductibility from $100 to $300, you will save money by doing so if you
have an accident less frequently than about every three years. If you are an
average driver and have a wreck, there is about a fifty-fifty chance it will be
the other person's fault, and his or her insurance company will pay. This improves
the odds; now the $75 you save per year will finance the $200 additional
deductibility about every year and a half. If you are quite sure you won't have
an accident very often, you might want to consider a $500 or even a $1,000
deductibility. Depending upon where you live and how expensive a car you
have, you can save from $100 to $200 per year in premiums by choosing a
$500 deductibility.

When to drop your collision insurance completely is a more difficult question.
Once the annual premiums plus the deductibility together amount to a substantial
percentage of the value of the car, you should consider dropping it. Suppose
your car is worth $1,000 and you have a $100 deductibility policy with an
annual premium of $100. If the car were totaled, your out-of-pocket cost would
be $200 (the premium plus the deductibility). You are paying $200 to protect
$800 of property (the car's value of $1,000 less $200 out-of-pocket cost). This
ratio is 25 percent, and you should consider dropping your collision insurance.
Your car will continue to decline in value as the years pass (your premiums may
too but probably by less). With the above ratio of 25 percent, if you totaled
your car less than every four years, you would be better off to drop the collision

insurance. This is especially true because the odds are improved by the possibility that the other driver's insurance will pay.

How Much Comprehensive Insurance?

You should decide your comprehensive needs in the same way you decide your collision needs. See how much money you can save by raising your deductibility to $100. On a new car you will want some comprehensive. As the car gets older, you will have to decide when the cost of protecting your property is costing more than it is worth, and give some thought as to how often you are likely to have a claim.

Medical Insurance and Uninsured Motorist Endorsement

Medical insurance is not expensive and you should seriously consider it. The same is true of the uninsured motorist endorsement. This also reimburses you for injuries suffered at the hands of a hit-and-run motorist even if he or she is not apprehended.

QUESTIONS FOR REVIEW

1. What is liability coverage?
2. What is the homeowner's policy?
3. What is the nature of the coverage one receives from personal property coverage under the homeowner's policy?
4. What is medical payments coverage?
5. How should a person who rents protect himself?
6. Where may you buy flood insurance? Why do most insurance companies not sell flood insurance?
7. What is the purpose of the apportionment clause in a fire insurance policy?
8. What is meant by coinsurance? Is a 90 percent coinsurance clause superior to an 80 percent clause? Explain why or why not.
9. If someone were to say that he or she had a "twenty/forty and ten" automobile policy, what would he or she mean?
10. Explain the difference between liability insurance, collision insurance, and comprehensive insurance as it applies to a car.
11. What is no-fault auto insurance? What benefits are claimed for it? Is there general agreement regarding what is meant by no-fault insurance?
12. In general, explain the financial responsibility laws as they appear on the statute books of those states having such laws.
13. Discuss the uninsured motorist endorsement, bringing out how it works.

14. What is meant by "basic sum" of insurance?
15. What is an assigned risk pool?
16. What are preferred risks?
17. How are automobile insurance rates determined?
18. Discuss the reforms that have been suggested for the fire and casualty insurance companies.
19. What is an umbrella policy?
20. Discuss property insurance programming.
21. How should you determine how much collision insurance you need?

CASES

1. Peter Green has a home valued at $80,000, and a few years ago he bought a homeowner's policy on it with an 80 percent coinsurance clause. Many of his friends have told him 80 percent is not enough and that he should have at least 90 percent. Do you agree? Explain why or why not.

2. Tom Singer is a traveling salesman who rents an apartment that, because of the nature of his work, is often unoccupied. Tom keeps a good many valuable personal items in it, and he is afraid of fire and theft. Can you give him advice with respect to insurance coverage?

3. Jim and Jean Sargeant have two cars—a new Ford and a ten-year-old Plymouth. Jean does not think they should spend money on insurance for their old car but is willing to pay for complete coverage on the new. Jim is not so sure. Can you explain Jim's reasoning? Jean's?

4. Carolyn Roundtree has a year-old car and carries $10,000/$20,000 liability insurance, $5,000 property damage, some comprehensive, and collision with $100 deductible. Is this a wise policy? Carolyn thinks her rates are high. Can you show her how to reduce them? Carolyn's sister believes she should carry more liability insurance. Do you agree?

5. Joan Rider has just purchased a $9,000 Ford sedan. She will use it to drive to and from her job and also for pleasure. She expects to drive about twelve thousand miles per year, and she has financed the car at the local bank where she keeps her checking account. Help her work out an insurance program on her car; advise her what kind of coverage she should get and how much.

6. Wanda Williams of western Walla Walla, Washington works as a willing worker at the Workington Western Westport Welding Works in western Walla Walla, Washington, while working her way through Witman College, also in western Walla Walla, Washington. She will need to buy a car but will use it only to drive to and from work. She also will need to finance it. Advise her about what kind of car to buy and what financing arrangements are available. Also, decide if she should buy insurance on her car.

SUGGESTED READINGS

Analysis of Automobile No-Fault Statutes. General Adjustment Bureau, Inc., 123 William Street, New York, N.Y. 10038.

Athearn, James L. *Risk and Insurance,* 2nd ed. St. Paul, Minn.: West Publishing Co., 1981.

Best's Review, Property-Liability Edition. Published monthly by A. M. Best Company, Oldwick, N.J. 08858.

Casualty Insurance Handbook. New York: Insurance Information Institute, 1982.

CPCU Journal. Published quarterly by the Society of Chartered Property and Casualty Underwriters (CPCU), Kahler Hall, Providence Road, Malvern, Pa. 19355.

Family Guide to Property and Liability Insurance. Published by the Insurance Information Institute, 110 William Street, New York, N.Y. 10038.

Gordis, Phillip. *Property and Casualty Insurance.* Indianapolis, Ind.: Rough Notes Company, 1980.

Greene, Mark. *Risk and Insurance.* Cincinnati: Southwestern, 1981.

Huebner, S. S., et al. *Property and Liability Insurance.* Englewood Cliffs, N.J.: Prentice-Hall, 1982.

Kohl, James A. *How to Save Money on Your Auto Insurance.* Helena, Mont.: Jaks Publishing Co., 1982.

Long, John O., and Davis, W. Gregg. *Property and Liability Insurance Handbook.* Homewood, Ill.: Irwin, 1965.

Mehr, Robert I., and Cammack, Emerson. *Principles of Insurance.* Homewood, Ill.: Irwin, 1980.

Riegel, Robert, Miller, Jerome S., and Williams, C. Arthur, Jr. *Insurance Principles and Practices: Property and Liabilities.* Englewood Cliffs, N.J.: Prentice-Hall, 1976.

Risk Management. Published monthly by the Risk and Insurance Management Society, Inc., 205 East 42nd Street, New York, N.Y. 10017.

Rokes, Willis P. *Human Relations in Handling Insurance Claims.* Homewood, Ill.: Irwin, 1981.

Statutes Affecting Liability Insurance; A Digest of State Statutes Relating to Negligence Actions and Liability Insurance Coverage, 15th ed. New York: American Insurance Association, 1981.

PART FOUR

MANAGING YOUR INVESTMENTS

CHAPTER FOURTEEN

SAVING AND INVESTING THROUGH THRIFT INSTITUTIONS

Personal Savings in the United States
Thrift Institutions
The Changing Legal Regulations
The Specific Deposits
The Various CDs
United States Savings Bonds
Some Notes on Interest
Appendix 14: Present and Future Values

Persons who manage their personal affairs well will probably have savings each month. Some of us have savings that appear as a residual after all our expenditures, whereas others have to budget and plan. Once we have put aside some money, we question what to do with it. It should be put to work so it will earn interest or dividends. It could be held in the form of idle cash in a mattress, but then it would not be working for us. This is referred to as hoarding. Individuals who hoard their savings are irrational because they forego investment income. In this chapter I will discuss putting savings in a thrift institution to be invested by someone else. This is indirect investing, where you earn interest via an institution. Later I will discuss investing in securities, or investing directly.

PERSONAL SAVINGS IN THE UNITED STATES

Savings come from earned income and represent that portion of income that individuals do not spend on consumption. The flow of savings from many small savers through thrift institutions, becoming indirect investments in American business (and governments), is depicted in Figure 14–1. Thrift institutions serve as a channel into which small savings flow from many individuals and out of which a large dollar volume of savings flows to the legitimate users of savings.

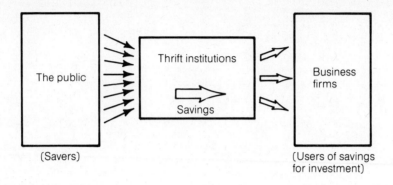

Figure 14–1 Dollar flows through the economy.

Personal or individual savings amounted to in excess of $142 billion in 1983, and many of these funds were channeled through thrift institutions.

Who Are the U.S. Savers?

Economists generally agree that there is a positive correlation between income and savings; the higher a person's income, the higher is the dollar volume of savings. There may also be a slight correlation between interest rate and savings; if interest rates are higher, there is a greater reward and greater incentive to save. But this theory is controversial and hard to prove. Studies at the University of Michigan Survey Research Center and elsewhere have suggested that there are a number of other factors influencing savings such as past income, direction of change in income, size of family, and age; but the effects of these variables are difficult to measure.

Most savings are generated by those whose income is high enough and who are over forty-five years of age. While many low-income groups save some money, the dollar volume is small. High savings among those over forty-five is related to the life cycle variation in the budget, discussed in Chapter 3. Up to about age forty-five or fifty are the high consumption years. After the children have left and the house is paid for and full of furniture and other consumer durable goods, more savings are generated out of any budget.

Why Save?

People save for all kinds of reasons, many to supplement their Social Security and other retirement plans, some for possible emergencies and the greater peace of mind savings provide, others save for a specific purpose: to send a child to college or for a future trip around the world. Still others save to acquire the down payment to buy a home or start a business. Some of the savings earmarked for a specific purpose, such as a college education or a vacation trip, will not become a permanent supply of capital for American business but will be liquidated and used for their intended purpose some day. The bulk of individual savings, however, can be looked upon as having been made for purposes of retirement or to provide greater security. They are not likely to be completely liquidated even after retirement and hence can be looked upon as semi-permanent sources of capital by American business firms. Moreover, much of this capital is made available for use through thrift institutions.

Volume and Classification of Savings

Individual (or personal) savings fluctuate greatly from year to year. Since 1975 they fluctuated from a high in 1975 of 8.6 percent to a 1977 low of 5.9 percent of after-tax income. Today's current low savings rate is often explained by the rapid rate of inflation. Inflation erodes savings and destroys the incentive to save. Also inflation creates a "buy now before prices rise" attitude. Many economic experts feel this low rate of saving is dangerous because it starves the economy of capital with which to grow (Table 14–1).

The savings you generate can be classified as "nest egg" or emergency funds, and others. The first should be considered emergency or "nest egg" and should be put in a safe place where they can be easily and quickly obtained, such as a thrift institution. How large your emergency supply of savings should be depends on your age, number of dependents, and so on, and is a personal judgment. Other savings may be invested differently from emergency savings.

Table 14–1   Personal savings

Year	Dollar savings in billions	Savings as % of income
1975	94.3	8.6
1976	82.5	6.9
1977	78.0	5.9
1978	89.4	6.1
1979	96.7	5.9
1980	106.2	5.8
1981	130.2	6.4
1982	139.1	6.6
1983*	145.0	6.7

* Estimate.
Source: Economic Indicators, July, 1983, Council of Economic Advisers, p. 6.

THRIFT INSTITUTIONS

Thrift institutions may be defined as one "designed either as repositories of assets used for short-term liquidity purposes or for accumulation of a fund of investment proportions."[1] The following institutions can be classified as thrift institutions:

1. Savings departments of commercial banks
2. Mutual savings banks
3. Savings and loan associations
4. Credit unions
5. Industrial banks
6. U.S. Series E and H savings bonds (since 1980 series EE and HH)[2]
7. Life insurance companies
8. Private pension plans

The first five institutions are also called depository institutions, because they serve as a depository for the public's savings. These deposits will be discussed in detail in this chapter; life insurance companies and pension plans will be discussed in separate chapters. While it might appear to many that U.S. savings bonds are not institutions, they are obligations of the U.S. government and they provide an outlet for individual savings. Indeed, they are safe and highly liquid and perform the same functions as institutions; hence logically they may be treated as such. This applies only to Series E and Series H bonds (and EE and HH), and not to other U.S. government bonds or to U.S. government securities that are not bonds. Consequently series EE and HH will also be discussed in this chapter.

There are a number of reasons why individuals place not only their nest egg but other surplus funds in thrift institutions.

1. The average person may have neither the skill nor the time to invest in other types of savings media, such as security markets.
2. Many savers want their savings to remain highly liquid, and feel that thrift institutions are the most liquid place.
3. Many savers feel they have insufficient funds to place in some other investment form, such as the stock market.
4. Most savers feel that the institutions can supply the investment judgment that they lack.
5. These institutions provide an extremely safe place to invest savings.
6. Most people do not wish to hold their savings in the form of idle cash (hoards).

1. Donald P. Jacobs et al., *Financial Institutions*, 5th ed. Homewood, Ill.: Irwin, 1972, p. 220.
2. In January, 1980 the Treasury stopped issuing series E and H bonds, and came out with series EE and HH. Of course, there are still a good many series E and H bonds outstanding.

The Various Depository Institutions

Commercial banks, savings and loan associations, and credit unions are found in all states; mutual savings banks are found in only seventeen of the fifty states and in Puerto Rico. They are located primarily in New England, the Middle Atlantic states, and on the West Coast. While there are some technical and legal differences between mutual savings banks and savings and loan associations, for all practical purposes they are the same.

Industrial banks are found in about twenty states. They are very much like commercial banks, but their powers are somewhat more limited. For example, they are not permitted to provide the trustee services that commercial banks and savings and loans may provide. (See Chapter 20 for a discussion of trusts.) However, they may make all kinds of loans and they do accept a variety of deposits.

Some of the above-mentioned thrift institutions provide the traditional checking account discussed in Chapter 4 that does not earn interest. In addition they all compete with each other for the public's savings dollars on which they do pay interest. Insofar as commercial banks are concerned, about 30 percent of their total deposits are noninterest-bearing whereas the other 70 percent pay interest. Figure 14–2 shows the growth of these deposits over the last few years.

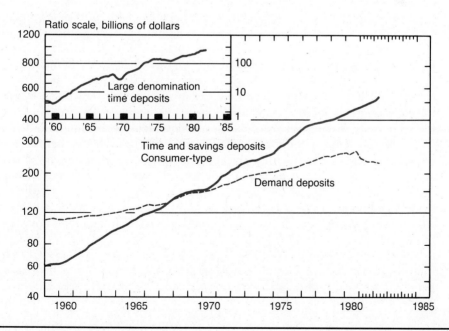

Figure 14–2   Principal liabilities of commercial banks, seasonally adjusted, quarterly averages. (*Source: 1982 Historical Chart Book*, Board of Governors of the Federal Reserve System, p. 79.)

Types of Interest-Bearing Deposits

All of the depository institutions offer a variety of interest-bearing deposits, but they can be classified into three main categories—the passbook savings account, the interest-bearing checking account,[3] and a number of different kinds of certificates of deposit (CDs).

If you invest your savings in the thrifts, the account is strictly a contract between you and the thrifts. In some cases, however, you are expected to pledge your funds for a specific period of time and not withdraw them before then. This is true in the case of certain CDs. If you withdraw them early, you must pay a penalty, as will be explained below.

THE CHANGING LEGAL REGULATIONS

Until recently the government imposed certain legal regulations regarding the maximum interest rates institutions could pay, the minimum dollar deposit required, and the length of time for which certain deposits had to be pledged. If the deposits were withdrawn early, certain penalties were assessed as required by federal law. Since the law did allow for some flexibility, a proliferation of deposits were developed in the late 1970s and early 1980s.

Most of these legal restrictions are now gone. In most cases, institutions are now free to set whatever interest rates they wish. They may also set their own minimum dollar amount of deposit if they wish, in most cases, and define for how long it must be pledged. Legal penalties for early withdrawals are still imposed, but they are much less severe than they were a year or two ago. Because of this new freedom, interest rates, types of deposit, minimum balances, and time to maturity vary among the institutions. Institutions are also free to compound the interest rate which they pay in any way they wish, and increasingly they are going to daily, or even continuous, compounding. Table 14-2 shows the true yield that results from daily, or continuous, compounding.

The few legal restrictions that still remain will be examined below. It should be noted, however, that within a year or so all legal restrictions will be removed and the free market will determine the interest rate, size of deposit, length to maturity, and so forth, on all deposits. Consequently, there will not be uniformity among the institutions and you will need to shop around to obtain the terms which are best for you. In summary, the legal restrictions today consist of (1) maximum interest rates which may be paid, but this applies only to passbook accounts, the interest-bearing checking (NOW) account, and any CD pledged for thirty-one days or less; and (2) the minimum deposit, in a few cases, and penalties for early withdrawal. Penalties for early withdrawal apply only to certain deposits, as will be noted below, along with a discussion of the actual penalty.

---

3. The interest-bearing checking accounts were originally called "negotiated order of withdrawal" (NOW) a few years ago when only a few institutions were offering them. Now they have a number of different names, but they actually are interest-bearing checking accounts.

Table 14–2   Real yield resulting from daily and continuous compounding* at various interest rates

Stated rate %	Yield due to daily compounding	Yield due to continuous compounding
5.00	5.13	5.20
5.25	5.39	5.47
5.50	5.65	5.73
5.75	5.92	6.01
6.00	6.18	6.27
6.50	6.72	6.81
7.00	7.25	7.36
7.50	7.79	7.90
8.00	8.33	8.45
8.50	8.88	9.00
9.00	9.42	9.55
9.50	9.96	10.11
10.00	10.52	10.67
10.50	11.07	11.23
11.00	11.63	11.80
11.50	12.19	12.37
12.00	12.75	12.94
12.50	13.31	13.51
13.00	13.89	14.09
13.50	14.45	14.67
14.00	15.02	15.25
14.50	15.60	15.84
15.00	16.18	16.43

* Continuous compounding is really a marketing device which permits the institution to say they are compounding more frequently than daily. Under daily compounding, simple interest for one year is calculated; that is then divided by 365 and added to the principal, and so on. Under continuous compounding, the year is simply broken down into a larger number of units, sometimes as many as 1000. This, of course, can be done with modern computers.

First, however, we will examine the more common of the various interest-bearing deposits. Keep in mind that there are some that must be pledged for as long as eight years. Moreover, as time passes, new accounts will no doubt be developed. Keep in mind that in most cases interest rates will vary with the amount of money you deposit and the length of time for which you pledge it. Generally speaking, deposits will vary positively with the amount of money you pledge — the larger the dollar amount, the higher the interest rate. However, this positive correlation will not necessarily exist with length of time for which the deposit is pledged.

Sometimes rates will be higher on short-term deposits; at other times, on longer-term. Which rate will be the higher is determined by the supply and demand conditions in the various maturities market, and rates will change as conditions change. The underlying conditions affecting the various rates are too complex to go into here; but because the free market will now determine most (and soon, all) rates, your task in selecting the proper maturity will become more complex. Not only will you need to examine which rate is higher, but also you will have to give some weight to what you believe market interest rates will be in the future because expected future interest rates will, of course, affect the rate on your deposit in the future when it matures and you wish to roll it over into a new deposit. One question you must consider is, do you wish to lock in on a longer-term basis at today's interest or to remain flexible and commit only on a short-term basis so that if rates rise in the future you may take advantage of them. As mentioned above, not only do rates vary from one type of deposit to another, but they may vary also from institution to institution for a similar deposit. Careful shopping, therefore, is now more important than ever.

THE SPECIFIC DEPOSITS

While the variety of deposits will no doubt change as the institutions develop under their new-found freedom, we will examine briefly those that are popular recently.

Passbook Savings Accounts

Passbook savings deposits are very liquid because they can be withdrawn at any time without a penalty. There are no service charges; and since, in many cases, funds can be transferred to an interest-bearing checking account by telephone, this is where you should keep your emergency funds if you are a modest investor. If you do not need a separate emergency fund, then you might want to keep your liquid assets in the interest-bearing checking account discussed in the next section. But since interest rates are low in both of these deposits, do not put extra or surplus funds in either of these accounts.

If your emergency funds are large enough to qualify for a higher-yielding deposit, which can be withdrawn free of penalty, you should consider putting them there.

Interest-Bearing Checking Accounts

These accounts can also be withdrawn without a penalty. Generally they earn the same interest as do passbook accounts, although some credit unions pay a little more than passbooks. However, there may be a service charge. Service charges vary from one institution to another, and they may also vary with the size of your average or minimum balance. While some credit unions do not assess a service charge under any circumstances, most other institutions require a fairly high minimum balance before they will forego service charges, which generally are only a few dollars per month. If you need a checking account, this is the one to choose. Unless your account is quite small, the interest you earn should more than offset your service charges. Some credit unions do not return your canceled checks. In this case your checks will come equipped with a carbon copy for your records, and you will get the regular monthly statements showing your transactions.

You should analyze your personal finances to see if you should transfer both your passbook and your old-fashioned checking (noninterest-bearing) account to this new checking account. If you need a separate depository for your emergency fund to lessen the likelihood of spending it, keep your passbook account. Otherwise, transfer it to the new interest-bearing checking account. You should almost surely eliminate your old-fashioned (noninterest-bearing) checking account, with one exception. If your account is quite small, it might be cheaper to select the noninterest account, because many institutions require a higher minimum balance on an interest than on a noninterest checking account before they waive monthly service charges. Analyze both accounts to see what your service charges, if any, would be in each of them. Remember—any money left in a traditional checking account is not working.

THE VARIOUS CDs

Different kinds of certificates of deposit (CDs) can be pledged for a specific period of time and some of them cannot be withdrawn early without a penalty. The time period (maturity) for traditional CDs varies from a few days to eight years or more. Historically, checks were not permitted to be written on any of these CDs, but recently checking privileges were authorized for some of them. From time to time, the institutions may impose minimum dollar amounts on some of these CDs, and a few still have legal minimums.

Credit unions, while they can offer CDs, are allowed to issue fewer varieties. In addition, federally chartered credit unions are generally not subject to any interest ceiling on deposits and may pay, in theory, then, any rate they wish on any of their deposits, including passbook accounts.

State-chartered credit unions may or may not be subject to legal ceilings depending on the state. However, federally chartered credit unions are regulated by the National Credit Union Administration; and, if they are paying a higher rate of interest than the regulators feel they can afford, they can be required to lower their rates.

Table 14-3 shows some of the more popular deposits that commercial banks, savings and loans, and mutual savings banks offered until late 1983. Now institutions are free to develop their own offerings and many will do so. Consequently there is now less uniformity among the various institutions, and not all of the CDs in the table are still being offered by all institutions. It should

Table 14—3   Various CDs offered by commercial banks, savings and loan associations, and mutual savings banks

	Interest rate[a] ceiling	Compounded[b]	Minimum legal deposit required[c]	Penalty for early withdrawal
Passbook	5 1/2%	yes	none	no
NOW Account	5 1/4%	yes	none	no
7–31 Day CD	tied to 91-Day Treasury Bill rate, if above 9%, no legal ceiling otherwise	yes	$2,500[d]	yes
91-Day CD	No legal ceiling; fluctuates with market conditions	yes	none	yes
6-Month Money Market CD	No legal ceiling; fluctuates with market conditions	yes	none	yes
30-Month Small Savers CD	No legal ceiling; fluctuates with market conditions	yes	none	yes
3.5-Year Wild Card CD	No legal ceiling; fluctuates with market conditions	yes	none	yes
18-Month IRA and Keogh CD	No legal ceiling; fluctuates with market conditions	yes	none	yes
Jumbo CD	No legal ceiling; fluctuates with market conditions	yes	$100,000	yes
Repurchase Agreement	No legal ceiling; fluctuates with market conditions	yes	none	no
Money Market Fund Account	No legal ceiling; fluctuates with market conditions	yes	$2,500[d]	no
Super NOW Account	No legal ceiling; fluctuates with market conditions	yes	$2,500[d]	no

[a] Savings and loan associations and mutual savings banks were permitted to pay 1/4 of 1 percent more than commercial banks, but since January 1, 1984 this has no longer been true. The interest which federally-chartered credit unions may pay is not regulated.

[b] If interest paid is compounded daily, it increases the real yield somewhat above the stated interest rate.

[c] While there are no longer any legal minimum requirements, some institutions impose their own minimums.

[d] If these accounts fall below $2.500, the maximum interest rate falls to 5 1/4 percent, the same interest as for the NOW account.

also be noted that a few institutions that are in fast-growth areas and short on capital have run advertisements in newspapers indicating that they will pay as high as 11 or 12 percent. Most of these advertisements are misleading; these high interest rates are only paid for one or two months in order to attract the funds. Note that savings historically and loan associations and mutual savings banks enjoy a quarter-of-a-percent preferential interest rate ceiling over banks in the case of passbook accounts only. The reason for this differential goes back many years, when it was used as a device to encourage the flow of savings into institutions that specialized in making mortgage loans. On January 1, 1984 this differential was eliminated. A number of these accounts are worthy of comment.

The Seven to Thirty-One-Day CD

This is the only CD that does not have checking privileges over which the federal government still exercises some control on the interest rate. If the balance falls below $2,500, the legal ceiling is 5 1/2 percent; if above that amount, the institutions are free to set their own rates.

The Ninety-One-Day and the Six-Month Money Market CDs

The interest rate on these two CDs reflected the free market short-term interest rate very closely during the early 1980s when it was tied to the treasury bill rate. Because of this and of their short-term maturities, these CDs became very popular. The rate on these CDs is now set by the free market and not by the government, and it reflects the free-market short-term rate.

The Small Savers' CD

During the period of intense regulation, this CD became very popular with the small investor because it was one of the first CDs for which no legal minimum dollar deposit was required. It is still a good vehicle to the investor who wishes to commit on a short-term basis. As noted above, some institutions set their own minimum, but often this is as low as $100 so it is especially designed for the small investor.

The Forty-Two-Month CD

This CD became popular with the intermediate-term investor. The interest on this CD is sometimes fixed for the entire forty-two-month period, and sometimes permitted to float up and down monthly and weekly as market interest rates change.

The Jumbo CD

For many years this was the only CD not regulated in any way by the government; all the terms (rates, deposit periods, etc.) were determined by negotiation between the depositor and the institution. For this reason they were very popular with the large investor. Now that virtually all rates are freely determined, the Jumbo may go the way of the dinosaur.

The Repurchase Agreement

As noted above, this was not a CD at all. Rather, it was a loan from the investor to the institution. As such, it was free of all regulation, but it was not insured as were other deposits. This arrangement is no longer used very much.

The Money Market Fund Account and the Super NOW Account

These were developed in 1983 to provide higher interest rates on checking accounts than the law then allowed on NOW accounts. They were authorized to permit thrift institutions to compete for funds with brokerage houses. The latter developed money market funds, which were similar to deposits, and drew a lot of money out of financial institutions in the early 1980s. A money market fund is a special type of mutual fund and is discussed in greater detail in Chapter 17 along with regular mutual funds. At this point, it is sufficient to note that a mutual fund is a device whereby many small investors pool their money with an institution which then invests it on their behalf. A money market mutual fund specializes in investing in short-term securities issued by the United States Treasury and by private corporations.

While checks may be written on both of these accounts, there is a monthly limit on the number of checks that may be written. In the money market fund account no such limit exists on the super NOW account. Since there is no limit on the dollar amount of these checks, there is no such thing as an early withdrawal penalty.

It should also be noted that a minimum balance of $2,500 must be maintained in both of these accounts to permit institutions to set interest rates as determined by the market. If the balance falls below this minimum, the maximum legal interest rate becomes the regular NOW account rate.

The IRA and Keogh CD

At one time this was a special account into which tax-free contributions were permitted if they were earmarked for retirement purposes. The funds in this account may also accumulate tax free. Now, however, tax-free IRA and Keogh contributions may now be placed into any CD that the institution offers.

The Sweep Arrangement

This is an arrangement whereby surplus funds in a lower interest-yielding account are periodically (say weekly or monthly) automatically swept into a higher-yielding account. For example, a NOW account may serve as a depository for transactions' balances, and may be balanced at say $2000. Funds in excess of that amount in multiples of $100 are swept out by computer on a periodic basis into a higher-yielding account. When the NOW account falls below $2000, multiples of $100 are swept in. The NOW account is therefore stabilized between $1900 and $2100.

The Phasing Out of Regulation Q

Regulation Q, which regulates the maximum interest rate which institutions may pay on deposits, is now almost gone. Maximum rates are now set only on (1) passbook accounts, (2) NOW accounts, (3) small CDs maturing in thirty-one days or less and (4) on money market fund and super NOW accounts if they are below $2,500. Even these restrictions will soon be eliminated.

All other rates are set by the institution in light of market forces. Because of this new freedom, most institutions now offer far fewer noninterest-bearing CDs. Interest rates vary with the dollar amount pledged and with the length of time for which it is pledged. Many institutions also give the depositor the choice of a fixed rate for the entire period for which the funds are pledged or a floating rate that is adjusted (up or down) periodically (usually monthly) as market interest rates vary. However, as noted before, interest rates now vary from one institution to another. Consequently you should shop around to obtain the best possible return on your money.

Safety of the Deposits; Deposit Insurance

All of the above-mentioned deposits, in most but not all of the depository institutions, are insured by an agency of the United States government up to $100,000. This is true of deposits in most commercial banks, savings and loan associations, mutual savings banks, and credit unions. There are, however, a few institutions that do not have deposit insurance, and you should probably avoid them. Those institutions that are insured will display a metal sign indicating this in a prominent place, usually near the teller's windows. Remember, too, that the $100,000 of insurance applies per person per institution, not per account. Hence, if you have several accounts, they are commingled, and all of them together come under the $100,000 protection if they are in the name of the same person in the same institution. However, you and your spouse may each have a separate account in the same institution, and each would be insured up to $100,000, for a total insurance coverage of $200,000. If you have funds in excess of that amount, you should split them between two or more insured institutions for complete coverage and safety.

Penalties for Early Withdrawal of CDs

While passbook savings deposits and regular checking, interest-bearing checking (NOW), money market fund, and super NOW accounts may be withdrawn without penalty at any time, this is not true of certain other CDs. There are two different penalties for early withdrawal of CDs: one on those issued prior to October 1, 1983 and another on those issued after that date.

If a CD issued prior to October 1, 1983 is withdrawn early, the penalty is the loss of three months' interest (at the CD's rate) if the deposit has a maturity of one year or less. If the CD has a maturity of more than a year, there is a loss of six months' interest, also at the CD's rate. On a $1000, two-year, 8 percent CD withdrawn after one year, the penalty would be $40. On CDs issued after October 1, 1983, the early withdrawal penalty is thirty days' loss of interest if the maturity is one year or less. If the CD has a maturity of more than a year, the penalty is a loss of ninety days' interest.

These penalties were imposed to discourage early withdrawal of CDs. The penalty is not assessed if a survivor withdraws the CD of a deceased person, or if the depositor is found to be mentally incompetent. It should also be noted that the above-mentioned penalties are legal minimums. Institutions are free to set higher penalties and some have done so.

UNITED STATES SAVINGS BONDS

United States government bonds can be classified into marketable and nonmarketable but redeemable. The marketable bonds are sold by brokers and appeal primarily to larger investors and institutions. They will be discussed in greater detail in Chapter 16. The nonmarketable bonds will be discussed here because they are designed for the small investor and because they are classified as thrift institutions. These bonds are issued in two different series; they were formerly called series E and series H, but in January, 1980, the Treasury made a few minor changes and the bonds are now called series EE and HH. The older series E and H bonds sold prior to 1980 are, of course, still outstanding.

Series EE

Series EE and HH bonds being nonnegotiable are also nonmarketable. They cannot be used as collateral for a loan nor can they be sold to a third party. However, they are redeemable, which means that they can be returned to the U.S. Treasury at the option of the bondholder. Because of this redeemability, their price is stabilized and they do not fluctuate inversely with changes in the interest rate.[4]

---

4. The reason Congress made these bonds nonnegotiable and redeemable was to protect the small investor from the unpleasant experience that took place regarding bonds sold during World War I. Those

Series EE bonds are discounted, whereas Series HH bonds are not. This merely means that Series EE bonds are sold below their face value and as time passes, their value rises to reflect accrued interest. These bonds come in denominations with face values of $50, $75, $100, $200, $500, and $1,000, $5,000, and $10,000. Since they are discounted, they are sold at a price below these figures.

Series EE bonds are sold at one-half of their face value and then appreciate as they approach maturity. On November 1, 1982, the U.S. Treasury changed the interest rate and hence the appreciation schedule of Series EE bonds. Bonds sold after that date have a floating interest rate that floats in accordance with the rate paid by the Treasury on five-year marketable securities. This variable rate works as follows. Every six months the Treasury Department compiles the average market interest rate on all Treasury marketable securities that are five years from their maturity during the previous half year. The rate on new Series EE savings bonds for the next six months is 85 percent of that market average. At the end of five years, the ten semiannual averages are added, averaged, and the average compounded on a semiannual basis to determine a bond's five-year yield. Series EE bonds held longer than five years have additional semiannual market averages computed in and compounded. This means, then, that since these bonds appreciate in value to accrue interest, their appreciation also varies; the appreciation is a function of the level of the interest rate. At maturity, the market value of these bonds may be at or above their face value. There is also a proviso in these Series EE bonds that guarantees a floor on the interest rate that the bondholder will receive if he or she holds these bonds for five years or more. This rate is 7 1/2 percent. If the interest rate were never to rise above 7 1/2 percent, these bonds' value would rise to their face value in ten years. If interest rates on them are above 7 1/2 percent, their value would rise above their face value.

The older Series EE bonds, purchased before November 1982, originally received a different interest rate and had a different appreciation schedule. They will now appreciate in accordance with their old appreciation schedule or the new one described above, whichever is more favorable to the bondholders. This means that the minimum guaranteed floor on Series EE bonds purchased before November 1, 1982, is 9 percent, since that was their rate when they were issued. At 9 percent these older EE bonds will reach their full face value in eight years, and their value, of course, can go higher. The interest (appreciation) on these Series EE bonds is not taxed until realized when the bonds are cashed in. This tax deferral makes the yield a little more attractive than their rate suggests. Interest on these bonds is not subject to state and local taxes.

The new Series EE bonds with a floating interest rate tied to the market

---

bonds were negotiable (and hence marketable). Many people bought bonds during the war but after the war their price fell drastically as interest rates rose. If people had to liquidate them due to an emergency, they suffered a substantial capital loss. Why the price of marketable bonds fluctuates inversely with changes in the interest rate is explained in Chapter 15.

rate are a more competitive investment. Before, many investors shunned them because of their relatively modest return.

Series HH

The interest on Series H and HH bonds, which are sold in units of $500, $1,000, $5,000, and $10,000, is payable semiannually beginning six months after issue date; it is paid on each interest date by check and mailed to the addressee of record. These bonds are always sold at their face value. They are not coupon bonds, however. They are registered bonds and the interest is automatically sent to the bondholder. Series HH (and the old H) bonds purchased before November 1982 yield 8.5 percent per year. This 8.5 percent is fixed for ten years and cannot float up as can Series EE. To receive the full 8.5 percent interest, however, the bonds must be held five years or more. If you redeem them sooner, they will be redeemed at less than face value, so the return drops below 8.5 percent.

The Treasury stopped selling Series HH over the counter on November 1, 1982. However, Series EE may be converted to Series HH. But since November 1982 Series HH bonds pay only 7.5 percent, having been reduced from 8.5. There is a limit to how many Series EE and Series HH a person may buy each year, $30,000 in the case of Series EE and $20,000 in the case of HH. A married couple may each purchase that amount, making the maximum annual investment $100,000. To do so, they would first need to buy $40,000 of Series EE, convert them to Series HH, and then buy $60,000 of Series EE.

You may obtain Series EE or HH bonds (or cash them in) at any large national bank. In addition, many employers have established a means whereby employees may buy Series EE bonds through payroll withholds.

Liquidity and Risk

All types of United States government securities are highly liquid. The marketable bonds (all but Series EE and HH) can be sold by telephoning a broker. A highly organized market exists for these bonds. The nonmarketable Series EE and HH bonds are redeemable at the option of the bondholder. Hence they, too, are very liquid. They can be redeemed at almost any commercial bank.

While there is absolutely no risk of default involved in holding any government bonds, there is a risk of possible capital loss involved in holding all government bonds except Series EE and HH. Since their market price is permitted to fluctuate freely with the forces of supply and demand, it is possible that, if a person wishes to sell bonds before they mature, he or she will have to accept a lower price than that paid. However, since Series EE and HH are redeemable by the Treasury, their price is in effect stabilized; there is no risk whatsoever attached to these bonds.

SOME NOTES ON INTEREST

Interest is mysterious to some people; it shouldn't be. Interest income is also sometimes looked upon as somehow being less virtuous than other income, an erroneous view. There is nothing mysterious about interest and there should be no stigma attached to receiving it. We shall next explore the theory of interest, simple interest, compound interest, the rule of 72, and how most thrift institutions calculate interest. Figure 14–3 shows how interest rates have changed over the years.

The Theory of Interest

Interest is the payment for the use of capital just as rent is the payment for the use of real property. Interest can be justified in several ways. Capital is productive and hence, like labor, it receives a return. Labor receives a wage; capital receives an interest payment. Liquid capital (money), however, must first be turned into real capital (plant and equipment) before it is productive.

Interest is also paid because the supplier of capital (the lender) assumes a risk (large or small) that the loan will not be repaid. This is the risk of default, and lenders must be paid a fee (interest) to entice them to assume that risk.

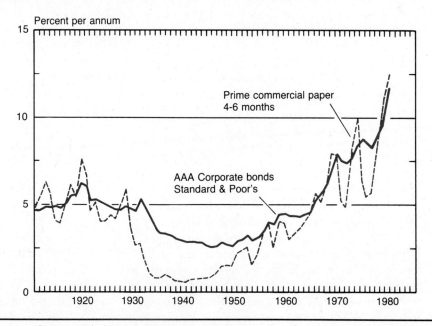

Figure 14–3 Long- and short-term interest rates, annually. (*Source: 1982 Historical Chart Book*, Board of Governors of the Federal Reserve System, p. 96.)

Moreover, the higher the risk of default, the higher the interest payment must be. If the risk is high enough, no one will advance the capital, and there is a fringe of unsatisfied would-be borrowers.

A third reason for the payment of interest is that most people prefer present dollars (or consumption) to future dollars. A lender gives up (it is hoped temporarily) present dollars, and hence present consumption, for future dollars, and hence future consumption. This is a personal sacrifice. For postponing consumption, the person must be given the reward of greater consumption in the future. Interest is a payment for abstinence, and is also called time preference. People prefer present consumption to future consumption; they have a positive time preference, and interest must be paid as a bribe to entice them to postpone consumption. Money or goods today is more valuable than the same money or goods in the future. The old saw perhaps explains interest best: "A bird in the hand is worth two in the bush."

Simple Interest

When a contract is made between a borrower and a lender, the borrower agrees to pay the lender a fixed percentage sum of the amount borrowed (called the principal) periodically. Usually the amount of interest to be paid is stated as so much per year. If the agreement calls for an 8 percent interest rate, then on a $1,000 loan the borrower must pay $80 per year. The contract could call for an $80 payment to be made every year, or it could stipulate a $40 payment every six months or $20 every three months. In each case, it would be 8 percent per year. If the interest payment is made each time it is due, the amount borrowed remains a constant ($1,000 in the case above), and the interest becomes a constant percentage of a constant principal sum. This is simple interest. However, this is not always what is done; and consequently, we also have compound interest.

Compound Interest

If the contract calls for the interest to be retained by the borrower, the principal sum grows as time passes. If a lender makes available to a borrower $1,000 to be compounded at 8 percent for a number of years, at the end of one year the $80 interest is added to the original loan of $1,000, which now becomes $1,080. The next year the interest is 8 percent of $1,080, or $86.40. The $86.40, instead of being paid to the lender, is again added to the principal sum of $1,080, now making it $1,166.40. Now interest will be calculated on $1,166.40, and so it goes year after year. This has been called paying interest on interest.

In the above case interest was compounded annually. Interest can also be compounded semiannually, quarterly, monthly, weekly, or even daily. Compounding semiannually would call for adding $40 to the principal sum at the end of six months and then figuring interest on $1,040 for the second six months and so on. Compounding results in a fixed percentage rate being calculated on an ever-increasing principal sum and becoming proportionately greater with each passing period.

The Rule of 72

If a dollar is earning compound interest, it will eventually double in value. How quickly a dollar will double is determined by the interest rate and by how frequently it is compounded (annually, semiannually, quarterly, monthly, or even daily) (see Table 1 in the appendix). If tables are not available you can approximate the time needed to double by applying the rule of 72. If you divide the interest rate into 72 you will get the approximate time needed for money to double, if earnings are compounded annually; for example, at 6 percent a dollar would double in 12 years ($72 \div 6 = 12$).

How Interest Is Calculated by Most Thrift Institutions

Not all thrift institutions calculate the interest that they pay the same way. But some general guidelines can be given. Some institutions have a rule that any deposits must be made by a certain date (most often the tenth of the month) to draw interest for that entire month. A few institutions still calculate interest on a quarterly basis. The funds must be on deposit by the tenth day of the quarter and remain there the entire quarter before interest is paid, a method being used by fewer and fewer institutions.

More institutions are now compounding interest daily. Interest is paid from the day the deposit is made until the day it is withdrawn. Modern computers make this possible. Daily calculation of interest permits banks to increase the real rate of return on deposits, and in recent years the growing competition for funds on the part of institutions has resulted in more daily interest computations. If, for example, interest is compounded daily at 5 percent, this makes the true yearly rate about 5.13 percent.

There are four general methods of calculating interest rates. The four methods are really means of establishing the balance upon which interest is to be computed.

First in first out (FIFO)
This method deducts all withdrawals from the interest period's beginning balance. If the interest period is quarterly and you have $1,000 in your account at the beginning of the quarter but sometime during the quarter you add another $1,000

(but too late to earn interest on it) and still later withdraw $100, the interest is calculated on $900. This is the least favorable method for the depositor.

Low balance

This method calculates interest on your minimum balance during the interest period. In the example immediately above, the interest would have been calculated on $1,000. This second method is not much better than the first one, and in the example above, if the $100 withdrawal had taken place before the $1,000 deposit, the two methods would have given the same result.

Last in first out (LIFO)

This method deducts withdrawals from the most recent deposits made during the period. In the example above, the $100 withdrawal would have been subtracted from the $1,000 deposit during the interest period. If the $1,000 deposit had come in early enough (generally before the 12th day of the interest period), the interest would be calculated on $1,900. If the deposit had not come in early enough, interest would be calculated on $1,000.

Day-in day-out (DIDO)

This method is also called the day of deposit to day of withdrawal and is the most favorable for the depositor. The interest period is one day, and a computer calculates and compounds interest daily. In the above example, with a beginning balance of $1,000, another deposit of $1,000, and a withdrawal of $100, interest would have been calculated on $1,000 for some days, $2,000 for some days, and $1,900 for some days. The day-in day-out method of calculating interest is now the most common, especially in metropolitan areas. Before you open a savings account you should check which method is used and choose the most favorable one. The difference in the interest that you will earn under the FIFO method and the day-in day-out method can be substantial.

There is a difference between daily compounding and the daily interest period. Only if the interest period is one day do you truly have a day-in day-out method. The interest period refers to the method of obtaining the balance on which interest is calculated. It is possible that under the first method (FIFO) the interest could be compounded daily; but it is on the beginning balance less withdrawal or $900 in our example, and not on each dollar for each day it was in the account.

In those cases where a method other than the day-in day-out method is used, the passbook holder should be careful not to withdraw funds a few days before the interest period ends because this could lose interest for a full quarter. It might be better to borrow money for a few days or weeks at, say, 9 or 10 percent until the interest payment is past in order to get 5 percent for a full three months. In some cases a depositor can do this from the same institution that has the deposit. This explanation generally applies only to passbook and NOW accounts; interest on CDs was discussed earlier in this chapter.

QUESTIONS FOR REVIEW

1. What is hoarding? Why is it irrational to hoard your savings? What else can you do with them?
2. What is meant by the term "investing indirectly"?
3. Who are the savers in the United States? Is there a correlation between savings and age?
4. Discuss some of the reasons for saving.
5. What are "nest egg" savings?
6. What are thrift institutions?
7. How do thrift institutions assist individuals in a savings program?
8. Why do many individuals place their savings in thrift institutions?
9. Distinguish between savings deposits and demand deposits.
10. What is a negotiated order of withdrawal (NOW)?
11. How do passbook savings deposits differ from a NOW account?
12. What is a certificate of deposit (CD)?
13. Discuss the money market CD.
14. What is the 30-month small savers CD?
15. Why may a repurchase agreement be withdrawn without a penalty?
16. What is the sweep arrangement?
17. Describe why most deposits in most institutions are very safe.
18. What is the penalty for early withdrawals of CDs?
19. What is the difference between Series EE and HH government bonds?
20. What are marketable bonds?
21. Why did Congress make Series EE and HH bonds nonnegotiable but redeemable?
22. What is the economic justification for the payment of interest?
23. Differentiate between compound interest and simple interest.
24. What is the rule of 72?

CASES

1. Lyndia Christensen, aged twenty-four, is a secretary in a large city and earns $450 per week. She would like to save as much as possible for her vacation, which she hopes to spend in Miami. She would also like to earn as much interest on her savings as possible but yet keep her principal liquid. By living on a tight budget, Lyndia is able to save $40 per week. Her vacation is still almost a year off, and she requests your advice as to where to invest her savings so as to achieve her objectives. Explain why you have selected certain institutions.
2. Keith Lawson works at the local foundry where he earns $500 per week. For the past several years, he has saved $50 per week, and he expects to

continue saving this amount in the future. In the past, he has invested his savings in U.S. Government Series E or EE bonds. Recently, however, the company where he works has started a credit union, and also the branch office of a savings and loan association has moved into town. Some of Keith's friends have suggested he should put his savings in these institutions. Keith is interested in yield and safety. Should Keith follow his friends' advice? Why?

3. Over the years Arthur Pedit has kept his savings in a savings deposit at the First National Bank in his town. He has accumulated almost $10,000 in his savings account, which is insured by the FDIC and on which he has been earning 5 1/4 percent interest. Can he earn more on his money by putting it in a mutual savings bank or a savings and loan association? Will his savings be as safe in these institutions? How would all of the above three compare with a credit union as to yield and safety?

4. Bernice Wilson has saved regularly and now has $5,000 in a Los Angeles savings and loan association. Recently she received notice from the institution that they are paying 5 1/2 percent. However, her friend Dorothy Jenkins told Bernice that she is receiving 7 percent on her savings in a branch of the same savings and loan association in Santa Ana where she lives. Can you explain the apparent discrepancy to Dorothy and Bernice?

5. What is likely to happen when regulation Q is eliminated?

6. Bob and Virginia Waring have a $1,000, two-year, 8 percent certificate of deposit in the Essex County Savings and Loan Association, which is only one month old. Because of an automobile accident, they need the money. Can they get it? What interest in dollar amounts will they get? What interest would they have received if the CD had been one year old?

SUGGESTED READINGS

The Bankers Magazine. A banking quarterly review, published by Warren, Gorham, and Lamont, Inc., 89 Beach St., Boston, Mass.

Carrol, Frieda. *The Joys of Saving and Economizing.* Atlanta, Ga.: Bibliotheca Press, 1981.

Credit Union National Association Yearbook. An annual publication by CUNA, P.O. Box 431, Madison, Wis. 53701.

Directors Digest. Published monthly by the United States League of Savings Associations, 111 E. Wacker Drive, Chicago, Ill.

Federal Home Loan Bank Board Journal. Published monthly by the Federal Home Loan Bank Board, 320 First Street N.W., Washington, D.C. 20552.

Finance Facts Yearbook. Washington, D.C.: National Consumer Finance Association. Annual publication.

Gough, T. J. *The Economics of Building Societies.* New York: Holmes and Meier Publishing, 1982.

Gup, Benton E. *Financial Intermediaries,* 2nd ed. Boston: Houghton Mifflin, 1980.

International Credit Union Yearbook. Washington, D.C.: CUNA International, Inc. Annual publication.

Lee, Elbert. *How to Make Money Twenty-Four Hours a Day.* Pinedale, Calif.: Positive Publishing, 1980.

Mutual Savings Banks National Fact Book. Published annually by the National Association of Mutual Savings Banks, 200 Park Avenue, New York, N.Y.

Mutual Savings Banks Annual Report. Published by the National Association of Mutual Savings Banks.

Sarnat, Marshall, and Szego, Giorgio. *Saving, Investment, and Capital Markets in an Inflationary Economy.* Cambridge, Mass.: Ballinger Publishing Co., 1982.

Savings and Loan Fact Book. Published annually by the United States Savings and Loan League, 221 North LaSalle Street, Chicago, Ill.

Savings and Loan Bulletin. Chicago: United States League of Savings Associations. Published monthly.

The Wall Street Journal. Published daily by Dow Jones and Company.

APPENDIX 14: PRESENT AND FUTURE VALUES

We discussed interest rates above; what they are, how they are calculated, and why they are paid. However, you do not have to laboriously calculate interest, because you can find out the interest from the tables shown in this appendix and from other sources mentioned below. The first table, *The future worth of a present dollar*, is ordinary compound interest. The second table, *The present worth of a future dollar*, is a sort of negative interest that is called discounting. Then comes *The future worth of an annuity*, which shows how your savings deposits would grow if you deposited a uniform amount each year and it grew by compound interest. The fourth table, *The present worth of a future dollar*, is the reverse of the third. It involves interest calculations, and shows the sum of money needed today to be equal in value to a given number of future payments.

Cases for Appendix to Chapter 14

The tables in this appendix, dealing with future worth and present worth, are used in finance. If a present-value calculator is available, you can calculate these as quickly and easily as you can look them up. Also, in some cases, there may be monthly payments rather than annual payments. Tables A14–1 and A14–2 are constructed for annual flows. There are also monthly tables available. In some cases, the yearly interest rate can be divided by 12 to get the monthly rate. If you have a monthly rate of less than one percent (1/2 of 1 percent, for example), you can approximate the answer by taking one-half of the sum under the column for 1 percent in Tables A14–3 and A14–4. To be accurate, however, you will need to use monthly tables or your present-value calculator.

The two cases illustrate two uses to which these tables can be put.

Cases

1. Cynthia Jean Reed recently signed a lease to rent a house for 12 months at $600 per month. Cynthia asked the landlady if she would give her a discount if she paid some or all of the rent in advance. Claire Baldwin, her landlady, told her she could pay the present value of any future rent discounted at 12 percent. What would Cynthia have to pay if she paid the entire twelve-months' rent in advance? What would her last six-months' rent be if she paid that in advance after having lived in the house six months?

2. Jim and Terry Chism established a college trust fund for their child at birth in the form of a deposit in a thrift institution. Terry deposits $20 per month into it, which earns 6 percent, but at the end of every year she transfers the funds into a 30-month Treasury Note CD that earns 12 percent. How much money will be on hand at the end of 18 years when the child is ready for college?

Table A14–1   Future worth of a present dollar $(1 + i)^N$

Years hence	1%	2%	3%	4%	5%	6%	7%	8%	9%	10%	12%
1	1.010	1.020	1.030	1.040	1.050	1.060	1.070	1.080	1.090	1.100	1.120
2	1.020	1.040	1.061	1.082	1.102	1.124	1.145	1.166	1.186	1.210	1.254
3	1.030	1.061	1.093	1.125	1.158	1.191	1.225	1.260	1.295	1.331	1.405
4	1.041	1.082	1.126	1.170	1.216	1.262	1.311	1.360	1.412	1.464	1.574
5	1.051	1.104	1.159	1.217	1.276	1.338	1.403	1.469	1.539	1.611	1.762
6	1.062	1.126	1.194	1.265	1.340	1.419	1.501	1.587	1.677	1.772	1.974
7	1.072	1.149	1.230	1.316	1.407	1.504	1.606	1.714	1.828	1.949	2.211
8	1.083	1.172	1.267	1.369	1.477	1.594	1.718	1.851	1.993	2.144	2.476
9	1.094	1.195	1.305	1.423	1.551	1.689	1.838	1.999	2.172	2.358	2.773
10	1.105	1.219	1.344	1.480	1.629	1.791	1.967	2.159	2.367	2.594	3.106
11	1.116	1.243	1.384	1.539	1.710	1.898	2.105	2.332	2.580	2.853	3.479
12	1.127	1.268	1.426	1.601	1.796	2.012	2.252	2.518	2.813	3.138	3.896
13	1.138	1.294	1.469	1.665	1.886	2.133	2.410	2.720	3.066	3.452	4.363
14	1.149	1.319	1.513	1.732	1.980	2.261	2.579	2.937	3.342	3.797	4.887
15	1.161	1.346	1.558	1.801	2.079	2.397	2.759	3.172	3.642	4.177	5.474
16	1.173	1.373	1.605	1.873	2.183	2.540	2.952	3.426	3.970	4.595	6.130
17	1.184	1.400	1.653	1.948	2.292	2.693	3.159	3.700	4.328	5.054	6.866
18	1.196	1.428	1.702	2.026	2.407	2.854	3.380	3.996	4.717	5.560	7.690
19	1.208	1.457	1.754	2.107	2.527	3.026	3.617	4.316	5.142	6.116	8.613
20	1.220	1.486	1.806	2.191	2.653	3.207	3.870	4.661	5.604	6.728	9.646
25	1.282	1.641	2.094	2.666	3.386	4.292	5.427	6.848	8.623	10.835	17.000
30	1.348	1.811	2.427	3.243	4.322	5.743	7.612	10.063	13.268	17.449	29.960

Future Worth of a Present Dollar

The present worth of $1 is, of course, $1. At 6 percent, however, $1 will grow to $1.06 in one year. Consequently, the future worth of a dollar in one year is $1.06 and in two years it is $1.124, if compounded at 6 percent. This is shown by the formula:

$$(1 + i)^N$$

where N is the number of years involved, and i is the going interest rate. This is the formula for calculating compound interest discussed above. Tables have been constructed taking the formula into account. One dollar compounded at 6 percent for ten years will be worth $1.791. Table A14–1 shows these values.

Present Worth of a Future Dollar

There is also the opposite of the future worth of a present dollar, i.e., present worth of a future dollar. The present worth of a future dollar is less than a dollar by whatever is the going interest rate. This is called discounting, and it

14%	15%	16%	18%	20%	24%	28%	32%	36%
1.140	1.150	1.160	1.180	1.200	1.240	1.280	1.320	1.360
1.300	1.322	1.346	1.392	1.440	1.538	1.638	1.742	1.850
1.482	1.521	1.561	1.643	1.728	1.907	2.067	2.300	2.515
1.689	1.749	1.811	1.939	2.074	2.364	2.684	3.036	3.421
1.925	2.011	2.100	2.288	2.488	2.932	3.436	4.007	4.653
2.195	2.313	2.436	2.700	2.986	3.635	4.398	5.290	6.328
2.502	2.660	2.826	3.185	3.583	4.508	5.629	6.983	8.605
2.853	3.059	3.278	3.759	4.300	5.590	7.206	9.217	11.703
3.252	3.518	3.803	4.435	5.160	6.931	9.223	12.166	15.917
3.707	4.046	4.411	5.234	6.192	8.594	11.806	16.060	21.647
4.226	4.652	5.117	6.176	7.430	10.657	15.112	21.199	29.439
4.818	5.350	5.926	7.288	8.916	13.215	19.343	27.983	40.037
5.492	6.153	6.886	8.599	10.699	16.386	24.759	36.937	54.451
6.261	7.076	7.988	10.147	12.839	20.319	31.961	48.757	74.053
7.138	8.137	9.266	11.974	15.407	25.196	40.565	64.359	100.712
8.137	9.358	10.748	14.129	18.488	31.243	51.923	84.954	136.97
9.276	10.761	12.468	16.672	22.186	38.741	66.461	112.14	186.28
10.575	12.375	14.463	19.673	26.623	48.039	86.071	148.02	253.34
12.056	14.232	16.777	23.214	31.948	59.568	108.89	195.39	344.54
13.743	16.367	19.461	27.393	38.338	73.864	139.38	257.92	468.57
26.462	32.919	40.874	62.669	95.396	216.542	478.90	1033.6	2180.1
50.950	66.212	85.850	143.371	237.376	634.820	1645.5	4142.1	10143.

Table A14–2   Present value of a future \$1 $(1 + i)^{-N}$

Years hence	1%	2%	4%	6%	8%	10%	12%	14%	15%	16%	18%
1	0.990	0.980	0.962	0.943	0.926	0.909	0.893	0.877	0.870	0.862	0.847
2	0.980	0.961	0.925	0.890	0.857	0.826	0.797	0.769	0.756	0.743	0.718
3	0.971	0.942	0.889	0.840	0.794	0.751	0.712	0.675	0.658	0.641	0.609
4	0.961	0.924	0.855	0.792	0.735	0.683	0.636	0.592	0.572	0.552	0.516
5	0.951	0.906	0.822	0.747	0.681	0.621	0.567	0.519	0.497	0.476	0.437
6	0.942	0.888	0.790	0.705	0.630	0.564	0.507	0.456	0.432	0.410	0.370
7	0.933	0.871	0.760	0.665	0.583	0.513	0.452	0.400	0.376	0.354	0.314
8	0.923	0.853	0.731	0.627	0.540	0.467	0.404	0.351	0.327	0.305	0.266
9	0.914	0.837	0.703	0.592	0.500	0.424	0.361	0.308	0.284	0.263	0.225
10	0.905	0.820	0.676	0.558	0.463	0.386	0.322	0.270	0.247	0.227	0.191
11	0.896	0.804	0.650	0.527	0.429	0.350	0.287	0.237	0.215	0.195	0.162
12	0.887	0.788	0.625	0.497	0.397	0.319	0.257	0.208	0.187	0.168	0.137
13	0.879	0.773	0.601	0.469	0.368	0.290	0.229	0.182	0.163	0.145	0.116
14	0.870	0.758	0.577	0.442	0.340	0.263	0.205	0.160	0.141	0.125	0.099
15	0.861	0.743	0.555	0.417	0.315	0.239	0.183	0.140	0.123	0.108	0.084
16	0.853	0.728	0.534	0.394	0.292	0.218	0.163	0.123	0.107	0.093	0.071
17	0.844	0.714	0.513	0.371	0.270	0.198	0.146	0.108	0.093	0.080	0.060
18	0.836	0.700	0.494	0.350	0.250	0.180	0.130	0.095	0.081	0.069	0.051
19	0.828	0.686	0.475	0.331	0.232	0.164	0.116	0.083	0.070	0.060	0.043
20	0.820	0.673	0.456	0.312	0.215	0.149	0.104	0.073	0.061	0.051	0.037
21	0.811	0.660	0.439	0.294	0.199	0.135	0.093	0.064	0.053	0.044	0.031
22	0.803	0.647	0.422	0.278	0.184	0.123	0.083	0.056	0.046	0.038	0.026
23	0.795	0.634	0.406	0.262	0.170	0.112	0.074	0.049	0.040	0.033	0.022
24	0.788	0.622	0.390	0.247	0.158	0.102	0.066	0.043	0.035	0.028	0.019
25	0.780	0.610	0.375	0.233	0.146	0.092	0.059	0.038	0.030	0.024	0.016
26	0.772	0.598	0.361	0.220	0.135	0.084	0.053	0.033	0.026	0.021	0.014
27	0.764	0.586	0.347	0.207	0.125	0.076	0.047	0.029	0.023	0.018	0.011
28	0.757	0.574	0.333	0.196	0.116	0.069	0.042	0.026	0.020	0.016	0.010
29	0.749	0.563	0.321	0.185	0.107	0.063	0.037	0.022	0.017	0.014	0.008
30	0.742	0.552	0.308	0.174	0.099	0.057	0.033	0.020	0.015	0.012	0.007
40	0.672	0.453	0.208	0.097	0.046	0.022	0.011	0.005	0.004	0.003	0.001
50	0.608	0.372	0.141	0.054	0.021	0.009	0.003	0.001	0.001	0.001	

is taking interest away rather than adding it. This is shown by the following formula:

$$(1 + i)^{-N}$$

Table A14–2 shows these values.

Future Worth of an Annuity

The concept of the future worth of an annuity is the amount of money that would exist at some future time if one added \$1 per year and it was growing

20%	22%	24%	25%	26%	28%	30%	35%	40%	45%	50%
0.833	0.820	0.806	0.800	0.794	0.781	0.769	0.741	0.714	0.690	0.667
0.694	0.672	0.650	0.640	0.630	0.610	0.592	0.549	0.510	0.476	0.444
0.579	0.551	0.524	0.512	0.500	0.477	0.455	0.406	0.364	0.328	0.296
0.482	0.451	0.423	0.410	0.397	0.373	0.350	0.301	0.260	0.226	0.198
0.402	0.370	0.341	0.328	0.315	0.291	0.269	0.223	0.186	0.156	0.132
0.335	0.303	0.275	0.262	0.250	0.227	0.207	0.165	0.133	0.108	0.088
0.279	0.249	0.222	0.210	0.198	0.178	0.159	0.122	0.095	0.074	0.059
0.233	0.204	0.179	0.168	0.157	0.139	0.123	0.091	0.068	0.051	0.039
0.194	0.167	0.144	0.134	0.125	0.108	0.094	0.067	0.048	0.035	0.026
0.162	0.137	0.116	0.107	0.099	0.085	0.073	0.050	0.035	0.024	0.017
0.135	0.112	0.094	0.086	0.079	0.066	0.056	0.037	0.025	0.017	0.012
0.112	0.092	0.076	0.069	0.062	0.052	0.043	0.027	0.018	0.012	0.008
0.093	0.075	0.061	0.055	0.050	0.040	0.033	0.020	0.013	0.008	0.005
0.078	0.062	0.049	0.044	0.039	0.032	0.025	0.015	0.009	0.006	0.003
0.065	0.051	0.040	0.035	0.031	0.025	0.020	0.011	0.006	0.004	0.002
0.054	0.042	0.032	0.028	0.025	0.019	0.015	0.008	0.005	0.003	0.002
0.045	0.034	0.026	0.023	0.020	0.015	0.012	0.006	0.003	0.002	0.001
0.038	0.028	0.021	0.018	0.016	0.012	0.009	0.005	0.002	0.001	0.001
0.031	0.023	0.017	0.014	0.012	0.009	0.007	0.003	0.002	0.001	
0.026	0.019	0.014	0.012	0.010	0.007	0.005	0.002	0.001	0.001	
0.022	0.015	0.011	0.009	0.008	0.006	0.004	0.002	0.001		
0.018	0.013	0.009	0.007	0.006	0.004	0.003	0.001	0.001		
0.015	0.010	0.007	0.006	0.005	0.003	0.002	0.001			
0.013	0.008	0.006	0.005	0.004	0.003	0.002	0.001			
0.010	0.007	0.005	0.004	0.003	0.002	0.001	0.001			
0.009	0.006	0.004	0.003	0.002	0.002	0.001				
0.007	0.005	0.003	0.002	0.002	0.001	0.001				
0.006	0.004	0.002	0.002	0.002	0.001	0.001				
0.005	0.003	0.002	0.002	0.001	0.001	0.001				
0.004	0.003	0.002	0.001	0.001	0.001					
0.001										

at an interest rate of 6 percent. If one added \$1 per year for twenty-five years and it was earning 6 percent, it would have grown to \$54.865; \$25 of this would have been the contribution and \$29.865 would have been interest. This is shown by the formula:

$$\frac{(1 + i)^{N-1}}{i}$$

Table A14–3 shows the various figures.

Table A14–3   Future worth of an annuity $\dfrac{(1 + i)^{N-1}}{i}$

Years hence	1%	2%	3%	4%	5%	6%	7%	8%	9%	10%	12%
1	1.000	1.000	1.000	1.000	1.000	1.000	1.000	1.000	1.000	1.000	1.000
2	2.010	2.020	2.030	2.040	2.050	2.060	2.070	2.080	2.090	2.100	2.120
3	3.030	3.060	3.091	3.122	3.152	3.184	3.215	3.246	3.278	3.310	3.374
4	4.060	4.122	4.184	4.246	4.310	4.375	4.440	4.506	4.573	4.641	4.770
5	5.101	5.204	5.309	5.416	5.526	5.637	5.751	5.867	5.985	6.105	6.353
6	6.152	6.308	6.468	6.633	6.802	6.975	7.153	7.336	7.523	7.716	8.115
7	7.214	7.434	7.662	7.898	8.142	8.394	8.654	8.923	9.200	9.487	10.089
8	8.286	8.583	8.892	9.214	9.549	9.897	10.260	10.637	11.028	11.436	12.300
9	9.369	9.755	10.159	10.583	11.027	11.491	11.978	12.488	13.021	13.579	14.776
10	10.462	10.950	11.464	12.006	12.578	13.181	13.816	14.487	15.193	15.937	17.549
11	11.567	12.169	12.808	13.486	14.207	14.972	15.784	16.645	17.560	18.531	20.655
12	12.683	13.412	14.192	15.026	15.917	16.870	17.888	18.977	20.141	21.384	24.133
13	13.809	14.680	15.618	16.627	17.713	18.882	20.141	21.495	22.953	24.523	28.029
14	14.947	15.974	17.086	18.292	19.599	21.051	22.550	24.215	26.019	27.975	32.393
15	16.097	17.293	18.599	20.024	21.579	23.276	25.129	27.152	29.361	31.772	37.280
16	17.258	18.639	20.157	21.825	23.657	25.673	27.888	30.324	33.003	35.950	42.753
17	18.430	20.012	21.762	23.698	25.840	28.213	30.840	33.750	36.974	40.545	48.884
18	19.615	21.412	23.414	25.645	28.132	30.906	33.999	37.450	41.301	45.599	55.750
19	20.811	22.841	25.117	27.671	30.539	33.760	37.379	41.446	46.018	51.159	63.440
20	22.019	24.297	26.870	29.778	33.066	36.786	40.995	45.762	51.160	57.275	72.052
25	28.243	32.030	36.459	41.646	47.727	54.865	63.249	73.106	84.701	98.347	133.334
30	34.785	40.568	47.575	56.805	66.439	79.058	94.461	113.283	136.308	164.494	241.333

Present Worth of a Future Annuity

Finally, there is the present worth of a future annuity, that is, the lump sum of money that today has the same value as periodic future payments, the total of which would be larger than the lump sum. For example, at 6 percent, $12.783 in hand is worth twenty-five annual payments of $1 each. This is shown by the formula:

$$\frac{1 - (1 + i)^{-N}}{i}$$

Table A14–4 can be used in lieu of the formula immediately above.

14%	16%	18%	20%	24%	28%	32%	36%	40%	50%
1.000	1.000	1.000	1.000	1.000	1.000	1.000	1.000	1.000	1.000
2.140	2.160	2.180	2.200	2.240	2.280	2.320	2.360	2.400	2.500
3.440	3.506	3.572	3.640	3.778	3.918	4.062	4.210	4.360	4.750
4.921	5.066	5.215	5.368	5.684	6.016	6.362	6.725	7.104	8.125
6.610	6.877	7.154	7.442	8.048	8.700	9.398	10.146	10.846	13.188
8.536	8.977	9.442	9.930	10.980	12.136	13.406	14.799	16.324	20.781
10.730	11.414	12.142	12.916	14.615	16.534	18.696	21.126	23.853	32.172
13.233	14.240	15.327	16.499	19.123	22.163	25.678	29.732	34.395	49.258
16.085	17.518	19.086	20.799	24.712	29.369	34.895	41.435	49.153	74.887
19.337	21.321	23.521	25.959	31.643	38.592	47.062	57.352	69.814	113.330
	23.044	25.733	28.755	32.150	40.238	50.399	63.122	78.998	98.739
									170.995
27.271	30.850	34.931	39.580	50.985	65.510	84.320	108.437	139.235	257.493
32.089	36.786	42.219	48.497	64.110	84.853	112.303	148.475	195.929	387.239
37.581	43.672	50.818	59.196	80.495	109.612	149.240	202.926	275.300	581.859
43.842	51.660	60.965	72.035	100.815	141.303	197.997	276.979	386.420	873.788
50.980	60.925	72.939	87.442	126.011	181.87	262.36	377.69	541.99	1311.7
59.118	71.673	87.068	105.931	157.253	233.79	347.31	514.66	759.78	1968.5
68.394	84.141	103.740	128.117	195.994	300.25	459.45	700.94	1064.7	2953.8
78.969	98.603	123.414	154.740	244.033	385.32	607.47	954.28	1491.6	4431.7
91.025	115.380	146.628	186.688	303.601	494.21	802.86	1298.8	2089.2	6648.5
181.871	249.214	342.603	471.981	898.092	1706.8	3226.8	6053.0	11247.0	50500.0
356.787	530.312	790.948	1181.882	2640.916	5873.2	12941.0	28172.0	60501.0	383500.0

Table A14–4   Present worth of a future $1 received annually for N years

$$\frac{1 - (1 + i)^{-N}}{i}$$

Years (n)	1%	2%	4%	6%	8%	10%	12%	14%	15%	16%	18%
1	0.990	0.980	0.962	0.943	0.926	0.909	0.893	0.877	0.870	0.862	0.847
2	1.970	1.942	1.886	1.833	1.783	1.736	1.690	1.647	1.626	1.605	1.566
3	2.941	2.884	2.775	2.673	2.577	2.487	2.402	2.322	2.283	2.246	2.174
4	3.902	3.808	3.630	3.465	3.312	3.170	3.037	2.914	2.855	2.798	2.690
5	4.853	4.713	4.452	4.212	3.993	3.791	3.605	3.433	3.352	3.274	3.127
6	5.795	5.601	5.242	4.917	4.623	4.355	4.111	3.889	3.784	3.685	3.498
7	6.728	6.472	6.002	5.582	5.206	4.868	4.564	4.288	4.160	4.039	3.812
8	7.652	7.325	6.733	6.210	5.747	5.335	4.968	4.639	4.487	4.344	4.078
9	8.566	8.162	7.435	6.802	6.247	5.759	5.328	4.946	4.772	4.607	4.303
10	9.471	8.983	8.111	7.360	6.710	6.145	5.650	5.216	5.019	4.833	4.494
11	10.368	9.787	8.760	7.887	7.139	6.495	5.988	5.453	5.234	5.029	4.656
12	11.255	10.575	9.385	8.384	7.536	6.814	6.194	5.660	5.421	5.197	4.793
13	12.134	11.343	9.986	8.853	7.904	7.103	6.424	5.842	5.583	5.342	4.910
14	13.004	12.106	10.563	9.295	8.244	7.367	6.628	6.002	5.724	5.468	5.008
15	13.865	12.849	11.118	9.712	8.559	7.606	6.811	6.142	5.847	5.575	5.092
16	14.718	13.578	11.652	10.106	8.851	7.824	6.974	6.265	5.954	5.669	5.162
17	15.562	14.292	12.166	10.477	9.122	8.022	7.120	6.373	6.047	5.749	5.222
18	16.398	14.992	12.659	10.828	9.372	8.201	7.250	6.467	6.128	5.818	5.273
19	17.226	15.678	13.134	11.158	9.604	8.365	7.366	6.550	6.198	5.877	5.316
20	18.046	16.351	13.590	11.470	9.818	8.514	7.469	6.623	6.259	5.929	5.353
21	18.857	17.001	14.029	11.764	10.017	8.649	7.562	6.687	6.312	5.973	5.384
22	19.660	17.658	14.451	12.042	10.201	8.772	7.645	6.743	6.359	6.011	5.410
23	20.456	18.292	14.857	12.303	10.371	8.883	7.718	6.792	6.399	6.044	5.432
24	21.243	18.914	15.247	12.550	10.529	8.985	7.784	6.835	6.434	6.073	5.451
25	22.023	19.523	15.622	12.783	10.675	9.077	7.843	6.873	6.464	6.097	5.467
26	22.795	20.121	15.983	13.003	10.810	9.161	7.896	6.906	6.491	6.118	5.480
27	23.560	20.707	16.330	13.211	10.935	9.237	7.943	6.935	6.514	6.136	5.492
28	24.316	21.281	16.663	13.406	11.051	9.307	7.984	6.961	6.534	6.152	5.502
29	25.066	21.844	16.984	13.591	11.158	9.370	8.022	6.983	6.551	6.166	5.510
30	25.808	22.396	17.292	13.765	11.258	9.427	8.055	7.003	6.566	6.177	5.517
40	32.835	27.355	19.793	15.046	11.925	9.779	8.244	7.105	6.642	6.234	5.548
50	39.196	31.424	21.482	15.762	12.234	9.915	8.304	7.133	6.661	6.246	5.554

20%	22%	24%	25%	26%	28%	30%	35%	40%	45%	50%
0.833	0.820	0.806	0.800	0.794	0.781	0.769	0.741	0.714	0.690	0.667
1.528	1.492	1.457	1.440	1.424	1.392	1.361	1.289	1.224	1.165	1.111
2.106	2.042	1.981	1.952	1.923	1.868	1.816	1.696	1.589	1.493	1.407
2.589	2.494	2.404	2.362	2.320	2.241	2.166	1.997	1.849	1.720	1.605
2.991	2.864	2.745	2.689	2.635	2.532	2.436	2.220	2.035	1.876	1.737
3.326	3.167	3.020	2.951	2.885	2.759	2.643	2.385	2.168	1.983	1.824
3.605	3.416	3.242	3.161	3.083	2.937	2.802	2.508	2.263	2.057	1.883
3.837	3.619	3.421	3.329	3.241	3.076	2.925	2.598	2.331	2.108	1.922
4.031	3.786	3.566	3.463	3.366	3.184	3.019	2.665	2.379	2.144	1.948
4.192	3.923	3.682	3.571	3.465	3.269	3.092	2.715	2.414	2.168	1.965
4.327	4.035	3.776	3.656	3.544	3.335	3.147	2.752	2.438	2.185	1.977
4.439	4.127	3.851	3.725	3.606	3.387	3.190	2.779	2.456	2.196	1.985
4.533	4.203	3.912	3.780	3.656	3.427	3.223	2.799	2.468	2.204	1.990
4.611	4.265	3.962	3.824	3.695	3.459	3.249	2.814	2.477	2.210	1.993
4.675	4.315	4.001	3.859	3.726	3.483	3.268	2.825	2.484	2.214	1.995
4.730	4.357	4.033	3.887	3.751	3.503	3.283	2.834	2.489	2.216	1.997
4.775	4.391	4.059	3.910	3.771	3.518	3.295	2.840	2.492	2.218	1.998
4.812	4.419	4.080	3.928	3.786	3.529	3.304	2.844	2.494	2.219	1.999
4.844	4.442	4.097	3.942	3.799	3.539	3.311	2.848	2.496	2.220	1.999
4.870	4.460	4.110	3.954	3.808	3.546	3.316	2.850	2.497	2.221	1.999
4.891	4.476	4.121	3.963	3.816	3.551	3.320	2.852	2.498	2.221	2.000
4.909	4.488	4.130	3.970	3.822	3.556	3.323	2.853	2.498	2.222	2.000
4.925	4.499	4.137	3.976	3.827	3.559	3.325	2.854	2.499	2.222	2.000
4.937	4.507	4.143	3.981	3.831	3.562	3.327	2.855	2.499	2.222	2.000
4.948	4.514	4.147	3.985	3.834	3.564	3.329	2.856	2.499	2.222	2.000
4.956	4.520	4.151	3.988	3.837	3.566	3.330	2.856	2.500	2.222	2.000
4.964	4.524	4.154	3.990	3.839	3.567	3.331	2.856	2.500	2.222	2.000
4.970	4.528	4.157	3.992	3.840	3.568	3.331	2.857	2.500	2.222	2.000
4.975	4.531	4.159	3.994	3.841	3.569	3.332	2.857	2.500	2.222	2.000
4.979	4.534	4.160	3.995	3.842	3.569	3.332	2.857	2.500	2.222	2.000
4.997	4.544	4.166	3.999	3.846	3.571	3.333	2.857	2.500	2.222	2.000
4.999	4.545	4.167	4.000	3.846	3.571	3.333	2.857	2.500	2.222	2.000

CHAPTER FIFTEEN

THE FUNDAMENTALS OF DIRECT SECURITY INVESTMENTS

Forms of Business Organization
Investment Objectives
Short-Run versus Long-Run Investments
Investment Risks
Reducing the Risk of Investments
Sources of Investment Information

In this chapter we will examine direct investments. We may invest directly in a business organization rather than in a financial institution, which would invest our dollars. A person can invest directly by becoming part owner of a business or by directly lending it money. There are three general forms of business organization to invest in. Before you invest in any of them you should determine your investment objectives, because that will influence the investment vehicle you choose. You must decide whether you wish to emphasize capital gains, income, or both; and whether to be a short-run or a long-run investor or both; and how much risk you are willing to take. When you invest directly, you are assuming more risk than when you invest indirectly via a financial institution.

FORMS OF BUSINESS ORGANIZATION

All persons should be familiar with how the businesses in which they may invest are organized. In our society we rely primarily on private individuals to own and utilize the means of production. Individuals do this through the ownership and operation of business firms. Generally, business firms are organized into single proprietorships, partnerships, and corporations. While partnerships and single proprietorships outnumber corporations in the United States, they are far less important by every other test. Noncorporate businesses have fewer employees, own fewer assets, and produce and sell much less. They are primarily small businesses owned by a few people, often family affairs. There also are some small family-owned corporations. While some corporations are small, nearly all partnerships and single proprietorships are; and all large business entities are corporations.

Noncorporate Forms

One noncorporate form is the *single proprietorship*, a business owned by one person, the simplest form of organization, and the easiest and quickest to enter. There need be no charter application or other papers to fill out to enter business. Business assets are commingled with the personal assets of the owner, as are business debt and personal debt. While there can be numerous employees, there can be only one owner. This form of business is fine for some small firms, but it cannot grow very large.

The other noncorporate form is the *partnership*, which can be comprised of two or more partners. It has some advantages over the single proprietorship. With several partners, usually more capital can be raised, and a number of varying talents may be brought together.

To form a partnership, a partnership agreement must be drawn up. All states have laws governing partnerships and the agreement spells out the duties, rights, and liabilities of each partner.

While a partnership has some advantages over the single proprietorship, it has some disadvantages as well. It is less flexible if several partners have to be consulted before a decision can be made. It is not permanent; the death of one partner dissolves the partnership. Perhaps the greatest single drawback of a partnership is that all partners are liable without limits for the debts of the business.[1] One partner can commit the others by the decisions he or she makes. Nevertheless, the partnership form of organization works well in many cases. If confidence exists between partners, it may be fine for a small business. But like the single proprietorship, it is virtually impossible for a partnership to grow into a truly big business firm.

Corporate Form

A corporation is a legal entity. It has been defined by Chief Justice Marshall as "an artificial being, invisible, intangible, and a device only in contemplation of law." It has many of the rights, duties, and powers of an individual. It can sue and be sued; it can sign contracts, borrow money, own property, and carry out regular business affairs. A corporation raises money by selling shares in itself

---

[1] There are limited partnerships, but generally all partners are liable for all business debts.

called stock. Because a corporation is artificial, it cannot do any of these things itself, but they are done in its name by the corporation's board of directors, elected by its owners.

The various states grant corporation charters, and a corporation comes into existence when the certificate of incorporation is accepted by the proper state agency, usually the secretary of state of the state in which incorporation takes place. The people who do the incorporating are the owners and are called the stockholders. They invest money by buying the corporation's stock which is then used to acquire business assets (capital) to carry out the business activity for which the corporation was organized.

Corporate bonds and stock

As noted above, corporations issue and sell shares in themselves called stock and also issue bonds. If you buy either, you are investing in a business directly.

Bonds are certificates of indebtedness; if you buy bonds you are lending the business money. You are a creditor. All of the terms of the loan are fixed; you will get a certain percentage interest rate on your money for a certain period of time after which the corporation must also repay the loan.

Corporate stocks are certificates of ownership (also called shares), and if you buy stock you become a part owner of the business (you in a sense join the club). However, you are promised no return on your money. If the corporation is successful, it will earn a profit and, as an owner, part of that will be yours. You will not necessarily receive it in the form of cash, because the corporation may retain it. Only if the board of directors decides to pay out all or part of the earnings in the form of dividends will stockholders receive cash. On the other hand, if the corporation is unsuccessful and suffers losses, you will share in those. There is no promise made that your stock will ever be redeemed. As a stockholder, the only thing you are promised is that you will be permitted to vote for the board of directors who will manage the corporation.

Stockholders, then, assume more risk than bondholders. Bondholders must receive their interest before stockholders may get anything. Stockholders are described as providing risk or venture capital.

There is also a special type of stock called preferred that stands between bonds and common stock and bonds. Preferred stockholders' claims are satisfied after bondholders' but before common stockholders'. We will discuss both bonds and stock in detail in Chapter 16.

Advantages of the corporate form of business organization

The advantages of the corporate form of organization include:

1.   One's liability is limited to his or her actual investment in the corporation, and one's personal assets cannot be used to pay the debts of the corporation. In a single proprietorship or partnership, personal assets are available to pay business debts. Since the corporation is a legal entity, only corporate assets may be used to satisfy claims against the corporation. The individual

stockholders can lose only what they paid for their own stock. This makes many people willing to invest in a corporation, which permits raising large aggregates of capital.

2.   Shares of stock (or ownership) in a corporation are easily transferred to another person. Corporate stock is negotiable, and can be sold to any other individual, or can be inherited by survivors. This gives a corporation an indefinite life and also contributes to raising large aggregates of capital. A partnership, in contrast, is dissolved upon the death of a partner, and if a partner wishes to sell his or her share to another person, the other partners must agree.

3.   The small as well as the large investor may easily invest in corporations. To be sure, most investors in partnerships are small, but the capital requirements of even partnerships are too large for many investors. Extremely small amounts of capital (as little as a few dollars) can be committed to the corporation by buying a single share of stock.

4.   A corporation may survive indefinitely. It may live for as long as it is successful. Because stock is easily transferable, the corporation may live through many generations and in theory never die. A partnership is dissolved on the death of any partner.

5.   Many thousands of individuals can collectively be the owners of a single business via the corporation, not the case with other forms of organization.

6.   The above advantages all contribute to the ability of the corporation to amass high sums of capital, to grow large, and to enjoy the benefits of greater efficiencies that often accompany greater size.

There may be other benefits that arise from the giant corporation. For example, if a firm is big it can hire better managerial and other specialized talent than can a small firm. On the other hand, some observers have expressed concern over the separation of ownership and control that a giant corporation makes inevitable. They state that the millions of stockholders who own (but are far removed from) the corporation cannot possibly influence the managers who control the corporation. The managers may or may not be stockholders, but in any event, they are not responsible to their constituents and this, it is alleged, is unhealthy in a democracy.

INVESTMENT OBJECTIVES

There are many different stocks to buy. You must decide your investment objectives before you select one. A wit once remarked that the objective of any investor is to make money, and the more the better. This generalization, however, does not tell us very much. The easiest way to make money is, of course, to inherit it. If you have to make it yourself, it is more difficult. Historically, one of the best ways to make money has been to invest in securities, especially common stock. But during the last decade this has become more difficult. The market did not rise a great deal during the 1970s as it did during the 1960s. In the first half of 1983 the stock market boomed, but who knows what the rest of the 1980s will bring. Some people feel stocks are no longer as popular as they once were. Others feel corporate stocks are today very good buys because they are unduly depressed. Indeed, some people say, in light of earnings, that corporate stocks are among the better investments available today, and that as soon as the general public discovers this, their prices will rise.

With 20-20 hindsight we can see what we would have if we had done this or that twenty or thirty years ago. For example, if you had purchased one hundred shares of IBM at $195 per share in 1946, your investment today would amount to about 25,558 shares because of stock splits and stock dividends over the years. Moreover, with IBM's recent market price of $120 per share, your $19,500 investment would be worth approximately $3,066,960, not including the dividend income you would have received over the years. But then perhaps you would have purchased LTV Corp. at its high price of $169 in 1967. Recently, its price was $10.

You need to select securities most likely to help you to achieve your objectives, which may be:

1.   Liquidity
2.   Income
3.   Capital gains or growth
4.   Security or principal
5.   Hedging inflation

or perhaps several or all of these.

Liquidity

Liquidity means how quickly and easily an asset can be turned into cash without a price concession. Money is 100 percent liquid, while other assets vary depending upon their relative "moneyness." Cash, the most liquid, is in general followed by certain U.S. government securities, high-grade corporate bonds, preferred and common stock traded on organized exchanges, over-the-counter securities, first mortgages on real estate, and real estate holdings. Generally, securities listed on organized exchanges are very liquid because they can be sold at the market price by making a telephone call. Selling real estate, on the other hand, takes time. Liquidity may not be a factor for some investors, but it is for others.

Income

Some companies achieve higher earnings (profits) than others, and they may pay out a high proportion of these earnings to the stockholder in the form of dividends. These are income stocks. Today, with high interest rates, bonds too yield a relatively high return. An investor with income as an objective would choose from among these higher yielding securities.

Capital Gains

Capital gains, or capital appreciation, is an important modern investment objective. This attitude has developed within the past thirty years. Before that, income, liquidity, and safety were stressed. This has been changed by higher individual income taxes. Long-term capital gains (assets held more than twelve months) are taxed more favorably than income (see Chapter 8). Therefore, many people invest in securities they believe will result in capital growth rather than income. This may involve investment in a firm that has growth possibilities or the purchase of a security the investor believes is depressed in value. Aside from the tax angle, capital gains—if one is successful in obtaining them—often give a greater return on investment. This, together with the tax consideration, has made capital gains very attractive.

Security of Principal

Security of principal means preservation of capital values through a conservative investment policy, the prime objective of any investor. Everyone desires to preserve the original principal. This can be done by good judgment, avoidance of highly speculative risks, and attempting to preserve capital from market fluctuations, but is easier said than done. Moreover, security of principal and liquidity are somewhat inconsistent with high yield. A person who wants high yield or rapid appreciation must assume more risk and accept a greater likelihood of no return or sometimes of actual loss. The risks associated with holding securities are examined below.

Hedging Inflation

Some investors may feel that prices will continue to rise. When prices rise, the real value of certain assets declines, whereas the value of others tends to rise with inflation. Historically, stock and real estate were considered the best hedges against inflation. Bonds, since they are fixed investments, are generally eroded by inflation. If the price level doubles, the value of the dollar falls by half. If prices rise, the person with fixed dollar assets suffers a loss in value of his or her assets. If one is dependent on fixed dollars for income—as, for example, are the retired—one's standard of living will decline. Historically, the price of common stock has at least kept up and in many periods surpassed the rate of inflation, but in recent years this has not been true. We noted above one reason for this may be because investors' attitudes and psychology have changed because of lack of much confidence in the future.

Common stock should be a good hedge against inflation because corporations often plow earnings back into the business. This means that new machinery, plants, and the like are purchased on behalf of the stockholder. As a result, the value of one's stock will rise. If the corporation is also providing goods or services, the demand for which is growing rapidly, its price may be outpacing inflation. If so, this will be reflected in corporate profits which should contribute to rising stock prices. Figures 15–1 and 15–2 illustrate how good an inflationary hedge stocks have been over the long run. One chart shows the cost of living and the Dow Jones Industrial stock average. The other shows the cost of living, Standard and Poor's 500 stock index, earnings, and dividends. These have more than held their own in the long run.

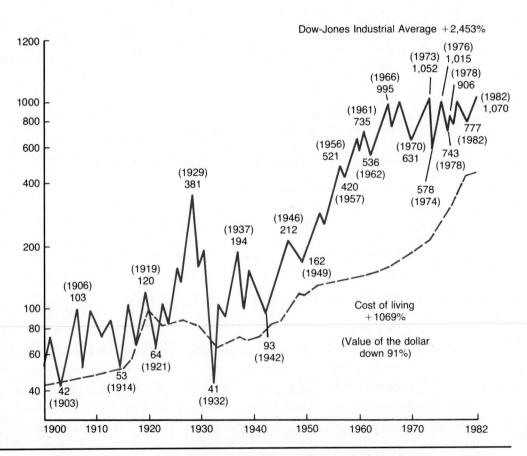

Figure 15–1   Common stocks and the cost of living, 1897–1982. (Source: Johnson's Investment Company Charts, 1983, Hugh A. Johnson Co., 2467 Homewood Avenue, Buffalo, New York, p. 5.)

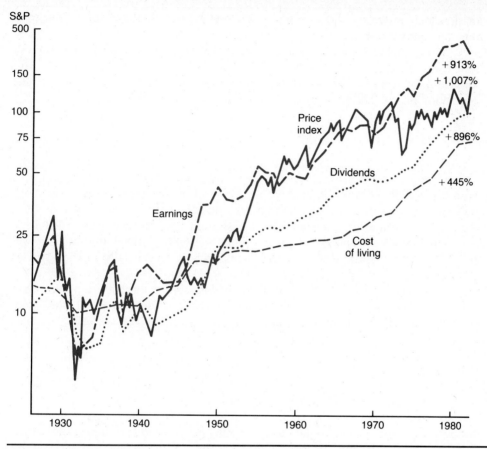

Figure 15–2 Cost of living, dividends, and Standard & Poor's 500 stock index, 1926–1982. (*Source: Johnson's Investment Company Charts, 1983*, Hugh A. Johnson Co., 2467 Homewood Avenue, Buffalo, New York, p. ix.)

SHORT-RUN VERSUS LONG-RUN INVESTMENTS

How short is the short run? Any definition is arbitrary but holding a security for less than a year or two is short run. Holding a security for twenty years or even five or ten is a long-run investment. It is generally conceded that the small investor should play largely in the long-run end of the field. If you are a large investor, it might be worthwhile to devote the energy, time, and perhaps money needed to make a short-term gain. The small investor may not have the time to watch an investment constantly and cannot hire expensive professional advice. Moreover, even if he or she does make a nice short-term gain, in absolute dollars it is likely to be small. A small investor who gets in and out of the market frequently on a short-term basis will pay commissions that may eat heavily into any profits earned.

Most small investors probably should buy securities to hold them for the long run. This does not mean that the investor can forget about them. Any long-term investment can also turn sour, and investors should review their portfolios periodically.

INVESTMENT RISKS

Our system is not a profit system as so many people like to claim. Rather it is a profit-and-loss system. Some firms prosper and show a profit, while others lag behind and have losses. No firm can have losses in the long run and survive. And indeed, some firms go out of business from time to time, and when they do, the stockholder absorbs the loss. Being an investor, then, is risky, but the reward for successfully assuming risk is financial gain, generally in the form of profits in some form.

Risk refers to the probability of future loss. Since there are different risks involved in any investment, investors must recognize those to which they may be exposed. There are six major types.

Risk of Business Failure

While some businesses prosper, others fail. In the event of business failure, a stockholder, having invested "equity" capital, may be entirely wiped out. Bond-holders who have loaned money to the company may also find themselves wiped out, but not as frequently as the stockholders. If the bonds are secured by certain specific corporate assets, the bondholders may sell these assets and sometimes recover all of the loan, though more often than not they recover less than the full amount. If the bonds are unsecured, the holder often collects much less.

Even investors in state or municipal bonds could find themselves in a precarious position in the event of a severe depression This has not happened on a widespread scale since the Great Depression of the 1930s. One way to lessen the likelihood of being wiped out is to diversify one's investments by types of securities and issuers, and to buy only the securities of financially strong firms.

Market Risk

This particular risk results from fluctuations in market prices of securities over time, which may or may not have to do with how well the business firm is doing. Stock prices may decline due to a lowering of earnings of a particular firm, such a decline stemming from poor management or even a change in the public's tastes. Or earnings may fluctuate due to the business cycle, which will cause the market price of securities to fluctuate.

Price fluctuations in securities may also arise as a result of investor psychology. Many persons may decide simply to stay out of the market, thus reducing demand for securities and consequently lowering prices, even though firms' profits may not have declined and may even have risen.

Price Level Risk

A change in purchasing power of money is particularly applicable to those assets whose value is stated as a fixed number of dollars. People who hold bonds and savings accounts are assuming this risk, as are people who hold idle cash, those who hold idle cash being the most vulnerable.

For example, if a person holds money and the value of the dollar falls—another way of saying that prices rise—then in real purchasing power the person who holds the money has lost. If the value of the dollar rises—another way of saying prices have declined—the real purchasing power of the dollar has risen and the person who holds the money gains. In a period of rising prices, the astute investor will try to move away from fixed assets into such items as common stock and real estate, which tend to appreciate with rising prices. In a period of falling prices (which we hardly see today), the investor should move from real estate and common stock into fixed assets yielding a fixed return, such as bonds.

While the person who holds idle cash is hurt the most by rising prices, bondholders also suffer, and we can roughly calculate their losses by the *nominal* rate of return and the *real* rate of return. The nominal rate of return is the money rate without an adjustment for inflation, and the real rate is after the inflationary adjustment. If you hold $1,000 in idle cash for one year during which the price level rises by 8 percent, your nominal rate of return is zero percent and your real rate is minus 8 percent. The value of your $1,000 has eroded to $920. If you hold a $1,000 bond paying 10 percent for one year during which prices rise by 8 percent, your nominal (money) rate of return is 10 percent and your real return is 2 percent. To convert the nominal rate to the real rate, subtract the rate of inflation from the nominal interest rate. In the above case, the real value of your $1,000 bond investment has grown only to $1,020.

Interest Rate Risk

This risk of loss results from changes in the price of bonds due to fluctuations in prevailing rates of interest. It is important only for investments in fixed obligations such as bonds and preferred stock. Even some U.S. government bond prices are affected by changes in the interest rates. When interest rates rise, bond prices fall; conversely, when interest rates go down, bond prices rise. There is nothing mystical about this process; it really makes sense. We will illustrate this with an example which, while using an unrealistic low interest rate, illustrates the principle because the interest rate doubles. Suppose a corporation issues a $1,000 bond at 5 percent. This is a contractual obligation and the corporation must pay the holder $50 per year. Later, if interest rates double to 10 percent, in theory—depending upon the date of maturity—the old bond would drop in price to about $500. The reason is that with rates at 10 percent, any new bond issues would have to be offered with this same 10 percent yield; investors with $1,000 can now expect to get a return of $100 on their investments. Therefore, the holders of the old bonds will attempt to sell them and attain the new rate, thus forcing the price down, until its market price is such that the fixed payment of $50 becomes closer to 10 percent of the bond's market price.

Actually the price of the old bond will not go down to $500, because the company still has an obligation to repay the original $1,000 loan on the due date. If the bond becomes due the year after the new interest rate, obviously it would be foolish for the holders of the bonds to sell at $500 when all they have to do is to wait a year and then demand $1,000 from the corporation. The bonds will nevertheless decline somewhat, and if they have twenty or more years to run, they will decline considerably.

If the interest rate declines, bond prices rise. Again suppose one holds a $1,000 bond paying 10 percent or $100 per year. If the interest rate declines to 5 percent, all a new investor can now expect as a yield on an investment of $1,000 is $50. Consequently, the demand for existing bonds paying $100 will increase and *theoretically* the older bond will rise to $2,000, again depending on maturity. Competition to obtain the older bond will theoretically bid its price up to the point where the $100 interest becomes 5 percent of the price of the bond, that is, $2,000. Again for practical reasons, however, it never goes that high.[2]

---

2. The longer the time to maturity, the greater the change in the price of a bond due to a given change in the interest rate. A bond would have to run to perpetuity (never become due) for a doubling of the interest rate to cut its market price in half. For example, if the interest rate rose from 12 to 15 percent, then a $1,000 bond maturing in twenty years would decline to $850, because in twenty years the bond would be redeemed at its face value of $1,000. Hence the $150 capital appreciation over this period must be prorated over twenty years and included in the $120 per year the bond pays. The bond would appreciate $7.50 per year; hence the total yield would be $127.50, which is 15 percent of $850.

The formula for determining the market price (P) of a bond is

$$P = I \left| \sum_{n=1}^{M} \frac{1}{\left(1 + \frac{i}{2}\right)^n} \right| + F \left| \frac{1}{\left(1 + \frac{i}{2}\right)^M} \right|$$

where

P = current market price
I = coupon interest payment in dollars
n = payment periods per year (2 in the case of most bonds)
M = total number of payments

Buying long-term bonds, then, is risky during periods when interest rates are volatile. You might think, however, that 12 percent is a fair return and you are willing to hold it until maturity. Then you may have paper losses, but no actual losses, and in 20 years you will get back your $1,000, but then you will be hurt by inflation; what do you think $1,000 will be worth in 20 years?

What causes changes in the interest rate? They are caused by changes in the demand for and in the supply of money. If money is thought of as any other commodity and interest as the price of the commodity, then when the demand is high and the supply constant, the price or interest rate will rise. When the demand is low, the price goes down, provided of course that the supply remains constant. The supply of money is to a degree regulated by the Federal Reserve System, and in this way so too is the interest rate. The basic reasons for this regulation of the interest rate are twofold. If the Federal Reserve had reason to fear deflation and recession, it would attempt to lower interest rates to make borrowing by businesspersons more attractive, with the idea that if interest rates are lowered and borrowing occurs, new capital will be created with a resulting upswing in the economy. On the other hand, if the Federal Reserve Board feared inflation, it would raise the interest rate, on the philosophy that if rates are high, businesspersons will be deterred from new capital formation to a certain degree and forces of inflation will be lessened.

Financial Risk

Financial risk is related to the debt (bond)-equity (common stock) ratio. A high debt-to-equity ratio means that the corporation has a large fixed obligation (interest) to pay each year. If sales and profits decline severely in any one year, this could cause a burden. It is even possible that the heavy interest payment could not be met, and the firm be forced into bankruptcy. The higher the debt-to-equity ratio then, the higher the financial risk. However, a business often has some control over this risk.

Political Risk

Political risk has to do with changes in the legal environment in which the business must operate. If the government changes taxes, tariffs, subsidies, or

---

i = market rate of interest
F = face value of the bond

In the case of a bond maturing in ten years paying $130 per year ($65 every six months) at a time when the market rate of interest is 12 percent, we would have

$$P = \$65 \times 11.4699 + 1000 \times 0.3118$$

and the market value of the bond would be $1,057.34.

imposes wage or price controls, this could have a bearing on political risk and affect profits.

Stampede or Overreaction Syndrome Risk

Related to, but somewhat different from, political risk and market risk is stampede or overreaction syndrome risk. Statements or forecasts by prominent individuals may cause a reaction on the part of many investors causing wide swings in security prices. What the President or the Chairman of the Federal Reserve says, or what Wall Street thinks and advises, affects this risk. These statements can set up expectations on the part of the investing public regarding future inflation, interest rates, and the economy, which may generate a herd psychology and may affect interest rates and security prices.

REDUCING THE RISK OF INVESTMENTS

Not much can be done about political risk and one must operate within the existing political environment. Interest rate risk is difficult to diffuse. If you can forecast changes in interest rates you can take advantage of this, but such forecasts are extremely difficult. When buying long-term bonds, one rule might be to buy them only if the yield is attractive enough to hold them to maturity, and then do so. Any future paper losses will not be achieved. To be sure, you may possibly be prevented from taking advantage of future higher yields. If you are concerned about future changes in the interest rates, buy only short-term fixed obligations so your risk of capital loss is smaller. You can invest for a year or two easily and hold your securities until they mature. Then you will have only temporary paper losses or gains. You may also get a higher interest return by going short, because during periods of very high interest rates, short-term rates are usually above long-term ones.

You can lessen financial risk (excess leverage in the firm's capital structure) by not buying the securities of highly leveraged firms. (See Chapter 16.) Study balance sheets and examine the stability of earnings. A firm that has good, stable earnings is able to service a higher debt-to-equity ratio than a firm whose earnings fluctuate.

In reducing the price level risk you should strive to invest in firms whose sales and product prices are likely to keep up with inflation. Their profits will probably keep up with inflation too, and, if profits keep up, the prices of their securities are more likely to rise.

The risk of business failure can be reduced by selecting companies that are financially strong, innovative, and whose products are presently in great demand and likely to remain so. With bonds, this risk can be reduced by investing only in A-rated bonds or better. For market risk, some companies are less vulnerable than others; for example, companies selling a product for which the demand is stable, such as food.

Reducing Risk by Business Trend Analysis

The trend of business conditions is indicated weekly and monthly by: figures on inventories, durable goods sales, price movements, employment, unemployment, industrial output, and GNP; figures that can give a clue as to whether the economy is moving up or down. There are cyclical movements up and down, but also broad overall long-run trends of economic expansion. By identifying broad upward or downward swings, and acting accordingly, risk can be reduced. If, for example, business conditions seem to be improving, one can buy securities with more confidence. If business conditions in general seem to be deteriorating, investors can reduce their risk by taking a more conservative stand regarding securities.

Specific industries and firms analysis and risk reduction

Industries are classified into groups for investment analysis—banks, food production, rails, and the like—and a movement either upward or downward of the business cycle may affect them in varying degrees. Although generally if there is an upward movement in business conditions, all groups move upward, and if there is a downward movement, all groups have a tendency to move downward; some groups move to a lesser degree in either direction. Utility company earnings and sales are relatively stable, although there has been a secular trend upward. Auto stock tends to be more volatile, moving more rapidly upward during periods of expansion and just as rapidly downward during periods of contraction. Within each group, there are individual firms whose performance may be quite different from that of the group as a whole. Even during periods of contraction some firms earn more than others. Generally this can be attributed to good management. Within any group, one can find firms that have consistently paid good dividends to investors even during periods of severe recession, while others dealing with the same products are able to pay earnings only during relatively good times.

One can reduce risk by investing mostly in those industries that typically have done well and whose future looks more promising than that of the economy as a whole. Finally, if investors select not only industries that have done well but firms that have the best records within good industries, they can generally reduce risk even more.

Reducing Risk by Diversification

Risk can be reduced by diversification, which is not putting all one's eggs in one basket. This is more difficult for a small investor than for a large one. But diversification is relative, and even a small investor should be able to obtain some. It can be achieved by firm, by industry, by type of security, and by investment objectives. If you decide to buy oil company stock, pick two or three or even four different companies; pick the ones you feel are best from history of the industry and firm analyses. Also, diversify by buying stock of firms in different industries. You might also diversify by different types of securities, say, bonds and stock. Finally, diversify by investment objective, that is, some investments for growth, some for income, and some for stability.[3] Diversification reduces risk by broadening your investment base, and your securities will probably include some that will fare better than average.

SOURCES OF INVESTMENT INFORMATION

Financial information can be obtained from newspapers, magazines, books, investment services, banks, brokers, investment counselors, and other sources.

Newspapers

Greater amounts of information about business conditions are now in the financial pages of any large city newspaper, but certain newspapers are superior to others. Any serious investor should probably subscribe to *The Wall Street Journal*, a financial paper published daily in six regional editions as a morning paper. This journal publishes articles on general business and economic conditions in the United States and abroad. It also has stories and articles on specific industries and corporations and news on labor and government relations. It is a treasure house of business and financial statistics, of past, present, and future trends. It also has complete stock market quotations, including the Dow-Jones Averages and bond quotations. *The New York Times* also has a good financial section, containing news articles and in-depth analyses of business conditions in general and of specific businesses and industries.

Magazines and Other Publications

The better business and financial magazines are *Barron's Weekly, Forbes, Business Week, U.S. News and World Report, Fortune Magazine,* and the *New York Stock Exchange Magazine*, published by the New York Stock Exchange. These publications have articles on business and finance. They analyze general economic conditions, industries, and specific firms. The *Federal Reserve Bulletin* and the monthly *News*

---

3. From a functional point of view, common stock can be classified into income, growth, cyclical, speculative, and defensive stock, classifications discussed in Chapter 16.

Letters published by the various district Federal Reserve Banks contain scholarly articles on business and finance and many useful financial statistics. The President's Council of Economic Advisers publishes its monthly *Economics Indicators*, which contains a wealth of statistical information. All of these, and, in addition, many books and pamphlets are available in any good library.

Brokerage Firms

Many large brokerage houses have libraries available to the public that contain many of the above publications. They also publish special studies and analyses made by their own research departments and provide their customers, free of charge, studies made by independent financial research services. One such study on Texas Instruments is shown in Figure 15–3. Many brokerage firms have their own weekly or monthly newsletter.

Additional information may be obtained from stockbrokers regarding both industries as a whole and individual corporations. Each industry is classified in relation to the general market as "relatively favorable," "average," or "relatively unfavorable." Individual securities are listed as "long-term investment," "liberal income," "good quality-wider price movement," or "speculative." Such listings are in accord with the various investment objectives.

Investment Services

Although there are a number of services from which one may obtain research and advisory services on whole industries and individual companies, the most popular are Standard and Poor's, Moody's Investors Service, Fitch Investors Service, the Value Line Investment Survey, and Argus Research Corporation. These services specialize in furnishing the public with the basic facts and figures on all securities publicly marketed and on the companies issuing them. From these services one may obtain information covering a period of many years on the assets, income, earnings, dividends, and stock prices of various corporations. The cost of these services is in many hundreds of dollars, but an interested individual may examine them free in a broker's office or at most large public and university libraries. These investment services make industry studies in which they appraise the future outlook at the various firms within each industry and their common stock. Standard and Poor's publishes their listed stock report, a one- or two-page summary of every company listed on the New York Stock Exchange that provides some vital statistics and analyzes recent developments and future prospects of the firm. This summary comes out periodically with a separate sheet for each listed firm. It is called the "Yellow Sheet" in brokerage offices because it is printed on yellow paper. A reproduction of Standard and Poor's Yellow Sheet on International Business Machines is shown in Figure 15–4.

INVESTMENT ANALYSIS
ARGUS RESEARCH CORPORATION ● NEW YORK, N.Y.

June 30, 1983
Vol. 8, No. 48

TEXAS INSTRUMENTS

SELL

HIGHLIGHTS

Texas Instruments' stock has attracted widespread attention recently because of its 25% price drop in one day following the announcement of an expected $100 million second-quarter loss caused by price cutting in the home-computer market. What caused the surprise was the enormous size of the loss, as the program was already known to be in trouble and had generated a $50 million charge in the first quarter because of a recall of defective transformers. The price drop raises the question as to whether the home-computer debacle can be ignored as regards Texas Instruments' prospects and whether the current price represents a buying opportunity.

● The home-computer episode indicates serious problems in internal corporate information and product quality control that may extend beyond the company's consumer-product lines.

● The company's performance in all its commercial product lines in the 1980-83 period has been notably inferior to those of other leaders in the same markets.

Price (NYSE): 119   12-Mo. Rge: 176-81
Symbol: TXN   Options Exch: C
DJIA: 1221.96   S&P 500: 167.56
Earnings:
1981: $4.62 1982: $6.10 1983E: $2.00
P/E Ratio (1982): 19.5   (1983E): NM
P/E vs. S&P 500 P/E:
(1982): 1.5   (1983E): NM
1978-82 Range: 2.9-1.0

Earnings Growth Rates:
(TXN) 1978-83E: (21%)   1983-88E: NM
(S&P 500) 1978-83E: 1%   1983-88E: 10%

Dividend: $2.00   Yield: 1.7%
Financial Strength: Medium-High

Expected 6-12 Month Price Behavior
Relative to S&P 500: Inferior
Portfolio Selector Status: None

RECOMMENDATION

Prices for the semiconductor stocks in the current market are based not on 1982 earnings or on estimated results for 1983, but rather on projected profits for 1984 and later years. Relative to potential 1984 earnings, Texas Instruments is priced lower than other semiconductor equities. Nevertheless it is still trading at a 10% premium over the S&P 500 based on projected 1984 earnings. Because of the company's unsatisfactory record as regards corporate information, and uncertainties about its ability to compete in some of its most important product lines as effectively in the future as it has in the past, we do not regard the stock as an attractive holding at current prices. The stock has rebounded 11% from its recent low of 107, and a further technical reaction is not unlikely. We would regard any periods of market strength as opportunities to sell the stock.

Figure 15–3   A sample brokerage analysis. (*Source:* Argus Research Corporation.)

Standard and Poor's also publishes a "Blue Sheet," an identical analysis for companies listed on the American Stock Exchange, and a "Green Sheet" for many over-the-counter securities, but only the better known ones.

The Stock Exchanges

The New York Stock Exchange has its own research department and makes available a number of publications free of charge, among them *The New York Stock Exchange Market* and the *New York Stock Exchange Fact Book*. The American

---

Int'l Business Machines   1210

NYSE Symbol IBM   Options on CBOE (Jan-Apr-Jul-Oct)

Price	Range	P-E Ratio	Dividend	Yield	S&P Ranking
May 2'83	1983				
115	118-92¼	15	3.80	3.3%	A+

Summary

IBM is the world's largest manufacturer of computers and information processing equipment and systems. A good earnings gain is expected for 1983, aided by continued strong demand for information processing, a better ratio of sales to rentals, and later in the year more favorable foreign exchange rates.

Current Outlook

Earnings for 1983 are projected at $8.50 a share, up from the $7.39 of 1982, which gives effect to new accounting rules for foreign currency translations.

Directors raised the quarterly dividend 10%, to $0.95 from $0.86, in April, 1983.

Gross income for 1983 is expected to advance on the order of 20%, reflecting continued growth in demand for information processing and an improving economy. Shipments of large scale processors, including the new 3084, the 3380 direct access storage device, and the IBM personal computer should remain strong. Margins are expected to widen on the higher volume, a better mix between sales and rentals, productivity improvements, and later in the year more favorable foreign currency exchange rates. IBM's leading position in the industry, together with its ongoing commitment to technological innovation, should enable it to maintain good long-term growth.

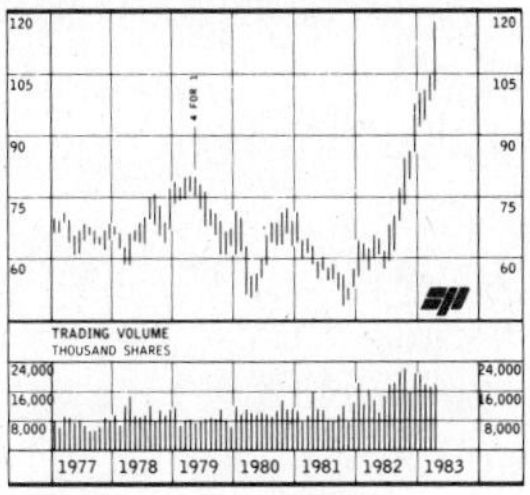

Gross Income (Billion $)

Quarter:	1983	1982	1981	1980
Mar.	8.29	7.07	6.46	5.75
Jun.		8.05	6.90	6.18
Sep.		8.17	6.72	6.48
Dec.		11.07	8.99	7.81
		34.36	29.08	26.21

Gross income for the three months ended March 31, 1983 rose 17%, year to year, reflecting gains of 45% in sales and 18% in services; rentals fell 9.4%. The better mix between sales and rentals as well as significant shipments of large scale processors and storage products aided margins, and pretax income advanced 27%. After taxes at 45.3%, versus 43.9%, net income increased 24%.

Per Share Data ($)

Yr. End Dec. 31	1982	1981	1980	1979	1978	1977	1976	1975	1974	1973
Book Value	33.13	30.66	28.18	25.64	23.14	21.39	21.15	19.05	17.05	15.02
Earnings	7.39	5.63	6.10	5.16	5.32	4.58	3.99	3.34	3.12	2.70
Dividends	3.44	3.44	3.44	3.44	2.88	2.50	2.00	1.62½	1.39	1.12
Payout Ratio	47%	62%	56%	67%	54%	54%	50%	49%	45%	42%
Prices—High	98	71⅛	72¾	80½	77⅜	71⅛	72⅛	56⅞	63½	91⅜
Low	55⅝	48⅜	50⅜	61⅛	58¾	61⅛	55⅞	38⅞	37⅜	58¾
P/E Ratio—	13-8	13-9	12-8	16-12	15-11	16-13	18-14	17-12	20-12	34-22

Data as orig. reptd. Adj. for stk. div(s). of 300% Jun. 1979, 25% May 1973.

Capital Share Earnings ($)

Quarter:	1983	1982	1981	1980
Mar.	1.62	1.33	1.25	1.17
Jun.		1.81	1.37	1.31
Sep.		1.75	1.18	1.51
Dec.		2.50	1.83	2.11
		7.39	5.63	6.10

Important Developments

Apr. '83—In releasing first quarter results, which were bolstered by greater outright purchases of new and installed equipment worldwide, IBM said that new display products, new models of the Personal Computer, Series/1 and System/38 processors, and a new tape subsystem should continue to aid order activity in 1983; it expected shipments of advanced, large scale processors and the 3380 direct access storage devices to remain strong.

Next earnings report due in mid-July.

Standard NYSE Stock Reports   May 9, 1983   Standard & Poor's Corp.
Vol. 50/No. 89/Sec. 17   25 Broadway, NY, NY 10004

1210   International Business Machines Corporation

Income Data (Million $)

Year Ended Dec. 31	Revs.	Oper. Inc.	% Oper. Inc. of Revs.	Cap. Exp.	Depr.	Int. Exp.	Net Bef. Taxes	Eff. Tax Rate	Net Inc.	% Net Inc. of Revs.
1982	34,364	11,199	32.6%	6,685	3,143	514	²7,930	44.4%	⁴4,409	12.8%
1981	29,070	8,926	30.7%	6,845	2,899	480	²5,988	44.8%	3,308	11.4%
1980	26,213	8,102	30.9%	6,592	2,362	¹325	²5,897	39.6%	3,562	13.6%
1979	22,863	7,215	31.6%	5,991	1,970	140	5,553	45.8%	3,011	13.2%
1978	21,076	7,265	34.5%	4,046	1,824	55	5,798	46.3%	3,111	14.8%
1977	18,133	6,657	36.7%	3,395	1,999	40	5,092	46.6%	2,719	15.0%
1976	16,304	5,928	36.4%	2,518	1,858	45	4,519	46.9%	2,398	14.7%
1975	14,437	5,245	36.3%	2,439	1,822	63	3,721	46.5%	1,990	13.8%
1974	12,675	4,871	38.4%	2,913	1,708	69	3,455	46.5%	1,838	14.5%
1973	10,993	4,363	39.7%	2,186	1,589	97	2,946	46.5%	1,575	14.3%

Balance Sheet Data (Million $)

Dec. 31	Cash	Current Assets	Current Liab.	Ratio	Total Assets	Ret. on Assets	Long Term Debt	Common Equity	Total Cap.	% LT Debt of Cap.	Ret. on Equity
1982	3,300	13,014	8,209	1.6	32,541	14.1%	2,851	19,960	23,134	12.3%	22.9%
1981	2,029	10,303	7,320	1.4	29,586	11.7%	2,669	18,161	21,082	12.7%	19.0%
1980	2,112	9,925	6,526	1.5	26,703	13.9%	2,099	16,453	18,734	11.2%	22.7%
1979	3,771	10,851	6,445	1.7	24,530	13.3%	1,589	14,961	16,690	9.5%	21.2%
1978	4,031	10,321	5,810	1.8	20,771	15.7%	286	13,494	13,889	2.1%	24.0%
1977	5,407	10,073	5,209	1.9	18,978	15.0%	256	12,618	12,962	2.0%	21.7%
1976	6,156	9,920	4,082	2.4	17,723	14.4%	275	12,749	13,088	2.1%	19.8%
1975	4,768	8,115	3,363	2.4	15,531	13.4%	295	11,416	11,756	2.5%	18.4%
1974	3,805	7,010	3,210	2.2	14,027	13.9%	336	10,110	10,482	3.2%	19.3%
1973	3,322	5,830	2,555	2.3	12,290	13.6%	652	8,812	9,496	6.9%	19.2%

Data as orig. reptd. 1. Reflects accounting change. 2. Incl. equity in earns. of nonconsol. subs.

Business Summary

IBM is primarily involved in information-handling systems, equipment and services.

Gross revenues (U.S. only)	1982	1981
Processors/peripherals	52%	50%
Office products	19%	20%
Programs/maint./other	24%	25%
Federal systems	5%	5%

Sales provided 49% of revenues in 1982, rentals 32%, and services 19%. Foreign operations contributed 45% of revenues and 37% of profits.

Processors manipulate data through the operation of a stored program. Peripherals include printers, copiers, and storage and telecommunication devices. Office products include small business computers, intelligent workstations and typewriters. IBM provides software, maintenance, data communications, remote computing, consulting, biomedical products, analytical instruments, and robots.

The Federal systems group serves U.S. government space, defense and other agencies.

IBM also provides education and testing materials and services for school, home and industrial use.

Dividend Data

Dividends have been paid since 1916. A dividend reinvestment plan is available.

Amt. of Divd. $	Date Decl.	Ex-div. Date	Stock of Record	Payment Date
0.86	Jul. 27	Aug. 5	Aug. 11	Sep. 10'82
0.86	Oct. 26	Nov. 4	Nov. 10	Dec. 10'82
0.86	Jan. 25	Feb. 3	Feb. 9	Mar. 10'83
0.95	Apr. 22	May 5	May 11	Jun. 10'83

Next dividend meeting: late Jul. '83.

Finances

A change in the method of accounting for foreign currency translation (FAS 52) increased 1982 earnings by $0.75 a share.

Capitalization

Long Term Debt: $2,851,000,000.

Capital Stock: 603,982,026 shs. ($1.25 par). Institutions hold approximately 52%. Shareholders: 725,745.

Office—Armonk, New York 10504. Tel—(914) 765-1900. Stockholder Relations Dept—590 Madison Ave., NYC 10022. Tel—(212) 407-4000. Chrmn & CEO—J. R. Opel. Pres—J. F. Akers. Secy—J. H. Grady. Treas—C. A. Northrop. Investor Contact—J. M. Heatley. Dirs—J. F. Akers, S. D. Bechtel, Jr. G. B. Beitzel, H. Brown, J. E. Burke, F. T. Cary, W. T. Coleman, Jr., P. R. Harris, C. A. Hills, A. Houghton, Jr., J. N. Irwin II, N. deB. Katzenbach, R. W. Lyman, M. McK. Moller, W. H. Moore, J. R. Munro, J. R. Opel, D. P. Phypers, P. J. Rizzo, W. W. Scranton, I. S. Shapiro, C. R. Vance, T. J. Watson, Jr. Transfer Agents—Company's NYC & Chicago offices. Registrars—Morgan Guaranty Trust Co., NYC; First National Bank, Chicago. Incorporated in New York in 1911.

Information has been obtained from sources believed to be reliable, but its accuracy and completeness are not guaranteed.   Christoper J. Pauley

---

Figure 15—4 Standard and Poor's "Yellow Sheet." (*Source:* Standard & Poor's Corporation. This report was up-to-date at the time of publication; subsequent changes are reflected in current Standard & Poor's reports.)

Stock Exchange makes available similar booklets called *Understanding the American Stock Exchange,* and *Amex Databook.*

Some of the smaller regional securities exchanges also have free publications. Some exchanges have libraries that contain extensive information and are open to the public. While many of the publications of the organized exchanges will not provide specific investment information, they provide good background information in the areas of business, finance, and economics.

Investment Counselors

Investment counselors will tailor an investment program for the individual investor according to the person's investment objectives. Investment counselors are professional investors and have their own skilled research departments. They, too, publish many studies, but these are available only to their customers. The services of investment counselors are expensive and hence not available to the small investor. The investor who has assets in excess of $100,000, however, and who wants investment advice might consider an investment counselor. Generally, large investment counselors will not accept clients with assets of less than $50,000 and some will require over $200,000. Their fees start at about .5 or 1 percent of the funds they manage and are scaled down from this level for really large accounts.

Investment counselors will first determine the investment objectives of their clients. If they are older retired persons, they may need income. If they are younger persons, the objective may be growth. Once the objectives have been determined, different portfolio questions are indicated. The counselors give their clients constant surveillance of their securities. Clients may give counselors authority to buy or sell on their behalf and instruct their brokers to execute their counselor's orders. Or they may wish to retain veto power over their counselor's advice and execute their orders themselves.

Corporation Reports

Before an investor buys any security, he or she may want to examine that corporation's financial reports—its balance sheet and income statement. Such reports give assets, liabilities, sales, expenses, earnings, dividends, and many more statistics, as well as top management's view concerning the future outlook of the business. Most corporations will send their balance sheet and income statement on request; brokerage houses also have many on file in their offices. (A sample balance sheet is shown in Figure 15–5.)

Many laypersons are overwhelmed by these reports and feel that since they cannot understand them, there is no need to read them. This attitude is nonsense. There is nothing difficult about either the balance sheet or the income statement. You learned about your personal balance sheet and income statement in Chapter

```
I. Assets

Current Assets
    Cash                                          $    200,000
    Accounts receivable                             14,600,000
    Inventory                                       10,200,000
        Raw materials
        Goods in process
        Finished goods
Fixed Assets
    Land                                          $  5,000,000
    Building and equipment                          20,000,000
        Total assets                              $50,000,000

II. Liabilities

Current Liabilities
    Accounts payable                              $13,500,000
    Short-term bank loan                            15,500,000
Fixed Liabilities
    Bonds outstanding (9%)                        $10,000,000
        Total Liabilities                         $39,000,000

III. Owner's Equity

Preferred Stock: 200,000 shares @ $10 per share   $  2,000,000
Common Stock Outstanding: 1,000,000 of par
    value $1                                          1,000,000
Amounts in Excess of Par Value Received for
    Stock (paid in surplus)                           7,000,000
Retained Earnings (Earned Surplus)                    1,000,000
    Total Owner's Equity                          $11,000,000
    Total Liabilities and Owner's Equity          $50,000,000
```

Figure 15–5 XYZ Corporation—year end balance sheet, December 31, 198X.

3. The corporate balance sheet and income statement are similar, except that different items and larger dollar amounts are involved. We shall work through both statements below.

The balance sheet

A balance sheet contains three major parts: assets, liabilities, and owner's equity—sometimes called net worth. Total assets are always equal to total liabilities plus net worth. Net worth, the difference between assets and liabilities, is the stockholder's equity.

Let us examine assets first. They are split into short-term assets (current assets) and long-term assets. Short-term assets include cash, which is self-explanatory; since it is a nonearning asset, firms try to keep cash amounts low.

Accounts receivable is the money owed the corporation because of sales that have been made and presumably will be collected within thirty days. Inventories, too, are self-explanatory. Fixed assets are valued at their cost less depreciation— the degree to which they are worn out. The company has total assets, with which it earns income. Assets permit the company to conduct its business.

To acquire these assets, however, the corporation had to assume some liabilities. Current liabilities are those due to be paid within a short time. Accounts payable come about because the firm buys, say, raw materials, which it will pay for within thirty days. They also include such things as accrued wages and taxes due but not yet paid. The short-term bank loans are money the company borrowed from a bank on a short-term basis. Fixed liabilities came about because when the present plant was built, the corporation sold $10,000,000 of bonds to finance it. Total liabilities represent the total amount the corporation owes, but some of these debts need not be paid for many years, although the interest on them must be paid annually.

The final item is net worth, and it belongs to the stockholders. It is the residual amount: the assets with which the company operates less the liabilities the company eventually will have to pay. Net worth is split into preferred stock, common stock at par on face value, amount of capital paid which was in excess of par value, and retained earnings. Preferred stock is generally listed first because it is closer to bonds. It must be first netted out before getting the book value of the common stock. The par or face value of the common stock is shown and, immediately below it, the amount in excess of par received for it. This third item is often referred to as paid-in surplus. The final item under net worth is retained earnings. It is also referred to as earned surplus, and it means profits the company earned in previous years but retained rather than paid out in dividends. Everything under net worth except the preferred stock belongs to the common stockholders. If that is divided by the number of shares of common stock outstanding, we obtain the book value per share of common stock (to be explained in Chapter 16).

The balance sheet shows how much capital the company has to work with as well as how much of it is represented by bonded indebtedness and how much by stock. By comparing assets and earnings, the reader can ascertain the return on invested capital and also the percentage return on stockholder's equity and the earning per share of common stock.

The income statement

While the balance sheet is a presentation of the company's affairs at a given moment in time, like a photograph, the income statement is a presentation of what happened to the company over a period of time, usually a year, like the flow of water during a year. A hypothetical income statement is shown in Figure 15–6.

The income statement, also called a profit and loss statement or an operating statement, shows the cash flows through the company during the year and also the company's earnings or profits. Cash inflows or sales increase the company's

Sales	$11,700,000
Selling costs (advertising, etc.)	350,000
Cost of raw materials	3,300,000
Labor costs	3,750,000
Interest cost (on bonds)	900,000
Other costs (utilities, telephone, etc.)	100,000
Depreciation	1,000,000
Total Cost	9,400,000
Income (before taxes)	2,300,000
Taxes	1,104,000
After-tax profits	1,196,000

Figure 15–6 XYZ Corporation—year end income sheet, December 31, 198X.

(and the stockholder's) well-being; cash outflows decrease it. Cash inflows or gross receipts are the same as sales, which were $11,700,000 for our company last year. Total costs are shown at $9,400,000 and are broken down into various components. For most manufacturing firms, labor costs are by far the largest item. The other costs are self-explanatory, with the exception of depreciation. Depreciation charges are made because fixed assets such as plant and equipment eventually wear out. When they do, the company must have the money on hand to replace them. In our case, the building and equipment is valued at $20,000,000. If we assume it has a useful life of twenty years with no scrap or salvage value, we must set aside one-twentieth of its value or $1,000,000 every year so that when it wears out we will be able to replace it. Depreciation is an expense and reduces profits by $1,000,000 per year. However, it is a unique kind of cost, one that does not cause a cash outflow from the company. While the $1,000,000 depreciation expense reduces profits by that amount, the company still has the money and will keep it invested somewhere and add to it every year until the time comes to replace the building and equipment.

After taxes, profits are $1.196 million, which is just over 10.8 percent return on total net worth. This sum of $1.196 million can be paid to the stockholders in the form of a cash dividend or it can be retained by the company, in which case it will go into the earned surplus account in the balance sheet for next year. Most companies split their after-tax profits, paying some to the stockholders and retaining some. However, in the above case there are 200,000 shares of preferred stock outstanding, and they must be paid a dividend before the common may receive anything. If we assume that they receive a 10 percent dividend on their par value of $2,000,000, this reduces profits by $200,000, which leaves a profit for the common stockholders of $996,000. This is a return of 11.07 percent on the common stockholders' equity of $9,000,000.

When analyzing balance sheets and income statements, it is often wise to read past reports to discover trends. Are sales rising and if so, how much? How have profits behaved over a number of years? Are the ratios of costs to sales rising or declining? These and many other important questions should be kept in mind when analyzing corporation reports. For example, when analyzing the balance sheet, we should also examine earnings per share. This is obtained by dividing earnings, after taxes and after making an allowance for a payment to the preferred stockholders, by the total number of shares of common stock outstanding. In our case we had after-tax earnings of $1.196 million. After the allowance shown above for preferred stockholders of 10 percent, there remains $996,000 which accrues to the common stockholder and amounts to 99.6 cents per share ($996,000 ÷ 1,000,000 shares).

Our company may or may not declare a dividend. If it does, we have a concept called *dividends per share*. By examining this over the years, we can determine if dividends per share are rising, falling, or remaining relatively constant. This may influence whether or not we wish to buy the stock.

We may also wish to compare earnings per share (99.6 cents in our case above) with the market price of the common stock. If we divide the market price of the common stock by the earnings, $.99 1/2, we get a concept called the *price earnings ratio*. This ratio may be ten or twenty; it varies from stock to stock. But it is an indicator of whether the stock might be priced too high or whether it is a genuine bargain. Finally, we may want to determine the yield of the common stock. This is simply the annual dividends per share divided by the market price of the stock and expressed in percentage terms.

Security analysts do not agree whether earnings per share or dividends (yield) per share are the best indicator of a stock's value, but all of these should be taken into account in making investment decisions.

QUESTIONS FOR REVIEW

1. How does the corporate form of business organization differ from that of a partnership or single proprietorship?
2. What is the difference between corporate stock and bonds?
3. One of the advantages of a corporation is said to be its limited liability. Explain.
4. Why may a corporation survive indefinitely?
5. What are the main objectives of most investors?
6. How do common stock investments help to hedge inflation?
7. What is the difference between a short-run and a long-run investor? Should the small investor be a short-run or a long-run investor?
8. Explain how holding your assets in the form of money or in an insured financial institution can possibly involve any risk of loss.
9. What is price level risk? What is interest rate risk?
10. Why does the price of a bond move down when the market rate of interest rises? What determines how much it comes down?
11. What is "market risk"?

12. Purchasing a number of issues of oil stock is a good example of reducing risk by diversification. Do you agree or disagree? Substantiate your position.
13. Outline the major sources of investment information.
14. How does an investment counselor operate?
15. The "net worth" figure on a balance sheet is said to belong to the stockholders. Explain in detail.
16. In examining corporate balance sheets and income statements, why is it important to examine both for several years past?

CASES

1. Jim and Mary McGovern are a young couple in their early thirties. Jim, a partner in a CPA firm, earns about $34,000 per year; Mary, a graphic artist, earns about $28,000. They believe they should start an investment program, and they have decided to save $500 per month for the purpose of purchasing securities. What do you feel their investment objectives should be? Why? Should Jim and Mary be long-run or short-run investors and why?
2. Bob and Virginia Carels have inherited $10,000, which they would like to invest. They know that they can earn about 6 or 7 percent on their money if they put it in a savings and loan association. However, they feel that prices will rise by about 7 to 10 percent per year on the average over the next few years and would like an investment that either yields substantially more or will provide them with a hedge against inflation. What are the better methods of hedging inflation? Why is this the case?
3. Bertha Underwood is a widow whose husband left her a nice nest egg. She has a $1,000 per month annuity and an additional $50,000 that she would like to invest. She is considering two alternatives: she could buy corporate securities or she could go into partnership with her brother, who is in the trucking business. She believes the return would be about the same in either case, but one of her friends has told her that it is riskier to invest in partnerships than in corporations. Bertha cannot understand this. Can you explain?
4. Kermit and Rita Jones recently purchased $5,000 worth of high-grade corporate bonds yielding 12 percent with a maturity of twenty years. They fully expected to leave their funds invested for twenty years and then use the proceeds to help pay for their children's college education. How much interest would they earn over the twenty years if they kept their investment?

    However, two years after the purchase Rita became sick and they were forced to sell the bonds to obtain emergency funds. They were surprised to find that their bonds were now worth $6,000. Can you explain this?
5. Edward and Marcella have over the past twenty years built up a portfolio of $50,000 in common stock. They were fortunate at first in that they

made good capital gains on their stock without a careful analysis; that is, almost everything they have bought appreciated in price during the decade of the 1960s. Then during the 1970s they lost some ground, but recently they have gained again. They would now like to minimize risk. Can you show them how? Why did they have such good fortune in the 1960s, and such bad fortune in the 1970s?

6. George Buck is a young Methodist minister who teaches philosophy of religion at the Southwest Theological Seminary in Dallas, Texas, and earns $26,000 per year. His wife, Marilyn, has her Ph.D. in social work from NYU and works as a consultant at the Texas School for the Blind and last year earned $41,600. Their combined salary provides a handsome surplus, and they would like your advice on how to invest it. They believe they have all the insurance they need; they already have $10,000 in a savings and loan association; and they own their own home. They are currently able to set aside $2,000 per month. What advice would you give them?

SUGGESTED READINGS

Altman, Edward I. *Financial Handbook*, 5th ed. New York: John Wiley and Sons, 1981.

American Stock Exchange Annual Report. New York.

Barron's Weekly. A weekly finance magazine.

Christy, G. A., and Clendenin, J. C. *Introduction to Investments*, 8th ed. New York: McGraw-Hill, 1982.

Engle, Louis. *How to Buy Stocks.* New York: Bantam Books, 1982.

The Exchange. Magazine published monthly by the New York Stock Exchange.

Financial Analysts Journal. New York: The Financial Analyst Federation. Published bimonthly.

Fisher, Lawrence, and Lorie, James H. *Rates of Return on Investments in Common Stocks.* New York: Merrill Lynch, Pierce, Fenner, and Smith. No date.

Fortune. A monthly magazine containing a great deal of information on business, economics, and finance.

Freund, William C., and Lee, Murray G. *Investment Fundamentals.* New York: American Bankers Association. No date.

How Over-the-Counter Securities Are Traded. Merrill Lynch, Pierce, Fenner, and Smith. 165 Broadway, New York, N.Y. 10006. Request copies from this firm.

How to Invest in Stocks and Bonds. New York: Merrill Lynch, Pierce, Fenner, and Smith.

How to Read a Financial Report. New York: Merrill Lynch, Pierce, Fenner, and Smith.

How to Understand Financial Statements. New York: New York Stock Exchange. Your broker can get this for you.

How You Get More Out of Financial News. Princeton, N.J.: Dow Jones and Company, The Educational Services Bureau.

Levine, Sumner N. *The Dow Jones-Irwin Business Almanac.* Homewood, Ill.: Dow Jones-Irwin, 1981.

The Market Place. Chicago: Chicago Board of Trade.

Nauheim, Fred. *Move Your Assets to Beat Inflation.* Englewood Cliffs, N.J.: Prentice-Hall, 1980.

Spiro, Herbert T. *Finance For the Non-Financial Manager*. New York: John Wiley and Sons, 1978.

Time. A weekly magazine that contains a good deal of information on business and finance.

Understanding the New York Stock Exchange. New York: New York Stock Exchange.

U.S. News & World Report. A weekly magazine that contains a good deal of information on business and finance.

The Wall Street Journal. Published daily by Dow Jones & Company.

Zahorchak, Michael G. *The Art of Low Risk Investing*. New York: Van Nostrand Reinhold, 1977.

CHAPTER SIXTEEN

THE ARRAY OF SECURITIES: STOCKS AND BONDS

The Array of Bonds—General Comments
The Array of Stocks—General Comments

In this chapter we will examine the wide variety of securities (obligations of issuers) available to the investor. The issuers of securities are, generally, business firms and government, and they represent the demand for savings or, in other words, the supply of securities.

The buyers of securities represent the supply of savings, or the demand for securities. The demand for securities can be further broken down into institutional demand and individual demand. Institutional demands stem from life insurance companies, corporate pension funds, mutual funds, and commercial banks. We will discuss securities pertinent to the individual investor.

THE ARRAY OF BONDS—GENERAL COMMENTS

Corporate bonds are certificates of indebtedness, credit instruments used in raising long-term funds. They are legal liabilities of the corporation. Bonds are long-term obligations, and the corporation is obligated to pay a fixed interest rate for so many years, then to redeem the bond at face value. This interest must be paid even if it is not earned. The interest on bonds must be paid before a payment can be made even to preferred stockholders (discussed below). In the event the corporation is liquidated, bondholders are repaid their capital before preferred stockholders. Bonds are considered senior securities: their needs must be taken care of first.

Corporate Bonds in General

Corporate bonds are nearly always issued in denominations of $1,000 face value, also referred to as par value. When the word *bond* is used, it is assumed to be of that denomination. The interest rate and maturity date are shown on the face of the bond. The interest rate shown thereon is called the coupon rate which, if 9 percent, obligates the corporation to pay $90 per year until the bond matures. Often, this would be paid as $45 every six months.

Bonds may be sold at their face value, above it, or below it. If a bond is sold below par, it is said to be at a discount; if above par, it is at a premium. If a bond sells at a premium and has a coupon rate of 10 percent, the yield is less than 10 percent. A bond sold at a discount has a yield greater than its coupon rate. Yields and the coupon rate, then, are not the same. Bond prices fluctuate in the market inversely with changes in the going market interest rate, as noted in the previous chapter. Generally, when corporations offer new issues of bonds, they are issued at par or close to it.

Most corporation bonds are coupon bonds, that is, they have interest coupons attached, and generally a coupon is due and payable every six months. The bondholder clips the coupon and mails it to the trustee for the interest. Often the coupons can be redeemed at banks. These bondholders are the people Thorstein Veblen had in mind when he referred to "the coupon clippers." Noncoupon bonds do exist, the interest on which is automatically mailed to the bondholder by the trustee.

Most bonds in the United States are registered. They have the name of the owner on the face of the instrument, and they cannot be transferred without endorsement. The corporation issuing the bond must have a trustee (usually a bank) who keeps the records and mails interest payments.

Some bonds, however, are bearer bonds, which means that they are not registered. These are rare in the United States. Bearer bonds are always coupon bonds, whereas registered bonds can be either coupon or noncoupon bonds.

In addition to corporate bonds, there are United States government bonds and state and local bonds, called municipal bonds. Each of these can be classified into subgroups. Figure 16–1 is a picture of a corporate bond.

Debentures

A debenture bond is issued by a corporation and no specific assets are pledged. The general credit rating of the corporation is at stake, and any and all assets can be seized if these bonds are in default. However, if first-mortgage bonds, collateral trust bonds, or equipment trust obligations are also outstanding for which specific assets have been pledged, these specific assets cannot be used to satisfy the claims of debenture bondholders until the other bondholders' claims have been met. Where the debentures were issued first, they usually have a clause in them that requires they have equal rights with any future mortgage bonds. There are, however, also subordinated debentures, which are like second mortgages and stand further back. They may be subordinated to regular debentures, to mortgage bonds, or to any other kind. Since they are riskier, they usually yield a higher return.

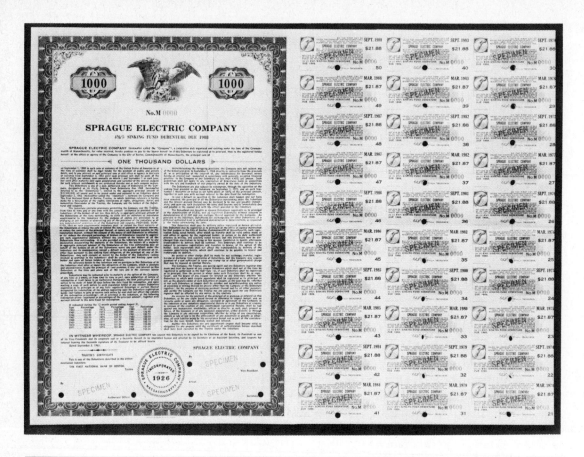

Figure 16–1   A corporate bond. (Courtesy Sprague Electric Company and the First National Bank of Boston.)

Convertible Bonds

Convertible bonds can be exchanged for a predetermined number of common stocks at the option of the bondholder. Convertible bonds are also usually debentures, but they need not be. The principle of convertible bonds is similar to that of convertible preferred stock. If the corporation does well, the convertibles take on the features of common stock, whereas if the corporation does poorly, the convertibles have the features of bonds. Convertible bonds pay a fixed interest rate like any bond and must be redeemed at maturity. However, they include a clause that permits the bondholder to convert them to common stock in the future at a rate determined when the bond is issued. If, for example, the common stock of the corporation were selling at $100 per share when the convertibles came out, the convertibility feature would permit one $1,000 bond to be converted to approximately ten shares of common stock at the option of the bondholder. If two or three years later the common stock were selling at $150 per share, the $1,000 bond could be converted into securities worth about $1,500. Thus, the market price of the bond would be bid up to about $1,500. Convertible securities, then, both preferred stock and bonds, may permit the holders to have their cake and eat it too. Corporations issue them for two reasons: (1) The corporation may be weak, or it may be issuing bonds at a time when savings are in short supply, and hence it must add the convertibility feature to sell them. (2) It may issue convertible bonds because this reduces the interest rate, say, from 12 to 11 percent.

Callable Bonds

Callable bonds might be debentures, mortgage bonds, or another kind, but in addition they can be called in and the principal repaid at the option of the corporation. The corporation will insert the call feature if it believes it can refinance later at a lower rate of interest or if it believes that it will be able in the future to operate with less bonded capital. Often they cannot be called in until a specific future time, but after that they may be redeemed at any time. The call provision usually states that if the bond is called, it will be at a premium above par. Generally, the call premium is one year's interest if the call is made a year or two from issue, and lesser amounts on later calls. You cannot be certain of locking yourself in on a long-term basis at high rate if you buy these.

Mortgage Bonds

These bonds are secured by a mortgage on all or part of the corporate property. A trustee, frequently a bank, is appointed to act for the bondholders. Title to the property is transferred to the trustee for the benefit of the bondholders. In the event that the corporation fails to pay either the interest or the principal when due, the trustee forecloses on the assets it holds and distributes the proceeds pro rata to the bondholders.

There are first-mortgage, second-mortgage, and sometimes even third-mortgage bonds. In these cases, first-mortgage bonds are the senior security and have a first claim to the assets if the company is to be liquidated.

Collateral Trust Bonds

These are corporate bonds secured by collateral other than real estate. The collateral may be stock in other corporations or other security owned by the corporations, such as promissory notes and accounts receivable. Often these bonds are issued by investment companies or other financial institutions that have securities of other companies but usually not much real estate. Often the securities used as collateral are held in trust by a third party.

Equipment Trust Obligations

These securities are issued by corporations with specific equipment of the corporation as security for the loan. Title to the equipment vests in a trustee, who holds it for the benefit of the owners of the bonds. This sort of security had its inception with the railroads, which pledged their rolling stock, but it has been extended to other types of corporate equipment as well. With railroads, an equipment trust bond is issued with rolling stock for security. In the event of default, the trustee sells the engines and box cars and pays the proceeds to the bondholders.

Income Bonds

Income bonds may be debentures or mortgage bonds or any other variety. Income bonds are unique because the interest on them does not have to be paid unless it is earned. Usually because of this qualification, they carry a higher rate of interest, but despite this are not very popular, and very few of them are issued.

Serial Bonds

Serial bonds can be debentures sometimes. Their unique feature is that an issue of serial bonds is numbered, and the different numbers mature at different times, permitting the corporation to redeem a few of these bonds each year according to a predetermined schedule.

Discount Bonds

Discount bonds have a market price below their face value. Since at maturity they must be redeemed at face value, the buyer will enjoy a capital gain, and hence favorable tax treatment.

There are two reasons why some bonds are sold at a discount. First, the corporation's credit rating may have worsened since the bonds were issued. Second, all bonds decline in value when the going market interest rate rises above the fixed stated interest (coupon) rate of any bond. The extent of the discount will be determined by the amount the market interest rate moves above the coupon rate and the length of time remaining until the bond matures. High discount, high quality bonds are a good buy when interest rates are at a peak and are expected to decline drastically.

The following example illustrates the tax benefits that may be obtained by investing in discount bonds. Suppose a bond was issued a few years ago at a 10 percent coupon rate, but now yields 14 percent due to its market price decline. The 10 percent is taxed as income as it is received, but the other 4 percent per year is realized as the bond appreciates toward its face value which it reaches at maturity. Not only are taxes deferred on the appreciation, but it is subject to a lower capital gains tax when the bond is redeemed or sold.

Zero Coupon Bonds

These bonds, which pay no interest but are deeply discounted when sold, have become popular recently. They are much like the Series EE U.S. government savings bonds, permitting investors to lock in at a yield that can be calculated for the entire period until maturity. Ordinary positive coupon bonds yield interest, usually semiannually, and it must be reinvested at whatever the going rate may be at that time. This may be beneficial or harmful depending on what happens to interest rates after buying the bonds. With zero coupon bonds, one does not have the reinvestment bother or reinvestment cost.

Unlike the other discount bonds described above, however, the annual market appreciation of these bonds is taxed as it occurs and as ordinary income. For this reason, the discount bonds discussed first are the better buys.

The major problem with long-term zero coupon bonds is the same as that with any long-term bond; interest rates could go even higher. There is also a second reason why you should think hard before you buy any long-term zero coupon bonds; in 20 or 30 years the issuing corporation may not even exist. With positive coupon bonds you would at least have received some interest along the way.

U.S. Government Marketable Securities

Three varieties of marketable securities will be discussed here. (Series EE and HH savings bonds were presented in Chapter 14.)

U.S. government bonds

Marketable U.S. Treasury Bonds are long-term obligations of five years or more and often run more than twenty years. Since they are marketable, they fluctuate in the market inversely with fluctuations in the interest rates. Some wealthy individuals buy them, but not many small investors; the latter usually buy the safer (in price stability) Series EE and HH bonds. Financial institutions, on the other hand, are important buyers of long-term government bonds. Insurance companies, investment companies, and private pension funds commit millions of long-term dollars in government bonds each year.

The bonds have a coupon and interest is paid every six months. To collect the interest, it is merely necessary to detach the coupon when the interest is due, take it to a bank, and deposit it. The bank will collect the interest.

Treasury notes

Treasury notes are similar to Treasury bonds but generally have shorter maturities: they run from two to as high as ten years. They have a coupon (are not discounted), which provides for an interest payment every six months; they are negotiable and marketable, so they fluctuate in the market inversely with fluctuations in their interest rate. These securities are like government bonds, except their maturities are shorter. These are not securities a small investor would buy; but institutions and wealthy individuals might.

Treasury bills

These bills are short-term bearer obligations of the United States government. Because they are discounted when issued, the interest is the difference between the price at which the Treasury sells them and their face value. The minimum amount that may be purchased is $10,000, and they can be obtained in multiples of that amount. They have a maturity of ninety days, six months, and sometimes one year. While some individuals buy them if they have funds temporarily idle while seeking long-term investments, Treasury bills are primarily purchased by financial institutions in order to put their funds to work immediately while they are seeking permanent long-term outlets for them. Sometimes, however, industrial corporations buy them with funds set aside for future tax or dividend payments.

There is one case when relatively small investors would buy these securities— during periods when interest rates are very high. This is especially true if their rates are higher than those of depository institutions.

Treasury bills can be purchased through a bank, which makes arrangements to buy them in a block and parcel them out to customers. Banks used to provide this service free, but in recent years they have begun to assess a fee. The cost varies from bank to bank, but is generally from $25 to $30 per transaction.

State and Local Securities

State and local government securities appeal to high-income investors because their interest income is exempt from federal taxation. Usually bonds of a state or a political subdivision of a state are exempt from state income taxes as well. Because of this exemption, municipal bonds often yield a lower return than United States government securities. Competition on the part of wealthy investors for these securities reduces the yield below that indicated by the risk and often below that of United States Treasury obligations. The justification given for tax exemption is that it reduces the cost of financing schools and other public institutions at the local level. The opponents of tax exemption argue that it is merely a loophole that enables high-income groups to avoid the payment of taxes. The average investor should probably never buy these securities. If you are in a high-income bracket, however, you should investigate them. Often one would have to get a 14 or 16 percent return on alternative investments to be as well off, after taxes, as one is with a 7 or 8 percent tax-exempt return. Table 16–1 below shows the tax-equivalent yield you would have to obtain on corporate securities to match various tax-free rates.

Not only do state and local governments issue these tax exempts, but so do their political subdivisions, such as schools, sewer and water districts, toll road commissions, and others. In recent years pollution control bonds have also been developed. These are issued by private corporations, are backed by the credit of the corporation, and are used to finance air or water pollution control devices. However, if they are issued under the auspices of a state or local government, they are tax exempt. There are different kinds of such tax-exempt securities, some of which are long-term securities (bonds) and some short-term notes. They may be classified as follows:

1.   General Obligation Bonds
2.   Special Tax Bonds
3.   Revenue Bonds
4.   New Housing Authority Bonds
5.   Pollution Control Bonds (also called Industry Revenue Bonds)
6.   Short-term Notes

General obligation bonds

Many municipal bonds are in this category. They are secured by the full faith and credit of the taxing entity issuing them, that is, the full and unlimited taxing powers of the issuing government are pledged to back them up. These presumably are the least risky municipal bonds (except for the new housing bonds which are guaranteed by the federal government) that can be issued by local governments. The risk, of course, varies from one government to another.

Special tax bonds

These bonds are secured not by the full faith and credit of the issuing government, but only by part of it. They are payable only from a specific and listed tax source. In some cases, a new and specific tax is imposed to support a new bond issue when it comes out. For example, a new sewer system may be financed by such bonds which are then to be repaid by a special tax levied on the citizens. These are riskier than full faith and credit bonds of the same entity, and hence their yield is higher.

Revenue bonds

These are not faith and credit bonds. These are frequently issued by certain political subdivisions such as a toll road commission or a state university which has no taxing powers. However, the interest and principal is to be repaid by the revenue (tolls from turnpikes or rent from college dormitories) to be raised by whatever the bonds finance. Sometimes municipal water and electric departments

Table 16-1 The tax-free equivalent

Taxable income ($000)		1984 Tax bracket	Tax-free yields										
Single return	Joint return	bracket	5.00%	6.00%	7.00%	8.00%	9.00%	10.00%	11.00%	12.00%	13.00%	14.00%	15.00%
$28.8 to 34.1	$35.2 to 45.8	33.0	7.46	8.96	10.45	11.94	13.43	14.93	16.42	17.91	19.40	20.90	22.39
34.1 to 41.5	45.8 to 60.0	34.0	7.58	9.09	10.61	12.12	13.64	15.15	16.67	18.18	19.70	21.21	22.73
41.5 to 55.3	60.0 to 85.6	38.0	8.06	9.68	11.29	12.90	14.52	16.13	17.74	19.35	20.97	22.58	24.19
	85.6 to 109.4	42.0	8.62	10.34	12.07	13.79	15.52	17.24	18.97	20.69	22.41	24.14	25.86
55.3 to 81.8		45.0	9.09	10.91	12.73	14.55	16.36	18.18	20.00	21.82	23.64	25.45	27.27
		48.0	9.62	11.54	13.46	15.38	17.31	19.23	21.15	23.08	25.00	26.92	28.85
	109.4 to 162.4	49.0	9.80	11.76	13.73	15.69	17.65	19.61	21.57	23.53	25.49	27.45	29.41
Over 81.8	Over 162.4	50.0	10.00	12.00	14.00	16.00	18.00	20.00	22.00	24.00	26.00	28.00	30.00

452

sell such bonds, which are to be repaid solely from the water and electricity rates which are charged. In recent years, some cities have established Industrial Development Authorities which then issue revenue bonds to finance the construction of hotels, warehouses, and industrial parks. Since no government's faith and credit are pledged, these revenue bonds are generally considered riskier, and their yield is higher than bonds of the same entity that have taxing power behind them.

New housing authority bonds

Public housing authorities may issue bonds to finance the construction of low-income housing projects. The rental income from the housing is earmarked to meet the obligation of the bonds. But if the rental income is insufficient to do so, the Federal Housing Assistance Administration makes up the difference with federal funds. In effect then, these bonds are backed by the federal government and they are virtually riskless. Because of this their yield is also low. In recent years some state and local governments have established Home Finance Agencies which sell tax-exempt bonds. The monies are then channeled into mortgage loans, some of which finance housing that cannot be considered low-income. These bonds are not guaranteed as are the low-income housing bonds.

Pollution control bonds

These are a special type of revenue bond issued by a government entity or at least under its auspices. They are the liability of a private corporation. The bonds are used to finance air or water pollution control facilities of the corporation. The entire credit of the corporation, or in some cases only the revenue of the plant that receives the pollution control equipment, is pledged. Because of this, these bonds are considered riskier and their yield is generally among the highest of all tax exempts. You should appraise these as corporate bonds. In some cases these may be among the better buys of the tax exempts if they are issued by a financially strong corporation. If the corporation defaults, it can at least be forced into bankruptcy. The trustee of the bondholders can seize the assets of the corporation, sell them, and pay off the bondholders. The bondholders will seldom lose, although the common stockholders likely will. On the other hand, when a government defaults, it may be more difficult to sell its assets. The trustee for the bondholders cannot seize Central Park and sell it.

Short-term tax exempt municipal notes

There are also short-term notes generally running from six months to two years which would appeal to you if you were uncertain about long-term interest rates and did not want to become locked in at a fixed rate for a number of years. If you buy these, you will be able to reappraise the situation a year hence.

These notes may be full faith and credit or revenue obligations. The full faith and credit are sometimes tax anticipation notes, that is, taxes due in six months or a year are pledged to pay off these notes. The revenue notes are backed by revenue expected some time in the near future.

Some of these short-term notes are construction notes, sometimes called bond anticipation notes. They are used to finance the construction of something that will take a year or two. When the construction is complete, long-term bonds are sold to pay off the short-term notes.

There are also some short-term project notes (for example, to finance construction of low-income housing) that are guaranteed by the federal government. These provide temporary funds to finance low-income housing. When the construction is complete, long-term housing authority bonds are sold to repay the short-term notes. Rental income is now earmarked to pay the interest and principal of the long-term bonds. These federally guaranteed notes are riskless, and hence the yield is lower.

State and Local Bond Trusts

Recently, a number of closed-end investment trusts have been established through which tax-exempt bonds can be purchased indirectly. These trusts work much like mutual funds. They can be purchased in multiples as low as $1,000. Most of the bonds in these trusts are A-rated or better. However, some of the trusts are spiced with some lower-rated bonds in order to increase the yield. There is, of course, a secondary market for these trust certificates, and hence they need not be held to maturity. These are discussed at greater length in Chapter 18.

Bonds and Credit Ratings

The amount of interest paid on corporate bonds is determined by the credit rating of the company, length of maturity of bonds, and demand for and supply of money at the time of the issuance of the bond. With United States government bonds, credit rating is not a factor; however, both length of maturity of bonds and demand and supply of money at the time of the issuance will determine the rate paid by the federal government. For example, if the supply of money is short, the rates of the "governments" will be forced up just as is the interest rate with any other borrower. However, because of the relatively riskless character of the government issues, the amount paid by the government in interest will be lower than that paid by corporations. The rate on state and local bonds, too, varies with the same factors, although, as noted above, the tax-free interest generally keeps the rate on these securities low.

Interest rates on all fixed obligations vary with the length of time the securities run to maturity. Generally when rates are relatively low, long-term bonds yield more than short-term debt obligation. However, when interest rates are relatively high, often short-term obligations yield a higher return than long-term.

With respect to credit rating, the higher the rating, the lower the interest rate on corporation bonds as well as on state and local bonds. There are services that assign a credit rating to bonds, these ratings being an attempt to measure the quality of bonds or their degree of "gilt-edgedness." Moody's, which is probably the most widely used bond rating service, has nine classifications of risk. Triple A bonds are the highest quality and C bonds the lowest. A triple A bond carries little risk of default, whereas a C bond is in default and has very little prospect of ever being paid off. If you buy a C bond, you are probably buying a lawsuit.

The accompanying list gives the nine ratings assigned by Moody's. Your broker can tell you which rating any coroprate bond has. Remember any bond below Baa (which is medium grade) is a speculative bond investment.

Moody bond ratings

- Aaa
- Aa
- A
- Baa ⎫
- Ba ⎪
- B   ⎬ Speculative Bonds
- Caa ⎪
- Ca ⎭
- C   In Default

Standard and Poor's, another service similar to Moody's, has slightly different symbols, and more classifications. Standard and Poor's ratings are shown below.

Standard and Poor's bond ratings

- AAA
- AA
- A
- BBB
- BB
- B   ⎫
- CCC ⎬ Speculative
- CC ⎪
- C   ⎭
- DDD ⎫ In Default. The different D bonds indicate that the bondholders
- DD ⎬ would get different amounts back upon liquidation, with the D
- D   ⎭ rating being the lowest.

Bonds and the Small Investor

Many financial experts consider that a small investor should not invest in corporate bonds. To have a subtantially safer investment than stock, one must select a triple or double A bond. The return on such high-grade bonds, however, is not much more than on other fixed assets such as savings and loan CDs. Why, then, go to the bother of buying bonds and paying brokerage fees, especially since corporation bonds come in denominations of $1,000? (State and local bonds normally come in minimum amounts of $5,000.00.) While there is some merit to this view, there is also another side.

One should not buy a bond unless one has $1,000 to put away as a long-term investment. If the investor can get an extra 1 or 2 percent yield on a high-grade bond and if it is to be invested to pay for a college education some years later, bonds are fine. However, the small saver should also have some fixed investments in safe and liquid assets such as deposits in a thrift institution or series EE or HH government bonds. Don't put your first savings in bonds.

Bond Yields

You have already learned that a bond has a coupon rate of interest and a market rate of interest, the latter also called the yield. For example, if a $1,000 bond has a coupon rate of 9 percent, this indicates that the corporation will pay a fixed dollar amount ($90) per year. But if you purchased such a bond that matures in one year at a discount (you paid, say, $990.90) the actual yield is equal to the $90 interest you will get plus the $9.10 capital appreciation. Your actual percentage yield is $99.10 ÷ 990.90 or 10 percent.

We should also recognize the following yield concepts:

1. Nominal Yield and Real Yield
2. Average Yield to Maturity
3. Annual Yield to Maturity
4. Tax-equivalent Yield of a Municipal Security
5. Tax-free Equivalent Yield of a Taxable Yield

Nominal yield and real yield

The nominal yield is stated in money terms and not adjusted for inflation. To convert the nominal yield to the real yield, we must subtract the rate of inflation from the money (nominal) yield. If, in the case discussed above, the price level had risen by 5 percent during the year, the real yield would, of course, be 5 percent.

Average yield to maturity

In a few cases (primarily U.S. Series EE bonds), the actual yield is not the same each year. U.S. Series EE bonds, you will recall, are discounted. In addition, the interest rate which they receive floats; it is tied to the rate of U.S. government marketable securities, and varies with that market rate. Consequently, you cannot calculate the average rate to maturity until you actually cash the bonds in. Nevertheless, it is a valid concept.

Annual yield to maturity

There is also the similar but slightly different concept of annual yield to maturity, which is important if the bond is sold at below (or above) par and has a number of years to run. This comes about because, in calculating yield to maturity, you must consider not only the dollar amount of interest you will receive each year but also the annual capital gain (or loss) as the bond matures and its market price moves toward its face value. The following formula approximates the yield to maturity:

$$\frac{\left(\begin{array}{c}\text{annual interest}\\ \text{payment}\end{array}\right) + \dfrac{\text{maturity value less market price}}{\text{years to maturity}}}{\dfrac{\text{maturity value} + \text{market price}}{2}}$$

For example, a bond with a face value of $1,000 paying a coupon interest rate of 8 percent running over 10 more years, and purchased at $800, will give us:

$$\frac{\$80 + \dfrac{(\$1,000 - \$800)}{(10)}}{\dfrac{\$1,000 + \$800}{2}} = \frac{\$80 + \dfrac{200}{10}}{\$900}$$

$$\frac{80 + 20}{900} = \frac{100}{900} = 11.1 \text{ percent}$$

Tax-equivalent yield of a municipal security

The tax-equivalent yield is the term used when discussing municipal bonds. Since interest on municipal bonds is not taxed, a 5 percent return there is also the after-tax yield. The tax-equivalent yield is that yield you would have to get on a corporate bond so that, after personal income tax on it, you would have the same amount left that you could have earned on a municipal bond. Consequently, the tax-equivalent yield will vary from person to person depending upon the individual income tax bracket. For a person in the 50 percent tax bracket, the tax-equivalent yield to a 5 percent municipal bond is 10 percent; for a person in the 33 percent tax bracket, it is 7.5 percent. The tax-equivalent yield, then, is that level to which the yield must be adjusted up to give you a sufficiently higher return so as to enable you to pay taxes and still be as well off as with a tax-exempt yield.

   To obtain the tax-equivalent yield, divide the tax-free yield by 1 minus your tax bracket; use the following formula:

$$\frac{\text{tax-free yield}}{1 - \text{your tax bracket}} \quad \frac{.05}{1 - .33} = \frac{.05}{.66} = .07575$$

The tax-equivalent yield of a 5 percent tax-free yield for a person in the 33 percent tax bracket is 7.58 percent.

A table showing the various tax-equivalent yields is shown above in Table 16–1.

Tax-free equivalent yield of a taxable yield

We can also go in reverse and find the tax-free equivalent of a taxable yield. We multiply the taxable yield by 1 minus the tax bracket. Or use the formula (taxable yield) × (1 − tax bracket). In the above case: .07575 × 1 − .33 = .07575 × .66 = .05

THE ARRAY OF STOCKS—GENERAL COMMENTS

Bonds, as you have seen, can be classified into several categories. Stocks have only two categories—common and preferred. Common stock represents the ultimate of risk capital; preferred stock is less so. Figure 16–2 is a picture of a common stock certificate.

Common Stock in General

For all practical purposes, there is only one kind of common stock. Common stockholders are the residual recipients of a corporation's income. Because they receive what is left after all others get their prior claim, common stockholders' futures are closely tied to that of the corporation. If the corporation does well, the common stockholders do well. If the corporation does poorly, the common stockholders suffer. Common stockholders are also the last to be paid off in the event the corporation must be liquidated and sell its assets. Owning common stock then is riskier than owning other securities, and thus the market value of common stock fluctuates more than that of other securities.

Common stock ownership conveys no rights except the right to vote at stockholders meetings, where the corporation's board of directors is elected and certain other corporate decisions are made. The common stockholder is never promised dividends. It is illegal for a corporation to pay dividends unless it earns them, and even then it is under no obligation to pay them. While there is nonvoting as well as voting common stock, the former is rare, and it may not be listed on the New York Stock Exchange.

Some Value Concepts of Common Stock

There are four general methods of valuing common stock: (1) par value, (2) book value, (3) market value, and (4) liquidation value. In most states it is

Figure 16—2 Common stock certificate. (Courtesy General Motors Corporation.)

now possible to issue a no-par-value common stock, and often this is done, although historically stock always had a par value. These terms can sometimes be confusing and need to be explained.

1. *Par value* is the face value of the stock printed on the certificate. A fixed and arbitrary value is assigned when the stock is issued; it has little financial significance. Even when the stock is issued, it may be at or above par. Today stock is usually sold substantially above par. Historically, par value was higher and a more meaningful indicator of what the stock was worth. If a stock was sold at below par, the stockholder was often held liable for the difference between the price paid for it and par value. Today this is no longer true because stock cannot legally be sold below par when it is first issued. Stock which has no printed face value is called no-par stock. The major significance of par value is for tax purposes. In some states, where corporate franchise taxes are based on par value, it is to the interest of the corporation to keep par value low. Also, par value has some meaning insofar as preferred stock is concerned because the dividend is often based on par value. Preferred stock is explained in greater detail below, where the importance of par value on preferred stock will become clear.

2. *The book value* of common stock is an accounting concept. It is what the stock is worth today from an accounting point of view. When you examined the corporate balance sheet you were introduced to the concept of net worth (assets minus liabilities). The net worth, less a possible allowance for preferred stock, belongs to the common stockholder. It is also called the stockholder's equity. Net worth (minus preferred stock outstanding, if any) divided by the total number of shares of common stock outstanding is the book value per share.

3. *Market value* is what you have to pay for the stock if you wish to buy it—or what you will get if you sell it. It is often above book value, and, if so, it is because the expected future income has been taken into account by investors, and their demand has bid up the market price. This process is sometimes referred to as discounting the future. During the 1960s some stocks had a market value so far above the book value that they seem to have discounted not only the future but the hereafter as well, but this is generally no longer true.

4. *Liquidation value* is a meaningful term only if the life of the corporation is likely to be terminated. This is generally only the case with unsuccessful corporations. If a corporation is to be liquidated, its assets will be sold and if there is anything left after all its legal bills have been paid, the remainder will be divided up among the stockholders. This part left for the stockholder divided by the number of shares outstanding is the liquidation value. It would first appear that liquidation value would be the same as book value (these could, of course, both be zero or negative). However, this is not necessarily so because the assets might be so highly specialized that no ready market for them exists.

Earnings, Yield, and Capital Gain on Common Stock

The earnings and yield on common stock vary greatly from firm to firm and from time to time. Earnings are simply the total earnings after taxes per share. The yield is less than earnings because an adjustment must be made to net out the corporation's retained earnings. Yield then is the actual dividends paid as a percentage of the price of the stock. An example of earnings and yield will clarify this.

$$\frac{\text{total after tax earnings}}{\text{total number of shares outstanding}} = \frac{\$7,500,000}{1,000,000 \text{ shares}} = \$7.50/\text{share}$$

In most cases part of this $7.50 is paid out in the form of dividends and part is retained and plowed back into the corporation for expansion. However, the entire $7.50 belongs to the stockholder, and that portion retained will increase the book value and hopefully the market value of the stock. Earnings per share is an important criterion in determining whether you might want to buy a given stock. A comparison of earnings with the market price of a given share gives us its price earnings ratio which is an important analytical tool. Let's assume our stock above, earning $7.50 per share, is selling at $75. We now may calculate its price earnings ratio (PER). It is

$$\frac{\text{market price}}{\text{earnings per share}} = \frac{\$75}{\$7.50} = 10$$

Other stock will have different price earnings ratios. To determine whether a given stock is a candidate for purchase, examine its P/E ratio and also how its earnings per share have grown over the years. If its earnings per share have grown at the rate of 10 percent per year and if you believe that rate of growth will continue into the future you can project its earnings into the future. If $7.50 is compounded at 10 percent for five years, earnings per share in five years should be about $12.08. If a PER of 10 seems valid, then in five years a PER of 10 would put the market price of the stock at $120. This would provide a nice capital gain. This is one way of seeking out good common stock investments. Compare various price earnings ratios, project future earnings, and locate stocks that are underpriced in today's market and whose prospects for growth are good. To calculate the percentage return the stock is earning, we simply reverse the above ratio; it is 10 percent.

Yield as noted above is simply the annual dividend payment per share divided by the market price. In our example above, assume that there is a 50 percent dividend payout rate. Then

$$\frac{\text{dividends per share}}{\text{market price per share}} = \frac{\$3.75}{\$75.00} = 5\% \text{ yield}$$

The next question is how much should the yield be; also how does the 5 percent yield compare with other stock in companies that provide the same or similar business risk and market risk. The investor must make a personal decision regarding how much of a yield he thinks he should have in light of alternative investment opportunities open to him that have comparable risk. Moreover, if a capital gain is also expected, a lower dividend yield is usually acceptable.

In the above case where, in addition to a $3.75 dividend, $3.75 is retained by the corporation, the market price (as well as the book value) of the stock will tend to rise. I say "tend to rise," but this is true only if the retained profits are successfully reinvested in expanding the business and its profits. In such a case the stockholders get part of their reward in the form of capital appreciation rather than in cash dividends. This may be to the investor's advantage taxwise because capital gains are taxed at a more favorable rate than are dividends.

Traditionally it has been felt by most investors that the dividend yield on a common stock should be higher than the yield on bonds—to compensate the investor for the greater risk associated with common stock. Traditionally the yield on common stock has been higher. But in recent years, due to high interest rates, bond yields have sometimes been higher. Even if stock yields were below bond yields, certainly earnings (dividends plus retained earnings) on common stock should be superior to bond yield. In many cases they are, but the retained earnings are not always reflected in common stock price appreciation, and in such a case, the yields and capital appreciation on stock combined might be below the yield on bonds. This has sometimes been the case recently.

However, investing in common stock has traditionally been one of the better ways to participate in the future economic growth of the country because profits rise with growth, and this often shows up in the form of capital gains on stock. Economic growth is a function of population growth and of technological change. Technological change will enhance profits either by reducing costs or by bringing forth new or improved products, or by some combination of the two. New and improved products enhance profits by increasing sales.

Figure 16–3 illustrates how dividends have risen over the past forty years in relation to the cost of living. If we considered the total earnings on common stock (dividends plus retained earnings), the record of common stock would look even better.

Perhaps the best measure of how good an investment a common stock has been is to take into account the total economic increment it has provided its owner. This includes cash dividends as well as capital gains, which are influenced by retained earnings but may very well be higher or lower than retained earnings indicate they should be. Suppose you had purchased a common stock for $50

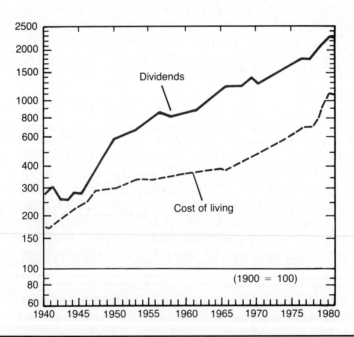

Figure 16–3 Industrial stock dividends vs. cost of living. (*Source: Investment Companies, Mutual Funds and Other Types, 1982*, Wiesenberger Financial Services, a division of Warren, Gorham & Lamont, Inc., p. 57.)

per share. Suppose too that its after-tax earnings were $5 per share and that it retained $2.50 and paid a cash dividend of $2.50. Clearly its dividend yield would be 5 percent but its total earnings 10 percent. But if the market price of the stock had increased over the year to $60 per share, the total economic increment it has provided is $12.50 (the $2.50 of retained earnings is included in the $10 capital gain, but the $2.50 dividend is not). A return of $12.50 on a $50 investment is 25 percent. To be sure, in order to realize this capital gain in the form of cash, the stockholder would have to sell the stock. Nevertheless, the capital gain cannot be ignored. The next year it may be more or less. Table 16–2 illustrates these ratios; Figure 16–4 shows how corporate dividends, profits, and taxes have fluctuated in recent years.

The Capital Structure of a Firm; One Reason Why Earnings Vary (Leverage)

Some firms have raised more capital via the sale of bonds both absolutely and relative to their total capital than other firms. This variation can be explained in part by management philosophy. However, it is also in part due to different kinds of business operations. Certain types of firms can safely raise a larger proportion of their capital by selling bonds than can others because their earnings are more stable from year to year. Such a firm may use more borrowed capital in the hope of increasing the earning (and yield) on their common stock. Raising capital via bonds imposes a fixed cost upon the corporation and introduces *leverage* into its earnings. Leverage can be positive or negative. Positive leverage comes about if a business can borrow capital at, say, 8 percent by selling bonds, and then earn 10 percent with it. The 2 percent differential accrues to the common stockholder. However, negative leverage will be generated if next year the firm earns only 6 or 7 percent on the capital it borrowed at 8 percent. Firms that have high and stable earnings can safely build more leverage into their capital structure than can low- and fluctuating-income firms. An illustration will make leverage clear.

Table 16–2   Possible returns on stock

ABC stock		Percent return on investment	
Purchase price		$50.00	
Earnings (per year)		5.00	10%
Dividend	$2.50		5%
Retained earnings			
Capital gains		10.00	20%
Due to retained earnings	2.50		
Due to other factors	7.50		
Economic increment		12.50	25%

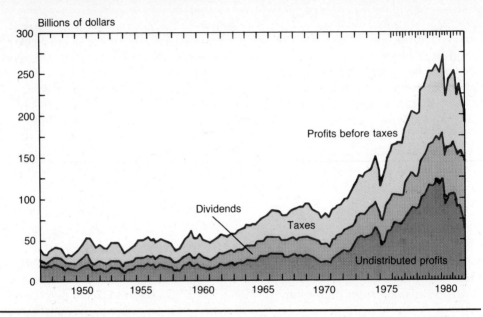

Figure 16—4 Corporate profits, taxes, and dividends. (*Source: 1982 Historical Chart Book,* Board of Governors of th Federal Reserve System, p. 60.)

Two hypothetical firms (see Tables 16–3 and 16–4); are identical to begin with and each earns a 10 percent return. Then they both expand, firm A by selling another million dollars of common stock and firm B by selling a million dollars of bonds. Both firms doubled in size and in sales and in profits before any interest was paid. However, the earnings return to common stock rose to 12 percent for one firm and remained unchanged for the other. This is an illustration of positive leverage.

If, next year, both firms' incomes before interest were to fall to $120,000, then firm A would be earning 6 percent for its stockholders while firm B would earn only 4 percent. This is an illustration of negative leverage. Certain firms whose incomes are more stable, like utilities, often are able to take greater advantage of leverage. This also explains why their incomes are often higher.

Table 16—3   Capital structure of a firm

Before expansion			
Firm A		Firm B	
Capital stock (20,000 shares at $50 per share)	$1,000,000	Capital stock (20,000 shares at $50 per share)	$1,000,000
After tax earnings	100,000	After tax earnings	100,000
Percentage return	10%	Percentage net	10%

Table 16–4   Capital structure of a firm

After expansion			
Firm A		Firm B	
Capital stock	$2,000,000	Capital stock	$1,000,000
(40,000 shares at $50		Bonds at 8%	1,000,000
per share)		After tax but before	
After tax earnings	200,000	interest earnings	200,000
Percentage return	10%	Interest	80,000
		Earnings for shareholders	120,000
		Percentage return	12%

While the amount of leverage a firm has built into its capital structure may influence earnings, it is by no means the only factor. The quality of management, the type of product it sells, how effectively it innovates and creates new and better products are equally important. Nevertheless, you should look at a firm's capital structure before you buy securities, especially if you are concerned that business conditions may worsen in the future and with them corporate profits. It may be a method of rejecting certain stocks if you are taking a defensive position.

Beta

A stock's beta is an indicator of its volatility relative to the market. The overall market has a beta of one. A stock's beta is the total return of that stock (both price appreciation and dividends received) relative to the return of the market— as measured by some index such as Standard and Poor's and some average of dividends for the market.

If a stock has the average beta of one, its return is proportionate to the market returns. If, on the other hand, a given stock generates a 20 percent return versus the market's 10 percent, its beta is 2. A 5 percent return versus a 10 percent return for the market indicates a beta of 0.5. Beta also measures declines. Beta is considered an indicator of risk. The higher the beta above one, the more it swings with market changes; the lower the beta is below one, the greater the stability of that stock relative to the market. To be sure, a stock's beta can change; any beta is only a reflection of what has happened in the past. Nevertheless, the past can be an indicator of what might happen in the future.

Rankings or Ratings of Common Stock

Bonds have long been rated as to their credit-worthiness, wth AAA being the highest quality, as explained above. Stock ratings, or rankings, have been developed in recent years. The best known of these is Standard and Poor's. Stocks are ranked somewhat differently than bonds, however—not ranked in degree of protection for principal and interest. The ranking services consider such things as the product produced, managerial capabilities, financial structure, and past earnings and dividends. In addition, growth and stability of earnings are assessed, and the long-run record of performance. Then a ranking is assigned with A+ being the highest. The following eight rankings are currently used:

- A+ Highest
- A   High
- A− Good
- B+ Median
- B   Speculative
- B− Highly speculative
- C   Marginal
- D   In reorganization

Classification of Common Stock

Common stock can be classified into a number of categories. It is possible to identify growth stock, income stock, cyclical stock, defensive stock, blue-chip stock, speculative stock, and others. Investment opportunities change as do people; so a stock that at one time may be considered a growth stock may at another time be regarded as an income stock. Also, some stock may have the characteristics of several classifications; defensive and income stocks, for instance, may in some cases be the same. Obviously some stock may have some of the attributes of all four. Income and growth stocks—indeed all stocks—have some cyclical aspects. Nevertheless, many stocks fall into patterns. You should select stock in accordance with your investment objectives, discussed in the previous chapter.

When stocks are classified as speculative or blue-chip, they are classified according to risk. These are relative terms, as there is an element of speculation in all stock and an element of investment in all. The least speculative (most blue-chip) stock over the years has probably been American Telephone and Telegraph. The most speculative (least blue-chip) stock is probably Dry Gulch Gold and Uranium, or some other stock like it. We shall examine all of these classifications.

Growth stock

Growth stocks are generally considered to be those that have good earnings but a very low dividend yield because the company is reinvesting the bulk of its earnings in expansion. This investment increases both the book value and the market value of the stock, and the stockholder's goal in such a case presumably is to achieve capital gains through the appreciation of the stock. A growth company, then, is one that has a good record of high and growing earnings per dollar invested, one that is doing better each year than the year before. Moreover, the company is using these earnings to expand its capacity. It is producing a product for which the demand is expected to increase greatly in the future.

To buy a growth stock, one may have to pay a high price, as many of them have excessively high price/earnings ratios, because the stock market is said to discount the future. If the company is earning a high rate of return per dollar invested and the rate is expected to increase further because the demand for the product is going to increase in the future, the market price of the stock will be bid up. Since the future profits of the company look good, up goes the market price of its stock. This process is called *discounting future profits*. In some cases it may be too late to buy such a stock; but, if the company continues expansion at its present rate, the stock will often continue to climb.

Let us assume that a given growth stock has discounted profits five years into the future and is selling for $100 per share. Its price/earnings ratio is out of line from an investment point of view; but if it is really a growth company, then five years from now it will still have discounted profits five years into the future (or perhaps seven) and may be selling for $200 per share. The opposite possibility is that its growth may be over or slowing down and that it may not rise much above $100. The secret to success in growth stocks is to find them first. This often means buying a speculative security. The investor wants the stock of a firm that will become the IBM of the space industry. If a person buys a proven growth stock, he or she pays for it, since it has already discounted the future. Some stocks that are typically looked upon as being growth stock include those of IBM, Coca Cola, and some of the newer, smaller, minicomputer companies. Growth stocks generally appeal to younger people who do not need income at the present time but who want capital gains they will take later.

Income stock

Income stocks are those in companies whose earnings are good but that either are not growing much or are growing with external funds.[1] They may be mature companies producing a product for which the demand has stabilized. They are companies, moreover, that pay out a large proportion of their earnings each year in the form of dividends. Utilities, tobacco, and food are considered such income areas. Not only are dividends fairly high but they are steady because the earnings of the companies are steady. AT&T for many years has been considered an income stock par excellence; it had for a long time yielded a steady return. Its current yield is about 9.5 percent. Income stocks in general appeal to older people who may need the income for retirement and who would benefit less from long-term growth. However, a good yield is one criterion that should be used by everyone in selecting stock for a well-balanced portfolio.

---

1. External funds are funds obtained by selling new issues of bonds or common stock.

Cyclical stock

Cyclical stocks fluctuate widely over swings in the business cycle and have high betas. They are the stocks of those companies whose sales and earnings vary greatly. The steel, nonferrous metals, and machine tool industry are examples. Because earnings fluctuate, so too do dividends and the market price of the stock. Nearly all stock fluctuates somewhat with swings in the business cycle, but cyclical stocks do so more than others.

Investors who buy a cyclical stock are betting that economic and business conditions will improve. In this connection, a word of warning is in order. The buyer should beware of selecting a cyclical stock after there has been an unusual jump in either sales or earnings unless the outlook is relatively certain that the up-trend will continue. Once sales and/or earnings have risen substantially, it is often already too late to buy cyclicals; now is the time to sell.

The Wall Street maxim in relation to cyclical stock is "Buy on bad news, sell on good." Investors in cyclical stock should buy when sales and earnings are down, sell when these figures are favorable. To do so one must, of course, be flexible and in a position to hold on to the stock for a considerable period of time, frequently for several years. However, this is true for any stock. No one but a professional speculator, and certainly no small investor, should go into the stock market on a short-term basis.

Defensive stock

Defensive stock is often income stock. It would probably be more accurate to say that most defensive stock is income stock but not as many income stocks could be classified as defensive. A defensive stock is one that declines less than most on a general downturn. By the same token, it may not rise as much in a general upturn. The stocks have low betas, because the company's sales and hence its income are more stable over the business cycle since the demand for its product is more stable. Such companies include some of the food and cigarette makers, but usually utilities are considered the best defensive stocks. Some utilities have been considered growth stock recently, especially if they are in an area that is growing rapidly, such as Florida or Arizona. Most utilities, however, pay out a considerable portion of their earnings as dividends and hence are more income and defensive than growth and defensive. Some analysts look upon defensive stock as the opposite of cyclical stock. If you expected the economy in general to be heading into a recession, you might well sell any cyclical stocks you had and buy either bonds or defensive stock. This is known as taking a defensive position.

Blue-chip stock

Blue-chip stock is the least risky—least risky both as to missing a dividend and to declining in price, although the price does decline when the market in general declines. Generally, however, the price of blue-chip stocks will decline less in a general downturn than the average. They are the stocks of the old well-established companies that have proved they can earn profits. They cannot be classified by industries at all, because some industries have both blue-chip companies and firms that either are not tested or that for other reasons are considered highly speculative.

A list of blue-chip stock would include General Electric, American Telephone and Telegraph, Exxon, Standard Oil of California, and other firms of similar financial strength.

Speculative stock

These stocks are untried securities, often stocks of new, small firms whose chances for success are not great or firms that at least are untested. Some of the small mining and uranium stocks are examples, as are the small electronics companies. Investors should not put any money in these stocks unless they can afford to lose it if the worst comes. The probability of gain is small, but the amount of gain would be great if it should come. One assumes a great risk in buying them. A small investor with few funds should probably never buy highly speculative securities. A person of means may want to invest in them occasionally.

Speculation is a relative term, as pointed out before, and some people take a chance on a mildly speculative stock. Of course, all stock has at least a slight element of speculation attached to it.

Incidentally, the investor can speculate with bonds as well as stock. One can buy bonds that are in default at a tremendous discount and hope for a substantial return when the firm is liquidated.

Preferred stock

Many investors consider preferred stock somewhere between bonds and stock, more risky than bonds but less so than common stock. As such, it appeals to certain moderately conservative investors.

Preferred stock is a special kind of stock issued by a corporation that gives a preference to the purchasers, generally a fixed return or dividend and a preference as to assets. For example, a preferred stockholder may be given a 9 percent return. This 9 percent is figured on the face or par value of the stock. Thus if a stock share were issued at $100 par and it were a 9 percent preferred, the stockholder would be entitled to $9.00 per annum on each share of stock he or she holds, provided there are enough profits to pay the $9. This $9 per share, moreover, is due and payable before any distribution can be made to the common stockholders.

In addition to the preference in the form of earnings, preferred stockholders are generally entitled to share in the assets of the corporation at dissolution before the common stockholders may receive any of the money. That is, if the corporation goes out of business either voluntarily or involuntarily, preferred stockholders will divide the assets and pay themselves off at par value before the common stockholders may receive any part of the assets. Some variations of preferred stock are examined below. Figure 16–5 shows a preferred stock certificate.

Cumulative and noncumulative preferred stock

A corporation issuing 9 percent cumulative preferred stock is liable to the preferred stockholders for past dividends that have not been paid. Suppose a company fails to pay dividends for three years, and the stock (with a $100 par value) calls for a payment of 9 percent and is cumulative; then the company must pay the cumulative preferred stockholders $27 at the end of the three years before any money is payable to the common stockholders.

Notice that corporations do not have to pay dividends to preferred stockholders even if they have the profits. They must merely pay the preferred before they may pay the common; and if the preferred is cumulative, they must pay all back dividends before common can be paid. Sometimes there are limits to how far back dividends have to be paid, such as three-year or five-year cumulative.

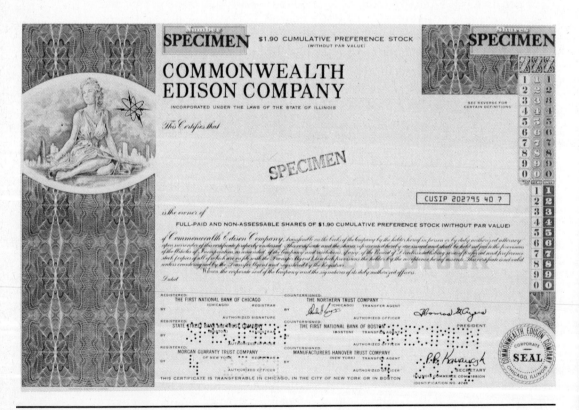

Figure 16–5   A preferred stock certificate. (Courtesy of Commonwealth Edison Company and the First National Bank of Boston.)

Other preferred cumulative stocks have no limits, and all back dividends have to be paid before common stockholders can receive anything. On noncumulative preferred stock the corporation need only pay the current year's dividends before it may pay dividends on the common stock.

Participating preferred

With this type of preferred stock, if the earnings are sufficient, preferred stockholders not only are given their agreed dividends but are entitled to share equally in the dividends paid to the common stockholders. Generally where there is a participating preferred stock, the preferred stockholders are paid their agreed-upon rate, say $9 per share, then the common stockholders are paid an equal dividend, or $9 per share, and after that the remainder of the money is distributed equally among the preferred and the common stockholders.[2]

Cumulative participating preferred

Obviously these two features can be combined, and we have then a preferred stock that must be paid past dividends before common is paid any dividends, and then will share equally with the common anything that remains.

Callable or redeemable preferred

Callable preferred stock is preferred stock issued by a corporation with a provision that the corporation has an option to buy the stock back from the preferred stockholders on terms specified at the time the stock is issued. For example, callable preferred stock may be issued at $100 per share and may be callable at $110. That is, if the corporation desires to exercise its option, it may buy back the stock at the call price of $110.

Corporations issue stock of this nature so that if the market is such that they could issue a new preferred at, say, 7 or 8 percent rather than at the old rate of 9, they can convert. Or they may wish to clean up their capital structure and eliminate the preferred. In the market seldom will the market price exceed the call price because of the possibility of redemption by the issuer.

Convertible preferred

This is preferred stock that can be exchanged for common stock by the stockholders at their option. The exchange ratio is determined at the time the stock is issued. Therefore, if the common stock of the corporation appreciates in the market, it will pull the preferred up with it. Convertible preferred stock has all the

---

2. The figure of $9 is not quite accurate because the price of the common and preferred stock is not usually the same. The common stock may be selling for $50 per share, whereas the preferred in this example has a face value of $100. Moreover, the price of the common stock often fluctuates widely over time. Therefore a participating agreement must be spelled out at the time the preferred stock is issued; generally it will give the common the same percentage return that the preferred has received, after which they share equally. But this means that the common must be evaluated at the time the preferred is issued, because its price fluctuates in the market. Usually the market price (or some price near it) of the common at the time the preferred is issued is taken; the common would get 9 percent of that, and then sharing would begin.

advantages of preferred, as well as of the common, just as in the case of convertible bonds, which were discussed above.

A footnote on preferred stock

Preferred stock may have the features of a bond or the features of common stock, or some of each. If it is participating preferred, it is a bit closer to common because it shares the good fortune of the common. However, it may not share as much of the bad. If it is noncallable and nonparticipating, it is closer to a bond. Its rate of return is fixed, and it will fluctuate in the market like a bond with variations in the interest rate. If it is convertible into common, it again shares in the good fortune of common but not necessarily in the bad because it will rise in price with the common but will not necessarily fall if the market price of the common declines.

QUESTIONS FOR REVIEW

1. How do bonds differ from common stock?
2. What is par value of a bond? What does it mean if a bond is sold at a premium?
3. What are registered bonds?
4. What is a debenture?
5. Explain convertible bonds.
6. What might lead a corporation to issue convertible bonds?
7. Explain the idea behind the equipment trust obligation.
8. What are discount bonds?
9. How do U.S. government marketable securities differ from Series EE and HH bonds?
10. Discuss state and local securities.
11. What is the difference between a Treasury note and municipal bond.
12. In the rating of bonds, how many classifications are there?
13. Should a small investor buy bonds? Why? If yes, what kinds of bonds would you recommend?
14. How does the nominal yield on a bond differ from its real yield?
15. What is meant by a stock's par value, book value, and market value?
16. What is the difference between earnings and yield, as most brokers define it, on common stock?
17. What is meant by total economic increment insofar as a common stockholder is concerned?
18. Why can some firms raise a larger percentage of their capital from the sale of bonds than can other firms?
19. What is meant by leverage?

20. What is a stock's beta?
21. Explain what is meant by a growth stock, an income stock, and a cyclical stock.
22. What are the advantages and disadvantages of preferred stock?
23. Distinguish between cumulative, noncumulative, and cumulative participating preferred stock.
24. The market price of callable preferred stock is said to have a "lid" on it. In short, there seems to be a top market price. Why is this so?

CASES

1. Janice Spier recently inherited some common stock. The par or face value on the stock is $10 per share, which gives Janice a total investment value of $5,000. Recently, however, she received from the corporation a report that gave the book value of the stock as $25 per share, which would make her investment $12,500. Then last night at a dinner party someone mentioned the same corporation and said he had just bought 100 shares of it at $102 per share. At this point Janice is confused. Could you straighten her out? What makes the par value, the book value, and the market value differ?

2. About a year ago Dale and Genevieve MacMasters purchased one hundred shares of participating preferred common stock yielding 8 percent on their investment of $150 per share. It was a new issue at the time of purchase, and the common stock at that time was selling for $50 per share. In the first year the company had a very good year and has announced that the final dividend on the preferred stock will be paid soon. What is the dividend (for the year) on the preferred?

   The company also announced that there would be a participating dividend later after the common stockholders had received their share. What is the dividend that must be paid on the common before the common and preferred stocks share equally that which remains?

3. Thomas and Rita Andrews purchased $5,000 face value of callable convertible bonds a year ago at par, paying 9 percent coupon rate. How much money did they invest, not counting brokerage fees? What is their annual dollar income from the bonds?

   The call feature provided for a call at the option of the company at $1,025. The convertible feature permitted Thomas and Rita to convert each bond into ten shares of common stock. What was the approximate price of the common stock at the time the convertibles were issued?

   Over the past year the company has been extremely prosperous, and the price of the common stock has risen to $200. What is the price of the convertible bonds? Explain.

4. Some time ago Gordon and Lillian Rider purchased a $1,000 face value

convertible bond having a coupon rate of 9 percent. They got the bond at a 5 percent discount. What is their total investment? What is their actual yield?

The bond is convertible into twenty shares of common stock. What was the approximate price of the common stock when the bond was issued? The present market price of the common stock is $160 per share. Should Gordon and Lillian convert? If they do, what will be the value of their investment? What is the present value of their convertible bond?

5. John Farely can truly be considered a small investor. While he has $3,000 in a savings and loan association and some life insurance, he has no other investments. He feels he should now start acquiring some securities directly. He can set aside $100 per month for this purpose. He is undecided between common stock, preferred stock, and bonds. Can you advise him? In so doing, bring out the differences between the three above-mentioned securities. Also state why he should buy what you recommend.

6. Judy Brown is saving a few dollars a month and wants to invest them in common stock. She has heard that certain firms like utilities have more leverage built into their capital structure than some other firms. She is unclear about what leverage means. Can you explain it to her? Also Judy would like to know why utilities generally have more leverage in their capital structure than most other firms.

SUGGESTED READINGS

Barron's Weekly. A weekly finance magazine.

Blodgett, Richard. *The Merrill Lynch Guide to Financial Planning.* New York: Simon and Schuster, 1983.

Dirks, Ray. *Heads You Win, Tails You Win.* New York: Bantam Books, 1980.

The Exchange. Magazine published monthly by the New York Stock Exchange.

Financial Analysts Journal. New York: The Financial Analyst Federation. Published bimonthly.

Haft, Richard A. *Investing in Securities: A Handbook for the 80's.* Englewood Cliffs, N.J.: Prentice-Hall, 1982.

Hedging Highlights. Chicago: Chicago Board of Trade.

How to Invest in Stocks and Bonds. New York: Merrill Lynch, Pierce, Fenner and Smith.

How You Get More Out of Financial News. Princeton, N.J.: Dow Jones & Company, Inc., The Educational Service Bureau.

Instruments of the Money Market. Richmond, Va.: Federal Reserve Bank of Richmond, 1981.

Jessup, Paul E. *Competing for Stock Market Profits.* New York: John Wiley and Sons, 1981.

The Kiplinger Washington Letter. A weekly newsletter with a good deal of material on business and finance.

Lee, Barbara. *The Women's Guide to the Stockmarket.* New York: Crown Publishers, 1982.

Levine, Sumner N., ed. *The Dow Jones-Irwin Business and Investment Almanac, 1983.* Homewood, Ill.: Dow Jones-Irwin, 1982.

New York Stock Exchange Fact Book. Published annually by the New York Stock Exchange.

Questions and Answers About the Stock Market. New York: Merrill Lynch, Pierce, Fenner and Smith.

Tax-Exempt Bonds and the Investor. Washington, D.C.: Investment Bankers Association of America.

U.S. News & World Report. A weekly magazine that contains a good deal of information on business and finance.

United States Government Securities: Basic Information. Federal Reserve Bank of Dallas. No date.

The Wall Street Journal. This is a daily financial newspaper, published by Dow Jones & Company.

Well Beyond the Average: The Story of Dow Jones. New Jersey: Dow Jones & Company, The Educational Service Bureau.

What Every Woman Investor Should Know. Washington, D.C.: Investment Bankers Association of America.

CHAPTER SEVENTEEN

THE INVESTOR AND THE SECURITIES MARKET

Securities Exchanges: Brokers and Dealers
Quoting Securities
Buying and Selling Securities
Distribution of Earnings from Stocks
Investment Strategies: Timing of Investment Decisions,
or When to Buy What
Appendix 17: Supplemental Material on Common Stock

An investor who wishes to buy or sell securities does so in the open market. The open market for securities is "the works." It consists of all the organized exchanges on which securities are listed and also the over-the-counter market. Broadly defined, it also includes the brokers and dealers who operate in the open market and make it go. In this chapter we shall examine the open market and the buying and selling of securities therein. We will also examine earning on stock and some supplemental material on securities.

Historically—over many years—common stocks have served as an excellent inflationary hedge. However, during the past decade this has ceased to be the case; stockholders lost some ground during the decade of the 1970s. Recently the market seems to have come back. Whether this is the start of a bull (long-term rising) market, only time will tell; but in light of historical and present stock prices and earnings, many brokers feel common stocks are an excellent buy.

SECURITIES EXCHANGES: BROKERS AND DEALERS

In the United States there are two major organized exchanges (the New York Stock Exchange and the American Stock Exchange) whose major function is to facilitate the sale of securities. In addition, there are a number of smaller regional exchanges. While the greatest volume of business on the organized exchanges takes place in the area of common and preferred stock, they also handle the sale of some bonds and warrants. To deal directly on an exchange, one must be a member or own a seat. Many of the members are security dealers as well as brokers; they are broker-dealers. Brokers are individuals who execute orders for third parties for a commission. Dealers, on the other hand, act as principals and buy for their own account and also sell from them, hoping for a profit margin between the buy and sell price. In doing this they are said to make a market in the securities they buy and sell.

The New York Stock Exchange

The New York Stock Exchange is by far the largest of the various exchanges in the United States. About 1,800 corporations have their common stock listed thereon. In addition, about 2,500 bonds and 500 preferred stocks are also listed, which makes the total listing on the "big board" almost 5,000 securities. To trade on the NYSE, one must own a seat, and obtaining a seat is not easy. The only way to do so is to buy one from a member willing to relinquish it. The exchange is a very exclusive club. Brokers who are not members must trade (buy and sell) through someone who is a member.

The members of the exchange are classified into a number of categories. About half the members are commission brokers; the rest are divided among floor brokers, specialists, registered traders, bond dealers, or a combination of the above capacities at different times.

1. *Commission brokers.* Some members act solely as commission brokers. These are the ones who are partners or officers of firms doing business with the public. They have offices where they contact the public (in the case of a large firm like Merrill Lynch they have many members and many offices throughout the country). They buy and sell securities for their customers in return for which they are paid a commission.

2. *Floor brokers.* These are the members of the exchange who assist commission brokers who are unable to handle all of the volume when trade is heavy. They ensure that orders are executed quickly. They used to be called contract brokers a few years ago, and before that "two-dollar" brokers because that was the fee they charged. Their fee is now higher and comes out of the regular fee paid to the commission broker.

3. *Specialists.* The physical area of the New York Stock Exchange being large, it is frequently impossible for a member to get around fast enough to execute customers' orders. Certain brokers therefore specialize in buying and selling certain stocks at certain posts on the exchange floor. Each security is sold at a given location, and the specialists stay at that post and execute orders for a few securities at the order of their fellow brokers. Also specialists are responsible for the execution of conditional orders.

Investors give an order to buy if the price drops to $34; this instruction goes into the specialists' books, and if and when the price reaches $34, they execute. The specialists also act as dealers and make a market in the stock in which they specialize. They are supposed to stabilize short-term movements in the market and in this way contribute to orderly conditions. However, specialists cannot buy or sell for their own accounts if there are unfilled orders from the public at the market price. If there are no unfilled orders or if the market is sluggish and buyers and sellers are having difficulty getting together on a price, the specialists are to enter the market on either the supply-sell or demand-buy side, whichever is necessary to help stabilize the market. Specialists are expected only to help stabilize short-term swings; they are not expected to take continued losses to stem long-term movements. Actually, the specialists will make rather than lose money by helping to stabilize short-term movements because they are in and out of the market frequently and if they make even a fraction of a point on many transactions, profits soon add up. Finally, some specialists will use their inventories to fill odd lot orders, discussed below.

4. *Registered traders or floor traders.* These are members who buy and sell on their own accounts; they deal in stocks themselves with the idea of making a profit on their purchases. They are able to do so because as members of the stock exchange they do not pay a regular commission, but a greatly reduced member commission. In addition, they are also professional traders, and they get in and out of the market on a short-run basis and take advantage of short-run price movements of common stock. Sometimes they also serve either as commission brokers for a few customers or as floor brokers for other commission brokers. They have been criticized because it is thought that they contribute to market instability in individual securities. For example, by becoming particularly active in an individual firm's stock, a floor trader might cause wide fluctuations in that particular issue.

The Historical Record of the NYSE

People have been buying and selling securities for many years, and the market has had many ups and downs, because the market is one of the most, if not the most, sensitive of all institutions in our society. It reacts to any and all news, good or bad. Bad news will nearly always send it down; what is considered good news may send it up or down. These are the short-run fluctuations. The long-run trend has been up more often than down.

While the deepest and most severe stock market decline took place with the crash in 1929, there have been other sharp declines as well. After the 1929 crash the market generally stayed depressed until the big bull market shortly after World War II.

At various times, different stocks have been popular. For a number of years after World War I, railroad stocks were the "in thing." While they made somewhat of a comeback after the Great Depression, they never regained their former popularity. More recently, electronics, computers, and other "hi-tech" firms have been the glamour items in the stock market. Much of the historical record of the stock market can be seen graphically in Standard and Poor's chart in Figure 17–1.

The American Stock Exchange (AMEX)

The second major stock exchange is the American Stock Exchange, called *Amex* for short. This market was originally outside in the street, but has been inside since 1921. There are fewer securities listed on the American Stock Exchange than on the New York Exchange, and the requirements for listing are less rigorous. To be listed in either exchange a company must meet certain tests as to dollar amount of assets, earnings, market value of its stock, and number of publicly held shares outstanding. In addition, the corporation must publish certain financial information about itself. About 1,500 securities are listed on the American Exchange. As for commission brokers, specialists, and so forth, the operation of the American Exchange is much like that of the New York Stock Exchange.

The Regional Exchanges

The New York and the American Stock Exchanges are national institutions. There are also a number of smaller stock exchanges that serve only the region in which they are located. The three major regional exchanges are the Midwest Stock Exchange, the Philadelphia-Baltimore-Washington Stock Exchange, and the Pacific Coast Stock Exchange. Many of the stocks listed for the regional exchanges are also listed on either the New York or the American Stock Exchange. The existence of the Pacific Coast Exchange permits trading in those dually listed stocks three additional hours after the close of the NYSE and AMEX. In addition, the regional exchanges list some securities of regional companies that are listed nowhere else.

Brokerage Commissions

There are brokerage commissions you must pay when buying or selling securities. On large orders the broker will negotiate commissions in advance with the buyer or seller. On most regular orders, however, brokers have a schedule they follow, and these schedules vary somewhat from broker to broker.

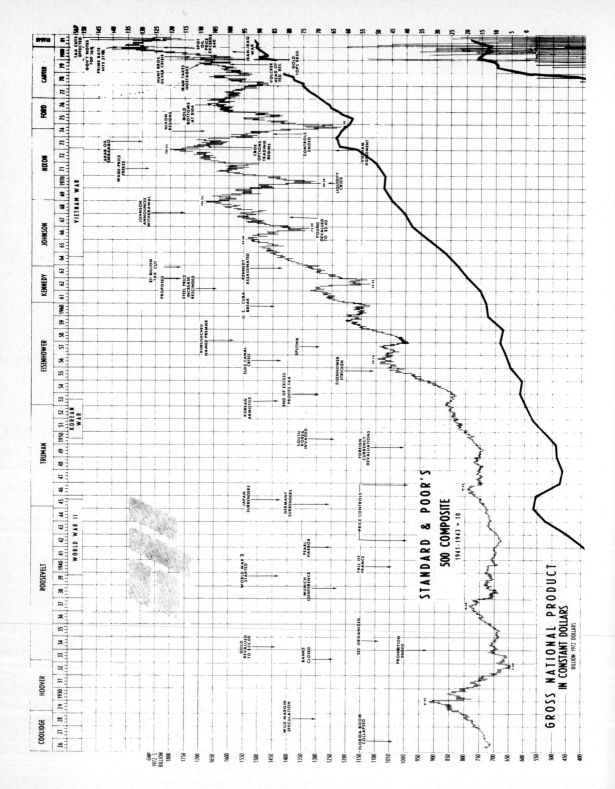

STANDARD & POOR'S
500 COMPOSITE
1941-1943 = 10

GROSS NATIONAL PRODUCT
IN CONSTANT DOLLARS
BILLION 1972 DOLLARS

480

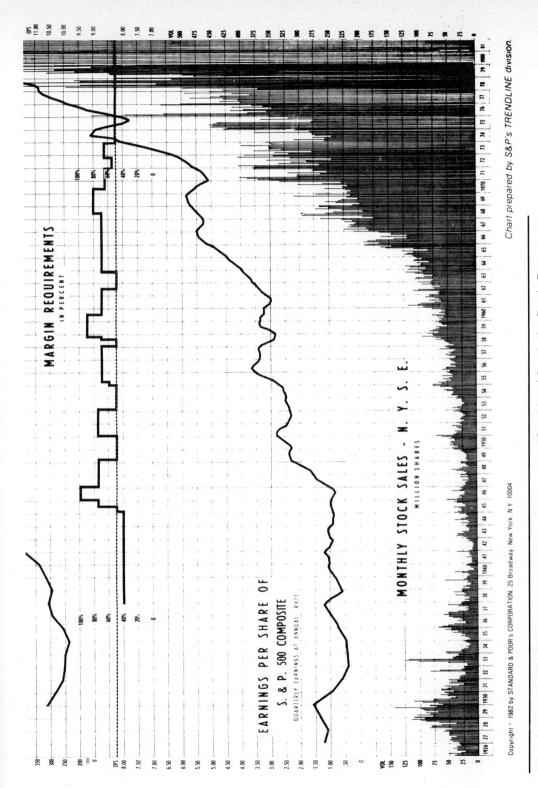

Figure 17–1 Stock market and business history since 1926. (Courtesy of Standard & Poor's Corporation.
This report was up to date at the time of publication; subsequent changes are reflected on current
Standard & Poor's reports.)

Copyright © 1982 by STANDARD & POOR's CORPORATION 25 Broadway New York N Y 10004

Chart prepared by S&P's TRENDLINE division.

The calculation of the commissions by the regular brokerage houses is complex and a table showing them is not possible. However, three variables are taken into account in setting them.

1. The dollar amount of money committed. Commissions decline, as a percent of the money committed, as the latter rises.
2. The number of shares purchased. Commissions per share decline as the number of shares purchased increases.
3. The price of shares. Commissions per share rise as the price of the shares selected declines. This one can offset the first two factors.

Most brokerage houses also have maximum and minimum commissions per 100-share orders. If, for example, you buy 100 shares priced at $50 (commit $5,000), one (typical) broker will charge you $92. If you purchase 200 shares priced at $25 per share (again commit $5,000), the same broker will charge you $112.49; and on 500 shares at $10 you would pay $140.96.

The above discussion applies to round lots of one hundred shares. If lesser amounts (odd lots) are traded, the commissions are calculated the same way, and then an additional odd-lot fee of one-eighth of one dollar ($.125) per share is added. Note that you pay these commissions when you buy as well as when you sell stock.

In recent years discount brokers (also called security discount houses) have sprung up. They charge commissions that are often substantially below those charged by regular brokerage houses. They can do this because they offer no investment advisory services and provide no research reports. They merely execute orders. You can find discount brokers by looking at advertisements in the financial papers. On the purchases discussed above, the commissions charged by a discount broker would often be as low as one-half of those charged by regular brokers.

Buying Odd Lots

On the organized exchange, transactions are usually carried out in round lots that consist of 100 shares. However, small investors would want lesser amounts. There used to be dealers who specialized in odd lots and who would maintain an inventory in stock and buy and sell in any amounts from 1 to 99, but these have passed from the scene. Odd-lot transactions are now carried out directly by some brokers who maintain an inventory of stock and stand willing to trade in any odd-lot amounts. Those (usually smaller) brokers who do not themselves maintain an inventory will fill their customer's odd-lot orders by going to members of the New York Stock Exchange (usually specialists or registered traders) who do carry an inventory and who do deal in odd lots, although this is a minor part of their business. On odd-lot purchases there is still the one-eighth of one dollar ($.125) per share odd lot fee, which is added to the price of stock (subtracted from it if you sell). This is over and above the regular commissions.

Securities Dealers

Securities dealers make a market in a security and buy and sell on their own account. They are not paid a commission but earn their living on the difference between what they pay for a security and what they sell it for. For example, a share of stock may be quoted as having an asked price of $11 and a bid price of $10. This means that the dealer will pay you $10 for the stock share if you wish to sell one; on the other hand, if you desire to purchase a share, you must pay $11. This leaves a spread of $1, out of which the dealers pay their expenses and receive their profits. Because dealers stand ready to buy and sell at all times, they are said to "make a market."

Stocks that are sold through dealers are usually "over-the-counter" securities. While many stock issues are listed on either the New York Exchange or the American Stock Exchange and are bought and sold by a broker acting as an agent, many other issues are not listed. The nonlisted stocks are the so-called over-the-counter stocks and are purchased and sold exclusively by dealers. In the final analysis, a securities dealer is a merchant whose stock in trade consists of stocks and bonds. In most instances, dealers specialize in a few lines of merchandise, that is, they handle only a relatively small number of unlisted stocks.

When an individual desires to purchase some shares of an unlisted stock, he or she contacts a broker. The broker checks the market for the unlisted stock designated. Actually, the broker contacts dealers who are making a market for that particular issue. Then the broker gets in touch with the purchaser to inform him or her of the lowest asked price. If the purchaser still wants the issue, a sale is made.

QUOTING SECURITIES

Almost every daily metropolitan newspaper has a financial page where securities prices are quoted, some of which are more elaborate and complete than others. Most of the more complete financial pages quote the price and the activity of the stocks and bonds *traded* the previous day, but some late evening papers have current day quotations. The emphasis here is on the word *traded*. If a particular security has not been traded, it is not listed. If ABC, Inc. has not been traded, for instance, the price is not given, obviously because no price has been set. In addition to the listed securities, the more complete financial pages carry the bid and asked prices of the over-the-counter securities.

The Listed Stock

Those issues traded the previous day are arranged in alphabetical order on the financial page of the more complete metropolitan newspapers, and appear under this arrangement:

52 weeks

High	Low	Stock	Div.	% yield	P/E ratio	Sales in 100s	High	Low	Close	Net change
129 1/2	73 1/4	IBM	3.80	3.0	16	5707	128 1/8	126 1/2	126 7/8	−1

The third column shows that the stock here is International Business Machines (IBM). Immediately to the left of that the high and low prices of that stock over the past 52 weeks are indicated. Moving now to the right, we will note all the other information the quotation conveys. Under "Div." we see 3.80 indicating that dividends of $3.80 were paid over the past year. The "% yield" column shows 3.0, the dividend yield as a percent of the market price of the stock. However, some earnings were retained by the company and hence the price-earnings ratio of 16 is shown in the next column. Then we see that sales for the day were 570,700 shares; that during the day's trade the stock of IBM fluctuated and reached a high of $128 1/8 per share, a low of $126 1/2; and that it closed at $126 7/8. On the basis of these figures, why was there a net change of −1 of a point? The net change figure is the difference between the closing price for that day and the closing price of the previous day, not the difference between the high and the low on the day in question. Obviously, yesterday's closing price can be either higher or lower than today's closing price. The preceding day's closing price in our example was 127 7/8. Note that stocks advance or decline in steps of one-eighth of one dollar.

Frequently there is a footnote in the quotations, a lower case letter. Footnotes that appear are explained at the bottom of the list of quotations under the heading of explanatory notes. A footnote under the explanatory notes may point out that the corporation is in bankruptcy or in receivership or one of a number of other valuable bits of information.

A portion of the NYSE market quotes for 7/11/83 appears in Table 17–1.

The Dow-Jones Averages

In addition to prices of individual stocks, most financial pages also publish the Dow-Jones Averages, which are supposed to indicate which way the market is going in general. The Dow-Jones Average is really four different averages: one for industrials, one for transportation, one for utilities, and one a composite of the other three. These averages date back to 1896.

The industrial average, based on the stock of thirty industrial companies, is calculated by adding the prices of these thirty stocks and then dividing by thirty. The transportation average with twenty transportation company stocks in it (this formerly included just rails, but now it has some airlines and trucking lines as well) is calculated in the same way, as is also the utility average, which contains the stock of fifteen utilities.

Table 17–1 A portion of the New York Stock Exchange market quotations for July 11, 1983

36 THE WALL STREET JOURNAL
Monday, July 11, 1983

Friday's Volume

79,645,560 Shares; 718,500 Warrants

TRADING BY MARKETS

	Shares	Warrants
New York Exchange	66,520,000	717,900
Midwest Exchange	5,561,600	....
Pacific Exchange	2,730,900	....
Nat'l Assoc. of Securities Dealers ...	2,767,160	600
Philadelphia Exchange	1,370,200	....
Boston Exchange	493,600	....
Cincinnati Exchange	145,300	....
Instinet System	56,800	....

NYSE – Composite

Volume since Jan. 1:	1983	1982	1981
Total shares	13,361,863,807	7,901,714,056	7,286,981,160
Total warrants .	87,172,400	19,911,450	25,933,300

New York Stock Exchange

Volume since Jan. 1:	1983	1982	1981
Total shares	11,476,864,552	6,796,497,086	6,360,424,680
Total warrants .	86,753,000	19,885,100	25,831,800

MOST ACTIVE STOCKS

	Open	High	Low	Close	Chg.	Volume
Chrysler	29⅞	30⅝	29⅛	29½	− ¾	1,250,000
Amer T&T	62½	62¾	62¼	62⅝	+ ⅜	1,126,400
WnAir Lin.........	5⅞	6⅜	5⅞	6⅜	+ ½	1,091,300
PrimeCm s.......	20⅝	20⅞	19⅝	19⅞	− ⅝	885,700
CinnGas El.......	18⅛	18⅜	18	18⅛	− ¼	826,600
Int T&T	44¾	45¼	44⅝	45¼	+1⅝	666,500
Citicorp	37¾	37¾	37⅜	37½	+ ½	660,400
Baker Intl	22⅝	23⅝	22½	23⅛	+ ½	597,000
Amer Can........	42⅝	43⅛	42⅜	43	+ ¼	559,200
EatonCp	43	43⅛	42¾	43	− ¼	532,800
ElPaso Co........	20⅝	20⅝	20	20⅜	− ⅜	510,200
FordMot	54⅜	55	54	55	+1⅛	497,300
Natomas	25	25	24⅝	24¾	− ¼	484,600
StdOilOh	53¼	54	53	53⅜	− ⅛	441,800
DartKraft	64¾	64¾	63⅛	64⅜	− ⅝	437,800

52 Weeks High	Low	Stock	Div.	Yld %	P-E Ratio	Sales 100s	High	low	Close	Net Chg.
		— A—A—A —								
17¾	5¾	AAR	.44	2.5	26	105	17⅝	17⅛	17⅜	− ⅛
37¾	27½	ACF	1.40	4.1	14	54	33⅞	33⅝	33¾	.....
20	12¼	AMF	.50	3.0	..	325	16⅞	16⅝	16⅝	.....
38¼	13¼	AMR Cp		..	..	2754	36⅝	35⅝	35¾	− ¾
24½	4	AMR wt		..	..	371	22½	21⅝	21⅝	− ½
18⅜	12⅞	AMR pf	2.18	12.	..	44	18	17⅞	17⅞	− ⅛
39⅜	24⅞	AMR pf	2.13	5.7	..	26	37⅝	37	37¼	+ ⅛
10½	2½	APL		..	..	67	10½	10¼	10⅜	.....
55	26	ARA	2.05	4.1	14	173	50¾	50¼	50¼	− ¼
79⅞	26	ASA	3a	4.4	..	448	68¾	67¼	68⅛	− ⅜
50	14½	AVX	.32	.8	67	324	41⅞	41⅝	41¾	− ⅛
48¾	27¾	AbtLab	1	2.1	19	622	48⅛	47¼	47⅜	− ⅜
30⅛	25¾	AccoW	n .50	1.8	22	382	28	27⅝	28	+ ⅛
27½	15⅝	AcmeC	.40	1.6	..	2	25	25	25	.....
14⅜	5¾	AcmeE	.32b	2.4	43	25	13¼	13	13¼	.....
19⅞	5½	AdmDg	.04	.2	15	45	18½	18⅛	18¼	+ ¼
17⅞	12½	AdaEx	1.73e	10.	..	64	17¼	17	17	− ¼
15¼	6½	AdmMI	.24	1.7	13	25	14½	14⅛	14⅛	− ⅛
28	12⅝	Advest	s .16	.6	13	71	24⅞	24⅝	24⅝	− ⅛

52 Weeks High	Low	Stock	Div.	Yld %	P-E Ratio	Sales 100s	High	low	Close	Net Chg
28½	18½	BeatFd	1.60	6.0	9	1527	26⅞	26½	26⅞	+ ⅝
52¾	35¾	Beat pf	3.38	6.8	..	8	49⅞	49	49⅞	+1⅛
53½	36	BectnD	1.15	2.5	13	652	45¾	45	45¼	− ¼
10⅛	3⅞	Beker		..	..	59	8½	8½	8½	.....
38¼	17⅛	BelcoPt	.80	2.1	9	48	37¾	37½	37½	− ¼
17	5⅜	BeldnH	.40	2.4	17	35	16⅞	16⅛	16¾	+ ⅜
49⅝	19½	BelHow	.96	2.0	..	104	46⅞	46	46⅞	+ ⅞
22⅞	13¼	BelCd	g2.08	..	..	399	21½	21⅜	21½	.....
39⅛	14	BellInd	.24	.7	25	56	36⅝	35⅝	35⅞	− ¾
40⅛	24⅛	Bemis	1.60	4.3	13	11	37⅝	37¼	37⅝	+ ¾
81½	39¾	Bndx pf	4.04	5.1	..	1	80	80	80	+ ¼
30	15¼	BenfCp	2	7.4	9	80	27¼	26⅞	27	.....
37½	26⅝	Benef pf	4.30	12.	..	24	35½	35	35½	+ ¼
133	74	Benef pf	5.50	4.6	..	z80	120	120	120	−1⅝
22½	15	Benef pf	2.50	13.	..	z100	19⅝	19⅝	19⅝	+ ⅛
11⅞	3	BengtB	.20e	2.3	15	395	8⅞	8¾	8⅞	− ⅛
7¾	3⅜	Berkey		..	93	109	6⅝	6½	6½	− ¼
36⅝	13¾	BestPd	.32	.9	14	710	35⅜	34¾	35⅛	− ⅛
26⅛	14½	BethStl	.60	2.7	..	1224	22⅞	22⅛	22⅛	− ⅝
54⅝	48½	BethSt pf	5	9.9	..	16	50⅞	50⅝	50⅝	− ¼
44¾	12⅞	Bevrly	s .28	.7	30	1481	44¼	41½	42	−2
28	15⅛	BigThr	.72	2.7	15	158	26¾	26	26¼	− ¼
39⅞	29⅜	Binney	1.28	3.2	14	81	u41½	39⅞	40⅛	+ ⅝
24	12	BlackD	.52	2.4	..	264	22⅛	21⅝	21¾	− ¼
19⅞	12	BlkHP	s	..	6	15	18½	18⅛	18⅛	− ⅜
40	15	BlairJ	s .56	1.4	17	134	39½	38⅜	39	+ ⅝
43¾	25¼	BlckHR	2.08	5.1	12	271	41	40¾	41	+ ¼
40	22½	BlueB	1.80	4.8	13	18	37⅛	37⅛	37⅛	.....
48¼	15¼	Boeing	1.40	3.1	14	2055	45½	44⅜	45¼	+ ⅞
47⅜	21½	BoiseC	1.90	4.9	97	2638	39¼	38⅝	38¾	− ¾
58¼	50⅝	BoiseC pf	5	9.4	..	216	53	52¾	53	.....
60⅝	29½	Borden	2.44	4.1	10	212	60⅜	59⅜	59½	− ⅝
55⅜	22⅝	BorgWa	1.52	3.1	13	431	49¼	48⅝	49⅛	+ ⅜
13¼	4	Bormns		..	6	64	9⅛	8⅞	9	− ⅛
28¾	21	BosEd	2.88	10.	8	44	27⅝	27⅜	27½	+ ⅛
10⅛	8¼	BosE pr	1.17	12.	..	11	9⅝	9⅝	9⅝	− ⅛
12¾	9¾	BosE pr	1.46	12.	..	10	11⅞	11¾	11⅞	+ ⅛
37¼	23⅞	BrigSt	1.36a	4.3	16	218	32	31¼	31½	− ¾
41½	26¾	BristM	s1.20	3.0	15	711	40⅜	39⅞	40	.....
86½	57¼	BrstM pf	2	2.4	..	2	83¾	83¾	83¾	− ½
27⅛	17½	BritPt	1.55e	6.3	10	43	25¼	24½	24⅝	−1⅛
14½	7½	Brock	.10	1.1	23	292	9	8⅞	8⅞	− ¼
19½	13¼	Brckwy	1.32	7.2	9	17	18⅝	18⅜	18⅜	− ⅛
31½	24	BkyUG	2.90	10.	6	52	29¼	29	29⅛	.....
23¼	17⅜	BkUG pf	2.47	11.	..	8	23¼	23	23¼	+ ½
19⅞	9¾	BwnSh	.20	1.2	..	40	16½	16⅜	16⅜	.....
39⅞	16⅜	BwnGp	s1.10	2.9	13	543	38¼	37¾	38	.....
47⅝	16¼	BrwnF	s .80	1.8	20	503	43¾	42¾	43¾	+ ¾
44¼	19	Brnswk	1	2.6	..	365	39¼	38¾	38¾	− ¼
65⅜	34¼	Brnsk pf	2.40	3.6	..	4	u67	67	67	+1⅝
55	23¾	BrshW	s .80	1.6	25	171	50⅜	49¾	49¾	− ¼
17	10¼	BucyEr	.44	2.7	16	2068	16⅝	16⅛	16½	.....
20½	7¼	Bundy	.60	3.1	18	19	19¾	19½	19½	+ ¼
18⅝	14⅞	BunkrH	2.16	12.	..	14	17¾	17⅜	17⅝	+ ⅜
40¼	17	BurlInd	1.52	3.9	24	318	39	38⅝	38⅞	− ⅛
91½	34¼	BrlNth	1.80	2.1	15	893	86½	85⅝	86	+ ¾
6¾	4⅞	BrlNo pf	.55	9.0	..	2	6¼	6⅛	6⅛	.....
21⅛	16¾	BrlN pf	2.13	10.	..	3	21	21	21	+ ⅛
26½	15⅝	Burndy	.76	3.1	24	44	24⅝	24¼	24½	+ ⅛
57⅝	29⅝	Burrgh	2.60	4.9	25	735	54⅜	53⅜	53½	− ½
24⅛	9	Butlrln	.52	2.2	20	204	u24¼	23¾	24	+ ⅛
12	7½	Buttes		..	14	498	12	11¼	11⅞	+ ¼
		— C—C—C —								
42⅞	26	CBI In	1.40a	3.9	8	115	37	36¼	36¼	− ¾
77⅝	36	CBS	2.80	4.3	16	508	65⅞	65	65½	− ⅜
52¾	25½	CBS pf	1	2.2	..	6	46	46	46	+1
9⅝	3½	CCX		..	..	467	9½	8½	9⅜	+ ¾
51½	31	CIGNA	2.48	5.1	7	419	48⅝	48⅛	48½	+ ¼
30½	21⅛	CIG pf	2.75	9.4	..	38	29½	29⅛	29¼	− ¼
12⅝	6¾	CLC		..	..	19	11	10¾	10¾	.....
22¾	12½	CNA Fn		..	15	64	21¼	21	21	− ¼
11	8½	CNAI	1.20a	11.	..	69	10⅝	10½	10⅝	+ ⅛
44⅞	29⅜	CPC Int	2.20	5.8	8	237	38	37⅝	37¾	− ¼
43	22⅝	CP Nat	2.44	6.3	9	21	39	38¾	38¾	− ⅜
73	36¼	CSX	3.12	4.6	10	681	67⅞	67⅛	67⅞	+1⅞
57¾	22	CTS	1	2.0	24	205	51⅜	50	50⅛	−1

Source: Reprinted by permission of *The Wall Street Journal,* © Dow Jones & Company, Inc., 1983. All rights reserved.

There are a number of criticisms of the Dow-Jones Averages, especially of the industrial average. First, it is argued that thirty stocks are not a large enough sample. Second, all of the stocks in the Dow-Jones Averages are blue chips such as General Motors, General Electric, Exxon, Du Pont, and American Telephone; such stocks as these, it is argued, are not representative of the market as a whole. Finally, the Dow-Jones Averages are only crudely adjusted for splits. Over the years many of the stocks have been split a number of times; moreover, not all of the thirty have been split the same amounts. Those companies that have never split their stock or have split it less have a greater weight in the averages than the others. The statistical formula used by the Dow-Jones publishing company to correct this has only partially done so.

The Dow-Jones industrial stock price averages are shown in Figure 17-2. The bar graph going back several months shows the high, low, and close for the day. There is also a market diary that indicates the number of issues traded,

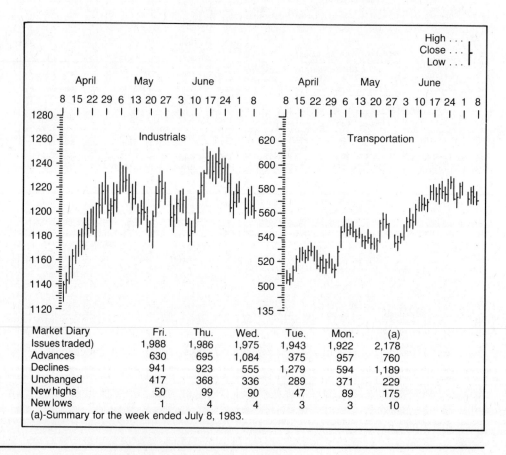

Market Diary	Fri.	Thu.	Wed.	Tue.	Mon.	(a)
Issues traded)	1,988	1,986	1,975	1,943	1,922	2,178
Advances	630	695	1,084	375	957	760
Declines	941	923	555	1,279	594	1,189
Unchanged	417	368	336	289	371	229
New highs	50	99	90	47	89	175
New lows	1	4	4	3	3	10

(a)-Summary for the week ended July 8, 1983.

Figure 17–2   The Dow-Jones averages—industrials and transportation. (Reprinted by permission of *The Wall Street Journal*, © Dow Jones & Company, Inc., 1983. All rights reserved.)

the number that advanced, the number that declined, and the number that remained the same.

Other Stock Market Indicators

There are a number of other indicators that attempt to show which way the market is going. These indicators, however, use index number devices (see Chapter 1). These index numbers measure movements in stock prices much like the cost of living was measured in Chapter 1. The best-known such stock indices are the Standard and Poor's and the New York Stock Exchange composite index of all common stocks that are traded on the New York Stock Exchange each day. About 1,800 stocks are listed, but a few are not traded each day. Therefore the number of stocks in the index varies from day to day but usually is close to 1,800. The New York Stock Exchange index was started in 1966, which is the base year; the prices of all stocks traded on a given day are added up on a computer, and then the figure is compared to the base year figure. The New York Stock Exchange also has an index for industrials, consisting of 1,000 stocks; one for utilities, which includes 136 stocks; one for transportation, made up of 76 stocks; and one for the stocks of 75 financial institutions of various kinds.

The Standard and Poor's index uses the average stock prices from 1941 to 1943 as the base year and that figure has been set to 10. The current figure, then, shows the increase since then. The Standard and Poor's index includes four hundred stocks in the industrial index, twenty stocks in the transportation industry, forty in the utility index, forty in the financial index, and a composite of all five hundred of these stocks. Both the Standard and Poor's and the New York Stock Exchange indices are considered more reliable indicators of which way the market in general is moving than the Dow-Jones Averages because they include more stocks. Table 17–2 shows the New York Stock Exchange and the Standard and Poor's indicator for July 11, 1983, and the same figure for a year earlier. Figure 17–3 shows the movement of the Standard and Poor's indicators over the past few years.

Bull and Bear Markets

Bull and bear markets are technical terms to indicate which way the market in general is going. If the market rises far enough and long enough, it is referred to as a bull market. If it falls far enough and long enough, it is referred to as a bear market. The stock averages discussed above are the tests used to determine whether the market is bullish or bearish. If the market just bounces around and moves up and down a bit from day to day, it is neither bearish nor bullish. To have a bull or bear market there must be a trend. The investors who buy heavily because they believe the market will rise in the future are called bulls. Those who are selling because they believe a decline is coming are called bears. And

Table 17–2   Market indicators other than the Dow-Jones averages and trading
activity July 11, 1983

	1983	Change		1982
N.Y.S.E. Composite	96.89	−0.31	−0.32%	62.54
Industrial	113.57	−0.43	−0.38%	71.06
Utility	46.29	...	%	37.05
Transp.	92.97	−0.42	−0.45%	53.92
Financial	99.42	−0.15	0.15%	61.05
Am. Ex. Mkt Val Index	245.72	−1.19	−0.48%	124.25
Nasdaq OTC Composite	319.57	−0.46	−0.14%	168.07
Industrial	393.93	−0.50	−0.13%	192.57
Insurance	267.93	−0.86	−0.32%	169.01
Banks	189.75	+0.37	+0.20%	128.96
Standard & Poor's 500	167.08	−0.48	−0.29%	108.83
400 Industrial	188.67	−0.61	−0.32%	121.76
Value Line Index	204.55	−0.62	−0.30%	120.61
Wilshire 5000 Equity	1,785.697	−5.209	−0.29%	1,104.077

Market value, in billions of dollars, on N.Y.S.E., Amex and actively traded OTC issues.
Volume of advancing stocks on N.Y.S.E., 21,289,600 shares; volume of declining stocks, 36,686,600. On American S.E., volume of advancing stocks, 2,882,700; volume of declining stocks, 3,993,300. Nasdaq volume of advancing stocks, 19,698,000; volume of declining stocks, 18,265,800.
Source: The Wall Street Journal, July 11, 1983. Reprinted by permission of *The Wall Street Journal,* © Dow Jones & Company, Inc., 1983. All rights reserved.

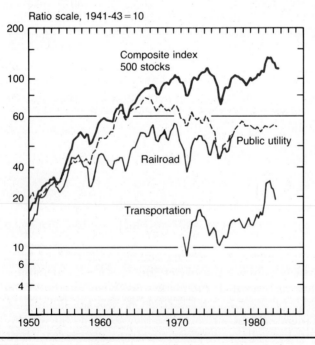

Figure 17–3   **Stock price indices.** (*Source: Federal Reserve Chart Book, May 1982,* Board of Governors of the Federal Reserve System, p. 92.)

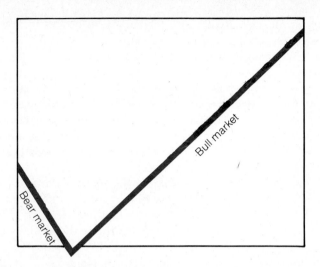

Figure 17–4 Ups and downs of the market

if the bulls outnumber the bears, the market will rise. If the reverse is the case, it will fall. (Figure 17–4 is a diagram of a bull and bear market.)

Quoting Over-the-Counter Stocks

Some people have the idea that if a stock is not listed and consequently is traded over the counter, there must be something wrong with it. This is just not true. Many over-the-counter stocks are as good as and frequently better than some of the securities listed on the organized exchanges. There are, however, some securities that do not qualify for listing, and these over-the-counter stocks are more risky.[1]

The over-the-counter prices are quoted by bid and asked prices. For example,

Stock & div.	Sales in 100's	Bid	Asked	Net chg.
Justin Ind.	32	19	19 1/4	—

In this case the stock is Justin Industries, a manufacturer of building materials; it pays no dividend; 3,200 shares changed hands on the day in question; the bid and asked prices were 19 and 19 1/4 respectively. The net change has to do with the change from the previous quotation. In this case there was no change.

1. In order to be listed, the firm must be of a certain size as measured by assets. It must also have a minimum number of common stocks outstanding and a minimum number of stockholders. And it must be willing to publish certain basic financial facts about itself. Some firms that qualify for listing prefer to remain unlisted.

This means in most cases that an individual who desires to sell a share of stock will receive $19 per share, less brokerage fees. An individual who desires to purchase the stock must, in most cases, pay $19 1/4 per share plus brokerage fees.

I say "in most cases," because these quotations are the current market quotations at which some dealer is willing to execute. But in the over-the-counter market your broker may wish to haggle and may make a counteroffer to buy at below the asked price, which may be accepted by one of several dealers who make a market in the stock in question. Moreover, the quoted bid and asked prices shown above are generally the lowest asked price and the highest bid price, and they may be those of two different dealers. In addition, the bid and asked prices are both subject to change without notice. However, all dealers have their own bid and asked prices at which they stand ready either to buy or to sell. The difference between the two figures is the dealers' spread and represents their profit margins. Dealers, as noted, are individuals or firms who buy and sell on their own accounts and may actively make a market in a number of stocks. The "Net Chg." merely indicates in which direction the last bid has moved and by how much. Often there is no entry in this column, which merely means that the bid price has not changed since the previous day. Commissions on over-the-counter securities are, generally speaking, the same as those on the listed securities.

Corporate Bonds Quotations

Corporate bonds are frequently listed on both the New York and the American exchanges. Those that are not so listed are traded over the counter. Bond quotations are not printed on the financial pages of all daily newspapers but may be found in financial papers such as *The Wall Street Journal*.

The quotations for bonds traded on the exchange are listed in alphabetical order. After the name of the company there appears the nominal coupon rate of interest paid per $1,000, which is the face value of the corporate bonds, and the maturity date. We will use as an example ATT (American Telephone and Telegraph). They have a number of different issues outstanding but one reads as follows:

Bonds	Cur. yield	Vol.	High	Low	Close	Net change
Att 8 5/8 07	11	100	77 1/4	76 1/2	77	− 1/4

The coupon rate of 8 5/8 percent ($86.25 per $1,000 bond) will be paid until the year 2007 when the bond matures. The current yield of 11 percent is shown next, then the sales volume, in thousands of dollars, followed by the high and low and closing price for the day, and finally the net change in the closing price from the previous day (note that the coupon rate of 8 5/8 provides a yield of 11 percent because the bond is selling at $770).

Corporate bonds always have a face value of $1,000, but the newspaper quotations drop the last digit. A quotation of under 100 means that the bond is selling at a discount, while over 100 indicates it is at a premium.

The closing price of the bond quoted above was 77. This indicates that it was selling at $770 and since this is at a discount of $230, the actual yield is 11 as shown and is above the 8 5/8 coupon rate. The easy way to get the market price of a bond is to convert the stock market page quote to decimals and then multiply by 10. For example, a quote of 84 3/8 would become $84.375 × 10 = $843.75.

The person buying corporate bonds must also pay brokerage commissions. These commissions also vary from broker to broker, but generally they are a certain percentage of the money committed together with a fixed fee. This percentage declines as the amount of money involved rises. In addition to the percentage fee, there is a flat per-bond fee which varies from $5 to $10. Where the fee is fixed within the $5 to $10 range is determined by the number of bonds purchased and the length of time to maturity, declining with the number of bonds bought and rising with the length of time to maturity.

Treasury Bond Quotations

Marketable United States Treasury bonds are quoted differently from corporate bonds. First, they are priced in thirty-seconds of a dollar. Second, there are bid and asked prices because they are all sold over the counter. Thus the following quotation means that this is a United States bond issue carrying a 9 1/4 percent coupon interest rate; it will mature in May, 1989. At the close of the trading day, the bid price was 91.12. Actually, 91.12 means 91 and 12/32 or $91.37. Since Treasury bonds are sold in units of $1,000, $91.37 × 10 = $913.70, the bid price. The asked price of 91.16 means 91 16/32 or $91.50 × 10 = $915.00. The bid change of −1.18 means that the price has gone down by 1 and 18/32 or about $1.56 since the previous day. At the current price the yield or return is 10.69 percent interest.

Rate	Mat.	Date	Bid	Asked	Bid. Chg.	Yield
9 1/4	1989	May	91.12	91.16	−1.18	10.69

BUYING AND SELLING SECURITIES

Securities can be purchased for cash or they can be purchased with borrowed funds, that is, on margin.

Cash Sales

In a cash sale when the transaction is completed, a bill is sent to the purchaser, who has five business days in which to pay for the stock. When selling, the seller also has five days in which to deliver the securities. The purchaser may actually take physical possession of the stock or he or she may instruct the broker to hold the stock for him or her in the purchaser's account. This is referred to as keeping in the street name and is discussed below.

Margin Purchases

Margin purchases are made with funds that are partly borrowed. The word *margin* refers to the percentage of the buyer's own funds needed to buy stock; the remainder may be borrowed from a broker. For example, if a share of stock is priced at $100 and the margin requirement is 75 percent, the purchaser must have that in cash, and may borrow no more than $25. Currently margin requirements are 50 percent; consequently, one half of the money for stock purchases may be borrowed. The Federal Reserve System sets margin requirements, and they have been as high as 100 percent in the past (no borrowed money may be used). The Federal Reserve raises margin requirements if it is believed there is excessive speculation in securities. If the market (and the economy in general) is in the doldrums, the Federal Reserve may lower margin requirements, thus making it easier for investors to enter the market with borrowed funds. This in turn, it is hoped, would increase the demand for stock and also create an environment more favorable to overall economic activity.

An investor has an incentive to buy on margin only if he or she feels the price of securities will rise by more than the interest cost of the loan. A problem could arise if the investor on margin is wrong and the market declines. Then the margin could be wiped out and the investor would have to cover. This works as follows: the rules require that the market price of the stock must be at least equal to the borrowed funds. In the case of a stock selling at $100 purchased with a 50 percent margin requirement, there would be no problem until and if the market price declined below $50. But if the price declined to $45, the borrowed funds ($50) would be $5 more than the market value of the stock. The investor would be called by the broker to "cover"; that is, come up with $5 more of his or her own funds (then the market price $45 is again equal to the loan). Today with relatively high margin, the market would have to come down a good deal before an investor would have to cover. However, in former days when margins were often much lower (sometimes only 10 percent) this was sometimes a problem. For example, a $100 stock would only have to decline below $90 before a 10 percent margin was wiped out and the broker would call for the investor to cover. If he or she could not, the stock would be sold. In those days during a declining market the inability of many margin investors to cover resulted in their stock being sold. This contributed further to the decline. This is another reason why relatively high margins are required today.

Short Sales

Short sales are the opposite of margin purchase. The investor has an incentive to sell short only if he or she believes the price of a stock will decline. When selling short the investor sells stock he or she does not own. Rather the stock is borrowed from a broker (stock can be borrowed just like money) and sold at its current price in the market. For example, if a stock is selling at $100 per share, you can borrow it from your broker and sell it. Then if, sometime later, its price declines to $80, you can buy it in the open market (from the same broker you borrowed it from), repay it, and pocket a profit of $20 less brokerage fees. You are also required to make up any dividend which was missed while you held a short position in the broker's stock. Selling short, then, is a speculative technique that enables persons to make a profit if they correctly forecast that the price of the security they purchased will decline. If those who have taken a short position are wrong and the security rises in price, they lose money.

Since both buying on margin and selling short are engaging in speculation, it is not recommended for the small investor, especially one who is a relative newcomer to security investments.

Types of Orders

There are a number of types of orders either to buy or to sell that an individual might place with a broker. These are the following:

1. Conditional buy order. An order to buy a certain number of shares under certain specific conditions. For example, you might order your broker to buy one hundred shares of ABC if the price declines from its present level of $50 to $45.
2. Conditional sell order. An order to sell a certain number of shares of a specific security under specific conditions, for example, if the stock rises to a certain level.
3. Market order. Either a buy or a sell order of a specific number of shares of a specific security at the current market price. It is left to the broker to obtain the best price possible for the client if it is an over-the-counter security and hence subject to haggling pricewise.
4. Good-till-canceled order. A type of order continuing in force until it is either executed or canceled. This applies to conditional orders. A new order at a different price cancels the former order if made by the same customer.

5. Stop order. An order to buy or sell conditioned upon a specific price. Frequently it is used as a selling device in order to prevent losses or as an attempt to ensure a profit. For example, an individual may have purchased at $10 a share of stock he believes will rise to about $15, and he puts in a stop order at $15. The stock will automatically be sold at $15. Or a person may have purchased a stock at $10 and it may have risen to $20. The purchaser may have reason to believe that it will advance even higher, but for protection in the event of a downward movement, he or she may place a stop order at $15. Thus if the stock does go down to $15 per share, the order will be executed immediately. This is sometimes called a stop loss order because it prevents the stock from falling below a certain price.

DISTRIBUTION OF EARNINGS FROM STOCKS

There are a number of reasons why people own common stock: capital gains, hedging inflation, and dividend income. Figure 17–5 illustrates how dividends, earnings, and stock prices have risen over the years. There are both cash dividends and stock dividends.

Cash Dividends

Dividends must be paid out of corporate earnings. The percentage of earnings distributed varies from company to company, but generally runs from 40 to 80 percent. However, in some cases cash dividends are zero; the corporation retains its entire earnings. Dividends do not have to be paid; rather they are declared at the discretion of the board of directors of the company. Most states have laws providing that dividends may be paid only out of current or past earnings. They may not be given out of paid-in capital.

1. *The declaration date and the announcement date.* The day the board of directors meets and declares a dividend is the declaration date. The day this declaration is announced to the press is the announcement date. Often these two dates may be the same, but sometimes the public announcement may be delayed a few days. Firms listed on the NYSE are required to send prompt notices of dividend declarations to the Exchange.

2. *The record date.* This is the date that the corporation counts heads to determine who owns how much stock. The NYSE rules require that the record date be at least ten days later than the announcement date. Owners as of this date, according to the corporation's records, will receive the dividends.

3. *The exdividend date.* The exdividend date is the first day that the purchaser of a stock does not receive the dividend that has been declared on it. Thus

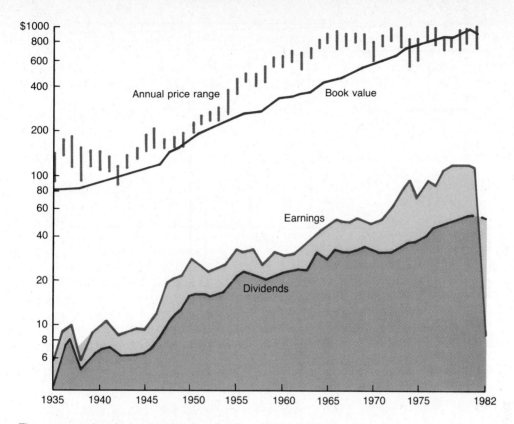

The accompanying chart and tables show that from 1935 to 1982, Dow-Jones Industrial Average:
- Dividends have increased +1,090%.
- Book values have increased +1,070%.
- Stock prices have increased 626% from the 1935 year-end to December 31, 1982.

Figure 17–5 Forty-seven-year performance of the Dow-Jones industrial average, 1935–1982. (*Source:* Johnson's Charts, Inc.)

when it is said that a stock is exdividend, it is being sold without the dividend. This is five business days before the record date, because the rules of the New York Stock Exchange allow five days in which to deliver stock one has sold or five days to pay for stock one has bought. The price of a stock often drops by the amount of the dividend when it goes exdividend.

4. *The payment date.* This is the date the dividends are actually paid. Established corporations with a good record of earning and a pattern of dividend payments usually pay dividends quarterly. The dividend checks are mailed to the stockholders of record by the trustee (usually a trust department of a bank) who keeps the stockholder records for the corporation. Figure 17–6 calendars these important dates.

SUNDAY	MONDAY	TUESDAY	WEDNESDAY	THURSDAY	FRIDAY	SATURDAY
			1	2	3 ABC Corp. met and declared dividend	4
5	6	7 ABC Corp. announced a dividend to be paid Sept. 30 to stockholders of record Sept. 22	8	9	10	11
12	13	14	15	16 Ex-dividend Date	17	18
19	20	21	22	23 Record Date	24	25
26	27	28	29	30 Payment Date		

Figure 17—6   Dividend dates calendar

Stock Dividends

Directors may avoid a cash distribution by using a stock dividend. For example, a 10 percent stock dividend would result in each stockholder receiving from the company one additional share for every ten shares currently held. If fractional shares are issued because the stockholder's holdings are not evenly divisible by ten, provisions are usually made for stockholders to buy (or sell) fractional shares from the corporation so they can come out even. While increasing the number of ownership shares, this policy leaves the owner with the same equity as formerly held in the corporation. Although theoretically such a device should cause a decline in the market because it has increased the supply of the stock, occasionally the reverse is true because it may cause more interest in that particular stock and thus create more demand for it.

INVESTMENT STRATEGIES; TIMING OF INVESTMENT DECISIONS, OR WHEN TO BUY WHAT

When it comes to making investment decisions, you have to decide not only what to buy, but when to buy. The importance of timing and the selection of securities is illustrated by the following example of what "might have been." Say you had invested $1,000 in Crown Cork in January, 1949. You held it until January, 1957, then sold it and bought Boeing with the proceeds, held Boeing until January, 1961, and then converted to Brunswick, which in turn was liquidated in December, 1969. How much money would you have? Exactly $145, a big loss over the years. By late in 1973 this would have declined further to $104. Now assume you bought the same securities but in a different order. First, you invest $1,000 in Boeing in January, 1949. Second, sell Boeing in January, 1957, and use the proceeds to acquire Brunswick. Third, sell Brunswick in January, 1961, and acquire Crown Cork. By December, 1969, your investment would have reached $2,607,210. Then you should have switched to bonds and preserved your capital and you could have been earning about 8 percent or more on it. However, had you continued to hold Crown Cork, by mid 1977, your $2,607,210 would have declined to about $750,000. "What the Lord giveth the Lord taketh away." Moreover, if you switched to long-term bonds in 1969 or 1970, you should have unloaded them in about 1976 and moved into short-term debt obligations like Treasury bills or commercial paper. You could have ridden up the rise in interest rate to its all-time high without a capital loss. Then in early 1982, you should have switched to long-term bonds when interest rates were at their peak. You would have enjoyed a nice capital gain as they declined. In late summer of 1982—back into common stock. If you had done that, you would be a very wealthy person today. What to do today? That depends on your appraisal of the future. If you think interest rates will remain where they are or go lower and the economy is going to recover, stay in stock. If you think the economy will not recover and that interest rates will rise again in the near future, move into short-term obligations. This is easy to say but hard to do because we are not sure what the future holds. Nevertheless, there are some techniques that will help you to decide when to buy what as well as what to buy. We will examine some of these below.

Defining Your Investment Objectives

First you must decide on your investment objectives such as growth, income, or any of the others discussed in Chapter 15. After you have made a choice you must identify the growth (or income) industries. Any competent brokerage house can help you do this. All industries' past records and future prospects are studied and analyzed periodically. Your broker will have these industry studies. If an industry has a good growth record, its management has proven itself, and its product is such that the demand for it will likely remain high or even rise, you have a growth area. Next you must compare the various growth industries and appraise their relative prospects for future growth. Some may be closer to maturity (end of growth) than others. Finally, after you have selected the industry (or industries), you must pick the firms within that industry that offer the best buys. This again necessitates a comparative appraisal of future prospects based in part on past records. The studies made by the investment services will often indicate which firm within an industry is the better buy, according to their view. They also sometimes list stocks in various industries in accordance with which seem best for income, appreciation, good quality, and speculative features. Figure 17–7 shows price variations of New York Stock Exchange–listed stocks without identifying them. Figure 17–8 illustrates the past performance of the stock of 65 different industries during the past ten years. The variation is remarkable.

If your goal is income rather than growth, follow the same procedure: selection of income industries, then comparative appraisal within the industry to identify the better buys, using industry studies and any other reliable information you or your broker can obtain. You will not always be right. But if you do your research carefully and make your decisions intelligently, you should be right more often than wrong.

If you wish to invest in stocks that swing more with the business cycle, your broker can help you select such stock. Steel and autos are good examples. Again you must make the industry and firm analysis. All stocks swing with the business cycle, but some swing more than others.

Diversification

After you have chosen your investment objectives, the watchword is "diversification"; indeed, you might want to diversify your objectives by choosing several, not

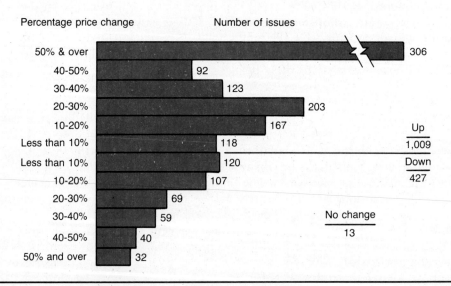

Figure 17–7   Percentage price changes of 1,449 New York Stock Exchange common issues in year ended December 31, 1982. (*Source: New York Stock Exchange 1983 Fact Book*, New York Stock Exchange, Inc., p. 25.)

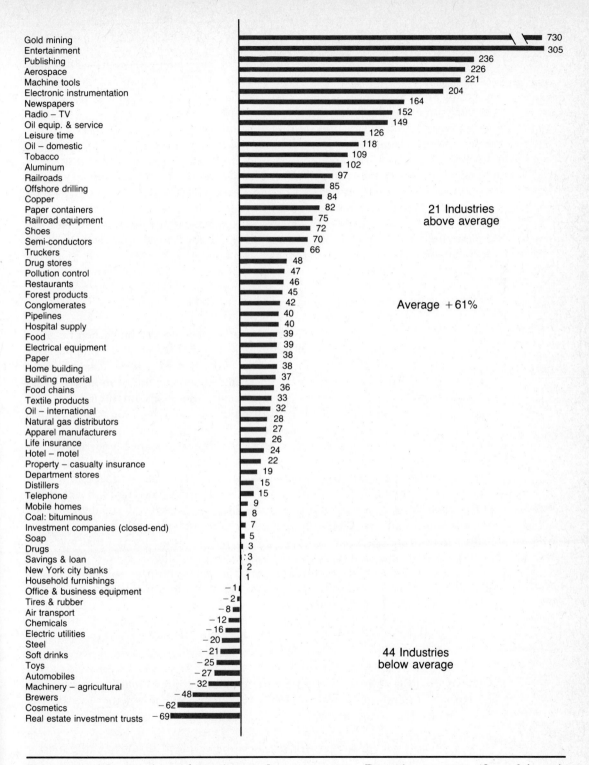

Industry	Value
Gold mining	730
Entertainment	305
Publishing	236
Aerospace	226
Machine tools	221
Electronic instrumentation	204
Newspapers	164
Radio – TV	152
Oil equip. & service	149
Leisure time	126
Oil – domestic	118
Tobacco	109
Aluminum	102
Railroads	97
Offshore drilling	85
Copper	84
Paper containers	82
Railroad equipment	75
Shoes	72
Semi-conductors	70
Truckers	66
Drug stores	48
Pollution control	47
Restaurants	46
Forest products	45
Conglomerates	42
Pipelines	40
Hospital supply	40
Food	39
Electrical equipment	39
Paper	38
Home building	38
Building material	37
Food chains	36
Textile products	33
Oil – international	32
Natural gas distributors	28
Apparel manufacturers	27
Life insurance	26
Hotel – motel	24
Property – casualty insurance	22
Department stores	19
Distillers	15
Telephone	15
Mobile homes	9
Coal: bituminous	8
Investment companies (closed-end)	7
Soap	5
Drugs	3
Savings & loan	3
New York city banks	2
Household furnishings	1
Office & business equipment	−1
Tires & rubber	−2
Air transport	−8
Chemicals	−12
Electric utilities	−16
Steel	−20
Soft drinks	−21
Toys	−25
Automobiles	−27
Machinery – agricultural	−32
Brewers	−48
Cosmetics	−62
Real estate investment trusts	−69

21 Industries above average

Average +61%

44 Industries below average

Figure 17–8   Stocks of sixty-five industries, January 1, 1973—December 31, 1982. (*Source:* Johnson's Charts, Inc.)

just one. Diversification—not putting all of your eggs in one basket—will reduce your risk. This is more difficult for a small investor to do than a large one. But diversification is a relative term and even a small investor should be able to obtain some by firm, by industry, by type of security, and by investment objectives. If you decide to buy oil company stock, pick two or three or even four different companies; pick the ones you feel are the best in light of the history of the industry and firm analyses. Also, diversify by buying stock of firms in different industries. You might also diversify by different types of securities, say, bonds and stock. Finally, give some thought to diversifying by investment objective; that is, some investments for growth, some for income, some for stability, and so on. Diversification reduces risk by broadening your investment base. If you broaden your base and are careful, your securities will include some that will fare better than average.

Investing with Cyclical Swings

This involves an analysis of business conditions. You should buy when business conditions are improving and sell when the economy seems to be slipping into a recession. You must decide what to buy and when to buy it. You can get a general feel for business conditions by following economic indicators and business statistics (discussed in Chapter 15), but making decisions on timing involves economic forecasting, and that is hard. Among the economic indicators to watch to get a clue on which way the economy is moving, is the stock market price level itself. Since the stock market is a lead indicator, when you decide the economy is finally moving strongly in one direction or the other, the stock market has already adjusted, at least in part, to take this into account. It is perhaps too late to benefit. On the other hand, while you may not get in on the ground floor, you may still benefit because the market will usually continue to move in its general direction. This is nebulous advice, but the best there is with regard to timing to benefit from cyclical swings. It is apparent that investing with cyclical swings is not for the small investor or for the newcomer to security investment. However, if you are a seasoned investor and have substantial assets and are of a special brave breed, you may wish to allocate a modest portion of your portfolio to cyclical stock.

Specific Security Analysis

Security analysis consists of examining yield and earnings, making an appraisal of expected future growth in these items, and then deciding whether the security is a candidate for acquisition.

1. *Yield analysis.* Yield, you will recall, is the dividend divided by the market price of the stock. A person may operate under the rule of thumb that

when the yield on a security reaches 8 or 9 percent it becomes a candidate for acquisition. Conversely, when the yield declines to less than say 6 percent it becomes a candidate for liquidation. This yield analysis has been given more weight recently because the American investor has become more yield-conscious in recent years. Examining yield also forces the investor to compare the yield on stock with that of alternative investments. Yield is more applicable if your objective is to acquire income stock.

2. *Price-earnings ratio.* Earnings are total earnings (or profits) after taxes per year. Dividing through, we get earnings per share. For example,

$$\frac{\text{total after tax earnings}}{\text{total number of shares outstanding}} = \frac{\$7,500,000}{1,000,000 \text{ shares}} = \$7.50/\text{share}$$

In most cases, part of this $7.50 is paid out in the form of dividends and part is retained and plowed back into the corporation for expansion. However, the entire $7.50 belongs to the stockholder, and that portion retained will increase the book value and hopefully the market value of the stock. A comparison of earnings with the market price of a given share is an important analytical tool and might be a factor in determining whether or not you buy a given stock. Let's assume our stock above earning $7.50 per share is selling at $50. We now may calculate its price-earnings ratio (PER).

$$\frac{\text{market price}}{\text{earnings per share}} = \frac{\$50}{\$7.50} = 6.66$$

Other stock will have different price-earnings ratios. Generally growth stock will have a higher PER than income stock. To determine whether a given stock is a candidate for purchase, examine its P/E ratio and also how its earnings per share have grown over the years. If its earnings per share have grown at the rate of 10 percent per year and if you believe that rate of growth will continue into the future, you can project its earnings into the future. If $7.50 is compounded at 10 percent for 5 years, earnings per share in 5 years should be about $12.08. If a PER of 6.6 seems valid, then in 5 years a P/E ratio of 6.66 would put the market price of the stock at about $80. This would provide a nice capital gain. You must now also look at how large a dividend this stock is paying, and compare the expected future dividends as well as expected future price appreciation, with alternative stock. This is one way of seeking out good common stock investments. Compare various price-earnings ratios, project future earnings, look at dividends, and locate stocks that are underpriced in today's market and have good growth prospects.

Formula Timing

Formula timing is the use of some predetermined signal or combination of signals to tell the buyer what to do. One of the more elementary methods of formula timing makes use of the price-earnings ratio, or yield analysis. A given price-earnings ratio is a buy signal and another is a sell signal. The investors may regard a selling price of ten to fifteen times earnings as the norm. If the stock is selling at less than ten times earnings, it is usually regarded as cheap and should be bought. If a stock is selling at more than fifteen times earnings, investors regard the price as inflated, and it should be sold. You would not buy indiscriminately within these P/E ratios, but rather selectively from certain stocks which become candidates when these ratios are achieved. The buy and sell limits would obviously be higher if you were buying growth rather than income securities. Nevertheless, this method will give you clues as to what to buy and when.

More elaborate formula timing plans have been developed for the investor with a large portfolio. Such a portfolio would be divided between stocks and bonds, and some ratio between the two would be selected to begin with, at whatever level stock prices were at that time. Let us assume we begin by having 50 percent of our assets in bonds and 50 percent in stocks, and our formula is tied to some average such as the Dow-Jones industrial stock average. When the price of stocks declines by a given amount—say 25 percent—the investor sells bonds and buys stocks to restore the 50/50 ratio. If stock prices rise by a predetermined amount, the investor sells stocks, takes the capital gain, and buys bonds to keep the market price ratio 50/50. Much more complicated formula timing plans have been developed, but the basic idea is the same. Plans that are split between bonds and stock in the manner described above answer only the question of timing. They do not tell us what to buy, and judgment has to be used. Moreover, while they are workable for the large investor, they are not as feasible for the small investor.

Another variation of formula timing calls for a gradual liquidation or acquisition of a given security once the formula has given the signal. For example, a person who has decided to sell a stock because the price-earnings ratio is too high might decide to liquidate one-tenth of his or her holdings per month until they are gone. The same is true of acquisitions. The investor phases into the market cautiously to test the validity of the formula.

Dollar Averaging

Dollar averaging, or more strictly speaking "dollar cost averaging," consists of purchasing a particular stock with a constant number of dollars at uniform intervals. The result is that the stock is fluctuating and the investor is purchasing more shares when it is depressed than when it is inflated. For example, $500 will purchase twelve shares when the market is down and eight when it is up. The investor is purchasing more than half of the shares at a favorable price, and in the long run the law of averages will work for the investor. Table 17–3 is an example of dollar averaging. The average cost is $400 divided by 39 or about $10.25 per share.

Table 17–3   Dollar averaging

Period of purchase	Amount	Price per share	Number of shares
1	$100	$10	10
2	$100	$ 5	20
3	$100	$20	5
4	$100	$25	4
	$400		39

The real difficulty with dollar cost averaging is that it assumes the investor will be able to have at hand a constant flow of dollars to invest over a given time period. In addition, there is the problem of bad timing or bad luck; the investor might happen to invest each time at the top of the market. In addition, it must be admitted that there is a certain psychological block in investing as the market is dropping.

Random Selection; The Random Walk

Recently, a school of thought has developed which suggests that a random selection of common stock may result in as fine a portfolio as will elaborate analysis. This view holds that a stock's future price movement cannot be predicted by an analysis of its past price movements. This is related to the efficient market hypothesis. In general, the efficient market hypothesis (EMH) states that the prices of securities traded in the market fully reflect all available information, and furthermore the market reacts instantaneously and in an unbiased manner to all new information. The EMH may be stated in its weak, semistrong, or strong form.

The weak form of the EMH suggests that current market prices fully reflect all possible pertinent historical information. Because of this, future stock prices cannot be predicted on the basis of past movements, cyclical swings, or past price highs and lows of stock prices.

The semistrong form of the EMH suggests that current market prices of securities fully reflect all *publicly* available information, such as annual reports and quarterly earnings announcements, that is, not just historical information but all pertinent information.

The strong EMH goes even further and gives the market even more credit. It states that current market prices reflect fully *all* information whether it is publicly available or not, such as insider's information.

The random walk hypothesis is a variation of the weak EMH, and states that at any time the next change (either up or down) in security prices and the magnitude of that change is random; that is, prices will move independently of past price movements.

If the random walk hypothesis is correct then one of its implications is to adopt a "buy-and-hold" strategy. This is because in the long run no historical analysis will permit the selection of a portfolio of stocks that will outperform a portfolio selected at random. A buy-and-hold strategy provides an added bonus; if adopted, investment and transaction costs of turning your portfolio over will be eliminated.

The semistrong and strong forms of the EMH, if correct, also suggest you might just as well select your stock at random.[2] Even if you use more than public information you cannot outperform the market consistently. That is, fundamental and statistical analyses regarding sales, earnings, expected future growth, and so on, are not helpful because the market knows more about these things than you do, and it will adjust to this information before you can act. While knowledge of an industry and of a company, and general know-how about the economy and the market, may permit successful prediction of the future value of a given stock from time to time, sheer statistical analysis will not provide better results than a random buy-and-hold selection strategy in the long run. The random walk theory and the EMH do not suggest that stock prices do not respond to changes in pertinent information. Rather they state the market is so efficient that it quickly adjusts to all information on all stocks so that the individual cannot benefit by trying to outdo the market.

This theory is highly controversial. First of all, one could challenge the view that the securities market, if sufficiently efficient, will discount all stocks to the point where they are all approximately equally good (or bad) buys. If an analysis is made, some obviously good and some obviously poor buys can no doubt be discovered from time to time. If we eliminate these extremes, perhaps a random selection will provide results that are as good as poor analysis will provide. But the analysis need not be poor; all investors can develop some degree of sophistication if they are willing to devote the time.

How to Do as Well as the Market

If you are a fairly large investor, you may do as well as the market in general by investing only in those securities that make up the market indicators. There are 30 stocks in the Dow Jones Industrial Averages. If you invest in most of these and nothing else, you will of course keep up with this indicator's market movement. There is also a Dow Jones average for transportation stock (20 stock), a 15-stock utilities average, and a composite average of all 65. A moderately large investor could look into this indicator.

---

2. Technically speaking, this is true only if your portfolio is large enough to enable you to obtain diversification by random selection. If you are a small investor, a random selection will not necessarily give you a well-diversified portfolio, and the strong and semistrong EMH suggests that diversification is also important and diversification should be given greater weight than random selection. For the small investor the answer is random selection tempered by diversification.

An even more broadly based market indicator is the Standard and Poor's index. While the Dow indicators are simple averages, each of the four Standard and Poor's indicators is a statistical device that measures the market's movement since a previous bench mark. This previous bench mark is the 1941 to 1943 market price level, which is set at 10, as noted earlier.

Standard and Poor's has an industrial index consisting of 400 stocks—one for transportation, which includes 20 stocks; one for utilities made up of 40 stocks; one for the stock of 40 financial institutions of various kinds; and a composite of all five hundred of these stocks. You cannot, of course, do as well as this market indicator unless you are a large investor.

Selecting What Stocks to Sell

If you buy stocks, you should perhaps also sell them from time to time. Some investors hold the view that if they buy the right stock, they need never sell. This view may have some merit if you buy only the bluest of the blue chips like AT&T, or G.E. (it also has some merit if you subscribe to the random walk theory). However, most stockholders should review their portfolios and weed out the weaker stocks from time to time.

The decision to sell a stock is similar to the decision to buy. You must review the firm whose stock you own and also compare it with other firms. Would you, for example, buy more of a given stock that you now have and are reviewing? Or is some other stock a better buy? If the answer to the first question is no and to the second yes, you should seriously consider selling the stock under review. If a stock has not done well or has had losses, the temptation might be to hold on to it in the hope that it will recover. This policy is not always sound; sometimes it is best to take your losses and admit your mistakes. Even if the stock does recover in the future, you would be better off to take your losses now if you can find a stock that will rise more.

Some people also feel that they should not sell a stock that has risen substantially since they purchased it. Why get off a winning horse? This is tempting reasoning, but again you should make the decision in light of your appraisal of what this stock will do in the future relative to others. Sometimes certain stocks are overpriced and if you own them you should sell and take your capital gain.

The small investor should be a long-run investor rather than a short-run investor, at least for the most part. This does not negate portfolio review, that is, not constantly getting in and out of the market, always seeking better buys, but that even the long-run investor should not go to sleep. How often should you review your portfolio? Some people keep it under review all the time. But if you do not, you should probably take a good look at your securities at least every six months. Again, this does not mean you should sell something every six months; rather that you should look.

QUESTIONS FOR REVIEW

1. Discuss the various types of brokers on the New York Stock Exchange.
2. How do brokers and dealers in securities differ?
3. Explain in general terms how brokerage commissions are established.
4. What is the Dow-Jones Average and what does it attempt to show?
5. What are some other stock market indicators besides the Dow-Jones? What are the weaknesses and strengths of the stock averages?
6. Explain briefly the differences between a bear market and a bull market.
7. On over-the-counter stock, what is meant by bid, asked, and net change?
8. Who controls margin requirements, and what is the purpose of this control?
9. When a person buys stock on margin and it declines, he or she may be required to "cover." What does this mean?
10. Explain a short sale and how it differs from a conditional sale.
11. Explain what is meant by exdividend date and how it is determined.
12. When determining your investment objectives, what are some of the major factors to consider?
13. What is meant by investing with cyclical swings?
14. Outline several techniques for reaching decisions with respect to timing of security purchases.
15. What is meant by *portfolio review*? Why should you review your portfolio periodically?
16. What is the "random walk" as applied to securities?
17. How can you as an investor do as well as the market?
18. What risks do you face if you simply buy good stocks and then forget them for twenty years?

CASES

1. Rodney and Melba Johnson are a young couple who have just inherited $20,000. They live comfortably on their modest salaries and since they do not need the money, they have decided to invest it in securities. Should they be long-run or short-run investors? Do you think now is a good time to buy common stock? If you advise buying, what kind of stock would you recommend?
2. Elmer and Susan Green are a couple in their middle thirties with twin boys aged six months. Elmer works in the local factory and makes just enough for the four of them to get along until Susan rejoins the work force. Last week Elmer heard that he will receive $5,000 from his father's estate. They have decided not to use the money to buy the house they have always

wanted but rather to save it for their children's college fund. How should they invest it? Elmer and Susan know that government bonds and banks are the safest but feel the return is too low. They are thinking about buying bonds and stocks. Should they? If so, what kind would you recommend?

3. Judy Smith is an elderly widow who has just received a check for $100,000 from a life insurance company in payment for her husband's death. Although she owns her own home, the $100,000 will be her sole support. She feels that she should invest the $100,000 and live off the income. Do you think she is wise? If she invests the money, what kind of securities would you recommend? Why?

4. Lydia de los Santos is a young college graduate who has her own CPA firm. She is single and has an income of $30,000 per year. She does not own any securities as yet, but would like to acquire some. Work out an investment program for her, and outline any investment advice you think appropriate.

5. Angela Thompson believes the market in general will rise by 10 percent per year over the next two years and that the stock of ABC Corporation will rise by twice that amount. While she has only a relatively small amount of money, she would nevertheless like to take a strong position in ABC stock, which is currently selling for $20 per share. If she has $5,000 to invest, what can she do to maximize the number of shares she may purchase? How many shares will that be? ABC is currently paying a dividend of $1.00 per year. How much will her shares have to appreciate before she breaks even?

6. Kate Brenchly has $40,000 to invest. She is 29 years of age and would like to invest her money on a long-term basis. She is not certain whether she is a big enough investor to invest via the random walk theory. Please advise her. She would also like to do as well as the market in general. How can she do that? Would a $40,000 portfolio be large enough to accomplish that goal?

SUGGESTED READINGS

Amex Databook. Fact book published annually by the American Stock Exchange.

Beadle, Patricia. *Investing in the Eighties: What to Buy and When.* San Diego, Calif.: Harcourt Brace Jovanovich, 1981.

Christy, George A., and Roden, Foster P. *Finance: Environment and Decisions.* New York: Canfield Press, 1981.

"The Dow Jones Averages." Education Service Bureau of Dow Jones & Company, P. O. Box 300, Princeton, N.J. 08540, 1977.

Engle, Louis. *How to Buy Stocks.* New York: Bantam Books, 1982.

"The Exchange Market and the Public Interest." The New York Stock Exchange Annual Report.

Farrell, James L. *Guide to Portfolio Management.* New York: McGraw-Hill, 1983.

Fogler, Russell H. *Analyzing the Stock Market*, 2nd ed. Columbus, Ohio: Grid Inc., Publishers, 1978.

Forbes Magazine. A weekly magazine with a great deal of material about business and finance.

Francis, Jack Clark. *Investments Analysis and Management.* New York: McGraw-Hill, 1980.

Geisst, Charles. *Guide to the Financial Markets.* New York: St. Martin's Press, 1982.

Hardy, C. Colburn. *Dun and Bradstreet's Guide to Your Investments: 1982.* New York: Harper and Row, 1982.

How Over-the-Counter Securities are Traded. Merrill Lynch, Pierce, Fenner and Smith. 165 Broadway, New York, N.Y. 10006.

"How to Read a Financial Report." New York: Merrill Lynch, Pierce, Fenner and Smith.

Market for Millions. New York: American Stock Exchange.

"Market Statistics." Chicago: The Chicago Board of Options Exchange.

The Merrill Lynch Guide to Writing Options. New York: Merrill Lynch, Pierce, Fenner and Smith. You can get this from your local Merrill Lynch broker.

New York Stock Exchange Fact Book. Published annually by the New York Stock Exchange.

The New York Stock Exchange Market. Princeton, N.J.: Education Service Bureau, Dow Jones & Company.

Radcliffe, Robert C. *Investments: Concepts, Analysis and Strategy.* Glenview, Ill.: Scott, Foresman, 1982.

Rates of Return on Investments in Common Stock. New York: Merrill Lynch, Pierce, Fenner and Smith.

Smith, Keith V., and Eiteman, David K. *Essentials of Investing.* Homewood, Ill.: Irwin, 1974.

Standard & Poor's Stock Guide. New York: Standard & Poor's Corporation, 1982.

Tax Considerations in Using CBOE Options. Chicago: The Chicago Board of Options Exchange, 1976.

Tuccille, Jerome. *Mind Over Money: Why Most People Lose Money in the Stock Market and How You Can Become a Winner.* New York: Morrow, 1980.

Understanding the New York Stock Exchange. New York: New York Stock Exchange.

Understanding Options. Chicago: The Chicago Options Exchange, 1977.

The Versatile Option. The American Stock Exchange, 86 Trinity Place, New York, N.Y. 10006.

Well Beyond the Average: The Story of Dow Jones. Princeton, N.J.: Dow Jones & Company, The Educational Service Bureau.

What Every Woman Investor Should Know. Washington, D.C.: Investment Bankers Association of America, undated.

APPENDIX 17: SUPPLEMENTARY MATERIAL ON COMMON STOCK

There are a number of other points on common stock with which you should be familiar, among them what to do if you lose securities, keeping securities in the street name, stock splits, preemptive rights, stock warrants, and the options market for common stock.

What to Do If You Lose Securities

If you take physical possession of securities, they should be kept in a safe place such as a safety deposit box at a bank. Since most securities are registered, they can be replaced, but this is neither easy nor cheap. If securities are lost, notify the transfer agent immediately. If you do not know the name of the agent, your broker may be able to tell you, although sometimes you may have to write to the company issuing the stock. The transfer agent will want the certificate numbers of the missing shares. Consequently, you should have a list of these numbers available.

Upon notification, the transfer agent puts a stop on the stock to prevent its sale. The next step is to get the company to issue new replacement shares. This costs money. Nearly all companies require an indemnity bond as protection against any possible future loss. While the corporation would not suffer a loss if the old securities reappeared and were successfully sold, a brokerage house would, and the bond is used to indemnify them. Generally a bond of 100 percent of the value of the securities is required. You can put up the bond in cash or have a bonding company do it for you. If you use a bonding company, you will have to pay premiums that generally amount to about 4 percent of the stock's value.

Keeping Securities in the Street Name

To eliminate the possibility of loss, some investors keep their securities in the street name. This merely means that the purchaser does not take physical possession, but rather leaves the securities with the broker, who stores them in a safe. This makes it easier to sell the securities. All that is required is a phone call; the owner need not sign them and deliver them to the broker. This also protects the individual from loss of the securities due to fire, theft, or misplacement. The reason securities held in the street name can be sold by making a phone call is that they are in the broker's name. The securities of hundreds of customers are all lumped together this way. While in theory there is some danger here, they are as safe as money in the bank. The brokers are subject to the regulations of the New York Stock Exchange and the Security and Exchange Commission. They cannot sell these securities without permission, nor may they borrow money on them. The brokers must carry a fidelity bond to cover losses due to fraud and insurance to cover theft.

There is some slight danger if the broker goes bankrupt, but there is protection even here. The federal government recently established a form of insurance for this purpose, similar to the insurance under the Federal Deposit Insurance Corporation (FDIC) to protect bank depositors. This insurance is more fully discussed at the end of this appendix.

Stock Gifts to Minors; Uniform Gifts to Minors Act

Most states have passed the Uniform Gifts to Minors Act, which makes it easier for a person to buy securities for his or her children. The security will be made out to "Jane Doe, Trustee for John Doe, Junior" under the Texas Uniform Gifts to Minors Act, or of whatever state you are a resident. The income is taxable only if the minor child has a high enough income to pay taxes. The gift is, and must be by law, irrevocable. However, the trustee can sell the security as long as he or she retains the principal on behalf of the child. The interest (or dividends) too must be retained for the child. The trustee may only manage the securities. No one, not even the child, can touch the fund until the child becomes twenty-one (now eighteen in many states), at which time he or she gains full control. Many people buy small amounts of high-quality securities for their children and build a portfolio to be used later to finance specific projects such as a college education.

Stock Splits

A stock split occurs when a corporation increases the number of shares of stock outstanding by sending additional shares of stock to existing stockholders without demanding additional payment. In so doing, the total net worth of the corporation is unaffected, and yet the book value of each individual share is reduced. Theoretically, the existing stockholders have received nothing that increases their share of the corporate assets. For purposes of illustration, assume a corporation with a net worth of $15,000,000 and one million shares, which would make the book value $15 per share. If the stock is split two for one—meaning that each shareholder is to receive two shares in exchange for each share now held—a shareholder who had one hundred shares before would now have a total of two hundred.[3] But the company, since it received no additional capital, would still have a net worth of $15,000,000. Since now twice as many shares have a claim on it, the book value of each share would drop from $15 to $7.50. If the market value had been $30 per share before the split, theoretically it would fall to $15. Often, however, the market value does not fall quite this much. The point is that the shareholders' positions would not be changed. The question then is, why do corporations split the stock?

The main reason is that lower-priced stock sometimes has a psychological attraction to investors. Then, too, lower-priced stocks are more accessible to more people. When the stock is split, more investors are attracted to the stock, and consequently there may be a tendency for market prices to be forced upward more rapidly from the lower price. Also many people, not knowing that theoretically

---

3. The stock must be exchanged because par value is cut in half. If the stock is no-par stock, a two-for-one split could be accomplished without an exchange. The company would simply mail the stockholder one additional share for each share owned.

they are no better off, think that somehow the stockholders have magically got something for nothing. Because this makes this corporation's stock more attractive to them, they buy it and bid up its price.

From a financial point of view, a stock split and a stock dividend are the same. A two-for-one split or a 100 percent stock dividend would double the number of shares a person had and would cut the book value in half. Theoretically, the market price would be cut in half, too. The two-for-one split discussed above and a 100 percent stock dividend would accomplish the same dilution per share. Generally stock dividends are used when smaller dilution is desired. (Many stock dividends are 10 to 20 percent.) Sometimes, however, stock dividends are used when a corporation cannot or does not want to pay a cash dividend but feels it must declare something to satisfy the stockholders. A stock dividend is not taxable as income.

From a technical accounting point of view, there is a slight difference between a stock split and a stock dividend. A stock dividend does not change the par value of the stock; a stock split might. Generally, a dividend reduces earned surplus, although on rare occasions it might reduce paid-in surplus. Moreover, a stock dividend does not require an exchange of stock; the company simply mails the increased shares to the stockholder. (Of course the same is true of a stock split, if it is a no-par stock.) As noted above, a stock dividend will dilute both the book value and the market price of the stock in the same manner as a stock split.

Preemptive Rights

The capital of a firm may be reduced or increased. A capital reduction is rare, and it would necessitate returning to the stockholder part of the stockholder's capital. This could happen in a government antimonopoly action against a company which was then required to divest itself of certain assets.

It is common, however, for a corporation to increase its capital; then the question is, what are the rights of the stockholders under such a situation? It can readily be seen that the relative strength of an individual stockholder could be affected if the capital of the corporation is increased. Suppose again that there are ten stockholders, each with one share, and the total assets of the corporation consist of $1,000. Thus each of the stockholders may be said to own 10 percent of the corporation and also 10 percent of the voting rights. Suppose further that the corporation desires to issue $1,000 in additional stock so that its asset cash will be $2,000. To accomplish this, it sells ten additional shares at $100 each. If an outsider buys all these shares, then his or her interest in the corporation will be 50 percent, and all old stockholders will have their interest reduced from 10 percent per share to 5 percent. Thus the old stockholders will be adversely affected by such a transaction.

To prevent this sort of imposition on the existing stockholders, the courts and the law have long since handled the situation by what are known as "preemptive rights," the right of the existing stockholders to purchase a proportionate share in the increase of the capital stock of the corporation. This right does not always exist. In some cases it exists because the corporate charter grants it and in some cases because the state law of the state of incorporation requires it. If neither state law nor corporate charter grants preemptive rights or if they are waived, then the corporation may go to the public or outside investors if it wants to expand its capital. A *right*, therefore, is defined as a privilege possessed by a stockholder to purchase a *pro rata share* of a new stock issue offered by the corporation at a specific price and for a specific time period.

Rights are issued by corporations that seek to raise additional capital. Suppose a corporation desires to raise about $7,500,000. It has outstanding one hundred thousand shares of common stock valued in the market at $100 per share. If it sells one hundred thousand new shares at $75 per share, it will have its $7,500,000. In accordance with preemptive rights it will give all existing stockholders the right to buy one new share for each share they already have. In this case, the company is increasing its capital by 75 percent. I have put the example this way to simplify calculations. Usually a firm will increase its capital by only 10 or 20 percent, and a person in such a case will have the right to buy a new issue for every ten or five shares he or she owns, respectively.

The firm usually sells the new stock at a price below the market price of the outstanding shares in order to expedite the sale. Since there cannot be two prices, when the new issue comes out, the market price of the old will fall and the new will rise; and the price, in the example above, will be approximately $87.50. Mr. X, who before had one share valued at $100, purchased a new one for $75. His total investment is $175 or $87.50 per share. If Mr. X had ignored his rights, he would now have only one share valued at $87.50. His equity would have been diluted by $12.50. The example also illustrates the value of rights; it is, in this case, $12.50.

If Mr. X could not afford to pay $75 for his new share, he could have sold his rights for $12.50 in cash and prevented a dilution of his equity in this way. That is to say, rights are valuable and if you do not have the money to exercise them, sell them. If you neither exercise nor sell them, they will expire after a time. Usually the company will offer to buy an investor's rights if he or she does not wish to exercise them. Sometimes if a large issue is coming out, an organized market develops in rights and one can both buy and sell them from a broker.

When rights are granted, the person who buys that stock in the market automatically gets the right, until the stock goes "ex-right." This is logically the same as a stock going "ex-dividend." For example, the company issuing the rights announces that stockholders of record on Wednesday, February 1, 1986, will receive the rights. The stock goes "ex-rights" in the market five days before this date because of the five day delivery rule. When a stock goes "ex-rights" its price in the market generally declines by the amount of the value of the right.

Companies issue rights because it is an easy way to raise capital, and it is also cheaper than to come out with a general public issue. It saves the corporation investment bankers' fees; the stockholders also receive their stock more cheaply because they don't have to pay commissions.

Since persons usually get a right for every ten or twenty shares they already have, there arises the problem of fractional rights. Suppose you had fifteen shares of stock and were given rights to buy one share of new stock for every ten of the old. Obviously you cannot buy 1 1/2 new shares. Usually the company will either buy back fractional rights or offer to sell the investor enough fractions for an even number of shares.

A formula can be used to calculate the value of a right, although ordinary logic and arithmetic are all that is needed in a simple case such as the one discussed above. However, if eight or ten shares of stock are required to obtain the right to buy one new share, the formula may be helpful. It is the market price less the subscription price divided by the number of old shares plus one, which are needed to get one of the new.

Or,

$$\frac{M - S}{N + 1} = V$$

Where

M = market value of old
S = subscription price
N = number of shares needed to
  buy one of the new
V = value of the right

In the case above we had,

M = $100
S =   75

and hence our formula tells us

$$\frac{\$100 - \$75}{2} = \$12.50$$

A second reason for preemptive rights—not very important in most cases—is to prevent dilution of control. For example, if you owned 10 percent of the stock in a given corporation, you would have 10 percent of the votes at the stockholders' meetings. If you were not permitted to continue to buy the same 10 percent of any new issues, your relative voting strength would decline. This is not important for most stockholders because they have so few shares that they don't really have any influence at corporate elections. However, for a few large stockholders it might be a factor.

Stock Warrants

A warrant is a certificate evidencing an option to purchase new securities, usually common stock, at a stated price for a stated time period. Sometimes, however, the time period is for perpetuity. The distinction between the right and the warrant is that the right is generally issued under the preemptive right privilege to existing stockholders, while a warrant may be issued aside from the preemptive rights to nonstockholders. Warrants are originally attached to other securities when they are issued and generally are attached to either bonds or preferred stock. Some warrants are not detachable, and hence they cannot be sold separately; but others are detachable, and a market exists for them.

When a corporation feels that it may have difficulty in selling a particular preferred stock or bond issue, it may offer warrants along with each security that will enable the purchaser to buy additional shares of common stock. These warrants, called "purchase warrants," are generally extended for relatively long periods of time or even perpetually. Thus the preemptive stock rights are different from warrants. The rights have a relatively short life (days or weeks). When a corporation attaches warrants to bonds or preferred stocks, it is able to sell them more easily. Since warrants permit the holder to purchase common stock at a predetermined price, they are a speculative device. They make the mother security more attractive, a fact best illustrated with an example.

Suppose the Adjax Corporation issues 9 percent bonds maturing in twenty years with detachable warrants on the bonds. Anyone who buys a bond also gets a warrant. The warrant permits the owner to purchase one share of common stock at, say, $30 per share at any time during the next three years. The common stock is presently selling for $20 per share, however, and hence the warrant has speculative value only. If it is detachable, it may sell for a dollar or $.50 or even less. But the $30 and the three-year period are fixed. If the common stock of the Adjax Corporation rises to, say, $40 before the three years have elapsed, the warrant will be worth $10; its price will have moved from $1 to $10. This is a tremendous percentage increase, but it is in the nature of warrants. They have great leverage. Once the stock rises above the warrant price, warrants have positive value and will appreciate by some multiple of the further appreciation of the common stock. Warrants also move downward with common stock but by greater magnitudes.

If you buy bonds with warrants attached, the warrant may have value in the future. If it does not, you simply remain a bond investor. Corporations attach warrants to bonds (or preferred stock) as "sweeteners"; it may reduce the interest that they have to pay. While not many corporations have issued warrants in recent years, there are still many detached ones outstanding, and they are traded almost daily. Don't take the plunge into warrants, because they are highly speculative, and I assure you, are only for the brave and those who can assume great risk.

What to Do with Rights and Warrants

Many investors have no idea what to do with either rights or warrants, some of which are destroyed physically and many of which are permitted to lapse. Three choices are open to the investor. One is to permit them to lapse; many people do just this. Another alternative is to exercise the right and the warrant if and when it has value; however, it may be that investors holding the warrants or rights are unable to do this because they lack available cash or are unwilling to because they lack any further interest in the particular stocks issued. The third alternative is to sell the rights, and the warrant if it is detachable, which can be done through any broker.

The Options Markets; Puts and Calls

Although there are a number of other stock options[4] the major ones are puts and calls, both of which are speculative devices.

Calls

A call option is a contractual and legal privilege for buying a given number (usually one hundred) of shares of a given common stock for a given period of time at a price determined at the time the call is purchased. For example, if you buy, say for $200, a thirty-day call on United States Steel at $25 this means that at any time during the next thirty days the seller is required to sell you one hundred shares of U.S. Steel for $25 per share if you request it. If U.S. Steel rises to $45 during this period, your $200 will have grown to $2,000. Your net return is $1,800 ($2,000 minus the $200 option price). This again is a tremendous percentage return on your money. If U.S. Steel does not move, on the other hand, you have lost $200. Options permit one to speculate in one-hundred-lot shares with only a relatively few dollars; they also hold out the possibility of a high rate of return on one's money; and the maximum amount that can be lost is the price of the option.

Puts

A put option is exactly the reverse of a call option. It is the privilege of selling 100 shares of a given stock for a given period of time at a price determined at

4. The various stock options one can buy in the options market should not be confused with the stock option plans many corporations make available to their key employees. In the case of corporate stock option plans, certain key executives are granted the privilege (option) of buying a certain number of shares of common stock from the corporation, usually at the market price of the stock at the time the option is granted. The option price is then, however, frozen for the executives for a period of time, usually several years or more. Then if the market price rises substantially, the option holders can execute and make a nice gain. The main justification for providing key executives stock options is to give them a vested interest in the corporation and hence a greater incentive to perform well.

the time the put is purchased. A person buying a put is speculating that the market price of that stock is going down.

Options may run up to nine months before they expire. A market in options is now being made on the Chicago Board of Options Exchange, the American Stock Exchange, the Philadelphia Stock Exchange, and the Pacific Stock Exchange. The Chicago exchange is by far the largest. It is to the options market what the New York Stock Exchange is to the stock market.

If you wish to buy (or sell) an option, your broker can make the arrangement through one of the organized options markets mentioned above. There are brokerage commissions for this that are similar to (but generally a little lower than) the stock commissions discussed above.

Table A17–1 shows some options listed on the Chicago Board of Options Exchange. An entry might appear as follows:

Option and N.Y. close	Strike price	Calls—last			Puts—last		
		Jul	Oct	Jan	Jul	Oct	Jan
IBM 123 1/8	120	5 5/8	10 5/8	13 5/8	1 13/16	4 3/4	7

It identifies first the corporation (IBM) on which there is an option and below it the price ($123 1/8) at which IBM stock closed on the New York Stock Exchange that day. Moving to the right we see the strike price at which the shares may be purchased by the option owner. Next comes the "Jul, Oct, and Jan Calls—last, which means it is a call option and the price of the last trade is quoted just below the months shown. The months refer to when the options on IBM will expire; buyers have some choice as to how long they want their option to run. The prices (5 5/8, 10 5/8, and 13 5/8) are the prices per share of the last option traded for each of the three expiration dates and are called the premium. However, since options are always for 100 shares, the prices are really $562.50, $1,062.50, and $1,362.50 respectively. The options will expire on the third Saturday of the month shown (options always expire on the third Saturday of the month shown).[5] If you want a call option for 100 shares that runs to the third Saturday of January, 1984, it will cost you $1,362.50, but will permit you to buy 100 shares of IBM at $120 per share even though its current price was 123 1/8 that day. Obviously, the buyers of this option believe the price of IBM will rise.

The next three quotations convey the same information on puts. The first quotation is for July and it is 1 10/16. This means the premium is $1 plus 1/16 of a dollar per share—option prices move in multiples of 1/16 of a dollar. This translates into $162.50 for 100 shares. The quotations also show that for $475 the buyer of that option has the right to sell 100 shares of IBM at $120

_____

5. Since the market is closed on Saturday, the options really expire on the third Friday of the month, but this is a technicality. The option will state that it will expire on the first Saturday after the third Friday of the month in question.

Table A17–1 Portion of the options listed on the Chicago Board of Options Exchange, July 11, 1983

Listed Options Quotations

Friday, July 8, 1983

Closing prices of all options. Sales unit usually is 100 shares. Security description includes exercise price. Stock close is New York or American exchange final price.

Most Active Options

CHICAGO BOARD OPTIONS EXCHANGE

	Sales	Last	Chg.	N.Y. Close
CALLS				
I B M Jul120	5753	2⅜	+ ¼	120⅝
SP100 Sep170	4556	4½	....	166.84
SP100 Sep175	3894	2 7-16	....	166.84
Gen El Sep47½	3601	6⅞	– ⅝	53¼
Gen El Sep42½	3600	11½	+ ¼	53¼
PUTS				
SP100 Sep165	3943	4⅛	– ⅛	166.84
I B M Jul120	2607	1 9-16	– ½	120⅝
SP100 Sep170	2377	6⅝	....	166.84
SP100 Sep160	2017	2½	+ 1-16	166.84
Honwll Aug110	1679	4⅞	+ ½	110½

AMERICAN STOCK EXCHANGE

	Sales	Last	Chg.	N.Y. Close
CALLS				
Merril Jul55	5469	1⅛	....	53⅞
MMIdx Jul125	4827	1-16	....	118.77
AmCan Aug35	4275	8⅛	+ ½	42⅞
Dr Pep Aug15	2244	1¼	+ 5-16	15⅞
MMIdx Jul120	2216	13-16	– 1-16	118.77
PUTS				
MMIdx Jul120	3033	2⅛	+ 3-16	118.77
Merril Jul50	1872	5-16	– 1-16	53⅞
MMIdx Jul115	1407	3-16	....	118.77
Dig Eq Jul110	1119	11-16	– ⅛	115⅝
Dig Eq Jul120	924	5	....	115⅝

PHILADELPHIA STOCK EXCHANGE

	Sales	Last	Chg.	N.Y. Close
CALLS				
Joy Aug20	1792	7⅞	– 2⅛	27½
Coleco Jul50	1087	7-16	– 3-16	44⅝
DomeM Aug20	1027	9-16	– 5-16	17¾
Coleco Jul45	1017	1 9-16	– ¼	44⅝
LaLnd o Aug25	881	6¼	– ⅜	24⅝
PUTS				
Coleco Jul45	587	1¾	+ 1-16	44⅝
Cmdrln Aug50	510	3¾	+ ¼	50½
Coleco Jul40	398	⅜	– ⅛	44⅝
Cmdrln Aug45	391	1 9-16	+ 3-16	50½
Comsat Jul40	361	3-16	....	42¾

PACIFIC STOCK EXCHANGE

	Sales	Last	Chg.	N.Y. Close
CALLS				
Travel Aug25	1210	5½	– ⅛	30¼
BakerIn Sep20	1124	3⅝	+ ⅜	23⅛
BakerIn Sep15	1120	8¼	+ ⅝	23⅛
SmkB Sep80	1018	1¾	+ ¾	75½
ResrtA Oct55	990	5⅜	+ ½	52
PUTS				
BakerIn Sep20	427	7-16	– ¼	23⅛
SmkB Sep70	372	1	– ⅝	75½
DataGn Sep50	326	3¼	+ ¾	53¾
DataGn Sep55	237	5½	+ ⅞	53¾
Pogo Jul25	181	¼	– 3-16	25

Chicago Board

S&P 100 INDEX

Strike Price	Calls–Last Sep	Calls–Last Dec	Calls–Last Mar	Puts–Last Sep	Puts–Last Dec	Puts–Last Mar
145	23	....	....	¼	1 1/16	....
150	....	....	....	½	....	....
155	....	....	....	1¼	....	....
160	10½	....	....	2½	4¼	....
165	7⅛	10½	....	4⅛	6⅞	....
170	4½	8	....	6⅝	9¼	....
175	2 7/16	5⅝	....	9⅞	....	....

Total call volume 10,520. Total call open int. 39,773.
Total put volume 9,801. Total put open int. 72,348.
The index closed at 166.84, –0.24.

Option & NY Close	Strike Price	Calls–Last Jul	Calls–Last Oct	Calls–Last Jan	Puts–Last Jul	Puts–Last Oct	Puts–Last Jan
Alcoa	30	7	r	r	r	r	¾
36⅝	... 35	1⅝	3¾	4½	⅜	1⅜	2⅛
36⅝	... 40	1-16	1 11-16	2½	3½	4	r
36⅝	... 45	s	11-16	r	s	8½	r
Am Tel	..55	7¾	s	s	r	s	s
62¼	... 60	2½	4⅝	5⅞	⅛	1	1⅞
36¾	... 45	r	¾	1½	r	r	r
Xerox	... 35	11¾	r	r	r	⅛	r
46⅝	... 40	6⅞	7½	r	r	⅜	13-16
46⅝	... 45	1 15-16	3¾	5⅛	1-16	1 11-16	r
46⅝	... 50	1-16	1 11-16	2⅞	3¼	4¾	5⅜
46⅝	... 55	s	¾	1⅝	s	r	r
		Aug	**Nov**	**Feb**	**Aug**	**Nov**	**Feb**
Amdahl	17½	9½	r	s	⅛	r	s
26¼	. 22½	4⅝	5¾	r	⅜	1⅛	r
26¼	. 27½	1¾	3½	r	2	3⅝	r
26¼	... 20	7⅛	r	s	3-16	¾	s
26¼	... 25	2⅞	4½	5½	1⅛	2⅜	r
26¼	... 30	13-16	2¼	3¼	4⅛	r	5⅞
A E P	...20	1-16	3-16	⅜	r	2	r
Am Hos	40	6	r	r	r	r	r
45½	... 45	2¼	4	5½	r	2⅛	2⅝
45½	... 50	7-16	2	r	r	r	r
A M P	.. 90	10	r	r	1	r	r
98½	... 95	6¼	r	r	2½	r	r
98½	.. 100	3⅝	r	r	5	r	r
Baxter	.. 55	4⅜	6¼	r	r	1¾	r
58½	... 60	1⅝	3⅝	5½	r	r	r
58½	... 65	r	1¾	r	r	r	r
Blk Dk	..20	r	3⅛	r	r	r	r

Option & NY Close	Strike Price	Calls–Last Sep	Calls–Last Dec	Calls–Last Mar	Puts–Last Sep	Puts–Last Dec	Puts–Last Mar
Celan	65	2¼	r	r	r	r	r
Chamln	. 20	r	r	r	⅜	9-16	r
23⅝	... 25	1¼	2¼	r	2	2⅝	3
23⅝	... 30	5-16	r	1¾	6	6¼	r
CompSc	. 20	1½	r	r	1⅜	1¾	r
19⅝	... 25	⅜	r	r	r	r	r
Dow Ch	. 30	4⅛	5¾	r	7-16	r	r
33⅛	... 35	1⅛	2¼	3	2½	r	r
33⅛	... 40	¼	¾	1⅜	r	r	r
Esmark	. 65	10¼	r	r	r	r	r
FBost	... 55	7⅞	10¼	s	1½	2½	s
59⅞	... 60	4½	7⅜	r	4	4¾	r
59⅞	... 65	3⅛	6	r	r	r	r
59⅞	... 70	1½	3½	r	r	r	r
Ford	 30	25	s	s	r	s	s
55	 35	20½	21⅝	s	r	3-16	s
55	 40	15	16½	s	⅛	r	s
55	 45	11⅛	12¾	s	3-16	1	s
55	 50	7	9½	10¾	1 7-16	2⅝	3⅛
55	 55	4¼	7	8½	3¾	4⅜	5
55	 60	2¼	4⅝	6⅝	6¼	7½	r
Gen El	42½	11½	s	s	r	s	s
53¼	. 47½	6⅞	r	s	r	r	s
53¼	... 45	9¼	s	s	r	s	s
53¼	... 50	5	6⅞	7½	15-16	2	2⅜
53¼	... 55	2¼	4¼	5⅝	3⅜	4¼	r

Source: Reprinted by permission of *The Wall Street Journal,* © Dow Jones & Company, Inc., 1983. All rights reserved.

per share until the third Saturday (Friday) of October. Obviously, the buyers of such an option believe that the price of IBM will decline. If you examine option quotations in *The Wall Street Journal*, you will note that sometimes an "r" or an "s" appears. An "r" means that no option for that stock was traded that day; an "s" means no option going out that far exists.

Straddles and combinations

There are also options involving straddles and combinations. A "straddle" consists of both a put and a call option on the same stock, with the same strike price, and the same expiration date. A "combination" is the same as a straddle except that the put and the call have a different strike price and/or expiration date. Straddles and combinations can become complex. However, if you operate in this market and the stock does not move in either direction, you will have earned a double premium if you sell rather than buy them.

Writing Options

Instead of thinking about buying options, sophisticated investors are thinking in terms of selling them (called "writing options"). There are two ways of writing call options: covered and uncovered. If you write a covered call option, this means you already have the stock; an uncovered call is on a stock you do not own and is a little more risky. Many financial advisers feel that writing covered options is a good strategy for conservative investors because it can increase their yield, as we shall see below.

Many option writers adhere to the following two rules of thumb. Never write a call on a stock you do not already own (write only covered options). Write calls only on stock you are thinking about selling anyway—or at least would not mind selling if the price went much higher, that is, on a stock that has risen about as much as you think it will and on which you are willing to take your capital gain or on a stock that has not done well and you are ready to sell for that reason. Some option writers, however, select what they think will be a good income stock and one that does not fluctuate much in price and then sell options on it. It is not unusual for option writers to double their yield on a stock by writing options. For example, if you own a stock providing you with a 9 percent dividend yield, writing several options per year on it could very well give you an additional 9 percent or even more. There are three ways in which you can benefit from owning a stock and writing options on it. There is, first, the dividend; second, possible capital appreciation (there is also the possibility of capital losses); and third, option income. All three should be netted to obtain your true economic improvement.

One final word on options, however. If you are a newcomer to security ownership and are just beginning to learn about them, or if you are a small investor, don't write options yet. Wait until you gain some experience and become more sophisticated.

The Government and Securities

There are some legal safeguards for securities that provide the investor with some protection. They include the following:

1. *Federal laws on securities.* Federal legislation dates from the financial reforms in the 1930s. Prior to 1933, there were some state laws regulating the sale of securities, the so-called "blue sky laws," but most of them were not very effective. They varied from state to state and were designed primarily to avoid the worst abuses of some traveling securities salespersons.

    In 1933 and 1934, the federal government passed legislation regulating the sale of securities. The Security Act of 1933 primarily regulated the sale of new securities issues; it applies primarily to investment bankers. The Security Act of 1934 was concerned primarily with the sale of outstanding securities; it applies to the operations of brokers and dealers. These acts as amended are the basis for our federal regulations today. The main protection provided by these acts is *full disclosure.* All pertinent financial information must be made public on all new securities sold to the public. This is generally done through the publication of a prospectus, which is a pamphlet available from any broker on any new issue.

    The second main provision of these acts is to prevent stock market manipulation. Prior to the coming of federal regulations in the 1930s there were a good many manipulative operations carried out by insiders to the detriment of the public. Stock prices were artificially manipulated up to attract the public; then the insiders quietly unloaded at a large gain, and let the prices fall back down, imposing large losses on the public. The law also established the Securities and Exchange Commission (SEC), which administers the law and serves as the watchdog for the public.

2. *Registration of security dealers.* The law also provides for the registration of securities, organized exchanges, and security dealers and brokers with the SEC, making available certain reports and more detailed information than might otherwise be available for full public disclosure of all pertinent financial information. Dealers and brokers must show, to the satisfaction of the SEC, that they are reputable, and in some cases they must meet certain capital requirements.

    There is also internal regulation. Members of the National Association of Security Dealers must adhere to a set of fair practices. The organized exchanges also have rules and regulations, designed to protect the public, that all members must observe.

3. *Securities insurance.* In 1970, Congress passed, and the President signed, a bill establishing the Securities Investor Protection Corporation (SIPC). It is to security buyers what the Federal Deposit Insurance Corporation (FDIC) is to bank depositors. It protects investors up to $500,000 per account against the loss of securities due to failure of broker-dealers. Many brokers have an additional $500,000 per account with private insurance companies.

This does not, of course, protect the investor from losses suffered by corporations that have issued the stock. Rather, it protects investors who keep their securities in the street name and have their broker keep physical possession of them. This protection was a result of the stock market crash in 1970 that caused some broker-dealers to fail.

All broker-dealers engaged in interstate security operations must join the SIPC. They are assessed an annual fee, which varies with the size of their operations. These fees go into a fund used to reimburse security owners who suffer losses when their broker goes into bankruptcy.

Questions for Review

1. What should you do if you lose securities?
2. What is meant by keeping securities in the street name? What are its advantages and disadvantages?
3. How does a stock split differ from a stock dividend?
4. What are preemptive rights? Discuss the differences between these rights and warrants.
5. Explain stock warrants.
6. Why do corporations use warrants?
7. What are puts and calls?
8. Would you recommend buying options or selling (called "writing") them?
9. What do legal regulations as applied to securities attempt to accomplish?
10. Are securities insured like bank deposits?

Cases

1. Alfred and Helen Walker own two different common stocks. They are one hundred shares of ABC corporation and one hundred shares of XYZ. Their ABC stock was recently split three for one, and before the split it was selling on the New York Stock Exchange for $120 per share. What, in theory, is the price now? Why may the price not fall that much? How many shares do they now own?

   The Walkers' XYZ stock was selling for $140 per share on the American Stock Exchange when they received a 100 percent stock dividend. How many shares do they now own? What is the theoretical price of the XYZ stock? How big a stock dividend would they have had to receive to have the same number of shares of XYZ stock as they have of ABC? What is the difference between a stock split and a stock dividend?

2. George Kennedy owns fifty shares of common stock, and the corporation has informed him he has preemptive rights on a new issue coming out. At present there are one million shares outstanding, and the new issue will consist of one hundred thousand shares. How many new shares can George

buy? Why? What is the idea behind preemptive rights? The market price of George's stock is $80 and the new issue is coming out at $75. If George decides to sell his preemptive rights rather than exercise them, what will he get for them?

3. Five years ago Bernice Edwards received 100 warrants attached to some convertible bonds she bought. These warrants entitled her to buy common stock on the same corporation at $15 per share. However, the common was selling in the market at the time for $5 per share. Yesterday, Bernice checked and found that the common is now selling at $35 per share. What are her warrants worth?

4. Sally Ann and Bill Herod purchased one hundred shares of ABC Corporation stock in 1946 for $195 per share. Since then the following stock splits and stock dividends have taken place:

1948   7 for 4 stock split
1949   5% stock dividend
1950   5% stock dividend
1951   5% stock dividend
1952   5% stock dividend
1953   5% stock dividend
1954   5 for 4 stock split
1956   2 1/2% stock dividend
1957   2 for 1 stock split
1958   2 1/2% stock dividend
1959   2 1/2% stock dividend and
       3 for 2 stock split
1961   3 for 2 stock split
1964   5 for 4 stock split
1966   3 for 2 stock split
1967   2 1/2% stock dividend
1968   2 for 1 stock split
1973   5 for 4 stock split
1978   4 for 1 stock split

Recently the market price of ABC was $101 per share. How many shares of ABC stock do Sally Ann and Bill own and what is their investment worth?

5. Bill and Betty Pasmack recently moved across country to Seattle, Washington, where Bill took a new job. After moving into their new home and unpacking, they couldn't find their securities. Betty said that since they were registered they had nothing to worry about; they would simply report it to the company and have new ones issued. Bill, however, is not sure that it is all as simple as that. Can you explain what they must do to have new securities issued? What if they do not have the serial number of their securities? What can people do to prevent or minimize the likelihood of losing securities?

CHAPTER EIGHTEEN

INVESTMENT COMPANIES (MUTUAL FUNDS) AND OTHER INVESTMENT VEHICLES

Some people do not care to buy common stock directly, either because they feel stocks are too risky or because they lack the time needed to review their portfolio frequently—and portfolio review is required. If you are in this category, you may wish to investigate investment companies, also sometimes called "mutual funds." If you invest in these companies, you are investing in common stock indirectly. An investment company is a financial intermediary (or financial institution) that collects, usually in small dollar amounts, the savings of many individuals. It then invests these funds in the securities of other corporations. The savings of many small savers are pooled to become one large fund to be managed collectively for the benefit of all of the participants. An investment company, therefore, is a specialized one-layer financial holding company. The persons who buy the securities of these investment companies are said to be investing indirectly. They own part of the investment company, and the investment

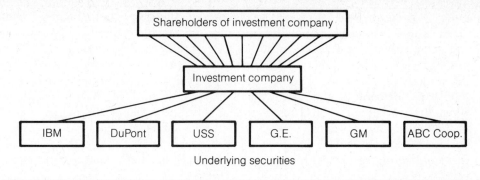

Figure 18–1   Investment company relationships

company owns the securities of other companies. The securities the investment company owns, on behalf of its owners, are referred to as the underlying securities, and it is the value of the underlyings that gives value to the shares of the investment companies. The relationship of the investment company, its owners, and the underlying securities is shown in Figure 18–1.

CLASSIFICATION OF INVESTMENT COMPANIES, AND NET ASSET VALUE

As noted above, certain types of investment companies are also called mutual funds. The terms *mutual funds, investment company,* and *investment trust* are used interchangeably to designate a variety of financial institutions that provide investors with the opportunity of investing indirectly in various corporations. In reality, however, only the open-end investment company (the open-end as opposed to the closed-end company will be explained below) is referred to as a mutual fund by the financial community. Generally, investment companies invest most funds they receive in common stock, but some companies buy substantial amounts of bonds and preferred stock. Any profits are shared among the shareholders of the mutual fund.

Investment companies can be classified as open-end and closed-end, and further classified according to their investment policies and objectives.

Closed-End Investment Companies

Closed-end investment companies have a relatively fixed amount of capital. To issue securities they need permission from the Securities and Exchange Commission (SEC), just like any corporation. They then have an authorized common stock issue, and when that is sold, they can sell no more unless another issue is approved. Once that issue is sold, therefore, you can no longer purchase it directly from the company but only from a broker in the open market. Moreover, closed-end investment companies do not stand ready to redeem their securities as do open-end companies. Shares in closed-end companies are frequently listed on the stock exchanges, although some are sold over the counter; when buying and selling them, one pays the brokerage fees described in Chapter 17. The price of closed-end shares is, therefore, determined not only by the price of the underlying securities, but by all the psychological factors that affect the supply and demand of closed-end shares in the market. There have been times when the market price of closed-end shares has been below the market price of the underlying securities. This is referred to as selling at a discount. In recent years some closed-end shares have been at a premium or above the value of their underlying securities, but most of them have been at a discount in recent years.

Closed-end investment companies sometimes also acquire capital by selling bonds to the public, a practice that introduces the element of leverage into their capital structure. (See Chapter 16.) Building a lot of leverage into a firm's capital structure can in some cases result in a sudden and rapid increase in earnings and hence in the price of the common stock, and the reverse can also happen. Closed-end investment companies have various amounts of leverage built into their capital structure, the amount varying from time to time, depending on their management's appraisal of what the future holds in store. Consult your broker if you wish to find a company with some leverage in its capital structure.

Open-End Investment Companies (Mutual Funds)

There is no legally set limit to the number of shares an open-end investment company (mutual fund) may sell. The number of shares is limited only by what investors will buy. Such a company issues its shares continuously as it sells them; it is called open-end because its capitalization is not fixed.

Open-end funds also stand ready to buy back their shares from investors at any time at a price determined by the price of the underlying securities. Their price is calculated daily by dividing the total number of shares outstanding into the market value of the portfolio of the underlying securities.

Since open-end funds raise no capital by selling bonds, their entire capital is equity capital. No leverage is built into capital structure, although it might be in their underlying securities. Many open-end companies charge what is known as a loading fee when they sell their shares, generally from 7 to 9 percent. The fee is paid only when the shares are purchased and not when they are redeemed. Open-end companies are much more popular than closed-end companies.

Net Asset Value

The term *net asset value* is used to indicate the price of mutual funds. It is calculated as follows: First, the market value of all the underlying securities in the fund's portfolio are added up. Then the liabilities are totaled and subtracted from the aggregate assets. Third, the result is divided by the number of mutual fund shares outstanding. This is done daily on a computer; mutual fund shares fluctuate daily with fluctuations in the price of their underlyings. Since the price of mutual fund shares is determined directly by the price of the underlying securities, they are never sold at a premium or discount as may be the case when closed-end company shares are involved. Moreover, the funds stand ready to buy back (redeem) their shares at the net asset value whereas closed-end companies do not.

OBJECTIVES OF INVESTMENT COMPANIES

The buyer of investment company shares faces the same problem as does the direct buyer of common stock: which one to buy? There are over seven hundred investment companies and several hundred well-known companies. Moreover, their records are not the same, and their objectives are not the same. Even among those with the same objectives, records vary. When you buy investment company (mutual funds) shares, you must first of all examine the ones with the same objectives as you have, and then choose what appears to be the best fund within that group.

All mutual funds state their objectives—for example, growth or income. Sometimes these objectives are broadly stated, and hence there is a good deal of overlap, and some funds admit that they have several objectives. Consequently, classifying investment companies in accordance with their objectives cannot be done with complete precision, but it can be done well enough to consider the following types of funds:

1. Growth funds
2. Income funds
3. Partially income, partially growth funds
4. Balanced funds
5. Tax-exempt funds
6. Money market funds
7. Other funds

Growth Funds

The objective of a growth fund's managers is to achieve long-term growth (or price appreciation) in the value of the securities in their portfolio. Certain growth industries would be selected for their portfolio and firms within those industries with a proven record of growth in sales and earnings and firms that typically plow a high percentage of their earnings back into the business are the target.

Income Funds

Funds with the objective of earning income would purchase more bonds and blue-chip stocks. They would select stocks in companies with a good record of earnings and a history of a high dividend payout. There are many income funds, and they appeal to older investors needing income perhaps for retirement purposes.

You may wish to review growth stock and income stock (discussed in Chapter 16) because those are precisely the stocks that these two types of funds would seek.

Partially Income, Partially Growth

Those funds striving for both income and growth could be the balanced funds mentioned below or widely diversified common stock funds with an emphasis on blue-chip stocks. These funds' portfolios would also probably include some utilities, which have a good record of earnings and some of them a good record of growth, especially if they are located in an area with heavy population growth.

Balanced Funds

A fund that has balanced objectives is one that usually emphasizes growth, income, and stability or maintenance of principal. However, these three objectives are given various weights or priorities at different times. The fund has bonds, common stock, and often preferred stock in its portfolio. The relative amounts of bonds and stock vary from time to time, depending on the fund's managers' appraisal of future conditions. If the future looks gloomy, they may take a more defensive position by increasing the proportion of bonds. Generally, the amount of bonds in a balanced fund varies from 20 to 80 percent. These balanced funds are also sometimes called diversified funds.

Tax-Exempt Funds

In recent years mutual funds have been established that buy only state and local bonds on which the interest is exempt from personal income tax. These appeal to investors in a high tax bracket. Many of these are more like a fixed investment trust. For example, one of them will buy, say, $10 million of various tax-exempt municipals on behalf of the fund shareholders. This $10 million package is then kept until maturity and there is no fund management fee because the fund need not be managed. Others buy and sell municipal bonds and turn their portfolio occasionally; they do charge a management fee.

In many cases, the minimum amount of state and local bonds that may be purchased directly is $5,000. Owning them indirectly through a fund makes it possible to own them in lesser amounts.

Tax-Managed Funds

In recent years, tax-managed funds have begun to appear. Unlike the tax-exempt fund, these funds invest in standard corporation securities, the income on which is taxable. However, it is taxable to the mutual fund shareholder when it is passed back to him or her by the mutual fund. The tax-managed funds do not pass their investment income back; they reinvest it, and the mutual fund shareholder receives more shares. Consequently, there is no tax due until the shareholder sells the shares; and if they have been held for more than a year, the capital gains tax (rather than the income tax) applies, and income is converted to capital gains.

Money Market Funds

A few years ago a number of money market funds were developed when interest rates, especially the rate for short-term notes, were very high. Money market funds specialize in buying very short-term securities in the money market. Such things as Treasury bills, commercial paper, and bankers' acceptances are selected. These are highly technical areas, and few individuals are able to buy these securities directly; it takes thousands of dollars to buy commercial paper, for example. These funds always become popular when short-term rates are high; later when rates come down, moneys are withdrawn. Consequently, the dollar volume of these funds fluctuates greatly. When interest rates are low, these funds are invested chiefly in bank certificates of deposit at perhaps 5 or 6 percent.

Money market funds were developed to enable the small investor to get into this high interest area. Most of them were established and are managed by the various brokerage houses. Generally, they do not charge a commission when the small investor buys or sells. Rather they take a fraction "off the top." For example, if they earn, say, 10 percent interest, they will keep about .4 or .5 percent, leaving 9.6 for the investor. The interest on these funds is very volatile and fluctuates daily. Historically, banks and savings and loan institutions could not compete with these funds by paying the same high interest rates. Consequently, these institutions lost money to the funds during periods of high interest rates. Recently, however, commercial banks and savings and loan associations have been given permission to establish money market accounts free of interest rate controls. Consequently, they are now able to compete interestwise with the brokerage house-managed money market funds. Moreover, the thrift institutions' accounts are insured (up to $100,000) by an agency of the U. S. government—the FDIC or the FSLIC. As a result, many observers believe that these brokerage-managed funds will be less able to drain funds out of banks and savings and loans during times of high interest rates in the future (see Chapter 14).

Other Funds

Other funds are less popular. One of these is the specialty fund, which invests only in, say, electronics; others specialize in some other industry or in foreign securities. Needless to say, a specialty fund may also be a growth, income, or balanced fund.

At one time the so-called "hedge" funds were popular, but recently they have fallen from favor. They would take a very aggressive position because their goal was short-term capital gains. They were highly leveraged and often purchased securities on margin.

There are also index funds, which invest only in securities that are included in the Dow-Jones averages or in the Standard and Poor's 400 industrial index. This will insure that they do as well as the market but no better. If a fund is willing to settle for performance equal only to the market averages, one may wonder about its "professional" management. Any investor can easily do this, if he or she has enough capital.

The real estate investment trust (REIT) is another special fund that was very popular a few years ago. Technically, the real estate investment company is a trust. Nevertheless, the result is the same as that of an investment company; a number of individuals provide the capital, which is then invested in real estate. The real estate company is subjected to certain legal restrictions to prevent speculation in land. Real estate investments in general are discussed below, as well as the real estate investment company.

Finally, there is the small business investment company (SBIC) very much like the investment companies described above except that, as the name implies, it invests solely in small business. These companies have received favorable tax treatment by Congress to encourage the flow of equity capital to small firms. These investment companies work closely with the Small Business Administration, which has some federal funds available to small business.

OTHER THINGS YOU SHOULD KNOW ABOUT INVESTMENT COMPANIES

You should know about the advantages and disadvantages of investing in investment companies. You will also need to learn where you can find information on investment companies to help you select what will be the better ones. Finally, you should be aware of the cost of buying mutual shares. These are primarily commissions for the salespersons and are called *loading fees*. They are not uniform, and there are some no-load funds.

Grouping of Funds

Many mutual funds, especially the larger and more well-established ones, are set up in what are referred to as *groups*. One management team will handle a growth fund or income fund and perhaps several more. This amounts to several funds with different investment objectives being brought under the same roof. This union broadens the appeal of the group and, for individual investors, provides greater flexibility since they can switch from one fund to another within the group, as their investment objectives change. Making such a change requires paying only a small transfer fee, usually $5 or $10.

Tailoring the Fund to the Investor

When buying mutual funds, then, individuals must decide what their investment objectives are and select a fund with the same objectives. A retired person will generally select an income fund, one that tries to select good income securities for the underlying securities in its portfolio. A younger person who has time to take advantage of growth and who perhaps does not need the income presently will be more attracted to a growth fund, which hopefully will be successful in selecting for its underlying securities the stock of corporations that will grow in the future. A person willing and able to take an aggressive stance might pick a hedge fund, a more conservative person perhaps a fund for maintenance of principal and income or a balanced fund.

Advantages and Disadvantages of Mutual Funds

Three advantages may accrue to the buyer of mutual funds, as opposed to the purchase of common stock directly, especially to a small investor. They are diversification, professional management, and constant surveillance. The major disadvantage is the high acquisition cost.

Diversification

The small investor, to be sure, finds it more difficult to diversify than the large investor. Diversification, as noted before, consists of investing in a number of different industries. Small investors with only a few thousand dollars cannot buy common stock of many different industries. They either have to assume the higher risk of "putting all of their eggs in one basket," or have to reduce the risk (and possibly the return) by investing conservatively. Mutual funds make a real contribution in aiding small investors to diversify.

Professional management

The management qualities of mutual funds vary greatly. If you select a good mutual fund, the added fees paid for management are probably well worth it.

On the other hand, you might get management that is professional only in the sense that they charge a fee.

Constant surveillance

This is probably a plus. Many small investors make excellent choices regarding the common stock they buy, but then forget about them. A given stock that is a good buy today may not be so six months or a year from now. Not only should you try to buy good stocks at the right time, but you should sell them at the right time, or at least before it is too late. Small investors may not have the time (even if they have the ability) constantly to watch and analyze their portfolio.

High cost

The major disadvantage of investing in mutual funds is the high acquisition cost. These loading fees, as they are called, vary from fund to fund, and there are some no-load funds (examined below). In addition to the loading fees that must be paid to acquire mutual funds, management charges fees to manage the funds, generally financed out of the dividends that the underlying securities provide. Nevertheless, it is another cost that comes out of income the mutual fundholder otherwise would get. Because of the relatively high acquisition cost, mutual funds are a poor vehicle for the short-term investor who wants to get in and out of the market periodically because his or her goal is a relatively short-term and possibly modest capital gain.

Management costs are a fraction of 1 percent of the total assets in the fund. Often this is .5 percent of the first $500,000 in the fund and is then scaled down in several steps as the size of the fund increases.

The acquisition costs of closed-end investment companies are the same as regular brokerage commissions charged when you purchase stock directly. Open-end companies (mutual funds), however, charge a loading fee that varies from 2 or 3 percent to as high as about 8 or 9 percent (except for the no-load funds). The acquisition cost (load) is shown in the mutual fund quotation on the financial pages of newspapers like *The Wall Street Journal*. It is the difference between the net asset value (NAV) and the offer price. It goes to the broker or other middleman from whom you buy the funds. To be sure, you pay this loading fee only once. Mutual fund shares are redeemable at the option of the holder and almost always without a redemption fee. Nevertheless, these high loading fees almost require that you become a long-run investor.

Some mutual funds will scale the loading fees down in a series of steps on large purchases. However, the first reduction does not usually apply until the amount purchased is about $10,000 or $15,000, depending on the fund.

No-load Funds

A growing number of open-end investment companies (mutual funds) sell their shares directly to the public at the asset value and do not have a loading charge.

These companies, however, do not solicit business as actively and if you want to buy their shares, you have to take the initiative. They do not have brokers actively selling their shares; hence there are no commissions and no loading fees. A few of the older and more well known no-load funds are the Rowe Price Fund; Scudder, Stevens and Clark Fund of Boston; and De Vegh Fund of New York. However, there are many others, a number of which are currently being organized. Investors have a growing interest in these funds.

Because they have no sales staff, it is a little more difficult for the potential investor to obtain pertinent information on no-load funds. You can write the company and get their literature and prospectuses. In addition, a No-Load Mutual Fund Association (NLMFA) was formed recently; located at 11 Pennsylvania Plaza, Room 2204, New York, New York 10001, (telephone 212-563-4540), it is a new and additional source of information.

If you write the NLMFA, they will send you a list of their members. This will include the size of each of the no-load funds, when it was organized, its investment objectives, and its address. You can then select those that have the same investment objectives you are seeking and contact them. Since there are no salespersons, you will have to contact the company itself to buy the shares.

You can identify the no-load funds in the financial pages easily. There is a NL in the column, "offer price." When you buy no-load funds, you buy them at the net asset value. Table 18–1 shows some mutual fund listings as they appear on the financial pages. "NAV" is the net asset value; the offer price is what you would have to pay. The difference between the two represents the loading fee, except where an NL appears under the offer price. "NAV chg." indicates the change in the net asset value from the previous day. Most of the early no-load funds developed out of the operations of the investment counselors; they developed their mutual fund operations to service smaller clients. Recently some no-load funds have been developed by some investment services, the incentive being the management fees they would get. The no-load funds generally charge the same management fees as the other mutual funds.

Liquidation or Withdrawal of Mutual Funds

Some people invest in mutual funds for a specific purpose such as retirement income or financing a child's college education. When you wish to withdraw, you may do so at the net asset value, and almost always no fees are charged. You may withdraw in a lump sum or in any one of a number of different installment plans, either monthly, quarterly, semiannually or annually. Further, you may withdraw only the income earned by the fund and leave the principal intact, or you may dip into the principal. If you withdraw from the fund for retirement purposes, you should consider converting the fund into an income fund if this has not already been done. If your fund is with a group system you may switch from, say, a growth fund to an income fund for only a nominal transfer fee of $5 or $10. Most of the larger funds are grouped, and have an

Mutual Funds

Friday, July 8, 1983

Price ranges for investment companies, as quoted by the National Association of Securities Dealers. NAV stands for net asset value per share; the offering includes net asset value plus maximum sales charge, if any.

Fund	NAV	Offer Price	Chg.
Acorn Fnd	32.62	N.L.	– .01
ADV Fund	21.91	N.L.	– .08
Afuture Fd	18.47	N.L.	– .01
AIM Funds:			
Conv Yld	14.67	15.69+	.03
Grnway	14.67	15.69–	.11
HiYld Sc	10.41	11.13–	.03
Alli Techn	(z)	(z)	...
Alpha Fd	26.82	28.23–	.29
Am Birthrt	17.44	19.06–	.08
AE Growth	15.44	N.L.–	.01
American Funds Group:			
Am Bal	11.01	12.03–	.02
Amcap F	8.73	9.54–	.04
Am Mutl	14.80	16.17–	.05
Bnd FdA	12.67	13.85–	.04
Fund Inv	11.72	12.81–	.02
Gth FdA	14.27	15.60–	.08
Inc FdA	10.41	11.38–	.02
I C A	11.22	12.26–	.03
Nw Prsp	8.83	9.65–	.02
Tax Ex	9.57	10.05–	.01
Wash Mt	9.79	10.70	...
American General Group:			
A GnCBd	6.96	7.61–	.02
AG Entp	16.58	18.12–	.01
Gn Exch	46.59	N.L.–	.14
Growth	33.58	N.L.–	.18
High Yld	10.15	10.88–	.02
A G Mun	17.58	18.46	...
A GnVen	33.75	36.89–	.04
Comstk	13.98	15.28–	.02
Fd Amer	14.79	16.16	...
Harbor	16.09	17.58–	.01
Pace Fd	20.58	22.49–	.04
Prov Inc	5.73	6.18	...
Am Grwth	9.89	10.81–	.05
Am Heritg	4.33	N.L.–	.02
Am Invest	12.25	N.L.+	.02
AmInv Inc	11.29	N.L.+	.03
Am MedAs	27.90	N.L.–	.09
AmNat Gw	6.28	6.86–	.04
AmNtl Inc	21.56	23.56–	.02
Amway Mt	7.06	7.55–	.01
Analytic	135.37	N.L.–	.77
Armstrng	10.20	N.L.–	.04
Axe-Houghton:			
Fund B	10.29	11.18–	.05
Income	4.63	5.03–	.01
Stock Fd	16.00	17.49–	.15
BLC Gwth	19.38	21.18–	.02
BLCInc Fd	16.56	18.10+	.01
Babsn Inc	1.52	N.L.	...
Babsn Inv	14.33	N.L.–	.04
Beacon Gr	14.66	N.L.–	.02
Beacon Hll	16.72	N.L.–	.05
Berger Group:			
100 Fund	22.30	N.L.–	.08
101 Fund	15.51	N.L.–	.05
Boston Company:			
Cap Apr	27.65	N.L.–	.08
Govt Inc	10.71	N.L.	...
Spcl Grw	20.10	N.L.–	.03
Bos Found	(z)	(z)	...
Bull & Bear Group:			
Cap Grw	17.33	N.L.–	.08
Eq Incm	11.31	N.L.–	.02
High Yld	4.72	5.16–	.03
Inc Bost	8.83	9.65–	.03
Invests	8.36	9.14–	.03
Spc Eqty	25.00	26.95–	.14
Tax Mge	12.40	13.55	...
VS Incm	(z)	(z)	...
VS Specl	15.02	16.42	...
Eberstadt Group:			
Chem Fd	x12.45	13.61–	.11
Enrgy R	12.25	13.39+	.12
Surveyr	x19.80	21.64–	.09
Energy Utl	20.88	N.L.–	.01
Evrgrn Fd	47.24	N.L.–	.06
Evrgrn TR	15.01	N.L.–	.02
Farm B Gr	16.06	N.L.–	.08
Federated Group:			
Am Lead	(z)	(z)	...
Exch Fd	(z)	(z)	...
Hi Incm	(z)	(z)	...
Tax Free	(z)	(z)	...
US Gvt S	(z)	(z)	...
Fidelity Group Funds:			
Asst Inv	25.25	N.L.–	.08
Bd Corp	6.75	N.L.–	.04
Congr St	53.03	N.L.–	.20
Contra	13.29	N.L.–	.07
Eq Incm	26.67	N.L.–	.05
Exch Fd	43.58	N.L.–	.23
Fidel Fd	20.38	N.L.–	.04
Freedm	12.91	N.L.+	.04
Govt Sec	9.35	N.L.–	.02
Hi Incm	8.85	N.L.–	.02
High Yld	11.28	N.L.	...
Ltd Muni	8.08	N.L.–	.04
Magein	38.57	39.76–	.16
Mercry	14.08	14.52–	.03
Muncpl	6.83	N.L.–	.02
Puritan	13.30	N.L.–	.02
Sel Ergy	10.40	10.61–	.07
Sel Finl	15.90	16.22–	.03
Sel Hlth	21.83	22.28–	.11
Sel Metl	15.39	15.70–	.02
Sel Tech	26.53	27.07–	.18
Sel Util	13.11	13.38+	.03
Thrift Tr	9.80	N.L.–	.03
Trend	38.31	N.L.–	.24
Fidu CapG	19.69	N.L.+	.03
Financial Programs:			
Bond Shr	6.86	N.L.–	.02
Dynam	10.68	N.L.–	.06
Industl	5.67	N.L.–	.01
Income	8.92	N.L.–	.01
Tax Free	14.39	N.L.	...
Wld Tch	9.22	9.71	...
First Investors Fund:			
Bond Ap	14.78	15.94	...
Discvr	20.67	22.59–	.04
Growth	11.86	12.96–	.04
Income	6.75	7.38–	.01
Intl Sec	15.32	16.74–	.06
Nat Resr	7.91	8.64–	.06
Optn Fd	6.30	6.79–	.01
Tx Exmt	8.76	9.44	...
Flex Fnd	12.36	N.L.–	.03
44 Wall St	21.87	N.L.–	.24
44 WS Eqt	13.70	14.97–	.08
F&M Grw	6.66	7.03–	.05
Muni Bd	7.96	8.36+	.02
Optn Inc	13.09	14.31–	.02
Summit	29.09	31.79–	.18
Technol	15.61	17.06–	.07
Total R	16.53	18.07–	.07
US GvSc	8.84	9.21–	.01
Keystone Mass Group:			
Cust B 1	16.02	N.L.–	.03
Cust B 2	19.65	N.L.–	.02
Disct B 4	8.58	N.L.+	.05
Cust K 1	9.26	N.L.	...
Cust K 2	9.30	N.L.–	.05
Cust S 1	21.64	N.L.–	.05
Cust S 3	10.75	N.L.–	.08
Cust S 4	8.50	N.L.–	.07
Intl Fnd	5.38	N.L.–	.04
Tax Free	7.83	N.L.–	.01
Mass Fd	13.99	15.29–	.04
Legg Masn	18.04	N.L.–	.03
Lehm Cap	25.44	N.L.–	.08
Leverage	11.91	N.L.–	.06
Lexington Group:			
Cp Ledrs	12.83	14.11–	.06
Gold Fd	4.65	N.L.–	.02
Gnma	7.69	N.L.	...
Growth	11.85	N.L.–	.02
Resrch	20.54	N.L.+	.05
Lindner Fd	18.62	N.L.–	.06
Loomis Sayles Funds:			
Cap Dev	27.13	N.L.–	.07
Mutual	18.71	N.L.–	.09
Lord Abbett:			
Affilatd	9.71	10.47–	.01
Bnd Deb	11.15	12.19–	.02
Devl Gro	10.58	11.56–	.02
Income	3.09	3.33–	.01
Value Ap	9.16	10.01–	.01
Lutheran Brotherhood:			
Broth Fd	(z)	(z)	...
Bro Inc	(z)	(z)	...
Bro MBd	(z)	(z)	...
Broth US	(z)	(z)	...
Mass Financial Services:			
MIT	(z)	(z)	...
MIG	(z)	(z)	...
MID	(z)	(z)	...
MCD	(z)	(z)	...
MEG	(z)	(z)	...
MFD	(z)	(z)	...
MFB	(z)	(z)	...
MMB	(z)	(z)	...
MFH	(z)	(z)	...
MFI	(z)	(z)	...
Mathers	24.50	N.L.–	.02
Merrill Lynch:			
Basc Val	14.75	15.78–	.07
Captl Fd	20.13	21.53+	.01
EquiBd 1	11.12	11.58–	.01
Hi Incm	8.25	8.60–	.01
Hi QualP	10.49	10.95–	.01
Int TPrt	10.53	10.74	...
Muni Ins	7.02	7.31	...
Mun HY	9.09	9.47–	.01
Ltd Mat	9.81	9.91	...
Pacific	13.20	14.12	...
Phoenx	11.79	12.61–	.02
Sci Tech	9.93	10.85–	.03
Sp'l Valu	14.28	15.27+	.02
Mid Amer	(z)	(z)	...
MidA HGr	(z)	(z)	...
Mdw Incm	10.11	N.L.–	.02
MSB Fund	22.15	N.L.–	.09
Mutl BnFd	14.17	15.49–	.01
Prec Metl	21.08	N.L.+	.04
Price Rowe:			
Growth	15.73	N.L.–	.06
Grw Inc	12.92	N.L.–	.07
Income	8.40	N.L.	...
Intl Fd	12.66	N.L.–	.08
New Era	18.17	N.L.–	.08
Nw Horz	20.75	N.L.–	.06
Tax Free	8.77	N.L.–	.01
Pro Services Funds:			
Med Tec	13.04	N.L.–	.04
Pro Fnd	10.65	N.L.–	.05
Pro Inco	8.82	N.L.–	.06
Prudential Bache:			
Equity	14.16	15.18–	.04
Govt Sec	x9.84	9.94–	.10
High Yld	10.23	10.97–	.03
HiY Mun	13.77	14.42–	.01
Option	15.60	16.73–	.09
Quality	x14.81	15.88–	.15
Resrch	9.76	N.L.–	.06
Prud SIP	14.12	15.43–	.04
Putnam Funds:			
Cal TxE	13.63	14.31–	.10
Captl Fd	22.87	(z)–	.06
Convert	15.91	17.39–	.03
George	14.98	16.37–	.06
Growth	13.02	14.23–	.05
Hlth Sci	21.07	23.03–	.08
High Yld	17.68	18.96–	.03
Income	6.80	7.29–	.02
Info Sci	13.64	14.91–	.04
Intl Equi	18.54	20.26–	.09
Investr	12.41	13.56–	.04
Option	12.98	14.13–	.01
Tax Ex	21.56	22.64–	.18
Vista Fd	20.41	22.31–	.10
Voyage	20.27	22.15–	.18
Quaser As	(z)	(z)	...
Rainbw Fd	4.19	N.L.–	.01
Roch TxM	14.38	15.72+	.01
Safeco Group:			
Equity	10.89	N.L.–	.09
Growth	20.32	N.L.	...
Income	13.11	N.L.–	.02
Safeco MB	11.62	N.L.–	.02
St Paul Funds:			
Captl Fd	14.74	15.68–	.04
Income	(z)	(z)	...
Growth	16.97	18.05–	.11
Specl Fd	26.53	N.L.–	.18
Scudder Funds:			
Cptl Gro	15.22	N.L.–	.07
Commn	15.53	N.L.–	.04
Devl Fd	70.33	N.L.–	.09
Income	11.86	N.L.–	.05
Intl Fnd	21.01	N.L.–	.05
Muni Bd	7.81	N.L.–	.02
Security Funds:			
Action	8.42	(z)–	.01
Bond Fd	8.10	8.50–	.02
Equity	8.78	9.60–	.09
Invest	11.27	12.32–	.02
Ultra Fd	11.53	12.60–	.03
Selected Funds:			
Selct Am	8.99	N.L.–	.04
Selct Spl	23.50	N.L.–	.06
Seligman Group:			
Captl Fd	15.03	16.20	...
Com Stk	14.10	15.20–	.01
Growth	8.24	8.88–	.05
Income	11.81	12.73–	.01
Sentinel Group Funds:			

income fund, growth fund, and balanced fund. This is another reason why the mutual fund you buy must be selected with care; selecting a good group provides greater flexibility.

If you switch from one fund to another within a group, in setting up a withdrawal program (or at any time) you may be realizing a substantial capital gain and have a tax problem. Hence taxes must be given some consideration when deciding whether to switch or not.

Information on Investment Companies

General information on investment companies can be obtained from the same sources that are available for any other type of investment information. The financial pages of most metropolitan newspapers carry price information and sometimes articles on certain companies. Papers like *The Wall Street Journal* and magazines like *Forbes, Business Week,* and *Barron's* are other good sources. *Forbes* and *Barron's* especially should be noted because they make special studies from time to time wherein they analyze and compare the past record of various investment companies. *Forbes* magazine has a special annual study of mutual funds every August, with articles and analyses of mutual funds and statistical data on each of the major funds. There are statistics on assets, sales charges (loading fees), expenses per $100 of fund assets, dividend returns, and average annual growth rates over a number of years, as well as the performance over the most recent twelve months. Various investment services, such as Moody's, Value Line Investment Services, and Standard and Poor's, publish information on investment companies. In addition, your broker may have a wealth of useful information.

Two investment company services specialize in analyzing and publishing information on investment companies. Two of these services publish their reports annually: *Investment Companies, Mutual Funds, and Other Types,* by Wiesenberger Financial Services, Inc., of 1633 Broadway, New York; and *Johnson's Investment Company Charts,* published by Hugh A. Johnson and Company, 246 Homewood Avenue, Buffalo, New York. These studies analyze most of the leading investment companies, appraise their various performances, and compare them with the performance of the stock market in general. The Wiesenberger Study and the Johnson Study can be purchased or can be perused at many brokerage houses and at any good library.

Which Funds Have Done Well?

When choosing what fund to buy, do so in light of your investment objectives. Even after choosing a growth fund or a balanced fund or an income fund, many choices are available. Not all funds perform the same, and differences in performance can be attributed primarily to the differences in management.

If you are buying a growth fund (and even some others with different objectives), it should be doing somewhat better than the Dow-Jones Industrial Averages. Otherwise you can buy common stock directly (choosing from the blue chips that make up the Dow-Jones) and save the extra cost of buying mutual funds. However, only some of the mutual funds have done better than the Dow-Jones Averages over the years, and some have not done as well.

Just as stock price averages have been constructed to show how stock prices are moving, averages or indexes can also be constructed of the price of mutual funds to show how mutual funds in general are performing. Two of the better-known mutual fund averages are published by Hugh A. Johnson and Company and by Wiesenberger Services, Inc. Figure 18–2 shows several mutual fund indexes. One is for a number of growth funds, one for growth/income funds, one for income funds, and one for a number of balanced funds. The growth fund has increased by about 57 percent since 1970. The income fund has outperformed the growth fund, having risen 85 percent during the same period, while the growth-income fund and the balanced fund are up 70 and 54 percent respectively. These records can be compared with that of Standard and Poor's industrial average which rose about 35 percent during this time.

We can also analyze the performance of the mutual funds with Johnson's statistics. Johnson has five mutual fund averages: (1) a growth fund average, (2) an aggressive growth fund average, (3) a growth and income fund average, (4) an income fund average, and (5) a balanced fund average. Table 18–2 shows these averages over the last few years and also the annualized rate of return. In

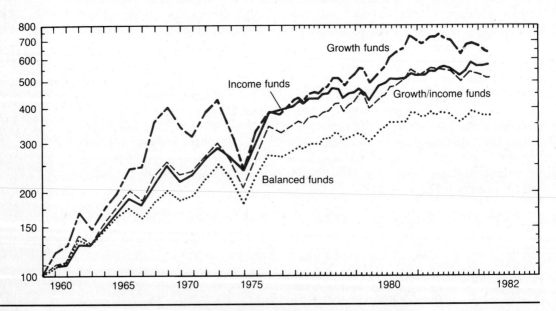

Figure 18–2 Wiesenberger mutual fund indexes. (*Source: Investment Companies 1982*, Wiesenberger Financial Services, a division of Warren, Gorham & Lamont, Inc., p. 104.)

Table 18–2 Johnson's charts, quarterly performance report, March 31, 1983

PERFORMANCE SUMMARY TABLES

	3 mos. 1983	1¼ Yrs. 1982-83	2¼ Yrs 1981-83	3¼ Yrs. 1980-83	5¼ Yrs. 1978-83	7¼ Yrs. 1976-83	8¼ Yrs. 1975-83	10¼ Yrs. 1973-83	15¼ Yrs. 1968-83
Dow-Jones Industrial Average	+ 9.3%	+ 37%	+ 32%	+ 61%	+ 83%	+ 95%	+183%	$18,914	$25,428
S & P 500 Stock Composite Index	+10.0	+ 32	+ 27	+ 67	+108	+140	+228	20,694	29,473
Cost of Living	+ 0.1	+ 4	+ 13	+ 27	+ 57	+ 76	+ 88	23,000	32,175
S & P High Grade Bonds	+ 2.0	+ 51	+ 46	+ 39	+ 32	+ 57	+ 71	17,136	21,012
S & P Municipal Bonds	+ 3.9	+ 61	+ 33	+ 6	+ 1	+ 34	+ 40	12,676	15,481
S & P Long-Term Government Bonds	+ 1.1	+ 51	+ 46	+ 40	+ 33	+ 34	+ 51	17,187	22,748
*Interest @ 5½%	+ 1.4	+ 7	+ 13	+ 19	+ 32	+ 48	+ 56	17,316	22,626
*Interest @ 7½%	+ 1.9	+ 10	+ 18	+ 27	+ 46	+ 69	+ 82	20,997	30,129
*Interest @ 10%	+ 2.5	+ 13	+ 24	+ 36	+ 65	+100	+117	26,586	42,780
Johnson Growth Fund Average	+ 9.4	+ 29	+ 25	+ 66	+136	+184	+276	21,915	27,358
Johnson Aggressive Grth. Fd. Avg.	+12.7	+ 40	+ 36	+ 92	+228	+399	+495	35,556	—
Johnson Growth & Income Fd. Avg.	+10.2	+ 39	+ 35	+ 72	+124	+178	+271	26,024	30,266
Johnson Balanced Fund Average	+ 6.9	+ 34	+ 32	+ 60	+ 89	+132	+193	20,947	29,366
Johnson Income Fund Average	+ 7.8	+ 39	+ 46	+ 57	+ 74	+122	+178	21,767	30,037

ANNUALIZED RATE OF RETURN

	3¼ Yrs.	5¼ Yrs.	7¼ Yrs.	10¼ Yrs.	15¼ Yrs.
Dow-Jones Industrial Average	15.8%	12.2%	9.6%	6.4%	6.3%
S & P 500 Stock Composite Index	17.1	15.0	12.8	7.4	7.3
Cost of Living	7.6	9.0	8.1	8.5	8.0
S & P High Grade Bonds	10.7	9.0	6.4	5.4	5.0
S & P Municipal Bonds	1.8	5.4	4.1	2.3	2.9
S & P Long-Term Government Bonds	10.9	0.2	4.1	5.4	5.5
*Interest @ 5½%	5.5	5.5	5.5	5.5	5.5
*Interest @ 7½%	7.5	7.5	7.5	7.5	7.5
*Interest @ 10%	10.0	10.0	10.0	10.0	10.0
Johnson Growth Fund Average	16.9	17.8	15.5	8.0	6.8
Johnson Aggressive Growth Fund Average	22.2	25.4	24.8	13.2	—
Johnson Growth & Income Fund Average	18.2	16.6	15.1	9.8	7.5
Johnson Balanced Fund Average	15.6	12.9	12.3	7.5	7.3
Johnson Income Fund Average	14.9	11.1	11.6	7.9	7.5

*Compounded annually

Source: Johnson's Charts, Inc., 246 Homewood Avenue, Buffalo, New York 14217.

addition, the table shows the Dow-Jones Industrial Averages, the Standard and Poor's composite stock index, and other financial indicators to compare with the mutual fund average.

While mutual fund averages are useful, the prospective buyer must also look at the record of individual companies. Some performed even better than the fund averages shown and some, not so well. You can get literature from the fund that you are interested in buying and compare their past record with both the fund averages, the Standard and Poor's average, and the Dow-Jones

Averages. This gives a clue to how well the fund is managed. A good past performance is no assurance of success in the future; however, it's probably better to bet (if bet you must) on a past winner.

You can also compare the growth of many individual funds with both the Standard and Poor's stock index and the Dow-Jones Averages by using Johnson's Charts, which you can find at many brokerage houses. Johnson has plotted the performance of individual funds and has included a transparent overlay of both the Dow-Jones and the Standard and Poor's market indicators. By comparing the two, you can see at a glance which funds have outdone the stock market indicators and which have not.

Who Should Buy Investment Company Shares?

To answer this question investors must analyze their personal affairs in light of the advantages and disadvantages of investment companies and how much time purchasers have to watch their investments (if they buy common stock directly) and how much skill they may have in selecting good securities. Some investment companies are better than others, and it may be almost as difficult to select a good investment company as it is to select a good common stock directly. A person who is building a portfolio of common stock must go through the analyzing and selecting process time and time again—a never-ending task. By choosing the investment company route, an investor has to make the selection decision only once.

Investment Company Legislation

With the stock market boom of the 1920s, investment companies became extremely popular and a large number of people invested in them. Unfortunately, many of the companies took unwarranted risks, and in the crash that followed large sums of money were lost by the shareholders. This situation led to an extensive study of investment companies by the Securities and Exchange Commission. Based on these studies, Congress passed the Investment Company Act of 1940 that requires that practically all investment companies register with the SEC, which to a certain extent regulates their activities. The act as amended sets up standards for such things as the statement of policies of the company, the number of shares authorized for closed-end companies, the sale of securities, and advertising standards. Generally when new shares are issued, a prospectus explaining the details of the issue must be published. Those companies that refuse to register are limited in the scope of their activity; they may not use the mails for the purchase or sale of securities and may not engage in interstate commerce. The companies that do qualify are called "registered investment companies."

In 1970, Congress passed an amendment to the Investment Company Act. The two main provisions of the amendment were to eliminate the front-end load and to see that other loading fees are not excessive. The amendment has virtually eliminated the front-end load, by providing for a partial or sometimes total refund of the loading fees if the shareholder withdraws from the fund contract within a specified period of time and if there is an excessive front-end load.

INTRODUCTION TO OTHER OUTLETS FOR SURPLUS FUNDS

In addition to mutual funds, a person may invest in commodities, real estate, and a number of unusual (sometimes called exotic) investments. Each of these will now be examined. We hasten to add, however, that, with the exception of real estate, these are not for the typical small investor because there is a larger element of speculation involved. Nevertheless, they may be right for some people.

Traditional Commodities[1]

Traditionally when one speaks of commodities, one has in mind such things as wheat, corn, sugar, sow bellies (bacon), and the like. In 1980 and early 1981 certain exotic items such as gold, diamonds, antiques, Chinese ceramics, and the like (which, with the possible exception of gold, aren't really commodities at all) gained some popularity. Then, in 1982 and 1983, they lost some of that luster, but in the future—who knows. While some people made money in commodities, this was more speculation than investing. Consequently, the small investor should probably steer clear of commodities. Probably so too should all but the professional speculator who makes a living through buying and selling commodities. Nevertheless, a few words on the commodity markets are in order.

The price of certain commodities fluctuates widely over short periods of time for a variety of reasons. The supply can change sharply due to crop failure caused by adverse weather or loss of production due to a strike. Demand for certain commodities, too, can fluctuate due to changed public tastes or governmental policies. These sharp changes in supply and demand can create sharp price changes. Because of these fluctuations, speculators have entered the market.

There are futures prices and spot or cash prices. The spot price is the price paid for delivery today, but the futures price is the price paid today for commodities to be delivered at a specified time in the future. There is a one-month, two-month, three-month futures price, and so on.

1. I wish to acknowledge the help I have received in developing the section on commodities from Professor Edna Villar of Pan American University.

If you believe the price of corn will rise and you buy corn futures, you are referred to as being "long." If you expect the price to decline and you sell, you are referred to as being "short." If your expectations come true, you make a profit. If prices turn against you, you suffer losses.

Since there are futures markets in commodities, and professional speculators that operate in them, business firms that use these commodities can hedge their operations and protect themselves from sharp price fluctuations. In the process, the speculator may make a lot of money. There is the so-called "short hedge" and the "long hedge."

The short hedge

The short hedge works as follows: Suppose a candy manufacturer has signed a contract to supply some candy. The price has been set, and it will take a month or more to make and deliver the candy. In the meantime, the manufacturer does not want to carry a large inventory of sugar but wants to protect itself against sharp price increases. He will buy sugar futures. This will freeze the price of sugar for, say, thirty days. While the future price may be slightly higher than the present or spot prices, it is known, and presumably the candy manufacturer negotiates the contract with future prices in mind. For the small price differential, he can avoid carrying a large inventory in sugar and also protect himself (hedge) against sharp price increases in sugar, his major input cost.

The long hedge

The long hedge involves holding an inventory and selling a contract for future delivery to hedge (protect) the inventory from a sharp change in prices. This is logically the same as a short sale in the case of securities. (See Chapter 17 above). For example, a miller, storage company, or exporter may have a large inventory of wheat that he would like to hedge against a price change. If he sells a contract for future delivery and the price falls, he will suffer a loss on his inventory, but it will be offset by a profit from his futures contract. If the price rises, exactly the reverse happens.

Business firms may hedge their operations only because there are speculators. My advice to virtually all investors is: don't speculate in commodities; don't buy or sell futures. Some people make money in commodities, or so they say, but few do, and most of those are brokers and a few professional broker-dealer speculators.

Commodity Market

There are speculators, hence a futures market, in certain foods, grains, fats and oils, textiles, and metals. Futures quotation may be found in the financial pages of large metropolitan newspapers. The Chicago Board of Trade is the largest commodities market in the nation. There are a number of others, including the Kansas City Board of Trade, the Minneapolis Board of Trade, the Chicago

Mercantile Exchange, the New York Coffee, Cocoa, and Sugar Exchange, the New York Cotton Exchange, and the New York Commodity Exchange. Table 18–3 shows the futures market prices for coffee and cotton as reported in *The Wall Street Journal* on July 11, 1983.

The Futures Market in Securities

There is also a futures market in Treasury bills, certain other short-term and intermediate-term and long-term U.S. government securities, and common stock which work much like commodity futures. If you believe interest rates are coming down in the future (government security prices are going to rise), you may buy security futures. If you are right, you will make money. If your view is that interest rates will rise (security prices will fall) and you are right, you could making money by selling futures.

The trading unit for Treasury bill futures is one million dollars and for longer-term securities $100,000. However, margins are very low and only a few

Table 18–3   Futures prices as published in *The Wall Street Journal*, July 8, 1983

Futures Prices

Friday, July 8, 1983

	Open	High	Low	Settle	Change	Lifetime High	Low	Open Interest
July	2,220	2,220	2,220	2,212	− 68	2,410	1,894	1,144
Sept	2,247	2,247	2,247	2,219	− 68	2,270	2,270	1
Dec	....	....	....	2,229	− 68	2,270	2,270	1

Est vol 3,455; vol Thur 4,484; open int 28,516, −376.

COFFEE (CSCE)−37,500 lbs.; cents per lb.

	Open	High	Low	Settle	Change	Lifetime High	Low	Open Interest
July	127.05	127.77	127.05	127.88	+ .53	135.50	102.00	302
Sept	128.00	128.75	127.61	127.89	− .11	131.75	101.00	4,578
Dec	126.40	126.75	126.00	126.15	− .10	130.00	98.00	2,174
Mar84	124.25	124.30	124.00	124.00	+ .12	127.65	110.50	558
May	122.25	122.25	122.10	121.75	....	126.00	108.50	146
July	....	....		119.88	− .17	124.00	106.25	173
Sept	118.00	118.00	118.00	118.13	....	123.00	110.50	229
Dec	116.60	116.60	116.40	116.00	− .90	117.50	116.40	12

Est vol 1,268; vol Thur 1,572; open int 8,172, +156.

COTTON (CTN)−50,000 lbs.; cents per lb.

	Open	High	Low	Settle	Change	Lifetime High	Low	Open Interest
July	....	....		....	....		....	385
Oct	77.40	78.00	77.20	77.63	− .20	82.20	65.65	2,996
Dec	78.70	79.45	78.60	79.12	− .07	82.85	65.50	23,838
Mar84	79.90	80.55	79.80	80.45	− .05	83.29	67.10	4,186
May	80.50	80.40	80.50	80.70	− .25	83.40	69.38	672
July	80.75	80.80	80.65	80.80	....	83.50	71.50	541
Oct	....	....		76.00	+ .10	79.00	74.25	223
Dec	75.00	75.05	74.60	75.02	+ .42	76.00	74.00	306

Est vol 5,800; vol Thurs 7,239; open int 33,148, −304.

thousand dollars are required to take a position. It is also possible to hedge with government securities, but only very large investors or institutions such as insurance companies are in a position to do so.

With stock market futures, trading is carried out in one of the stock indexes, such as Standard and Poor's 500, the Value Line Index, or the New York Stock Exchange Composite Index. For example, if you buy (or sell) the Standard and Poor's index futures, you are speculating on the future prices of 500 different stocks. If the Standard and Poor's index is 165, but you expect it to rise to 175 and buy, you would make money if correct and lose if wrong. If you expect it to decline, you do the reverse.

The minimum dollar amount you may buy, however, is the index level times 500. Therefore, if the index level stands at 165, the minimum dollar amount is $82,500, so it is definitely not for the small investor; it is also highly risky. You may also buy common stock indexes on margin, generally ranging from 5 to 25 percent.

It is also possible to hedge via common stock indexes—just as in the case of commodities or government securities. However, this would be of interest primarily to institutional investors and wealthy individuals. While these futures markets are in securities, the actual operations are carried out not in the security exchange, but on the commodities exchange.

There are now also stock index options—that is, you may buy puts and calls on the indexes and not buy the index itself. (Puts and calls on stock were discussed in Chapter 17.) Several exchanges are offering options on the index futures. Again, this is not for the small investor.

REAL ESTATE INVESTMENTS

There are two major ways of investing in real estate, first, investing in mortgages, and second, owning real property outright. If you invest in mortgages you are lending money to a homeowner to help finance a home; on this loan you receive interest.

Mortgages[2]

A mortgage is a legal document given by the prospective homeowner (borrower) to the lender. The borrower who gives the mortgage is called the mortgagor,

2. In early 1980 interest rates on mortgages (and other investments as well) rose greatly. One reason mortgage interest rates rose is because in 1980 the federal government nullified all state mortgage usury laws. However, this nullification applied only to mortgage lending financial institutions. Individuals making mortgage loans *are still subject* to state usury laws, which vary from a low of 9.5 percent to a high of 21 percent, although several states do not have a usury limit. If you as an individual decide to invest in mortgages, be sure to check the usury law in your state. *You are still subject to it.*

and the lender who receives the mortgage is called the mortgagee. The mortgage stipulates the terms of the loan such as: the interest rate, the monthly payments, and the length of time over which the loan is to be repaid. In addition, the borrower agrees to pay all taxes, assessments, and other charges levied against the property, also to keep it in good repair and fully insured against fire and other hazards.

The mortgage also provides for foreclosure and repossession of the home by the mortgage lender in the event that the homeowner defaults. In some states a deed of trust is used in place of a mortgage but it provides for the same arrangements.

Most mortgage loans are made by financial institutions such as savings and loan associations and mutual savings banks, but there is no reason why an individual with surplus funds cannot make such a loan to a homeowner. When a person makes a mortgage loan, he or she in effect pays off the seller of the home (sometimes the builder if it is a new home) and the purchaser gives the lender a mortgage as described above.

If you wish to make a mortgage loan, see a realtor or a builder, who can put you in contact with a prospective mortgagor. You should probably retain an attorney to draw up the mortgage, at least the first time.

Mortgages are negotiable just like corporate bonds, and can be sold just like corporate bonds. The interest rate on a mortgage is fixed for the duration of the loan, and hence if interest rates rise after a given mortgage has been agreed upon, the market price of the mortgage declines. The market price of mortgages, then, fluctuates inversely with changes in the going interest rate, and consequently mortgages may be sold at a premium or at a discount from their face value, just as in the case of corporate bonds. (See Chapter 15 for a discussion relative to bonds.)

Determination of Mortgage Yields

Since the price of mortgages, purchased from another mortgagee, fluctuates, the yield is not necessarily the same as the fixed interest rate specified in the mortgage itself. Also, mortgages are not as liquid as corporate bonds; it takes time to sell them to someone else. For this reason, the yield on mortgages is generally higher than that on corporate bonds. The true yield on a mortgage, of course, is determined by how much above or below face value it is sold. To determine the approximate yields, the following formula is used.[3]

---

3. Note the word "approximate." The reason for approximation is that the components of the problem are themselves only averages. The figures used are generally average interest earned per year. This is true where monthly payments are made (this is not the case, however, in this oversimplified problem). To be strictly accurate, yields must be figured using compound interest functions.

$$Y = \frac{R(P) + \left(\dfrac{P - C}{N}\right)}{\left(\dfrac{P + C}{2}\right)} \times 100$$

Y = approximate yield
P = principal balance of the mortgage
C = the cost to the investor of the mortgage
N = number of years the mortgage runs until paid
R = coupon rate of interest the mortgage carries

Assume, for example, a ten-year-old mortgage with an unamortized face value of $50,000 running over ten years, bearing a fixed interest rate of 10 percent which you can purchase for $35,000.

$$(1) \qquad Y = \frac{.10(\$50,000) + \left(\dfrac{\$50,000 - \$35,000}{10}\right)}{\left(\dfrac{\$50,000 + \$35,000}{2}\right)} \times 100$$

$$(2) \qquad Y = \frac{5,000 + \left(\dfrac{\$15,000}{10}\right)}{\dfrac{85,000}{2}} \times 100$$

$$(3) \qquad Y = \frac{\$5,000 + \$1,500}{\dfrac{85,000}{2}} \times 100$$

$$(4) \qquad Y = \frac{\$6,500}{\$42,500} \times 100 =$$

$$(5) \qquad Y = 15.29 \text{ percent approximate yield}$$

We noted above that a mortgage is less liquid than corporate bonds, and hence the yield should be higher. Mortgages also generally are riskier than corporate bonds, which also will increase their yield above bonds. However, the degree of risk varies with the credit rating of the mortgagor. When making a mortgage loan, you must appraise the credibility of the mortgagor. You must also consider the age and the condition of the house, and what portion of its total value you are financing. The general rule is that the individual should not make a mortgage loan in excess of 75 percent of the value of the house. You should also remember that some costs are involved if you have to foreclose and repossess the home. All this will have a bearing on the yield on mortgage loans.

You must also decide whether the yield on a given mortgage is sufficiently higher than your alternative investment opportunities. If it is not, you can bargain to increase it by asking for a larger discount. Whether the above 15.29 percent yield is adequate depends on the investor's alternative investment opportunities.

Second Mortgages

In the above discussion we had in mind first mortgages. There are also second mortgages, which are riskier. In the event of a foreclosure and sale of a house on which the mortgagor has defaulted, the second mortgage is not paid off until after the first mortgagee has been completely repaid. Assume a home valued at $100,000 with a $60,000 mortgage. If the home is sold, the buyer would need a $40,000 down payment to take over the existing mortgage. If he had only $25,000, he could offer a second mortgage for $15,000, and he would now have two mortgages to pay. Second mortgages are for smaller dollar amounts and run over fewer years than firsts, generally from five to twelve years. While riskier, second mortgages provide a higher yield; and if the mortgagor has a sufficiently high income and a good enough credit rating, many mortgage lenders will assume the higher risk in order to obtain the higher yield. Second mortgages generally have a maximum amortization period of twelve years and yield as high as 20 percent. The yield on discounted second mortgages is calculated by using the above formula just as in the case of the first mortgages. Be sure and check your state's usury laws before investing in mortgages; they may apply to you.

Reasons for (or for Not) Buying Mortgages

If you are willing to buy corporate bonds and other fixed investments, why not mortgages—if you can get a higher yield? Obviously if you think interest rates will not rise in the future, you should consider them. If you think interest rates will go higher, then you should not. There may be the problem of finding a mortgagor willing to lock in at high rates for 20 or 30 years. You, too, may be unwilling to lock in for 20 years, even at higher rates, because, mortgages are not very liquid. However, you need not accept the conventional long-term fixed mortgages. You may invest in an innovative mortgage and not lock yourself in for a long period of time (see Chapter 9).

A Final Word of Caution

When accepting a mortgage be sure that the mortgagor has a strong credit rating. This is especially true in an innovative mortgage. If you escalate interest on him and create a hardship for him it may also be unpleasant for you. If a mortgagor's income rises substantially over the years, your investment is probably safe; otherwise it might not be. If the mortgages in your portfolio have balloon payments, you may have to refinance them in order to avoid a default. To be sure you can foreclose on the loan if necessary, but that is a lengthy and expensive process. The best advice is caution—make loans only to the strong.

Real Estate Investment Trusts

Another possible outlet for surplus funds is the real estate investment trust, which generally resembles the mutual fund. It is a specialized holding company that sells stock in itself to the public. However, instead of investing in stocks as the mutual fund generally does, the investment is in real estate. The main inducement for the real estate investment is that it is exempt from paying the corporate income tax provided it distributes at least 90 percent of its income to the holders of the trust certificate of ownership.

For the trust to be exempt from the corporate income tax, it must strictly follow the law, which requires:

1. That there be more than one hundred shareholders
2. That no five persons directly or indirectly own 50 percent or more of the shares
3. That 90 percent of its taxable income must be distributed to the shareholders
4. That it derive at least 75 percent of its gain from rents, capital gains, or mortgage income
5. That it derive no more than 25 percent of its income from dividends and interest in other concerns (provided that only 75 percent of its income results from investments outlined in point 4; For example, if 85 percent of the income were from rents, then only 15 percent would have to come from dividends and interest in other concerns).
6. That it hold property for a minimum of four years
7. That it be separate from the management of the real estate it holds.

The trust provides more liquidity than most real estate investments. For example, if you own a trust certificate, you may sell it. If you wish to become part of a trust, you may purchase a certificate.

Real estate investment trusts are specialized closed-end investment companies. In addition, some of them borrow money and have leverage built into their capital structure just as do some closed-end investment companies. In recent years, they have become an additional source of substantial mortgage capital, and this capital does not seem to dry up as much during periods of extremely tight credit as is the case with more traditional sources.

Real estate investment trusts (REIT) have also begun to specialize to some extent. There are now about five types: (1) equity, (2) short-term mortgage construction, (3) long-term mortgage, (4) hybrid, and (5) specialized. Most of them can be classified as those that buy securities representing real estate investments (mortgages) and receive a fixed-interest income and those that buy the real estate directly and receive a rental (and perhaps a capital gain) income.

Many individuals who invest in real estate shy away from the real estate investment trust because of the lack of individual control and the fact that the investment must be in income-producing property. For example, the trust cannot purchase a piece of raw land for development purposes or for capital gains. These two facts have prevented the trust from becoming as successful as it might have.

Owning Real Estate Directly

So far I have discussed primarily buying securities that represent real estate investments. It is also possible to own and manage real estate directly, primarily for income purposes, but also for capital gains, as a hedge against inflation, or for tax reasons.

Income properties are generally divided into two categories: residential income properties, including individual homes, duplexes, and apartment houses, and nonresidential, including commercial space, office space, and industrial or warehouse space.

Single family, duplexes, or multifamily (apartments) residentials
When you buy rental property, you must choose whether to buy a single family dwelling, a duplex, a triplex, or an apartment. How much money you are able to invest will be a constraint that may rule out everything but a single family unit. If you are able to invest more and have a choice, you must come to grips with the following questions:

1. What type of residential unit is in the greatest demand? Indeed, what is the demand for all of the various types of units?
2. What is the supply of currently available rental units of the various types which would compete with you in providing housing? It is possible that the demand for apartments is greater than for single family units, but nevertheless apartments may be overbuilt while single family rentals are very scarce.
3. What size of family unit (small or large house) is in greatest demand relative to the available supply?
4. What part of the community is the best location for various types of residential units?
5. What is the cost of acquiring a residential unit? (Generally, the cost per square foot is less on a multifamily than on single units.)
6. What are maintenance costs and rental incomes?

All this will require an analysis of population growth in the area, residential values, monthly rents, construction rates, rental unit vacancy rates, yield on capital invested, whether the population is in large part transient or permanent, and personal income.

In recent years, residential rental property has been an excellent investment. It has provided an inflationary hedge, a tax shelter, capital gains in excess of the rate of inflation, and a fairly good investment return. Recently some analysts have maintained that real estate is no longer a superior investment outlet. It is certainly no longer a viable vehicle for achieving all of the above goals; high interest rates and high construction costs have pushed prices to the point that rental income, at the time of purchase, cannot even come close to amortizing the mortgage. In the past there was usually at least a small positive cash flow on rental property. Recently, however, rental prices have not kept up with the price of houses. In some sections of the country they have not even kept up with inflation. If you buy residential rental property there, you will almost certainly have to accept a negative cash flow, at least temporarily.[4]

While housing prices may not rise as rapidly in the future as they have in the past, they should at least keep up with inflation, especially in growth areas. It has also been stated that the future housing market will be soft, because more and more people have been (and will remain) priced out of home ownership. But these people will have to live somewhere and will become renters. (There will also be more doubling up—that is, two or more unrelated individuals buying or renting a home jointly; this is already happening to some degree.) Also there is a growing number of persons approaching first-time homeownership age because of the 1950s baby boom. There was also a decline in construction in 1980 and 1981. What does the combination of these factors suggest? The supply of housing is down—or at least new construction is—and the demand for it is up. Will this increase or decrease the price of homes? This factor alone should tend to increase the price of homes in the future. If many people can't afford these homes or there is little mortgage money to finance them, we will become more a nation of renters again, as we once were, so rentals should be a good investment. If you can afford to buy a house, you can rent it to someone who cannot. Rents may rise relative to housing costs to the point where the monthly rent again becomes about equal to the traditional 1 percent of the house's value.

Calculating the yield on direct real estate investments

To analyze rental property as an investment, you must look at the cash flow, the tax consequences, expected future cash flow, and expected price appreciation of the property. Table 18–4 provides a starting point. An investor purchases a duplex for $150,000; makes a down payment of $40,000; and finances the remainder at 14 percent over 30 years. The net rental income amounts to $15,800, which after taxes, insurance, and interest generates a negative cash flow of $3,840. In earlier days, an investor could expect a positive yield, but this is virtually impossible today. However, depreciation laws have recently been liberalized, and real estate may now be depreciated (now called "cost recovery")

---

4. A negative cash flow merely means that the mortgage payments are in excess of rental income.

Table 18–4   Rental property as a tax shelter

Duplex:		$150,000
Downpayment		40,000
Mortgage at 14 percent interest–thirty years		110,000
Rental Income:		
Two units at $700 per month	$16,800	
Maintenance, repairs, and vacancy	1,000	
Net Rental Income		$15,800
Taxes and Insurance		4,000
Mortgage Payment (about $1,303 per month)		15,640
Cash Flow (negative)		($ 3,840)
Equity Buildup First Year (about ($12.50 per month)	$150	$ 150
Cash Flow Less Equity Buildup		($ 3,690)
Depreciation over fifteen years at 175 percent of straight line ($130,000 × 11.66), first year		$ 15,158
Interest First Year (Mortgage payment less equity buildup)		$ 15,490
Taxes and Insurance		$ 4,000

Source: Calculated by author.

over fifteen years at 175 percent of the straight-line method. In our example, accelerated depreciation comes to $15,158 during the first year and provides that much of a tax shelter—it can offset that much of other income and shield it from taxes. Is this duplex, then, a good investment? It depends on one's tax bracket, among other things. In the 50 percent tax bracket, this investment will save $7,579 in taxes. In the 40 percent bracket, the tax savings will be $6,063; and in the 35 percent bracket, $5,305. The cost of this tax shelter is your negative cash flow of $3,690. Is it worth it? You must also remember that your interest payments and property taxes (totaling $19,490) are also tax deductible. If you are in the 50 percent bracket, $9,745, or half of these two payments, are shifted to the government. Also, in the future, rents will probably rise, and your cash flow may become positive. Finally, you have what may be a good inflationary hedge. Whether the above duplex is a good investment, then, depends on personal circumstances, and what you think future rent increases and price appreciation will be. With respect to these latter two points, *where* your rental property is located may be crucial. If it is in a fast-growth area (e.g., certain cities in the Sun Belt), the risk would be less than if it is in a low-growth or declining area.

Nonresidential real estate

Logically, investing in nonresidential property is similar to investing in residential—there is a rental cash inflow, as well as maintenance, taxes, insurance, mortgage payments, and depreciation. More money is usually needed to invest in nonresidentials.

Nonresidential property may be classified as commercial and business, office and professional, and industrial and warehouse. When investing in any of these, you must, among other things, analyze population and business growth and their patterns, vacancy rates, parking facilities, transportation arteries, and zoning ordinances.

Older buildings

Sometimes if you invest in older real estate, you may also be able to take an investment tax credit. Generally when you invest in real estate, you may not take this credit, but if you buy and rehabilitate older buildings, in addition to the favorable depreciation (cost recovery) allowance described above, you may be eligible. A tax credit is better than an expense because, after taxes have been calculated, the credit reduces taxes dollar for dollar.

If the building is 30 to 39 years old, the credit is 15 percent. If the building is 40 or more years old, the credit is 20 percent. In these two cases, however, the building must be a nonresidential one. In the case of a building certified by the IRS as being an historical structure, the investment tax credit may be as much as 25 percent, and the building may be either residential or nonresidential. The investment tax credit applies only to the rehabilitation cost, not the acquisition cost. If you buy a building certified as an historical structure for $60,000 and spend $40,000 rehabilitating it, the rehabilitation investment tax credit would be $10,000.

Undeveloped (raw) land

Be careful with raw land. Some people feel undeveloped land is a superior investment to rental property. Sometimes it is, and sometimes it is not. To be sure, you do not have to worry about leaky roofs, broken furnaces, or poor tenants who pay the rent late and are complainers. On the other hand, it yields no income, and there are taxes to pay plus interest on the loan, which can use up your money quickly. There is also no depreciation to provide a tax shelter. Your land would have to appreciate in value by substantially more than enough to offset these factors to make the investment worthwhile. If you buy land in a fast-growing area, this may happen, but such land has already been discounted into the future for a number of years, and hence is very expensive. If you buy land that is not in a growth area that becomes a growth area, you have made a shrewd investment, or were lucky and will probably have a nice capital gain.

Be wary of raw land in general. Check it out carefully with respect to taxes, interest on the loan, expected future growth in the area, and present and possible future zoning restrictions.

COLLECTIBLES AND OTHER EXOTIC INVESTMENTS

Collectibles became popular during 1980 and early 1981. Because of rapid inflation, many people bought them believing they were a good inflationary hedge, and their prices rose dramatically. The same is true of certain other exotic "investments" which are, generally speaking, not considered collectibles. These items often become a panic haven during periods of rapid inflation. Since inflation has slowed, the prices of most of these items have come down a great deal, and many people lost money. Here is a word of warning: anything that can go up in price drastically and rapidly can come down drastically and rapidly. Approach all collectibles carefully. Most people probably should not buy them except under the most extraordinary circumstances.

Collectibles generally include the following:

1. any work of art,
2. any rug or antique,
3. any stamp or coin,
4. any alcoholic beverage,
5. any metal or gem,
6. any other tangible personal property specified by the Secretary of the Treasury.

Paintings and Other Works of Art

Paintings

We have all read about an unusual case where someone has purchased a work of art at a relatively low price and then found some years later it was worth a fortune. Such a case is extremely rare and fortuitous. There are also a few instances of a wealthy individual buying an expensive painting, not as an investment, only to find out that it has indeed been a good one. This is not for the average person. Occasionally a person may buy an original by a young and unknown artist for a few hundred dollars, to discover it is worth substantially more as time passes and the artist becomes more famous. But you cannot tell which unknown is going to become famous. Works of art are not very liquid, and when you wish to sell a painting, you may have difficulty finding a buyer.

Chinese ceramics

These are not for the amateur, perhaps not even for the experts. They were a fad for a time in recent years—highly speculative and highly illiquid.

Rugs and Antiques

Antiques

Investing in antiques might be a possible investment outlet for a few—but only if you are an antique dealer or other expert in your own right. Even then, buy only on a modest scale. Buying a few antiques because you like them and can afford them is fine. After a time you might even develop enough expertise to become a part- (or full-) time dealer in them. Then you might invest a modest amount in an inventory of antiques and hope for a capital gain. There is often a fine line between antiques and junk, and many of us cannot tell one from the other. Also, antiques are not very liquid. To sell (and buy) them at a decent price you would have to go to antique shows, or scour the countryside for items in old homes. If you buy and sell through a dealer, you will buy retail and sell wholesale—almost always a losing game.

Antique cars

Antique cars are much like other antiques. Their supply is fixed, and as the demand for them increases, their price will rise. They are also expensive to maintain. Spare parts are hard to find and often must be handmade. Unless you are rich and can afford this expensive hobby, do not invest money in a 1929 Duesenberg or Packard convertible.

Rugs

Oriental and Persian rugs, too, appreciated pricewise in recent years; then the price came down. They are not liquid and no market for them exists. Do not buy them as an investment.

Stamps, Coins, and Rare Books

Everything said earlier about paintings and other works of art applies to stamps, coins, and rare books. These items you buy retail and sell wholesale—a losing game. Stamp and coin prices especially rose greatly in 1980 and they have since fallen.

Alcoholic Beverages

Scotch whiskey

Scotch whiskey is another item that became popular for investment a few years ago. The idea was that the investor would purchase raw whiskey, hold it until properly aged, and then sell it. Actually, only warehouse receipts for whiskey were delivered, and later these were then sold. As in the case of commodities, actual delivery was almost never taken.

You should be careful about buying Scotch. Its price can fluctuate much like that of other commodities. It is a myth that a person can always buy raw whiskey, hold it until it ages, and then sell it at a good profit. If it were that easy, the distilleries would store it all themselves and keep the profit. The price of both raw and aged whiskey fluctuates. Sometimes aged whiskey is even cheaper than raw. Buying whiskey is a high-risk, speculative undertaking and the small nonprofessional should refrain from investing in it.

Wine

Buy wine only to drink, never for an investment. Wine has become more popular recently, and if you ever have an opportunity to buy a (or part of a) winery, investigate it. But analyze this as you would buying into any business.

Precious Metals and Gems

Gold, silver, and platinum

The price of precious metals is highly volatile. Metals are a high-risk, very speculative investment, and you should steer clear of them except in the most extraordinary circumstances.

Some feel that gold is an inflationary hedge. It is really not, and there is no logical or rational reason why it should be. Gold yields no interest or dividend return; for it to be an inflationary hedge, it would have to rise steadily at a rate in excess of the rate of inflation. That has happened during only a relatively few periods over the long run. Then the price often falls drastically.

Gold, for psychological and historical reasons, is really a panic haven. To the extent that near panic is induced by inflation, gold prices are related to the rate of inflation. Gold prices rose to a high of $884 per ounce in early 1980, because of mild panic, which in turn was the result not only of inflation of 18 percent in the spring of 1980 but also a weakening of the dollar internationally. Middle East money drove gold prices to their 1980 high when, due to loss of confidence in the dollar, Arabs bought gold. The price soon fell from its $884 high to less than $400, then rose somewhat again. The price of gold can fluctuate wildly.

If the present (Reagan) administration can control inflation, the case for gold will be weak. If the administration's policy fails and panic or near panic sets in, gold prices may soar again. Because of this, some financial planners are advising wealthy clients to buy small amounts of gold merely to diversify their investments, as insurance. But the small investor should be wary.

There are costs involved in holding gold. First, there are the premiums or commissions paid to dealers. These vary depending on how much you buy. In addition, most states have sales taxes, and often these must be paid on gold purchases. (In this sense, it is considered a consumer item rather than an investment.) However, you may often avoid sales taxes if, instead of taking delivery, you let your broker store the gold. There are also shipping charges, insurance charges, and storage charges which can add another one percent or so to the cost of the gold. Then when you wish to sell it, you need to have it assayed to determine its quality and fineness. All these costs, together with the fact that gold yields no interest return, suggest that the small or modest investor should be wary of gold bullion.

If the small investor insists on buying gold, he or she should probably select one of four gold coins: the South African Krugerrand, the Canadian Mapleleaf, a special Mexican gold Peso, or the Austrian Corona. Each of these coins contains about one ounce of gold so their price fluctuates with the daily market price of gold. You can buy these from various brokers, coin dealers, and a few banks; the commissions (if you buy from brokers) are generally about the same as those on gold bullion.

You should shop around when buying gold coins, because commissions will vary. As in the case of bullion, there may be a sales tax, shipping, and insurance costs; if you have a safe deposit box, there will be no storage costs. Since they are stamped, they do not have to be assayed when sold. If you commit some funds to gold, be a long-run investor—don't get in and out of the market because of wild swings in the short run. In the long run, the price of gold will probably rise; at least it probably won't fall much. However, commit yourself only if you are brave, and then only a small amount of your total investment assets.

Silver and platinum prices, too, can fluctuate wildly. Silver, being much cheaper than gold, has often been called "poor man's gold." It fell from its high of over $50 per ounce in early 1980, and recently has been selling at about $11.00 per ounce.

Some brokers set a minimum on the amount of silver bullion they will sell—usually about 10 ounces. You can also buy silver coins. Commissions, shipping charges, insurance, storage fees, and sales taxes on silver are similar to those on gold.

Platinum is the other precious speculative metal. Its recent price of about $400 per ounce is also lower than its high of around $800 early in 1980. The same commissions, insurance, and so on, paid when buying gold, apply to platinum. Everything said about investing in gold applies to silver and platinum. They are high-risk, speculative ventures.

Precious stones—diamonds, emeralds, and rubies

Most people who invest in precious stones choose diamonds, but some select emeralds, rubies, or other rare gems. In the case of diamonds, only high quality ones are appropriate for investment purposes. The price of high quality diamonds rose substantially during 1980; since then, like gold, the price has come down again. Many gems are never made into jewelry, but rather are held by investors.

Adam Smith said many years ago that diamonds have no *use* value but a very high *market* value; air, on the other hand, has a very high *use* value, but no *market* value. That is, air is free. This is no longer completely true, because a good deal of money is spent keeping the air clean, and industrial diamonds are used as cutting tools. Generally, however, diamonds are of value because they are extremely rare and because people want them, at least in part, for psychological reasons.

Since diamonds rose greatly in value in 1980, some investors chose them as an inflationary hedge. If an investor buys a $5,000 diamond from a retail jeweler, it may be worth $10,000 or $15,000 five years from now—but only if you buy it, not if you want to sell it.

With diamonds there are the wholesale market and the retail market. The markup at the retail level is 50, 60, 70, and up to 100 percent. Therefore, unless you can buy in the wholesale market, don't buy; because when you sell, you will sell at the wholesale price. Buying retail and selling wholesale will nearly always be a losing game. There is also the problem of finding a buyer if you wish to sell. Many wholesale dealers will sell, but will not necessarily buy. They can acquire their supply of new diamonds directly or indirectly through the DeBeers Network. Those dealers who buy back diamonds from the public buy them at the wholesale price less a discount.

You have to face two other problems when investing in diamonds. First, you need to determine a diamond's grade or quality, and then its fair value. While related, these are not the same. Until recently, ascertaining the quality of a diamond was somewhat subjective, and no uniform criteria existed. Now, however, there are four independent professional diamond grading laboratories, and more uniform criteria exist for determining a diamond's grade and quality These are The American Gemological Laboratories (AGL), The Gemological Institute of American (GIA), The International Gemological Institute (IGI), and The European Gemological Laboratory (EGL). Most high-quality diamonds are now traded almost exclusively on the basis of what the certificate issued by one of these independent grading organizations says. Only if you buy a diamond which has a certificate issued by one of the four laboratories are you certain you will get a diamond of the quality it is reputed to be. Be sure to get a genuine certificate from one of these; be wary of some other certificate that states the diamond has been graded "in accordance" with the standards established by The Gemological Institute of America (GIA).

It is important to emphasize that grading and appraising are not the same thing, although there is a relationship between the grade of a diamond and its value. The four grading laboratories do not appraise diamonds; they only grade them. But once a grading certificate has been issued for any given diamond, expert diamond dealers are able to appraise it. The best way to obtain a diamond's true wholesale value is to get its grading certificate and then find out at what price a diamond dealer will buy that stone from you.

The trade and hence the value of a diamond are determined by its carat weight, color, clarity, and cut quality. These are the four Cs of diamond valuation. The test for weight is simple: the diamond is weighed.

Color quality is designated by assigning a letter grade (D through Z), with D the highest quality and Z the lowest. (The reasons A, B, and C are not used to measure color is because many retail jewelers use these three letters to value their diamonds, and they represent nonstandardized scales.) The test for color is really a test for the *absence* of color. The lower the level of color the higher the rating, and ideally a diamond should have no color, because it breaks up and reflects light without imparting any of its own color to that light. However, if a diamond has enough natural color in it, it may be considered a "fancy color diamond" and is rated beyond Z, and is valued more highly because of its color. Although very rare, diamonds come in green, red, blue, yellow, and brown. Most diamonds, however, contain faint tinges of yellow; and the less yellowness there is, the higher the value and the rating. A "D" rating has virtually no yellow (is colorless).

Clarity has to do with the absence of impurities and imperfections, such as carbon spots, gas bubbles, hairline cracks, and natural blemishes. The size and location of these imperfections are considered when assigning a clarity grade.

The following grades are used:

> FL   — Flawless
> IF   — Internally Flawless
> VVS — Very, Very Slightly Imperfect
> VVS_1 (There are two subclassifications in this grade.)
> VVS_2
> VS   — Very Slightly Imperfect
> VS_1 (There are two subclassifications in this grade.)
> VS_2
> SI   — Slightly Imperfect
> SI_1 (There are two subclassifications in this grade.)
> SI_2
> I   — Imperfect
> I_1 (There are three subclassifications in this grade.)
> I_2
> I_3

Good quality investment diamonds are considered to be VS or better; diamonds graded below I_3 are considered industrial diamonds.

The test for cut quality is subjective, but there are three major factors to consider: (1) the shape, (2) the style, and (3) the quality of the cut.

1. A round cut is generally superior to a pear, marquise, oval, or emerald cut, all else being the same. A round cut is best at reflecting light, and hence is more valuable. (All diamonds are not cut round because sometimes their color, clarity, or net size can be improved by choosing a different cut.) A round cut, if viewed from the top, appears as a circle.

2. The style of the cut is virtually always the "American cut" (sometimes also called the "Brilliant cut," because it reflects more light than any other style of cut).

The area of maximum width of a diamond is called a "girdle." It is analogous to the equator of a sphere. The upper half is called the "crown" (Northern Hemisphere); the lower half is referred to as the "pavillion" (Southern Hemisphere); both of them have facets cut into them. The top of the diamond is flat and is called the "table" (or the Arctic Ocean). The bottom of the diamond comes to a tip and is called the "culet" (or South Pole).

3. A number of measurements are made to determine the quality of the cut, including:

a. The *table percentage*, the ratio between the table diameter and the diamond's diameter at the girdle.

b. The *depth percentage*, or the relationship between the total depth of the diamond and its diameter at the girdle.

c. The *pavillion depth*, or the relationship between the pavillion depth and the total depth of the diamond.

d. The *crown angle* is the angle of the upper (crown facets away from the horizontal girdle.

e. The *girdle* (equator) around the diamond can be thick or thin.

f. The *symmetry* has to do with the geometry of the cut. If you look at a diamond from the top, how perfect a circle is formed by the girdle? The table top and girdle should both be horizontal if viewed from the side. An imaginary line drawn from the middle of the table top should hit the culet. The symmetry of the cut can be rated from poor to excellent.

g. The *finish* refers to the quality of the diamond's polish, which can be poor to excellent.

h. The *fluorescence*, which refers to the glow some diamonds give under fluorescent light; the less the glow, the higher the quality.

i. The *culet*, which is the bottom tip of the diamond, should not come to a sharp tip but rather to a tiny leveled-off area.

Diamond experts suggest certain guidelines be followed by investors buying diamonds, especially for the first time. Some have even suggested that some diamonds could be considered "blue-chip" diamonds—the term is used just as in the case of common stock. Blue-chip diamonds are considered to have the following characteristics:

1. 1/2 carat to 3 carat
2. top 5 color grades
3. top 5 to 6 clarity grades
4. round American (or Brilliant) cut
5. certified by one of the four grading labs mentioned above
6. meets the quality cut outlined in the following table:

Table percentage	53–65 percent
Depth percentage	57–63 percent
Pavillion depth	41–45 percent
Crown angle	30–35 degrees
Girdle	Avoid gems with an extremely thin or extremely thick girdle.
Symmetry	Any stone rated good or better
Finish	Any gem rated good or better
Fluorescence	If the rating states the diamond has strong fluorescence,

	it is of lower quality. Anything less than strong is satisfactory.
Culet	If the grading laboratories do not mention the culet in the certificate that they issue, it is acceptable. All comments about the culet such as "large culet" or "no culet" are negative comments.

The range in the quality of a diamond that is considered investment grade seems to be widening. For example, a few years ago when someone said "investment quality," it often was taken to be "d" flawless. If this widening trend continues, it could be good strategy to buy diamonds just inside or just outside the lower end of the investment quality range.

Since the supply of new diamonds is controlled, and since the DeBeers Consolidated Mines, Ltd. has a vested interest in a stable but rising price level for diamonds, some investors feel that diamonds are a good long-run inflationary hedge.

There is no doubt, however, that the spectacular increase in diamond prices during late 1979 and 1980 was brought about by speculative demand. People were desperately looking for an inflationary hedge. Diamonds are akin to gold in that they have become a panic—or high uncertainty—haven. If the present administration controls inflation, the speculative demand for diamonds is likely to lessen greatly—indeed by mid-1981 it already had somewhat, and the diamond prices came down greatly. Then, in late 1982 and early 1983, their prices, like that of gold, rose modestly once more. If the inflation level stays as low as it now is, or goes even lower, the price of diamonds will rise only modestly, if at all; but if inflation reignites, who knows.

Diamonds are not for everyone. The small investor should stay away from them. If you buy diamonds, remember they have to be considered high risk. Buy only graded diamonds with a certificate issued by one of the four reliable laboratories. Be sure you get them at the wholesale price from a reputable dealer (there will be a 10–20 percent commission when you buy and sell). Expect to hold them for the long run. You probably should not invest in diamonds unless your after-tax income is at least $50,000 and your personal net worth (not counting your home and personal property) is at least $250,000. Then perhaps for purposes of diversification, possible insurance against what the future holds in store, or a haven for panic, you might want to consider holding a small portion of your total assets in diamonds.

One of the problems of investing in diamonds is that historically they were not very liquid; some dealers would *sell* but would not *buy back*. This lack of liquidity may be changing. As diamonds have become more popular, diamond trading companies and diamond dealers have begun to make a market in diamonds and trade them for the commissions. Diamonds may soon be traded much like securities in the over-the-counter market with all diamond dealers tied together by a computer network. Diamonds that have been graded by one of the four diamond grading laboratories may even be quoted both price- and quality-wise. A newly established firm, Polygon Corporation, in a joint venture with the Xerox Corporation, is developing a computer system to do this. Then diamonds could be quoted over the counter like securities.

What is true about diamonds is also true of other precious stones such as rubies, sapphires, and emeralds. Their prices have risen greatly recently, and they too are high-risk investments. Like diamonds, they too can be graded as to color, clarity, and the like; but the criteria used for evaluation have not yet become as standardized as those in diamond grading. Nevertheless, some investors prefer them to diamonds.

MORE EXOTIC INVESTMENTS

There are a few other unusual investments (speculations) that you should keep away from. Some people have invested in these believing they were a possible inflationary hedge.

Furs

Buy as a consumer item if you can afford them, but not as an investment. A $5,000 fur coat today might be worth $10,000 in a few years; but only if you buy it, not if you try to sell it. There is no used fur coat market; and any fur coat you buy is used, even if you have never worn it. You would be better off to buy and stockpile blue jeans. Their price has risen from $10 to over $40 during the last few years, and there are still some used clothing stores in big cities where you can sell used clothes. However, don't buy blue jeans as an investment; you will probably lose money if you do.

Foreign Currency

You will gain by holding foreign currency only if the dollar (exchange rate) declines relative to foreign currency. Looking at the record of the 1970s, it appears that the German mark and the Swiss franc would be prime candidates for acquisition. But no one knows what the valuable currency will be by the mid- and late 1980s. The rate of inflation in the U.S. relative to that abroad is one of the factors determining the exchange rate, but it is not the only factor. The rate of interest in the U.S. relative to other countries is another. If you think rapid inflation will continue, you might want to consider buying some marks and francs as an insurance policy—that is, diversifying your assets widely. In buying them, you are attempting to hedge against inflation. While there are costs involved in buying, foreign currency may in some cases also earn interest.

Horses

Investing in horses is another exotic investment. Traditionally, this has been reserved for wealthy individuals, but more recently less affluent—but well off—individuals have moved into this area. Horses may be a tax shelter, and they also have proven a fairly good inflationary hedge in recent years. Investing in horses, however, is a high-risk venture, and you should not consider it unless you can afford to lose what you venture.

There are three general kinds of horses the investor may choose: racehorses, quarter horses (a kind of racehorse), and cutting horses. Cutting horses, more popular in the West, are horses that display great skill in cutting a steer out of a herd; in a sense they are show animals.

A horse may generate a cash flow for its owner from prize moneys, stud fees, and the sale of foal. But price winnings are the key. If a horse does well at winning, his stud fees will rise, and winning mares can be bred and their foals will sell for more money. If a horse is really good it may be retired from competing and be used exclusively for breeding purposes. The market value (price) of such a horse will also rise, providing a nice capital gain.

If you invest in a horse, all the expenses associated with this may be deducted—such things as feed, veterinarians' fees, training expenses, interest on the loans, and the like. A horse may also be depreciated over either three or five years depending on its type. While a horse is not eligible for the investment tax credit, certain property associated with horses, such as barns and trailers, may be.

To receive these tax benefits as business expenses, you must invest in horses with the intent of making a profit. If it is a hobby, the tax benefits do not apply. If you actually make profits in some years, it is, of course, easier to persuade the Internal Revenue Service (IRS) that your intent is to make a profit, even though you may have losses in some years. The important thing is "profit intent," not "actual profits," and that is what the taxpayer must show in order to deduct expenses and offset losses against other income. Whether or not an individual is engaged in an activity for profit or for personal satisfaction as a hobby is a question to be determined by the facts in each case.

If you do not wish to invest in an entire horse, you might purchase part of one through a limited partnership. If you do, make certain the managing partner knows horses. Investments in horses are high risk and are not for everyone. However, if you are knowledgeable about horses and are a rancher—with cattle—and have substantial income, owning a few horses might become a profitable sideline.

When Is a Hobby Also a Business?

If you collect, buy, sell, or trade stamps, coins, antiques, or other items, or if you are an amateur magician and put on displays, any income received is subject to tax. However, any expenses connected with any of these activities are first deductible. Expenses in excess of this income are not deductible from other income unless you convert your hobby to a business. You may be able to do so.

If your activity resulted in net profits in two of the last five years, it may be classified as a business. Or if you are just starting out you may be able to count the coming five years. If you are listed in the telephone Yellow Pages, have a business telephone, and a separate bank account, this strengthens the case that your activity is a business. The real test is that you must intend to make a profit.

If the activity qualifies as a business, not only may you offset any losses against other income, but you may also be able to depreciate assets and take an investment tax credit on the acquisition of new assets. This too would shelter other income.

Yachts

Some people buy yachts (and other boats) believing they will appreciate in price just like a house. This is not always true. Some very expensive yachts are worth much more today than three or four years ago when they were built, but this is generally not true of cheaper boats. Also in the case of yachts, there are high maintenance and insurance costs, so unless you are rich, do not invest.

ONE FINAL COMMENT

One final word—stay clear of all of these exotic investments discussed in this chapter, except in the most unusual circumstances. The small investor should stay clear in all cases. If you do buy, probably gold or diamonds are the best investment. If your view of the economy is very gloomy and you feel inflation will reignite and go out of control, then a small proportion of your total assets might be placed in gold or diamonds as insurance against inflation and panic.

QUESTIONS FOR REVIEW

1. What are mutual funds and what is the underlying rationale for the existence of mutual funds?
2. Distinguish between a closed-end investment company and an open-end investment company.
3. What is net asset value?
4. What are some of the objectives of investment companies?

5. Suppose a mutual fund salesperson were selling a balanced fund. What does this mean?
6. What is a hedge fund; an income fund?
7. How do the objectives of various mutual funds differ?
8. What is a tax-managed fund?
9. Why should a mutual fund do at least somewhat better than the Dow-Jones Averages before becoming a candidate for acquisition?
10. What are some of the advantages that one receives when one buys mutual funds? Are there any disadvantages?
11. How is the value of a share in an open-end company determined?
12. What are loading charges as related to mutual funds?
13. What is a no-load fund? How can no-load funds stay in business?
14. Where can you obtain information about mutual funds?
15. What factors should be considered before a person buys mutual funds?
16. Discuss the commodities markets. Would you recommend investing in commodities? Why or why not?
17. Discuss the short hedge, the long hedge.
18. What is the futures market in securities?
19. What is a discounted first mortgage?
20. What factors must be taken into account when calculating the yield on a mortgage?
21. What is a second mortgage?
22. What is a real estate investment trust?
23. Discuss the advantages and disadvantages of owning real estate directly.
24. How is the yield calculated on direct real estate investments?
25. Discuss art, painting, and the like, as investment outlets.
26. Why is it that dealers in art, and so on, are in a better position than the rest of us to make investments in art?
27. What has been the recent history of gold as an investment?
28. What is the cost of holding gold?
29. Are diamonds a risky investment in your opinion? Why?

CASES

1. Bill and Nancy Greenwood have over the years accumulated $10,000 of savings that are in a savings and loan association earning 5 3/4 percent compounded semiannually. Bill and Nancy feel that now is a good time to take $5,000 of it and invest it in common stock. They think they should be getting more than 5 3/4 percent. Recently somebody told them they should investigate mutual funds rather than invest in common stock directly. Is this a good time to buy stock? Can they expect to receive more then 5 3/4 percent by going into equities? Would you recommend mutual funds or buying common stock directly? Explain your answer.

2. Rita Roundsetter has just inherited $25,000 and is undecided how to invest it. She has never owned common stock and is inexperienced with respect to securities. Nevertheless, she thinks she should buy equities. Is she wise? Would you recommend buying common stock directly or mutual funds? Rita is thirty-four and has no dependents. What kind of stocks (or mutual funds) would you recommend?

3. Ruben Haywood has an income of $30,000 per year and has decided to set aside $100 per month to buy equities. However, since he has had very little experience with securities, and since he does not have the time to watch his portfolio carefully, he considers that he should own commmon stock indirectly through an investment company. Do you agree?

   Ruben is also undecided between open-end and closed-end investment companies and owning stock directly. As far as investment companies are concerned, which stock do you think Ruben should buy?

4. Robert Shafer works in the trust department of the Bank of America and is earning $28,000 per year. He is twenty-eight, married, and has one child. He expects his income to be rising over the years and thinks it is time for him to acquire some equities. Since he is not going to be able to invest very much at first, he cannot get much diversification. Nevertheless, he still thinks it would be foolish for him to buy mutual shares and pay someone to handle his investments for him. Do you agree? What kind of stock (or mutual shares) would you recommend for Robert?

5. Joan Rider is a twenty-four-year-old school teacher who has her own car fully paid for and $1,000 in the bank. She wants to invest in equities but is undecided whether to buy common stock directly or indirectly through a mutual fund. One of the things she dislikes about mutual funds is the high acquisition costs. Would you advise her to invest directly or indirectly? Specifically what kind of direct or indirect investments would you advise?

6. Jim and Virginia Hansen are in their early thirties and have a combined income of $24,000 per year. They have two children—six and four years old—and want to start saving now for their college education. They are able to save $25 per month for each child and will earmark it for a college fund. How should they invest it? Can you make specific recommendations?

7. Clem Kensington has inherited $50,000 and has savings of $20,000 in a savings and loan association that is paying 5 3/4 percent. It seems to him that he should be getting at least 8 percent, and therefore he is thinking about taking $20,000 out of the savings and loan association, putting it with $50,000 he inherited, and buying a mortgage. The other alternative is to buy a duplex, live in one unit, and rent out the other.

   Clem has found out that he can get a mortgage that will yield him a 12 percent return. He has also found a duplex he can buy for $70,000 that has a net rental income of $4,200 per year. Which is the better investment? Explain fully.

8. Billie Stewart is a young lawyer with $50,000 to invest. She has decided to invest it in some real estate venture, but is uncertain what type of venture she should choose. She has investigated first mortgages and has discovered

she can obtain a 12 percent yield. Now she learns that second mortgages are available. Most of these are $3,000 to $5,000 and will yield her about 15 percent return on her money. Why is the yield difference so great on first and second mortgages? Would you recommend that she buy first or second mortgages? Why? Why are the second mortgages usually only for several thousand dollars while first mortgages run up to $50,000 and more?

9. Joe and Dorothy Jenkins have $500,000 that they wish to invest in various real estate ventures. They have considered buying both first and second mortgages, buying land on the edge of the city in which they live and holding it for capital gain, and buying shares in a real estate investment trust. What would you advise?

10. John and Mary Whippet decided to retire from their ranch near Aspen, Colorado, and move to Denver. Consequently, they sold their ranch for $250,000, which they hope to invest in the Denver area in order to live off the income. They have decided to invest in income-producing property rather than in securities, and they are thinking in terms of either an apartment building, which they could manage, or an office building. How much yield would they need on their investment to make it superior to corporate bonds? Advise them regarding the merits of investing in an apartment versus an office building.

11. After living in Denver for several years, John and Mary Whippet found time on their hands; therefore, they decided to go into an additional part-time business for themselves. Mary has always liked antiques and has suggested they become antique dealers. John is not so sure. They seek your advice.

12. Bill Bryant and his wife believe that inflation may return to double digit levels soon and would like an inflationary hedge. They are considering investing the royalties from a book Bill and his wife wrote, which will be about $20,000, in gold because they have heard that gold is a good inflationary hedge. Advise them about investing in gold, pointing out the dangers, and make a recommendation regarding whether or not to invest in gold, and if so, how much.

SUGGESTED READINGS

"Before you Speculate." The Chicago Mercantile Exchange, 444 West Jackson Boulevard, Chicago, Ill. 60606.

Donoghue, William E., and Tilling, Thomas. *William E. Donoghue's No-Load Mutual Fund Guide: How to Take Advantage of the Investment Opportunity of the 80's.* New York: Harper and Row, 1983.

"Forbes Mutual Fund Survey." *Forbes Magazine.* This is an annual survey that comes out every August.

Green, Fred T. *Thrift and Home Ownership,* Chicago: United States Savings and Loan League, no date.

Hedging Highlights. Chicago: Chicago Board of Trade.

Heflebower, R. B. *Cooperatives and Mutuals in the Market System*. Madison: University of Wisconsin Press, 1980.

Herzfeld, Thomas J., and Drach, Robert F. *High Return, Low-Risk Investment: Combining Market Times, Stock Selection and Closed-end Funds*. New York: G. P. Putnam's Sons, 1981.

Hoagland, Henry E., and Stone, Leo D. *Real Estate Finance*, 6th ed. Homewood, Ill.: R. D. Irwin, 1981.

How to Buy and Sell Commodities. New York: Merrill Lynch, Pierce, Fenner and Smith.

Investment Companies, Mutual Funds and Other Types. Latest edition of this annual publication by Wiesenberger Financial Services, Inc., 870 7th Avenue, New York, N.Y. 10019.

Johnson's Investment Company Charts. Latest edition of this annual publication by Hugh A. Johnson Investment Company, 246 Homewood Avenue, Buffalo, N.Y. 14217.

Mutual Fund Fact Book. Investment Company Institute, 1775 K St. N.W., Washington, D.C. This is an annual publication.

Rugg, Donald D., and Hale, Norman B. *The Dow Jones-Irwin Guide to Mutual Funds*, revised ed. Homewood, Ill.: Dow Jones-Irwin, 1982.

SBA, What It Is, What It Does; SBIC Financing for Small Business; SBIC Industry Review; SBIC Industry Trends. Washington, D.C.: Small Business Administration. The Small Business Administration (SBA) is a government agency and it publishes numerous pamphlets on small business management. It also publishes a *Handbook of Small Business Finance*. Its address is 1441 L Street N.W., Washington, D.C. 20416.

Speculating on Inflation: Future Trading in Interest Rates, Foreign Currencies, and Precious Metals. New York: Merrill Lynch, Pierce, Fenner and Smith, 1979.

U.S. News & World Report. A weekly magazine that contains a good deal of information on business and finance.

Well Beyond the Average: The Story of Dow Jones. Dow Jones & Company, Princeton, N.J.: The Educational Service Bureau.

Wendt, Paul, and Cerf, Alan R. *Real Estate Investment Analysis*, 2nd ed. New York: McGraw-Hill, 1979.

Wiedemer, John P. *Real Estate Investments*. Reston, Va.: Reston Publishing Company, 1982.

————. *Real Estate, the Money Angle: A Realistic Guide to Real Estate Investments*. Reston, Va.: Reston Publishing Company, 1983.

APPENDIX 18: THE ACQUISITION OF YOUR PERSONAL INVESTMENTS; THE ORDER OF PRIORITIES IN ACQUIRING ASSETS

You have studied a number of different investment outlets. In building your portfolio, the watchword should be diversification. You might want to acquire stocks and bonds, life insurance, savings accounts, perhaps a home, rental real estate, and possibly a number of other assets. The portfolio will, of course, differ for different people. Some people will want to own a home of their own; others, because of temperament, will not. Younger investors will no doubt lean more heavily toward growth stock, older ones toward income. The newcomer to security investing should invest relatively conservatively; so too should the small investor. A person with substantial securities and experience can afford to take more risk—once in a while, perhaps, even a flyer on a higher-risk security. One rule to follow in buying long-term bonds is buy them only if you believe interest will not rise. If you expect rates to increase wait until they do.

In what order should you acquire the various assets? The first savings generated should be invested differently than certain later ones. Certain assets are high-priority assets like, for example, life insurance, and a highly liquid savings deposit that is available in the case of an emergency. Assets that serve as tax shelters should also be given a high priority in some cases. Other assets have lower priorities, which will vary from individual to individual. Nevertheless, assets can be grouped into three general categories of priorities as shown below. Some investors may not acquire enough assets to consider the acquisition of the third category. Also there may be some overlap in that some investors will begin acquiring assets in the middle priority range before they completely satisfy their highest priority requirement.

1. Highest priority (to be acquired first)
    Liquid savings deposits
    A higher-yielding CD
    Life insurance
    A home (if this fits your temperament)
    A Keogh Plan (if you qualify)
    An Individual Retirement Account (IRA)
    College trust fund for the children

There will be individual differences even within the highest priority categories. If you have substantial assets and a good credit rating so that you are able to borrow in the event of an emergency, you may refrain from having a relatively low-yielding savings deposit. Insurance needs will vary. If you have a good group plan and low insurance needs, individual insurance may be given less weight.

2. Middle priority
    Stock
    Bonds
    Mutual funds
    Rental property
    Tax-exempt state and local bonds (only if you have a tax problem)

As you acquire more assets, begin acquiring them from the middle group. Even here there will be variations based on age and temperament. Some rental tenants can be troublesome, and some investors do not have the personality to be landlords.

3. Lower priority
    Raw land

Gold and diamonds (only small proportion of your total assets)
Speculative stock
Exotic tax shelters such as equipment leasing and cattle feedlot operations

The third group of assets is not for everybody, but some or all of them may be right for you. Gold and diamonds, for example, should be avoided unless you have a net worth of at least $250,000, not counting your home, and an after-tax income of at least $50,000. Even then, probably only if you believe the dollar will be ravaged further by rapid inflation should you invest in these.

PART FIVE

RETIREMENT AND ESTATE PLANNING

CHAPTER NINETEEN

SOCIAL SECURITY, ANNUITIES, AND OTHER PENSION PLANS

Social Security
Private (Life Insurance) Annuities
Private (and Government) Pension Plans
Individual Tax-Sheltered Retirement (Pension) Plans

This chapter deals with retirement income. Social Security, private insurance annuities, and certain pension plans are the trinity of retirement programming. Pension plans may, in turn, be broken down into corporate pension plans (or government plans for government employees) and individual pension plans. In addition, some people have other assets (for example, bonds, stock, and rental real estate), which will also yield income during retirement. Stocks, bonds, real estate, and the like, were discussed in previous chapters; in this chapter we will discuss formal retirement plans—Social Security, life insurance annuities, and corporate and individual pension plans.

SOCIAL SECURITY

Social Security will provide you with some tax-free retirement income.[1] That tax-free income is also indexed—at least currently—to protect the recipient from inflation. You Social Security benefits will vary depending in part on your income while you were working; but even if you are drawing the maximum benefits, it by itself will not provide a decent retirement standard of living, and you will

---

1. In most cases this is taxed. In a few cases benefits are taxed. See page 477.

need to supplement it. Indeed Social Security never was—and is not now—intended to provide an adequate retirement income. Rather it was intended to provide a minimum base or starting point on which to build and which, if supplemented, could provide for an adequate retirement. It was believed that with Social Security as a base most people could provide for their retirement years.

In addition to retirement benefits, Social Security provides for certain other benefits.

1. Old-Age Retirement
2. Survivors' Benefits
3. Disability Benefits, and
4. Medicare. (Medicare was discussed in Chapter 12; the other three will be discussed here.)

Who is Covered?

Almost everyone in the labor force, including self-employed persons, is included under Social Security, including members of the armed forces. Today the only exceptions are certain federal employees, some state and local employees, and ministers and other members of religious orders who file a form stating they are conscientiously opposed to receiving Social Security benefits because of religious convictions.

Prior to January 1, 1984, federal employees were not covered by Social Security. They had their own alternative pension system. In 1983, however, Congress provided for coverage for federal workers effective in 1984 and later years, but applying only to workers hired after that time. For state and local workers, coverage was voluntary prior to 1984; now it is mandatory. Moreover state and local employees could drop out before 1984. Now state and local employees may no longer terminate their participation in the Social Security system.

Social Security Taxes

Everyone under Social Security must pay Social Security taxes (also called payroll taxes). In 1983 this was 6.70 percent on the first $35,700 of earnings. In January, 1984, this rises to 7.00 percent on a base which will be higher, but which has not yet been set. This is matched by the employer, and the sum is paid to the Social Security Administration.

The self-employed pay a higher tax because there is no matching contribution. In 1983, the self-employment tax was 9.35 percent on a base of $35,700, and in 1984 this tax rose to 14 percent. In 1983, Congress amended the Social Security tax and raised sharply the tax which the self-employed pay. They now pay exactly double what people who work for others pay. Part of the Social Security tax is earmarked to finance Medicare, and the remainder finances retirement benefits, disability benefits, and survivors' benefits.

Both the Social Security tax and the base income to which it is applied are scheduled to rise in future years in accordance with a law already passed by Congress. The income base (taxable wage) will be adjusted upward to take into account average wage level increases throughout the U.S. Table 19–1 shows the future increases in the tax rate. Since Social Security taxes are withheld through payroll deductions, they are automatically stopped when the maximum base income is reached. However, if you have two or more employers, you may have a tax withheld in excess of the maximum because each employer is required to withhold the maximum amount. If so, you can get it back by taking it as a credit against your personal income tax when you file your annual return.

Building Protection; Quarters of Coverage

To build up Social Security benefits, you must earn what are called *quarters of coverage*. A person receives one quarter of coverage for every $370.00 of earned income on which he or she pays Social Security taxes. Therefore, four quarters of coverage—the maximum that may be earned for the year—are obtained in any year during which you pay Social Security taxes on $1,480.00 of earned income. (Income from dividends, interest, rent, or capital gains is not subject

Table 19–1   Social Security taxes

| Year | Taxable wage | Employed | | Self-Employed | |
		Tax rate	Maximum tax	Tax rate	Maximum tax
1978	$17,700	6.05%	$1,070.85	8.10%	$1,433.70
1979	$22,900	6.13%	$1,403.77	8.10%	$1,854.90
1980	$25,900	6.13%	$1,587.67	8.10%	$2,097.90
1981	$29,700	6.65%	$1,975.05	9.30%	$2,762.10
1982	$32,400	6.70%	$2,170.80	9.35%	$3,029.40
1983	$35,700	6.70%	$2,391.90	9.35%	$3,337.95
1984	——	7.00%	——	14.00%	——
1985	——	7.05%	——	14.10%	——
1986	——	7.15%	——	14.30%	——
1987	——	7.15%	——	14.30%	——
1988	——	7.51%	——	15.02%	——
1989	——	7.51%	——	15.02%	——
1990	——	7.65%	——	15.30%	——

Note: By law, the taxable wage will be increased automatically every year to take into account average wage-rate increases in the U.S.
Source: U.S. Department of Health, Education & Welfare, Social Security Administration

to Social Security taxes and hence does not count.) It does not matter when during the year you earn this $1,480.00; even if you earn it all in one day, you will receive four quarters of coverage. This quarters-of-coverage base will be adjusted upward to take into account average wage-level increases in future years.

Quarters of coverage are important because this determines whether you are eligible to receive benefits. The amount of benefits is determined by your income while employed. That is, there is a loose and indirect connection between what a person earns (and pays in the form of Social Security taxes) and benefits received.

The number of quarters of coverage needed to qualify for Social Security benefits varies with the year in which you become 62, in the case of retirement benefits, and with the age when you die or become disabled in the case of those benefits. These variations range from a minimum of 30 quarters to a maximum of 40 for retirement benefits, and 6 to 40 quarters in case of survivors' or disability benefits.

To calculate the quarters of coverage you need to qualify permanently for Social Security retirement benefits, work through the following three steps.

1.   Take the year in which you were born
2.   Add 62 to it
3.   Subtract 1951 from the result

For example

$$
\begin{array}{r}
1923 \\
+\,62 \\
\hline
1985 \\
-\,1951 \\
\hline
34 = \text{quarters of coverage needed.}
\end{array}
$$

Social Security Trust Funds; What Happens to Money Collected?

Social Security taxes go into a special Social Security trust fund. The moneys are then invested in a special issue of U.S. government securities from which the money earns interest. Since Social Security taxes flow into the fund and Social Security benefits flow out of the trust fund, in any one year the fund may be built up or depleted. In recent years the fund has been depleted to the extent that Congress raised taxes periodically.

A few years ago Congress created several new trust funds; there is now a separate one for disability payments, hospital benefits, and medical benefits (see Figure 19–1). In recent years much more money has been flowing out in the form of benefits than has been flowing in in the form of taxes, and the trust funds have become dangerously depleted. Because of this in late 1983 Congress

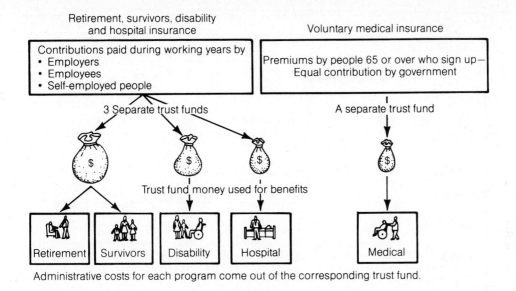

Figure 19–1   Trust fund money can be used only for benefits and for the costs of administering the corresponding programs. (*Source:* U.S. Department of Health, Education and Welfare.)

changed the Social Security laws. We will discuss this in Chapter 14. It should be noted that the Social Security taxes you pay are not earmarked to pay your benefits when you retire. Rather they are commingled and used to pay benefits to those presently retired. Later when you are retired, the members of the labor force at that time will be paying Social Security taxes that will be used to provide for your benefits. In this way an intergeneration transfer takes place.

The Wage Statement Request

Once a year anyone may check his or her records by filling out a wage statement request, as illustrated in Figure 19–2, and sending it to the Social Security Administration, P.O. Box 57, Baltimore, Maryland 21203. This should be done at least every three years because that is the limit for correcting errors. A wage statement request card can be obtained from any Social Security district office, and there is one in all large cities. Look in the telephone directory under United States government for the address and phone number of the field office nearest you.

When you hear from Social Security headquarters, you can check their figures with the amount your employer claims to have reported, shown on your W2 income tax forms. The Social Security Administration's records you will receive will not show what your tax deductions have been, but rather whether your income has been reported and its dollar amount. That is the only important

REQUEST FOR STATEMENT OF EARNINGS

SOCIAL SECURITY NUMBER →			
DATE OF BIRTH →	MONTH	DAY	YEAR

Please send a statement of my social security earnings to:

NAME ______________________________

STREET & NUMBER ______________________________

CITY & STATE ______________________ ZIP CODE __________

Print Name and Address In Ink Or Use Typewriter

SIGN YOUR NAME HERE (DO NOT PRINT) ______________________________

Sign your own name only. Under the law, information in your social security record is confidential and anyone who signs another person's name can be prosecuted. If you have changed your name from that shown on your social security card, please copy your name below exactly as it appears on your card.

Figure 19–2 Request for statement of earnings. (*Source:* U.S. Department of Health, Education and Welfare.)

item to verify because your future Social Security payments will not be based directly on your taxes but rather on your income reported to the Social Security Administration. If the figures are not in agreement, contact your Social Security field office right away.

Retirement Benefits

When you reach age 65 you may receive full benefits (and remember full benefits vary with your earned income) if you have the proper quarters of coverage. You may retire any time after the age of 62; but if you retire before 65, you will receive permanently reduced benefits, as explained below.[2]

Your benefits are determined, among other things, by your income during your working years, but the actual dollar level is calculated by applying a complex formula. Visit your local Social Security Field Office if you are near retirement age. While they cannot calculate your benefits precisely until you retire, they can, and will, give you an accurate approximation. When you do retire and

2. It should be noted that in 1983, Congress changed the Social Security law, and provided, among other things, that the eligibility age for retirement be increased. However, it will be a number of years before this provision of the law will become effective. See the section on "The Future of Social Security" below for a more complete discussion of the changes Congress made in the Social Security law.

receive your benefits, they are adjusted every January to offset cost-of-living increases.

Married couples both of whom work are discriminated against by the Social Security law. Both pay taxes, but when they retire they get only one benefit. If the husband's and wife's benefits are not the same, they get the larger of the two, but they can in no circumstances get both. The same is true of a widow or widower; each can choose his or her own benefits, or the spouse's, whichever is the higher.

The law also discriminates against some two-income married couples in another way. In some cases there is a dollar-for-dollar Social Security benefit payment reduction for any public pension (federal, state, or local) received. Affected are benefits based on a spouse's Social Security. Moreover, for the reduction to be made, you must have a non-Social Security type public pension in your own right. This discriminates against couples of whom both work but only one has Social Security, and the one that does not has a public pension plan other than Social Security. An example will clarify this. A and B are a married couple both of whom work. A has Social Security, and B has a pension plan under a state or local government. When they retire, the Social Security benefits to be paid because B is a dependent of A will be reduced because B has a pension from a state or local government. While this provision of the law was passed in 1977, it will not apply to spouses who become eligible for public pensions before 1983.

Early or Late Retirement

You may retire as early as age 62, but if you do benefits are reduced. Benefits are calculated in the regular way and are then reduced by five-ninths of 1 percent for each month you are under 65 at the time you retire. If you retire at 62, you are 36 months under 65 and hence your retirement benefits are 80 percent of what they would be at age 65 ($36 \times 5/9 = 180/9 = 20$).[3]

Delaying retirement beyond age 65 will increase your regular benefits by 3 percent for each year up to age 70, the maximum increase being 15 percent.

Limits to Earnings

The law requires that one dollar of Social Security benefit payments be withheld for every two dollars of earned income above a certain amount (income from investments are excluded). In 1983 the maximum amount you may earn and not lose any benefits is $6,600, if you are between the ages 65 and 70, and $4,920 if under 65. The exempt amount is increased yearly to offset increases in the

3. Beginning in the year 2000, early retirement benefits will be reduced by 15/18 of 1 percent for each month that you are under 65. At 62, then, your retirement benefits would be 70 percent of what they would be at age 65 ($36 \times 15/18 = 540/18 = 30$).

cost of living. This provision of the law no longer applies when the recipient reaches age 70; he or she can then earn as much as desired and still receive full benefits.

Disability Payments

Disability payments dollarwise are calculated exactly the same way as retirement benefits, and dollarwise they are the same amount as retirement at age 65 benefits. To qualify you must be unable to engage in any substantial gainful activity. Merely being unable to perform your regular work is not enough to qualify, if you can do other work. Moreover, your disability must be expected to last at least twelve months. Disability payments start after a five-month waiting period.

The amount of work credit (quarters of coverage) needed to qualify for disability benefits varies with your age when you become disabled. Before age 24, you need one and a half years (six quarters) during the three-year period just before your disability started. During ages 24 through 31, you need credit for one-half the time between age 31 and the time you become disabled. After age 31, the amount of credit needed varies with your age from a low of five years (20 quarters) between the ages of 31 to 42, to a high of ten years' coverage for a person becoming disabled at age 62 and older.

Survivors' Benefits; Family Benefits

In the case of death, the survivors receive a lump-sum settlement as well as a monthly payment. The lump-sum settlement is $255.00. The monthly benefit varies with the income of the deceased as well as with the number of dependents.

Normally these dependents are unmarried children under the age of eighteen— up to 19 if still in high school—and a spouse. Furthermore, the Social Security recipient may also count as a dependent child one over eighteen who becomes severely disabled before reaching twenty-two and who continues to be disabled. A surviving spouse under 60 without dependent children does not qualify as a dependent until reaching age 60. Regardless of a widower or widow's age, he or she is considered a dependent while caring for a child under eighteen, and receives payments for herself or himself and the child based on the worker's Social Security account.

Student's Benefits

Some students receive benefits because of the death, disability, or retirement of a parent who worked long enough to be eligible for Social Security. At one time, this included college students, but the college student Social Security program is being phased out in 1983, 1984, and 1985. To be eligible the student must be unmarried; enrolled full time in a high school, or trade or vocational school; and under age nineteen.

The Future of Social Security

During any given year the Social Security trust fund may be reduced. In the past, there were other years during which the trust funds would be built up again. Recent years have virtually all been deficit years, and this has caused some concern. The major reason for the decline of the funds is that Congress has raised the benefits without a commensurate increase in Social Security taxes. In addition, retirees are living longer than formerly. Then, as noted above, a few years ago Congress added an escalator clause to the Social Security law, providing for an automatic cost-of-living adjustment for all recipients. Every January all benefits are adjusted upward automatically to offset inflation. As early as 1981, some critics maintained that because of the escalator clause and other provisions added by Congress, the trust funds would run out of money in a few years. By late 1982, it became apparent to nearly everyone that if Congress did not act, the fund would indeed be exhausted soon. Consequently, in March 1983, a new Social Security law was passed, increasing the retirement age by two months per year beginning in the year 2000. In 2022 the full retirement age will be 67. The early retirement age will remain 62, but early retirement benefits would be reduced to 70 percent of full benefits, in effect in the year 2000. It is hard to see how these age increases will help the trust fund very much very soon.

As noted above, the new law also brought all federal employees hired after January 1984 under the law, which will bring in more revenue.

The law also increased Social Security taxes for everyone, but the increase was particularly severe for the self-employed. To soothe the pain of this, Congress authorized a Social Security tax credit which could be used to reduce personal income taxes a bit beginning in 1984. (See Chapter 8 for a discussion of how the investment tax credit works.) The credit for employed people is 0.3 of one percent—exactly equal to the tax increase for 1984. For the self-employed this tax credit is 2.7 percent in 1984, 2.3 percent in 1985, and 2 percent in 1986 through 1989. This tax credit will fund Social Security indirectly from general revenues. The law also postponed until January 1984 the cost-of-living benefit increase which was scheduled to go into effect on July 1, 1983. These increases will then be made every January.

The new law also made a portion of Social Security benefits taxable, in some cases, for the first time. The law defines a base amount of income, which is $25,000 ($32,000 on a joint return). If one-half of benefits, together with adjusted gross income and interest income on tax exempt bonds, exceeds the base amount, a tax is due. The tax would be due on the lower of two items:

1.   one-half of Social Security benefits
2.   one-half of the excess of the combined income over the base amount.

Whether these changes solve Social Security's problems remains to be seen. Some observers remain skeptical and maintain that Congress has again applied a Band-Aid to a massive hemorrhage. Increasing the retirement age will not aid the trust fund for many years; the other changes, these critics maintain, are only marginally beneficial. Only time will tell. Congress may have to act again in a few years, and it will because it will not permit Social Security to go bankrupt. The funds will be there when you retire.

PRIVATE (LIFE INSURANCE) ANNUITIES

An annuity is a contract with a life insurance company in which the company agrees to pay the annuitant an income stream for a specific period of time. The income stream may be fixed in dollar amounts per month or per year, or it may be variable. The specific period of time for which the payment is to be made may be for a given number of years, or it may be for life. If it is for life, the annuitant cannot outlive his or her income. An annuity then is a device to enable a person to retire. Annuities are sold by life insurance companies because life contingencies are involved. Life insurance protects your beneficiaries from having the income stream cut off due to a premature death. An annuity can protect you from outliving your accumulated assets due to a lengthy retirement period.

The Annuity Principle

To be sure, if your assets are large enough, and you can live on your investment income and never dip into the principal, you cannot outlive your income. But an annuity will enable you to dip into your principal and still not outlive it. This is because, as with life insurance, the insurance company applies the law of averages to large numbers of individuals. If each individual from among a large group of people of the same age were to rely on his or her individual accumulated assets, some would outlive their principal; others would not. Insurance companies, however, can guarantee that none will outlive their principal. While the company does not know which individuals in a large group will die at what age, the company does know how many will die at each age. The insurance company can scientifically liquidate the principal sum of all the individuals. Those who live to a ripe age will be drawing on the funds of those who die earlier.

Annuities are the opposite of life insurance, but life contingencies are involved. As with life insurance, the law of averages is applied to large numbers.

Instead of using mortality tables as with life insurance, annuity tables are used, which indicate how many individuals out of a large group will still be alive at the end of each year.

Uses of Annuities

Generally annuities are used to provide retirement income. However, they can also be used to free capital and hence increase your retirement income and sometimes to save taxes. For example, if you had accumulated assets of $200,000 over the years, you could invest this conservatively at, say, 8 percent and have an annual income of $16,000 to supplement other retirement income you might have. An annuity could increase this. A man age 65 can buy a single-premium straight-life annuity paying $10,741 per year for about $100,000. The other $100,000 could be invested to yield $8,000 or $9,000. The total income on your $200,000 is enlarged because you are scientifically liquidating part of the principal. To be sure, there would be less left for your heirs, and hence it might not appeal to you. However, for people without heirs it is a possibility. Also, in the above case, 64.7 percent of the $10,741 would not be taxable because it is a return of premiums rather than interest income.

Annuities may also reduce capital gains taxes in some cases. Suppose you have an duplex valued at $100,000, of which the rental income is earmarked for your retirement. Now that you retire, however, you no longer want to be bothered managing the apartment. You would like to sell the building and invest the funds in good quality securities. However, you purchased the building some years ago, at $50,000, and if you sell it you will have a capital gains tax which could run as much as $10,000.[4] An annuity might help you in such a case. The prospective new owner might be willing to buy whatever annuity $50,000 would provide as partial payment for the apartment. If the annuity were a private annuity, capital gains taxes would not apply on the $50,000 capital gain. Income taxes would apply to the annual income from the annuity as it was received, but they might be lower since they would be spread out over more years. In order to obtain this tax benefit it must be a private annuity, that is, not with an insurance company, and be an unsecured (no specific assets pledged) annuity. This does not mean it cannot be in writing and legally binding. In the above case the annuity could be underwritten by a trust company, if the buyer of the apartment transferred property to the trust company. Moreover, such a private annuity could be a temporary annuity, technically called an annuity certain (5 or 10 years). This would then be a means of converting a large capital gain into an income stream over a period of years in order to minimize taxes.[5]

---

4. A capital gains tax is a special tax on assets (wealth such as stocks, bonds, or real estate) which have risen in value over the years. This was discussed in detail in Chapter 8.

5. Using a private annuity this way to avoid taxes is a complex and intricate maneuver, and you should seek competent tax counsel beforehand.

Annuity Premiums

Annuity premiums can be paid monthly, quarterly, semiannually, or annually, just like life insurance. Premiums are paid over the years, and a principal sum is accumulated on behalf of the individual. These premiums are invested by the company and earn interest on behalf of the individual. Over the years the annuity builds up a cash surrender value just like permanent life insurance. In the case of annuities this is called account value. Again as in the case of life insurance, a person can turn in an annuity at any time and take the account value. If the individual dies prior to when the payments are to begin, the beneficiaries generally receive the principal sum. However, some insurance companies pay either the account value or the sum of all premiums paid in, whichever is the greater. This method of buying an annuity is a planned savings program.

It is also possible to buy an annuity in one lump-sum payment. People of some means may do this. Also people may use the cash surrender value of their paid-up life insurance policy to buy a single premium annuity when they wish to retire. This is generally one of the settlement options of life insurance policies.

Annuity Benefit Payments

The annuitant selects when he or she wants the annuity payments to begin—monthly, quarterly, semiannually, or annually. The dollar amount of the payment an annuitant will receive is determined by several factors: first, the principal sum built up on his or her behalf. This sum is dependent on the total dollars in premiums paid, plus the interest earned over the years. Then an allowance must be made for expenses by the insurance company. Finally, the amount of the annuity is determined by the age and sex of the annuitant, and the type of annuity selected.

The older you are when you start receiving payments, the higher the payment for any principal sum. Women, since they live longer than men, on the average, receive a slightly lower payment than men of the same age with the same principal sum, because a woman will receive the payment for a longer period of time.

Classification of Annuities by Benefit Payments

Most annuities are deferred annuities; that is, premiums are paid over the years and benefits are deferred until later in life. But there are also immediate annuities, where one lump sum premium is paid and benefits begin immediately. Whenever payments begin, there are a number of options from which to choose.

Straight life annuity

A straight life annuity provides for a periodic payment until the annuitant dies. This could be for one month or for thirty years or more, depending on how long the individual lives. If the annuitant dies after even only one monthly payment has been made, the insurance company keeps the remainder of the principal sum built up on the annuitant's behalf. There is nothing left for his or her heirs. For this reason such an annuity guarantees the annuitant the largest possible payment. For this same reason this type of annuity is not very popular.

Life annuity with guaranteed minimum installments

This annuity pays an income to the annuitant for life, with a minimum number of payments guaranteed. If the annuitant dies before the guaranteed payments have been made, they continue to be made to the beneficiary until the guaranteed minimum has been made. Quite often a 10- to 20-year (120–240 months) period is selected. The insurance company must make payments until the annuitant dies or until ten (or twenty) years have passed, whichever occurs last.

Such an annuity is more expensive than the straight life annuity, or, putting it another way, an individual of a given age with a given principal sum built up, will receive a smaller yearly payment with this guarantee than without it.

A variation of this guaranteed minimum installment annuity is the guaranteed lump-sum annuity. In such a case, if the annuitant dies prior to the guaranteed number of payments the difference is paid to his or her beneficiary in one lump sum.

Guaranteed premium refund annuity

This annuity is also called the installment refund annuity. It will pay an income for life with a guarantee that the total amount to be paid will be at least equal to the total premiums paid. If the person dies before collecting all the premiums he or she has paid over the years, the beneficiaries receive the difference. This difference can be taken in installments or in one lump sum.

Annuity certain, or temporary annuity

The annuity certain is not really an annuity because life contingencies are not involved. In this case the insurance company will pay an income for a specific period of time, say ten years, and that is all. The payments continue for ten years—to the annuitant if he or she is alive and otherwise to the beneficiaries. At the end of ten years the payments stop even if the annuitant is still alive. This is the only so-called annuity that may expire even though the annuitant may still be alive.

The Joint and Survivorship Annuity

The joint or survivorship annuity guarantees a payment for the entire life of two individuals. Since two individuals are involved, the risk to the insurance company is greater, and hence a given principal sum will provide a smaller benefit payment than will an annuity on one individual. The premiums needed to guarantee a given income are higher on a joint and survivorship annuity than on a single annuity. Often, but not always, the joint annuity is written so that when one member dies the payments, while they continue, decrease in amount. Generally this reduction is to 75 percent, 66.6 percent, or even to 50 percent of what the two individuals were receiving, which lowers the cost somewhat.

Joint annuities are always more expensive than an annuity on a single life, all other factors being equal. However, the dollar amount of an annuity that may be obtained with a given sum of money on a joint basis declines even more as the age gap between the husband and wife increases. This assumes, of course, that the wife is younger than the husband. For instance, if the husband is ten years older than his wife, the joint annuity would provide less than if he is only two years older—if in both cases it is to start when he reaches sixty-five and if the annuity is purchased at the same time and costs the same dollar amount. This is obvious because if an old man has a young wife, on the average she will be alive a long time after he is dead. If, on the other hand, the wife is sufficiently older than the husband, then it would appear that a joint annuity should be the same as a single annuity dollarwise. It does not work out that way, however, because on a joint annuity the life insurance company takes a risk on two lives, always greater than a risk on one life only.

Most annuity contracts (as well as life insurance contracts with a cash surrender value) permit the option of converting to a joint annuity at the time payments are to begin.

The Fixed Annuity

Traditionally, annuities were nearly always fixed annuities, contracts in which everything was determined and agreed to in advance. The only thing the insurance company did not know was the dollar amount of interest the annuity would earn over the years on future premiums, but a conservative assumption was made. The premiums were invested in bonds or mortgages that yielded a known return for a known period of time. The insurance company then could calculate accurately how large a principal sum would be generated for any annuitant. When the annuitant retired, the insurance company would be able to guarantee a fixed dollar payment per month or per year for life. Actuaries have constructed tables that deplete the principal sum actuarily but also make an allowance for interest to be earned on the declining principal.

The major problem with fixed annuities is that inflation erodes the principal sum both while it is being built up and also while it is being paid out. Consequently, fixed annuities have become somewhat less popular in recent years and interest has been stimulated in the variable annuity.

The Variable Annuity

The variable annuity was developed in an attempt to protect the annuitant against inflation both during the premium-paying years and during retirement. Premiums on variable annuities are invested in common stock. Historically the price of common stock has more than kept pace with inflation, and consequently premiums invested in common stock would protect the principal sum against erosion. When the annuitant retired, enough additional dollars would have been generated to pay increased benefits taking inflation into account. Unfortunately, in recent years common stocks have not been a good inflationary hedge, but they have been over the long run, and one day they may again serve this purpose. Indeed in 1982 and 1983 this began to happen.

Under a variable annuity contract the premiums you pay are used to buy a block of stock called an accumulation unit. For example, if your premiums are $600 per year, this $600 may buy ten units in one month and fifteen units in another as the price of the stock fluctuates. Your principal sum being built up would accumulate more and more units as time passed. These units, and hence your principal sum, would fluctuate in value. Hopefully, however, each unit would rise in the long run and this, together with the new units you purchase, would provide protection against inflation.

When you retire, your accumulation units are converted into annuity units. You are then guaranteed a retirement income equal to the value of a fixed number of annuity units, as follows: First, the value of your accumulation units is calculated at their market value to obtain your principal sum. Your first annual payment is then calculated in the same way as a fixed annuity would be. If, for example, your principal sum is $200,000, and the actuarial tables indicate that for a person of your age a $10,000 annual payment could be made on a fixed annuity of the type you had chosen, then the first payment on your variable annuity would also be $10,000. The initial payment ($10,000) is then divided by the present market value of one accumulation unit. This indicates how many accumulation units are currently required to meet the $10,000. Suppose the market value of one accumulation unit is $50; then two hundred units are needed to make the first payment, and future payments will always be equal to the fluctuating value of two hundred units. It is expected that the value of the units will rise in the long run, increasing your $10,000 annual retirement income.

Most variable annuity contracts will give you the option to convert your variable annuity into a fixed annuity when you retire. In such a case the $10,000 initial payment described above would become fixed and guaranteed. The insurance company would simply convert the $200,000 principal sum in the accumulation units into fixed obligations in order to finance this. In such a case you would have hedged against inflation during the accumulation period but not after retirement.

Combination Fixed Variable Annuity

It is possible to hedge by buying both a fixed and a variable annuity in one package. The most popular combination is a 50–50 split between a fixed and variable; half of your premiums would be invested in common stock and half in fixed obligations. However, 25–75 fixed variable or 75–25 are also popular, and a number of other combinations are also available.

The Cost of Annuities

Several factors determine the cost of an annuity:

1. The age of the person receiving the annuity figured at the time the annuity is to begin
2. The age of the person when he or she begins paying premiums
3. The type of annuity selected
4. The monthly annuity payment you want
5. Your sex (on old contracts only). The courts desexed annuities in late 1983.

Since annuities are the opposite of life insurance, the older you are when your payments are to begin, the lower the cost of a given payment. This is obvious, for the older a person is, the fewer the payments will be, on the average.

Insofar as annuity premium payments are concerned, they also vary with the age of the person when he or she buys the annuity, if it is a deferred annuity. A younger person will pay premiums for more years than an older person, and hence the yearly premium will be lower.

The cost also varies with the type of annuity. The straight life annuity, where the payments continue until the death of the annuitant with no guaranteed number of payments, is the least costly.

The larger the monthly payments you want, the higher the cost.

Since women live longer than men, a fixed monthly payment for a woman will be larger than it will for a man of the same age. Or a fixed sum of money will buy a smaller annuity income for a woman. Insurance companies do not have separate annuity tables for women but charge women the same rate as for a man five years younger. This sex variation, however, was eliminated by the courts for new annuities.

PRIVATE (AND GOVERNMENT) PENSION PLANS

Most corporations of any size have developed pension plans for their employees to provide a retirement income when they retire from the labor force, usually at age sixty-five. Such plans are designed to supplement Social Security retirement benefits. Regular money contributions are paid into the fund and are invested to earn interest. The fund then is available upon retirement. In some cases, deductions are withheld from the employee's wages, matched by the employer, and paid into the fund. In other cases, the employer makes the entire contribution. More and more of the plans are of the noncontributory type wherein the employer makes the entire contribution.

How good a plan you have is determined by the retirement benefits it promises, its vesting provisions, and the extent to which it is funded. You should investigate your plan to determine these things. How much your plan promises in the way of retirement benefits is obvious, but you should also consider what happens to the funds built up in your behalf if you terminate your employment prior to retirement, and how sound your plan is—that is, how likely it will be able to deliver what it promises.

Vesting of Interest and Portability

Vesting of interests concerns what happens to the funds built up on your behalf, if you should terminate your employment prior to retirement. If your plan is vested, you take your funds with you; if it is not vested, you will lose them. A few plans are immediate and fully vested, but most plans provide for partial delayed vesting; that is, a portion of the funds are vested every so many years until eventually full vesting is achieved.

Since there is bound to be some turnover, lack of immediate vesting permits higher benefits to those who do retire, with a given cost, or reduces the cost of a pension plan with a given retirement program. Some employers also feel that lack of vesting reduces labor turnover. It is debatable whether this in itself is desirable, because it reduces the mobility of labor; mobility of both labor and resources is required, many argue, to keep our economy dynamic. In any event, those workers who leave the firm before vesting occurs subsidize those who stay and finally retire. Federal regulations that now require certain vesting provisions as well as other matters are spelled out below.

Some vested plans are also portable; if so, the funds are combined with the funds of any new employer's plan. If they are vested but not portable, the employee usually gets his funds in one lump sum when he or she moves. In such a case, he can roll them over into an IRA (see below). If this applies to you, consider such a rollover; otherwise there can be complex tax problems.

Funding

Funding is another technical term with which you should be familiar. A pension plan can be 100 percent funded, partially funded, or zero percent funded. If a plan is not at all funded (zero percent), it is referred to as a pay-as-you-go plan. In such a case, an employer takes whatever money is needed out of operating revenue and pays retired employees a pension; the employee contributes nothing. This, of course, reduces profits. A pay-as-you-go plan is considered actuarially unsound and there are very few of them.

At the other extreme are the fully funded plans (100 percent funded). A fully funded pension plan is one where assets are accumulated each year in an amount equal to the future pension benefits earned that year. Actuarially the future cost of a pension plan can be predicted with great accuracy. If the pension plan is then designed so that the annual buildup of future benefits (discounted to present value) is always equal to the annual buildup of assets, there is 100 percent funding. In such a case, every employee could be paid his pension at any and all times. One hundred percent funding can be achieved by keeping the benefits lower than in a partially funded plan, or the contributions (cost of the pension fund) higher.

Funding and vesting are somewhat related. If a plan is not vested, then many of the contributions made for personnel who leave the company will be left in the fund. They can be used to pay benefits to employees who actually do retire, hence full funding is unnecessary. The same can be said in reverse. If a plan is fully funded, it might just as well be fully and immediately vested because the moneys are available.

Employee Retirement Income Security Act (ERISA)

Prior to the passage of the Employee Retirement Income Security Act (ERISA) of 1974, there were no federal controls over private pension funds and only loose, haphazard regulations at the state level. The act was passed in response to complaints that many workers were not obtaining their benefits upon retirement. Generally this was because either their pension funds were not adequately funded and moneys for retirement payments were not available or the plan was not vested and the employee left prior to retirement.

The federal act's main purpose was to establish minimum requirements regarding vesting and funding, but it contained some other provisions as well. For example, the act provides that each fund make an annual report to the Secretary of Labor and provide all employees covered with full information regarding their benefits, including access to financial records.

The act also established the Public Pension Benefit Guarantee Corporation (PPBGC). This is a government corporation and operates much like the FDIC. It guarantees pension rights, and if a pension fund collapses and cannot pay pension benefits the PPBGC could pay eligible retirees up to $750 per month. The PPBGC is to be financed with premiums collected from the employer amounting to $1 per worker per year ($.50 per worker in the case of multiemployer plans).

The act established minimum vesting procedures. Employers may choose one of three alternative methods of allowing workers to obtain vesting. First, they may decide to grant full vesting after ten years and provide nothing until then. Second, the employer may grant 25 percent vesting after five years, 50 percent after ten years, and full (100 percent) after fifteen years.

The third method of providing for vesting is to grant 50 percent vesting when the worker's age and years on the job total forty-five, providing the worker has been employed at least five years. This rule would then provide gradual increases until full vesting was achieved at the end of fifteen years.

If pension plans are vested, the matter of funding becomes very important. The 1974 act requires certain minimum funding provisions for all future pension fund obligations. The law also requires the employers to build up a fund over a period of thirty to forty years to make possible some funding of past nonfunded pension obligations.

Pension Benefits

When you retire you will receive pension benefit payments in accordance with the provisions of your plan. These vary. In some cases, your fund will simply buy you an annuity from a life insurance company. In such a case, you will have to consider all types of annuities discussed above.

Your pension plan will also build up a cash value, but you cannot generally get this prior to retirement. It is, however, paid to your beneficiaries if you die prior to retirement. In such a case, they might have to choose one of the annuities noted above, or the options discussed below. Some pension funds will allow you to withdraw your benefits upon retirement in one lump sum rather than in installments. Others do not give you this option. If you withdraw in one lump sum there could be a complex tax problem. The same is true if you withdraw this entire sum over, say, ten years, rather than over a longer period. Generally, a lump-sum withdrawal can be averaged and taxed over a ten-year period, but you should seek competent tax counsel on this problem for your specific case.

Some pension plans provide that the contributions made on your behalf are earmarked for you, are invested on your behalf, and then when you retire, the money built up is yours. This is sometimes called a *money purchase plan*. The amount of your benefit is determined by how much was paid in and how successful the fund managers were in investing the funds. Nothing is guaranteed while the fund is being built up. When you retire, you can usually take your benefits in one lump sum or in installments. A money purchase plan is really a fully funded plan.

There are other so called *"fixed benefit"* plans. Under these plans, the funds contributed on your behalf are commingled with those of your fellow employees. While you have a claim, there are no specific dollars you can call your own. Instead of an individual fund for each employee, there is a collectively owned group fund.

When you retire, your benefits are calculated by a formula that usually takes into account your salary and the length of time you have been with the company. For example, you might receive 1 percent of your average salary over your last five years for every year with the company. If your average salary over the last five years was $30,000 and you were with the company thirty years, your pension would be $9,000 per year.

Under the fixed benefit plan your benefits then are not as directly tied to your contributions as is the case in the money purchase plans. Under this fixed plan, the group fund could be used to provide you with your monthly payment or the fund could buy you an annuity with a life insurance company; the practice varies.

Most fixed benefit plans are not fully (100 percent) funded. The law requires some funding, enough to make it actuarily sound. Also the fixed benefit plan must belong to the Public Pension Benefit Guarantee Corporation (PPBGC) discussed above; the money purchase plan does not.

Tax Benefits of Private Pension Plans

There are some tax benefits that can be obtained with private pension plans. To obtain these benefits the plan must be what is called *qualified*, that is, it must be approved by the Internal Revenue Service. If the plan is nondiscriminatory in that all employees participate in it on the same basis and is in compliance with the Employee Retirement Income Security Act discussed above, it will be approved.

The funds going into an approved plan are tax sheltered; that is, a tax is not paid on them. In addition, the interest and dividends which they earn are not taxable, nor is any capital gain which may accrue. They are taxed as income upon retirement as an individual withdraws funds. It should also be noted that any contributions made by employees are fully deductible for them on their tax returns.

Government Pension Plans

All government-sponsored (administered) pension plans are exempt from the 1974 Federal Employee Retirement Income Security Act. This includes all local government plans as well as state plans. There are hundreds of government pension plans, some of which are very good and some of which are rather poor. Consequently, only certain generalizations can be made. Even though government plans are exempt from the 1974 act, they can be approved by the IRS, and if they are, the tax benefits discussed above apply.

Some government plans are managed by life insurance companies. Those are actuarily and financially very sound. Other government funds are managed by trust departments of commercial banks and are generally fairly high quality plans.

Still other government plans are managed by the governing unit itself or an agency established by the government for that purpose. In such a case, funding varies from plan to plan; it ranges from fairly high to virtually zero. Vesting provisions vary from relatively early and complete vesting to no vesting whatsoever until the employee retires. If you are a government employee and have a pension plan with your employer, it is suggested that you investigate your plan closely to determine just what benefits you have.

INDIVIDUAL TAX-SHELTERED RETIREMENT (PENSION) PLANS

If you are self-employed, you have to make your own plans for your retirement and accumulate assets on your own. This has always been the case, but there are now six different vehicles for building a retirement fund that utilizes tax shelters. Some of these are only for the self-employed, and some are for salaried individuals who qualify. These plans are:

1. The Simplified Employee Pension Plan (SEP)
2. The Individual Retirement Account (IRA)
3. The Keogh Plan
4. The Personal Service Corporation (sometimes called the Professional Corporation)
5. Individual Tax-Sheltered Annuities
6. Deferred Compensation Plans

The Simplified Employee Pension Plan (SEP)

Corporations that do not have a regular qualified pension plan discussed above may establish an SEP for their employees. There is less red tape involved in establishing an SEP, and fewer reports must be filed with the IRS and Department of Labor. Because of this, they appeal to smaller businesses. The employer must sponsor the plan but need not be involved in administering it; the employee may choose the custodian. Moreover, it may be a self-directed plan in which the individual has some control over the investment decisions. Under an SEP, 15 percent of the person's salary, up to a maximum of $15,000 annually, may be put away tax free during 1983. The maximum contribution will be increased beginning after December 31, 1983, to 25 percent of a person's salary up to a maximum of $30,000. The earnings and capital gains that accrue are also tax free until the person retires and begins drawing benefits. The funds cannot be withdrawn until the year in which the individual becomes 59-1/2 years of age, and the person must start withdrawing funds when he or she reaches age 70 1/2. There is a special 10 percent penalty tax (which is over and above the regular income tax) for early withdrawal of funds. This penalty for early withdrawals is waived if you become totally disabled. Or if you die prior to taking your funds, your dependents may withdraw them without penalty.

SEP contributions are fully and immediately vested. Any self-administered plan may not invest in collectibles such as coins, stamps, works of art, and so on, on a tax-free basis. (Technically speaking, you may put collectibles into your SEP; but if you do, their value will be taxed as income, and they will also be subject to the 10 percent penalty tax.) Regular qualified corporate pension plans discussed above administered by third parties, and over which the employee or employer have no investment control, may invest in collectibles.

The Individual Retirement Account (IRA)

The tax law passed in 1981 allows almost everyone to establish an IRA. The only qualification is that the person have earned income, that is, wages, salaries, or income from self-employment. Income in the form of interest, dividends, rent, or other property income does not qualify.

If you establish an IRA, you may put away $2,000 per year of earned income tax free. If you are employed part-time and earn $2,000 or less per year, you may place your entire earnings into an IRA. Your spouse may set up a separate IRA if he or she has earned income. A two-income couple may then put away, tax-free, $4,000. They must be *separate* accounts and not commingled. If your spouse has no earned income, you may set up what is called a "spousal IRA" and contribute an additional $250 on her or his behalf, for a total of $2,250. A spousal IRA must also be set up as two separate accounts. You may split the funds equally into two separate $1,125 accounts or you may choose different amounts. The only rule is that no one of the accounts may receive more than $2,000 per year.

If you are self-employed and your spouse has no earned income, you might want to consider employing him or her at least until $2,000 is earned, so that each of you may establish a $2,000 IRA. In addition, you may deduct the wages you paid your spouse as a business expense. If you do this, however, be sure your spouse's work is bona fide work, contributes to the business, and is paid for at reasonable rates.

Your IRA may then accumulate earnings and capital gains tax free; regular income taxes will be due when you retire and draw money out. You may not touch the funds in your account until you are 59 1/2 years of age without a penalty and you must begin withdrawals at age 70 1/2, just as in the case of a SEP. The penalty for early withdrawals is also the same and the disability waiver applies; and dependents have the same rights in the event of your death. When you withdraw your funds, you may take them all in one lump-sum payment, convert them to an annuity, or choose an income stream spread over the number of years equal to your life expectancy. (If you are married, you may even spread them over your joint life expectancy. See the section "When You Withdraw Your Funds" below for a more detailed discussion of this.) If you choose one lump sum, you may choose to average them together with any other income over five years for tax purposes, just as you can average any large increase in income.

It should be noted that if you have both a corporate pension plan and an IRA, and you retire and take your corporate pension in one lump sum and are not yet 70.5 years of age, you may roll your pension payment over into your IRA tax free and let it accumulate tax free until you are 70 1/2. Look this over carefully, however, because if you withdraw your pension funds in one lump sum, you can average them forward over ten years for tax purposes. If you roll them over into an IRA, then, although you can postpone taxes until you are

70.5 years of age, when you do withdraw them, you will have lost the ten-year averaging for one lump-sum withdrawal and will have to settle for five-year backward averaging. To be sure, you need not draw them out on a one-lump-sum basis, but rather over a number of years based upon your life expectancy.

If you established an IRA in 1982 or later, and if you have a regular corporate pension plan, a SEP, or a Keogh Plan (see below for a discussion of the Keogh Plan), you need not establish a separate account for your IRA. Rather, you may add an additional $2,000 to any of the above-mentioned plans. If your IRA was established in 1981 or earlier, it must remain as a separate account; it cannot be rolled over into one of the others. Only a relatively small number of people qualified for an IRA prior to 1982. It should also be noted that the IRA contribution is over and above the corporate or SEP pension plan. That is to say, after you have saved the maximum in your other plans, you may add $2,000 ($4,000 if you have a working spouse) more via an IRA.

The Keogh Plan

If you are self-employed, you may not have a corporate pension plan, but you may establish your own personal retirement fund. These are called Keogh Plans, and the only requirement for establishing one is to be self-employed. This includes people who work for a corporation and have a corporation pension plan, if they are self-employed on the side (moonlighting).

If you establish a Keogh Fund, you may put 15 percent of your net self-employment income—not to exceed $15,000 per year—into it tax free, and it can accumulate tax free. These limits will be increased beginning in 1984 to 25 percent and $30,000; the $30,000 maximum is then frozen until 1986 when it will be adjusted upward to reflect inflation. The words *net self-employed* are important, because you will no doubt have some business expenses. Consequently, you may not know exactly how large a Keogh contribution you may make until you calculate your taxes. But contributions for any year may be made up until you file your return—normally April 15 of the following year. If you have overpaid, you may withdraw the funds until you file your tax return, or you may treat them as a contribution for the following year. If you do the latter, it is recommended that you actually withdraw the excess and then put it back in again immediately.

The Keogh Plan permits more generous tax-free contributions than the IRA, but virtually everything else we said about the IRA applies. Both you and your spouse may have a separate one if both qualify; the 59 1/2 and 70 1/2 ages and the penalty for early withdrawals apply. There are, however, three differences: you may not add $250 for a nonworking spouse to your Keogh and the "15 percent of net earned income" rule (25 percent beginning in 1984) is firm; you may not contribute 100 percent of the first $2,000 of self-employed income. Finally, if you withdraw your funds in one lump sum, you average them over ten years for tax purposes, whereas with an IRA you may not.

After-Tax Contributions, and the Defined Keogh Plan

There are two ways in which you may increase your Keogh contributions above the maximum discussed above. First, you may add an additional amount over and above the maximum (but not to exceed 10 percent or $2,500 of your net earned income), but this would consist of after-tax dollars. However, the investment income and the capital gains accruing to these after-tax contributions are not taxable until the person retires and receives his or her benefits.

Second, you may establish a defined benefit Keogh Plan (or modify an existing one) and then make tax-free contributions substantially in excess of the above-mentioned maximum. Under a defined plan you must define specifically what you want your future retirement benefit payments from your Keogh Plan to be. There is a limit to how large a sum you may designate, and the limit is determined by your age and your net self-employed income. The limit is reduced somewhat the older you are when you make the designation because there are fewer years to accumulate the needed funds. However, at any age, the limit rises with the level of net self-employed income.

There is also an overall limit (or maximum) that you may set as your benefits under a defined plan. This maximum was set several years ago at $75,000 per year. This sum, however, is subject to cost-of-living adjustments annually, and by early 1982, it had grown to $136,425. There is also a second overall limit to the benefit you may define; it may be no larger than the average of your last three years of consecutive self-employment income. This upper limit of $136,425, then, would apply only to a person with a very large self-employed income. There are other guidelines for establishing your defined benefits, and they must be approved by the Internal Revenue Service. Once your defined benefits have been established (and they may vary from year to year as your income varies), you may make tax-free Keogh contributions of whatever is necessary to fund your Keogh Plan to the extent needed to provide for the benefits you have chosen. This involves making some complex actuarial calculations. If you wish to establish a defined benefit plan, you will need to see a trust officer of a commercial bank or a qualified estate or financial planner.

The defined limit of $136,425 applied only for the year 1983. The Tax Equity and Fiscal Responsibility Act of 1982 (TEFRA) reduced that figure to a maximum of $90,000 beginning in 1984. It will remain at that level until 1986, when it will again be adjusted for inflation. TEFRA implemented certain reforms and also eliminated some of the differences between the benefits available under a Keogh Plan and a Personal Service Corporation (see below).

There is one drawback in starting a defined Keogh Plan. If you treat yourself more generously than under the regular Keogh, you must do the same for your employees and this can become expensive.

The Personal Service Corporation (PSC)

In recent years many self-employed, especially professionals—such as doctors and lawyers—have chosen the corporation rather than a Keogh Plan to provide for their retirement. If a doctor (or a group of them) incorporates, his fees flow into the corporation, which now pays him a salary. The corporation may now establish a pension fund for him. A corporation may in some cases permit a larger tax-free donation to a pension fund than a Keogh Plan, and this will continue through 1983.

The sub-chapter S corporation

You may incorporate as a traditional corporation or you may incorporate as what is known as a "sub-chapter S" corporation, in which case all corporate income is taxed as personal income even if not passed through. In such a case, however, no corporation income taxes need be paid. It should be noted, too, that you may not have both a Keogh Plan and a corporation for the same income stream. However, it is theoretically possible that say a self-employed doctor could have a professional corporation for his income from the practice of medicine, then write a book and put some of his royalty income into a Keogh fund. However, the funds going into both of them are counted together in determining the maximum that could be set aside tax free.

If you incorporate as a sub-chapter S corporation, the funds you may set aside tax-free are identical to those permitted under a Keogh Plan (15 percent up to $15,000 through 1983, and 25 percent and $30,000 after 1983). Or a defined benefit plan may be chosen; and again, it works just like a defined benefit Keogh Plan. In addition, the corporation may pay your life, health, and disability insurance premiums and deduct them even though they are tax free to you. (This will change in 1984; then you will have to report the premiums as income and pay a tax on them.)

You may also borrow from the corporation pension plan at reasonable interest rates. The new tax law passed in 1982 restricted these loans to $10,000 or one-half of your vested benefits up to $50,000. You can deduct the interest or the loan from your taxes while it accumulates tax free in the pension fund.

Under the old rules, a sub-chapter S corporation could not have more than 20 percent of its total income in the form of passive income—that is, interest and dividends on stock it owns. This has been changed; there is now no limit. In addition, a sub-chapter S corporation may now have 35 stockholders instead of the previous 25. Because of these two factors, a wealthy family may transfer securities to the corporation and make their children stockholders. The children's share of the investment income would be taxed at the children's—presumably lower—rate.

Regular corporation

If you incorporate as a regular corporation, the benefits may be even larger, but only through 1983. However, you are now subject to the corporate income tax. Under the traditional corporation, you would pay yourself a salary—which might be all or nearly all of your corporation's income. You may then choose between a defined benefit pension plan and a defined contribution plan. The defined benefit plan is much like the defined benefit Keogh Plan discussed above, the maximum defined benefit not exceeding \$136,425 (\$90,000 beginning in 1984). Actuarial calculations would be necessary, but whatever contributions were needed to fund the benefits would be permitted.

Under the defined contribution plan, you set the amount of money going into the pension fund on your behalf. This may be as high as \$45,475 per year or 25 percent of your income, whichever is less, through 1983. As before, the corporation could pay your insurance premiums. You may borrow from it, and transfer other property to it.

A corporation pension plan may be set up so that part of the 25 percent is profit sharing and part is a mandatory annual contribution; most frequently 15 percent is profit sharing, and 10 percent is a mandatory contribution. The profit-sharing contributions need not be made even if there are profits, and of course they may be made partially, or made in some years but not in others.

Whether a defined benefit plan or a defined contribution plan would be best for you is impossible to say. It depends on your age, number of employees, and other factors. You should seek professional help to find the answer to that question.

In August, 1982, a law was passed that eliminated the differences in the dollar amount that may be sheltered through four of the above-discussed plans, beginning in 1984. After that date, the SEP, the Keogh Plan, the sub-chapter S corporation, and the regular corporation will all be able to shelter the same amount: 25 percent of net income up to \$30,000 per year. The IRA was left unchanged at \$2,000 per year. Many financial planners expect to see less emphasis on incorporating and more and more self-employed adopting the Keogh Plan.

What about Your Employees?

If you are self-employed and establish a Keogh account or a personal corporate pension plan, your plan must be nondiscriminatory. You must provide for all of your employees as soon as they qualify on the same basis as for yourself. "As soon as they qualify" are the crucial words, because the law permits you to require that they work for you for three years before they become eligible to participate. Once they are eligible, however, you must make the contribution on their behalf, and it must be the same percentage of their salary as the contribution on your behalf is of yours.

Where to Invest Your Retirement Funds

If you have an individual retirement program (either a Keogh Plan, Personal Service Corporation, a self-directed SEP, or an IRA), you may choose from a number of different investment outlets. You may put your funds in any of the following:

1.   Thrift institutions
2.   Annuities from a life insurance company (you cannot buy life insurance, only annuities)
3.   Mutual funds
4.   The trust department of a commercial bank
5.   Brokerage firms
6.   An IRA established in 1982 or after may also be commingled with a Keogh Plan, a SEP, or a corporate pension plan.

If your account is relatively small and you wish to eliminate investment fees, you should consider thrift institutions. If you choose the thrifts, you may select any of the various CDs they offer. One was developed especially for the IRA and Keogh accounts, free of all interest rate controls; the rate is subject to negotiation. This special CD requires that IRA and Keogh funds be pledged for 18 months. You may have the choice of an interest rate fixed for the entire 18 months or one that floats. If it floats, it is usually tied to the Treasury bill rate or the prime rate (or something like it), and is then adjusted every few weeks or every month. While the people who establish an IRA or Keogh account cannot touch their funds without paying the tax penalty established by the IRS, they can avoid the CD early withdrawal penalty if they roll over their account into another custodial account when the CD matures. This is why you should not use IRA or Keogh funds to purchase a CD with more than an 18-month maturity. Remember, you may roll your IRA and Keogh over into another institution without penalty. The 1982 Act also allows partial IRA rollovers. Before, you had to roll the entire amount over to another custodian.

If you choose annuities, you will have to pay commissions, which will vary from company to company. You should check this out carefully. If you buy mutual funds, you may also have to pay commissions, but now there is the possibility of capital gains. You may also buy no-load mutual funds on which there are no investment costs. If you select a trust department of a commercial bank, you will have to pay a management fee. This will generally be about one-half or three-fourths of 1 percent of the first $50,000 of your account and lesser amounts on larger accounts. However, trust departments also have a minimum management fee (generally about $150). For small accounts, a trust department may not be the best; but for a larger account, it provides greater flexibility than some of the other outlets. If you select a brokerage firm, you will also have substantial flexibility, but there will be investment fees. If you choose a brokerage

Table 19–2   Buildup of assets with a tax-exempt IRA and $2,000 of savings in which both the principal and interest are diluted by taxes—both yielding 10 percent

| Year end | IRA | Taxable deposits | |
		40% bracket	50% bracket
1	$ 2,200	$ 1,272	$ 1,050
5	13,421	7,170	5,804
10	35,062	16,765	13,210
15	69,898	29,605	22,662
20	126,004	46,791	34,729

Source: Calculated by author.

firm, you may invest in stock, bonds, mutual funds, money market funds, and in some cases even in real estate or gas and oil investments.

A vehicle that provides great flexibility is worth considering. Then you may switch from bonds to stock, from short-term to long-term securities, or vice versa, and also into and out of a number of other outlets as conditions change. Investigate all of the possible custodians of your retirement funds carefully before you choose one.

Whatever vehicle you choose, benefits are substantial. Table 19–2 shows the differences over the years between the account of a person in either the 40 or the 50 percent tax bracket who saves $2,000, pays a tax on it, and puts the remainder into a regular savings account on which the interest is taxed, and another person who puts $2,000 per year in an IRA or Keogh account. In both cases, they are earning 10 percent. Table 19–3 shows the buildup if the taxed account receives the same yearly cash inflow.

Table 19–3   Buildup of assets with tax-exempt IRA and taxable deposits—both yielding 10 percent

| Year end | IRA | Taxable deposits | |
		40% bracket*	50% bracket**
1	$ 2,200	$ 2,120	$ 2,100
5	13,431	11,949	11,605
10	35,062	27,941	26,661
15	69,898	49,342	45,628
20	126,004	77,986	69,840

* $3,335 of taxable income is needed to generate $2,000 after taxes to put into this account.
** $4,000 of taxable income is needed to generate $2,000 after taxes to put into this account.

A Final Note on Pension Plans and Individual Retirement Accounts

Generally speaking, there are five different pension plans: the regular corporation (or government) pension plan, the SEP, the IRA, the Keogh Plan, and the Personal Service Corporation.

A person who is employed may have a corporate pension plan where he or she works or an SEP, but not both. Self-employed individuals may choose either a Keogh Plan or a Personal Service Corporation. Everyone who has earned income may establish an IRA, which is over and above the others. An IRA, moreover, as noted above, may be tied in (commingled) with a corporate pension plan, an SEP, a Keogh Plan, or a Personal Service Corporation.

While many people want to save the maximum amount possible in their various plans, there may be some exceptions. If you are relatively young, and if your income is relatively modest but is expected to grow substantially in the future, you might consider waiting before you set up an IRA. First, you may not be able to afford to save as much as the law allows. Second, if you are in your twenties, putting money aside and not being able to touch it without paying a heavy penalty for 30 years or more is also something to ponder.

The acquisition of certain other assets should perhaps be given a higher priority than an IRA if you are quite young. For example, buying a house, buying some life insurance, and acquiring an emergency fund held in a highly liquid form might be given a higher priority.

When You Withdraw Your Funds

If you work for a corporation, the corporate plan itself will spell out your withdrawal options. Some corporate plans permit a lump-sum withdrawal, and some do not. If you have an SEP, an IRA, a Keogh Plan, or a Personal Service Corporation, you will be able to select one of several options when you reach age 59 1/2. You may elect a lump-sum withdrawal, you may convert the funds to an annuity, or you may take an income stream spread over the number of years equal to your life expectancy at that time. You may choose a combination of the three. If you choose an annuity, you pay income taxes on the funds as you receive them. The same is true if you take an income stream based on your life expectancy. If you take a lump-sum distribution, you may average the funds over ten years spread forward for tax purposes, if you have a Keogh Plan. You may not do this, however, with an IRA. A lump-sum IRA distribution is considered income when received for tax purposes. However, as with any big increase in income, the tax laws allow five-year backward averaging.

If you withdraw your funds over the life expectancy years and you have a spouse, you may draw them out over the joint life expectancy.[6] This will

6. For actuarial reasons, and because the figures are based on averages, the joint life expectancy is somewhat longer than the longest single life expectancy of the couple. It is not, of course, the sum of the two.

increase the number of pull-out years, and will postpone and almost certainly reduce taxes. As you pull your funds out over your life expectancy, the balance remaining will continue to grow, tax free. However, you have to develop a plan that will exhaust the fund at the end of the life expectancy years. This will necessitate some complex calculations, and you should seek professional help. This also means that you could outlive your funds.

If you are over 70 1/2, you may not skip a year and then make it up by withdrawing a larger amount the following year. If you fail to take out at least the minimum required each year, the IRS will assess a 50 percent excise tax penalty on the difference between what you took out and what the withdrawal should have been.

If you start drawing out funds and are under 70 1/2 years of age, (but over 59 1/2) you may stop withdrawals. You may even be withdrawing funds and putting funds in during the same year. However, you may put in only the amount for which you are eligible: $2,000 of earned income in an IRA and 15 percent (25 percent in 1984 and after) of your net self-employed income in a Keogh Plan. You may not make up by putting in an amount to offset that which you took out earlier.

Even if you are over 70 1/2, you may still make contributions to a Keogh Plan (but not to an IRA) if you are eligible—i.e., have earned self-employed income—while depleting the fund. In such a case, you would have to recalculate yearly the withdrawals needed to exhaust the fund over your life expectancy.

If you withdraw funds prior to age 59 1/2, there is, as noted above, a penalty in the form of a 10 percent surtax on the funds withdrawn. This penalty is waived if you become totally disabled.

If a joint survivorship annuity had not been selected before the individual's death, a surviving spouse may immediately withdraw any remaining funds in one lump sum, or in installments, but not in excess of five years. There is also a $100,000 estate tax exemption.[7]

Tax-Sheltered Annuities (TSA)

Certain people are permitted under the Internal Revenue Code to purchase tax-sheltered annuities. These are also sometimes referred to as tax deferred annuities (TDA) and supplemental retirement annuities (SRA). People who work for tax-exempt organizations, including schools and colleges, are eligible; people who work for profit-making corporations are not. Congress authorized these tax-sheltered annuities some years ago because tax-exempt institutions have less of an incentive to establish a pension plan for their employees, since there are no tax benefits available to institutions that are already exempt. Even if these

---

7. The estate tax is discussed in Chapter 20. In the case of a surviving spouse, this $100,000 estate tax exemption may be meaningless because of the unlimited estate tax-free transfers between spouses. However, if someone else is the beneficiary, it may be important.

institutions have since established pension plans for their employees (and most have), their employees may still purchase tax-sheltered annuities.

The amount of dollars you may commit (if eligible) to such tax-sheltered annuities depends on what other types of tax-sheltered fringe benefits you may have with your employer. Generally speaking, the amount of dollars you may commit to a tax-sheltered annuity, together with dollars going into another tax-exempt plan with your employer, may not exceed 20 percent of your salary. Note the words "with your employers"; moneys going into a Keogh or IRA are not included in the 20 percent. There are, however, exceptions to this 20 percent rule. For example, if you have sheltered less than 20 percent in previous years, you may recapture that in future years and in this way often exceed 20 percent by a substantial margin. If you cannot afford to shelter all of the income that the law allows during your thirties and forties, you may wish to recapture all or part of that during your fifties when your income does permit this. See your personnel department or other qualified expert, if you are planning to buy such an annuity.

If you buy such an annuity, neither the premium you pay nor the annuity's earnings are taxed until you retire and receive the benefits. One advantage of the tax-sheltered annuity over the IRA is that you may withdraw it at any time without penalty; you do not need to wait until you are 59 1/2 years of age like the IRA. You pay taxes only as you withdraw the funds.

Partially Tax-Sheltered Annuities

The annuities described immediately above are completely tax-sheltered. However, anyone may buy an annuity with after-tax dollars, and then defer the interest it earns or the capital gain that may accrue to it, until receiving the benefits. If you are concerned that inflation will erode fixed-dollar annuities, you might consider a variable annuity in which the premiums are invested in common stock. You may also arrange to have your annuity premiums invested in money market funds. Then your savings can accumulate tax free at short-term interest rates.

In 1982, the Tax Act changed slightly the treatment of these annuities. Before that time funds could be withdrawn at any time without a penalty. Now there is, in some cases, a 5 percent penalty (as opposed to 10 percent in the case of a Keogh or IRA account). There is no penalty if your contract with the life insurance company is ten years old regardless of your age. There is also no penalty if you are 59 1/2 years of age, regardless of how old the contract is. If you are under 59 1/2 and your contract is less than ten years old, the penalty applies.

When you withdraw the funds, you pay taxes, but only on the accumulated interest. Before the 1982 Tax Act, it was assumed that the principal came out first and the interest last, if you withdrew in installments. This deferred taxes a bit longer. Now it is assumed that interest comes out first insofar as taxes are concerned.

Deferred Compensation Plans

You may be able to defer part of your income until later and, hence, defer taxes. There are two general types of deferred compensation plans. There are the so-called "mass plans" (also called qualified plans), which virtually any employer may make available to all employees. Under these plans a person may defer up to 25 percent of his salary or $7,500, whichever is less. (Other tax-exempt plans, including the tax-sheltered annuity, with your employer, are counted within this 25 percent limit, but the Keogh and IRA funds are not.) Neither the deferred income nor its earnings or capital gains are taxed until you receive it. The employer withholds this deferred income and invests it on the employee's behalf, and takes a tax deduction. Currently these funds may be invested in life insurance policies, annuities, mutual funds, or in thrift institutions.

Insofar as the IRS is concerned, you may take your deferred funds at any time without extra penalty; you need only pay taxes on them as you draw them. In actual practice, however, the plans are often set up in a way that you cannot withdraw the funds until you retire or otherwise terminate your employment.

There is also the nonqualified deferred compensation plan which is designed primarily for highly paid individuals. These plans are not funded with a third party, and the employer does not receive a tax deduction at that time. Rather, the employee enters into a contract with his employer to receive moneys some time in the future when he will be retired. (Or the heirs receive the funds in the event of death prior to retirement.) The value of such a contract, then, is a function of the financial strength of the employer. Later, when the funds are paid, the employer does receive a tax deduction. In theory there is no limit to how much income may be deferred under these individual nonqualified plans, but the IRS has established certain guidelines that must be adhered to. Consequently, each plan is scrutinized by the IRS, and it must be considered reasonable. Hence, informal limits may be imposed this way.

QUESTIONS FOR REVIEW

1. Social Security is now said to be a matter of right. How is this different from a "needs" test, which is often a necessary prerequisite for welfare payments?
2. What are the different kinds of benefits that the federal government administers under the Social Security Act?
3. Who is covered under the Social Security law?
4. What is meant by quarters of coverage?

5. How are Social Security Funds invested, and how may these funds have an impact upon the economy?
6. How are ministers and the clergy covered by Social Security?
7. At present retired persons drawing social security cannot earn more than $6,600 per year. Suppose they earn $6,800 per year. How does this affect the total payment paid to them?
8. What is the future of Social Security, in your opinion?
9. How may it be said that the annuity is, in the final analysis, an insurance problem?
10. Explain the three major purposes for which annuities are used.
11. Distinguish between the single-premium annuity and the annual-premium annuity.
12. Why are straight-life annuities often difficult to sell?
13. What is an annuity certain?
14. Under what circumstances may it be desirable to purchase a joint survivorship annuity?
15. Why is a straight-life annuity cheaper than a joint and survivorship annuity?
16. Explain briefly any three of the general types of annuity that life insurance companies sell.
17. What are the similarities and differences between the conventional or fixed annuity and the variable annuity?
18. What is portability as the term applies to pension funds?
19. What is the difference between "vesting" and "funding"?
20. Discuss the tax benefits Congress has provided for the self-employed if they establish a retirement program.
21. What is a simplified employee pension plan?
22. What is the individual retirement account?
23. What provision for retirement may a self-employed person undertake?
24. What happens if you withdraw funds from an IRA prior to age 59 1/2?
25. May you borrow from your Keogh Fund?
26. How can it be stated that your insurance program and your retirement program are tied together?

CASES

1. John Fisher, aged sixty-five with no dependents, has been working off and on as a farm laborer all his life. Although he has never worked the year around, he has worked some each year. During the last five years, which were the best years of his life incomewise, John has never earned less than $3,000 nor more than $8,000. John is not certain whether he is eligible for retirement under Social Security. Is he eligible?
2. George Adams and Pete Gerrard are two elderly widowers drawing Social Security benefits. George is seventy-three years of age and Pete is sixty-

six. Both have part-time jobs, and last year each made about $7,000. Pete lost some of his Social Security benefits, but George did not. Why? Can you calculate how much Pete lost? Pete found out that his twin brother earned $10,000 last year on some investments he had as well as $5,000 because of a part-time job. Pete wonders how much Social Security benefits his brother lost. Can you explain it to him?

3. Jane Stodard, thirty-two, has worked for a large manufacturing firm in Detroit for the last ten years and is currently earning $500 per week. Five years ago the union and the company agreed on a pension plan. The plan is partially funded and fully vested but only after ten years. Each week $20 is deducted from Jane's check and is matched by the company, hence $40 per week goes into the fund on Jane's behalf. Explain funding and vesting to Jane.

    Recently Jane was offered another job, which pays $550 per week. Should she take it? How much of her pension will she lose if she does take the new job? How much cash will she take with her if she makes the move?

4. George and Esther Gant are both fifty-five and are looking forward to retiring when they reach sixty-five. They would like to begin planning now so that they will have about $1,600 per month at that time. They know that Social Security will provide them with about $900 per month and that George will get a pension from his employer of about $550 per month. They own their own home and a $25,000 whole life insurance policy. Can you help them with their retirement plan?

5. Tom and Mary Brown are reaching retirement age and seek your help in converting life insurance to annuities. The only other retirement income they will have is $950 from Social Security. They are both the same age and are unclear whether they should convert their life insurance to a single or a joint and survivorship annuity. What is your advice?

6. John Green is a man of substantial means with all of his funds invested either in securities or in property. He feels he can retire on his investment income, but recently he has heard he might want to consider annuities for other reasons. What would you advise?

7. Bob Price is self-employed. He earns $48,000 as an insurance agent. He is thirty-four years old, has a wife, Evelyn, and two children ages six and eight. He has $50,000 of life insurance. Bob saves regularly for the children's college education by putting $25 per month into a savings and loan association on their behalf. He now wants to start accumulating assets for his own retirement. He doesn't want to buy an annuity from an insurance company, but he is in a position where he can put aside about $3,000 per year. How should he invest it? Bob has heard that in some cases he receives tax benefits if he sets aside savings for his retirement. Can you explain how this works?

8. Cynthia Jean Reed is a 39-year-old college professor and has a pension plan with her university. Recently she heard that she is eligible for a tax-

sheltered annuity over and above the pension benefits she has with the university. Is this true? Currently Cynthia is contributing 7 percent of her salary to a pension plan, and this is matched by the university. Explain how a tax-sheltered annuity works and calculate how much more Cynthia could set aside for retirement purposes, tax-free.

SUGGESTED READINGS

Allen, Everett T., et al. *Pension Planning: Pensions, Profit Sharing and Other Deferred Compensation Plans*, 4th ed. Homewood, Ill.: Irwin, 1981.

Carrigan, Arnold. *How to Get the Most from Your IRA*. New York: Crown Publishers, 1982.

Dickson, David T. *Tax Shelters for the Not-So-Rich*. Chicago, Ill.: Contemporary Books, 1981.

Drollinger, William C., and Drollinger, William C., Jr. *Tax Shelters and Tax-Free Income for Everyone*, 4th ed., Vol. II. Orchard Lake, Mich.: Epic Publications, 1981.

Egan, Jack. *Your Complete Guide to IRA's and Keogh's: The Simple, Safe Tax Deferred Way to Future Financial Security*. New York: Harper and Row, 1982.

"Financing Your Social Security Benefits; If You Become Disabled." Washington, D.C.: U.S. Department of Health, Education and Welfare. (SSA)-79-10029. This is an annual publication.

"If You Work While You Get Social Security Payments." Washington, D.C.: U.S. Department of Health, Education and Welfare, Social Security Administration. This is an annual publication.

Krass, Stephen J., and Keschner, Richard L. *The Pension Answer Book*. Greenvale, N.Y.: Panel Publishers, 1981.

Life Insurance Fact Book. Published annually by the Institute of Life Insurance, 277 Park Avenue, New York, N.Y.

Munnell, Alicia H. *The Economics of Private Pensions*. Washington, D.C.: The Brookings Institution, 1982.

Myers, Robert. *Social Security*, 2nd ed. Homewood, Ill.: Irwin, 1981.

Nauholm, Fred. *The Retirement Money Book: New Ways to Have More Income When You Retire*. Washington, D.C.: Acropolis Books, 1982.

"Pension Facts." American Council of Life Insurance, 1850 K Street, Washington, D.C. 20006.

Questions and Answers on Retirement Plans for the Self-Employed; Retirement Plans for Self-Employed Individuals. Washington, D.C.: Internal Revenue Service. No date.

Shapiro, Ruth G., ed. *Tax Shelters*, 3rd ed. New York: Practicing Law Institute, 1983.

"Social Security," and *Supplement to Social Security Handbook*, Washington, D.C.: U.S. Department of Health, Education and Welfare. This is an annual publication. You can get it free by writing or calling your local social security field office. Offices are located in all big cities.

"Social Security Information for Young Families." (SSA 10033). Washington, D.C.: U.S. Department of Health, Education and Welfare.

"Social Security in Your Financial Planning." Washington, D.C.: U.S. Department of Health, Education and Welfare. This is an annual publication.

Swanson, Robert E., and Swanson, Barbara M. *Tax Shelters: A Guide for Investors and Their Advisors*. Homewood, Ill.: Dow Jones-Irwin, 1982.

Tanner, Beverly, et al. *Shelter What You Make; Minimize the Take: Tax Shelters for Financial Planning.* San Francisco, Calif.: Harbor Publishing, 1982.

"A Woman's Guide to Social Security." Washington, D.C.: U.S. Department of Health, Education, and Welfare. Publication No. (SSA) 79-10127.

"Your Medicare Handbook." Washington, D.C.: U.S. Government Printing Office.

"Your Social Security." Washington, D.C.: U.S. Department of Health, Education, and Welfare. Publication No. (SSA) 05-10035, 1980.

"Your Social Security Earnings Record." U.S. Department of Health, Education and Welfare. This is an annual publication.

"Your Social Security Rights and Responsibilities." Washington, D.C.: U.S. Department of Health, Education, and Welfare. Publication No. 05-10077.

CHAPTER TWENTY

ESTATE PLANNING: WILLS, GIFTS, AND TRUSTS

No one cares to discuss his or her own death. However, it is inevitable. Consequently, you should think about the disposition of your estate, with some sort of deliberate plan or method. The major reason is inheritance, estate, and gift taxes. Suppose a small business owner or a farmer desires to leave property to a son or daughter. Without a plan it might be necessary to dispose of the business or the farm to pay taxes. The simplest plan would call for a will passing the business or the farm to the offspring and life insurance sufficiently large to cover the tax. If the individual failed to make a will, the property possibly would not pass as wished but instead in a manner prescribed by the state's statutes. Even in the absence of taxes, it might be desirable, because of certain state statutes, to set up means of providing for a surviving husband or wife to prevent the business or the farm from being liquidated, which would defeat the intention to pass the property on to others. Additionally, if the son or daughter were a minor, one would want to designate the person who would act as guardian for the child and the estate.

PREPARING A WILL

Gathering the Facts

Since every individual and every family are unique, each estate plan will be unique. There is, however, some basic information that is important to every estate plan, and your attorney must have the information to plan the best estate for your needs.

Residence and domicile

Your residence and domicile are important to your plan. Domicile is the name given to a person's permanent home, and residence is the place where one lives without the intention of making a permanent home. (They may be the same place, but if not, the site of the domicile is where the person's will is to be probated.) In addition, any marital rights that may attach to the property, such as dower or community-property rights, are determined by the domicile, as are state inheritance taxes.

Family status

Your family status is very important. A prior marriage or a separation from your present spouse can have an effect on your legal ability to make gifts of property in your will. A prior spouse may have a claim against an estate. Your attorney will want to know whether you plan to have more children and whether your children are dependent on you. Your attorney will also want to know whether you have other living relatives from whom you may expect an inheritance. This is important in developing an estate plan that will best conserve your assets, since inheritances often constitute a large portion of the assets of an estate.

Safe deposit box

If you have a safe deposit box, where are the box and the key? On your demise it is necessary for the attorney to obtain a court order to open the box, and it is simpler if the location of the box is immediately known.

Beneficiaries

Your attorney will want to know about your beneficiaries, their names, addresses, relationship to you, financial needs, and character traits. The reason for wanting to know financial needs is that you may wish to provide financial means to enable them to live at the same standard as at present or even better. The character traits of the proposed beneficiaries are also important. Perhaps one of the proposed beneficiaries gambles or indulges in some vice; the attorney may then think of establishing a trust that would provide funds over time rather than funds in a lump sum that might be gambled away or spent in loose living.

Taking a Financial Inventory

The first step in estate planning and in making a will is to take a financial inventory. List all of your assets and liabilities at their fair market value, and then determine your net worth. The following personal balance sheet (Table 20–1) is a beginning. We have added hypothetical figures for some of the entries, and there are some blanks for you to fill in, also a blank to show the

Table 20–1   Personal (or family) balance sheet

Assets	Example	Your personal entry	% return	Liabilities	Example	Your personal entry
Cash (inc. checking accounts)	$ 750	____	____	Mortgage on owner-occupied home	$ 30,000	____
Savings deposits (inc. certificates of dep.)	5,000	____	____	Other mortgages	—	____
Life insurance (estimated cash surrender value)	15,000	____	____	Notes & loans payable (inc. installments)	2,000	____
Annuities (est. cash surrender value)	5,000	____	____	Other unpaid bills	300	____
Gov. sec. of all kinds	—	____	____	Long-term business debts	—	____
Tax exempt state and local securities	—	____	____	Short-term business liabilities (inc. accounts payable)	—	____
Corporation bonds	—	____	____			
Common Stock	—	____	____	Loans against life insurance	—	____
Mutual funds	5,000	____	____	Other liabilities	—	____
Vested corp. pension benefits (exclude Soc. Sec.)	10,000	____	____	Total Liabilities	$32,300	____
Individual pension benefits (inc. Personal Service Corp., Keogh, and IRA)	—	____	____	Net Worth	$118,450	
Stock options and profit sharing benefits	—	____	____			
Real estate (owner occupied)	100,000	____	____			
Rental property	—	____	____			
Other long-term business assets	—	____	____			
Short-term business assets (e.g., accts. receivable)	—	____	____			
Personal assets (furniture, car, jewelry, etc.)	10,000	____	____			
Other assets	—	____	____			
Total Assets	150,750	____	____			

yield on your earning assets. Now that your assets and liabilities are outlined, your attorney may proceed to draw up a will.

Modern Wills

There are a number of types of wills and a number of things that wills can accomplish. There are also, of course, many legal technicalities one should know about wills. While this book will not make you an expert able to draw up your own will, it should give you an appreciation for the problems involved and convince you to see an experienced and competent attorney.

General definitions

A will is ordinarily a writing that provides for the distribution of property on the death of the writer but confers no rights prior to that time. In short, the will is ineffective prior to the death of the writer of the will. Moreover, the writer may destroy or cancel the will at any time. The person making the will is known as the testator, if a man, or the testatrix, if a woman. If a person dies leaving a will, he or she is said to have died testate. One who dies without a will is said to have died intestate. A gift of land by way of a will is known as a devise, and the person receiving the gift, a devisee. A bequest, or legacy as it is sometimes called, is a gift of personal property, and the person to whom the personal property has been given is called a legatee. To be valid, a will must satisfy the requirements as to both the *intention* of the testator and the *formality* of expression of the intention.

Intention

There can be no will unless the testator manifests an intention in writing and in the will to make a provision that will be effective on his death. This is called a *testamentary intent*. There likewise can be no will unless the testator has testamentary capacity (generally the requirement that the testator be of sound mind). He need not possess superior or even average intelligence. He is only required (1) to plan conceptually the distribution of his property, (2) not to execute the will as a fraud, and (3) not to be under the undue control of some other person in the execution of the will.

Attestation

Wills must be witnessed. The act of witnessing the will, known as attestation, generally includes the signing of the will by the witnesses after a clause that states that the witnesses have observed the testator sign the will. Publication is the act of the testator's informing the attesting witnesses that the document he is signing before them is his will. The person making the will need not inform the witnesses of its contents. He merely announces that the document is his will and that he requests the witnesses to attest to his signature. This constitutes the publication. In a few states, witnesses are not required but in general two or three witnesses are necessary. In those states where witnesses are required, it is generally specified that they are credible or competent and that they have no interest in the will.

Probating the Will; the Executor

Upon the death of the testator or testatrix, the will must be probated. Probate means to prove. It is the job of the executor named in the will to go to court, prove that the will is valid, and carry out its terms. When specific pieces of property are to go to named persons, the executor transfers the property to those persons. Where specific property is not designated to go to named persons, it is the function of the executor to obtain a court order, sell the property, and distribute the proceeds. The first thing that the executor is bound to do is to pay off the debts of the estate and settle taxes.

Executors are paid a fee for their services. If the testator or testatrix appoints an executor, the fee is generally agreed on in advance. Since probating a will is a complex and technical operation, probably an experienced attorney should be appointed. If no executor has been designated, the court will appoint one, and his or her fees will be determined in accordance with state law. Fees vary from state to state and with the size of the estate. Generally, however, executor's fees range from 4 to 5 percent of the first $5,000 or $10,000 of the estate and are then scaled down in a series of steps to about 1 to 2 percent of that portion of an estate in excess of $200,000 or $250,000.

The probation of the validity of the will is not always simple. Some states require the witnesses who attested the execution of the will to testify at probation the validity of the execution. Frequently, the witnesses are dead or for some other reason unable to testify. To forestall the possibility of preventing the probation of many wills, most states permit a will to include a self-proving clause. The will is signed and attested in the usual manner. The writer and witnesses then execute an affidavit before a notary public acknowledging their acts. The affidavit is appended to the will, which may then be admitted to probate without the testimony of these witnesses.

The General Contents of a Will

No one should attempt to draw a will without the assistance of an experienced attorney except under extraordinary circumstances. Even lawyers sometimes cause a certain amount of confusion, as was expressed by Mr. Justice Cullen in *Moneypeny v. Moneypeny*, 202 NY 90: "The will is drawn with a prolixity of language and confusion in thought and in expression approximating to genius." The good judge, it seems, also had difficulty with words. However, in general, wills contain the following items:

1. A statement of the domicile of the testator or testatrix.
2. A statement revoking prior wills: "I hereby revoke all wills and codicils by me at any time heretofore made."
3. A provision for payment of debts and funeral expenses. This may read, "I direct that all my just debts and funeral expenses be paid as soon after my death as may be practicable or as they come due." The testator should communicate to the attorney his idea of the just debts that he intends the executor to pay or add the clause as they become due. A simpler "just debts" clause may be interpreted as "all debts." Consider the plight of the widow who learns that the residence she expects to live in for the rest of her life must be sold for its equity value to pay off a mortgage on it—a just debt. The experienced attorney will draft this clause carefully.
4. Funeral and burial directions may sometimes be included but need not be; they may read, for instance, "I direct that my body be cremated."
5. A provision for the disposition of property. This may read, "I give and bequeath to my beloved wife Jane DeFoe all property which I shall own or be entitled to at my death." More than one person may, of course, be named as beneficiaries.
6. A secondary provision for the disposition of property to a secondary heir in the event the first-named person predeceases the testator or testatrix.
7. A statement about legacies. These are usually of two types: the general legacy and the specific legacy. The general legacy is a gift of money to an individual, paid out of the general assets of the estate. It is not a bequest of a particular thing or a particular fund designated from all others of the same kind.[1] The general legacy may read, "I give and bequeath to my dear friend Howard G. Jensen the sum of $1,000." The specific legacy is a bequest of a particular thing, which is a specified part of the estate, distinguished from all other property of the same kind.[2] If there were inadequate assets to pay all the bequests, the general legacy would be scaled down, but a specific legacy may read, "I give and bequeath to my dear friend James G. Richardson my entire stamp collection."
8. Charitable or religious bequests. Such a statement may read, "I give and bequeath the sum of $1,000 to the Lord Nelson Home for Wayward Boys."
9. A statement concerning the residual estate. This includes all of the remaining items that have not yet been disposed of by the will and is dealt with by means of a so-called residuary clause giving away or disposing of all that remains in the testator's estate. This may read, "All the rest, residue, and

1. *Armstead v. Union Trust Co.*, 61 F2d 677.
2. *Byrne v. Hume*, 86 Mich. 546.

remainder of my estate, of whatsoever kind and nature, and wheresoever situated, of which I may be seized or possessed or to which I may be entitled at the time of my death, not hereby otherwise effectually disposed of (including any property over which I have the power of appointment), I direct my executor, hereinafter named, to devise and bequeath to my beloved wife, Jane DeFoe."

10. A statement naming the executor who will probate the will. Generally anyone not specifically disqualified by law will be permitted to be the executor. Often this is the surviving spouse, an adult child, or some other blood relative or close friend of the family. However, if there is a large estate and probate may be technically complex, an experienced attorney or the trust department of a bank may be named executor. Many states require that an executor furnish a bond to assure that he or she will faithfully carry out his or her duties. A will may, however, contain a statement requesting that no bond need be furnished.

11. Frequently a will appoints a guardian if there are minor children. Normally if there is a surviving spouse, no other guardian is needed; hence this provision appoints a guardian only if the spouse predeceases the testator or testatrix.

12. A statement about the witnesses and a place for them to sign their names.

13. A statement regarding the notary public who must see that the witnesses sign the will in the presence of the testator or testatrix and then notarize and sign the document. Sometimes a self-proving affidavit is added, to ease probate by vouching for the validity of the signatures.

The Joint Will

A joint will is defined as a single testamentary instrument that contains the wills of two or more persons, is in common, or in severalty, by them. Typically, it is executed by husband and wife, and typically each leaves his or her property to the other; and only when they are both gone will the children inherit anything. These are the so-called "Ma and Pa" wills. Many authorities feel that the joint will should not be used because it can lay the groundwork for future litigation.

Essentially the joint will contains the same general type of clauses with regard to burial instructions and appointments of executors as does the will made by an individual. However, the residuary clause in a joint will gives the residue of the estate to each other. Another important clause in this joint or mutual will is the following:

We do hereby declare that the mutual and reciprocal dispositive provisions [this is the clause in a will providing for the disposition of the property] herein for the benefit of the other have been made pursuant to an understanding and agreement that each has made the provisions herein in consideration of the other similarly providing, and upon condition that neither of us will during our lives alter, amend, or revoke such provisions without the written consent of the other, nor will the survivor alter, amend, or revoke the same, after the death of the first of us to die.

Such a statement is important because it expresses the intent of the parties that neither will revoke or alter the will without notice to the other. In the absence of this clearly expressed intent, it may be held that the execution of the joint will without reference to the terms of the instrument is not sufficient evidence of an enforceable contract to devise between the testator and testatrix. In short, either of the parties may subsequently make another will that is likely to take precedence over the joint will.

The Common Disaster Clause

All wills should have a common disaster clause. Otherwise if a husband and wife have an automobile accident and both are killed, there might be litigation to determine who died first. If the wife died first and the wife had a will leaving the property to her husband, her property, together with what he owned, would pass according to the terms of his will. However, with his wife dead, the property cannot pass to her. If there were children, the will would probably provide for them. But if there were no children and the husband's will did not specifically state who was next in line, all of the property might go to the husband's relatives and the wife's kin would receive nothing. To provide against this, a common catastrophe clause is frequently inserted in a will. This clause may read as follows:

> Any person who shall have died at the same time as I, or in a common disaster with me, or under such circumstances that it is difficult or impossible to determine which died first, shall be deemed to have predeceased me.

Both the husband's and wife's will would then pass property as if each had died last. Each person's property would then pass according to his or her will, and if there were no children, each side's relatives would get something.

Protection of Dependents

There is also the problem of the testator who is the all-time villain who would disinherit his wife or children. Every state has some method by which it attempts to protect widows. Forty-two states retain a facet of medieval England called the *right of dower*. The disappointed or disinherited widow can elect to take the bounty provided in her spouse's will, can elect to receive the share of the estate that would have been hers if her spouse had died without a will, or can elect to take her right of dower. Dower simply means that she has the use for life of one-third of all that was her husband's. In the eight remaining states, the law generally provides that one-half of all property that she and her husband acquired after marriage is hers in her own right. Her husband cannot deprive her of her ownership, even if he attempts to do so by distributing more than his one-half of the community property in his will.

No state requires that children must be provided for in a parent's will. There are two types of relevant laws, however, and each state has one. The first requires that all children must be mentioned or acknowledged in the parent's will. This does not mean that any type of gift must be made to them. The second requires that children to be born after the execution of the will must be provided for by reference in the will. The effect of these laws is that an after-born child or one not mentioned in the will is entitled to the share that would have been his or hers if the parent had died intestate.

The Codicil

A codicil to a will is defined as an addition or change executed with the same formalities as required in the will itself. Generally it is better to draw a new will than to have a codicil. The codicil may, for instance, eliminate a person already designated as a beneficiary under the terms of the will; if so the door is left open for that beneficiary to contest the will, which is extremely costly to the estate and may end up with property not being disposed of in accordance with the intention of the testator or testatrix.

The codicil refers to the will and is dated. It contains a dispositive provision and is attested to by the number of witnesses required in accordance with the state statute. Above the signatures of the witnesses is the following clause:

> The foregoing instrument consists of one page and was made on the third day of July 1984, signed and sealed at the end thereof, and at the same time published and declared by James J. DeFoe, the above named Testator, as and for a Codicil to his Last Will and Testament dated the third day of June 1984, in the presence of each of us, who, this attestation clause having been read to us, did at the request of said testator, in his presence and in the presence of each other sign our names as witnesses thereto.

Holographic Wills

Holographic wills are instruments that are wholly drafted by the testator as a will and meet only some of the formal requirements of a will. They must always be signed and dated, but witnesses are not necessary. Not all states recognize holographic wills, and those that do may recognize them to pass property only up to a given amount of value. Typically, a holographic will is written at the time when the testator becomes aware of impending death and decides to alter completely his or her will or suddenly realizes there is none. Holographic wills written on envelopes, napkins, and even clothing have been admitted to probate in many states.

Why is not every codicil a holographic will? A codicil acknowledges the basic existence of a preexisting will and is written only to supplement that will. A holographic will supersedes an existing will and often is the only will a testator has written. Why isn't every note a person would write concerning the distribution of property designated to be a holographic will? This type of will, like any other, must meet certain minimal formal requirements. More importantly, the writing must express a testamentary intention in its author. The student can readily foresee the amount of litigation this type of instrument might cause.

What to Do with a Will

If a will cannot be found after the death of the testator or testatrix, it is presumed that he or she destroyed it with the intent of revoking it. This presumption can be overcome only by proving fraudulent destruction or by showing that the person was mentally incapable of possessing the intention to revoke.

There are generally four things that can be done with the will once it has been written:

1. In the majority of cases, the will is left with the attorney who drew it, who either puts it in an office safe or places it in a safe deposit box in a financial institution.
2. Where a financial institution has been named as one of the executors, the will is generally placed with that institution for safekeeping.
3. The will can be placed in the person's own safe deposit box. This is sometimes objected to on the grounds that it takes a court order for the box to be opened after death. However, the box must be opened in any case, and the state tax department officials who are present when the box is opened will have no objection to the removal of the will after an inventory has been taken of the contents of the box.
4. The will may be kept in the home in a strongbox. This is the least recommended place, because it is too easily accessible to destruction by persons other than the testator and it may easily be lost or mislaid.

It is best to make several copies of the will and keep them in all of the above places.

A sample of a modern will is shown in Figure 20–1. Figure 20–2 is a sample of the oldest known will in existence today. It was written by the Egyptian Pharaoh, Uah, and was executed in 2548 B.C. We have also found what is believed to be the shortest will ever probated. It contained just ten words: "Being of sound mind and body, I spent it all."

The Last Letter of Instructions

Every person should write a letter of last instructions and leave it in an easily accessible place as well as with every member of the family. A copy should also

KNOW ALL MEN BY THESE PRESENTS:

That I, _____ of Travis County, Texas, being of sound and disposing mind and memory, and above the age of eighteen years, do make and publish this my last will and testament, hereby revoking all wills heretofore made by me.

I.

I direct that all my just debts shall be paid.

II.

Should my beloved wife, _____, survive me, I give to her all property which I shall own or be entitled to at my death.

III.

Should my said wife not survive me, I give all property which I shall own or be entitled to at my death to my son, _____.

I hereby appoint my wife, _____, independent executrix of this my last will and testament, and I direct that no bond shall be required of her as such executrix, and I further direct that no action shall be had in the County Court or any other court in relation to the administration and settlement of my estate other than the probating and recording of this my last will and testament and filing of an inventory and list of claims in the manner provided by law.

If my said wife does not survive me, I appoint my son _____, independent executor of my will without bond under the same terms and conditions which would have obtained had my wife served as independent executrix.

IN TESTIMONY WHEREOF, I have hereunto set my hand, this the _____ day of _____, in the presence of _____ _____ and _____, who witness my signature and attest this my last will and testament at my request as attesting witnesses.

(name) _____

The above instrument was now here on the date hereinabove set forth, subscribed by _____, the testator, in our presence and in the presence of each other, and we, as attesting witnesses at his request and in his presence and in the presence of each other, sign our names hereto as attesting witnesses.

_____

_____

Before me, the undersigned authority, on this day personally appeared

_____,

_____, and

_____ known to me to be the testator and the witnesses, respectively, whose names are subscribed to the annexed or foregoing instrument in their respective capacities, and, all of said persons being by me duly sworn, the said

_____, testator, declared to me and to the said witnesses in my presence that said instrument is his last will and testament, and that he had willingly made and executed it as his free act and deed for the purposes therein expressed; and the said witnesses, each on his oath stated to me, in the presence and hearing of the said testator, that the said testator had declared to them that said instrument is his last will and testament, and that he executed same as such and wanted each of them to sign it as a witness; and upon their oaths each witness stated further that they did sign the same as witnesses in the presence of the said testator and at his request; that he was at that time nineteen years of age or over and was of sound mind; and that each of said witnesses was then at least fourteen years of age.

Testator _____

Witness _____

Witness _____

Subscribed and acknowledged before me by the said _____, testator, and subscribed and sworn to before me by said _____ and _____, witnesses, this the _____ day of _____, 1984.

_____
Notary Public, Travis County, Texas

Figure 20–1 Sample of a modern will

be given to the family lawyer, if there is one, and another copy should be placed in a safe deposit box. This letter should probably be rewritten and updated every year or two as the individual's assets and other conditions change.

It should be noted that a letter of last instructions is not a will or a substitute for a will; both are needed. A letter of last instructions is a supplementary document to a will. This letter should, among other things, include a list of all the individual's assets and liabilities and indicate where the documents are located.

As a minimum, it should include the following:

1. A statement of where the will, if any, may be found.
2. Funeral instructions, if necessary. Some people wish to be cremated, others, buried. Some wish to donate certain organs (e.g., eyes) to others after death. In any case all members of the family should have general knowledge in advance of future funeral arrangements.
3. A statement regarding a safe deposit box—where it and the key are located.
4. A list of all life insurance policies and their location.
5. An inventory of all stocks and bonds, and where they are kept.
6. A list of all other property such as real estate, mutual funds, and business property, and their location.
7. The person's Social Security number should be recorded.
8. A statement indicating what benefits the deceased may have from his or her employer. There may be pension benefits, death benefits, profit-sharing plans, and other benefits to which the deceased's estate or survivors may have a claim.
9. A list of all deposits in banks, savings and loan associations, mutual savings banks, or credit unions.

AMENEMHAT IV,

Year 2, Month Paophi, Day 18

I, Uah, am giving a title to property to my wife SHEFTU, the woman of Gesab who is called Teta, the daughter of Sat Sepdu, of all things given to me by my brother Ankh-ren. She shall give it to any she desires of her children she bears me.

I am giving to her the Eastern slaves, 4 persons, that my brother Ankh-ren gave me. She shall give them to whomsoever she will of her children.

As to my tomb, let me be buried in it with my wife alone.

Moreover as to the house built for me by my brother Ankh-ren, my wife shall dwell therein without allowing her to be put forth on the ground by any person.

It is the deputy Gebu who shall act as guardian of my son.

Done in the presence of these witnesses:

KEMEN, Decorator of Columns.

APU, Doorkeeper of the Temple.

SENB, son of Senb, Doorkeeper of the Temple.

Figure 20–2. Will from 2548 B.C., translated by the American University at Cairo.

10. A list of memberships in all unions, professional associations, lodges and fraternal organizations, and veterans groups. There may be financial benefits because of memberships in some of these organizations.

11. A list of all just debts owed you and accounts receivable, the interest rate they bear, the terms of payment, and where to locate the documents to prove their validity.

12. A list of all the just debts owed by the individual, the interest rate they bear, the terms of their repayment, and the location of the pertinent documents.

Living Wills

In recent years, there has been some litigation over life-support systems being used to continue the life of terminally ill people who are often in great pain or in a vegetative state. Recently California passed a right-to-die-in-dignity law, and other states are likely to follow. This permits life-support systems to be withdrawn in such cases. Also some people have written living wills which a person authorizes, permits, and requests that the life-support system be withdrawn if he or she is in a situation such as that described above. Sometimes the deceased wishes to become a donor of certain transplantable organs. If so, this should be spelled out in the living will, because eyes and certain other organs must be removed immediately upon death.

Property Transfer in the Absence of a Will

If you do not have a will, the state in which you reside has drawn up one for you. The person who dies without a will is said to have died intestate, and his property will be disposed of in accordance with the laws of his state. These vary some from state to state, but generally they distribute property in the following order of priority of claims.

1. *Spouses and children.* Surviving spouses and children are first in line and they generally receive the main share of the estate and perhaps all of it. In some states the surviving spouse will receive the bulk of the estate, but in others the children will receive a substantial amount. It is possible, then, that without a will a widow might have insufficient assets.

2. *Lineals.* Lineals or lineal descendants are blood descendants of the deceased. The major portion of an estate not distributed to the surviving spouse and children is generally distributed to lineals (brothers and sisters) although sometimes parents also have a claim to part of it.

3. *Parents.* If the estate has not been exhausted by this time, the remainder is commonly distributed to the decedent's parents.

4.   *Collateral heirs.* These are persons who are not descendants of the decedent but who are related through a common ancestor. Such more distant relatives with a common ancestry are considered. Cousins, uncles, and the like are next in line. Usually there is not much left by now.

Distant relatives will exhaust any estate if it gets that far, but one more step is provided by law in most states. It takes effect in the very rare case when a person dies intestate and has no heirs—no surviving spouse, children, or parents; also no cousins or other blood relatives, and no one with a common ancestry. Where does his property go? It goes to his or her state tax collector.

Administration of Estates

Administration of estates is the means of distributing property of a decedent who died intestate. When no will is left, the court or an officer designated by law appoints one or more persons who are then entitled to administer the estate of the decedent. More often than not, close relatives of the deceased make application to the court for the so-called letter of administration. Such a letter gives the administrator the obligation of gathering the assets of the deceased, paying off the debts and taxes of the estate, and then distributing the assets in accordance with the statute pertaining to distribution of the estate. Generally, the letter of administration is granted to the first relative or person who applies. In some cases where there are creditors of the deceased and no previous application for letter of administration has been made, the letter may be granted to a creditor. In the absence of creditor, applications, or known relatives, the letter may be issued by the court to a public administrator. In any event, once the letter has been granted to the administrator, the job becomes much the same as that of the executor of an estate.

HOW TO HOLD CERTAIN PROPERTY; NONPROBATE PROPERTY

The question immediately arises: "How should major assets be held?" This is important for married couples with respect to such assets as checking accounts, savings deposits, real estate, securities, and perhaps some others. There are four legal forms of ownership:

1.   Tenancy by the Entirety
2.   Joint Tenancy with Right of Survivorship
3.   Tenancy in Common
4.   Community Property

How to hold property will vary from state to state depending on the laws of that state.

Tenancy by the Entirety

Only two people married to each other are able to hold real property in the form of tenancy by the entirety, and personal property cannot be held in this form. They are both equal owners. This is the one way in which you could own your home in most cases in many common law states. The deed is made out to both parties, and when one dies the deed passes cleanly to the other. Both signatures must be obtained when selling the property. Some community property states do not permit property ownership in the form of tenancy by the entirety.[3]

Joint Tenancy with Right of Survivorship

Joint tenancy can involve more than two owners. If it is between a husband and wife, it should spell out, "with rights to survivorship," under which the surviving spouse takes full title to the property on the death of the other. This type of ownership is not possible in some community property states. Hence, in states like Texas or California a husband and wife can enter into such an ownership agreement with their separate property only but not with their community property unless they first partition their community into separate property. The one exception to this is U.S. Government securities. They can be community property and still be held in the form of a joint tenancy with right of survivorship because they are governed by federal law which takes precedence.

Tenancy in Common

This can also involve more than two owners. The ownership interest of the survivors of property held in common is not changed by the death of one owner. In community property states, only separate property of either spouse can be held in the form of tenancy in common.

Community Property

Community property is a legal concept valid only in community property states. Under the law, most property acquired during a marriage is owned 50 percent by each spouse. However, each member of a married couple can have separate property. This would include property acquired prior to marriage, that acquired after marriage through a gift or inheritance, and possibly previous community property that was partitioned earlier. In a community property state, on the

3. The community property states are Arizona, California, Idaho, Louisiana, Nevada, New Mexico, Texas, and Washington.

death of one spouse one-half of all community property passes to the deceased's estate. If there is no will spelling out who is to receive it, the property passes in accordance with the law of inheritance, and the surviving spouse and the children usually are the heirs. However, the surviving spouse may not get it all or even the main share; the children may get as much as one-half. This is true of personal as well as real property.

Real estate, securities, and bank accounts should be held jointly with rights to survivorship in most common law (based on English law) states insofar as married couples are concerned. Then, on the death of one, the survivor acquires it automatically and directly without the necessity of probating a will. In community property states, this cannot be done, and a will may be the only way to assure that the survivor will get all of the estate. In the absence of a will, the children might get some of it in certain community property states.

TRUSTS

Gifts and trusts are useful in estate planning because both of them can reduce taxes, i.e., gift and estate taxes—not income taxes. Gift taxes are paid by the giver, not the recipient; estate taxes are taxes on the assets left by the deceased.

Equally important, the use of the trust allows the creators some control over their assets even after they die. The trust can also provide financial security to those who are inexperienced or incapable of managing their financial affairs, such as minor children.

Creation of the Trust

The trust is an arrangement whereby title to property is transferred by the creator or settlor to another person (trustee) for the benefit of a third party (beneficiary or *cestui que* trust). The property placed in trust is called the corpus, the trust *res*, the trust fund, or the trust property. The title to the corpus is split, with the trustee holding the property for an ascertainable length of time, and all benefits from the corpus go to the beneficiaries. The beneficiaries who receive the income from the trust during their lifetime are known as *life tenants;* those beneficiaries who receive the corpus (principal) of the trust upon the death of the last of the life tenants are known as the *remaindermen.*

Generally, a trust may be created for any purpose that is not against public policy. For instance, a trust created from funds obtained from the commission of a felony is void, as is a trust created to encourage divorce. There are other prerequisites that each state imposes for the creation of a valid trust. Two of the most important are *intention* and *capacity.*

There must be an intention on the part of the settlor, declared in writing, to convey property to a trust for the benefit of beneficiaries. Secret, unexpressed intentions will not effectively create a trust. There must also be a manifest intent to impose enforceable duties on the trustee to manage the property for the benefit of another.

In addition to intent, there must be capacity among all the parties involved to create a trust. The settlor must have the capacity to convey property. Thus, insane persons and minors, who cannot validly convey property, lack the capacity to create a trust. The trustee must be capable of owning property and meeting the requirements of being a fiduciary. For example, no person convicted of a felony is capable of being a fiduciary. While settlors can name themselves as beneficiaries, they cannot be their own trustee. (There are exceptions to this in some states.) Finally, a definite beneficiary who is capable of owning property is required. The beneficiary must be named or, as will be discussed later, capable of being determined under a definite standard.

The *Inter Vivos* and *Causa Mortis* Trust

The *inter vivos* trust, or so-called living trust, is one created by the grantor during his or her lifetime. The grantor also may be the beneficiary. In general, the *inter vivos* trust may be either irrevocable or revocable. The *causa mortis* trust (also called testamentary trust) is one set up through a will, and it becomes effective upon the death of the grantor.

The Revocable Trust

The revocable trust can be terminated by the creator at any time. It can also be set up to terminate automatically at a specific time in the future. If you make the beneficiary someone other than yourself (for example, a minor child), gift taxes do not apply. It is not a gift; you still have full control over it. You can even tell the trustee how to invest the funds, and you can change these managerial instructions from time to time. Generally the creator will give only broad general investment instruction and leave wide discretion with the trustee. The major reason some people set up such trusts is to turn day-to-day management decisions over to someone else because they do not want to be bothered, they feel they can increase the return on their assets through a trust, or the beneficiary may be a minor or otherwise inexperienced in finance. The income earned by such a trust may be disbursed to the beneficiary or left to accumulate in the trust. In either case, it is taxable income. The trustee will report it to the beneficiary, and he or she must then declare it on the tax return.

Irrevocable Trusts

The creator can never terminate (revoke) an irrevocable trust. He also usually gives up all income earned by it, but this need not be so. The creator gives up the right not only to revoke but also to alter or amend the trust. You can put some loose control into the trust agreement—such as, for example, it will be invested only in bonds, or at least 50 percent in bonds—or you can give the trustee complete discretion.

You may set up an irrevocable (living) trust and name yourself as the beneficiary with the right to receive the income from it. You would probably name someone else to become the beneficiary after your death, or stipulate that the trust then be dissolved and someone receive the corpus. A reason for making yourself the beneficiary would be to achieve the peace of mind of having someone competent manage your financial affairs, and also to protect your assets from being dissipated due to possible loss of financial sophistication in the future from illness or the like. Such a trust, however, would not be protected from claims of creditors; an irrevocable trust which made someone else the beneficiary would be protected from your creditors. The property of a trust in which the grantor is also the beneficiary would also be includable in the grantor's estate upon his death. Estate taxes would have to be paid at that time. Whoever received the corpus of the trust when it was dissolved (called vesting) would also be subject to estate taxes upon his or her death.

An irrevocable trust may, however, name someone other than the grantor as the beneficiary. This is looked on as a gift, and gift taxes might be due (see below) rather than estate taxes on the death of the grantor.

There are several ways in which an irrevocable trust may reduce income taxes. A person might create an irrevocable trust for the benefit of a child with the idea of creating an educational fund. In such a case the income from the corpus might not be passed through to the beneficiary until he or she had enrolled in a university. The income earned by the trust fund would be taxable to the trust, at a relatively low rate, and not to the father or mother, who might be at a high tax bracket. Thereby the grantor could accomplish two things: (1) reduce the total amount of tax paid, and (2) provide a fund for the education of his or her child. If the trust passes its earnings through to the beneficiary, he or she would pay the taxes, presumably again at a lower rate. How a trust can reduce future estate taxes is explained below.

The Testamentary Trust

A testamentary trust is one that is created by a provision in a will. The trust agreement would have to be written in advance, and on the death of the grantor, it would become effective. Such a trust would be subject to estate taxes, but, as we shall see below, it could reduce later estate taxes of the beneficiaries. A testamentary trust is irrevocable, and much of what was said immediately above applies. In addition to tax reduction, a reason for the creation of such a trust is to protect the beneficiary who is inexperienced. It may be undesirable, for instance, to leave a large estate consisting of investments in securities to a person lacking experience in investments. Or it may be desirable to leave property to a trustee in order to provide income for a wife for life, and at her death to provide that the corpus of the trust pass on to the children or their heirs. Often, too, property is left to a trustee to hold and to invest and to pay the income to minor children, with the corpus passing to them when they become of age.

Simple and Complex Trusts

A trust may be simple or complex. A simple trust is one in which all of the income from the trust is given to the beneficiary; a complex trust is one that retains the income at least until some predetermined time in the future, which must be spelled out in the trust agreement, if it is an irrevocable trust. The beneficiary is liable for the taxes on the income he receives from a simple trust. With a complex trust, the trustee pays the taxes, using some of the income for this purpose, in accordance with whatever tax bracket the income of the trust indicates.

With the simple trust where the beneficiary pays the tax on the income earned, if the beneficiary is a student and is claimed as a dependent on another return (for instance, a parent's) as well as on his or her own, he or she is able to take only the $1,000 exemption; the zero bracket amount of $2,300 ($3,400 for marrieds filing jointly) does not apply to unearned (for example, investment) income in the case where a person is used as a double exemption.[4] With the complex trust, neither the $1,000 exemption nor the zero bracket amount may be taken; the complex trust has a special tax exemption of only $300. All income retained by the trust above that amount is taxed at the appropriate rate beginning at 14 percent on the first $1,050 above the $300 exemption.

A complex trust may also be set up so that part of the income is passed through to the beneficiary and part is retained. In such a case, that portion passed through is taxed as described above under the simple trust, and that part retained is taxed as described under a complex trust.

Clifford Trusts; Temporary Trusts

This is a specialized trust that could save personal income taxes. A Clifford trust must be a simple trust and its investment income given yearly to the beneficiary. It is irrevocable for a time, and then it revokes automatically and the principal reverts to the creator. The minimum time period is ten years and one day, but it can be set up for longer. It also revokes automatically if the beneficiary dies prior to ten years and one day. It is useful if you are supporting (or contributing to the support of) a parent or other relative. An example will make this clear. Suppose you are contributing $2,000 to supplement the Social Security payments of your parents. This $2,000 is not a tax deductible item to you. If you are in

4. Students may sometimes serve as a double exemption. See Chapter 8 on taxes.

the 50 percent tax bracket, it takes $4,000 of your income to provide your parents with $2,000.

If you were to set up a Clifford trust today for $21,000 it could earn about 10 percent or about $2,100. After trustee fees of about $100 (tax deductible) the beneficiary would have $2,000. The beneficiary might have to pay a tax on part of that $2,000 but presumably at a much lower rate than you. In ten years and one day or on the death of the beneficiary, the entire $21,000 would revert to you. If after ten years and one day the trust were still needed, you would have to set up another one. Setting up a Clifford trust is a one-shot affair. You must put in the entire principal sum in one payment and then cannot add to it. However, you can set up more than one such trust, and when the one you have revokes, you can establish another one. Also the beneficiary can invade the trust up to 5 percent or $5,000 per year if done on a noncumulative basis (invasion is spelled out in greater detail below).

You can also use the Clifford trust to pay your child's college expenses in a way that will save you taxes. Make him or her the beneficiary of a Clifford trust. Its earnings are then taxed at his or her lower rate. However, to make absolutely certain that you are not personally vulnerable to pay the tax on the trust's income, the trust plan must avoid any mention of distribution for the purpose of a child's education. (In many states parents who can afford it are legally obligated to provide a college education as part of the child's support.) As noted above, if you also take the $1,000 exemption because you provide more than one-half of your child's support and, therefore, he or she provides a double exemption, the zero bracket amount does not apply to investment income. You might still take him or her as an exemption, however, depending upon your tax bracket and on the child's tax, if any. For example, if you are in the 50 percent bracket, the $1,000 exemption will save you $500. If the child's added tax due to losing the zero bracket amount is more than this, then don't take the double exemption; if not, take it. Insofar as the child's higher tax results in a hardship, you could give the child a gift equal to his or her added tax liability, if it were less than $500, and both of you would still be better off.

The Power of Invasion

Unfortunately, one cannot predict the future, even in economic terms. A man may believe that he has provided sufficient cash assets to maintain his wife and child; he has established a testamentary trust and provided that the income therefrom shall go to the support of his wife and child. However, as the years pass, the cost of living may rise by far more than was anticipated. It may be then that the income from the trust fund will be insufficient to support his wife and child. In practice, therefore, a statement is frequently inserted to provide that the trust fund itself may be used to support the beneficiaries if the need arises. This dipping into the principal is called the *power of invasion*. It may be unlimited, with the amount to be taken from the fund left to the best judgment and discretion of either the beneficiary or the trustee, or it is sometimes limited to a certain percentage of the trust fund over the annual income per year. For example, if the fund is $100,000 and the income is $10,000 in any one year, the trustee may be permitted to pay out a maximum of 3 percent, 4 percent, or even 10 percent of the principal annually, depending on how the clause is drawn.

Needless to say, the importance of the clause cannot be stressed too strongly if the purpose of the trust is for the support and maintenance of the beneficiaries. Although the courts can authorize the reformation of the trust agreement to allow dispersal of a portion of the corpus as long as no one beneficiary is deprived of his or her rightful share, this is undesirable for the beneficiaries since litigation is a costly and time-consuming process. If the principal is dipped into, the trust's future earnings are likely to decline, which may necessitate dipping into the principal even further. In such a case, it is possible that the beneficiary could outlive his or her principal sum.

The Rule Against Perpetuities

This rule prevents even irrevocable trusts from going on and on. That is, while an irrevocable trust cannot be revoked by its grantor, it must eventually be liquidated. Or in legal terms, it must *vest*, that is, it must be liquidated and pass to someone. Of course, the person or persons receiving the property can immediately set up another trust. However, when a trust vests, the people receiving it must pay an estate tax when they die.

When a trust must finally be liquidated varies from state to state. Generally it must vest 21 years after the death of the "lives in being" at the time the creator dies and those who are mentioned in the trust. Unborn heirs who might be referred to in the trust do not count. You may set up a trust that can continue during the lives of all your children, grandchildren, and great-grandchildren, if any, that were mentioned in your will and were alive on the day of your death, plus 21 years. Only 21 years after the death of the last survivor of the above group would the trust have to be liquidated.

In some states, this "lives in being" has been modified, and the trust must vest after the death of not more than two lives mentioned in the trust and who are living at the testator's death—the plus 21 years being removed. This is the so-called "measured lives" doctrine.

A well-drawn trust, then, must provide for a method of determining who gets what, when it is finally liquidated. If a trust spans two or more generations before liquidation, there may be grandchildren and even great-grandchildren of the creator who will finally share in the distribution of the property. A simple equal per capita distribution for all claimants would be unfair because some grandchildren might be alive and others dead, and also some grandchildren would have produced more heirs than others. Because of this, most trusts provide *per stirpes* distribution.

A *per stirpes* distribution dilutes the principal along ancestral lines. In the above case, for example, the great-grandchildren whose parents are dead should get all of their parents' share. The great-grandchildren of living parents should get nothing, or at least no more than a portion of their parents' share. (They would get their parents' share later.) Also, an only great-grandchild of one of the creator's grandchildren should get more than each of the two great-grandchildren of another one of the creator's grandchildren. Figure 20–3 illustrates a *per stirpes* distribution.

Assume those nine without crosses are alive and have a claim. In some cases the law (or proviso in the trust) would provide for nothing for the children of C and D (that is, nothing to I, J, and K, the great-grandchildren of the creator); they would get their share later through their parents when the parents die. However, the only child of D would eventually get twice what each of the two children of C would eventually get. (This assumes D has no children in the future and that both C and D neither add to nor deplete the principal). The four offspring of A and B have claim to exactly 50 percent of the trust; if the trust were $1,000,000, they would each get $125,000. C and his offspring together would have a claim to $250,000 but the offspring might have to wait. The same is true of D and his offspring. If D were dead, his child (K, the great-grandchild of the creator) would get $250,000.

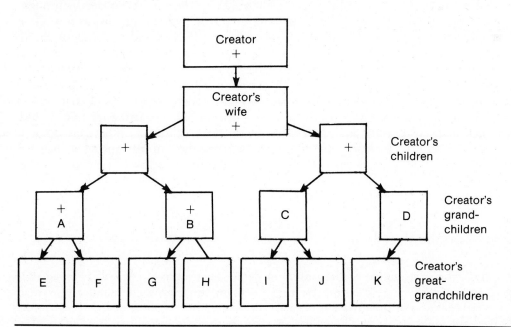

Figure 20–3   Per stirpes distribution of property.

A trust that continues through two or more generations before it vests, with the heirs along the way receiving only the income, is often called a "generation-skipping" trust, and at one time it postponed taxes. There were no further estate taxes due until the death of the people into whom the trust finally vested. This will now soon be changed. Trusts created by wills are exempt from the generation-skipping transfer tax if the will was written before June 11, 1976 and if the grantor dies before January 1, 1983. So, too, are irrevocable living trusts established on or before June 11, 1976. They will be taxed under the old rules. But trusts that do not qualify as noted above will be taxed more severely. For example, if you establish a trust in a way so that it vests, not in your children but rather in your grandchildren or even your great-grandchildren—a generation-skipping trust—estate taxes are due when your children die, in whom the trust would normally have vested.

The Power of Appointment

A power of appointment is defined as a device by which the owner of property grants to another person or persons the power to designate, within whatever limits he or she wishes, how the property shall be distributed after the original beneficiary dies.

In other words, it is a device giving the beneficiary of a trust the right to alter the disposition of the trust *res* or trust fund on his or her death through his or her will. For example, A by will leaves property to his son, in trust, the income from the trust fund to be paid to the son for life, and the property upon the death of the son to pass to his son's children. If the son dies before his wife, it may be that his widow will have no means of support; consequently there may be included in A's will a provision giving his son the power of appointment. This would mean that the son through his will could change the distribution of the property by providing that on his death the income should go to his widow for life and on her death to his children. What this does is to enable A to look into the future through the eyes of his son; what may be considered wise today may be considered absurd tomorrow. The main reason for including the power of appointment in a trust agreement, then, is to protect the fund for the several life beneficiaries.

The Trustee—The Role of the Fiduciary

It is the prerogative of the settlor to name the trustee for the trust. Since this person is to be responsible for the corpus of the trust for a number of years, the selection of the trustee is critical. Although a private individual can be named as trustee if he or she is willing to take on the responsibilities and duties of a fiduciary for the nominal fee involved in managing the trust, the settlor generally finds it more satisfactory to name an organized trust corporation or trust department of a bank as the trustee. The settlor could expect trust companies and banks to have a larger and more experienced staff to administer the trust and a greater willingness to take on the strict liabilities of being fiduciary than could generally be found from an individual.

Trustees owe the highest loyalty to the trust fund and the beneficiaries, and their role is spelled out by the law. As fiduciaries, they have a duty to act primarily for the benefit of the trust property. In investing or managing the property of the trust, they are held accountable, within limits, by the prudent person standard. This is to say, they must act as a reasonable and prudent person investing the funds of another. Because they cannot be engaged in anything that resembles speculation, the trustees attempt to manage the assets of the corpus in order to preserve capital and provide income. In addition to investing the assets of the corpus, the trustees must also handle all legal disputes concerning the trust, pay any tax liabilities the trust generates, and handle any other responsibility resulting from the operation of the trust. Generally speaking, for their services, the trustees will receive less than 1 percent of the assets of the corpus each year.

GIFT AND ESTATE TAXES

Gift taxes are imposed on the giver (the recipient need not pay), and estate taxes are imposed on the estate (property) of the deceased before the heirs may receive the residual. These used to be separate taxes with separate rate schedules. Recently, however, Congress combined the gift and estate tax rate into one common schedule—the unified gift and estate tax. This tax is applicable to all taxable transfers, either through gifts while living or through an estate after death. Indeed, dying and leaving an estate are now considered as making one final gift. However, there are exclusions and exemptions before either gift or estate taxes need be paid.

Many states also have gift and estate taxes. Some even have inheritance tax, a tax on the recipient of an estate. Practices vary so much from state to state that little can be said about them except for two general comments. First, most state taxes of this sort are less severe than the federal taxes, and even the federal estate and gift taxes do not bring in vast sums. For example, in fiscal 1982, total gift and estate tax receipts at the federal level were just over $7.9 billion.[5] Second, the severity of the state taxes and exemptions varies with the closeness of the kin. Spouses are taxed less severely than children, and children less severely than other relatives. Moreover, the Federal Tax Code allows a tax credit for a large proportion of all state inheritance and estate taxes. Therefore, for all practical purposes, one need pay the amount the federal government demands.

5. *The United States Budget in Brief, Fiscal Year 1983*, Office of Management and Budget, p. 30.

Annual Gift Tax Exclusions

Every individual has an annual gift tax exclusion and a lifetime gift tax exemption. The annual exclusion is $10,000 per year per recipient. You could give away $1 billion without paying a gift tax if you gave $10,000 to 100,000 people. More realistically, if you have four children, you could give each $10,000 tax free annually, for a total of $40,000 per year. In addition, the law allows gifts to pay for qualified medical expenses or school tuition tax free.

Split Gifts

The split gift is sometimes referred to as a joint gift made by the husband and wife. It, too, can result in tax savings. The law provides, among other things, that a gift made by one person to any person other than his or her spouse shall be considered as having been made one-half by him and one-half by her. This is true even if only one of them has an income.

The net effect is that the annual exclusion may be doubled, and a husband and wife may make an annual gift of $20,000 times the number of donees without paying any gift tax whatsoever.

Lifetime Gift or Estate Tax Exemption

There is also an overall lifetime gift or estate tax exemption. For 1984, this exemption is $325,000, but Congress has already provided for it to rise each year until 1987 when it will stabilize at $600,000. Everyone has this lifetime exemption; hence a married couple together may give away (or leave an estate of) $1,200,000 tax free by 1987. This is above the $10,000 per year ($20,000 in the case of a joint gift) exclusion per recipient. It should be noted, however, that while the $10,000 exclusion applies only to gifts, the $600,000 exemption is unified and can be taken in the case of a gift, or left through an estate, or some combination of the two—*but not both*. To the extent that it is used through a gift, it cannot be taken later when estate taxes are due.

In reality, however, the exemption is converted to a tax credit. The tax is calculated as if there were no exemption, and then the tax credit is subtracted from the tax so calculated. Table 20–2 shows how the lifetime tax exemption will rise over the years through 1987 with the tax credit equivalent.

The Marital Deduction

The marital deduction refers to transfers between spouses. The marital deduction applies to both gifts and estates, and it is 100 percent. All gifts to spouses and all estates left to spouses are now completely tax free.

Table 20–2   Lifetime unified gift and estate tax exemption

Year	Amount of credit	Exemption equivalent	Lowest tax bracket rate (%)
1983	$ 79,300	$275,000	34
1984	96,300	325,000	34
1985	121,800	400,000	34
1986	155,800	500,000	37
1987 and later	192,800	600,000	37

How Gift and Estate Taxes Are Calculated

The unified gift and estate tax is progressive and varies from 18 to 60 percent. The maximum rate will decline in a series of steps to 50 percent by 1986, as shown in Table 20–3. After 1985 rates will range from 37 to 50 percent.[6] The tax is also cumulative, and because of this, each future taxable gift is taxed at a higher and higher rate. For example, if a person makes a $100,000 taxable gift, the proper tax rate is applied; if then the next year another $100,000 taxable gift is made, the tax on it is calculated as if it were a $200,000 gift. The actual tax so obtained is then reduced by the amount of the tax paid on the previous $100,000 gift.

The estate tax is calculated just like the gift tax, by applying the proper tax rate to the sum of all previous cumulative lifetime taxable transfers plus the deceased's estate. That is, all previous taxable gifts are added to the estate before calculating the tax on it. You will recall the government now looks on leaving

Table 20–3   Reduction in top-bracket rates

Transfers made and decedents dying in	Top-bracket rate	Top-bracket amount in excess of
1982	65%	$4,000,000
1983	60	3,500,000
1984	55	3,000,000
1985 and later	50	2,500,000

Thus when fully implemented after 1985 transfers will be taxable at progressive marginal rates ranging between 37 percent and 50 percent.

6. Technically speaking, rates will still range from 18 to 50 percent, but the unified gift and estate tax exemption provides everyone with some relief at the lower end of the scale. That is, the exemption (which is converted to credit) exempts enough dollars so that the minimum rate becomes 37 percent. For example, if a person had made enough taxable gifts during his or her lifetime to have used up the entire credit, then the estate tax would apply to the first dollar and would begin at 18 percent.

an estate as one final gift—and gift and estate taxes are the same. By including all previous transfers, the estate is pushed into a higher tax bracket. To be sure, a credit is given for previous gift taxes paid.

How Gifts Can Save Taxes

Gifts can save taxes for three reasons. First, the $10,000 ($20,000 on joint gifts) annual exclusion for a recipient, as noted above, is above the $600,000 unified gift and estate tax exemption. In addition, gifts made more than three years prior to death are treated differently. These gifts are in the final estate for the tax computation (which pushes it into a higher tax bracket), but the taxes on them are not. The taxes on more recent gifts are in the estate as well as the gifts themselves.

This may sound confusing, but an example will make it clear. Suppose A gave his child a $100,000 taxable gift more than three years ago and another $100,000 taxable gift this year. He then dies. The tax on the first $100,000 taxable gift is $23,800. (This is at the 1984 rate and assumes that the unified credit was saved for the estate tax). The tax on the second $100,000 gift is $31,000. Remember, the tax is progressive, and the second gift is taxed as if it were a $200,000 gift, which makes the tax $54,800, but that is reduced by the tax on the first gift. In the final estate tax computation, both of the $100,000 gifts, but only the second $31,000 tax, are included in the estate for the tax computation. When the final tax is arrived at, it is of course reduced by $54,800 due to the two gift taxes paid.

Third, gifts prevent appreciable assets from being evaluated at a higher level later when an estate is probated.

How a Trust Can Save Taxes

An irrevocable trust can also be used to reduce estate taxes, because the surviving spouse will not inherit the deceased's property. Rather the property goes into an irrevocable trust with the survivor receiving the income from it. While the surviving spouse could inherit the entire estate tax free, there would be more taxes to pay when she died; the marital deduction could become a trap. To achieve the tax savings, one-half of the couple's assets must be placed in trust. Then, her taxable estate would be smaller, thus saving taxes. Consider the following example of a couple who have $500,000 of assets.

Without a trust

1.   First spouse dies, and $250,000 passes tax free—there is no tax on transfers between spouses.
2.   Survivor dies and leaves an estate of $500,000, which is taxed.
3.   The tax on a $500,000 estate is $155,800; but after the 1984 unified credit of $96,300, the tax is $59,500.

With a trust

1. First spouse dies and leaves nothing to the survivor. Rather, $250,000 goes into an irrevocable trust established by the deceased's will, and the survivor gets the income from it.[7]
2. There is a $70,800 tax on this $250,000 going into the trust, but after the unified credit of $76,300, it became zero. The tax is on the property of the deceased for the privilege of passing property to, in this case, the trust.
3. Survivor dies and leaves an estate of $250,000, not $500,000—the $250,000 in trust on her behalf is not hers.
4. Second partner's estate tax after the unified credit is also zero.
5. Total tax with trust is zero.
6. Tax savings: $59,500.

The tax savings from a trust will decline as the 1981 tax reduction act is fully phased in; and after 1987, the estate would need to be in excess of $600,000 before tax savings would be achieved through the use of a trust.

QUESTIONS FOR REVIEW

1. How may a person's domicile and residence differ, and what is the importance of this distinction from the point of view of estate planning?
2. Why is it important to draw up a personal balance sheet when planning a will?
3. What is the major purpose of a will?
4. Why is it important to have an experienced attorney draft a will or trust arrangement? Why should the executor of a will also be experienced?
5. What does probating a will entail?
6. What are the relative merits of appointing a private individual to act as trustee as opposed to a trust corporation or trust department of a bank?
7. List what you think are the most important contents of a will.
8. What is a joint will? Would you recommend its use?
9. What is the common disaster clause? Should each will have one? Why or why not?
10. What is a codicil to a will? Would you recommend its use? Explain why or why not?
11. Why should a last letter of instructions be written?

---

7. If we are assuming a community property state, each member already owns one-half of the property and the deceased cannot put his or her spouse's property into a trust. In a noncommunity property state, the entire $500,000 could be put into trust, but then the tax would be on $500,000 just as in the case of not having a trust. The community property states are Arizona, California, Idaho, Louisiana, Nevada, New Mexico, Texas, and Washington. Property rights in these states are based on Spanish law that assumes that a man and wife are one person. In the remainder of the states—called common law states—property rights are based on English common law.

12. What are the adverse possibilities of dying intestate? Would a person ever want to die intestate?
13. When is a joint tenancy a desirable form of property distribution?
14. Differentiate between the *inter vivos* trust, the irrevocable trust, the revocable trust, and the testamentary trust.
15. Differentiate between a simple and complex trust.
16. Explain the Clifford trust.
17. What is the power of invasion?
18. Explain the rule against perpetuities.
19. How does a *per stirpes* distribution of an estate differ from a *per capita* distribution?
20. What is the idea behind the power of invasion? Do you think it is wise? Why?
21. What are split gifts?
22. What is the annual gift tax exclusion?
23. Explain how gifts can reduce total taxes.
24. What is the marital deduction and how does it work?
25. How can a trust reduce taxes?
26. Can you think of any nontax reasons for making gifts?

CASES

1. Jack McCarthy and his wife Bette are in their early thirties and have two children, four and six. Jack earns $30,000 per year. He has $50,000 worth of life insurance. Bette earns $20,000 per year. They have $20,000 equity in their $60,000 house, $5,000 in cash in a savings and loan association, and $10,000 worth of personal assets including a car. Both Jack and Bette are in excellent health. A few evenings ago a lawyer friend of theirs told them everyone should have a will. Jack and Bette have always believed wills were for older people and probably for older people of means. Jack feels that because they are young and do not have many assets, they do not need a will. What do you think?

2. Peter Geldsack is an extremely wealthy man. He is a vigorous widower in his early sixties and has the following assets.

Assets	Value
1. Farm in Connecticut	$ 450,000
2. Ski Lodge in Aspen, Colorado	75,000
3. House in Bergen County, N.J.	200,000
4. Department Store in Newark, N.J.	1,600,000
5. Common Stock	3,452,000
6. Corporate Bonds	2,500,000
7. Municipal Bonds	2,000,000
Total	$10,277,000

Peter has two children to whom he would like to leave the bulk of his estate in equal parts. However, he would also like to leave approximately $100,000 to his faithful butler, and to do so in such a way that he will be well cared for during the rest of his life. The butler, moreover, knows little of investments, and Peter is afraid he might lose any outright cash grant. Peter would also like to leave his ski lodge to his dear friend and ski companion Grover Attwater of Glenwood Springs, Colorado.

Could you give Peter advice on drawing up a will that will carry out his wishes? If Peter died without a will, what would happen to his estate?

3. Wally and Dorothy Brown are in their middle sixties and have assets totaling close to one million dollars. They have two children to whom they wish to leave their estate split equally between them. They propose to do this in a will, but each wishes that the surviving spouse first get the entire estate and that the children have it only when they are both gone. How can this be arranged in a will? Should they draw up a joint will? Why or why not?

4. Bernice Wilson inherited a substantial sum of money when her husband died last year. She has two children and has provided that they will share her estate equally when she is gone. However, she has recently become concerned over the high taxes, which will diminish the amount her children will receive. What taxes does she have in mind? Can you help her plan her affairs so as to minimize these taxes?

5. Joseph Horohan is a wealthy elderly widower, with only one child who knows nothing about investments. Joe knows his child would lose his money if he left it to him. He would also like to minimize taxes. Can you advise him?

6. Bill and Sara Smith, an elderly couple, have just over $1,000,000 of tax-exempt municipal bonds yielding 8.1 percent. They also own a home free and clear and have no other substantial assets. They have three grown children to whom they will leave their estate in equal parts in their will. Recently they have heard they can reduce taxes by giving part of their assets away prior to death. Is this true? How does it work? What is one of the pitfalls to be avoided if they decide to give some of their assets away?

7. Spencer D'Orsey, an exceptionally well-to-do man, has recently died. His will created a testamentary trust for his four children—Bob, Carol, Ted, and Alice. While he was alive, D'Orsey was an exceptionally opinionated man. For example, he detested Carol's husband Abby Rubin, a professional union organizer, and could not understand why Alice would not marry Richard Starkley, a young attorney employed as a trust officer in a local bank. Because of these situations, D'Orsey had some unusual provisions written into the trust. One of thes provisions was that Carol would not receive her share as a beneficiary unless she divorced her husband. In addition, Alice could not receive her share until she married Starkley. To complicate affairs, Starkley's bank was named trustee. Can D'Orsey do this to his daughters? What conflicts does Starkley face if he marries Alice?

8.   Don Price drafted a will in which he distributed every item of property he owned, naming each piece. Several years later, Don became wealthy and held a large number of valuable stock certificates. When he reached the age of seventy, Don realized he should provide for the distribution of his stocks. Never an inefficient man, Don reached into the wastebasket and withdrew a sheet of butcher paper that had the words "Joe's Meat Market—Baloney" stamped on one side. On the other side, Don wrote a holographic will bequeathing his stocks to the local Catholic church. Don suffered a heart attack one week later and, as the local priest was administering Don's last rites, Joe (from the meat market) entered the room. Don looked at Joe and produced a small key. "Here, Joe, you take this. This key will open up a new way of life for you." Don soon died and his executors found that the key unlocks a small strongbox in which Don kept his stock certificates. Who gets what?

9.   Howard Johnson is a wealthy land owner in Massachusetts. In response to his wife's obvious interest in becoming the owner of some of Howard's country mansions, Howard drafts a will that devises his property "To my loving wife, Louise Johnson, for her years of devotion to our family." When Howard learns that he has terminal cancer, he executes a deed to these estates to Robert Gunsel, a friend. Robert then executes a deed to these estates "To Howard Johnson and Dottie Carter, as joint tenants and not as tenants in common, and to the survivor of them and his heirs." What may Louise do to protect herself against Dottie, Howard's paramour of thirty years?

SUGGESTED READINGS

Ashley, Pritcher B. *You and Your Will; The Planning and Management.* New York: McGraw-Hill, 1977.

Cantor, Gilbert M. *How to Avoid Estate Taxes.* Wilmington, Del.: Enterprise Publishing, 1981.

Clay, William C. *The Dow Jones-Irwin Guide to Estate Planning,* 5th ed. Homewood, Ill.: Dow Jones-Irwin, 1982.

Crumbley, D. L., and Milam, Edward E. *Estate Planning in the 80's.* New York: American Management Association, 1983.

Drollinger, William C. *Tax Shelters and Tax Free Income for Everyone.* Ann Arbor, Mich.: Epic Publications, 1981.

Estate Planners Quarterly. Published by Farnsworth Publishing Co., Inc., New York.

Farr, James A., and Wright, Jackson. *Estate Planners Handbook.* Boston: Little, Brown, 1982.

Federal Estate and Gift Taxes. Chicago: Commerce Clearing House.

Fundamental Concepts of Estate Planning. New York: Practicing Law Institute, 1982.

Guilfoyle, A. P., Fossett, Alice W., Thomas, William W., and Scoville, Samuel S. *Tax Facts on Life Insurance.* Cincinnati, Ohio: The National Underwriter Company. An annual publication.

Harmon, Susan M., ed. *Readings in Estate and Gift Tax Planning.* Bryn Mawr, Pa.: American College, 1982.

Holzman, Robert S. *Encyclopedia of Estate Planning,* revised ed. New York: Boardroom Books, 1982.

Internal Revenue Service. *A Guide to Federal Estate and Gift Taxation.* U.S. Treasury Department, Internal Revenue Service. This pamphlet can be obtained from the local IRS office.

Journal of the American Society of Chartered Life Underwriters. Published quarterly by the American Society of Chartered Life Underwriters, 270 Bryn Mawr Avenue, P. O. Box 59, Bryn Mawr, Pa.

Kahn, Arnold D. *Family Security Through Estate Planning,* 2nd ed. New York: McGraw-Hill, 1983.

Kahn, Waggoner. *Provisions of the Internal Revenue Code and Treasury Regulations Pertaining to the Federal Taxation of Gifts, Trusts, and Estates, 1983.* Boston: Little, Brown, 1983.

Lippett, Peter. *Estate Planning After the Reagan Tax Cut.* Reston, Va.: Reston Publishing Co., 1982.

Magee, David S. *Everything Your Heirs Need to Know About You.* Aurora, Ill.: Caroline House Publishers, 1982.

McCord, John H. *Estate and Gift Tax.* New York: Harcourt Brace Jovanovich, 1980.

————. *Estate and Gift Tax Reform.* St. Paul, Minn.: West Publishing, 1979.

Trusts and Estates, The Journal of Estate Planning and Administration. Published monthly by Communication Channels, Inc., 461 Eighth Ave., New York, N.Y.

Use of Trusts in Estate Planning Nineteen Eighty. New York: Practicing Law Institute, 1980.

APPENDIX 20: TECHNICAL APPENDIX

(Glossary of Terms)

Administrator:	One who administers a decedent's estate during probate. He or she differs from the executor in that the administrator is appointed by the judge of the probate court when no executor is named by a will or when the appointed executor is unable to perform the duties.
Attestation:	The witnessing of a paper's execution and a signed statement to that effect.
Bequest:	A gift of personal property or money under a will.
Cestui que trustent:	The beneficiaries of a trust. (Called cetty for short).
Codicils:	Writings executed subsequent to a will and forming a part thereof.
Collateral heirs:	Persons who are not descendants of the decedent but who are related through a common ancestor. Generally they include cousins and aunts and uncles of the decedent.
Corpus, trust res:	The body of the trust; the assets.
Decedent:	A deceased person.
Devise:	A gift of real property by the last will and testament of the donor. In contrast, a bequest or legacy is a gift of personal property or money.

Devisee:	Person receiving a gift of land by way of will.
Domicile:	The place of the permanent home of a person. The place of domicile is largely a matter of intention, though declarations of intention contrary to the actions of a person do not always control. A person has only one domicile at one time. It is not necessarily the same place as one's residence because domicile is the home, the fixed place of habitation, whereas residence is a transient place of dwelling. The domicile is where wills are probated.
Donor:	The person who holds the legal title to trust property for the purposes as stated by the terms of the trust. The person for whose benefit the trust is created is called a beneficiary or *cestui que* trustent.
Escrow:	An agreement under which certain executed documents, e.g., deeds, are delivered into the hands of a third person to be held until specified conditions are fulfilled and then delivered to the person so performing or, in the case of default, returned to the person executing the document.
Estate:	The interest that anyone has in property, being used particularly in connection with the interests owned by a person in real property. Also the total property of whatever kind owned by a decedent before the property is distributed according to the terms of a will, or by the laws of inheritance if the owner died intestate.
Estate in severalty:	An estate that is held by a person in his or her own right only, without any other person being joined or connected.
Executor:	The personal representative of a testator, appointed by the testator and approved by the judge of a probate court to take charge of the testator's estate, pay the debts, and distribute the balance of the property to the beneficiaries of the will pursuant to the order of the probate court.
Fee simple:	The highest in dignity and the greatest in extent of the estates in real property.
Fiduciary:	The person or institution who manages the financial affairs of a trust.
Gift causa mortis:	An unrevoked gift of personal property made in expectation of death.
Grantee:	One to whom a conveyance is made by deed.
Grantor:	One who makes a conveyance. Also the person who creates a trust.
Holographic will:	A will written entirely by the testator with his own hand.
Inter vivos gift:	A gift among the living, in contrast to a gift by will or in anticipation of death.
Inter vivos trust:	A trust created during the lifetime of the grantor.
Intestate:	Having no will. An intestate is a decedent who left no will or a defective will. Property not included in a will is often called intestate property.
Joint tenancy:	Two or more persons owning the same land and having the same unity of interest, time, title, and possession together with the right of survivorship.
Legacy:	Specific legacy: a gift of personal property, generally a specific item

	of value, under a will. General legacy: a gift of a certain sum, but no specific asset cited.
Legatee:	Person receiving a legacy or bequest.
Lineals:	Blood descendants of a decedent.
Per stirpes:	The method of distribution of the assets of a grant after the death of the original beneficiary. The children (grandchildren) share in the same proportions that their parents did (or would have).
Probate:	The procedure of proving a will before a court having jurisdiction over the administration of the estate of a deceased person.
Settlor:	The creator of a trust; also called grantor, trustor, and donor.
Spendthrift trust:	A trust created to provide a fund for the maintenance of a beneficiary and at the same time to secure it against his or her improvidence or incapacity. Generally, the trust principal is beyond the reach of creditors.
Tenancy by the entirety:	Title in real property held by husband and wife together; based on the common-law concept that provides rights to survivorship. Property held by the entirety can only be disposed of by the joint action of the husband and wife.
Tenancy in common:	A type of co-ownership of property by which the owners have undivided interests in the property. The interests may be unequal in quantity, may have been created at different times, and may have been derived from different sources. The co-owners are also known as cotenants. A cotenant may sell or otherwise dispose of his or her interest without consent of the other cotenants, and the new owner takes the right of the cotenant from whom he or she took interest. There is no survivorship right as between co-tenants, and the undivided interest may be disposed of by will or, in the absence of a will, descends to the heirs of the deceased cotenant, as would other property of the same kind. All of the tenants, in the absence of agreement between them to the contrary, have equal rights of possession regardless of inequality in their undivided interests.
Testamentary instrument:	A legal document such as a will or trust bestowing certain rights to certain individuals after the death of the person making the instrument.
Testamentary trustee:	A trustee appointed by or acting under a will in order to carry out a trust created by a will.
Testate:	A testate is a decedent who left a will. Property included in the will is often called testate property.
Testator:	The term may be used to describe either a man who has made a will or a decedent who left a will.
Testatrix:	A female testator.
Trustee:	The person who holds the legal title to trust property for the purposes as stated by the terms of the trust.

GLOSSARY

Accidental death benefits:	A provision that may be put into a life insurance policy calling for the payment of double benefits in the case of death by accidental means. See also *"Double Indemnity."*
Actual cash value clause:	Clause in a homeowner's policy that states the insurer pays the actual cash value of the loss on the building insured, provided the loss does not exceed the face value of the policy. Thus the face value of the policy defines the maximum liability of the insurance company.
Actuary:	A person professionally trained in the mathematics and other technical aspects of life insurance.
American Stock Exchange (AMEX):	The second major stock exchange (after the New York Stock Exchange) in the U.S.A.
Amortization:	A method of paying off a home mortgage.
Annuitant:	The person who has a contract with a life insurance company to receive periodic payments for a specific number of years, or perhaps for life.
Apportionment clause:	An insurance policy clause that is effective in preventing a homeowner from collecting more money than a house is worth (if the homeowner had more than one policy on the house).
Asked price:	The price at which a dealer will sell a nonlisted or over-the-counter security.
Assets:	Anything of value. (There are also *"Earning Assets"* and *"Non-Earning Assets."* See below.)
Assigned risk plans:	Plans developed to take care of those drivers who cannot obtain liability insurance because of their driving record but still wish to show financial responsibility.
Assigning wage clause:	A clause that allows the creditor to go directly to the debtor's employer and get a portion of the debtor's wages without first having to obtain a court order.
Automated teller:	A machine that will accept deposits or allow withdrawals from an account in a depository institution.
Automatic funds transfer (AFT):	Funds can be transferred automatically from savings accounts to checking accounts and vice versa.
Automatic premium loan (APL):	Provision in an insurance policy that grants the insured an automatic loan that is used to pay the premiums after the grace period has expired if the policy has a cash value.
Balance sheet:	The method of showing all the assets and liabilities of a corporation.

Balanced fund: An investment company that holds varying proportions of bonds, preferred stocks, and common stocks from time to time in order to maintain relatively greater stability of both capital and income.

Balloon clause: A clause in an installment loan contract calling for a final payment substantially larger than the earlier payments.

Bankruptcy: The state in which a person is legally declared unable to pay his debts.

Bear market: Technical term for a long-run downward-moving securities market.

Beneficiary: The person who receives certain benefits as spelled out in a will or a life insurance contract.

Better business bureaus: Organizations established by the business community, whose goal is to provide better relations between businesses and the public.

Bid price: The price at which a dealer will buy nonlisted or over-the-counter securities.

Blue-chip stock: The common stock of large, well-known, financially strong corporations with good records of earnings and dividend payments over many years.

Blue Cross: Insurance policy designed to cover hospitalization costs (i.e., hospital room and supplies).

Blue Shield: Insurance policy designed to cover physician's fees, whether surgical, surgical-medical, or general medical.

Blue sky laws: The laws of the various states regulating the sale of securities and the activities of security salespersons, brokers, and dealers.

Bond: A certificate of indebtedness that represents a loan from the bondholder to the corporation.

Book value: The accounting concept of the value of a share of common stock. It is equal to assets minus liabilities divided by the number of shares outstanding.

Broker: A person in the business of buying and selling securities for another party for which he or she receives a commission.

Budget: A financial plan in the form of an income statement which uses current and future operations to achieve certain goals. Very often it must be an estimate of future receipts and disbursements.

Bull market: Technical term for a long-run upward-moving securities market.

Call option: A contract giving the holder the privilege of purchasing a given security at a specific price for a specific period of time.

Call price: As applied to bonds, the price at which a corporation can prematurely retire bonds.

Callable bonds: Bonds that can be called in at the option of the corporation and on which the principal will be repaid.

Callable preferred stock: Preferred stock with a provision that the corporation has an option to buy back the stock on terms specified at the time the stock is issued.

Capital: Total assets of a business.

Capital gains: The market appreciation in the value of securities or other assets.

Capital gains tax: A special tax that must be paid by those who receive capital gains.

Capital loss: The decline in the market value of securities or other assets.

Capital structure: The relative proportions of capital represented by bonds, preferred stock, and common stock.

Cash discount: When the customer receives a discount off the purchase price if cash is paid for the purchase.

Cash surrender value: The amount of cash a person may obtain by voluntarily surrendering a life insurance policy.

Cashier's check: A check that the bank will write on itself. Cashier's checks may be bought from a bank by a depositor or nondepositor to make payments to a designated payee.

Certificate of deposit (CD):   A deposit account into which funds are placed at a specified time, not to be withdrawn until a specified time. CDs vary in terms of their maturities and yields.

Certified check: A means of assuring the payee that the check is good in cases where the payee may lack confidence in the drawer. The sum is deducted from the drawer's account before the check is issued.

Check: A bill of exchange. A written order drawn on a bank by a depositor, ordering the bank to pay on demand, and unconditionally, a definite amount of money to bearer or to the order of a specified person. A sight bank draft used to make payments with funds held in demand deposits.

Clifford trust: A specialized trust that can save one money on personal income tax. It is a simple trust, and the investment income is given yearly to the beneficiary. It is a temporary trust that reverts to the creator at the end of ten years and one day.

Closed-end investment company: A company that has a definite limit to the number of shares in itself that it may sell.

Closing costs: Cost incurred when closing a real estate sale between two parties. Included in these costs are title insurance, attorney's fees, recording fees, and the like.

Collateral trust bonds: Corporate bonds secured by collateral that consists of other corporations' stocks or bonds. Often the securities used as collateral are held in trust by a third party.

Commercial banks: Institutions that perform a wide variety of financial services, differentiating them from more specialized savings banks.

Commission brokers: Brokers who buy and sell securities for their customers, for which they receive a commission.

Common stock: Represents the residual interest in a corporation's income. Common stockholders (owners of the corporation) are the last to be paid off in the event the corporation must be liquidated.

Common stock equities: Certificates of ownership in a corporation.

Comptroller of the currency:	An office of the United States Treasury that charters, supervises, and examines national banks.
Conditional buy (sell) order:	An order to buy (sell) a certain number of shares under certain specific conditions, for example, at a certain expected future price.
Consumer credit:	Credit extended to individuals for the purchase of final consumer items.
Consumer finance company:	A firm specializing in loans to consumers, generally at higher interest rates than those charged by other lenders.
Consumer Leasing Act:	Federal consumer credit law that requires disclosure of information that helps the consumer compare the cost and terms of one lease with another.
Consumer price index:	A statistical device that measures the increase in the cost of living for consumers. Sometimes used to illustrate the extent that prices in general have risen or the amount of inflation.
Consumption expenditures:	Expenditures by individuals on final goods and services.
Contract brokers:	Brokers who assist the commission brokers who are unable to handle the entire volume of business by themselves. Contract brokers do not deal with the public.
Conventional mortgage:	Mortgage arrangement solely between the lending institution and the buyer of the home. These are mortgages that are neither guaranteed by the VA nor insured by the FHA, but they may be insured by various private mortgage insurers.
Convertible:	A bond or preferred stock that may be, under specific circumstances, exchanged for a certain number of shares of common stock.
Convertible preferred stock:	Preferred stock that can be exchanged for common stock at the stockholder's option.
Corporation:	A legal entity that has many of the rights, duties, and powers of an individual. The corporation raises capital by selling shares in itself called stock. Corporations come into existence when the proper state agency grants the corporation its charter. The owners of the corporation are the stockholders and have liability to the extent of their investment.
Credit card:	A card that permits consumers to obtain merchandise without paying at the time of purchase, receiving one bill at the end of the month for all purchases.
Credit life insurance:	Special term life insurance purchased when borrowing money on an installment loan basis, which is then used to pay off the loan in the event of the borrower's death before he or she pays it off.
Credit scoring:	A method of appraising the credit-worthiness of potential borrowers where numerical values are assigned to various factors.
Credit unions:	A cooperative type of depository institution designed to make loans to members for any reasonable purpose.
Cumulative preferred stock:	Preferred stock that requires corporations to pay all back dividends (dividends missed in prior years) before dividends on common stock can be paid.

Cyclical stock:
Stock of those companies whose sales and earnings vary greatly with swings in the business cycle; thus the stock's price fluctuates widely over swings in the business cycle.

Dealer:
A person or firm who stands ready to buy or sell securities at given prices. Dealers differ from brokers in that they make the market in certain securities by being willing simultaneously either to buy at a given price or to sell at a different given price.

Debenture:
A type of bond secured by no specific assets but by the general credit and all assets of the corporation.

Debit card:
A card used to make automatic fund transfers from the account of a buyer of merchandise to that of the seller. It eliminates the need for checks or cash by initiating automatic transfer of funds via a computer.

Decreasing term rider:
A type of term insurance in which the contract payout by the insurance company (or face value) decreases as time passes.

Deed of trust:
A special kind of mortgage, conveying title of property to a third party (trustee) rather than to the lender.

Defensive stock:
A stock that usually declines less than most securities in a downward movement of the market because of the nature of the business it represents.

Deflation:
A continuous decrease in the overall price level (an appreciation in the value of the dollar).

Demand deposits:
Deposits payable to the depositor upon demand. Funds placed in checking accounts are demand deposits.

Depreciation:
The expense allowance on capital goods that is allowed because capital will wear out. The depreciation expense permits the recapture of dollars invested in capital goods, so that they can be replaced after they wear out.

Disability insurance:
Insurance that generally provides for payments if the policyholder's income is cut off due to disability from an accident or illness.

Discount house:
Stores that achieve savings in their operating costs and pass them on to their customers in lower prices.

Discounted loan:
A loan on which the interest is deducted from the principal before it is made.

Diversification:
Investing in the securities of a number of different firms and a number of different industries in an attempt to spread the risk and lessen the likelihood of losses.

Dividend:
Payment made to the owners of common stock.

Dollar cost averaging:
Buying securities at regular intervals with specific and equal dollar amounts. This results in lowering the average price of securities because more are purchased when the prices are depressed than when they are high.

Double indemnity:
A clause in a life insurance contract that requires a double payment in the case of an accidental death. See also "Accidental Death Benefits."

Dow-Jones averages:
A statistical service that shows the general level and movement of security prices.

Drafts:

Specialized checks written by one bank on its account in another bank. Usually utilized for payments made long distance.

Drawee:

The party requested to pay the stated amount of the check, usually the bank or other savings institution.

Drawer:

The person drawing the bill of exchange instrument (check). Person writing a check against his checking account, and ordering that a payment be made.

Earnest money:

A deposit made by a purchaser of real estate as evidence of his good faith.

Earning assets:

Those assets that yield a return such as stocks, bonds, savings accounts, and rentable real estate. These assets may yield a return in the form of interest, dividends, or rent.

Earnings:

A corporation's income after all expenses, including preferred dividend payments.

Efficient market hypothesis (EMH):

States that the prices of securities traded in the market fully reflect all available information and that the market reacts instantaneously and in an unbiased manner to all new information. The EMH may be stated in its weak, semi-strong, or strong forms. One could conclude from the EMH that, if one is big enough and diversified enough, one would do as well by picking common stock at random as by analysis.

Electronic funds transfer systems (EFTS):

Involves advanced communication systems that use electronic impulses to facilitate fund transfers among accounts. *See also* automatic funds transfer.

Endowment life insurance policy:

A policy that provides protection for a specified number of years, at the end of which the insured will have cash value equal to the face amount of the policy.

Equal Credit Opportunity Act:

Federal consumer credit law that prohibits discrimination against an applicant for credit because of age, sex, marital status, race, color, religion, national origin, or receipt of public assistance.

Equipment trust obligations:

Securities (bonds) issued by corporations with specific equipment of the corporation used as security for the loan.

Estate taxes:

Taxes that come from the estate of the deceased and hence reduce the amount the heirs may inherit.

Ex dividend:

Without dividend. This means that the stock, if purchased, does not include the most recent dividend that has been declared.

Ex-dividend date:

The first day that the purchaser of a stock does not receive the dividend that has been declared on it.

Extended term insurance:

Insurance policy that includes a provision stating that if the holder fails to pay the premiums during the grace period, the policy automatically will remain in force as a term policy for as long as the cash surrender value of the policy will permit.

Fair Credit Billing Act:

Federal consumer credit law that sets up a procedure for the prompt correction of errors on a credit account and prevents damage to a credit rating while settling a dispute.

Fair Credit Reporting Act:	Federal consumer credit law that sets up a procedure for the prompt correction of mistakes on the consumer's credit record and requires that the record be kept confidential.
Federal Deposit Insurance Corporation (FDIC):	A federal regulatory authority, which began operating in 1934, that provides insurance protection for small deposits (i.e., those $100,000 or less), and supervises state-chartered banks who are not members of the Federal Reserve System but insured by the FDIC.
Federal Home Loan Bank Board (FHLBB):	Federal agency that regulates savings and loan associations.
Federal Reserve:	The central bank of the United States, established by Congress in 1913. The Federal Reserve is one of the regulatory agencies that oversees and supervises commercial banks.
FHA mortgage:	A mortgage loan made by an approved lending institution, the loan being insured by the Federal Housing Administration. Borrowers, property, and lenders must all meet FHA standards for the FHA to insure the mortgage loan.
Fiduciary:	A person who has certain legal rights and powers relating to financial matters to be exercised for the benefit of another person.
Finance company:	A financial institution specializing in making small loans to consumers.
Financial assets:	Includes such things as stocks, bonds, bank accounts, and cash or currency.
Financial responsibility laws:	Laws designed to protect the victims of automobile accidents by encouraging people to have at least the minimum amount of insurance to compensate a victim for damages.
Financial risk:	Risk related to the debt-equity ratio. With a high debt-equity ratio a corporation has large fixed obligations to pay each year, and there is the possibility creditors may force the firm into bankruptcy if the firm cannot pay.
Fixed annuity:	A contract with a life insurance company that provides the periodic payment of a fixed number of dollars for a specific period of time or for life.
Fixed income security:	A preferred stock or a bond that has a stated or fixed percentage income return.
Floor brokers:	Members of the exchange who assist commission brokers, who are unable to handle all the volume when trading is heavy.
Floor traders:	Members of the New York Stock Exchange who buy and sell securities for their own account.
Formula timing:	A method of buying securities in accordance with a formula that will tell you when to buy and when to sell. For example, a price earnings ratio of ten may be a signal to buy and one of fifteen or twenty a signal to sell.
Funding:	Technical term that refers to the buildup of assets of a pension fund.
General obligation bonds:	Municipal bonds that are secured by the full faith and credit of the taxing entity issuing them.

Gift taxes:	Taxes imposed on the giver; taxes on the privilege of giving something away.
Good-till-canceled order:	A type of conditional order that continues in force until it is either executed or canceled.
Grace period:	The period, usually thirty days, following the premium due date of a life insurance policy during which an overdue premium may be paid without penalty.
Graduated payment mortgage (GPM):	Under this mortgage the payments start out substantially below what they should be and then increase as time goes on. GPMs are often utilized by young people who expect their income to rise.
Gross national product (GNP):	The market value of all final goods and services produced in the United States per year.
Group life insurance:	Generally, insurance sold to a business firm, the firm providing each insured employee with an insurance certificate. The business firm usually withholds the premiums from the employees' salaries, and the employees are provided with an insurance package that consists of some term life insurance and some medical insurance.
Growth stock:	A stock that has shown a better than average growth in earnings, hence, a better than average appreciation in its market price. Moreover, there are expectations that it should continue to do so.
Health maintenance organizations (HMOs):	A type of medical expense protection method. HMOs provide medical care for their members, for a fixed fee per month, by owning and operating clinics and hospitals and hiring doctors, nurses, and technicians.
Hedge fund:	A mutual fund (or investment company) that hedges its market commitments by holding certain securities it believes are likely to increase in value and, at the same time, sells others short because it believes they are likely to decline in value. Its main objective is capital appreciation.
Holder-in-due-course doctrine:	Formerly a legal concept that if a merchant entered into a credit relationship with a consumer to finance purchased goods and then sold the installment contract to a third party (say, a finance company), a legally binding contract existed between the consumer and the third party. Previously this doctrine forced consumers to pay for goods even if they were defective. Today consumers can withhold payment for defective goods.
Home Mortgage Disclosure Act:	Federal consumer credit law that requires most lending institutions in metropolitan areas to let the public know where they make their mortgage and home improvement loans.
Homeowner's insurance policy:	Insurance policy that provides for property insurance on the home, personal property insurance, liability insurance, and medical payment insurance.
Income averaging:	A method of figuring out one's tax liability that can save a taxpayer money if his or her income fluctuates sharply or rises rapidly from

a relatively low level. Income is averaged over several years for tax purposes.

Income bonds: Bonds on which the interest is paid only if earned.

Income statement: Depicts the financial position over a period of time, for example, a year. A flow concept. Measures dollar income inflows and dollar expenditure outflows.

Income stock: Stock of a corporation that has a historical record of above average earnings and dividends and that is likely to continue performing favorably.

Individual retirement account (IRA): Salaried individuals may place a portion of their earnings, tax free, into a special account where principal, interest, and capital gains are not taxable until the account is drawn upon.

Inflation: An overall general upward price movement of all goods and services that results in the decline in the value of a dollar.

Inheritance tax: A tax imposed on the privilege of inheriting something, imposed on the person receiving the property. There are no federal inheritance taxes, but some states impose them.

Installment credit: Consists of all credit extended to individuals that is to be repaid in two or more installments.

Insurance dividend: The payment made to owners of mutual life insurance policies. Part of this must be looked upon as a return of premiums, part of it as earnings.

Interest rate risk: The risk of loss that results from the changes in the market price of bonds due to changes in the prevailing rates of interest. A risk relevant only with regard to investments in fixed obligations such as bonds and preferred stock.

Investment company: A corporation that sells stock of itself to the public and then uses the funds to buy the securities of many other firms. There is no limit to the number of shares an open-end investment company may sell of itself whereas a closed-end investment company definitely has a limit on the number of shares it may sell.

Investment service: Service from which one may obtain research and advisory information about whole industries and individual companies that one may wish to invest in.

Investment tax credit (ITC): The reduction in the final tax liability that may be taken if certain investments are made. Dollar-wise it is a certain percentage of the investments made.

Irrevocable trust: A trust in which the grantor gives away the property without any right to or control over the income. Moreover, the grantor may never reclaim the property.

Itemized deductions: Deductions that can only be used to offset income if they exceed the zero bracket amount. These include interest expenses on personal debts, state and local taxes, charitable contributions, and the like.

Joint account:	A checking account that allows two people to write checks against the account.
Keogh Bill:	The bill that allows most self-employed persons to set up their own retirement programs with generous tax savings.
Keogh Plan:	The self-employed individual's tax retirement plan. Under this tax provision, self-employed individuals earmark savings for retirement and receive certain tax benefits. Interest and capital gains which the investments earn are not taxed until they are withdrawn.
Lessee:	One who holds a leasehold estate (a tenant).
Lessor:	One who grants a leasehold estate (a landlord).
Level premium life insurance:	Life insurance policy with fixed insurance premiums over the life of the policy. Premiums are used to build up reserves in the early years of the policy to be used in the later years. This amounts to averaging the premiums for individuals over the period of their insurance contracts.
Leverage:	The use of borrowed money to increase the earnings of the common stockholder. If money is borrowed at 6 percent and the corporation earns 12 percent with it, the extra 6 percent accrues to the common stockholder.
Liabilities:	Amounts owed to others.
Life insurance trust:	A trust created by a life insurance policy upon the death of the insured. A trustee (i.e. a bank) then administers the funds on behalf of someone else.
Limit order:	An order to a broker to buy a certain stock only if its price falls to a specified level or to sell a stock only if the price rises to a specified level.
Limited payment life insurance policy:	A type of whole life insurance that provides for permanent protection, with the premiums paid only for a certain number of years.
Liquid:	Anything easily and quickly convertible to cash without a substantial price concession.
Liquidation value:	In the event a corporation is liquidated, the amount left after all debts are paid is divided by the number of shares outstanding to derive liquidation value per share.
Liquidity:	Refers to how quickly assets can be converted into cash without making a price concession (or at least not a substantial price concession). Liquidity is a relative term.
Load:	The fees that must be paid when buying mutual funds. These generally range from 7 to 9 percent; some are more and some are less, and some funds have no load.
Loan shark:	A person who makes loans and illegally charges interest rates in excess of what the law allows.
Major medical insurance:	A medical insurance policy that pays large medical bills. There is a deductible feature, with the insurance company paying medical expenses beyond that.

Malpractice insurance:	Primarily designed to protect doctors and nurses against personal liability damage suits arising out of actual or alleged professional carelessness.
Management fees:	The fees charged by the managers of investment companies for their services in managing the portfolio.
Margin purchases:	Purchases of securities with money that is partially borrowed.
Margin requirement:	The percentage of the price of a security that must be paid with the buyer's own money. The remainder may be borrowed.
Market order:	Either a buy or sell order of a specific number of shares of a specific security at the current market price.
Market risk:	Risk resulting from fluctuations in market prices of securities over time. This applies primarily to common stock but not to bonds.
Market value:	The price the investor must pay for the stock if he wishes to buy, or the amount received if the stock is sold.
Measure of economic welfare (MEW):	A measure that attempts to refine income into a meaningful concept of how well off we are.
Money market funds:	Mutual funds that specialize in buying very short-term securities in the money market. These funds were developed to enable the small investor to enter the money market.
Money market instruments:	Short-term credit instruments such as Treasury bills and commercial paper. Investors who buy them are lending their money on a short-term (one year or less) basis.
Monthly investment plan:	An arrangement for regular purchases of stock listed on the New York Stock Exchange. These arrangements can be made with most member firms.
Moody's:	A bond rating service that assigns credit ratings to bonds to permit investors to assess the risk associated with buying them.
Mortality tables:	Tables indicating the number of deaths per thousand at various ages, which have been developed from past experience by life insurance companies.
Mortgage:	Instrument used to finance real estate. Security for debt. It gives the lender the legal right to sell the property in order to repay the loan should the borrower default.
Mortgage banker:	An individual or firm that primarily originates real estate loans and then sells them to institutional lenders and other investors.
Mortgage bonds:	Bonds behind which specific assets of a corporation have been pledged as collateral.
Mortgagee:	One to whom a mortgage is given as security for a loan (i.e., the lender).
Mortgagor:	One who gives a mortgage to secure a loan (i.e., the borrower).
Municipal securities:	Debt obligations of state and local governments. These securities appeal to high-income investors because their interest income is exempt from federal taxation.
Mutual fund:	The more popular name for an open-end investment company. See also "*Open-end Investment Company.*"

Mutual life insurance company:	An insurance company that is owned by the policyholders.
Mutual savings banks:	Financial institutions similar to savings and loan associations in that they accept deposits and make primarily mortgage loans.
National Auto Dealers Association (NADA):	This group publishes the "Blue Book," a guide containing information on the value of used cars.
National health insurance:	Federal government medical insurance programs designed both to supplement and to replace various private health insurance plans.
National income:	The total of all the income of all the people in the United States for a given accounting period.
Net asset value:	As applied to mutual funds, this is the market value of underlying securities divided by the number of mutual fund shares outstanding.
Net worth:	Assets less liabilities. Net worth is the best measure of what a person or business is worth.
New York Stock Exchange:	The largest organized stock exchange in the U.S., accounting for 78% of the total dollar volume of securities transactions on all stock exchanges.
No-load funds:	Mutual funds that do not charge any commissions on their sales. To buy these, you may have to contact the company directly.
Nominal yield:	Yield stated in money terms and not adjusted for inflation.
Nonearning assets:	Personal assets, such as your watch or automobile, that do not earn income.
Nonfinancial assets:	Such things as clothes, automobiles, and jewelry.
Nonforfeiture options:	The options available to holders of life insurance policies if they discontinue the payment of premiums. Generally the policy value is taken in the form of cash, as extended term insurance, or as reduced paid-up insurance.
NOW Account (Negotiated order of withdrawal):	A specialized checking account that bears interest.
Odd lot:	A block of stock consisting of fewer shares than the number customarily traded at one time, which is known as a round lot of one hundred shares.
Odd-lot dealer:	A dealer who buys and sells odd lots exclusively.
Open-end investment company (Also called mutual fund):	A company that has no limit as to the number of shares in itself that it may sell.
Open order:	An order to buy or sell securities at a stipulated price that remains in effect until it is executed or canceled.
Option:	See "Puts" and "Call Option."
Overdrafts:	Checks written for amounts in excess of the funds in the account. In such a case the bank will usually make the full payment for a fee later charged to the depositor.

Over-the-counter:	The market for those securities not listed on any organized exchange.
Paid-up insurance:	Insurance on which premiums are no longer due but which is still in force.
Par value:	The face or stated value of a bond or a stock. In the case of a stock, this is meaningless. However, in the case of a bond or a preferred stock, the par value generally indicates the dollar value on which the annual interest or dividends are to be paid.
Participating preferred:	Type of preferred stock in which, if the corporation's earnings are sufficient, the preferred stockholders not only are given their agreed dividends but also are entitled to share equally in the dividends paid to the common stockholders.
Partnership:	Noncorporate form of business organization comprised of two or more partners. All partners are liable for the debts of the business. Partnership agreements are drawn up that spell out the duties, rights, and liabilities of each partner.
Payee:	The person to whom a check is made payable.
Plain English policies:	Insurance policies that are written in language the layman can understand. Legal terminology has been removed, and simple phraseology has been developed.
Points:	A point is one percentage point of the mortgage loan. The lender usually receives this points sum, and it is considered additional compensation to offset the fact that the regular interest rate charged to the buyer (borrower) is below the market rate.
Policy loan:	A loan made by an insurance company to a policyholder on the cash surrender value of the policy.
Political risk:	Has to do with the legal and political environment in which the business must operate.
Portfolio:	The securities owned by an individual or corporation.
Preemptive rights:	The rights of existing stockholders to buy a prorated share of a new issue of common stock that a corporation may issue.
Preferred stock:	Stock that receives preferential treatment over common stock with respect both to dividends and to claims on assets in the event that the corporation goes out of business.
Price-earnings ratio:	The market value of a common stock divided by its earnings.
Price-level risk:	Risk associated with inflation. This risk is particularly applicable to those assets whose value is stated in terms of a fixed number of dollars.
Prospectus:	The official document that describes the shares of a new security being issued.
Proxy statement:	The written permission that one stockholder gives to another person to vote his stock for him.
Purchase money mortgage:	A mortgage that is taken by a seller from a buyer in lieu of purchase money (i.e., the seller helps finance the purchase). Usually takes the form of a second mortgage when the buyer cannot come up with a first mortgage loan to cover the purchase price.

Puts:	Contracts that give a holder the right to sell a particular security at a specified price for a specific period of time.
Random walk:	Theory that holds that a stock's future price movement cannot be predicted by an analysis of its past price movements. It means that a large diversified investor can do as well by selecting stock at random as by analysis.
Real estate investment trust (REIT):	An institution that pools capital for the purpose of investing in real estate or in mortgages.
Real Estate Settlement Procedures Act:	Federal consumer credit law that requires the consumer to be given information about the services and costs involved in a settlement when real property transfers from seller to buyer.
Real income:	Income derived by adjusting money income to take into account the effects of inflation.
Real yield:	Yield derived by adjusting the nominal yield for inflation.
Regional exchanges:	A number of smaller stock exchanges that serve only the region in which they are located and not the whole nation as does the New York Stock Exchange.
Registrar:	The institution (usually a bank) that maintains a list of the common stockholders of a corporation and the number of shares that they hold.
Regulation Q:	The Federal Reserve's regulation that sets interest rate ceilings payable on various deposits. The Monetary Control Act of 1980 calls for the phasing out of these regulations by 1986.
Remedial loan society:	A nonprofit organization designed to loan cash on the pledge of watches, diamonds, and other articles one typically finds in a pawnshop.
Revenue bonds:	Municipal bonds that are repaid by the revenue generated from whatever the bonds finance (e.g., tollways or power plants).
Reverse mortgage:	Used when one has paid off a mortgage and sells back a home to a lending institution. Monthly payments are received, and as time passes equity declines.
Round lot:	The fixed number or block of shares, usually one hundred, that is the commonly traded unit on the organized exchanges.
Safety deposit box:	Steel box inside a bank vault that may be rented by bank customers in which to store valuables.
Sales credit:	Credit extended by a merchant in which the customer gets the goods and promises to pay later.
Sales finance companies:	Companies primarily engaged in the purchase of merchant's time-sales contracts arising out of the sale of goods to consumers.
Savings accounts:	Accounts on which banks pay interest to the depositor and upon which checks cannot be written.
Savings and loan associations:	Financial institutions in the business of accepting deposits and making primarily mortgage loans.
Second mortgage:	A mortgage recorded after the first mortgage, where both mortgages are on the same property. In the event of a foreclosure and sale

of a house on which the mortgagor has defaulted, the second mortgage is not paid off until after the first mortgagee has been completely repaid. This usually comes into existence when the purchaser does not have sufficient funds to pay the owner his or her equity in an existing (not new) home.

Securities and Exchange Commission (SEC): An agency of the United States government that administers the various federal security laws.

Senior securities: Securities such as bonds and preferred stock that have a higher claim than common stock on earnings as well as on assets on liquidation.

Serial bonds: Bonds that are numbered according to their issue groupings, and are retired at various times in accordance with their numbers.

Short sales: Selling securities you do not own. You borrow them from a broker, and later (hopefully when the price falls) you buy them back and repay the broker.

Sight draft: A bank draft (check) payable on demand.

Small claims courts: Courts able to handle claims effectively, quickly, and at a much lower cost than by regular legal action. The amount of damages for which a person may sue is limited in a small claims court to about $500 usually.

Social Security: The nation's basic method of providing family income when earnings are reduced or stopped because of death, retirement, or disability.

Sole proprietorship: A business owned by one person where the business assets are commingled with the personal assets of the owner. The business has no charter and is the simplest form of organization.

Specialists: Members of the exchange who specialize in buying and selling only certain specific securities that are traded at a specific location on the exchange. The commission broker, or the contract broker, will go to whatever specialist is required to execute an order.

Speculative stocks: These stocks are untried securities, often stocks of new, small firms, whose chances for success are not great. The probability of gain is small, but the amount of gain might be great if there is one.

State and local bond trust: A closed-end investment trust established through which tax-exempt bonds can be purchased indirectly.

Stock: Certificate of ownership in a corporation. Also called "shares of ownership."

Stock dividend: A dividend paid to the shareholders in the form of additional shares of stock.

Stock exchanges: Organizations that provide their members with a place and the facilities to buy and sell securities.

Stock split: An increase in the number of shares of a corporation brought about by division of existing shares. A two-for-one split, for example, will result in two new shares for each old share that previously existed, making a total of three.

Stock warrant: A certificate authorizing the owner to buy a specific company's stock

	at a specific price for a specific period of time, or perhaps in perpetuity.
Stop order:	An order to buy or sell conditioned upon a specific price. This order is very often referred to as a "stop loss" order, because it prevents the stock from falling below a certain price.
Straight life policy:	A type of whole life insurance policy that builds up a cash surrender value and pays dividends. If the dividends are left with the insurance company, the straight life policy may eventually become a paid-up policy.
Suggested list price:	Legally required price tag on an automobile. It is not the hard and fast price because there is room for bargaining over a final price.
Tax credit:	A tax credit reduces the actual tax. Some of the common tax credits are for political contributions, investment tax credits, and child or dependent care credits.
Tax shelter:	In the broadest sense, any deduction from income or credit against tax. More narrowly, certain investments permit tax write-offs by generating deductible expenses such as depreciation, which can be used to offset other income. In other cases, investments will qualify for an investment tax credit (ITC). An ITC is better than depreciation expense because after the final tax liability has been calculated, the tax may be reduced dollar for dollar by the ITC.
Tenant:	One who rents an apartment or a house from the owner (Landlord). A tenant holds a leasehold estate.
Term insurance:	The simplest type of ordinary life insurance. Term insurance provides only protection over the contract period and has no savings feature or so-called *living benefits*.
Thin market:	A market in which there are few offers either to buy or sell. The term can be applied to a single security or to the entire market.
Thrift institutions:	Financial intermediaries whose principal source of funds is the savings of the public. Thrift institutions are credit unions, mutual savings banks, savings and loan associations, industrial banks, life insurance companies, private pension plans, and commercial banks.
Time draft:	A bank draft (check) payable at some predetermined future time.
Treasury bills:	Short-term obligations of the U.S. government. Treasury bills are sold at a discount from face value with maturities of three months, six months, and one year.
Treasury notes:	Similar to Treasury bonds but generally with shorter maturities. They are marketable and negotiable and have coupons that provide for an interest payment every six months.
Trust:	An arrangement whereby title to property is transferred by the creator or settlor to another person (trustee) for the benefit of a third party (beneficiary).
Trustee service:	A service that looks after the financial affairs (manages assets) of someone for a fee.

Truth-in-Lending Act:	Federal consumer credit law that requires disclosure of the finance charge and the annual percentage rate of interest charged.
U.S. government bonds (Treasury bonds):	Marketable long-term obligations of five years or more of the U.S. government. These bonds have coupons, and interest is paid every six months.
United States savings bonds:	Generally nonmarketable U.S. government bonds designed for the small investor.
Usury:	Interest in excess of what the law allows.
VA-guaranteed mortgage:	A mortgage loan on which the Veteran's Administration guarantees payment to the lending institution in the event of default by the veteran-buyer.
Variable annuity:	An annuity contract with a life insurance company under which the dollar payments received are not fixed but vary (or fluctuate), usually with the price of common stock.
Variable rate mortgage (VRM):	A mortgage that carries an interest rate that may move either up or down depending on market conditions.
Vesting of interests:	Concerning the legal ownership of certain benefits of a pension fund. Important if persons leave their employer prior to retirement.
Warrant:	A certificate authorizing the owner to buy a specific company's stock at a specific price for a specific period of time, or perhaps in perpetuity.
Warranty:	A guarantee of the integrity of a product or service and of the maker's responsibility to repair or replace the defective product (or perform the service again if necessary).
Wrap-around mortgage:	A form of mortgage financing in which the face amount of the second (wrap-around) loan is equal to the balance of the first loan plus the amount of the new financing.
Yield:	Income received on investments. Usually expressed as a percentage of the market price of the security.
Zero bracket amount:	The amount of income (depending on marital status) upon which no federal income tax need be paid.

INDEX

666   Index